NEW WEBSTER'S

ENGLISH

SPANISH

DICTIONARY

elair new york
Consolidated
A DELAIR PUBLISHING COMPANY

ISBN: 0-8326-0050-4

A

a, *prep.* to; at
a·ba·ce·rí·a, *f.* grocery
a·ba·ce·ro, *m.* grocer
a·ba·dí·a, *f.* abbey
a·ba·jo, *adv.* below; down; beneath. *prep.* down
a·ban·do·na·do, *a.* forlorn; derelict
a·ban·do·nar, *v.* abandon; desert; maroon; forsake
a·ban·do·no, *m.* abandonment; dereliction
a·ba·ni·car, *v.* fan
a·ba·ni·co, *m.* fan
a·ba·ra·tar, *v.* make cheaper; lower
a·bar·car, *v.* encompass; embrace; comprise
a·bas·te·ce·dor, *m.* caterer
a·ba·ti·do, *a.* dejected; downcast; glum
a·ba·ti·mien·to, *m.* dejection
a·ba·tir(se), *v.* depress; knock down; fall
ab·di·car, *v.* abdicate
ab·do·men, *m.* abdomen
a·be·dul, *m.* birch
a·be·ja, *f.* bee
a·be·jo·rro, *m.* bumblebee
a·be·rra·ción, *f.* aberration
a·ber·tu·ra, *f.* opening; aperture; breach; gap
a·be·to, *m.* fir
a·bier·ta·men·te, *adv.* outright
a·bier·to, *a.* open
a·bi·ga·rra·do, *a.* motley; many-colored
a·bis·mo, *m.* abyss
ab·ju·rar, *v.* abjure
a·blan·dar(se), *v.* soften
a·bo·fe·tear, *v.* cuff; slap
a·bo·ga·do, *m.* lawyer; attorney; advocate; counsel
a·bo·gar, *v.* advocate; plead
a·bo·len·go, *m.* ancestry
a·bo·lir, *v.* abolish
a·bo·lla·du·ra, *f.* dent
a·bo·mi·nar, *v.* loathe; abominate
a·bo·nar, *v.* fertilize; credit
a·bo·no, *m.* fertilizer; pass
a·bo·rí·ge·nes, *m. pl.* aborigines
a·bo·rre·cer, *v.* abhor; hate
a·bo·rre·ci·mien·to, *m.* hatred
a·bor·to, *m.* abortion
a·bo·to·nar, *v.* button up
a·bo·za·lar, *v.* muzzle
a·bra·sión, *f.* abrasion
a·bra·za·de·ra, *f.* brace; clamp
a·bra·zar(se), *v.* embrace; hug; cuddle
a·bra·zo, *m.* embrace; hug
a·bre·via·ción, *f.* abbreviation
a·bre·viar, *v.* abbreviate; abridge

condense; curtail
a·bri·gar(se), *v.* harbor; shelter
a·bri·go, *m.* overcoat; coat; shelter
a·bril, *m.* April
a·bri·llan·tar, *v.* brighten; cut into facets
a·brir(se), *v.* open; open up; spread out
a·bro·char, *v.* fasten; button up
a·bro·gar, *v.* repeal; abrogate
a·bru·ma·dor, *a.* crushing
a·brup·to, *a.* blunt; steep; abrupt
abs·ce·so, *m.* abscess
ab·so·lu·to, *a.* absolute; complete
ab·sol·ver, *v.* absolve; acquit; clear
ab·sor·ber, *v.* absorb; soak up; engross
ab·sor·to, *a.* intent; absorbed
abs·te·mio, *a.* abstemious
abs·te·ner·se, *v.* refrain; abstain
abs·trac·to, *a.* abstract
abs·traer, *v.* abstract
ab·sur·do, *a.* absurd; silly; preposterous
a·bue·la, *f.* grandmother
a·bue·lo, *m.* grandfather; grandparent
a·bun·dan·cia, *f.* abundance; amplitude
a·bun·dan·te, *a.* abundant; plentiful; ample; bounteous
a·bun·dar, *v.* abound
a·bu·rri·mien·to, *m.* boredom
a·bu·rrir, *v.* bore
a·bu·sar, *v.* abuse; misuse; maltreat
a·bu·so, *m.* abuse; encroachment
a·byec·to, *a.* abject
a·cá, *adv.* here; hither
a·ca·ba·do, *a.* finish; end; conclusion. *a.* finished
a·ca·bar, *v.* finish; end; accomplish; achieve; fail
a·ca·de·mia, *f.* academy
a·ca·dé·mi·co, *a.* academic
a·ca·li·zar, *v.* alkalize
a·cam·par, *v.* camp
a·ca·ri·ciar, *v.* fondle; pet; pat
a·ca·rrear, *v.* cart
a·ca·rreo, *m.* cartage
ac·ce·der, *v.* accede
ac·ce·si·ble, *a.* accessible
ac·ce·so, *m.* access; approach; fit
ac·ce·so·rio, *a.* accessory; subordinate; *pl.* accessories
ac·ci·den·ta·do, *a.* broken; uneven; eventful
ac·ci·den·te, *m.* accident; casualty
ac·ción, *f.* action; movement; share of stock
a·ce·bo, *m.* holly
a·ce·char, *v.* lurk; spy on
a·cei·te, *m.* oil
a·cei·to·so, *a.* oily
a·cei·tu·na, *f.* olive

a·ce·le·rar(se), v. accelerate; speed up; expedite

a·cen·to, m. accent; stress; emphasis

a·cen·tuar(se), v. accent; stress; emphasize

a·cep·tar, v. accept; adopt; agree to; allow

a·ce·ra, f. sidewalk

a·cer·car(se), v. approach; near

a·ce·ri·co, m. pincushion

a·ce·ro, m. steel

a·cer·ti·jo, m. riddle

a·cé·ti·co, a. acetic

a·ce·to·na, f. acetone

á·ci·do, m. acid

á·ci·do bó·ri·co, m. boric acid

á·ci·do cí·tri·co, m. citric acid

á·ci·do sul·fú·ri·co, m. sulphuric acid

a·cla·ma·ción, f. acclaim

a·cla·mar, v. acclaim

a·cla·ra·ción, f. clarification

a·cla·rar, v. clarify; clear; rinse

a·cli·ma·tar, v. acclimate

ac·né, m. acne

a·co·bar·dar(se), v. cringe; flinch; quail; unnerve

a·co·gi·da, f. welcome; reception

a·co·la·da, f. accolade

a·col·char, v. pad

a·có·li·to, m. acolyte

a·co·me·ter, v. assail; attempt

a·co·mo·da·di·zo, a. obliging; easygoing

a·co·mo·da·dor, m. usher

a·co·mo·dar, v. accommodate; suit; fit; adjust; usher

a·com·pa·ñan·te, m. escort; (mus.) accompanist

a·com·pa·ñar, v. accompany; escort; go with; attend

a·con·di·cio·na·dor de ai·re, m. air conditioner

a·con·se·jar(se), v. advise; take advice

a·con·te·cer, v. happen; chance

a·con·te·ci·mien·to, m. happening; occasion

a·cor·dar(se), v. agree; agree on; harmonize; remember

a·cor·de, m. chord

a·cor·de·ón, m. accordion

a·cor·near, v. gore

a·co·rra·lar, v. corral; corner

a·cor·tar, v. clip; shorten

a·co·sar, v. pursue; harass; beset

a·cos·tar(se), v. lie down; go to bed

a·cos·tum·brar(se), v. habituate; accustom oneself to

a·cre, m. acre. a. acrid; sour

a·cre·cen·tar, v. increase

a·cree·dor, m., a·cree·do·ra, f. creditor

a·cri·mo·nia, f. acrimony; bitterness

a·cró·ba·ta, m., f. acrobat

ac·ti·tud, f. attitude; pose; position

ac·ti·var, v. activate

ac·ti·vi·dad, f. activity; movement; briskness

ac·ti·vo, a. active; alive; brisk. adv. astir. m. pl. assets

ac·to, m. act

ac·tor, m. actor

ac·triz, f. actress

ac·tual, a. actual; instant

ac·tual·men·te, adv. actually; now

ac·tuar, v. act; perform

a·cua·rio, m. aquarium

a·cuá·ti·co, a. aquatic

a·cu·chi·llar, v. knife; slash; hack

a·cue·duc·to, m. aqueduct

a·cueo, a. aqueous; watery

a·cuer·do, m. agreement; accord; resolution. es·tar de a·cuer·do, concur

a·cu·mu·lar, v. accumulate; cumulate; amass; stockpile; congest; fund

a·cu·ña·ción, f. coinage

a·cu·ñar, v. mint; coin

a·cu·sar, v. accuse; charge; impeach; indict

a·cús·ti·ca, f. acoustics

a·chi·ca, v. bail; humble; diminish

a·chi·co·ria, f. chicory

a·chis·pa·do, a. tipsy

a·da·gio, m. adage; proverb; (mus.) adagio

a·dap·ta·ble, a. versatile; adaptable

a·dap·tar, v. adapt; adapt oneself to; adjust

a·de·cua·do, a. adequate; fit; suitable

a·de·ha·la, f. bonus; tip

a·de·lan·ta·do, a. advanced; fast

a·de·lan·tar(se), v. proceed; further; go ahead; advance; gain upon

a·de·lan·te, adv. forward, forwards; forth; onward

a·de·lan·to, m. advance; progress

a·del·ga·zar(se), v. slim down; lose weight; taper

a·de·mán, m. gesture; attitude

a·de·más, adv. moreover; besides; furthermore; also. prep. besides

a·de·re·zar, v. garnish; adorn; dress

a·de·re·zo, m. adornment

ad·he·rir(se), v. adhere; cling; cohere; cleave to; espouse

ad·he·si·vo, a. adhesive. m. adhesive

a·di·ción, f. addition; increment; annex

a·di·cio·nal, a. additional; more; extra

a·dies·trar(se), v. train; exercise

a·diós, m. farewell. int. farewell; goodby, goodbye

a·di·vi·nar, v. guess; divine; foretell

ad·je·ti·vo, m. adjective

ad·ju·di·ca·ción, *m.* adjudgment; award

ad·ju·di·car(se), *v.* award; allot

ad·jun·tar, *v.* annex

ad·mi·nis·tra·ción, *f.* administration; management

ad·mi·nis·tra·dor, *m.*, **ad·mi·nis·tra·do·ra**, *f.* administrator; manager; steward

ad·mi·nis·trar, *v.* administer; manage; dispense

ad·mi·ra·ble, *a.* admirable; fine; excellent

ad·mi·rar(se), *v.* admire; wonder

ad·mi·si·ble, *a.* admissible; acceptable

ad·mi·tir, *v.* admit; receive; permit

a·do·be, *m.* adobe

a·do·les·cen·cia, *f.* adolescence

a·dop·tar, *v.* adopt; embrace

a·do·rar, *v.* adore; worship

a·dor·me·cer(se), *v.* drowse; fall asleep

a·dor·mi·de·ra, *f.* poppy

a·dor·nar, *v.* decorate; adorn; deck; bedeck; grace

a·dor·no, *m.* ornament; adornment; array; *pl.* finery

ad·qui·rir, *v.* acquire; secure; obtain

a·dre·na·li·na, *f.* adrenaline

ads·cri·bir, *v.* ascribe; assign

a·dua·na, *f.* custom-house; *pl.* customs

a·du·ja·da, *a.* coiled

a·du·la·ción, *f.* adulation; flattery; blarney

a·du·la·dor, *m.*, **a·du·la·do·ra**, *f.* sycophant; flatterer

a·du·lar, *v.* flatter

a·dul·te·rio, *m.* adultery

a·dul·to, *m.* adult; grownup. *a.* grown-up

ad·ver·bio, *m.* adverb

ad·ver·sa·rio, *m.* adversary; opponent

ad·ver·si·dad, *f.* adversity

ad·ver·so, *a.* adverse; averse; unfavorable

ad·ver·tir, *v.* caution; notify; take notice of

ad·ya·cen·te, *a.* adjacent

aé·reo, *a.* aerial

ae·ro·náu·ti·ca, *f.* aeronautics

ae·ro·puer·to, *m.* airport

a·fa·ble, *a.* affable; kind; genial

a·fán, *m.* travail; anxiety

a·fec·ción, *f.* affection; fondness

a·fec·ta·ción, *f.* affectation; pretense

a·fec·tar, *v.* affect

a·fec·to, *m.* affection. *a.* affectionate

a·fec·tuo·sa·men·te, *adv.* affectionately; fondly

a·fei·ta·do, *m.*, **a·fei·ta·da**, *f.* shave. *a.* shaven

a·fe·rrar(se), *v.* furl; grasp

a·fian·zar, *v.* guaranty; bail; clinch

a·fi·cio·na·do, *m.*, **a·fi·cio·na·da**, *f.* amateur; fancier; fan

a·fi·jo, *m.* affix

a·fi·lar(se), *v.* hone; sharpen

a·fi·liar(se), *v.* affiliate; join

a·fín, *a.* related

a·fi·na·ción, *f.* refining; (*mus.*) tuning

a·fi·nar, *v.* tune; polish

a·fi·ni·dad, *f.* affinity

a·fir·mar(se), *v.* affirm; assert; contend; aver; make fast

a·fir·ma·ti·vo, *a.* affirmative

a·flic·ción, *f.* affliction; anxiety; bereavement

a·fli·gi·do, *a.* stricken

a·fli·gir(se), *v.* afflict; grieve

a·flo·jar(se), *v.* slacken; loosen; weaken

a·fluen·cia, *f.* affluence

a·fo·ris·mo, *m.* aphorism

a·for·tu·na·do, *a.* fortunate; prosperous; lucky

a·fren·ta, *f.* affront; insult

a·fren·tar(se), *v.* affront; insult; be affronted

a·fro·di·sía·co, *m.* aphrodisiac

a·fue·ra, *adv.* out; outside. *f. pl.* suburbs

a·ga·char(se), *v.* crouch; bow down; squat

a·ga·lla, *f.* gill

a·ga·rrar(se), *v.* seize; grasp; grapple; clinch; clutch

a·ga·rro, *m.* grab; clutch; grip

a·gen·cia, *f.* agency; bureau

a·gen·te, *m.* agent; officer. **a·gen·te de po·li·cía**, cop

á·gil, *a.* agile; nimble; active; lithe; lithesome

a·gi·li·dad, *f.* agility

a·gi·ta·ción, *f.* agitation; excitement; stir; flutter; flurry

a·gi·tar(se), *v.* agitate; stir up; churn; shake; flutter

a·glo·me·ra·do, *a.* agglomerate

a·glo·me·rar, *v.* agglomerate

ag·nós·ti·co, *m.*, **ag·nós·ti·ca**, *f.* agnostic

a·go·nía, *f.* agony; pain

a·gos·to, *m.* August

a·go·ta·mien·to, *m.* depletion; exhaustion

a·go·tar(se), *v.* exhaust; drain; deplete; give out; tire

a·gra·da·ble, *a.* agreeable; pleasant; delightful; gracious; nice; genial

a·gra·de·cer(se), *v.* acknowledge; thank; appreciate

a·gra·de·ci·do, *a.* grateful; thankful

a·gra·rio, *a.* agrarian

a·gra·var(se), *v.* aggravate; get or

make worse; burden
a·gra·vio, *m.* grievance
a·gre·gar(se), *v.* aggregate; join together
a·gre·miar(se), *v.* unionize
a·gre·sión, *f.* aggression
a·gre·si·vo, *a.* aggressive
a·griar(se), *v.* sour; acetify
a·gri·cul·tor, *m.* farmer
a·gri·cul·tu·ra, *f.* agriculture; farming
a·grie·tar(se), *v.* chap
a·gri·men·sor, *m.* surveyor
a·grio, *a.* sour; acid; acrid; bitter; surly
a·gro·no·mía, *f.* agronomy
a·gru·par(se), *v.* group; bunch; cluster
a·gua·ca·te, *m.* avocado; avocado tree
a·gua·fuer·te, *f.* etching
a·gua·ma·nil, *m.* ewer
a·gua·nie·ve, *f.* sleet
a·guan·tar(se), *v.* endure; put up with; support
a·gu·de·za, *f.* acuity; acumen; keenness; brightness; witticism
a·gu·do, *a.* keen; sharp; acute; quick-witted; exquisite
a·güe·ro, *m.* omen; augury
a·gui·ja·da, *f.* goad
á·gui·la, *f.* eagle
a·gui·le·ño, *a.* aquiline
a·gui·lón, *m.* gable
a·gui·lu·cho, *m.* eaglet
a·gu·ja, *f.* needle; pin; spire
a·gu·je·ro, *m.* hole
ah, *int.* ha, hah
a·he·cha·du·ra, *f.* chaff; winnowing
a·he·rrum·brar(se), *v.* rust
a·hí, *adv.* there
a·hi·ja·da, *f.* goddaughter
a·hi·ja·do, *m.* godson; godchild
a·ho·gar(se), *v.* suffocate; choke; drown; smother; stifle
a·ho·ra, *adv.* now. **has·ta a·ho·ra**, heretofore
a·hor·car, *v.* hang
a·ho·rrar, *v.* save; economize
a·ho·rros, *m. pl.* savings
ai·re, *m.* air; manner; aspect; tune. **al ai·re li·bre**, outdoors
ai·rear(se), *v.* aerate; air; cool oneself
ai·ro·so, *a.* airy; jaunty
ais·la·mien·to, *m.* isolation; insulation
ais·lar, *v.* isolate; seclude; sequester; insulate
a·jar, *v.* crumple; rumple
a·je·drez, *m.* chess
a·je·no, *a.* alien
a·jo, *m.* garlic
a·jus·ta·do, *a.* snug; tight-fitting
a·jus·tar, *v.* adjust; settle; bargain

a·jus·te, *m.* settlement; fitting; fit; accommodation
a·la·ban·za, *f.* praise
a·la·bar, *v.* praise; extol; commend
a·la·bas·tro, *m.* alabaster
a·la·cri·dad, *f.* alacrity
a·lam·bre, *m.* wire. **a·lam·bre de púas (de espino)**, barbed wire, barb wire
a·lar·de, *m.* boast; review
a·lar·gar(se), *v.* elongate; extend; prolong; reach; hand
a·lar·ma, *f.* alarm; alert
a·lar·mar, *v.* alarm; startle
a·lar·mis·ta, *m.* alarmist
al·ba, *f.* dawn
al·ba·cea, *m. f.* executor
al·ba·ha·ca, *f.* basil
al·ba·ñal, *m.* sewer
al·ba·ñil, *m.* mason
al·ba·ñi·le·ría, *f.* masonry; brick work
al·ba·ri·co·que, *m.* apricot
al·ba·tros, *m.* albatross
al·ber·gar(se), *v.* lodge; shelter
al·bi·no, *m.* albino. *a.* albino
al·bón·di·gas, *f.* meatballs
al·bo·ro·tar, *v.* brawl; riot
al·bo·ro·to, *m.* brawl; uproar; disturbance; turmoil; *inf.* ruckus
ál·bum, *m.* album
al·bu·men, *m.* albumen
al·bú·mi·na, *f.* albumin
al·ca·hue·ta, *f.* bawd; procuress
al·ca·hue·te, *m.* pimp
al·ca·hue·tear, *v.* procure
al·cal·de, *m.* mayor
ál·ca·li, *m.* alkali
al·can·ce, *m.* scope; range; reach; extent
al·can·cear, *v.* spear
al·can·ta·ri·lla, *f.* culvert; sewer
al·can·zar(se), *v.* overtake; gain; reach; attain; achieve
al·ca·ra·vea, *f.* caraway
al·ce, *m.* moose; elk
al·co·ba, *f.* bedroom; alcove
al·co·hol, *m.* alcohol
Al·co·rán, Co·rán, *m.* Koran
al·dea, *f.* village
al·de·hue·la, *f.* hamlet
a·lea·ción, *f.* alloy
a·le·ga·ción, *f.* allegation
a·le·ga·do, *a.* alleged
a·le·gar, *v.* allege; argue
a·le·go·ría, *f.* allegory
a·le·grar(se), *v.* cheer; rejoice; exhilarate
a·le·gre, *a.* happy; joyous; glad; cheerful; gay; convivial; jolly; hilarious; jocund; light-hearted; blithe; airy
a·le·gre·men·te, *adv.* happily; gaily
a·le·grí·a, *f.* joy; gladness; cheer; gaie-

ty; mirth; hilarity

a·le·jar(se), v. recede; move away; separate

a·le·lu·ya, int. hallelujah

a·len·ta·dor, a. encouraging

a·len·tar, v. hearten; animate; raise (the spirits of); get well

a·ler·gia, f. allergy

a·le·ro, m. overhang; pl. eaves

a·ler·ta, a. alert. f. watchword

a·ler·tar, v. alert; put on guard

a·le·ta, f. fin

a·le·te·o, m. flutter of wings

al·fa·be·to, m. alphabet

al·fal·fa, f. alfalfa

al·fa·re·ría, f. pottery

al·fé·rez, m. ensign; subaltern

al·fi·ler, m. pin. al·fi·ler de pe·cho, broach

al·fom·bra, f. rug; carpet

al·fom·brar, v. carpet

al·for·fón, m. buckwheat

al·ga, f. alga. al·ga ma·ri·na, seaweed

ál·ge·bra, f. algebra

al·go, m. aught; something. pron. anything. adv. somewhat

al·go·dón, m. cotton. dril de al·go·dón, denim

al·gua·cil, m. bailiff; constable; marshal

al·guien, pron. somebody; someone; anybody; anyone

al·gu·no, al·gún, pron. any; anybody; anyone; pl. some. a. any; some

a·lia·do, m., a·lia·da, f. ally

a·lian·za, f. alliance; coalition; covenant

a·liar(se), v. align; ally

a·lias, m. alias. adv. alias

a·li·ca·tes, m. pliers

a·lien·to, m. breath; respiration. sin a·lien·to, breathless

a·li·ge·ra·mien·to, m. alleviation

a·li·ge·rar(se), v. lighten; relieve; leviate

a·li·men·tar(se), v. nourish; feed

a·li·men·ti·cio, a. alimentary; nutritious

a·li·men·to, m. aliment; food; pl. alimony

a·li·near(se), v. range; line; align

a·lis·ta·mien·to, m. enlistment

a·lis·tar(se), v. enlist; join up

a·li·viar, v. relieve; alleviate; ease; allay

a·li·vio, m. relief; alleviation

al·ma, f. soul; spirit

al·ma·cén, m. store; storehouse; warehouse

al·ma·na·que, m. almanac

al·me·ja, f. clam

al·me·na·ra, f. beacon

al·men·dra, f. almond; kernel

al·miar, m. haystack

al·mí·bar, m. syrup

al·mi·dón, m. starch

al·mo·ha·da, f. pillow; cushion

al·mo·ha·di·lla, f. pad; pin cushion

al·mol·dar, v. mold, mould

al·mor·zar, v. lunch

al·muer·zo, m. lunch; luncheon

a·lo·ja·mien·to, m. lodging; housing; billet; quarters

a·lo·jar(se), v. lodge; house; billet; room

al·que·ría, f. farmhouse

al·qui·lar(se), v. rent; hire; charter

al·qui·ler, m. rent; wages

al·qui·mia, f. alchemy

al·qui·trán, m. tar

al·qui·tra·nar, v. tar

al·re·de·dor, adv. around; round. prep. about; round. m. pl. outskirts; surroundings

al·ta·ne·ro, a. haughty; proud; disdainful

al·tar, m. altar

al·ta·voz, m. loudspeaker

al·te·ra·ción, f. alteration

al·te·rar(se), v. alter; change; pervert

al·ter·ca·ción, f. altercation; quarrel

ál·ter e·go, m. alter ego

al·ter·nar, v. alternate; rotate; take turns

al·ter·na·ti·va, f. alternative

al·ter·no, a. alternate

al·tí·me·tro, m. altimeter

al·ti·tud, f. altitude

al·to, a. high; tall; upper; loud. adv. aloud; high. m. height; half; (mus.) alto

al·truís·mo, m. altruism

al·tu·ra, f. height; elevation; altitude

a·lu·ci·na·ción, f. hallucination

a·lud, m. avalanche

a·lu·dir, v. allude; hint at; refer to

a·lu·mi·nio, m. aluminum

a·lum·no, m., a·lum·na, f. scholar; student; pupil; alumnus

a·lu·sión, f. allusion; reference

al·za·mien·to, m. lift; insurrection

al·zar(se), v. lift; hoist; raise; arise; rebel

a·llá, adv. there; in or to that place; thither. más a·llá, beyond

a·lla·nar, v. level; even; smooth

a·llí, adv. there; in or to that place

a·ma, f. owner; mistress

a·ma·ble, a. amiable; nice; kindly; goodhearted; lovable, loveable

a·ma·do, m., a·ma·da, f. dear; sweetheart. a. beloved; darling

a·ma·dri·gar(se), v. burrow

a·mal·ga·ma, f. amalgam

a·mal·ga·mar(se), v. amalgamate

a·ma·ne·cer, v. dawn; daybreak

a·man·te, m., f. lover

a·mar, v. love

a·mar·go, a. bitter; tart; acrid

a·mar·gu·ra, f. bitterness; sharpness

a·ma·ri·llo, a. yellow. m. yellow

a·ma·rra·de·ro, m. berth; fastening

a·ma·rrar, v. moor; fasten; tie up

a·mar·ti·llar, v. cock a gun; hammer

a·ma·sar, v. mash; knead; mix

a·ma·tis·ta, f. amethyst

a·ma·to·rio, a. amatory

a·ma·zo·na, f. amazon; horse-woman

ám·bar, m. amber

am·bi·ción, f. ambition

am·bi·cio·so, a. ambitious

am·bi·dex·tro, a. ambidextrous

am·bien·te, a. atmosphere; environment

am·bi·güe·dad, f. ambiguity

am·bi·guo, a. ambiguous; equivocal; uncertain

am·bi·va·len·cia, f. ambivalence

am·blar, v. amble

am·bos, a. both. pron. both

am·bri·no, a. amber

am·bu·lan·te, a. ambulatory; mobile; traveling

a·mén, int. amen

a·me·na·za, f. threat; menace

a·me·na·zar, v. threaten; menace; loom

a·me·ni·dad, f. amenity; pleasantness

a·me·ri·ca·na, f. jacket

a·me·ri·ca·no, a. American

a·mi·ba, m. amoeba, ameba

a·mi·ga, f. friend; girl friend

a·míg·da·la, f. tonsil

a·mig·da·li·tis, f. tonsillitis

a·mi·go, m. friend, boyfriend; pl. archaic. kith

a·mis·tad, f. friendship

a·mis·tar(se), v. befriend; become friends

a·mis·to·so, a. friendly; amicable

am·ne·sia, f. amnesia

am·nis·tía, f. amnesty

a·mo, m. employer; boss; master; owner

a·mo·nes·tar, v. caution; warn; admonish

a·mo·ni·a·co, m. ammonia

a·mon·to·nar(se), v. heap; amass; mound; hoard; bank up; drift; huddle

amor, m. love; lover. **a·mor pro·pio**, conceit

a·mo·ral, a. amoral

a·mor·da·zar, v. gag; muzzle

a·mor·fo, a. amorphous

a·mo·río, m. romance; love affair

a·mo·ro·so, a. amorous

a·mor·ti·guar, v. deaden; cushion; buff

a·mor·ti·za·ción, f. amortization; redemption

a·mor·ti·zar, v. amortize

a·mo·ti·nar(se), v. mutiny; riot; incite to revolt

am·pe·rio, m. ampere

am·plia·ción, f. enlargement

am·pli·fi·car, v. amplify

am·plio, a. ample; extensive; broad

am·pli·tud, f. amplitude; fullness

am·po·lla, f. blister

am·pu·lo·si·dad, f. bombast; verbosity

am·pu·ta·ción, f. amputation

am·pu·tar, v. amputate

a·mu·le·to, m. amulet; charm

a·na·car·do, m. cashew

a·na·con·da, f. anaconda

a·na·cro·nis·mo, m. anachronism

a·na·gra·ma, m. anagram

a·nal, a. anal

a·na·les, m. pl. annals

a·nal·fa·be·tis·mo, m. illiteracy

a·nal·fa·be·to, m., **a·nal·fa·be·ta**, f. illiterate. a. illiterate

a·nal·gé·si·co, m. analgesic. a. analgesic

a·ná·li·sis, m. analysis; review; breakdown

a·na·li·za·dor, m. analyst

a·na·li·zar, v. analyze

a·na·lo·gía, f. analogy

a·na·quel, m. ledge; shelf

a·na·ran·ja·do, a. orange

a·nar·quía, f. anarchy

a·nar·quis·mo, m. anarchism

a·nar·quis·ta, m., f. anarchist

a·na·te·ma, m. anathema

a·na·to·mía, f. anatomy

an·ca, f. haunch; rump

an·cia·no, a. old; aged. m. old man

an·cla, f. anchor

an·co·ra, m. anchor

an·cho, a. broad; wide; roomy; loose

an·choa, f. anchovy

an·chu·ra, f. width; breadth; fullness

an·da·mio, m. scaffold; stage

an·dar, v. walk; ambulate; go; work, as machines. m. gait

an·dén, m. platform; sidewalk

an·do·rrear, v. gad about; wander about

an·dra·jos, m. pl. tatters

a·néc·do·ta, f. anecdote

a·nea, f. bulrush

a·ne·gar(se), v. drown; flood

a·ne·mia, f. anemia, anaemia

a·ne·mó·me·tro, m. anemometer

a·nes·te·sia, f. anesthesia

a·nes·té·si·co, a. anesthetic. m. anesthetic

a·ne·xar, v. annex; append

a·ne·xión, f. annexation

an·fi·bio, a. amphibious. m. amphibian

an·fi·tea·tro, *m.* amphitheater

an·fi·trión, *m.* host

án·gel, *m.* angel

an·gé·li·co, *a.* angelic

an·glo·sa·jón, *m.,* **an·glo·sa·jo·na,** *f.* Anglo-Saxon. *a.* Anglo-Saxon

an·go·ra, *f.* angora

an·gos·to, *a.* narrow

an·gui·la, *f.* eel

an·gu·lar, *a.* angular

án·gu·lo, *m.* angle; corner

an·gu·lo·so, *a.* angular

an·gus·tia, *f.* agony; anguish; woe; heart break; heartache

an·gus·tio·so, *a.* harrowing; anguished

an·he·lar, *v.* long for; crave; hanker

an·he·lo, *m.* longing; hankering; aspiration

an·hi·dro, *a.* anhydrous

a·ni·dar, *v.* nest; shelter

a·ni·llo, *m.* ring

a·ni·ma·ción, *f.* animation; life; vivacity

a·ni·ma·do, *a.* animated; lively; sprightly; animate

a·ni·mad·ver·sión, *f.* animadversion

a·ni·mal, *m.* animal. *a.* animal. **a·ni·mal do·més·ti·co,** pet

a·ni·mar(se), *v.* animate; liven; rouse; encourage

á·ni·mo, *m.* spirit; courage; resolution

a·ni·mo·si·dad, *f.* animosity

a·ni·ña·do, *a.* childish

a·ni·qui·la·ción, *f.* annihilation

a·ni·qui·lar(se), *v.* annihilate; destroy; decline; waste away

a·nís, *m.* anise

a·ni·ver·sa·rio, *m.* anniversary

a·no, *m.* anus

a·no·che, *adv.* last night

a·no·che·cer, *v.* get dark. *m.* nightfall; evening

á·no·do, *m.* anode

a·no·ma·lía, *f.* anomaly

a·nó·ma·lo, *a.* anomalous

a·nó·ni·mo, *a.* anonymous. *m.* anonymity

a·nor·mal, *a.* abnormal; unnatural; subnormal

a·no·tar, *v.* annotate; note down; enter

an·sia, *f.* anxiety; anguish; worry; eagerness; thirst; longing

an·sio·so, *a.* anxious; eager

an·ta·go·nis·ta, *m., f.* antagonist

an·tár·ti·co, *a.* antarctic

an·te, *prep.* before. *m.* suede; buckskin; buff

an·te·bra·zo, *m.* forearm

an·te·cá·ma·ra, *f.* anteroom

an·te·ce·den·te, *m.* antecedent; *pl.* background. *a.* previous

an·te·ce·der, *v.* antecede; precede

an·te·da·tar, *v.* antedate

an·te·di·lu·via·no, *a.* antediluvian

an·te·ma·no, *adv.* beforehand. **de an·te·ma·no,** in advance

an·te·me·ri·dia·no, *a.* antemeridian. Abbr. a.m.

an·te·na, *f.* antenna; aerial; feeler

an·te·o·jo, *m.* eyeglass; *pl.* goggles

an·te·pa·sa·do, *m.* forefather; ancestor

an·te·ra, *f.* anther

an·te·rior, *a.* anterior; former; prior; above; preceding; fore

an·tes, *adv.* before; heretofore. **an·tes de,** before. **an·tes de que,** before; ere

an·ti, *prefix.* anti

an·ti·á·ci·do, *m.* antacid

an·ti·bió·ti·co, *m.* antibiotic. *a.* antibiotic

an·ti·ci·pa·ción, *f.* anticipation

an·ti·ci·par(se), *v.* advance; anticipate

an·ti·clí·max, *m.* anticlimax

an·ti·con·cep·cio·nal, *a.* contraceptive

an·ti·con·cep·cio·nis·mo, *m.* contraception; birth control

an·ti·cua·do, *a.* antiquated; old-fashioned; obsolete; *inf.* square

an·ti·cuar, *v.* antiquate

an·ti·cuer·po, *m.* antibody

an·tí·do·to, *m.* antidote

an·ti·fo·na, *f.* anthem; antiphony

an·ti·gua·men·te, *adv.* formerly; in old times

an·ti·güe·dad, *f.* antiquity; antique

an·ti·guo, *a.* antique; old; ancient; erstwhile

an·tí·lo·pe, *m.* antelope

an·ti·pa·tía, *f.* antipathy; dislike

an·tí·po·das, *m. pl.* antipodes

an·ti·se·mi·tis·mo, *m.* anti-Semitism

an·ti·sép·ti·co, *a.* antiseptic. *m.* antiseptic

an·ti·so·cial, *a.* antisocial

an·tí·te·sis, *f.* antithesis

an·ti·to·xi·na, *f.* antitoxin

an·to·lo·gía, *f.* anthology

an·tó·ni·mo, *m.* antonym

an·tor·cha, *f.* torch

an·tra·ci·ta, *f.* anthracite

an·tro·poi·de, *a.* anthropoid

an·tro·po·lo·gía, *f.* anthropology

an·tro·pó·lo·go, *m.* anthropologist

a·nual, *a.* annual. *a.* annual

a·nu·blar(se), *v.* cloud; blight; get dark

a·nu·dar, *v.* knot

a·nu·la·ción, *f.* annulment; repeal

a·nu·lar, v. annul; cancel; undo

a·nun·cia·ción, f. annunciation; announcement

a·nun·ciar, v. advertise; announce; annunciate; forbode

a·nun·cio, m. announcement; notice; bulletin

a·ña·di·du·ra, f. addition

a·ña·dir, v. add; increase; affix

a·ñil, m. indigo; bluing

a·ño, m. year. a·ño bi·sies·to, leap year. a·ño de luz, light year

a·ño·ran·za, f. yearning; hankering

aor·ta, f. aorta

a·pa·ci·ble, a. gentle

a·pa·ci·guar(se), v. placate; appease; calm down

a·pa·ga·do, adv. out; dull; spiritless

a·pa·gar(se), v. quench; muffle; put out; go out

a·pa·la·brar, v. bespeak; engage; agree

a·pa·lear, v. batter; beat

a·pa·ra·dor, m. dresser; buffet

a·pa·ra·to, m. apparatus; device; gadget

a·par·car, v. park

a·pa·rear(se), v. mate; pair

a·pa·re·cer(se), v. appear; show up; come; haunt

a·pa·re·jar(se), v. prepare; rig out; get ready

a·pa·ren·te, a. apparent; ostensible

a·pa·ri·ción, f. appearance

a·pa·rien·cia, f. appearance; guise; pl. looks

a·par·ta·men·to, m. apartment

a·par·tar(se), v. separate; divide; avert; remove; estrange

a·par·te, adv. apart; asunder. m. aside. a·par·te de, apart from

a·pa·sio·na·do, a. passionate; ardent; fiery; vehement

a·pa·tía, f. apathy

a·pe·la·ción, f. appeal

a·pe·lan·te, m., f. appellant

a·pe·lar, v. appeal

a·pe·lli·do, m. name; surname

a·pe·nar(se), v. pain; grieve

a·pe·nas, adv. hardly; barely; just

a·pen·dec·to·mía, f. appendectomy

a·pén·di·ce, m. appendix; appendage

a·pen·di·ci·tis, f. appendicitis

a·peo, m. survey

a·pe·ten·cia, f. appetite; relish

a·pe·ti·to, m. appetite

a·pe·ti·to·so, a. appetizing

á·pi·ce, m. apex; top; vertex

a·pi·ñar(se), v. jam; crowd together

a·pio, m. celery

a·pi·so·na·do·ra, f. steamroller

a·plas·tan·te, a. crushing

a·plas·tar(se), v. crush; flatten

a·plau·dir, v. applaud; clap; cheer

a·plau·so, m. applause; cheer

a·pla·za·mien·to, m. deferment; adjournment

a·pla·zar, v. postpone; procrastinate; delay; defer

a·pli·ca·ción, f. application

a·pli·car(se), v. apply; devote to

a·plo·mo, m. poise; aplomb

a·po·ca·lip·sis, m. apocalypse

a·po·dar, v. nickname

a·po·de·ra·do, m. proxy; commissioner

a·po·de·rar(se), v. seize; empower; grant power of attorney

a·po·do, m. nickname

a·po·geo, m. apogee; inf. heyday; heydey

a·po·lo·gía, f. apology; defense

a·po·ple·jía, f. apoplexy

a·po·plé·ti·co, a. apoplectic

a·po·rrear(se), v. club; cudgel; beat; toil

a·po·si·ción, f. apposition

a·pos·tar, v. bet; station

a·pós·ta·ta, m., f. apostate

a·pós·tol, m. apostle

a·pos·tó·li·co, a. apostolic

a·pós·tro·fo, m. apostrophe

a·po·yar(se), v. prop; support; rest on; bolster; back; second

a·po·yo, m. support; prop

a·pre·ciar, v. appreciate; value; regard

a·pre·cio, m. estimation; appraisal; appreciation

a·pre·hen·sión, f. apprehension

a·pren·der, v. learn. a·pren·der de me·mo·ria, memorize

a·pren·diz, m., a·pren·di·za, f. apprentice. po·ner de a·pren·diz, apprentice

a·pre·sa·dor, m., a·pre·sa·do·ra, f. captor

a·pre·sar, v. capture; seize

a·pre·su·ra·do, a. hasty

a·pre·su·rar(se), v. hurry; quicken; bustle

a·pre·tar, v. push; press; crowd; clench; clutch

a·pre·tón, m. grip; squeeze; tighten. a·pre·tón de ma·nos, handshake

a·prie·to, m. fix

a·pro·ba·ción, f. approbation; approval

a·pro·ba·do, a. approved; inf. O.K.

a·pro·bar, v. approve; pass. no a·pro·bar, flunk

a·pro·pia·do, a. appropriate; proper; suitable

a·pro·piar(se), v. appropriate; fit; borrow

a·pro·ve·char(se), v. avail; utilize; take advantage of; benefit; profit

a·pro·xi·ma·ción, f. approximation;

approach

a·pro·xi·ma·do, *a.* approximate

a·pro·xi·mar(se), *v.* approximate; approach

ap·ti·tud, *f.* aptitude; ability

ap·to, *a.* apt; suitable

a·pues·ta, *f.* bet

a·pun·tar(se), *v.* point; aim; note; jot down

a·pun·te, *m.* cue; memorandum; *pl.* notes

a·pu·ña·lar, *v.* stab; thrust

a·pu·rar(se), *v.* fret; worry; refine; verify

a·pu·ro, *m.* hardship; predicament; plight; *pl.* straits; *inf.* jam

a·quel, *a., m.*, **a·que·lla**, *a. f.* that; *pl.*, **a·que·llos**, *m.*, **a·que·llas**, *f.* those

a·quél, *pron. m.*, **a·qué·lla**, *pron. f.* that one; *pl.*, **a·qué·llos**, *m.*, **a·qué·llas**, *f.* those

a·quí, *adv.* here. **de a·quí en a·de·lan·te**, henceforth, henceforward

a·quie·tar, *v.* lull; quiet; tranquilize; still; allay

á·ra·be, *a.* Arab; Arabian. *m., f.* Arab

a·ra·do, *m.* plow

a·rán·da·no, *m.* cranberry

a·ra·ña, *f.* spider. **a·ra·ña de lu·ces**, chandelier

ar·bi·tra·je, *m.* arbitration

ar·bi·trar(se), *v.* arbitrate; umpire; manage

ar·bi·tra·rio, *a.* arbitrary

ár·bi·tro, *m.* referee; umpire; arbiter

ár·bol, *m.* tree

ar·bo·le·da, *f.* grove

ar·bó·re·o, *a.* arboreal

ar·bus·to, *m.* bush; shrub; *pl.* shrubbery

ar·ca, *f.* ark; box; chest

ar·ca·da, *f.* arcade

ar·cai·co, *a.* archaic

ar·cán·gel, *m.* archangel

ar·ci·lla, *f.* clay

ar·ci·pres·te, *m.* archpriest

ar·co, *m.* arc; arch; bow. **ar·co i·ris**, rainbow

ar·chi·du·que, *m.* archduke

ar·chi·du·que·sa, *f.* archduchess

ar·chi·pié·la·go, *m.* archipelago

ar·chi·var, *v.* file

ar·chi·vo, *m.* archive(s); file; *pl.* records

ar·der(se), *v.* blaze; burn; burn up. **ar·der sin lla·mas**, smolder

ar·did, *m.* ruse

ar·dien·do, *a.* afire. *adv.* afire

ar·dien·te, *a.* ardent; aglow; burning; fiery

ar·dor, *m.* ardor; fire; heat

ar·duo, *a.* arduous

á·rea, *f.* area

a·re·na, *f.* sand; grit. **a·re·na mo·ve·di·za**, quicksand

a·ren·ga, *f.* harangue

a·ren·gar, *v.* harangue

a·re·nis·ca, *f.* sandstone

a·re·no·so, *a.* sandy; gritty

ar·ga·ma·sa, *f.* plaster

ar·go, *m.* argon

ar·go·lla, *f.* ring

ar·got, *m.* slang

ar·gu·men·ta·dor, *a.* argumentative

ar·gu·men·to, *m.* argument

a·ria, *f.* aria

a·ri·dez, *f.* aridity; dryness

á·ri·do, *a.* arid; dry

a·ris·to·cra·cia, *f.* aristocracy

a·ris·tó·cra·ta, *m., f.* aristocrat

a·ris·to·crá·ti·co, *a.* aristocratic

a·rit·mé·ti·ca, *f.* arithmetic

a·rit·mé·ti·co, *m.* arithmetician. *a.* arithmetic

ar·ma, *f.* arm; weapon. **ar·ma de fue·go**, firearm; gun

ar·ma·da, *f.* armada

ar·ma·di·llo, *m.* armadillo

ar·ma·du·ra, *f.* armor; frame

ar·ma·men·to, *m.* armament

ar·mar(se), *v.* arm; get ready

ar·ma·rio, *m.* armoire; buffet; cupboard; closet

ar·ma·zón, *f.* bedstead; skeleton

ar·me·ría, *f.* armory; gunsmith

ar·mi·ño, *m.* ermine

ar·mis·ti·cio, *m.* armistice

ar·mo·nía, *f.* harmony; accord

ar·mó·ni·ca, *f.* harmonica

ar·mo·nio·so, *a.* harmonious

ar·mo·ni·zar, *v.* harmonize

a·ro, *m.* rim; ring; hoop

a·ro·ma, *m.* aroma; bouquet; fragrance

a·ro·má·ti·co, *a.* aromatic

ar·pa, *f.* harp

ar·peo, *m.* grapple; grappling iron

ar·pía, *f.* shrew; vixen

ar·pi·lle·ra, *f.* burlap; sackcloth

ar·pis·ta, *m., f.* harpist

ar·pón, *m.* harpoon; grapple; gaff

ar·po·near, *v.* harpoon

ar·quear(se), *v.* arch; retch

ar·queo·lo·gía, *f.* archaeology; archeology

ar·que·ro, *m.* archer

ar·que·ti·po, *m.* archetype

ar·qui·tec·to, *m.* architect

ar·qui·tec·tó·ni·co, *a.* architectural

ar·qui·tec·tu·ra, *f.* architecture

a·rran·car, *v.* rip out; pull up; wrest; start

a·rras·trar(se), *v.* draw; pull; drag; trail; creep; crawl

a·rre·ba·tar(se), *v.* grab; snatch; get carried away

a·rre·ba·ti·ña, f. scrimmage

a·rre·glar(se), v. arrange; order; fix; set; settle; marshal

a·rre·glo, m. arrangement; compromise

a·rre·mo·li·nar(se), v. swirl; crowd

a·rren·da·jo, m. jay

a·rren·dar, v. lease; rent

a·rreos, m. pl. paraphernalia; trappings; harness

a·rre·pen·ti·do, a. sorry; contrite

a·rre·pen·ti·mien·to, m. contrition; repentance

a·rre·pen·tir·se, v. repent; regret

a·rri·ba, adv. up; above; upstairs. de a·rri·ba a·ba·jo, upside down

a·rrien·do, m. lease

a·rries·ga·do, a. venturesome; daring; dangerous; hazardous; desperate

a·rries·gar(se), v. risk; venture; dare; hazard; jeopardize

a·rri·mar(se), v. stow; bring close; snuggle; nestle

a·rrin·co·nar(se), v. corner; lay aside; retire

a·rro·di·llar(se), v. kneel; kneel down

a·rro·gan·cia, f. arrogance; hauteur; haughtiness

a·rro·gan·te, a. arrogant; supercilious; haughty; proud

a·rro·jar(se), v. throw; fling; hurl; pelt; emit; expel

a·rro·llar(se), v. curl; coil; roll up

a·rro·yo, m. stream; brook; gutter

a·rroz, m. rice

a·rru·gar(se), v. pucker; rumple; crinkle; wrinkle

a·rrui·nar(se), v. ruin; destroy; spoil; wreck

a·rru·llar(se), v. coo; rock to sleep

ar·se·nal, m. arsenal

ar·sé·ni·co, m. arsenic

ar·te, m., f. art; craft; skill. be·llas ar·tes, fine arts

ar·te·ria, f. artery

ar·te·rial, a. arterial

ar·te·sa·nía, f. handicraft; craftsmanship

ar·te·sa·no, m. craftsman

ár·ti·co, a. arctic

ar·ti·cu·la·ción, f. articulation

ar·ti·cu·la·do, a. articulate

ar·ti·cu·lar, v. articulate

ar·tí·cu·lo, m. article; item. ar·tí·cu·lo de fon·do, editorial

ar·ti·fi·cial, a. artificial

ar·ti·lle·ría, f. artillery

ar·tis·ta, m., f. artist

ar·tís·ti·co, a. artistic

ar·trí·ti·co, a. arthritic

ar·tri·tis, f. arthritis

ar·zo·bis·po, m. archbishop

as, m. ace

a·sal·tan·te, m. assailant

a·sal·tar, v. attack; molest; inf. mug

a·sal·to, m. assault; attack

a·sam·blea, f. assembly; meeting

a·sar(se), v. roast. a·sar en·te·ro, barbecue. a·sar a la pa·rri·lla, broil; grill

as·bes·to, m. asbestos; asbestus

as·cen·der, v. ascend; advance; promote

as·cen·sión, f. ascension; ascent

as·cen·sor, m. elevator

as·ce·ta, m., f. ascetic

as·cé·ti·co, a. ascetic

as·ce·tis·mo, m. asceticism

as·co, m. disgust; revulsion

a·sea·do, a. cleanly

a·se·diar, v. besiege

a·se·gu·rar(se), v. secure; fasten; insure; assure; anchor

a·se·me·jar(se), v. resemble; make similar

a·sen·tar(se), v. sit down; seat

a·sen·ti·mien·to, m. assent

a·sen·tir, v. assent

a·se·si·nar, v. assassinate; murder

a·se·si·na·to, m. assassination; murder

a·se·si·no, m. assassin; cutthroat

a·se·ve·rar, v. asseverate

a·se·xual, a. asexual

as·fi·xia, f. asphyxiation

as·fi·xiar(se), v. asphyxiate; suffocate

as·fal·to, m. asphalt

a·sí, adv. so; thus. a·sí a·sí, so-so

a·si·dua·men·te, adv. assiduously

a·si·duo, a. assiduous; diligent

a·sien·to, m. seat

a·sig·na·ción, f. assignment

a·sig·nar, v. assign; allocate; allot

a·si·lo, m. sanctuary; asylum; haven

a·si·mien·to, m. seizure; grasp

a·si·mi·la·ción, f. assimilation

a·si·mi·lar(se), v. assimilate

a·si·mis·mo, adv. likewise

a·sir(se), v. grab; grip; take hold of

a·sis·ten·te, m. assistant; helper; orderly

a·sis·tir, v. attend

as·ma, f. asthma

as·má·ti·co, a. asthmatic

a·si·nal, a. asinine

a·so·cia·ción, f. association; society; combine

a·so·cia·do, a. associate; fellow. m. associate

a·so·ciar(se), v. associate; consort with; pool

a·so·mar(se), v. loom; show

a·som·brar(se), v. astonish; amaze; astound

a·som·bro, m. amazement; astonish-

ment
a·so·nan·cia, *f.* assonance
as·pec·to, *m.* aspect; configuration; *usu. pl.* looks
as·pe·re·za, *f.* asperity; severity
ás·pe·ro, *a.* harsh; rough; sour; brusque, brusk; surly
ás·pid, *m.* asp
as·pi·ra·ción, *f.* aspiration; breath
as·pi·ra·dor de pol·vo, *m.* vacuum cleaner
as·pi·ran·te, *m.* candidate; applicant
as·pi·rar, *v.* inhale; breathe; aspire to
as·pi·ri·na, *f.* aspirin
as·que·ro·so, *a.* nasty; disgusting
as·ta, *f.* antler; flagstaff
ás·ta·co, *m.* crayfish
as·ter, *m.* aster
as·te·ris·co, *m.* asterisk
as·ti·lla, *f.* splinter; chip
as·ti·llar, *v.* chip
as·tro·lo·gía, *f.* astrology
as·tró·lo·go, *m.* astrologer
as·tro·nau·ta, *m., f.* astronaut; spaceman; spacewoman
as·tro·na·ve, *f.* spaceship
as·tro·no·mía, *f.* astronomy
as·tró·no·mo, *m.* astronomer
as·tu·cia, *f.* craftiness; cunning; guile
as·tu·to, *a.* astute; sly; artful; crafty; foxy; canny; knowing; subtle; cunning
a·su·mir, *v.* assume; don
a·sun·ción, *f.* assumption
a·sun·to, *m.* matter; affair; issue; business; concern
a·sus·tar(se), *v.* scare; frighten; be startled
a·ta·car, *v.* attack; assault; sic; strike; charge
a·ta·jo, *m.* shortcut
a·ta·que, *m.* attack; seizure. **a·ta·que aé·re·o,** airraid. **a·ta·que ful·mi·nan·te,** stroke
a·tar(se), *v.* bind; tie; rope; lash; lace; brace
a·tar·de·cer, *v.* get dark. *m.* dusk
a·tas·car(se), *v.* clog; stop up; stall
a·taúd, *m.* coffin; casket
a·ta·viar(se), *v.* array
a·teís·mo, *m.* atheism
a·te·mo·ri·za·do, *a.* afraid
a·ten·ción, *f.* attention; notice; kindness
a·ten·der, *v.* attend to; heed; cater
a·ten·to, *a.* attentive; intent; considerate
a·teo, *m.*, **a·tea,** *f.* atheist
a·te·rrar(se), *v.* terrify; appall, appal; land
a·te·rri·za·je, *m.* touchdown; landing
a·te·rri·zar, *v.* land
a·te·rro·ri·zar, *v.* terrorize; terrify

a·tes·tar(se), *v.* clutter; stuff
a·tes·ti·guar, *v.* testify; attest
a·te·za·do, *a.* swarthy
a·tie·sar(se), *v.* stiffen; tighten
a·tí·pi·co, *a.* atypical
a·ti·zar, *v.* poke; stoke
at·las, *m.* atlas
a·tle·ta, *m., f.* athlete
a·lé·ti·co, *a.* athletic
at·mós·fe·ra, *f.* atmosphere
at·mos·fé·ri·co, *a.* atmospheric
a·to·lón, *m.* atoll
a·to·lon·dra·do, *a.* reckless; stunned
a·tó·mi·co, *a.* atomic
a·to·mi·zar, *v.* atomize
á·to·mo, *m.* atom
a·tor·men·tar, *v.* harass; torment; anguish; tantalize; bait
a·tor·ni·llar, *v.* screw on
a·trac·ción, *f.* attraction
a·trac·ti·vo, *a.* attractive; fetching; engaging
a·traer, *v.* attract; engage; draw; lure; appeal to; allure
a·trás, *adv.* back; aback; backward; behind
a·tra·sa·do, *a.* late; behind hand; backward(s)
a·tra·ve·sar, *v.* traverse; cross; go through
a·tre·ver·se, *v.* dare
a·tre·vi·do, *a.* daring; forward
a·tre·vi·mien·to, *m.* daring; audacity
a·tri·bu·ción, *f.* attribution
a·tri·buir, *v.* attribute to; ascribe
a·trin·che·rar(se), *v.* entrench
a·tro·ci·dad, *f.* atrocity; outrage; cruelty; enormity
a·tro·fia, *f.* atrophy
a·troz, *a.* atrocious; heinous
a·tún, *m.* tuna
a·tur·dir(se), *v.* stun; daze; bewilder; fluster; muddle
au·daz, *a.* audacious
au·daz·men·te, *adv.* boldly
au·di·ción, *f.* audition; concert
au·dien·cia, *f.* audience
au·di·to·rio, *m.* auditorium
au·gus·to, *a.* grand; august
au·llar, *v.* howl; bay
au·lli·do, *m.* howl; bay
au·men·tar(se), *v.* increase; augment; grow; magnify; enhance
au·men·to, *m.* increase; raise; enlargement
aun, *adv.* even
aún, *adv.* yet; still
aun·que, *conj.* though; although; albeit
áu·reo, *a.* aureate
au·reo·la, *f.* halo
au·ri·cu·la, *f.* auricle
au·ri·ga, *m.* charioteer
au·ro·ra, *f.* aurora; dawn

au·sen·te, *a.* absent; missing. *m., f.* absentee

aus·pi·cio, *m.* auspice

aus·te·ri·dad, *f.* austerity

aus·te·ro, *a.* austere; stern; dour

au·ten·ti·car, *v.* authenticate

au·ten·ti·ci·dad, *f.* authenticity

au·tén·ti·co, *a.* authentic; genuine

au·to·bio·gra·fía, *f.* autobiography

au·to·bió·gra·fo, *m.* autobiographer

au·to·bús, *m.* bus; omnibus

au·to·cra·cia, *f.* autocracy

au·tó·cra·ta, *m., f.* autocrat

au·tó·gra·fo, *m.* autograph

au·tó·ma·ta, *m.* robot; automaton

au·to·má·ti·co, *a.* automatic

au·to·ma·ti·za·ción, *f.* automation

au·to·mó·vil, *m.* automobile; car; *inf.* auto

au·to·no·mía, *f.* autonomy; self-government

au·tó·no·mo, *a.* autonomous

au·to·pis·ta, *f.* freeway; highway.
au·to·pis·ta de pea·je, turnpike; tollroad

au·top·sia, *f.* autopsy; post-mortem

au·tor, *m.* au·to·ra, *f.* author; writer

au·to·ri·dad, *f.* authority

au·to·ri·za·ción, *f.* authorization

au·to·ri·zar, *v.* authorize; sanction; empower

au·xi·liar, *a.* auxiliary. *m., f.* assistant. *v.* help

au·xi·lio, *m.* aid

a·van·ce, *m.* advance

a·van·za·do, *a.* advanced; early

a·van·zar(se), *v.* advance; promote

a·va·ri·cia, *f.* avarice; greed; cupidity

a·va·ro, *m.* miser. *a.* greedy; avaricious

a·ve, *f.* bird; fowl. a·ves de co·rral, poultry

a·ve·lla·no, *m.* hazel

a·ve·na, *f.* oats

a·ve·ni·da, *f.* avenue; boulevard

a·ven·ta·jar(se), *v.* excel; surpass

a·ven·tu·ra, *f.* adventure; escapade.
a·ven·tu·ra a·mo·ro·sa, affair

a·ven·tu·re·ro, *a.* adventuresome

a·ven·tu·rar(se), *v.* venture; dare; stake

a·ven·tu·re·ro, *a.* venturesome

a·ver·gon·za·do, *a.* ashamed

a·ver·gon·zar(se), *v.* shame; abash; be embarrassed

a·ve·ría, *f.* damage; breakdown

a·ve·ri·guar, *v.* ascertain; find out

a·ver·sión, *f.* aversion; distaste

a·ves·truz, *m.* ostrich

a·via·ción, *f.* aviation

a·via·dor, *m.* aviator; flyer, flier

á·vi·do, *a.* avid

a·vión, *m.* airplane; plane; aircraft

a·vión a reac·ción, jet

a·víos, *m. pl.* kit

a·vi·sar, *v.* advise; inform; counsel

a·vi·so, *m.* notice; announcement; warning; tip

a·vi·var(se), *v.* enliven; brighten

a·xio·ma, *m.* axiom

a·xio·má·ti·co, *a.* axiomatic

a·xis, *m.* axis

a·yu·da, *f.* help; assistance; aid

a·yu·dan·te, *m.*, a·yu·dan·ta, *f.* adjutant; assistant

a·yu·dar, *v.* help; aid; assist; abet

a·yu·nar, *v.* fast

a·yu·no, *m.* fast

a·za·ba·che, *m.* jet

a·za·dón, *m.* hoe

a·za·do·nar, *v.* hoe

a·za·fa·ta, *f.* stewardess

a·za·frán, *m.* crocus

a·zar, *m.* chance; luck; hazard. al a·zar, at random

a·za·ro·so, *a.* risky; eventful

a·zo·ga·do, *a.* a fidgety

a·zo·tar, *v.* flog; lash

a·zú·car, *m.* sugar

a·zu·ca·rar, *v.* sweeten; add sugar to

a·zue·la, *f.* adz, adze

a·zu·fre, *m.* brimstone

a·zul, *a.* blue. *m.* blue. a·zul ma·ri·no o de mar, navy, also navy blue

a·zu·lar, *v.* color blue

B

ba·bear, *v.* slobber; drool

ba·bel, *m.* babel; confusion. Also Babel

ba·be·ro, *m.* bib

ba·bor, *m.* port

ba·bo·sear, *v.* slobber

ba·ca·lao, *m.* codfish; cod

ba·ca·nal, *a.* bacchanalian. *f.* bacchanalia

ba·ci·lo, *m.* bacillus

bac·te·ria, *f.* bacterium

bac·te·rio·lo·gía, *f.* bacteriology

bac·te·rió·lo·go, *m.* bacteriologist

ba·chi·lle·ra·to, *m.* baccalaureate

ba·ga·je, *m.* baggage; luggage

ba·ga·te·la, *f.* trifle; trinket

ba·hía, *f.* bay

bai·la·dor, *m.*, bai·la·do·ra, *f.* dancer

bai·lar, *v.* dance

bai·la·ri·na, *f.* ballerina

bai·le, *m.* dance; ball

ba·ja, *f.* casualty; drop

ba·jar(se), *v.* lower; subside; fall; descend; alight

ba·jo, *adv.* lowly; below. *a.* small; short; low; deep; bass. *prep.* underneath; under. *m.* bass

ba·jón, *m.* (*mus.*) bassoon; decline;

slump
ba.la, *f.* bullet; bale
ba.la.da, *f.* ballad
ba.la.dro.na.da, *f.* boast
ba.lan.cear(se), *v.* teeter; swing balance
ba.lan.za, *f.* balance; scale
ba.lar, *v.* baa; bleat
ba.laus.tra.da, *f.* balustrade
bal.bu.cear, *v.* stutter; babble
bal.cón, *m.* balcony
bal.da.quín, *v.* canopy
ba.li.do, *m.* baa; bleat
ba.lís.ti.ca, *f.* ballistics
ba.lís.ti.co, *a.* ballistic
bal.nea.rio, *m.* spa
ba.lon.ces.to, *m.* basketball
ba.lo.ta, *f.* ballot
bal.sa, *f.* raft; balsa
bál.sa.mo, *m.* balsam; balm
ba.luar.te, *m.* bulwark; bastion
ba.lle.na, *f.* whale
ba.lles.te.ría, *f.* archery
ba.llet, *m.* ballet
bam.bo.lear(se), *v.* sway; wobble
bam.bú, *m.* bamboo
ba.na.na, *f.* banana
ban.ca, *f.* banking
ban.ca.rro.ta, *f.* bankruptcy
ban.co, *m.* bank; bench; stripe; strip; band; pew
ban.da.da, *f.* bevy; flock
ban.de.ra, *f.* flag; ensign; colors
ban.di.do, *m.* bandit
ban.jo, *m.* banjo
ban.que.ta, *f.* stool
ban.que.te, *m.* banquet; feast
ban.que.tear, *v.* feast; banquet
ba.ñar(se), *v.* bathe; suffuse
ba.ñis.ta, *m., f.* bather
ba.ño, *m.* bath; bathtub
bar, *m.* bar
ba.ra.ja, *f.* deck of cards
ba.ra.jar, *v.* shuffle (cards)
ba.ra.to, *a.* cheap; inexpensive. *adv.* cheap; cheaply
bar.ba, *f.* chin; beard; stubble; *pl.* whiskers
bar.ba.coa, *f.* barbecue
bar.ba.do, *a.* bearded
bar.ba.ri.dad, *f.* barbarity; outrage
bár.ba.ro, *m., bár.ba.ra,* *f.* barbarian; savage. *a.* barbaric
bar.bear, *v.* shave
bar.be.ro, *m.* barber
bar.bi.tu.ra.to, *m.* barbiturate
bar.co, *m.* boat; vessel; ship
bar.dar, *v.* thatch
bar.do, *m.* bard
ba.rio, *m.* barium
ba.ri.to.no, *m.* baritone
bar.niz, *m.* glaze; varnish
bar.ni.zar, *v.* glaze; varnish

ba.ro.mé.tri.co, *a.* barometric
ba.ró.me.tro, *m.* barometer
ba.rón, *m.* baron
ba.ro.ne.sa, *f.* baroness
ba.rra, *f.* bar
ba.rra.ca, *f.* hut; booth
ba.rran.ca, *f.* gully; ravine
ba.rrer, *v.* sweep
ba.rre.ra, *f.* barrier; barricade; barrage
ba.rri.ca.da, *f.* barricade
ba.rri.ga, *f.* belly
ba.rril, *m.* cask; barrel
ba.rrio, *m.* neighborhood; quarter
ba.rro, *m.* mud; clay; pimple
ba.ro.co, *a.* baroque
ba.sal.to, *m.* basalt
ba.sar, *v.* base
ba.se, *f.* base; foundation; basis
bá.si.co, *a.* basic; basal
ba.sí.li.ca, *f.* basilica
bás.quet.bol, *m.* basketball
bas.tan.te, *a.* enough; sufficient. *adv.* enough
bas.tar, *v.* suffice; be enough
bas.tar.dear, *v.* bastardize; debase
bas.tar.do, *m.,* **bas.tar.da,** *f.* bastard. *a.* bastard
bas.tar.di.lla, *f.* italics
bas.ti.dor, *m.* wing of a theater; frame
bas.to, *a.* coarse; rough
bas.tón, *m.* cane; stick; baton
bas.tos, *m. pl.* clubs
ba.su.ra, *f.* garbage; rubbish
ba.su.re.ro, *m.* dump; garbage man
ba.ta, *f.* bathrobe; negligee; smock
ba.ta.lla, *f.* battle
ba.ta.llar, *v.* battle; struggle
ba.ta.llón, *m.* battalion
ba.ta.ta, *f.* sweet potato
ba.te.ría, *f.* battery
ba.ti.do, *m.* batter. *a.* beaten
ba.tir(se), *v.* beat; churn; clash; fight
ba.tu.ta, *f.* baton
baúl, *m.* trunk
bau.tis.mo, *m.* baptism; christening
bau.ti.zar, *v.* christen; baptize
bau.ti.zo, *m.* baptism; christening
ba.ya, *f.* berry
ba.yo, *a.* bay
ba.yo.ne.ta, *f.* bayonet
ba.zar, *m.* bazaar
ba.zo, *m.* spleen
ba.zo.fia, *f.* swill
ba.zu.ca, *f.* bazooka
bea.ti.fi.car, *v.* beatify
bea.tí.fi.co, *a.* beatific
bea.ti.tud, *f.* beatitude
be.bé, *m.* baby
be.ber, *v.* drink
be.bi.da, *f.* drink; beverage. **be.bi.da al.co.hó.li.ca,** liquor; *inf.* booze
be.ca, *f.* scholarship

be·ce·rro, *m.* calf
be·far, *v.* jeer; taunt
beige, *m.* beige. *a.* beige
béis·bol, *m.* baseball
be·li·cis·ta, *m., f.* warmonger. *a.* warmongering
be·li·co·so, *a.* bellicose; warlike
be·li·ge·ran·cia, *f.* belligerency
be·li·ge·ran·te, *a.* belligerent. *m., f.* belligerent
be·lle·za, *f.* beauty
be·llo, *a.* beauteous; beautiful
be·mol, *m.* (*mus.*) flat
ben·de·cir, *v.* bless
ben·di·ción, *f.* benediction; blessing. **ben·di·ción de la me·sa,** grace
ben·di·to, *a.* blessed; holy
be·ne·fi·ciar(se), *v.* benefit
be·ne·fi·cia·rio, *m.,* **be·ne·fi·cia·ria,** *f.* beneficiary
be·ne·fi·cio, *m.* benefaction; benefit; profit; interest; behalf
be·ne·fi·cio·so, *a.* beneficial
be·né·fi·co, *a.* beneficent; charitable
be·ne·vo·len·cia, *f.* benevolence; kindness
be·né·vo·lo, *a.* benevolent
ben·ga·la, *f.* flare
be·nig·ni·dad, *f.* benignity; kindness
be·nig·no, *a.* benign; kind; mild
be·ren·je·na, *f.* eggplant
ber·ga·mo·ta, *f.* bergamot
be·rrin·che, *m.* tantrum
be·sar(se), *v.* kiss; *inf.* smooch
be·so, *m.* kiss
bes·tia, *f.* beast; animal
bes·tial, *a.* bestial
bes·tia·li·dad, *f.* beastliness; bestiality
Bi·blia, *f.* Bible
bí·bli·co, *a.* Biblical
bi·blio·gra·fía, *f.* bibliography
bi·bliografo, *m.* bibliographer
bi·blio·te·ca, *f.* library
bi·blio·te·ca·rio, *m.,* **bi·blio·te·ca·ria,** *f.* librarian
bí·ceps, *m.* biceps
bi·ci·cle·ta, *f.* bicycle; *inf.* bike
bi·ci·clis·ta, *m., f.* bicyclist
bi·cho, *m.* bug
bien, *m.* good; advantage; *pl.* goods. *adv.* well; quite; fully; gladly
bie·nal, *a.* biennial
bie·na·ven·tu·ra·do, *a.* blissful; happy; blessed
bien·he·chor, *m.* benefactor. *a.* beneficial
bien·ve·ni·da, *f.* welcome; greeting
bien·ve·ni·do, *a.* welcome
bi·fur·car·se, *v.* fork
bi·ga·mia, *f.* bigamy
bí·ga·mo, *m.,* **bí·ga·ma,** *f.* bigamist
bi·go·te, *m.* mustache
bi·la·te·ral, *a.* bilateral

bi·lio·so, *a.* bilious
bi·lis, *f.* gall; bile
bi·llar, *m.* billiards
bi·lle·te, *m.* ticket; bill
bi·llón, *m.* trillion (*Br.* billion)
bi·men·sual(mente), *adv.* bimonthly
bi·mes·tral(mente), *adv.* bimonthly
bi·na·rio, *a.* binary
bio·gra·fía, *f.* biography
bio·grá·fi·co, *a.* biographic
bió·gra·fo, *m.* biographer
bio·lo·gía, *f.* biology
bio·ló·gi·co, *a.* biological
bió·lo·go, *m.* biologist
biop·sia, *f.* biopsy
bió·xi·do, *m.* dioxide, **bió·xi·do de car·bo·no,** carbon dioxide
bi·pe·do, *m.* biped
bi·sa·bue·la, *f.* great-grandmother
bi·sa·bue·lo, *m.* great-grandfather; *pl.* great-grandparents
bi·se·car, *v.* bisect
bi·sec·ción, *f.* bisection
bi·se·xual, *a.* bisexual
bis·mu·to, *m.* bismuth
bi·son·te, *m.* bison
bi·tu·mi·no·so, *a.* bituminous
biz·que·ar, *v.* squint
blan·co, *a.* white; blank. *m.* white; blank; target; aim; mark. **cen·tro del blan·co,** bull's-eye
blan·dir, *v.* brandish; flourish
blan·do, *a.* soft; supple; bland; mild
blan·que·ar, *v.* bleach; whiten; blanch
blas·fe·mar, *v.* blaspheme; swear; curse
blas·fe·mia, *f.* blasphemy; profanity; oath
blin·da·do, *a.* armored
blo·que, *m.* block; bloc
blo·que·ar, *v.* blockade; block
blo·queo, *m.* blockade
blu·sa, *f.* blouse; smock
bo·bo, *a.* silly; stupid. *m.* ninny; fool; clown
bo·ca, *f.* mouth; muzzle; opening. **bo·ca de rie·go,** hydrant
bo·ca·ca·lle, *f.* intersection
bo·ca·di·llo, *m.* sandwich
bo·ca·do, *m.* morsel; bite
bo·chas, *f.* bowling. **ju·gar a las bo·chas,** bowl
bo·chor·no·so, *a.* sultry
bo·da, *f.* wedding; marriage
bo·de·ga, *f.* bar; wine cellar
bo·fe·ta·da, *f.* slap; buffet
boi·co·tear, *v.* boycott
boi·co·teo, *m.* boycott
boi·na, *f.* beret
bo·la, *f.* ball. fib. **bo·la de me·sa,** dumpling
bo·ie·tín, *m.* bulletin
bo·li·che, *m.* bowling
bo·li·ta, *f.* pellet

bol·sa, f. pouch; bag; pocket
bol·si·llo, m. pocket
bol·sis·ta, m. stockbroker
bol·so, m. purse; handbag; bag
bo·llo, m. bun; bump; dent
bom·ba, f. bomb; pump. **bom·ba de in·cen·dios**, fire engine
bom·bar·dear, v. bomb; shell; bombard
bom·bar·deo, m. bombardment
bom·bar·de·ro, m. bomber; bombardier
bom·bear, v. pump; pad; shell
bom·bi·lla, f. bulb
bom·bón, m. sweet; pl. sweets. **bombón de me·ren·gue**, marshmallow
bon·dad, f. goodness; kindness
bon·da·do·so, a. good; kindly; kind-hearted
bo·ni·to, a. pretty
bo·quea·da, f. gasp
bo·quear, v. gasp
bo·quia·bier·to, a. agape
bo·qui·lla, f. nozzle; mouthpiece
bó·rax, m. borax
bor·da·do, m. embroidery
bor·de, m. border; edge; lip; brim; brink; verge
bor·di·llo, m. curb
bor·la, f. tassel
bo·rra·che·ra, f. spree
bo·rra·cho, a. drunk; drunken. m. drunkard
bo·rra·dor, m. draft; eraser
bo·rra·du·ra, f. deletion
bo·rrar, v. erase; rub out; blur
bo·rras·co·so, a. boisterous; stormy
bo·rrón, m. blot; blur
bos·que, m. forest; woods
bos·que·jar, v. outline; sketch
bos·que·jo, m. outline; sketch; delineation
bos·te·zar, v. yawn
bo·ta, f. boot; wine bag
bo·tá·ni·ca, f. botany
bo·tá·ni·co, m., bo·tá·ni·ca, f. botanist. a. botanical. **jar·dín bo·ta·ni·co**, arboretum
bo·te, m. canister; jackpot; kitty; bounce; boat. **bo·te sal·va·vi·das**, life boat
bo·te·lla, f. bottle
bo·ti·ca·rio, m. apothecary; druggist
bo·tín, m. plunder; loot; booty; pl. spoils
bo·tón, m. button; stud
bo·to·nes, m. bellboy, bellhop
bó·ve·da, f. vault
bo·vi·no, a. bovine
bo·xea·dor, m. boxer
bo·xear, v. box
bo·xeo, m. boxing
bo·ya, f. buoy
bo·yan·te, a. buoyant

bo·zal, m. muzzle
bra·man·te, m. string; twine
bra·mar, v. bellow; bluster
bra·mi·do, m. bellow
bra·va·ta, f. bravado; brag
bra·vo, a. brave; stormy; wild. *int.* bravo
bra·za, f. fathom
bra·za·do, m. armful
bra·zo, m. arm
brea, f. tar
bré·col, m. broccoli
bre·cha, f. breach
bre·ve, a. brief; short; terse
bre·ve·dad, f. brevity; conciseness
bre·zal, m. heath
bri·bón, a. lazy. m. knave; rogue; rascal
bri·da, f. bridle
bri·ga·da, f. brigade
bri·llan·te, a. brilliant; shiny; bright. m. diamond
bri·llan·tez, f. brilliance
bri·llar, v. shine; glow; gleam; beam; blaze; flare
bri·llo, m. shine; glow; glare; burnish
brin·car, v. leap; jump; caper about; gambol
brin·dar, v. toast
brin·dis, m. toast
brío, m. spirit; jauntiness; vitality; verve
brio·so, a. spirited
bri·sa, f. breeze
briz·na, f. blade; thread
bro·ca·do, m. brocade
bro·cha, f. brush
bro·che, m. clasp; brooch
bro·ma, f. joke; prank
bro·mear(se), v. joke
bro·mis·ta, m., f. joker
bro·mu·ro, m. bromide
bron·ce, m. bronze
bron·cea·do, m. suntan. a. bronze; tanned
bron·cear, v. bronze; tan
bron·quial, a. bronchial
bro·que·ta, f. skewer
bro·tar, v. sprout; bud; spring up
bro·te, m. bud; outbreak
bru·ja, f. witch; hag; harridan
bru·ñir, v. burnish
brus·co, a. brusque, brusk; sudden; curt
bru·se·las, f. pl. tweezers
bru·tal, a. brutal. m. brute
bru·ta·li·dad, f. brutality
bru·to, a. brute; gross; rough; raw. m. brute; beast
bu·ca·ne·ro, m. buccaneer
bu·cle, m. lock; curl
bu·dín, m. pudding
bue·no, a. good; sound; fine; kind

buey, *m.* ox
bú·fa·lo, *m.* buffalo
bu·fan·da, *f.* muffler; scarf
bu·fi·do, *m.* snort
bu·fón, *m.* buffoon; clown. *a.* comical
bú·ho, *m.* owl
bu·ho·ne·ro, *m.* peddler, pedler, pedlar
bui·tre, *m.* vulture
bu·jía, *f.* taper; candle
bul·bo, *m.* bulb
bu·le·var, *m.* boulevard
bul·to, *m.* bulk; mass; lump; heft; parcel; ticket
bu·lla, *f.* fuss; uproar; crowd; brawl
bu·lli·cio, *m.* bustle; riot; racket
bu·me·rang, *m.* boomerang
bu·ñue·lo, *m.* fritter
bu·que, *m.* ship. bu·que de car·ga, freighter
bur·bu·ja, *f.* bubble
bur·bu·jear, *v.* bubble
bur·del, *m.* brothel; bagnio
bur·gués, *m.*, f. bur·gue·sa, *f.* bourgeois. *a.* bourgeois
bur·gue·sía, *f.* bourgeoisie
bur·la, *f.* banter; taunt; ridicule; joke
bur·lar(se), *v.* hoax; gibe; jibe; joke; mock; *inf.* roast
bur·lón, *m.*, bur·lo·na, *f.* joker. *a.* mocking; quizzical
bu·ro·cra·cia, *f.* bureaucracy
bu·ró·cra·ta, *m.*, f. bureaucrat
bu·rro, *m.* burro; donkey; ass; jackass
bur·sa, *f.* rubbish
bus·ca, *f.* pursuit; search
bus·car, *v.* look for; seek
bús·que·da, *f.* quest; search
bus·to, *m.* bust
bu·zo, *m.* diver
bu·zón, *m.* mailbox

C

cá·ba·la, *f.* cabal
ca·bal·ga·ta, *f.* parade; cavalcade
ca·ba·lle·ría, *f.* cavalry
ca·ba·lle·ro, *m.* gentleman; cavalier; knight
ca·ba·lle·ro·si·dad, *f.* chivalry
ca·ba·lle·ro·so, *a.* chivalrous
ca·ba·lle·te, *m.* easel
ca·ba·llo, *m.* horse. ca·ba·llo de fuer·za, horsepower
ca·ba·llón, *m.* ridge
ca·ba·ña, *f.* cabin
ca·ba·ret, *m.* cabaret; bistro
ca·be·cear, *v.* nod the head
ca·be·ci·lla, *m.* ringleader
ca·be·llo, *m.* hair
ca·ber, *v.* fit
ca·bes·tri·llo, *m.* sling

ca·bes·tro, *m.* halter
ca·be·za, *f.* head. do·lor de ca·be·za, headache
ca·be·zu·do, *a.* heady
ca·bil·dear, *v.* lobby
ca·ble, *m.* cable
ca·ble·gra·fiar, *v.* cable
ca·ble·gra·ma, *m.* cable; cablegram
ca·bo, *m.* cape; corporal; end; butt; stub
ca·bra, *f.* goat
ca·bria, *f.* hoist
ca·brio, *m.* rafter. ma·cho ca·brío, *m.* billy goat
ca·brio·la, *f.* caper; antic
ca·bri·to, *m.* kid
ca·ca·hue·te, *m.* peanut
ca·cao, *m.* cocoa; cacao
ca·ca·rear, *v.* cackle; crow
ca·ca·túa, *f.* cockatoo
ca·ce·ro·la, *f.* pan; casserole
ca·ci·que, *m.* chief; party boss
ca·co·fo·nía, *f.* cacophony
cac·to, *m.* cactus
ca·cha·lo·te, *m.* sperm whale
ca·chi·po·rra, *f.* bludgeon; blackjack
ca·cho·rro, *m.* cub; puppy
ca·da, *a.* each; every. ca·da u·no, each one
ca·dá·ver, *m.* corpse; body; cadaver; *inf.* stiff
ca·da·vé·ri·co, *a.* cadaverous
ca·de·na, *f.* chain
ca·den·cia, *f.* cadence; rhythm
ca·de·ra, *f.* hip
ca·de·te, *m.* cadet
caer(se), *v.* fall; tumble down. caer en·fer·mo, sicken; fall ill
ca·fé, *m.* coffee; cafe, café
ca·fei·na, *f.* caffeine
ca·fe·te·ría, *f.* cafeteria
cai·da, *f.* fall; tumble; downfall
cai·mán, *m.* alligator
ca·ja, *f.* case; box. ca·ja de car·tón, carton. ca·ja de cau·da·les, safe. ca·ja de em·ba·la·je, crate
ca·je·ro, *m.*, ca·je·ra, *f.* teller; cashier
ca·jón, *m.* case; drawer; till
cal, *f.* lime
ca·la, *f.* cove
ca·la·ba·za, *f.* pumpkin; gourd
ca·la·bo·zo, *m.* jail
ca·la·fa·tear, *v.* caulk, calk
ca·la·mar, *m.* squid
ca·lam·bre, *m.* cramp
ca·la·mi·dad, *f.* calamity
ca·la·mi·to·so, *a.* calamitous; baleful
ca·lar(se), *v.* swoop; soak; penetrate
cal·ce·te·ría, *f.* hosiery
cal·ce·tín, *m.* sock
cal·ci·fi·ca·ción, *f.* calcification
cal·ci·fi·car(se), *v.* calcify
cal·cio, *m.* calcium

cal·cu·lar, v. calculate; estimate; reckon

cál·cu·lo, m. calculus; calculation

cal·de·ra, f. boiler; cauldron, caldron

cal·do, m. soup; stock; broth; bouillon

ca·le·fac·ción, f. heating

ca·len·da·rio, m. calendar

ca·len·ta·dor, m. heater

ca·len·tar(se), v. warm; heat up

ca·le·ta, f. bight

ca·li·bra·ción, f. calibration

ca·li·brar, v. calibrate

ca·li·bre, m. caliber, calibre

ca·li·có, m. calico

ca·li·dad, f. quality; importance

cá·li·do, a. hot; warm

ca·li·dos·co·pio, m. kaleidoscope

ca·lien·te, a. hot; warm

ca·li·fa, m. caliph, calif

ca·li·fa·to, m. caliphate, califate

ca·li·na, f. haze

ca·lip·so, m. calypso

ca·lis·te·nia, f. calisthenics

cá·liz, m. calyx; chalice

cal·ma, f. calm

cal·man·te, a. sedative. m. tranquilizer

cal·mar(se), v. calm; soothe; compose; alleviate; settle; pacify

ca·lor, m. heat; warmth

ca·lo·ría, f. calorie

ca·ló·ri·co, a. caloric

ca·lum·nia, f. calumny; slander

ca·lum·niar, v. slander; libel; slur; traduce

ca·lu·ro·so, a. warm

cal·vi·cie, f. baldness

cal·vo, a. bald

cal·za·da, f. drive; causeway

cal·za·dor, m. shoehorn

cal·zo·nes, m. pl. trousers; breeches. **cal·zo·nes cor·tos**, shorts

ca·lla·do, a. quiet; silent

ca·llar(se), v. hush; stop talking; keep quiet

ca·lle, f. street. **ca·lle sin sa·li·da**, dead-end

ca·lle·jue·la, f. alley

ca·llo, m. corn; callus

ca·ma, f. bed. **ro·pa de ca·ma**, bedding; bedclothes

ca·ma·da, f. brood; litter

ca·ma·león, m. chameleon

cá·ma·ra, f. chamber; room; camera

ca·ma·ra·da, m., f. comrade

ca·ma·re·ra, f. waitress; barmaid; chambermaid

ca·ma·re·ro, m. waiter; steward

ca·ma·rón, m. shrimp

ca·ma·ro·te, m. cabin

cam·biar(se), v. change; shift; alter; switch; vary; exchange

cam·bio, m. change; shift; alteration; switch; exchange

ca·me·lia, f. camellia

ca·me·llo, m. camel

ca·mi·lla, f. stretcher

ca·mi·nar, v. walk; trek

ca·mi·na·ta, f. hike

ca·mi·no, m. road; route; way. **a me·dio ca·mi·no**, halfway

ca·mión, m. truck. **ca·mión de mu·dan·zas**, van

ca·mio·ne·ro, m. truckdriver; teamster

ca·mio·nis·ta, m. truckdriver; teamster

ca·mi·sa, f. shirt

ca·mi·se·ta, f. T-shirt, tee-shirt; undershirt

cam·pa·men·to, m. camp

cam·pa·na, f. bell

cam·pa·na·rio, m. steeple; belfry

cam·pa·ña, f. campaign; expedition

cam·peón, m., **cam·peo·na**, f. champion

cam·pe·si·no, a. peasant; country. m. peasant

cam·pis·ta, m. camper

cam·po, m. country; field; camp

ca·mu·fla·je, m. camouflage

ca·mu·flar, v. camouflage

ca·nal, m. canal; channel; pipe

ca·na·le·te, m. paddle

ca·na·lla, m., f. scoundrel; swine

ca·na·rio, m. canary

ca·nas·ta, f. basket; hamper

can·ce·la·ción, f. cancellation

can·ce·lar, v. cancel

cán·cer, m. cancer

can·ci·ller, m. chancellor

can·ción, f. song. **can·ción de cu·na**, lullaby

can·da·do, m. padlock

can·de·la, f. candle

can·de·la·bro, m. candelabrum

can·di·da·to, m. candidate; candidacy

cán·di·do, a. unsophisticated; naive

ca·ne·la, f. cinnamon

can·gre·jo, m. crab

can·gu·ro, m. kangaroo

ca·ní·bal, m. cannibal. a. cannibal

ca·ni·ba·lis·mo, m. cannibalism

ca·ni·ca, f. marble

ca·ni·no, a. canine

can·je, m. exchange

ca·noa, f. canoe

ca·non, m. canon

ca·no·ni·za·ción, f. canonization

ca·no·ni·zar, v. canonize

can·sa·do, a. tired; weary; tiresome; rundown

can·sar(se), v. tire; weary; jade

can·ta·lu·po, m. cantaloup, cantaloupe, cantalope

can·tan·te, *m., f.* singer

can·tar, *v.* sing; chant. *m.* song

can·te·ra, *f.* quarry

can·ti·dad, *f.* quantity; sum; amount; deal

can·tim·plo·ra, *f.* canteen

can·ti·na, *f.* canteen; barroom

can·to, *m.* rim; singing; croak

can·tu·rrear, *v.* hum; croon

ca·ña, *f.* reed; cane. **ca·ña de pes·car,** fishing rod

cá·ña·mo, *m.* hemp

ca·ño, *m.* spout; pipe

ca·ñón, *m.* cannon; canyon; barrel; pipe

cao·ba, *f.* mahogany

caos, *m.* chaos

caó·ti·co, *a.* chaotic

ca·pa, *f.* layer; stratum; cloak; cape; coating

ca·pa·ci·dad, *f.* capacity; competence; capability

ca·pa·taz, *m.* taskmaster; foreman

ca·paz, *a.* capable; roomy

ca·pe·llán, *m.* chaplain

ca·pi·lla, *f.* chapel

ca·pi·tal, *m.* capital. *a.* capital

ca·pi·ta·lis·mo, *m.* capitalism

ca·pi·ta·lis·ta, *m., f.* capitalist. *a.* capitalistic

ca·pi·ta·li·zar, *v.* capitalize

ca·pi·tán, *m.* captain

ca·pi·to·lio, *m.* capitol

ca·pi·tu·lar, *v.* capitulate

ca·pí·tu·lo, *m.* chapter

ca·pri·cho, *m.* caprice; whim; fancy; quirk; vagary

ca·pri·cho·so, *a.* capricious; temperamental

cáp·su·la, *f.* capsule

cap·tu·ra, *f.* catch; capture

cap·tu·rar, *v.* capture

ca·pu·cha, *f.* hood

ca·pu·llo, *m.* cocoon

ca·qui, *m.* khaki

ca·ra, *f.* face; countenance. **ca·ra in·fe·rior,** underside

ca·ra·bi·na, *f.* carbine

ca·ra·col, *m.* snail

ca·rác·ter, *m.* character; nature

ca·rac·te·rís·ti·ca, *f.* characteristic; trait

ca·rac·te·rís·ti·co, *a.* characteristic; typical

ca·rac·te·ri·zar, *v.* characterize

ca·rám·ba·no, *m.* icicle

ca·ra·me·lo, *m.* caramel; taffy; toffee

ca·ra·va·na, *f.* caravan

car·bón, *m.* coal. **pa·pel car·bón,** carbon paper. **car·bón ve·ge·tal,** charcoal

car·bo·na·to, *m.* carbonate

car·bo·ni·llo, *m.* cinder

car·bo·no, *m.* carbon

car·bun·co, *m.* carbuncle

car·bu·ra·dor, *m.* carburetor

car·ca·ja·da, *f.* guffaw

cár·cel, *f.* jail; prison; *inf.* calaboose

cár·cel mi·li·tar, guardhouse

car·ci·no·ma, *m.* carcinoma

car·de·nal, *m.* cardinal

car·día·co, *a.* cardiac

car·di·nal, *a.* cardinal

car·do, *m.* thistle

ca·re·cer, *v.* lack

ca·ren·cia, *f.* need

ca·res·tía, *f.* dearness; shortage

car·ga, *f.* load; burden; tax; charge

car·ga·men·to, *m.* cargo

car·gar(se), *v.* load; burden; charge

car·go, *m.* burden; office; charge; care

ca·riar·se, *v.* decay

ca·ri·bú, *m.* caribou

ca·ri·ca·tu·ra, *f.* caricature

ca·ri·dad, *f.* charity

ca·ri·llón, *m.* carillon

ca·ri·ño, *m.* love; affection

ca·ri·ño·so, *a.* loving; affectionate; fond

ca·ri·ta·ti·vo, *a.* charitable

car·me·sí, *a.* crimson. *m.* crimson

car·nal, *a.* carnal

car·na·li·dad, *f.* carnality

car·na·val, *m.* carnival

car·ne, *f.* meat; pulp; flesh. **car·ne de va·ca,** beef

car·ne·ro, *m.* ram

car·ni·ce·ría, *f.* butcher shop; carnage; bloodshed; slaughter

car·ni·ce·ro, *m.* butcher

car·ní·vo·ro, *a.* carnivorous. *m.* carnivore

ca·ro, *a.* dear; expensive

car·pa, *f.* carp

car·pe·ta, *f.* folder

car·pin·te·ría, *f.* carpentry

car·pin·te·ro, *m.* carpenter

ca·rre·ra, *f.* race; career

ca·rre·ro, *m.* carrier

ca·rre·ta·je, *m.* cartage

ca·rre·te, *m.* spool; reel; coil

ca·rre·te·ra, *f.* highway; road

ca·rri·llo, *m.* jowl

ca·rro, *m.* cart; chariot

ca·rro·ña, *f.* carrion

ca·rro·za, *f.* chariot; coach; float

ca·rrua·je, *m.* carriage

car·ta, *f.* letter; card. **car·ta ad·jun·ta,** enclosure. **car·ta de na·ve·gar,** chart

car·tel, *m.* poster; placard

car·te·le·ra, *f.* billboard

car·te·ra, *f.* wallet; billfold; portfolio

car·te·ro, *m.* mailman; postman

car·tí·la·go, *m.* cartilage; gristle

car·to·gra·fía, *f.* cartography

car·tó·gra·fo, *m.* cartographer

car.tón, m. cardboard
car.tu.cho, m. cartridge
ca.sa, f. house; home
ca.sa.men.te.ro, m., ca.sa.men.te.ra, f. matchmaker
ca.sar(se), v. marry; wed; mate
cas.ca.bel, m. bell
cas.ca.da, f. cascade
cás.ca.ra, f. shell; hull; husk
cas.co, m. helmet; skull; hoof
cas.co.te, m. rubble
ca.si, adv. almost
ca.si.mir, m. cashmere
ca.si.no, m. casino
ca.so, m. case; happening. ha.cer ca.so de, heed
cas.pa, f. dandruff
cas.ta, f. caste; breed; cast
cas.ta.men.te, adv. chastely
cas.ta.ñe.tear, v. chatter; snap
cas.ta.ñue.las, f. pl. castanets
cas.ti.dad, f. chastity
cas.ti.gar, v. castigate; punish; chastise
cas.ti.go, m. castigation; discipline; penalty
cas.ti.llo, m. castle
cas.tor, m. beaver
cas.tra.ción, f. castration
cas.trar, v. castrate; geld
ca.sual, a. accidental; incidental
ca.sua.li.dad, f. chance; coincidence
ca.ta.clis.mo, m. cataclysm; upheaval
ca.ta.cum.bas, f. usu. pl. catacomb
ca.ta.le.jo, m. spyglass
ca.ta.li.za.dor, m. catalyst
ca.tá.lo.gar, v. catalog, catalogue
ca.tá.lo.go, m. catalog, catalogue
ca.ta.pul.ta, f. catapult
ca.ta.ra.ta, f. cataract; waterfall
ca.ta.rro, m. catarrh; cold
ca.tar.sis, f. catharsis
ca.tás.tro.fe, f. catastrophe
ca.tas.tró.fi.co, a. catastrophic
ca.te.dral, f. cathedral
ca.te.drá.ti.co, m., ca.te.drá.ti.ca, f. professor
ca.te.go.ría, f. category; standing
ca.te.gó.ri.co, a. categorical
ca.te.quis.mo, m. catechism
Ca.to.li.cis.mo, m. Catholicism
Ca.tó.li.co, m., Ca.tó.li.ca, f. Catholic. a. catholic
ca.tor.ce, a. fourteen
ca.tre, m. cot
cau.ce, m. channel
cau.ción, f. bail
cau.cho, m. rubber
cau.di.llo, m. leader; head of state
cau.sa, f. cause. a.cau.sa de, because of

cau.sar, v. cause; produce; make
cáus.ti.co, a. caustic
cau.te.la, f. caution; stealth
cau.te.lo.so, a. cautious; wary
cau.te.ri.zar, v. cauterize
cau.ti.var, v. captivate; capture
cau.ti.ve.rio, m. captivity
cau.ti.vo, a. captive
ca.var, v. dig; delve
ca.ver.na, f. cavern
ca.ver.no.so, a. cavernous
ca.viar, m. caviar, caviare
ca.vi.dad, f. cavity
ca.za, f. hunt; hunting; game
ca.za.dor, m., ca.za.do.ra, f. hunter
ca.zar, v. hunt; bag
ca.zue.la, f. pan
ce.ba.da, f. barley
ce.bar, v. prime; feed; bait
ce.bo, m. bait
ce.bo.lla, f. onion
ce.bra, f. zebra
ce.cear, v. lisp
ce.der, v. give in; relent; cede
ce.dro, m. cedar
cé.du.la, f. warrant, certificate; charter
ce.gar, v. blind
ce.gue.ra, f. blindness
ce.ja, f. eyebrow
cel.da, f. cell
ce.le.bra.ción, f. celebration
ce.le.brar(se), v. celebrate; solemnize
cé.le.bre, a. celebrated; famous
ce.le.bri.dad, f. celebrity
ce.les.tial, a. celestial; heavenly
ce.li.ba.to, a. celibate. m. celibacy
ce.lo.fán, m. cellophane
ce.lo.sí.a, f. jalousie; jealousy
ce.lo.so, a. jealous; zealous
cé.lu.la, f. cell
ce.lu.lar, a. cellular
ce.lu.lo.sa, f. cellulose
ce.men.tar, v. cement
ce.men.te.rio, m. cemetery; graveyard
ce.men.to, m. cement
ce.na, f. dinner; supper
ce.nar, v. dine; eat dinner; sup
ce.ni.za, f. ash; pl. cinders
cen.so, m. census
cen.sor, m. censor
cen.su.ra, f. censure; blame; stricture; censorship
cen.su.ra.ble, a. censurable
cen.su.rar, v. censure; blame; censor
cen.tau.ro, m. centaur
cen.ta.vo, m. penny; cent
cen.te.llear, v. twinkle; sparkle
cen.te.lleo, m. twinkle
cen.te.na.rio, a. centennial. m. centenary
cen.te.no, m. rye

cen·té·si·mo, a. hundredth
cen·ti·gra·do, a. centigrade; Celsius
cen·tí·me·tro, m. centimeter
cen·ti·ne·la, m., f. sentry; sentinel
cen·tral, a. central
cen·tra·li·zar, v. centralize
cen·trar, v. center
cén·tri·co, a. central
cen·tro, m. center; middle; core
cen·tu·rión, m. centurion
ce·ñir(se), v. encircle; gird
ce·ño, m. frown; scowl
ce·pi·llo, m. brush. ce·pi·llo de dien·tes, toothbrush
ce·ra, f. wax
ce·rá·mi·ca, f. ceramics
ce·rá·mi·co, a. ceramic
cer·ca, adv. close; near; nearby; by. prep. beside; near; toward
cer·ca, f. fence
cer·ca·no, a. close; near
cer·car, v. surround; enclose; fence; encompass
cer·co, m. siege
cer·da, f. bristle; pig
cer·do, m. pig
cer·do·so, a. bristly
ce·real, m. cereal. a. cereal
ce·re·bral, a. cerebral
ce·re·bro, m. brain
ce·re·mo·nia, f. ceremony; formality; pl. solemnities
ce·re·mo·nial, m. ceremonial. a. ceremonial
ce·re·za, f. cherry
ce·ri·lla, f. match
ce·ro, m. zero; naught; cipher
ce·rra·do, a. shut; closed
ce·rra·du·ra, f. lock
ce·rrar(se), v. close; shut; turn off; seal
ce·rro·jo, m. bolt
cer·te·za, f. certitude
cer·ti·dum·bre, f. certitude; certainty
cer·ti·fi·ca·do, m. certificate; a. certified
cer·ti·fi·car, v. certify
cer·va·to, m. fawn
cer·ve·ce·ría, f. brewery
cer·ve·za, f. beer; ale. cer·ve·za de jen·gi·bre, gingerale
ce·sa·ción, f. cessation; stoppage
ce·sar, v. cease
ce·se, m. cessation
ce·sión, f. cession; grant
cés·ped, m. lawn; grass; sod; turf
ces·ta, f. basket
ce·tri·no, a. sallow
cia·nu·ro, m. cyanide
cla·la·mi·no, m. cyclamen
cí·cli·co, a. cyclic
ci·clis·ta, m., f. cyclist
ci·clo, m. cycle; circle

ci·clón, m. cyclone
ci·clo·trón, m. cyclotron
ci·cu·ta, f. hemlock
cie·go, a. blind; sightless
cie·lo, m. sky; heaven; usu. pl. heavens
cien (cien·to), a. hundred
cié·na·ga, f. swamp
cien·cia, f. science
cien·tí·fi·co, m. scientist. a. scientific
cien·to (cien), a. hundred. m. hundred
cie·rre, m. snap
cier·ta·men·te, adv. certainly
cier·to, a. sure; certain
cier·vo, m. stag; hart
ci·fra, f. cipher; figure; code
ci·frar, v. code; cipher
ci·ga·rri·llo, m. cigarette, cigaret
ci·güe·ña, f. stork
ci·lín·dri·co, a. cylindric(al)
ci·lin·dro, m. cylinder
ci·ma, f. top; crest; summit; acme
ci·mi·ta·rra, f. scimitar, simitar, scimiter
cin·cel, m. chisel
cin·co, a. five. m. five
cin·cuen·ta, a. fifty. m. fifty
cin·cha, f. cinch; girth
ci·ne, m. cinema; movies
cí·ni·co, a. cynical. m. cynic
ci·nis·mo, m. cynicism
cin·ta, f. ribbon; reel; tape. gra·bar en cin·ta, tape
cin·to, m. girdle
cin·tu·rón, m. belt
ci·prés, m. cypress
cir·co, m. circus
cir·cui·to, m. circuit. cor·to cir·cui·to, short-circuit
cir·cu·la·ción, f. circulation; currency
cir·cu·lar, a. circular. v. circulate
cír·cu·lo, m. circle
cir·cun·ci·dar, v. circumcise
cir·cun·ci·sión, f. circumcision
cir·cun·fe·ren·cia, f. circumference
cir·cun·lo·cu·ción, f. circumlocution
cir·cun·na·ve·gar, v. circumnavigate
cir·cuns·cri·bir, v. circumscribe
cir·cuns·pec·to, a. circumspect
cir·cuns·tan·cia, f. circumstance
ci·rio, m. taper; candle
ci·rro, m. cirrus
ci·rro·sis, f. cirrhosis
ci·rue·la, f. plum. ci·rue·la pa·sa, prune
ci·ru·gía, f. surgery
ci·ru·ja·no, m. surgeon
cis·ma, f. schism
cis·ne, m. swan
cis·ter·na, f. cistern
ci·ta, f. assignation; meeting; appointment; date; tryst; quotation;

extract; citation
ci·ta·ción, f. citation; subpoena, subpena; summons
ci·tar(se), v. summon; quote; cite
ciu·dad, f. city; town
ciu·da·da·no, m., **ciu·da·da·na**, f. citizen; citizenry
ciu·da·de·la, f. citadel
cí·vi·co, a. civic
ci·vil, a. civilian; civil. m. civilian
ci·vi·li·dad, f. civility
ci·vi·li·za·ción, f. civilization
ci·vi·li·zar(se), v. civilize; become civilized
cla·mor, m. noise; clamor; outcry
cla·mo·ro·so, a. clamorous
clan, m. clan
clan·des·ti·no, a. clandestine
cla·ra·men·te, adv. clearly
cla·re·te, m. claret
cla·ri·dad, f. clarity; clearness
cla·ri·fi·ca·ción, f. clarification
cla·ri·fi·car, v. clarify; light up
cla·rín, m. bugle
cla·ri·ne·te, m. clarinet
cla·ri·vi·den·cia, f. clairvoyance
cla·ro, a. bright; light; clear; transparent; articulate; lucid; apparent. m. clearing; glade
cla·se, f. class; grade; sort; order. **de pri·me·ra cla·se**, first-rate
clá·si·co, a. classic, classical; vintage. m. classic
cla·si·fi·ca·ción, f. classification
cla·si·fi·car(se), v. classify; class; categorize; sort; grade
claus·tro, m. cloister
cla·var(se), v. stick; nail; thrust
cla·ve, a. key. f. key; gist; clef
cla·vel, m. carnation
cla·vi·za, f. peg
cla·vo, m. nail; spike
cle·men·cia, f. clemency; mercy
cle·men·te, a. clement
cle·ri·cal, a. clerical
clé·ri·go, m. parson; priest
cle·ro, m. clergy; ministry
clien·te, m., f. client; customer; patron
cli·ma, m. climate
clí·max, m. climax
clí·ni·ca, f. clinic
clí·ni·co, a. clinical
clo·quear, v. cluck
clo·ro, m. chlorine
clo·ro·fi·la, f. chlorophyll, chlorophyl
coac·ción, f. compulsion; constraint
coac·ti·vo, a. coercive
coa·gu·la·ción, f. coagulation
coa·gu·lar(se), v. coagulate; clot
coa·li·ción, f. coalition
coar·ta·da, f. alibi
co·bal·to, m. cobalt

co·bar·de, a. cowardly. m. coward; dastard
co·bar·día, f. cowardice
co·bra, f. cobra
co·bra·dor, m., **co·bra·do·ra**, f. conductor
co·brar(se), v. cash; charge; receive; recover
co·bre, m. copper
co·bro, m. collection; recovery
co·caí·na, f. cocaine
co·cer, v. cook; bake. **co·cer en hor·no**, bake
co·cien·te, m. quotient
co·ci·na, f. kitchen; stove
co·ci·nar, v. cook
co·ci·ne·ro, m., **co·ci·ne·ra**, f. cook; chef
co·co, m. coconut, cocoanut
co·co·dri·lo, m. crocodile
coc·tel, m. cocktail
co·che, m. car; automobile; coach. **co·che·co·me·dor**, diner. **co·che fú·ne·bre**, hearse
co·di·cia, f. greed; covetousness; cupidity
co·di·ciar, v. covet
co·di·cio·so, a. greedy; covetous
co·di·fi·car, v. codify
có·di·go, m. code
co·do, m. elbow
co·dor·niz, f. quail
co·e·du·ca·ción, f. coeducation
coer·cer, v. coerce
coer·ción, f. coercion
coe·tá·neo, m. contemporary. a. contemporary
co·fra·día, f. fraternity; gang
co·fre, m. chest
co·ger, v. take; get; pick; choose; cull; pluck; catch; net; inf. nab; cop
co·gi·da, f. catch; toss
co·gu·lla, f. cowl
co·he·char, v. bribe
co·he·cho, m. bribery
co·he·ren·cia, f. coherence
co·he·ren·te, a. coherent
co·he·si·vo, a. cohesive
co·he·te, m. rocket; skyrocket
co·hor·te, f. cohort
coin·ci·den·cia, f. coincidence
coin·ci·den·te, a. coincidental
coin·ci·dir, v. coincide; agree
coi·to, m. coitus; intercourse
co·jear, v. limp; hobble
co·je·ra, f. limp
co·jín, m. cushion
co·jo, a. lame
col, f. cabbage. **en·sa·la·da de col**, coleslaw
co·la, f. tail; queue; line; glue
co·la·bo·ra·ción, f. collaboration
co·la·bo·rar, v. collaborate
co·la·de·ra, f. sieve

co·la·dor, *m.* strainer

co·lap·so, *m.* collapse

co·la·te·ral, *a.* collateral

col·cha, *f.* quilt; comforter; spread

col·chón, *m.* mattress

co·lec·ción, *f.* collection; batch

co·lec·cio·nar, *v.* collect

co·lec·ti·vo, *a.* collective

co·le·ga, *m.* colleague

co·le·gio, *m.* academy; high school; college

có·le·ra, *f.* choler; anger; cholera

co·lé·ri·co, *a.* choleric; irate; angry

co·le·ta, *f.* pigtail

col·ga·du·ra, *f.* drape; hangings

col·gar, *v.* hang; suspend; dangle

co·li·brí, *m.* hummingbird

có·li·co, *m.* colic

co·li·flor, *f.* cauliflower

co·li·na, *f.* hill

co·li·seo, *m.* coliseum

col·me·na, *f.* beehive; hive

col·me·nar, *m.* apiary

col·mi·llo, *m.* tusk; fang; eyetooth

col·mo, *m.* climax; height; culmination

co·lo·ca·ción, *f.* location; placing; situation

co·lo·car(se), *v.* put; place; locate; lay; settle; pose; range; array

co·lon, *m.* colon

co·lo·nia, *f.* colony

co·lo·nial, *a.* colonial

co·lo·ni·za·ción, *f.* colonization; settlement

co·lo·ni·za·dor, *m.* colonist

co·lo·no, *m.* settler

co·lor, *m.* color; hue

co·lo·re·te, *m.* rouge

co·lo·sal, *a.* colossal; gargantuan. *m.* colossus

co·lum·na, *f.* column; pillar

co·lum·na·ta, *f.* colonnade

co·lum·nis·ta, *m., f.* columnist

co·lum·piar(se), *v.* swing

co·lum·pio, *m.* swing

co·lu·sión, *f.* collusion

co·ma, *f.* comma; coma

co·ma·dre, *f.* gossip

co·man·dan·te, *m.* commander; major

co·man·dar, *v.* command

co·ma·to·so, *a.* comatose

com·ba, *f.* bend; warp; sag

com·bar(se), *v.* sag; bend

com·ba·te, *m.* combat; fight

com·ba·tien·te, *m.* combatant

com·ba·tir(se), *v.* combat; fight; struggle

com·bi·na·ción, *f.* combination; blend; slip

com·bi·na·do, *a.* joint; combined

com·bi·nar(se), *v.* combine; blend; unite

com·bus·ti·ble, *a.* combustible. *m.* fuel

com·bus·tión, *f.* combustion

co·me·dia, *f.* comedy

co·me·jén, *m.* termite

co·men·ta·dor, *m.* commentator

co·men·tar, *v.* comment on

co·men·ta·rio, *m.* commentary; observation

co·men·zar, *v.* start; begin; commence

co·mer(se), *v.* eat; consume; eat up

co·mer·cial, *a.* commercial

co·mer·cian·te, *m.* merchant

co·mer·ciar, *v.* trade

co·mer·cio, *m.* trade; commerce; business; intercourse

co·mes·ti·ble, *a.* edible; eatable. *m. pl.* groceries

co·me·ta, *m.* comet. *f.* kite

co·me·ter, *v.* commit; make

có·mi·ca, *f.* comedienne

có·mi·co, *a.* comical; funny; burlesque. *m.* comic; comedian

co·mi·da, *f.* meal; fare; keep

co·mien·zo, *m.* start; beginning; commencement

co·mi·llas, *f. pl.* quotation marks

co·mi·sa·rio, *m.* commissioner; commissary

co·mi·sión, *f.* commission

co·mi·té, *m.* committee

co·mi·ti·va, *f.* train; retinue

co·mo, *adv.* as; like. *conj.* as

có·mo, *adv.* how? what? why?

co·mo·di·dad, *f.* comfort; coziness; convenience

co·mo·dín, *m.* (*cards*) joker

có·mo·do, *a.* comfortable; snug; cozy; convenient; *inf.* comfy; homey, homy

com·pac·to, *a.* dense; compact

com·pa·de·cer, *v.* pity

com·pa·dre, *m.* friend; godfather

com·pa·ñe·ris·mo, *m.* fellowship

com·pa·ñe·ro, *m.* companion; associate; mate; buddy; *inf.* side-kick

com·pa·ñía, *f.* company; troupe

com·pa·ra·ble, *a.* comparable

com·pa·ra·ción, *f.* comparison

com·pa·rar, *v.* compare; contrast; liken; equate

com·pa·ren·do, *m.* subpoena, subpena

com·par·sa, *m., f.* supernumerary

com·par·ti·mien·to, *m.* compartment; division

com·par·tir, *v.* share

com·pás, *m.* compass; measure

com·pa·sión, *f.* compassion; sympathy

com·pa·si·vo, *a.* compassionate; sympathetic

com·pa·ti·ble, *a.* compatible

com·pa·trio·ta, *m., f.* compatriot

com·pe·ler, *v.* compel
com·pen·sa·ción, *f.* compensation; *pl.* amends
com·pen·sar, *v.* compensate
com·pe·ten·cia, *f.* competence; competition
com·pe·ten·te, *a.* competent; able
com·pe·ti·dor, *m.*, **com·pe·ti·do·ra**, *f.* rival; competitor
com·pe·tir, *v.* compete; vie
com·pi·la·ción, *f.* compilation
com·pi·lar, *v.* compile
com·pin·che, *m.* chum
com·pla·cer(se), *v.* humor; please; gratify
com·ple·ji·dad, *f.* intricacy; complexity
com·ple·men·to, *m.* complement
com·ple·ta·men·te, *adv.* completely; fully; quite
com·ple·tar, *v.* complete
com·ple·to, *a.* complete; thorough; absolute; full
com·pli·ca·ción, *f.* complication
com·pli·car(se), *v.* complicate; involve
cóm·pli·ce, *m.* accessory; accomplice
com·po·ner(se), *v.* compose; make; constitute; compound
com·por·ta·mien·to, *m.* behavior; deportment
com·por·tar(se), *v.* behave
com·po·si·ción, *f.* composition
com·pra, *f.* purchase; buy. **ir de compras**, to shop
com·pra·dor, *m.*, **com·pra·do·ra**, *f.* buyer; shopper
com·prar, *v.* buy; purchase; trade
com·pren·sión, *f.* comprehension
com·pren·der, *v.* understand; comprehend; grasp; see; comprise
com·pren·si·vo, *a.* comprehensive; broad
com·pre·sión, *f.* compression
com·pri·mir, *v.* compress
com·pro·ba·ción, *f.* proof; substantiation
com·pro·bar, *v.* verify; substantiate
com·pro·me·ter(se), *v.* compromise; involve
com·pro·mi·so, *m.* predicament; obligation
com·pues·to, *m.* compound. *a.* compound; composite
com·pul·sión, *f.* compulsion; stress; coercion
com·pu·ta·dor, *m.* computer
com·pu·tar, *v.* compute
co·mún, *a.* common
co·mu·ni·ca·ción, *f.* communication; message
co·mu·ni·car(se), *v.* impart; communicate
con, *prep.* with; towards. *adv.* along

con·ca·vi·dad, *f.* hollow
con·ce·bi·ble, *a.* conceivable
con·ce·bir, *v.* conceive
con·ce·der, *v.* concede; allow; accord; grant; give
con·ce·jo, *m.* council
con·cen·tra·ción, *f.* concentration
con·cen·trar(se), *v.* concentrate
con·cep·ción, *f.* conception
con·cep·to, *m.* concept; notion
con·ce·sión, *f.* concession; allowance
con·cien·cia, *f.* conscience
con·cien·zu·do, *a.* thorough; conscientious
con·cier·to, *m.* concert
con·ci·liar(se), *v.* conciliate; reconcile
con·ci·so, *a.* concise; terse
con·cluir(se), *v.* conclude; end
con·clu·sión, *f.* conclusion; end
con·cor·dar, *v.* agree; tally
con·cor·dia, *f.* concord
con·cre·to, *a.* concrete
con·cu·bi·na, *f.* concubine
con·cu·rren·cia, *f.* turnout; concurrence
con·cu·rrir, *v.* concur; meet
con·cur·san·te, *m.*, *f.* participant
con·cur·so, *m.* contest
con·da·do, *m.* county
con·de, *m.* count; earl
con·de·co·rar, *v.* decorate
con·de·na, *f.* sentence
con·de·na·ción, *f.* condemnation
con·de·nar(se), *v.* condemn; convict; doom; damn
con·den·sa·ción, *f.* condensation
con·de·sa, *f.* countess
con·di·ción, *f.* condition; state
con·di·cio·nal, *a.* conditional
con·di·cio·nar, *v.* condition
con·di·men·to, *m.* condiment; flavoring; seasoning
con·do·len·cia, *f.* condolence
con·do·nar, *v.* condone
con·du·cir(se), *v.* drive; steer; lead; conduct
con·duc·ta, *f.* behavior
con·duc·to, *m.* conduit; duct
co·nec·tar, *v.* connect; (*elec.*) switch on
co·ne·je·ra, *f.* warren
co·ne·ji·to, *m.* bunny
co·ne·jo, *m.* rabbit
co·ne·xión, *f.* connection
con·fa·bu·la·ción, *f.* collusion
con·fec·ción, *f.* confection
con·fec·cio·nar, *v.* concoct; make up
con·fe·de·ra·ción, *f.* confederacy; confederation
con·fe·de·ra·do, *a.* confederate. *m.* confederate; ally
con·fe·ren·cia, *f.* conference; lecture
con·fe·rir, *v.* bestow; grant

con·fe·sar(se), v. confess; acknowledge; admit

con·fe·sión, f. confession; admission; avowal

con·fe·sio·na·rio, m. confessional

con·fe·so, m. confessor

con·fe·ti, m. confetti

con·fia·ble, a. reliable

con·fian·za, f. trust; dependence, dependance; confidence

con·fiar, v. entrust; trust; rely; confide

con·fi·den·cial, a. confidential; private

con·fi·gu·ra·ción, f. configuration

con·fín, m. usu. pl. bound; confines

con·fir·ma·ción, f. confirmation; corroboration

con·fir·mar, v. confirm; ratify

con·fis·ca·ción, f. confiscation

con·fis·car, v. confiscate

con·fla·gra·ción, f. conflagration

con·flic·to, m. conflict; clash

con·for·mar(se), v. conform; adjust

con·for·me, a. agreeable; similar

con·for·mi·dad, f. conformity

con·for·tar, v. comfort

con·fron·ta·ción, f. confrontation

con·fron·tar, v. confront

con·fun·dir(se), v. confound; confuse; perplex; puzzle; baffle; bemuse; mix

con·fu·sión, f. confusion; mess; jumble

con·fu·tar, v. confute; disprove

con·ge·la·ción, f. frostbite

con·ge·lar(se), v. freeze; congeal

con·gé·ni·to, a. congenital

con·ges·tión, f. congestion

con·glo·me·ra·ción, f. conglomeration

con·glo·me·ra·do, m. conglomerate

con·gre·gar(se), v. congregate; assemble; flock

con·gre·so, m. congress; convention

co·ní·fe·ra, f. conifer

con·je·tu·ra, f. conjecture; guess; surmise

con·je·tu·rar, v. conjecture; surmise

con·ju·gar(se), v. conjugate

con·jun·ción, f. conjunction

con·jun·to, m. ensemble; whole

con·ju·rar, v. conjure

con·me·mo·ra·ción, f. commemoration

con·me·mo·rar, v. commemorate

con·me·mo·ra·ti·vo, a. memorial

con·mo·ción, f. commotion; stir; concussion

con·mo·ve·dor, a. stirring

con·mo·ver(se), v. move; thrill; shake

con·no·ta·ción, f. connotation

con·no·tar, v. connote

co·no, m. cone

co·no·cer(se), v. know; recognize

co·no·ci·do, m., co·no·ci·da, f. acquaintance. a. familiar; known

co·no·ci·mien·to, m. knowledge; pl. ken; lore

con·quis·ta, f. conquest

con·quis·ta·dor, m. conqueror

con·quis·tar, v. conquer; vanquish

con·sa·gra·ción, f. consecration

con·sa·grar, v. consecrate

con·scien·te, a. conscious

con·se·cuen·cia, f. consequence; result; consistency

con·se·cuen·te, a. consistent

con·se·cu·ti·vo, a. consecutive

con·se·je·ro, m., con·se·je·ra, f. counselor

con·se·jo, m. counsel; advice; board. con·se·jo de gue·rra, court-martial

con·sen·so, m. consensus

con·sen·ti·mien·to, m. consent

con·sen·tir, v. consent; accede; acquiesce; indulge

con·ser·va, f., usu. pl. preserve

con·ser·va·ción, f. conservation

con·ser·var(se), v. conserve; save; preserve

con·ser·va·to·rio, m. conservatory

con·si·de·ra·ble, a. considerable; goodly

con·si·de·ra·ción, f. consideration; regard; sake; account; thought

con·si·de·rar, v. consider; entertain; regard; take into account

con·sig·na·ción, f. consignment

con·sig·nar, v. consign

con·si·go, pron. with him, her, you, etc.

con·si·guien·te, a. consequent

con·sis·ten·cia, f. consistency

con·sis·tir, v. consist of

con·so·lar(se), v. comfort; console; solace

con·so·li·da·ción, f. consolidation

con·so·li·dar, v. consolidate; fund

con·sor·te, m., f. consort

cons·pi·cuo, a. visible

cons·pi·ra·ción, f. conspiracy; plot

cons·pi·ra·dor, m., cons·pi·ra·do·ra, f. conspirator

cons·pi·rar, v. conspire

cons·tan·cia, f. constancy

cons·tan·te, a. constant; steady; uniform

cons·tan·te·men·te, adv. constantly

cons·te·la·ción, f. constellation

cons·ter·na·ción, f. consternation

cons·ter·nar(se), v. dismay

cons·ti·tu·ción, f. constitution

cons·ti·tuir(se), v. constitute; form

cons·truc·ción, f. construction; structure

cons·truc·ti·vo, *a.* constructive

cons·truir, *v.* construct; build; structure

con·sue·lo, *m.* consolation

cón·sul, *m.* consul

con·su·la·do, *m.* consulate

con·sul·ta, *f.* consultation

con·sul·tar, *v.* consult

con·su·mar, *v.* consummate; carry out

con·su·mi·dor, *m.*, **con·su·mi·do·ra**, *f.* consumer

con·su·mir(se), *v.* consume; waste away

con·su·mo, *m.* consumption

con·sun·ción, *f.* consumption

con·tac·to, *m.* contact

con·ta·giar(se), *v.* infect; catch

con·ta·gio, *m.* contagion

con·ta·gio·so, *a.* contagious; catching

con·ta·mi·na·ción, *f.* contamination; pollution

con·ta·mi·nar(se), *v.* contaminate

con·tar(se), *v.* count; number; tell; relate. **con·tar con**, depend on; rely on

con·tem·pla·ción, *f.* contemplation

con·tem·plar, *v.* contemplate; meditate; view

con·tem·po·rá·neo, *a.* contemporary

con·ten·der, *v.* contend; strive; contest

con·ten·dien·te, *m.*, *f.* contestant

con·te·ner(se), *v.* contain; hold; include; suppress

con·te·ni·do, *m. usu. pl.* content

con·ten·to, *a.* contented; happy

con·tes·ta·ción, *f.* answer

con·tes·tar, *v.* answer; reply

con·tien·da, *f.* strife; struggle; contest

con·ti·guo, *a.* adjacent. *prep.* next

con·ti·nen·tal, *a.* continental

con·ti·nen·te, *m.* continent; mainland; container

con·tin·gen·cia, *f.* contingency

con·ti·nua·ción, *f.* continuation

con·ti·nuar, *v.* continue

con·ti·nuo, *a.* continuous; constant; perpetual

con·to·near(se), *v.* strut

con·tor·no, *m.* contour; outline

con·tra, *prep.* against; versus. *adv.* against

con·tra·ba·jo, *m.* bass

con·tra·ban·dis·ta, *m.*, *f.* smuggler

con·tra·ban·do, *m.* contraband; smuggling

con·trac·ción, *f.* contraction

con·tra·de·cir, *v.* contradict; gainsay

con·tra·dic·ción, *f.* contradiction

con·traer(se), *v.* contract

con·tra·fuer·te, *m.* buttress

con·tra·ha·cer, *v.* counterfeit; *inf.* fudge

con·tral·to, *m.*, *f.* contralto; alto

con·tra·rie·dad, *f.* vexation; snag

con·tra·rio, *a.* contrary; adverse; opposite. **lo con·tra·rio**, reverse

con·tras·tar, *v.* contrast

con·tras·te, *m.* contrast

con·tra·tiem·po, *m.* mishap; upset

con·tra·to, *m.* agreement; contract

con·tra·ven·ta·na, *f.* shutter

con·tri·bu·ción, *f.* contribution; tax

con·tri·buir, *v.* contribute

con·trol, *m.* control

con·tro·lar, *v.* control

con·tro·ver·sia, *f.* controversy

con·tu·sión, *f.* contusion; bruise

con·va·le·cen·cia, *f.* convalescence

con·va·le·cer, *v.* convalesce

con·va·le·cien·te, *m.*, *f.* convalescent

con·ven·cer, *v.* convince; satisfy

con·ven·ción, *f.* convention

con·ven·cio·nal, *a.* conventional

con·ve·nien·cia, *f.* expediency; *pl.* amenities

con·ve·nien·te, *a.* convenient; handy; fitting; expedient

con·ve·nir(se), *v.* befit; agree; go with

con·ven·to, *m.* convent; abbey. **con·ven·to de mon·jas**, nunnery

con·ver·gir, *v.* converge

con·ver·sa·ción, *f.* conversation

con·ver·sar, *v.* converse

con·ver·sión, *f.* conversion

con·ver·so, *m.*, **con·ver·sa**, *f.* convert

con·ver·tir(se), *v.* convert; turn into

con·ve·xo, *a.* convex

con·vic·ción, *f.* conviction

con·vi·da·do, *m.*, **con·vi·da·da**, *f.* guest

con·vi·dar(se), *v.* invite; volunteer

con·vi·te, *m.* invitation

con·vo·ca·ción, *f.* convocation

con·vo·car, *v.* convene; summon

con·voy, *m.* convoy

con·vul·sión, *f.* convulsion

co·ñac, *m.* cognac; brandy

co·o·pe·ra·ción, *f.* cooperation; teamwork

co·o·pe·rar, *v.* cooperate

co·or·di·na·ción, *f.* coordination

co·or·di·nar, *v.* coordinate

co·pa, *f.* glass; goblet

co·pe·te, *m.* tuft

co·pia, *f.* copy; imitation; duplicate

co·piar, *v.* copy

co·pio·so, *a.* copious

co·pu·lar·se, *v.* copulate

co·que, *m.* coke

co·que·ta, *f.* flirt; coquette

co·que·tear, *v.* flirt

co·ral, *a.* choral. *m.* chorale; coral

Co·rán, *m.* Koran

co·ra·zón, *m.* heart; core

co·ra·zo·na·da, *f.* hunch
cor·ba·ta, *f.* tie; cravat
cor·cel, *m.* steed
cor·che·te, *m.* clasp; *pl.* brackets
cor·cho, *m.* cork
cor·del, *m.* string
cor·de·ro, *m.* lamb
cor·dial, *a.* cordial; hearty
cor·dia·li·dad, *f.* cordiality
cor·do·bán, *m.* cordovan
cor·dón, *m.* shoelace; cord
co·reó·gra·fía, *f.* choreography
co·reó·gra·fo, *m.,* **co·reó·gra·fa,** *f.*
 choreographer
co·ris·ta, *m., f.* chorister
cor·ne·ta, *m.* bugler
cor·ni·sa, *f.* cornice
cor·nu·co·pia, *f.* cornucopia
co·ro, *m.* choir; chorus
co·ro·la, *f.* corolla
co·ro·la·rio, *m.* corollary
co·ro·na, *f.* crown; corona
co·ro·na·ción, *f.* coronation
co·ro·nar, *v.* crown; top
co·ro·na·ria, *f.* coronary
co·ro·nel, *m.* colonel
cor·pi·ño, *m.* bodice
cor·po·ra·ción, *f.* corporation
cor·po·ral, *a.* corporal
cor·po·ra·ti·vo, *a.* corporate
cor·pó·reo, *a.* bodily
corps, *m. pl.* corps
cor·pu·len·to, *a.* stout
cor·pús·cu·lo, *m.* corpuscle
co·rral, *m.* corral; barnyard; pen
co·rrea, *f.* strap
co·rrec·ción, *f.* correction; propriety
co·rrec·to, *a.* correct; right; seemly
co·rrec·tor de prue·bas, *m.,* **co·rrec·to·ra de prue·bas,** *f.* proofreader
co·rre·dor, *m.* broker
co·rre·gir(se), *v.* correct; revise; amend
co·rre·la·ción, *f.* correlation
co·rreo, *m.* mail; post. **co·rreo aé·reo,** airmail
co·rre·o·so, *a.* tough
co·rrer(se), *v.* run; stream; move along
co·rre·ría, *f.* foray
co·rres·pon·den·cia, *f.* correspondence
co·rres·pon·der(se), *v.* correspond; concern
co·rre·ta·je, *m.* brokerage
co·rrien·te, *a.* running; current; regular; common; ordinary. *s.* current; flow; stream
co·rro·bo·rar, *v.* corroborate
co·rroer(se), *v.* corrode; erode
co·rrom·per(se), *v.* corrupt; rot; taint
co·rro·sión, *f.* corrosion
co·rro·si·vo, *a.* corrosive
co·rrup·ción, *f.* corruption

cor·sé, *m.* corset
cor·ta·do, *a.* cut; abrupt
cor·ta·du·ra, *f.* cut; slit
cor·tan·te, *a.* sharp; edged
cor·tar(se), *v.* cut; chop; slit; clip; crop; sever; pare
cor·te, *m.* cut; court
cor·te·jar, *v.* court
cor·tés, *a.* polite; courteous; civil; courtly; gracious
cor·te·sía, *f.* courtesy; civility
cor·te·za, *f.* bark; rind; peel; crust
cor·ti·jo, *m.* grange
cor·ti·na, *f.* curtain. **cor·ti·na de fue·go,** barrage
cor·to, *a.* short; brief
co·sa, *f.* thing; affair
co·se·cha, *f.* harvest; crop
co·se·char, *v.* harvest
co·ser, *v.* sew; stitch
cos·mé·ti·co, *a.* cosmetic. *m.* cosmetic
cós·mi·co, *a.* cosmic
cos·mo·po·li·ta, *a.* cosmopolitan. *m., f.* cosmopolitan
cos·mos, *m.* cosmos
cos·qui·llear, *v.* tickle
cos·qui·llo·so, *a.* ticklish
cos·ta, *f.* coast; cost
cos·tar, *v.* cost
cos·te, *m.* cost; price
cos·ti·lla, *f.* rib
cos·to·so, *a.* costly; expensive; valuable
cos·tra, *f.* scab
cos·tro·so, *a.* crusty
cos·tum·bre, *f.* custom; practice; habit; usage
cos·tu·ra, *f.* seam; joint
cos·tu·re·ra, *f.* seamstress
co·ti·dia·no, *a.* daily
co·ti·za·ción, *f.* quotation
co·yo·te, *m.* coyote
co·yun·tu·ra, *f.* juncture
crá·neo, *m.* skull
cra·so, *a.* crass; thick
crá·ter, *m.* crater
crea·ción, *f.* creation
crea·dor, *m.* creator
crear, *v.* create; make; launch; establish
cre·cer(se), *v.* grow; increase
cre·cien·te, *m.* crescent. *a.* increasing
cre·ci·mien·to, *m.* growth
cre·den·cial, *f.* credential; *pl.* credentials
cré·di·to, *m.* credit
cre·do, *m.* creed; credo
cré·du·lo, *a.* gullible; credulous
creen·cia, *f.* belief; faith
creer(se), *v.* believe; think; credit
creí·ble, *a.* believable; plausible
cre·ma, *f.* cream

cre·ma·lle·ra, *f.* zipper
cre·pús·cu·lo, *m.* twilight; dusk
cre·sa, *f.* maggot
cres·po, *a.* crisp
cres·ta, *f.* crest
cre·ta, *f.* chalk
cria·da, *f.* maid; handmaiden
crian·za, *f.* upbringing; breeding
criar(se), *v.* rear; raise; breed; nurse; nurture
cria·tu·ra, *f.* creature; infant
cri·men, *m.* crime; felony; offense
cri·mi·nal, *a.* criminal. *m., f.* criminal; felon
crin, *f.* mane
crip·ta, *f.* crypt
cri·sá·li·da, *f.* chrysalis; pupa
cri·san·te·mo, *m.* chrysanthemum
cri·sis, *f.* crisis; breakdown; emergency
cri·sol, *m.* crucible
cris·par(se), *v.* twitch
cris·tal, *m.* glass; crystal; window pane
cris·ta·li·zar(se), *v.* crystallize
cris·tian·dad, *f.* Christendom
cris·tia·nis·mo, *m.* Christianity
cris·tia·no, *m.,* cris·tia·na, *f.* Christian. *a.* Christian
Cris·to, *m.* Christ
cri·te·rio, *m.* criterion
crí·ti·ca, *f.* criticism; censure; stricture
cri·ti·car, *v.* criticize; *inf.* knock
crí·ti·co, *a.* critical. *m.* critic
croar, *v.* croak
cro·má·ti·co, *a.* chromatic
cro·mo, *m.* chrome
cro·mo·so·ma, *m.* chromosome
cró·ni·ca, *f.* chronicle
cró·ni·co, *a.* chronic
cro·nis·ta, *m., f.* chronicler; reporter
cro·no·lo·gía, *f.* chronology
cro·no·ló·gi·co, *a.* chronological
cro·no·me·trar, *v.* time
cro·nó·me·tro, *m.* chronometer
cro·quet, *m.* croquet
cro·que·ta, *f.* croquette
cru·ce, *m.* crossing; intersection
cru·ce·ro, *m.* cruiser
cru·ci·fi·car, *v.* crucify
cru·ci·fi·jo, *m.* crucifix
cru·ci·fi·xión, *f.* crucifixion
cru·do, *a.* raw; crude
cruel, *a.* cruel; heartless; ruthless; inhuman
cruel·dad, *f.* cruelty
cru·jía, *f.* ward
cru·ji·do, *m.* creak; crack
cru·jir, *v.* creak; crunch; swish
crus·tá·ceo, *m.* crustacean
cruz, *f.* cross
cru·za·da, *f.* crusade
cru·za·do, *m.* crusader. *a.* crossed

cru·zar(se), *v.* cross; intersect; bridge; span
cua·der·no, *m.* workbook
cua·dra, *f.* stable
cua·dra·do, *m.* square. *a.* square
cua·dra·gé·si·mo, *a.* fortieth
cua·dran·te, *m.* dial; quadrant
cua·drar(se), *v.* square; tally
cua·dri·lá·te·ro, *m.* quadrilateral
cua·dri·lon·go, *m.* oblong. *a.* oblong
cua·dro, *m.* picture; square; check
cua·drú·pe·do, *m.* quadruped
cua·dru·pli·car(se), *v.* quadruple
cua·ja·da, *f. (often pl.)* curd
cua·jar(se), *v.* curdle; jell; clot; set
cual, *adv.* as. *prep.* like. *a.* such as. *pron.* which
cuál, *pron.* which (one)? what?
cua·li·dad, *f.* quality
cual·quier(a), *a.* either; any; whichever. *pron.* any; anybody; anyone
cuán, *adv.* how
cuan·do, *adv.* when. *conj.* when; although. *prep.* when
cuán·do, *adv.* when? *conj.* when?
cuan·to, *a.* as much as. *pron.* all that; *pl.* as many as
cuán·to, *a.* how much? *pron.* how many? *adv.* how
cua·ren·ta, *a.* forty
cuar·to, *a.* fourth. *m.* fourth; quarter; room; chamber
cuar·zo, *m.* quartz
cua·si, *a.* quasi
cua·tro, *a.* four. *m.* four
cu·ba, *f.* vat; barrel
cu·be·ta, *f.* tray
cu·bi·car, *v.* cube
cú·bi·co, *a.* cubic
cu·bier·ta, *f.* cover; casing; deck
cu·bil, *m.* lair
cu·bo, *m.* pail; pailful; bucket; cube
cu·brir(se), *v.* cover; conceal; bank
cu·ca·ra·cha, *f.* cockroach; roach
cu·co, *m.* cuckoo
cu·cha·ra, *f.* spoon; ladle
cu·cha·ra·da, *f.* spoonful; tablespoonful
cu·cha·ra·di·ta, *f.* teaspoonful
cu·cha·ri·lla, *f.* teaspoon
cu·cha·ri·ta, *f.* teaspoon
cu·cha·rón, *m.* ladle
cu·chi·lla·da, *f.* gash; slash
cu·chi·lle·ría, *f.* cutlery
cu·chi·llo, *m.* knife
cue·llo, *m.* neck; collar
cuen·ca, *f.* basin
cuen·ta, *f.* bill; check; count; tally; score; account. **dar·se cuen·ta de,** realize
cuen·ta·ki·ló·me·tros, *m.* speedometer
cuen·tis·ta, *m., f.* storyteller
cuen·to, *m.* story; tale

cuer·da, *f.* rope; cord. **cuer·da de tri·pa**, catgut

cuer·do, *a.* sane

cuer·no, *m.* horn; antler

cue·ro, *m.* leather; hide. **cue·ro ca·be·llu·do**, scalp

cuer·po, *m.* body; force; corpse

cuer·vo, *m.* raven

cues·ta, *f.* ascent; slope

cues·tión, *f.* question

cues·tio·na·rio, *m.* questionnaire

cue·va, *f.* cave

cui·da·do, *m.* care; heed; keep

cui·da·do·so, *a.* careful

cui·dar(se), *v.* care for; look after; mind; conserve

cu·le·bra, *f.* snake

cu·li·na·rio, *a.* culinary

cul·mi·na·ción, *f.* culmination

cul·mi·nar, *v.* culminate

cul·pa, *f.* fault; guilt; *inf.* rap

cul·pa·bi·li·dad, *f.* guilt

cul·pa·ble, *a.* guilty; blameworthy

cul·par, *v.* blame; accuse; censure

cul·ti·va·ble, *a.* arable; cultivable

cul·ti·var, *v.* cultivate; farm; culture

cul·ti·vo, *m.* cultivation

cul·to, *m.* cult; worship

cul·tu·ra, *f.* culture

cul·tu·ral, *a.* cultural

cum·bre, *f.* top; peak; crown

cum·plea·ños, *m.* birthday

cum·pli·do, *m.* compliment. *a.* complete

cum·pli·men·tar, *v.* compliment

cum·pli·mien·to, *m.* fulfillment, fulfilment

cum·plir, *v.* comply with; accomplish; discharge; fulfill; serve; observe

cu·na, *f.* cradle; bassinet

cu·ña·da, *f.* sister-in-law

cu·ña·do, *m.* brother-in-law

cu·ñe·te, *m.* keg

cuo·ta, *f.* quota

cu·po, *m.* quota; allocation

cu·pón, *m.* coupon

cú·pu·la, *f.* dome

cu·ra, *m.* priest. *f.* cure

cu·ran·de·ro, *m.* quack

cu·rar(se), *v.* cure; heal; treat; recover

cu·rio·si·dad, *f.* curiosity

cu·rio·so, *a.* curious; inquisitive; *inf.* nosy

cur·si, *a.* cheap; vulgar

cur·si·llo, *m.* short course

cur·so, *m.* course

cur·tir(se), *v.* tan; coarsen

cur·va, *f.* curve; bend; crook

cus·to·dia, *f.* custody; keeping

cus·to·dio, *m.* custodian; caretaker

cu·tí·cu·la, *f.* cuticle

cu·tis, *m.*, *f.* skin

cu·yo, *a.* whose

CH

cha·cal, *m.* jackal

chal, *m.* shawl

cha·le·co, *m.* vest

cha·let, *m.* chalet

cham·pán, cham·pa·ña, *m.* champagne

cham·pi·ñón, *m.* mushroom

cham·pú, *m.* shampoo

cha·mus·car, *v.* singe; scorch

chan·clo, *m.* overshoe; *pl.* galoshes; rubbers

chan·ta·je, *m.* blackmail

chan·za, *f.* jest; joke

cha·pa, *f.* veneer; plate

cha·pi·tel, *m.* spire

cha·po·tear, *v.* splash

cha·pu·cear, *v.* bungle

cha·pu·ce·ría, *f.* botch; mess

cha·pu·ce·ro, *m.* bungler. *a.* shoddy

cha·pu·rreo, *m.* jabber

cha·pu·zar(se), *v.* duck

cha·que·ta, *f.* jacket

cha·ra·da, *f.* charade

char·ca, *f.* pond

char·co, *m.* puddle

char·la, *f.* chat; talk; gossip

char·lar, *v.* chat; talk; gossip; *inf.* jaw

char·la·tán, *m.* charlatan; quack

cha·rro, *a.* flashy; tawdry; ill-bred

cha·sis, *m.* chassis

chas·quear, *v.* snap; click

cha·to, *a.* snub-nosed; squat

che·que, *m.* check

chi·ca, *f.* girl; lass

chi·cle, *m.* gum

chi·co, *m.* boy; lad. *a.* small

chi·fla·do, *a.* cranky. *m. inf.* crank

chi·le, *m.* chili, chilie, chile

chi·llar, *v.* shriek; screech; scream

chi·llón, *a.* gaudy; shrill

chi·me·nea, *f.* chimney

chim·pan·cé, *m.* chimpanzee; chimp

chi·na, *f.* china; (*cap.*) China

chin·chi·lla, *f.* chinchilla

chi·qui·tín, *a.* tiny

chi·ri·pa, *f.* fluke

chi·rriar, *v.* chirp; squeak

chi·rri·do, *m.* squeak

chis·me, *m.* gossip

chis·mear, *v.* blab; gossip

chis·pa, *f.* spark; drop

chis·po·rro·tear, *v.* sizzle; hiss; sputter

chis·te, *m.* joke; quip; *inf.* gag

chis·te·ra, *f.* top hat

chis·to·so, *a.* facetious; funny

cho·car, *v.* collide; hit; bump; knock; clash; conflict

cho·co·la·te, *m.* chocolate; cocoa

cho·chez, *f.* dotage

chó·fer, *m.* chauffeur
cho·que, *m.* collision; crash; clash; shock
chor·rear, *v.* spout; jet; gush
cho·rro, *m.* spout; spurt; jet
cho·za, *f.* shack; shanty
chu·bas·co, *m.* shower
chu·che·ría, *f.* bauble; knickknack
chu·le·ta, *f.* cutlet; chop
chu·par(se), *v.* suck; sip
chu·pe·chup, *m. inf.* lolipop, lollypop
chus·ca·da, *f.* drollery

D

da·do, *m.* die; *pl.* dice
da·ma, *f.* lady. **da·ma de ho·nor,** bridesmaid
dan·za, *f.* dance
da·ñar(se), *v.* hurt (oneself); damage; harm
da·ño, *m.* injury; damage
dar(se), *v.* give; bestow; allow. **dar·se cuen·ta**, realize. **dar·se pri·sa,** hurry
dá·til, *m.* date
de, *prep.* from; of; with; to. *conj.* than
de·ba·jo, *adv.* under; underneath
de·ba·tir, *v.* debate
de·be, *m.* debit
de·ber, *aux.* v. ought; must. *m.* duty
de·bi·do, *a.* due
dé·bil, *a.* weak; dim; feeble
de·bi·li·dad, *f.* weakness
de·bi·li·tar(se), *v.* weaken
de·bu·tan·te, *f.* debutante
de·ca·den·cia, *f.* decadence; decline
de·ca·den·te, *a.* decadent
de·caer, *v.* decay; ebb
de·ca·no, *m.* dean
de·ca·pi·tar, *v.* behead
de·cen·cia, *f.* decency
de·ce·nio, *m.* decade
de·cen·te, *a.* decent; proper
de·ci·di·da·men·te, *adv.* decidedly
de·ci·dir, *v.* decide; resolve
de·ci·mal, *a.* decimal. *m.* decimal
de·ci·moc·ta·vo, *a.* eighteenth
de·ci·mo·quin·to, *a.* fifteenth
de·cir, *v.* say; state; speak; tell; mean
de·ci·sión, *f.* decision
de·ci·si·vo, *a.* decisive; crucial
de·cla·ra·ción, *f.* declaration
de·cla·rar(se), *v.* declare; propose; allege; pronounce
de·cli·nar, *v.* decline
de·cli·ve, *m.* slope; drop
de·co·ra·ción, *f.* decoration
de·co·ra·dor, *m.*, **de·co·ra·do·ra**, *f.* decorator
de·co·ro, *m.* propriety
de·cré·pi·to, *a.* decrepit

de·cre·tar, *v.* decree; enact
de·cre·to, *m.* decree
de·dal, *m.* thimble
de·di·car(se), *v.* devote
de·do, *m.* finger; digit. **de·do del pie,** toe
de·du·cir, *v.* deduce
de·fa·mar, *v.* defame
de·fec·ción, *f.* defection
de·fec·to, *m.* defect; fault; shortcoming
de·fen·der, *v.* defend; uphold; plead; contest
de·fen·sa, *f.* defense, defence; plea
de·fen·si·vo, *a.* defensive
de·fen·so, *m.* advocate
de·fen·sor, *m.* supporter
de·fe·ren·cia, *f.* deference
de·fi·cien·cia, *f.* deficiency; shortage
de·fi·cien·te, *a.* wanting
dé·fi·cit, *m.* deficit
de·fi·ni·ción, *f.* definition
de·fi·nir, *v.* define
de·fi·ni·ti·vo, *a.* definitive
de·for·mar(se), *v.* deform; loose shape
de·for·mi·dad, *f.* deformity
de·frau·dar, *v.* defraud; cheat
de·ge·ne·rar, *v.* degenerate
de·gra·da·ción, *f.* degradation
de·gra·dar(se), *v.* degrade; demean; demote
dei·dad, *f.* deity
de·jar(se), *v.* let; quit; leave; lay. **de·jar de**, cease
de·lan·tal, *m.* apron
de·lan·te, *adv.* before; ahead. **de·lan·te de**, before
de·lan·te·ro, *a.* front; forward
de·le·ga·do, *a.* delegate
de·le·gar, *v.* delegate
de·lei·ta·ble, *a.* delectable
de·lei·tar(se), *v.* delight
de·lei·te, *m.* joy
de·le·trear, *v.* spell
del·ga·do, *a.* slender; slim; thin
de·li·be·rar, *v.* deliberate
de·li·ca·de·za, *f.* delicacy; sensitivity
de·li·ca·do, *a.* delicate; sensitive; dainty; ticklish
de·li·cio·so, *a.* delicious
de·lin·cuen·cia, *f.* delinquency
de·lin·cuen·te, *a.* delinquent. *m., f.* delinquent
de·li·near, *v.* delineate
de·li·ran·te, *a.* delirious
de·li·rar, *v.* rave
de·li·rio, *m.* delirium
de·li·to, *m.* misdemeanor
del·ta, *m.* delta
de·ma·cra·ción, *f.* emaciation
de·ma·go·gis·mo, *m.* demagoguery
de·ma·go·go, *m.* demagogue, demagog

de·man·da, *f.* claim; challenge
de·man·dan·te, *m., f.* claimant
de·man·dar, *v.* demand; sue
de·ma·sia·do, *adv.* too
de·men·te, *a.* demented
de·mé·ri·to, *m.* demerit
de·mo·cra·cia, *f.* democracy
de·mó·cra·ta, *m., f.* democrat
de·mo·crá·ti·co, *a.* democratic
de·mo·ler, *v.* demolish
de·mo·nio, *m.* demon; devil; fiend
de·mo·rar(se), *v.* delay
de·mos·tra·ción, *f.* demonstration
de·mos·trar, *v.* demonstrate; display
de·no·mi·na·ción, *f.* denomination
de·no·mi·na·dor, *m.* denominator
de·no·tar, *v.* denote
den·si·dad, *f.* density
den·so, *a.* dense; thick; close
den·ta·du·ra, *f.* denture
den·tis·ta, *m., f.* dentist
den·tro, *adv.* inside; within; in; indoors. den·tro de, inside
de·nun·cia, *f.* denunciation
de·nun·ciar, *v.* denounce
de·par·ta·men·to, *m.* department; office
de·pen·den·cia, *f.* dependence; dependency
de·pen·der, *v.* depend
de·pen·dien·te, *m., f.* dependent, dependant. *a.* subordinate
de·plo·ra·ble, *a.* deplorable
de·po·ner, *v.* depose
de·por·ta·ción, *f.* deportation
de·por·tar, *v.* deport
de·por·te, *m.* sport
de·por·tis·ta, *m., f.* sportsman; sportswoman
de·po·si·tar, *v.* deposit; bank
de·pó·si·to, *m.* deposit; depot; *vat.* de·pó·si·to de ca·dá·ve·res, morgue
de·pra·va·ción, *f.* depravity
de·pra·var, *v.* deprave
de·pre·cia·ción, *f.* depreciation
de·pre·sión, *f.* depression; slump
de·pri·mi·do, *a.* depressed
de·pri·mir, *v.* depress
de·re·cho, *a.* standing; straightforward; upright; right. *m.* law; fee; right. de·re·cho de au·tor, royalty
de·ri·va·do, *a.* derivative. *m.* by-product
de·ri·var(se), *v.* derive; drift
de·rra·mar(se), *v.* spill; overflow
de·rre·tir(se), *v.* melt
de·rri·bar(se), *v.* prostrate; fell; floor
de·rro·ta, *f.* defeat; checkmate
de·rro·tar(se), *v.* rout; ruin
de·rrum·ba·mien·to, *m.* collapse
des·a·co·plar, *v.* disconnect
des·a·cos·tum·bra·do, *a.* unaccustomed

des·a·cre·di·tar, *v.* discredit
des·a·cuer·do, *m.* disagreement; variance
des·a·fiar, *v.* defy; brave
des·a·fio, *m.* defiance; challenge
des·a·gra·da·ble, *a.* disagreeable; unpleasant
des·a·gra·dar, *v.* displease
des·a·gre·ga·ción, *f.* disintegration
des·a·güe, *m.* drain; drainage
des·a·hu·ciar, *v.* evict
des·ai·rar, *v.* snub
des·ai·re, *m.* snub; slight
des·a·len·tar, *v.* dishearten
des·a·lien·to, *m.* discouragement
des·a·li·ña·do, *a.* squalid
des·am·pa·ra·do, *a.* destitute; underprivileged
des·a·ni·mar(se), *v.* discourage; dismay
des·á·ni·mo, *m.* depression; *pl.* doldrums
des·a·pa·re·cer, *v.* disappear; vanish
des·a·pa·ri·ción, *f.* disappearance
des·a·pro·bar, *v.* disapprove
des·ar·mar, *v.* disarm
des·a·rrai·gar, *v.* uproot; eradicate
des·a·rre·glar(se), *v.* disarrange; derange
des·a·rre·glo, *m.* disorder
des·a·rro·llar(se), *v.* develop; unfold; evolve
des·a·rro·llo, *m.* development
des·a·so·sie·go, *m.* unrest
de·sas·tre, *m.* disaster
de·sas·tro·so, *a.* disastrous
des·a·tar(se), *v.* loosen; undo
des·a·ten·der, *v.* disregard
des·a·ten·to, *a.* unthinking
des·a·yu·nar(se), *v.* breakfast
des·a·yu·no, *m.* breakfast
des·ba·ra·tar(se), *v.* thwart; spoil
des·ca·li·fi·car, *v.* disqualify
des·can·sar, *v.* rest
des·can·so, *m.* rest
des·ca·ra·do, *a.* bold; brazen; insolent; sassy
des·car·gar(se), *v.* discharge; unload; vent
des·ca·ro, *m.* gall; *inf.* nerve
des·car·tar, *v.* discard
des·cas·ca·rar, *v.* shell ...
des·cen·den·cia, *f.* offspring; origen
des·cen·den·te, *a.* downward
des·cen·der, *v.* descent
des·cen·dien·te, *m., f.* descendant
des·cen·so, *m.* decline; descent
des·ci·frar, *v.* decipher
des·co·lo·rar(se), *v.* fade
des·com·po·ner(se), *v.* decompose; unsettle
des·com·po·si·ción, *f.* decomposition

des·con·cer·tar(se), *v.* disconcert; embarrass
des·con·fi·ar, *v.* distrust
des·co·no·cer, *v.* disown; disavow
des·co·no·ci·do, *a.* unknown; strange. *m.* stranger
des·con·ten·to, *m.* discontent
des·con·ti·nuar, *v.* discontinue
des·cor·tés, *a.* discourteous; impolite
des·co·ser(se), *v.* rip; come apart
des·cri·bir, *v.* describe
des·crip·ción, *f.* description
des·cu·bri·mien·to, *m.* discovery
des·cu·brir, *v.* discover; find
des·cuen·to, *m.* discount; deduction
des·cui·da·do, *a.* careless; remiss; reckless
des·cui·dar, *v.* neglect
des·de, *prep.* from; since. *conj.* since.
des·de lue·go, certainly
des·dén, *m.* scorn
des·de·ñar, *v.* disdain
des·de·ño·so, *a.* disdainful
des·di·cha, *f.* unhappiness
des·di·cha·do, *a.* unlucky; unhappy
de·sea·ble, *a.* elegible
de·sear, *v.* desire; hope; wish; want
des·e·char, *v.* reject
des·em·bo·car, *v.* land
des·em·bol·sar, *v.* disburse
des·en·can·tar, *v.* disenchant
des·en·cor·var, *v.* unbend
des·en·chu·fa·do, *a.* off
des·en·fre·na·do, *a.* unbridled; rampant; wanton
des·en·la·ce, *m.* end; ending
des·en·mas·ca·rar, *v.* unmask
des·en·re·dar(se), *v.* unravel; unsnarl; extricate
des·en·ro·llar(se), *v.* unroll
de·seo, *m.* wish; craving; *inf.* yen
des·e·qui·li·bra·do, *a.* unbalanced
de·ser·tar, *v.* defect
de·ser·tor, *m.* deserter
des·es·pe·ra·ción, *f.* desperation
des·es·pe·rar, *v.* despair
des·fal·car, *v.* embezzle
des·fi·gu·rar, *v.* disfigure; blemish; deface
des·fi·lar, *v.* march
des·fi·le, *m.* parade
des·ga·rrar(se), *v.* tear
des·gas·tar(se), *v.* wear; weather
des·gas·te, *m.* wear; waste
des·gra·cia, *f.* trial; misfortune
des·gra·cia·do, *a.* unlucky; miserable. *m.* unfortunate
des·ha·cer(se), *v.* undo; unwrap
des·ha·rra·pa·do, *a.* seedy
des·he·lar(se), *v.* thaw
des·he·re·dar, *v.* disinherit
des·hi·dra·ta·ción, *f.* dehydration
des·hi·dra·tar, *v.* dehydrate
des·hi·la·char(se), *v.* fray

des·hi·lar(se), *v.* ravel
des·hon·ra, *f.* dishonor; disgrace
des·hon·rar, *v.* dishonor; disgrace; shame
de·sier·to, *m.* desert
des·i·gual, *a.* uneven; irregular
des·i·lu·sio·nar(se), *v.* disillusion
des·in·fec·tan·te, *m.* disinfectant
des·in·flar, *v.* deflate
des·in·te·rés, *m.* disinterest
de·sis·tir, *v.* desist
des·leal, *a.* disloyal
des·li·zar(se), *v.* slide; glide; slip
des·lo·car·se, *v.* dislocate
des·lu·ci·do, *a.* dingy
des·lum·bra·mien·to, *m.* daze
des·lum·brar, *v.* dazzle; blind
des·lus·trar(se), *v.* tarnish; dull
des·lus·tre, *m.* tarnish
des·ma·yar·se, *v.* faint; swoon
des·ma·yo, *m.* faint
des·mi·ga·jar(se), *v.* crumble
des·mon·tar(se), *v.* dismantle
des·mo·ra·li·zar, *v.* demoralize
des·mo·ro·na·do, *a.* dilapidated
des·na·tar, *v.* skim
des·nu·dar(se), *v.* undress; strip
des·nu·dez, *f.* nudity
des·nu·do, *a.* naked; nude; bare
des·nu·tri·ción, *f.* malnutrition
des·o·be·de·cer, *v.* disobey
des·o·be·dien·cia, *f.* disobedience
des·o·cu·pa·do, *a.* empty; free
des·o·do·ran·te, *m.* deodorant
des·o·do·ri·zar, *v.* deodorize
de·so·la·ción, *f.* desolation
des·or·den, *m.* disorder; mess
des·or·de·nar, *v.* mess up
des·or·ga·ni·zar, *v.* disrupt
des·pa·bi·la·do, *a.* wide-awake
des·pa·cio, *adv.* slowly
des·pa·char, *v.* dispatch; speed
des·pe·di·da, *f.* parting. *f.* farewell
des·pe·dir(se), *v.* say goodbye; discharge; fire
des·pe·gue, *m.* takeoff
des·pei·na·do, *a.* unkempt
des·pen·sa, *f.* pantry; larder
des·per·di·ciar, *v.* squander; waste; trifle
des·per·tar(se), *v.* wake up; awaken; arouse; rouse
des·pia·da·do, *a.* pitiless
des·pier·to, *a.* awake
des·pis·tar, *v.* mislead
des·plan·ta·dor, *m.* trowel
des·ple·gar(se), *v.* unfold
des·po·jar(se), *v.* despoil; strip
des·po·sar(se), *v.* get engaged; marry
dés·po·ta, *m.* despot
des·po·tis·mo, *m.* despotism
des·pre·cia·ble, *a.* despicable; vile; worthless
des·pre·ciar(se), *v.* despise; scorn

des·pro·vis·to, *a.* devoid of
des·pués, *adv.* later; after. *prep.* since
des·te·llar, *v.* sparkle; glint
des·te·rra·do, *m.* exile
des·te·rrar, *v.* exile; banish
des·te·tar(se), *v.* wean
des·tie·rro, *m.* exile; banishment
des·ti·lar, *v.* distill
des·ti·le·ría, *f.* distillery
des·ti·no, *m.* destiny; fate; destination
des·tre·za, *f.* skill; dexterity; workmanship
des·tri·par, *v.* gut
des·truc·ción, *f.* destruction
des·truir, *v.* destroy
des·u·nir, *v.* disunite
des·va·lo·ri·zar, *v.* devaluate
des·ván, *m.* attic; loft
des·va·ne·cer(se), *v.* vanish
des·ven·ta·ja, *f.* disadvantage; drawback; handicap
des·ver·gon·za·do, *a.* shameless; unabashed
des·viar(se), *v.* deviate; divert; deflect; wander
de·ta·lla·do, *a.* detailed; elaborate
de·ta·llar, *v.* detail; itemize
de·ta·lle, *m.* detail
de·tec·ti·ve, *m.*, *f.* detective; sleuth
de·ten·ción, *f.* arrest
de·te·ner(se), *v.* detain; arrest
de·ten·te, *f.* détente
de·ter·gen·te, *a.* detergent. *m.* detergent
de·te·rio·rar(se), *v.* deteriorate; decay
de·ter·mi·na·ción, *f.* determination
de·ter·mi·nar, *v.* determine; decide
de·tes·tar, *v.* detest; hate
de·trás, *adv.* behind; aback. de·trás de, after
deu·da, *f.* debt
deu·dor, *m.*, deu·do·ra, *f.* debtor
de·va·lua·ción, *f.* devaluation
de·va·nar, *v.* wind
de·vas·ta·ción, *f.* devastation
de·vas·tar, *v.* devastate
de·vo·ción, *f.* devotion
de·vol·ver, *v.* return; refund; restore
de·vo·rar, *v.* devour
de·vo·to, *a.* devout
día, *m.* day; daytime. ca·da día, daily. día de fies·ta, holiday
dia·be·tes, *f.* diabetes
dia·bé·ti·co, *a.* diabetic
dia·blo, *m.* devil
dia·bó·li·co, *a.* diabolic(al); devilish
diá·co·no, *m.* deacon
dia·frag·ma, *m.* diaphragm
diag·nos·ti·car, *v.* diagnose
diag·nós·ti·co, *m.* diagnosis
dia·go·nal, *a.* diagonal. *m.* diagonal
dia·gra·ma, *m.* diagram

dia·lec·to, *m.* dialect
dia·man·te, *m.* diamond
diá·me·tro, *m.* diameter
dia·po·si·ti·va, *f.* slide
dia·rio, *a.* daily. *m.* daily; journal
dia·rrea, *f.* diarrhea
di·bu·jan·te, *m.*, *f.* designer; cartoonist
di·bu·jar, *v.* draw; sketch
di·bu·jo, *m.* drawing; cartoon
dic·cio·na·rio, *m.* dictionary. dic·cio·na·rio geo·grá·fi·co, gazetteer
di·ciem·bre, *m.* December
dic·ta·do, *m.* dictation
dic·ta·dor, *m.* dictator
dic·tar, *v.* dictate
di·cho, *m.* saying
die·ci·nue·ve, *a.* nineteen
die·cio·cho, *a.* eighteen
die·ci·séis, *a.* sixteen
die·ci·sie·te, *a.* seventeen
dien·te, *m.* tooth
dies·tro, *a.* dexterous; adroit
die·té·ti·co, *a.* dietary
diez, *a.* ten
diez·mo, *m.* tithe
di·fa·ma·ción, *f.* defamation; libel
di·fe·ren·cia, *f.* difference
di·fe·ren·ciar(se), *v.* differ
di·fe·ren·te, *a.* different
di·fe·rir, *v.* defer
di·fí·cil, *a.* difficult; hard; trying
di·fi·cul·tad, *f.* difficulty
dif·te·ria, *f.* diphtheria
di·fun·dir(se), *v.* diffuse
di·fun·to, *a.* deceased
di·fu·sión, *f.* diffusion
di·fu·so, *a.* diffuse; widespread
di·ge·rir, *v.* digest
di·ges·tión, *f.* digestion
di·ges·to, *m.* digest
dí·gi·to, *m.* digit
dig·nar·se, *v.* deign; condescend
dig·ni·dad, *f.* dignity
dig·no, *a.* worthy
di·gre·sión, *f.* digression
di·la·tar(se), *v.* dilate; procrastinate
di·le·ma, *m.* dilemma
di·li·gen·cia, *f.* diligence
di·li·gen·te, *a.* diligent
di·lu·ción, *f.* dilution
di·luir, *v.* dilute
di·lu·viar, *v.* pour
di·lu·vio, *m.* deluge; flood
di·men·sión, *f.* dimension
di·mi·nu·to, *a.* diminutive
di·ná·mi·co, *a.* dynamic(al)
di·na·mi·ta, *f.* dynamite
dí·na·mo, di·na·mo, *f.* dynamo
di·nas·tía, *f.* dynasty
di·ne·ro, *m.* money. di·ne·ro con·tan·te, cash
di·no·sau·rio, *m.* dinosaur

dió·ce·sis, f. diocese

dios, m. god; (cap.) God; Lord

dio·sa, f. goddess

di·plo·ma, m. diploma

di·plo·ma·cia, f. diplomacy

di·plo·má·ti·co, a. diplomatic. m. diplomat

dip·ton·go, m. diphthong

di·pu·ta·ción, f. delegation

di·que, m. dike

di·rec·ción, f. direction; address; control

di·rec·ta·men·te, adv. directly; straight

di·rec·to, a. direct; straight

di·rec·tor, m., di·rec·to·ra, f. director; conductor

di·ri·gir(se), v. direct; lead; control; send; operate

dis·cer·ni·mien·to, m. discernment; discrimination

dis·cer·nir, v. discern

dis·ci·pli·na, f. discipline

dis·ci·pli·nar, v. discipline

dis·cí·pu·lo, m. disciple

dis·co, m. disc, disk; dial; record

dis·cor·dia, f. discord

dis·cre·ción, f. discretion

dis·cre·pan·cia, f. discrepancy

dis·cre·par, v. differ; disagree

dis·cre·to, a. discreet

dis·cri·mi·na·ción, f. discrimination

dis·cul·pa, f. apology; excuse

dis·cul·par, v. excuse

dis·cur·so, m. speech

dis·cu·sión, f. discussion

dis·cu·tir, v. discuss; argue

di·se·car, v. dissect

di·se·mi·nar, v. spread

di·sen·sión, f. dissension

di·sen·te·ría, f. dysentery

di·se·ñar, v. design

dis·fraz, m. disguise; costume; mask

dis·fra·zar, v. disguise

dis·fru·tar, v. enjoy

dis·gre·gar(se), v. disintegrate

dis·gus·tar(se), v. disgust; annoy

dis·gus·to, m. displeasure

di·si·den·cia, f. nonconformity

di·si·mu·la·do, a. sly

di·si·par(se), v. dissipate

dis·lo·ca·ción, f. dislocation

dis·mi·nuir(se), v. diminish; decrease; abate; dwindle

di·so·lu·to, a. loose

di·sol·ver(se), v. dissolve

di·so·nan·cia, f. dissonance

dis·pa·rar(se), v. fire; go off

dis·pa·ri·dad, f. disparity

dis·pen·sa, f. dispensation

dis·per·sar(se), v. disperse; dispel

dis·po·ner(se), v. dispose; prepare

dis·po·ni·ble, a. available

dis·po·si·ción, f. layout; temperament

dis·pues·to, a. ready; willing

dis·pu·ta, f. argument; dispute

dis·pu·tar, v. dispute; quarrel

dis·tan·cia, f. distance

dis·tan·te, a. distant

dis·tin·ción, f. distinction

dis·tin·gui·ble, a. distinguishable

dis·tin·guir, v. distinguish

dis·tin·to, a. distinct; separate

dis·trac·ción, f. distraction

dis·traer(se), v. distract; beguile

dis·traí·do, a. distracted

dis·tri·bu·ción, f. distribution

dis·tri·buir, v. distribute; issue

dis·tri·to, m. district

dis·tur·bio, m. disturbance; trouble

di·sua·dir, v. dissuade; deter

di·ver·gen·cia, f. divergence; deviation

di·ver·gir, v. diverge

di·ver·si·dad, f. diversity

di·ver·sión, f. diversion; amusement

di·ver·so, a. diverse; varied; pl. several; sundry

di·ver·ti·do, a. merry

di·ver·tir(se), v. amuse oneself

di·vi·den·do, m. dividend

di·vi·dir(se), v. divide; portion; split

di·vi·ni·dad, f. divinity

di·vi·no, a. divine

di·vi·sa, f. badge

di·vi·sar, v. espy

di·vi·sión, f. division; split; section

di·vor·ciar(se), v. divorce; get divorced

di·vor·cio, m. divorce

di·vul·gar(se), v. divulge; circulate; blab

do·bla·di·llar, v. hem

do·blar(se), v. double; fold; bend; crease. m. turn

do·ble, a. double. m. double

do·ce, a. twelve

do·ce·na, f. dozen

dó·cil, a. docile; meek

do·cu·men·to, m. document

doc·to, a. learned

doc·tor, m., doc·to·ra, f. doctor

doc·tri·na, f. doctrine

doc·tri·nar, v. indoctrinate

dog·ma, m. dogma; tenet

dog·má·ti·co, a. dogmatic

do·lar, m. dollar

do·len·cia, f. ailment

do·ler(se), v. hurt; pain; ache; grieve

do·lor, m. pain; ache; distress

do·lo·ri·do, a. sore

do·mes·ti·ca·do, a. tame

do·mes·ti·car(se), v. domesticate

do·més·ti·co, a. domestic

do·mi·ci·lio, m. abode

do·mi·na·ción, f. domination

do·mi·nar(se), v. dominate; master

do·min·go, *m.* Sunday
do·mi·nio, *m.* domain; dominion
don, *m.* gift
do·nan·te, *m., f.* donor
do·nar, *v.* donate
don·ce·lla, *f.* maiden; maid
don·de, *adv.* where
dón·de, *adv.* where?
don·de·quie·ra, *adv.* anywhere
do·rar, *v.* gild
dor·mir(se), *v.* sleep
dor·mi·tar, *v.* nap; doze; snooze
dor·mi·to·rio, *m.* dormitory
dos, *a.* two. *m.* two
do·sis, *f.* dose. **do·sis ex·ce·si·va**, overdose
do·tar, *v.* endow
dra·gar, *v.* dredge
dra·gón, *m.* dragon
dra·ma, *m.* drama
dra·má·ti·co, *a.* dramatic
dra·ma·ti·zar, *v.* dramatize
dra·ma·tur·go, *m.* playwright; dramatist
drás·ti·co, *a.* drastic
dre·na·je, *m.* drainage
dro·ga, *f.* drug
dual, *a.* dual
du·ca·do, *m.* dukedom
du·cha, *f.* shower
du·char·se, *v.* shower
du·da, *f.* doubt
du·dar, *v.* doubt; query
du·do·so, *a.* doubtful; dubious
due·lo, *m.* duel
duen·de, *m.* bogy, bogey; elf
due·ña, *f.* owner; duenna
due·ño, *m.* master; proprietor
duer·me·ve·la, *f.* catnap
dul·ce, *a.* sweet. *m.* candy; *pl.* sweets
du·na, *f.* dune
dúo, *m.* duet
duo·dé·ci·mo, *a.* twelfth
du·pli·ca·ción, *f.* duplication
du·pli·car(se), *v.* duplicate
du·pli·ci·dad, *f.* duplicity
du·que, *m.* duke
du·que·sa, *f.* duchess
du·ra·ción, *f.* duration; standing
du·ra·de·ro, *a.* lasting; durable
du·ran·te, *prep.* during; in
du·rar, *v.* endure; last
du·re·za, *f.* hardness
du·ro, *a.* hard; stern; stiff; severe; tough

E

é·ba·no, *m.* ebony
e·cle·siás·ti·co, *a.* ecclesiastic. *m.* ecclesiastic; minister
e·clip·se, *v.* eclipse
e·co, *m.* echo
e·co·lo·gía, *f.* ecology

e·co·ló·gi·co, *a.* ecologic
e·có·lo·go, *m.* ecologist
e·co·no·mía, *f.* economy; thrift; *pl.* economics
e·co·no·mis·ta, *m., f.* economist
e·co·no·mi·zar, *v.* economize
e·cua·ción, *f.* equation
e·cua·dor, *m.* equator
e·cua·ni·mi·dad, *f.* equanimity
e·cu·mé·ni·co, *a.* ecumenical
ec·ze·ma, e·cze·ma, *m.* eczema
e·cha·da, *f.* throw; toss
e·char(se), *v.* toss; throw; eject; cast; lie
e·dad, *f.* age
e·di·ción, *f.* edition; issue
e·dic·to, *m.* edict
e·di·fi·ca·ción, *f.* edification
e·di·fi·car, *v.* edify
e·di·fi·cio, *m.* edifice
e·di·tar, *v.* edit
e·di·tor, *m.* editor; publisher
e·di·to·ria·lis·ta, *m., f.* editorialist
e·du·ca·ción, *f.* education
e·du·car, *v.* educate
e·fec·to, *m.* effect; *pl.* goods
e·fec·tuar, *v.* accomplish; contrive
e·fi·caz, *a.* effective
e·fí·me·ro, *a.* ephemeral
e·go·cén·tri·co, *a.* self-centered
e·goís·ta, *m., f.* egoist
e·je, *m.* axle; axis; shaft
e·je·cu·ción, *f.* execution
e·je·cu·tar, *v.* execute
e·je·cu·ti·vo, *a.* executive
e·jem·plar, *a.* exemplary
e·jem·plo, *m.* example; sample
e·jer·cer, *v.* exert; exercise; practice
e·jer·ci·cio, *m.* exercise; drill
e·jér·ci·to, *m.* army
el, *def. art. m., pl.* los. the
él, *pron. m.* he; *(neuter)* it
e·la·bo·ra·ción, *f.* elaboration
e·la·bo·rar, *v.* elaborate
e·lás·ti·co, *a.* elastic
e·lec·ción, *f.* election
e·lec·to, *a.* elect
e·lec·to·ral, *f.* precinct
e·lec·tri·ci·dad, *f.* electricity
e·lec·tri·cis·ta, *m., f.* electrician
e·lec·tro·cu·tar, *v.* electrocute
e·lec·tro·do, *m.* electrode
e·lec·trón, *m.* electron
e·lec·tró·ni·ca, *f.* electronics
e·le·fan·te, *m.* elephant
e·le·gan·cia, *f.* elegance; grace
e·le·gan·te, *a.* elegant; chic; smart
e·le·gía, *f.* elegy; lament
e·le·gi·ble, *a.* eligible
e·le·gi·do, *a.* elect; chosen
e·le·gir, *v.* pick; choose; select; elect
e·le·men·to, *m.* element
e·le·va·ción, *f.* elevation
e·le·va·do, *a.* high; lofty; overhead

stately
e·le·var(se), v. raise; elevate; lift; heighten
e·li·mi·nar, v. eliminate
e·lip·se, f. ellipse
e·líp·ti·co, a. elliptical
e·li·xir, m. elixir
e·lo·cu·ción, f. elocution
e·lo·cuen·cia, f. eloquence
e·lo·giar, v. eulogize
e·lo·gio, m. eulogy
e·lu·ci·dar, v. elucidate
e·lu·di·ble, a. avoidable
e·lu·dir, v. elude
e·lla, pron. f. she; (neuter) it. e·lla mis·ma, herself
e·llas, pron. f. pl. they; them
e·llo, neuter pron. it
e·llos, pron. m. pl. they; them
e·ma·nar, v. emanate
e·man·ci·pa·ción, f. emancipation
e·man·ci·par(se), v. emancipate
em·ba·ja·da, f. embassy
em·ba·ja·dor, m. ambassador
em·ba·lar, v. bale
em·bal·sa·mar, v. embalm
em·ba·ra·za·da, a. pregnant
em·ba·ra·zo, m. pregnancy
em·bar·ca·de·ro, m. pier
em·bar·car(se), v. embark
em·bar·go, m. embargo. sin em·bar·go, nevertheless
em·bau·car, v. fool; dupe
em·be·lle·cer, v. embellish
em·ble·ma, m. emblem
em·bo·rra·char(se), v. get drunk
em·bos·ca·da, f. ambush
em·bo·ta·do, a. blunt; dull
em·bo·tar, v. blunt; dull
em·bo·te·lla·dor, m. bottler
em·bo·te·llar, v. bottle
em·bra·gue, m. clutch
em·bre·ar, v. tar
em·bria·gar(se), v. intoxicate
em·bria·guez, f. drunkenness
em·brión, m. embryo
em·bro·llo, m. muddle
em·bru·te·cer(se), v. brutalize
em·bu·do, m. funnel
em·bus·te, m. lie; inf. story
em·bu·ti·do, m. sausage
e·mi·gran·te, m., f. emigrant
e·mi·grar, v. emigrate
e·mi·nen·cia, f. eminence
e·mi·nen·te, a. eminent
e·mi·sa·rio, m. emissary
e·mi·sión, f. emission; issue; broadcast
e·mi·tir, v. emit; issue
e·mo·ción, f. emotion; feeling; excitement
e·mo·cio·nar(se), v. thrill
em·pa·car, v. bale
em·pa·cho, m. surfeit

em·pa·la·gar, v. cloy
em·pa·ñar(se), v. film over; steam; swaddle
em·pa·pa·do, a. sodden; soggy
em·pa·par(se), v. soak; drench
em·pa·que·tear, v. package
em·pa·ren·ta·do, a. related; kindred
em·pas·te, m. filling
em·pa·tar, v. tie
em·pa·te, m. tie; draw
em·pe·drar, v. pave
em·pei·ne, m. instep
em·pe·ñar, v. pledge; pawn
em·peo·rar(se), v. worsen
em·pe·ra·dor, m. emperor
em·pe·ra·triz, f. empress
em·per·nar, v. bolt
em·pe·zar, v. begin; start
em·plea·do, m. employee
em·plear(se), v. employ; use
em·pleo, m. work; employment; use
em·po·bre·cer(se), v. impoverish
em·po·llar, v. hatch; brood
em·pren·der, v. undertake
em·pre·sa, f. business; enterprise; undertaking
em·prés·ti·to, m. loan
em·pu·jar, v. push; poke; shove; thrust
em·pu·je, m. push; thrust
e·mu·lar, v. emulate
e·mul·sión, f. emulsion
en, prep. in; into; within; at; on; onto
e·na·je·nar, v. alienate
e·na·mo·rar(se), v. enamor; fall in love
e·na·no, m. dwarf; midget
en·ca·be·za·mien·to, m. caption
en·ca·de·nar, v. enchain; shackle
en·ca·jar, v. encase; foist
en·ca·jo·nar, v. box; case
en·can·ta·do, a. delighted; winning
en·can·ta·dor, a. enchanting; delightful
en·can·tar, v. enchant; charm; bewitch
en·can·to, m. enchantment; charm; captivation
en·ca·rar(se), v. face
en·car·ce·lar, v. jail
en·car·gar(se), v. commission; order
en·car·go, m. task
en·car·na·ción, f. incarnation
en·cen·der(se), v. light; ignite; kindle
en·ce·rrar(se), v. enclose; confine; encase
en·cí·a, f. gum
en·ci·clo·pe·dia, f. encyclopedia
en·cie·rro, m. custody; constraint
en·ci·ma, adv. above; atop; overhead. en·ci·ma de, upon; over
en·cin·ta, a. pregnant
en·claus·trar, v. cloister
en·co·ger(se), v. shrink. en·co·ger·se

de hom·bros, shrug
en·co·lar, v. glue
en·co·le·ri·zar(se), v. incense; anger
en·co·men·dar(se), v. commend
en·co·mio, m. commendation
en·co·nar·se, v. fester
en·con·trar(se), v. encounter; meet; find; discover
en·cor·va·do, a. bent; crooked
en·cor·var(se), v. curve; bend
en·cru·ci·ja·da, f. crossroads
en·cua·der·nar, v. bind
en·cu·brir, v. cloak; hide; inf. whitewash
en·cuen·tro, m. encounter; meeting
en·cur·ti·do, m. pickle
en·chu·fe, m. plug; socket
en·de·cha, f. dirge
en·de·re·zar(se), v. straighten
en·dia·blar, v. bedevil
en·do·sar, v. endorse
en·do·so, m. endorsement
en·dul·zar, v. sweeten
en·du·re·cer(se), v. harden; toughen; cake
e·nel·do, m. drill
e·ne·mi·go, m. enemy; foe
e·ne·mis·tad, f. enmity
e·ner·gía, f. energy; spirit; drive
e·ne·ro, m. January
en·fa·da·do, a. angry; mad
én·fa·sis, m. emphasis; stress
en·fá·ti·co, a. emphatic
en·fer·me·dad, f. illness
en·fer·me·ra, f. nurse
en·fer·me·ría, f. infirmary
en·fer·mi·zo, a. unhealthy
en·fer·mo, a. sick; ill
en·fla·que·cer(se), v. emaciate
en·fo·car(se), v. focus
en·fre·nar, v. bridle
en·fu·re·cer(se), v. enrage; anger
en·gan·char(se), v. catch; hook
en·ga·ñar(se), v. deceive; trick; fool; hoax
en·ga·ño, m. trick; deceit
en·gas·te, m. setting
en·ga·tu·sar, v. wheedle; blandish; coax
en·gen·drar, v. father; breed
en·go·mar, v. gum
en·gor·dar, v. fatten
en·gra·sar, v. grease
en·gu·llir, v. gobble; guzzle
en·he·brar, v. thread
e·nig·ma, m. enigma
e·nig·má·ti·co, a. enigmatic(al)
en·ja·bo·nar, v. soap
en·jam·brar, v. swarm
en·jau·lar, v. cage
en·jua·gar, v. rinse out
en·ju·gar, v. wipe dry
en·la·ce, m. liaison; link

en·la·zar(se), v. link
en·mas·ca·rar(se), v. mask
en·ne·gre·cer(se), v. blacken
en·no·ble·cer, v. ennoble
e·no·ja·do, a. inf. sore
e·nor·me, a. enormous; huge
en·ra·ma·da, f. bower
en·re·dar(se), v. tangle; mesh; involve
en·re·do, m. intricacy; jam
en·re·ja·do, m. trellis
en·ri·que·cer(se), v. enrich; prosper
en·ros·car(se), v. twist; twine
en·sa·la·da, f. salad. en·sa·la·da de col, coleslaw
en·san·char(se), v. widen
en·san·gren·tar, v. bloody
en·sar·tar, v. string
en·sa·yar(se), v. rehearse
en·sa·yis·ta, m.; f. essayist
en·sa·yo, m. essay; theme; test
en·se·na·da, f. inlet
en·se·ñan·za, f. teaching; tuition
en·se·ñar, v. teach; instruct; show
en·se·res, m. pl. chattel
en·si·llar, v. saddle
en·si·mis·ma·do, a. withdrawn
en·sor·de·cer, v. deafen
en·su·ciar(se), v. soil
en·sue·ño, m. daydream
en·ta·pi·zar, v. upholster
en·ten·der(se), v. understand; interpret
en·ten·di·mien·to, m. understanding
en·te·ra·do, a. aware
en·te·ra·men·te, adv. entirely
en·te·rar(se), v. learn; acquaint
en·te·ro, a. entire; whole; total
en·te·rrar, v. bury
en·ti·dad, f. entity
en·tie·rro, m. funeral
en·ton·ces, adv. then
en·tra·da, f. entry; entrance; ticket; inlet
en·tram·par, v. trap
en·tra·ñas, f. pl. entrails
en·trar, v. enter. en·trar sin de·re·cho, trespass
en·tre, prep. between; among; amid
en·tre·a·bier·to, a. ajar
en·tre·ga, f. delivery; installment
en·tre·gar(se), v. entrust; give in; deliver
en·tre·nar, v. train
en·tre·pa·ño, m. panel
en·tre·puen·te, m. steerage
en·tre·sue·lo, m. mezzanine
en·tre·te·jer(se), v. intertwine
en·tre·te·ner(se), v. entertain; amuse; dally
en·tre·vis·ta, f. interview
en·tris·te·cer(se), v. sadden
en·tro·me·ter·se, v. meddle

en.tu.sias.mo, *m.* enthusiasm
e.nu.me.ra.ción, *f.* enumeration
e.nu.me.rar, *v.* enumerate
e.nun.ciar, *v.* enunciate
en.ve.je.cer(se), *v.* age
en.ve.ne.nar, *v.* poison
en.via.do, *m.* envoy
en.viar, *v.* send; dispatch
en.vi.dia, *f.* envy; jealousy
en.vi.diar, *v.* envy
en.vío, *m.* shipment
en.vol.ver(se), *v.* envelop; wrap
en.zi.ma, *f.* enzyme
é.pi.ca, *f.* epic
e.pi.de.mia, *f.* epidemic
e.pi.der.mis, *f.* epidermis
e.pi.lep.sia, *f.* epilepsy
e.pí.lo.go, *m.* epilogue, epilog
e.pis.co.pal, *a.* episcopal
e.pi.so.dio, *m.* episode
e.pís.to.la, *f.* epistle
e.pi.ta.fio, *m.* epitaph
e.pí.te.to, *m.* epithet
e.pi.to.mar, *v.* epitomize
é.po.ca, *f.* epoch; age; period
e.po.pe.ya, *f.* epic
e.qui.dad, *f.* equity
e.qui.li.brar(se), *v.* balance
e.qui.li.brio, *m.* equilibrium; poise
e.qui.noc.cio, *m.* equinox
e.qui.pa.je, *m.* luggage
e.qui.par, *v.* equip
e.qui.po, *m.* equipment; team
e.qui.ta.ti.vo, *a.* equitable
e.qui.va.len.te, *a.* equivalent
e.qui.vo.ca.ción, *f.* mistake; *inf.* slip-up
e.qui.vo.ca.do, *a.* wrong
e.qui.vo.car(se), *v.* mistake; err
e.ra, *f.* era
e.ri.gir, *v.* erect
er.mi.ta.ño, *m.* hermit
e.ro.sión, *f.* erosion
e.ró.ti.co, *a.* erotic
e.rran.te, *a.* errant
e.rrar(se), *v.* err; miss; wander
e.rrá.ti.co, *a.* erratic
e.rró.neo, *a.* wrong; erroneous
e.rror, *m.* error
e.ruc.tar, *v.* belch
e.ru.di.ción, *f.* erudition; scholarship
e.ru.di.to, *a.* erudite. *m.* scholar
e.rup.ción, *f.* eruption; rash; outbreak
e.sa, *a.* that; *pl.* those
é.sa, *pron. f.* that; that one; *pl.* those
es.bel.to, *a.* svelte; slender
es.bo.zo, *m.* sketch
es.ca.be.char, *v.* marinate
es.ca.bel, *m.* hassock
es.ca.bro.so, *a.* rocky; rugged
es.ca.la, *f.* ladder; scale
es.ca.lar, *v.* scale

es.cal.dar(se), *v.* scald
es.ca.le.ra, *f.* steps; stairs; staircase; stairway; ladder. **es.ca.le.ra de ti.je.ra**, stepladder. **es.ca.le.ra mó.vil**, escalator
es.cal.far, *v.* poach
es.ca.lo.frío, *m.* chill
es.ca.lo.nar, *v.* stagger
es.cal.pe.lo, *m.* scalpel
es.ca.ma, *f.* flake; scale
es.can.da.li.zar(se), *v.* shock
es.ca.par(se), *v.* escape; flee; leak; slip
es.ca.pe, *m.* escape; leak
es.ca.ra.ba.jo, *m.* beetle
es.ca.ra.mu.za, *f.* skirmish
es.car.cha, *f.* frost
es.car.nio, *m.* taunt
es.car.pa.do, *a.* abrupt; sheer; craggy
es.ca.sez, *f.* shortage
es.ca.so, *a.* scarce; stingy
es.ca.ti.mar, *v.* spare; stint
es.ce.na, *f.* scene; stage; view
es.cép.ti.co, *m.* skeptic; unbeliever. *a.* skeptical
es.cla.vi.tud, *f.* slavery; bondage
es.cla.vi.zar, *v.* enslave
es.cla.vo, *m.* slave
es.co.ba, *f.* broom
es.co.ger, *v.* choose; pick; opt; select
es.co.gi.do, *a.* chosen
es.co.lar, *a.* scholastic
es.col.tar, *v.* escort
es.co.llo, *m.* reef
es.com.bro, *m.* mackerel; *pl.* debris
es.con.der(se), *v.* hide; screen
es.con.di.te, *m.* cache
es.co.pe.ta, *f.* shotgun
es.co.plear, *v.* chisel
es.co.ria, *f.* slag
es.cor.pión, *m.* scorpion
es.co.ti.lla, *f.* hatch; hatchway
es.co.ti.llón, *m.* trap door
es.cri.bir, *v.* write; correspond
es.cri.to, *m.* writing; brief
es.cri.tor, *m.*, es.cri.to.ra, *f.* writer
es.cri.to.rio, *m.* desk
es.cri.tu.ra, *f.* writing
es.crú.pu.lo, *m.* scruple; qualm
es.cru.ti.nio, *m.* scrutiny
es.cua.dra, *f.* squad
es.cua.dri.lla, *f.* squadron
es.cu.char, *v.* listen to; heed
es.cu.di.lla, *f.* bowl
es.cu.do, *m.* shield
es.cu.dri.ñar, *v.* scrutinize
es.cue.la, *f.* school
es.cul.pir, *v.* sculpture; carve
es.cul.tor, *m.*, es.cul.to.ra, *f.* sculptor
es.cul.tu.ra, *f.* sculpture
es.cu.pir, *v.* spit
e.se, *a.* that; *pl.* **e.sos.**

é·se, *pron.* that; that one; *pl.* é·sos. those

e·sen·cia, *f.* essence

e·sen·cial, *a.* essential; necessary. *m.* essential

es·fe·ra, *f.* sphere; field

es·for·zar(se), *v.* endeavor; strive

es·fuer·zo, *m.* effort; attempt; struggle; exertion

es·gri·ma, *f.* fencing

es·la·bón, *m.* link

es·mal·te, *m.* enamel

es·me·ral·da, *f.* emerald

es·me·ril, *m.* emery

es·nob, *m., f.* snob

e·so, *neuter pron.* that

e·só·fa·go, *m.* esophagus, oesophagus; gullet

e·so·té·ri·co,a. esoteric

es·pa·ciar(se), *v.* space; spread

es·pa·cio, *m.* space

es·pa·da, *f.* sword

es·pa·da·chín, *m.* swashbuckler; swordsman

es·pa·gue·ti, *m.* spaghetti

es·pal·da, *f.* back

es·pan·to·so, *a.* frightful

es·par·cir(se), *v.* scatter; litter

es·pá·rra·go, *m.* asparagus

es·pas·mo, *m.* spasm

es·pas·mó·di·co, *a.* spasmodic

es·pás·ti·co, *a.* spastic

es·pá·tu·la, *f.* spatula

es·pe·cia, *f.* spice

es·pe·cial, *a.* special; especial

es·pe·cia·li·dad, *f.* specialty

es·pe·cia·lis·ta, *m., f.* specialist

es·pe·cia·li·za·ción, *f.* specialization

es·pe·cia·li·zar(se), *v.* specialize; major in

es·pe·ciar, *v.* spice

es·pe·cie, *f.* species, *pl.;* sort

es·pe·ci·fi·ca·ción, *f.* specification

es·pe·ci·fi·car, *v.* specify

es·pé·ci·men, *m.* specimen

es·pec·ta·cu·lar, *a.* spectacular

es·pec·tá·cu·lo, *m.* spectacle; pageant; show; sight

es·pec·ta·dor, *m.,* es·pec·ta·do·ra, *f.* spectator; witness

es·pec·tro, *m.* ghost; specter; *inf.* spook; spectrum

es·pe·cu·lar, *v.* speculate

es·pe·jis·mo, *m.* mirage

es·pe·jo, *m.* mirror

es·pe·ra, *f.* wait

es·pe·ran·za, *f.* expectation; hope

es·pe·rar, *v.* wait; hope for; expect

es·pe·so, *a.* thick; bushy

es·pe·tar, *v.* spit; pierce

es·pía, *m.; f.* spy

es·piar, *v.* spy; *inf.* snoop

es·pi·ga, *f.* spike; ear

es·pi·na, *f.* thorn; spine

es·pi·na·ca, *f.* spinach

es·pi·na·zo, *m.* spine; backbone

es·pi·ni·lla, *f.* shin

es·pio·na·je, *m.* espionage

es·pi·ral, *f.* spiral. *a.* spiral

es·pi·rar, *v.* exhale

es·pi·ri·tis·mo, *m.* spiritualism

es·pi·ri·tis·ta, *m., f.* spiritualist. es·pi·ri·tis·ta, *n.; f.* spiritualist. sesión de es·pi·ri·tis·tas, séance

es·pí·ri·tu, *m.* spirit

es·pi·ta, *f.* spigot

es·plén·di·do, *a.* splendid

es·plen·dor, *m.* splendor

es·plie·go, *m.* lavender

es·po·le·ta, *f.* fuse

es·pon·ja, *f.* sponge

es·pon·jo·so, *a.* spongy

es·pon·tá·neo, *a.* spontaneous

es·po·ra, *f.* spore

es·po·rá·di·co, *a.* sporadic

es·po·sa, *f.* wife; *pl.* handcuffs

es·po·so, *m.* husband; spouse

es·pue·la, *f.* spur

es·pu·ma, *f.* foam; lather; froth

es·que·le·to, *m.* skeleton; framework

es·quí, *m.* ski

es·quiar, *v.* ski

es·qui·na, *f.* corner

es·qui·var(se), *v.* shirk; dodge

es·qui·vo, *a.* elusive

es·qui·zo·fre·nia, *f.* schizophrenia

es·ta(s), *a. f.* this; *pl.* these

és·ta(s), *pron. f.* this; this one; *pl.* these

es·ta·bi·li·dad, *f.* stability

es·ta·ble·cer(se), *v.* establish; form; settle

es·ta·ble·ci·mien·to, *m.* establishment; recovery

es·ta·blo, *m.* stable; stall

es·ta·ca, *f.* stake; peg

es·ta·ca·da, *f.* stockade

es·ta·car, *v.* stake out

es·ta·ción, *f.* season; station; depot

es·ta·dio, *m.* stadium; furlong

es·ta·dis·ta, *m.* statesman

es·ta·dís·ti·ca, *f.* statistics, *pl.*

es·ta·dís·ti·co, *m.* statistic; statistician

es·ta·do, *m.* state; status. es·ta·do de cuen·ta, statement

es·ta·fa, *f.* swindle; gyp

es·ta·far, *v.* swindle; defraud; *inf.* gyp

es·ta·fe·ta, *f.* courier

es·ta·lac·ti·ta, *f.* stalactite

es·ta·lag·mi·ta, *f.* stalagmite

es·ta·llar, *v.* explode

es·tam·bre, *m.* stamen; worsted

es·tam·par, *v.* impress; stamp

es·tam·pi·da, *f.* stampede

es·tam·pi·do, *m.* boom

es·tan·car(se), *v.* stagnate; stem

es·tan·cia, *f.* stay; stanza; farm

es·tan·co, a. watertight
es·tan·dar·te, m. standard
es·tan·que, m. pond; pool
es·tan·te, m. shelf
es·tar, v. be; lie; be present
es·tar·cir, v. stencil
es·tá·ti·co, a. static
es·ta·tua, f. statue
es·ta·tuir, v. charter; establish
es·ta·tu·ra, f. height; stature
es·ta·tu·to, m. statute
es·te, a. east. m. east; Orient
es·te, a. this; pl. es·tos, these
és·te, pron. this; this one; pl. és·tos, these
es·te·la, f. trail; wash
es·te·pa, f. steppe
es·te·ra, f. mat
es·te·reo·fó·ni·co, a. stereophonic
es·te·reo·ti·pa·do, a. stereotyped
es·té·ril, a. sterile
es·te·ri·li·dad, f. sterility
es·te·ri·li·za·ción, f. sterilization
es·te·ri·li·zar, v. sterilize
es·ter·li·na, a. sterling
es·ter·nón, m. sternum; breastbone
es·te·ta, m. f. aesthete
es·té·ti·co, a. esthetic, aesthetic
es·te·tos·co·pio, m. stethoscope
es·te·va·do, a. bandy-legged
es·ti·ba, f. stowage
es·ti·ba·dor, m. stevedore
es·ti·bar, v. stow
es·tiér·col, m. manure; dung
es·tig·ma, m. stigma
es·ti·le·te, m. stiletto
es·ti·lo, m. style; fashion
es·ti·ma, f. esteem
es·ti·ma·ble, a. estimable
es·ti·ma·ción, f. esteem; value
es·ti·mar(se), v. estimate; value; esteem
es·ti·mu·lan·te, m. stimulant; stimulus
es·ti·mu·lar, v. stimulate; inspire
es·ti·mu·lo, m. stimulation; stimulus
es·ti·pen·dio, m. stipend
es·ti·pu·lar, v. stipulate
es·ti·rar, v. stretch; strain
es·to, neuter pron. this; pl. these
es·to·fa·do, m. stew
es·to·far, v. stew
es·toi·co, m. stoic. a. stoical
es·tó·ma·go, m. stomach
es·tor·bar, v. obstruct; impede; interrupt
es·tor·nu·dar, v. sneeze
es·tor·nu·do, m. sneeze
es·tra·bis·mo, m. squint
es·tra·do, m. podium
es·tra·go, m. havoc; ravage
es·tran·gu·la·dor, m. strangler
es·tran·gu·lar, v. strangle; choke
es·tra·ta·ge·ma, f. stratagem; device

es·tra·te·ga, m. strategist
es·tra·te·gia, f. strategy
es·tra·té·gi·co, a. strategic
es·tra·ti·fi·car(se), v. stratify
es·tra·to, m. stratum; layer; bed
es·tra·tos·fe·ra, f. stratosphere
es·tre·char(se), v. narrow; shake
es·tre·cho, a. narrow; parochial. m. strait
es·tre·lla, f. star. es·tre·lla de mar, starfish. es·tre·lla fu·gaz, shooting star
es·tre·llar(se), v. crash; smash
es·tre·me·cer(se), v. shudder; tremble; shake
es·tre·me·ci·mien·to, m. shiver
es·tre·no, m. premiere; debut
es·tre·ñi·mien·to, m. constipation
es·tre·ñir(se), v. constipate
es·tré·pi·to, m. racket
es·tri·a, f. groove
es·tri·bi·llo, m. refrain; chorus
es·tri·bo, m. stirrup
es·tri·bor, m. starboard
es·tric·ni·na, f. strychnine
es·tric·to, a. strict
es·tri·den·te, a. shrill; strident
es·tro·fa, f. stanza; stave
es·tro·pa·jo, m. mop
es·tro·pear(se), v. spoil; mar; ruin
es·truc·tu·ra, f. structure; frame
es·truen·do, m. thunder; roar
es·tru·jón, m. squeeze
es·tua·rio, m. estuary
es·tu·che, m. case
es·tu·dian·te, m. f. student
es·tu·diar, v. study
es·tu·dio, m. study; studio; den
es·tu·dio·so, a. studious
es·tu·fa, f. stove
es·tu·pe·fac·ción, f. stupefaction
es·tu·pen·do, a. stupendous; stunning
es·tu·pi·dez, f. stupidity
es·tú·pi·do, a. stupid
es·tu·por, m. stupor; lethargy
e·ta·pa, f. stage
et·cé·te·ra, f. etcetera
é·ter, m. ether
e·té·reo, a. ethereal
e·ter·ni·dad, f. eternity
e·ter·no, a. eternal; timeless
é·ti·ca, f. ethics
é·ti·co, a. ethical
e·ti·mo·lo·gí·a, f. etymology
e·ti·mo·lo·gis·ta, m. f. etymologist
e·ti·que·ta, f. tag; label; etiquette
ét·ni·co, a. ethnic(al)
et·no·lo·gí·a, f. ethnology
Eu·ca·ris·tí·a, f. Eucharist
eu·fe·mis·mo, m. euphemism
eu·fo·ní·a, f. euphony
eu·fo·ria, f. euphoria
eu·nu·co, m. eunuch

eu·ta·na·sia, f. euthanasia
e·va·cua·ción, f. evacuation
e·va·cuar, v. evacuate
e·va·dir, v. evade; dodge
e·va·lua·ción, f. evaluation
e·va·luar, v. evaluate
e·van·gé·li·co, a. evangelical
e·van·ge·lio, m. gospel
e·van·ge·lis·ta, m. evangelist
e·va·po·ra·ción, f. evaporation
e·va·po·rar(se), v. evaporate
e·va·sión, f. evasion
e·va·si·va, f. evasion
e·ven·tua·li·dad, f. eventuality
e·vi·den·cia, f. evidence
e·vi·den·te, a. evident; plain; obvious
e·vi·tar, v. avoid; shun
e·vo·car, v. evoke
e·vo·lu·ción, f. evolution
ex·ac·ción, f. levy; extortion
ex·ac·ta·men·te, adv. exactly; right
ex·ac·to, a. exact; precise
ex·a·ge·ra·ción, f. exaggeration
ex·a·ge·rar, v. exaggerate
ex·al·tar, v. exalt; elevate
ex·a·men, m. examination; test
ex·a·mi·nar(se), v. examine; inspect; test
ex·as·pe·ra·ción, f. exasperation
ex·as·pe·rar(se), v. exasperate
ex·ca·va·ción, f. excavation; dig
ex·ce·der(se), v. exceed; surpass
ex·ce·len·cia, f. excellence
ex·ce·len·te, a. excellent
ex·cen·tri·ci·dad, f. eccentricity
ex·cén·tri·co, a. eccentric. m. eccentric
ex·cep·to, prep. except; but; unless. conj. save
ex·ce·si·vo, a. excessive; undue
ex·ce·so, m. excess; surfeit
ex·ci·tar(se), v. excite; arouse
ex·cla·ma·ción, f. exclamation
ex·cla·mar, v. exclaim
ex·cluir, v. exclude; bar
ex·clu·sión, f. exclusion
ex·co·mu·nión, f. excommunication
ex·cre·men·to, m. excrement; pl. feces
ex·cur·sión, f. excursion; outing; tour
ex·cu·sa, f. excuse; alibi
ex·cu·sar, v. excuse
ex·ha·lar, v. exhale
ex·hor·ta·ción, f. exhortation
ex·hor·tar, v. exhort
ex·i·gen·te, a. exacting; exigent
ex·i·gir, v. demand; exact; require
ex·i·la·do, m., ex·i·la·da, f. exile
ex·i·lio, m. exile
ex·is·ten·cia, f. existence; life
ex·is·tir, v. exist; live
éx·i·to, m. success; hit
éx·o·do, m. exodus

ex·ó·ti·co, a. exotic
ex·pan·sión, f. expansion
ex·pec·ta·ción, f. expectation
ex·pe·di·ción, f. expedition
ex·pen·der, v. expend
ex·pe·rien·cia, f. experience
ex·pe·ri·men·tal, a. experimental
ex·pe·ri·men·tar, v. experiment; test
ex·pe·ri·men·to, m. experiment
ex·per·to, a. expert; adept. m. expert
ex·pia·ción, f. atonement
ex·piar, v. atone for
ex·pli·ca·ción, f. explanation
ex·pli·car(se), v. explain
ex·plí·ci·to, a. explicit
ex·plo·ra·ción, f. exploration
ex·plo·ra·dor, m. explorer; scout; pioneer
ex·plo·rar, v. explore
ex·plo·sión, f. explosion
ex·plo·ta·ción, f. exploitation
ex·por·ta·ción, f. export; exportation
ex·por·tar, v. export
ex·po·si·ción, f. exhibition; show; exposure
ex·po·si·tor, m. exhibitor
ex·pre·sar(se), v. express; voice
ex·pre·sión, f. expression
ex·pri·mir, v. wring; squeeze
ex·pul·sar, v. expel
ex·qui·si·to, a. exquisite
éx·ta·sis, f. ecstasy
ex·ten·der(se), v. extend; expand; enlarge
ex·ten·sión, f. extension; range
ex·ten·so, a. extensive; wide
ex·te·rior, a. exterior. m. exterior; outside
ex·ter·mi·nar, v. exterminate
ex·ter·no, a. external
ex·tin·ción, f. extinction
ex·tin·guir(se), v. extinguish
ex·tin·to, a. extinct
ex·traer, v. extract; dig
ex·tran·je·ro, m., ex·tran·je·ra, f. foreigner; alien. a. foreign. en el ex·tran·je·ro, abroad; overseas
ex·tra·ño, a. strange; weird
ex·tra·or·di·na·rio, a. extraordinary
ex·tra·viar(se), v. mislay; stray
ex·tre·mi·da·des, m. pl. extremities
ex·tre·mo, a. extreme; radical. m. extreme; end
ex·ul·ta·ción, f. exultation

F

fá·bri·ca, f. factory; mill
fa·bri·ca·ción en se·rie, mass production
fa·bri·car, v. manufacture
fa·bu·lo·so, a. fabulous
fac·ción, f. faction; feature
fa·ce·ta, f. facet

fá·cil, *a.* easy; simple
fa·ci·li·dad, *f.* facility; ease
fa·ci·li·tar, *v.* facilitate; expedite
fac·sí·mi·le, *m.* facsimile
fac·ti·ble, *a.* feasible
fac·tor, *m.* factor
fac·tu·rar, *v.* bill; invoice
fac·tó·tum, *m.* handyman
fa·cul·tad, *f.* faculty; power
fa·cha·da, *f.* facade
fa·chen·da, *f. inf.* splurge
fai·sán, *m.* pheasant
fa·ja, *f.* girdle; sash; band
fa·la·cia, *f.* fallacy
fal·da, *f.* skirt
fal·dón, *m.* gable; flap
fa·li·ble, *a.* fallible
fa·lo, *m.* phallus
fal·sear, *v.* forge
fal·se·dad, *f.* falsity; untruth
fal·si·fi·ca·ción, *f.* forgery; counterfeit
fal·si·fi·car, *v.* falsify; misrepresent
fal·so, *a.* false; dishonest; unsound
fal·ta, *f.* lack; deficiency; want; fault
fal·tar, *v.* lack; fail. **fal·tar a,** neglect
fal·to, *a.* lacking
fa·llar, *v.* fail; (*cards*) trump
fa·lle·cer, *v.* decease; die
fa·lle·ci·mien·to, *m.* demise
fa·llo, *m.* verdict; failure
fa·ma, *f.* fame; name
fa·mi·lia, *f.* family
fa·mi·liar, *a.* familiar; family
fa·mi·lia·ri·dad, *f.* familiarity
fa·mo·so, *a.* famous; well-known
fa·ná·ti·co, *a.* fanatic(al). *m.* fanatic; zealot
fa·na·tis·mo, *m.* fanaticism; bigotry
fan·fa·rro·near, *v.* swagger
fan·ta·sía, *f.* fantasy
fan·tas·ma, *m.* phantom; ghost; apparition; spirit
fan·tás·ti·co, *a.* fantastic; fanciful; bizarre
fa·raón, *m.* pharaoh
far·do, *m.* pack
far·fu·llar, *v.* jabber
far·ma·céu·ti·co, *m.* druggist. *a.* pharmaceutical
far·ma·cia, *f.* pharmacy
fa·ro, *m.* headlight; beacon; lighthouse
far·sa, *f.* farce
fas·ci·nar, *v.* fascinate; intrigue
fas·cis·mo, *m.* fascism
fas·cis·ta, *m., f.* fascist
fa·se, *f.* phase
fas·ti·diar(se), *v.* pester; bother; hassle; *inf.* bug
fas·ti·dio, *m.* annoyance
fas·ti·dio·so, *a.* bothersome; wearisome
fa·tal, *a.* fatal; mortal

fa·ta·li·dad, *f.* fatality
fa·ta·lis·mo, *m.* fatalism
fa·ta·lis·ta, *m., f.* fatalist
fa·ti·ga, *f.* fatigue
fa·ti·gar(se), *v.* tire; fatigue; fag
faus·to, *m.* ostentation; pomp
fa·vor, *m.* favor
fa·vo·ra·ble, *a.* favorable
fa·vo·re·cer, *v.* favor; become
fa·vo·ri·tis·mo, *m.* favoritism
fa·vo·ri·to, *a.* favorite; pet. *m.,* **fa·vo·ri·ta,** *f.* favorite
fe, *f.* faith; belief
fe·bre·ro, *m.* February
fe·bril, *a.* feverish; hectic
fé·cu·la, *f.* starch
fe·cun·di·dad, *f.* fertility
fe·cun·do, *a.* fertile; fecund
fe·cha, *f.* date
fe·char, *v.* date
fe·de·ra·ción, *f.* federation
fe·de·ral, *a.* federal
fe·li·ci·dad, *f.* felicity; bliss; good fortune
fe·li·ci·ta·ción, *f. usu. pl.* congratulation
fe·li·ci·tar, *v.* congratulate
fe·li·no, *a.* feline
fe·liz, *a.* happy; felicitous
fel·pu·do, *m.* mat
fe·me·ni·no, *a.* female; feminine
fe·mi·nis·mo, *m.* feminism
fé·mur, *m.* femur
fe·nó·me·no, *m.* phenomenon
feo, *a.* ugly; unsightly
fé·re·tro, *m.* bier
fe·ria, *f.* fair
fer·men·ta·ción, *f.* fermentation
fer·men·tar, *v.* ferment
fe·ro·ci·dad, *f.* ferocity
fe·roz, *a.* ferocious; fierce
fe·rre·te·ría, *f.* hardware
fe·rro·ca·rril, *m.* railroad
fe·rro·pru·sia·to, *m.* blueprint
fér·til, *a.* fertile; rich
fer·ti·li·zar, *v.* fertilize
fér·vi·do, *a.* fervid
fer·vor, *m.* fervor
fer·vo·ro·so, *a.* ardent; fervent
fes·te·jar, *v.* entertain; celebrate; fete
fes·ti·vo, *a.* festive; merry
fes·tón, *m.* festoon; scallop
fe·ti·che, *m.* fetish
fé·ti·do, *a.* fetid
fe·to, *m.* fetus
feu·dal, *a.* feudal
feu·da·lis·mo, *m.* feudalism
fia·dor, *m.* sponsor; guarantor
fian·za, *f.* security
fias·co, *m.* fiasco
fi·bro·so, *a.* fibrous; stringy
fic·ción, *f.* fiction
fic·ti·cio, *a.* fictitious
fi·cha, *f.* token

fi·de·dig·no, *a.* trustworthy
fi·dei·co·mi·sa·rio, *m.* trustee
fi·dei·co·mi·so, *m.* trust
fi·de·li·dad, *f.* fidelity; loyalty
fie·bre, *f.* fever; temperature. **fie·bre ti·foi·dea**, typhoid fever
fiel, *a.* faithful; loyal; true; devoted. *m. pl.* congregation
fiel·tro, *m.* felt
fie·ra, *f.* virago; wild beast
fie·ra·brás, *m.* spitfire
fies·ta, *f.* party; feast; celebration; festival
fi·gu·ra, *f.* figure
fi·gu·rar(se), *v.* figure
fi·gu·rín, *m.* figurine; model
fi·jar(se), *v.* fix; determine; assess; set
fi·jo, *a.* fixed; stated; confirmed; set; static
fi·la, *f.* file; row; rank; line; tier
fi·lan·tro·pía, *f.* philanthropy
fi·le·te, *m.* fillet; steak
fi·li·gra·na, *f.* filigree; watermark
fil·mar, *v.* film
fi·lo, *m.* edge
fi·lón, *m.* vein; lode
fi·lo·so·fía, *f.* philosophy
fi·ló·so·fo, *m.* philosopher
fil·trar(se), *v.* filter; strain
fil·tro, *m.* filter
fin, *m.* end; finish; purpose
fi·nal, *a.* final; last. *m.* end; finale
fi·na·li·dad, *f.* finality
fi·na·lis·ta, *m.*, *f.* finalist
fi·nal·men·te, *adv.* finally; lastly
fi·nan·ciar, *v.* finance
fi·nan·cie·ro, *a.* financial. *m.* financier
fi·nan·zas, *f. pl.* finance
fin·ca, *f.* estate
fin·gi·do, *a.* sham; feigned
fin·gir(se), *v.* feign; pretend; fake; sham
fi·ni·to, *a.* finite
fi·no, *a.* fine; delicate; acute; nice; polite
fir·ma, *f.* firm; signature
fir·ma·men·to, *m.* firmament
fir·mar, *v.* sign; autograph
fir·me, *a.* firm; hard; adamant; fast; steady; strong
fir·me·za, *f.* firmness; decision
fis·cal, *a.* fiscal
fis·gón, *m.* snoop
fis·go·near, *v.* pry
fí·si·ca, *f.* physics
fí·si·co, *a.* physical
fla·co, *a.* thin; skinny; lean; gaunt; spare
fla·mear, *v.* flame
flá·mu·la, *f.* streamer
fla·quear, *v.* weaken
flau·ta, *f.* flute
fle·cha, *f.* arrow. **pun·to de fle·cha**, arrowhead

fle·ma, *f.* phlegm
fle·xi·ble, *a.* flexible; pliant; supple
flir·tear, *v.* flirt
flo·jo, *a.* loose; slack; limp; weak
flor, *f.* flower; blossom
flo·re·cer, *v.* flower; blossom; bloom; flourish; prosper
flo·reo, *m.* flourish
flo·re·ro, *m.* vase; florist
flo·re·te, *m.* foil
flo·ri·do, *a.* florid
flo·ris·ta, *m.*, *f.* florist
flo·ta, *f.* fleet
flo·tar, *v.* float
flo·ti·lla, *f.* flotilla
fluc·tua·ción, *f.* fluctuation; vacilation
fluc·tuar, *v.* fluctuate; bob
flui·dez, *f.* fluency
flúi·do, *a.* fluid. *m.* fluid
fluir, *v.* flow
flu·jo, *m.* flow; flux
fluo·res·cen·te, *a.* fluorescent
fluo·ri·za·ción, *f.* fluoridation
fo·bia, *f.* phobia
fo·ca, *f.* seal
fo·co, *m.* focus; spotlight; floodlight
fo·gón, *m.* galley; stove
fo·lí·cu·lo, *m.* follicle
folk·lo·re, *m.* folklore
fo·lla·je, *m.* foliage; leafage
fo·lle·to, *m.* booklet; brochure; pamphlet
fo·men·tar, *v.* foment; promote; encourage
fon·do, *m.* depth; bottom; background; *pl.* funds
fon·ta·ne·ro, *m.* plumber
fo·ra·ji·do, *m.* outlaw
fo·ras·te·ro, *m.*, **fo·ras·te·ra**, *f.* stranger; outsider
fór·ceps, *m.* forceps
for·ja·do, *a.* wrought
for·jar, *v.* forge
for·ma, *f.* form; shape; build; method
for·ma·ción, *f.* formation; array
for·ma·li·dad, *f.* formality
for·mar(se), *v.* form; make; shape; fashion
for·ma·to, *m.* format
for·mi·da·ble, *a.* formidable; tremendous
for·món, *m.* chisel
fór·mu·la, *f.* formula
for·ni·car, *v.* fornicate
fo·ro, *m.* forum
fo·rra·je, *m.* forage; fodder
for·ta·le·cer(se), *v.* strengthen; fortify
for·ta·le·za, *f.* fortress
for·ti·fi·ca·ción, *f.* fortification
for·tui·to, *a.* fortuitous; casual; haphazard

for·tu·na, *f.* fortune

for·zar, *v.* force; coerce; strain; violate

fo·sa, *f.* socket; cavity

fos·fa·to, *m.* phosphate

fos·fo·res·cen·cia, *f.* phosphorescence

fós·fo·ro, *m.* phosphorus

fó·sil, *a.* fossil. *m.* fossil

fo·so, *m.* moat; trench

fo·to, *f.* photograph; snapshot

fo·to·co·pia, *f.* photocopy

fo·to·gé·ni·co, *a.* photogenic

fo·to·gra·fía, *f.* photography; photograph

fo·tó·gra·fo, *m.*, fo·tó·gra·fa, *f.* photographer

fra·ca·sar, *v.* fail; flop; break down

fra·ca·so, *m.* failure; debacle

frac·ción, *f.* fraction

frac·tu·ra, *f.* fracture; breakage

frac·tu·rar(se), *v.* fracture

fra·gan·cia, *f.* fragrance

frá·gil, *a.* fragile; frail; breakable

frag·men·to, *m.* fragment; shred

fra·gor, *m.* clash; uproar

fra·gua, *f.* forge

frai·le, *m.* friar

fram·bue·sa, *f.* raspberry

fran·ca·che·la, *f. inf.* jamboree

fran·ca·men·te, *adv.* frankly

fran·cés, *a.* French

fran·co, *a.* frank; candid; open; direct

fran·co·te, *a.* bluff; blunt

fran·quear, *v.* frank

fran·queo, *m.* postage

fran·que·za, *f.* frankness

fras·co, *m.* flask; flagon

fra·se, *f.* phrase; sentence

fra·seo·lo·gía, *f.* wording

fra·ter·nal, *a.* fraternal

fra·ter·ni·dad, *f.* fraternity; brotherhood

frau·de, *m.* fraud; deception

frau·du·len·to, *a.* fraudulent

fre·cuen·cia, *f.* frequency

fre·cuen·tar, *v.* frequent; haunt

fre·cuen·te, *a.* frequent

fre·ga·de·ro, *m.* sink

fre·gar, *v.* scour; scrub; wash

freír(se), *v.* fry

fre·nar, *v.* brake

fre·ne·sí, *m.* frenzy

fre·né·ti·co, *a.* frantic; frenetic

fre·no, *m.* brake; curb

fren·te, *f.* brow; forehead; front. *al frente*, ahead. *en frente*, opposite

fre·sa, *f.* strawberry

fres·ca·chón, *a.* buxom; healthy

fres·co, *m.* fresco. *a.* fresh; cool; smart

fres·cu·ra, *f.* coolness; nerve

fres·no, *m.* ash tree

fre·za, *f.* spawn

frial·dad, *f.* coldness; aloofness

fric·ción, *f.* friction

frío, *a.* cold; cool; chilly; frigid. *m.* cold

fris·co, *m.* frieze

frí·vo·lo, *a.* frivolous; trivial

fron·tal, *a.* frontal

fron·te·ra, *f.* frontier; border; boundary; limit

fro·tar(se), *v.* rub; chafe

fro·te, *m.* friction

fru·gal, *a.* thrifty; frugal

frun·ce, *m.* gather; tuck

frun·cir, *v.* gather; purse

frus·tra·ción, *f.* frustration

frus·trar(se), *v.* frustrate; defeat; foil; thwart

fue·go, *m.* fire. *al·to el fue·go*, cease-fire. *ar·ma de fue·go*, firearm; gun. *cor·ti·na de fue·go*, barrage. *fue·gos ar·ti·fi·cia·les*, fireworks

fue·lle, *m.* bellows

fuen·te, *f.* fountain; spring; source

fue·ra, *adv.* away; outside; off; abroad

fuer·te, *m. fort. a.* strong; sturdy; potent

fuer·za, *f.* force; power; might; strength

fu·ga, *f.* escape; elopement

fu·gar·se, *v.* flee; abscond

fu·gaz, *a.* fleeting

fu·gi·ti·vo, *a.* fugitive; runaway

ful·cro, *m.* fulcrum

ful·gu·rar, *v.* flare; gleam

fu·mar, *v.* smoke

fu·mi·gar, *v.* fumigate

fun·ción, *f.* function; show; performance

fun·cio·nar, *v.* function; work

fun·da·ción, *f.* foundation

fun·da·dor, *m.* founder

fun·da·men·tal, *a.* fundamental

fun·dar(se), *v.* found; establish

fun·di·ción, *f.* foundry

fun·dir(se), *v.* fuse; cast

fú·ne·bre, *a.* funeral

fu·nes·to, *a.* baneful

fur·gón, *m.* wagon. *fur·gón de co·la*, caboose

fu·ria, *f.* fury

fu·rio·so, *a.* furious

fu·ror, *m.* furor

fur·ti·vo, *a.* furtive

fu·rún·cu·lo, *m.* boil

fu·sión, *f.* coalescence; fusion

fút·bol, *m.* football; soccer

fu·tu·ro, *a.* future. *m.* future

G

ga·bar·di·na, *f.* gabardine

ga·ba·rra, *f.* barge

ga·bi·ne·te, *m.* cabinet; study
ga·ce·la, *f.* gazelle
ga·ce·ta, *f.* gazette
ga·fas, *f. pl.* glasses; spectacles. ga·fas de sol, sunglasses
ga·fe, *m.* jinx
gai·ta, *f. usu. pl.* bagpipe
ga·lan·te·ría, *f.* gallantry
ga·la·xia, *f.* galaxy
ga·le·ra, *f.* galley
ga·le·ría, *f.* gallery; arcade; veranda
ga·li·ma·tías, *m.* gibberish
ga·lón, *m.* gallon
ga·lo·par, *v.* gallop
gal·va·ni·zar, *v.* galvanize
ga·lle·ta, *f.* biscuit; cookie
ga·lli·na, *f.* chicken; hen
ga·lli·ne·ro, *m.* coop
ga·llo, *m.* rooster; cock
ga·ma, *f.* doe; gamut
gam·bi·to, *m.* gambit
ga·mu·za, *f.* chamois
ga·na, *f.* appetite; desire
ga·na·de·ro, *m.* cattleman; rancher
ga·na·do, *m.* cattle; livestock
ga·na·dor, *m.*, ga·na·do·ra, *f.* winner
ga·nan·cia, *f.* gain; profit
ga·nar, *v.* win; gain; earn; profit
gan·cho, *m.* hook
gan·du·lear, *v.* lounge; loaf
gan·ga, *f.* bargain; *inf.* steal
gan·gre·na, *f.* gangrene
gáng·ster, *m.* gangster
gan·so, *m.* goose; gander
ga·ñir, *v.* yelp; yip
ga·ra·je, *m.* garage
ga·ran·te, *m.* surety
ga·ran·tía, *f.* guarantee, guaranty; surety; warrant; warranty
ga·ran·ti·zar, *v.* guarantee; vouch for; pledge
ga·ra·pi·ña, *f.* icing
gar·ban·zo, *m.* chickpea
gar·gan·ta, *f.* throat; neck
gár·ga·ras, *f.* gargle
gar·ga·ri·zar, *v.* gargle
ga·rra, *f.* talon; claw
ga·rra·fa, *f.* decanter
ga·rra·pa·tear, *v.* scribble
ga·rro·te, *m.* cudgel; club
gá·rru·lo, *a.* garrulous
gar·za, *f.* heron
gas, *m.* gas
ga·sa, *f.* chiffon; gauze
ga·so·li·na, *f.* gasoline; gas
gas·ta·do, *a.* worn-out; trite
gas·tar(se), *v.* spend; use up; eat up; consume; wear out
gas·to, *m.* expense; expenditure
gás·tri·co, *a.* gastric
gas·tro·no·mía, *f.* gastronomy
gas·tró·no·mo, *m.* gourmet
ga·ti·llo, *m.* trigger
ga·ti·to, *m.* kitten; kitty; pussy

ga·to, *m.* cat; jack
ga·vio·ta, *f.* gull
ga·za, *f.* loop
gaz·mo·ño, *m.*, gaz·mo·ña, *f.* prude; hypocrite
géi·ser, *m.* geyser
ge·la·ti·na, *f.* gelatin
ge·ma, *f.* gem
ge·me·lo, *a.* twin. *m.*, ge·me·la, *f.* twin; *m. usu. pl.* binoculars
ge·mi·do, *m.* groan; wail
ge·mir, *v.* groan; moan; wail
gen, *m.* gene
ge·nea·lo·gía, *f.* genealogy
ge·ne·ra·ción, *f.* generation
ge·ne·ra·dor, *m.* generator
ge·ne·ral, *m.* general. *a.* general; common. por lo ge·ne·ral, usually
ge·ne·ra·li·dad, *f.* generality
ge·ne·ra·li·zar(se), *v.* generalize; become known
ge·ne·rar, *v.* generate
ge·né·ri·co, *a.* generic
gé·ne·ro, *m.* gender; genus; nature; kind; type; sort. gé·ne·ros di·ver·sos, sundries
ge·ne·ro·si·dad, *f.* generosity
ge·né·si·co, *a.* genetic
gé·ne·sis, *f.* genesis. *m. (cap.)* Genesis
ge·né·ti·ca, *f.* genetics
ge·nio, *m.* temper; nature; genius
ge·no·ci·dio, *m.* genocide
gen·te, *f.* people; folk; nation
gen·til, *a.* comely; graceful
gen·ti·le·za, *f.* gentility; gracefulness; courtesy
ge·nui·no, *a.* genuine; true; real
geo·fí·si·ca, *f.* geophysics
geo·gra·fía, *f.* geography
geo·grá·fi·co, *a.* geographic, geographical
geó·gra·fo, *m.* geographer
geo·lo·gía, *f.* geology
geo·ló·gi·co, *a.* geologic, geological
geó·lo·go, *m.* geologist
geo·me·tría, *f.* geometry
geo·mé·tri·co, *a.* geometric
ge·ren·te, *m.* manager
ge·ria·tría, *f.* geriatrics
ger·men, *m.* germ
ger·mi·na·ción, *f.* germination
ger·mi·nar, *v.* germinate
ge·run·dio, *m.* gerund
ges·ti·cu·lar, *v.* gesticulate
ges·tio·nar, *v.* negotiate; work towards
ges·to, *m.* gesture; face; expression
gi·ba, *f.* hump
gi·bón, *m.* gibbon
gi·gan·te, *m.* giant
gi·gan·tes·co, *a.* gigantic; giant
gim·na·sia, *f.* gymnastics
gim·na·sio, *m.* gymnasium; *inf.* gym

gim·nas·ta, *m. f.* gymnast
gi·mo·tear, *v.* whine
gi·ne·bra, *f.* gin
gi·ne·co·lo·gía, *f.* gynecology
gi·ra, *f.* circuit; tour
gi·rar, *v.* turn; rotate; revolve; gyrate; twirl; spin; swivel
gi·ra·sol, *m.* sunflower
gi·ro, *m.* turn; twirl; draft
gi·ros·co·pio, *m.* gyroscope
gi·ta·no, *m.* **gi·ta·na**, *f.* gipsy, gypsy
gla·cial, *a.* arctic; glacial; icy; wintry
gla·ciar, *m.* glacier
gla·dio·lo, **gla·dío·lo**, *m.* gladiolus, gladiola
glán·du·la, *f.* gland
glan·du·lar, *a.* glandular
glau·co·ma, *m.* glaucoma
glo·bo, *m.* globe; balloon
gló·bu·lo, *m.* corpuscle; globule
glo·ria, *f.* glory
glo·ri·fi·car(se), *v.* glorify; glory in
glo·sa·rio, *m.* glossary
glo·tis, *f.* glottis
glo·tón, *m.* glutton
gno·mo, *m.* gnome
go·ber·na·dor, *m.* governor; ruler
go·ber·nar, *v.* govern; rule
go·bier·no, *m.* government; guidance
golf, *m.* golf
gol·fo, *m.* gulf
go·lon·dri·na, *f.* swallow
go·lo·si·na, *f.* dainty; tidbit; *inf.* goody
gol·pa·zo, *m. inf.* wallop
gol·pe, *m.* hit; blow; band; stroke; coup
gol·pear, *v.* hit; slug; strike; beat; knock; buffet; rap; jab
gol·pe·ci·to, *m.* pat; flick; dab
go·ma, *f.* gum; rubber band. **go·ma la·ca**, shellac, shellack
gón·do·la, *f.* gondola
gon·do·le·ro, *m.* gondolier
go·no·rrea, *f.* gonorrhea
gor·do, *a.* fat; corpulent; overweight
gor·go·tear, *v.* gurgle
gor·go·teo, *m.* gurgle
gor·jear, *v.* twitter
gor·jeo, *m.* twitter; chirp; warble
go·rra, *f.* cap
go·ta, *f.* drop; drip; bead; gout. **caer go·ta a go·ta**, dribble
go·tear, *v.* drip; trickle
go·te·ra, *f.* leak
go·zar(se), *v.* enjoy
goz·ne, *m.* hinge; hinge joint
gra·ba·do, *m.* engraving; print
gra·ba·dor, *m.* engraver
gra·ba·do·ra, *f.* stapler; recorder
gra·bar, *v.* engrave; record
gra·cia, *f.* grace; *pl.* thanks

gra·cio·so, *a.* graceful; funny; droll
gra·da, *f.* step; *pl.* bleachers
gra·da·ción, *f.* gradation
gra·do, *m.* grade; degree
gra·dua·ción, *f.* graduation; rank
gra·dua·do, *m.*, **gra·dua·da**, *f.* graduate
gra·dual, *a.* gradual
gra·duar(se), *v.* graduate
grá·fi·ca, *f.* graph
grá·fi·co, *m.* chart; graph. *a.* graphic; vivid
gra·fi·to, *m.* graphite
gra·má·ti·ca, *f.* grammar
gra·ma·ti·cal, *a.* grammatical
gra·mo, *m.* gram
gra·na·da, *f.* shell; **gra·na·da de ma·no**, hand grenade
gra·na·te, *m.* garnet
gran·de (gran), *a.* great; big; large
gran·dio·so, *a.* grand; grandiose
gra·ne·ro, *m.* granary; barn
gra·ni·to, *m.* granite; pimple
gra·ni·zar, *v.* hail
gra·ni·zo, *m.* hail. **pie·dra de gra·ni·zo**, hailstone
gran·ja, *f.* farm
gra·no, *m.* grain; cereal; pimple
gra·nu·lar, *v.* granulate
grá·nu·lo, *m.* granule
gra·pa, *f.* staple; clamp
gra·sa, *f.* fat; grease
gra·sien·to, *a.* greasy; oily
gra·ti·fi·ca·ción, *f.* gratification
gra·tis, *a.* free; gratis. *adv.* gratis
gra·tui·to, *a.* gratuitous; complimentary; free
gra·var, *v.* encumber
gra·ve, *a.* grave; serious; grievous; dignified
gra·ve·dad, *f.* gravity
gra·vi·ta·ción, *f.* gravitation
graz·nar, *v.* squawk
graz·ni·do, *m.* squawk. **graz·ni·do del pa·to**, quack
gre·ga·rio, *a.* gregarious
gre·mio, *m.* guild; union
grie·ta, *f.* fissure; rift; crack
gri·fo, *m.* faucet; tap; griffin, griffon
gri·lle·te, *m.* shackle
gri·llo, *m.* cricket; *pl.* fetters
gri·pe, *f.* grippe; *inf.* flu
gris, *a.* gray; grizzled. *m.* gray
gri·tar, *v.* shout; cry; yell; *inf.* holler
gri·to, *m.* shout; yell; outcry; scream
gro·se·lla, *f.* currant
gro·se·ría, *f.* vulgarity; rudeness
gro·se·ro, *a.* gross; vulgar; uncouth; coarse
gro·tes·co, *a.* grotesque
grúa, *f.* crane
grue·sa, *f.* gross
grue·so, *a.* gross; thick; heavy
gru·lla, *f.* crane

gru·mo, *m.* clot
gru·ñi·do, *m.* grunt
gru·ñir, *v.* grunt; growl
gru·ñón, *a.* grumpy
gru·po, *m.* group; bunch
gru·ta, *f.* grotto
gua·da·ña, *f.* scythe
guan·te, *m.* glove
guan·te·le·te, *m.* gauntlet
gua·po, *a.* good-looking
guar·da·es·pal·das, *m.* bodyguard
guar·da·fan·go, *m.* fender
guar·dar(se), *v.* guard; keep; watch; beware
guar·da·rro·pa, *f.* wardrobe
guar·dia, *f.* guard. *m.* guard; sentry
guar·dián, *m.* guardian; caretaker; warden
guar·di·lla, *f.* garret
gua·ri·da, *f.* den
guar·ne·cer, *v.* man; adorn
guar·ni·ción, *f.* garrison; adornment; fittings
gua·són, *m.* tease
gu·bia, *f.* gouge
gue·rra, *f.* war; warfare. **gue·rra ci·vil,** civil war. **gue·rra fría,** cold war
gue·rre·ro, *m.* fighter; warrior
gue·rri·lle·ro, *m.* guerrilla
guía, *f.* guidebook; guide. *m.* guide
guiar, *v.* guide; lead; steer
gui·ja·rro, *m.* pebble
gui·llo·ti·na, *f.* guillotine
gui·ñar, *v.* wink
gui·ño, *m.* wink
guión, *m.* hyphen; dash
guir·nal·da, *f.* garland; wreath
gui·san·te, *m.* pea
gui·ta, *f.* twine
gui·ta·rra, *f.* guitar
gu·la, *f.* gluttony
gu·sa·no, *m.* worm. **gu·sa·no de tie·rra,** earthworm
gus·tar, *v.* like; please; relish
gus·to, *m.* taste; pleasure; gusto; zest. **con mu·cho gus·to,** gladly; with pleasure. **dar gus·to,** please
gu·tu·ral, *a.* guttural

H

ha·ba, *f.* bean
ha·ber, *aux. v.* used in compound tenses. *m. pl.* assets; goods
há·bil, *a.* dexterous; adroit; knowing
ha·bi·li·dad, *f.* skill; ability; craft; workmanship
ha·bi·li·tar, *v.* qualify
ha·bi·ta·ble, *a.* habitable
ha·bi·ta·ción, *f.* habitat; habitation; room; lodging
ha·bi·tan·te, *m., f.* inhabitant
ha·bi·tar, *v.* inhabit; dwell

há·bi·to, *m.* habit
ha·bi·tual, *a.* habitual; usual
ha·bi·tuar(se), *v.* inure; accustom to
ha·bla, *f.* speech
ha·bla·dor, *a.* talkative; voluble
ha·blar, *v.* speak; talk. **ha·blar en·tre dien·tes,** mumble
ha·ce, *a.* ago. *adv.* ago
ha·cer(se), *v.* do; make; act; perform; become
ha·cia, *prep.* to; towards; about. **ha·cia a·de·lan·te,** onward(s). **ha·cia ca·sa,** homeward(s). **ha·cia den·tro,** inward. **ha·cia fue·ra,** outward(s)
ha·cien·da, *f.* ranch
ha·cha, *f.* ax; axe
ha·da, *f.* fairy
ha·do, *m.* fate
ha·la·gar, *v.* cajole; allure
ha·la·go, *m.* cajolery
hal·cón, *m.* hawk; falcon
ha·lo, *m.* halo
ha·llar(se), *v.* find; locate; find oneself
ha·llaz·go, *m.* discovery
ha·ma·ca, *f.* hammock
ham·bre, *f.* hunger; famine
ham·brien·to, *a.* hungry; starving
ham·bur·gue·sa, *f.* hamburger
ha·ra·ga·near, *v.* loaf; idle
ha·ra·pien·to, *a.* tattered
ha·rén, *m.* harem
ha·ri·na, *f.* flour; meal
har·tar(se), *v.* sicken; satiate; glut; gorge
has·ta, *adv.* to. *prep.* till; as far as. *conj.* until
ha·ya, *f.* beech
haz, *f.* sickle. **haz de le·ña,** fagot
ha·za·ña, *f.* exploit; deed
he·bi·lla, *f.* buckle
he·bra, *f.* strand; thread
he·chi·ce·ra, *f.* witch; sorceress
he·chi·ce·ría, *f.* sorcery
he·chi·ce·ro, *m.* sorcerer; wizard; warlock
he·chi·zar, *v.* bewitch; entrance; charm
he·chi·zo, *m.* charm; spell
he·cho, *a.* done; ready-made. *m.* deed; fact; act
he·der, *v.* stink
he·dor, *m.* stench; stink
he·la·da, *f.* frost
he·la·do, *m.* ice cream. *a.* icy
he·lar(se), *v.* freeze; ice
hé·li·ce, *f.* propeller; helix; spiral
he·li·cóp·te·ro, *m.* helicopter
he·lio, *m.* helium
he·mis·fe·rio, *m.* hemisphere
he·mo·rra·gia, *f.* hemorrhage
he·mo·rroi·des, *f.* hemorrhoids
he·nal, *m.* loft

hen·der(se), v. split; crack; rend; gash

he·no, m. hay

he·rál·di·ca, f. heraldry

her·cú·leo, a. herculean

he·re·dad, f. domain; landed property

he·re·dar, v. inherit

he·re·de·ra, f. heiress

he·re·de·ro, m. heir

he·re·di·ta·rio, a. hereditary

he·re·je, m. f. heretic

he·re·jía, f. heresy

he·ren·cia, f. heredity; heritage; inheritance

he·ri·da, f. hurt; wound

he·ri·do, a. wounded; stricken

he·rir, v. wound; injure

her·ma·na, f. sister

her·ma·nas·tra, f. stepsister

her·ma·nas·tro, m. stepbrother

her·man·dad, f. brotherhood

her·ma·no, m. brother

her·mo·so, a. lovely; beautiful; handsome

her·nia, f. hernia; rupture

hé·roe, m. hero

he·roí·na, f. heroine; heroin

he·rois·mo, m. heroism

he·rra·du·ra, f. horseshoe

he·rra·mien·ta, f. tool; implement; pl. gear

he·rre·ro, m. blacksmith; smith, smithy

he·rrum·bro·so, a. rusty

her·vir, v. boil; seethe

he·te·ro·gé·neo, a. heterogeneous

hex·á·go·no, m. hexagon

hí·bri·do, a. hybrid

hi·dal·go, m. nobleman

hi·dráu·li·co, a. hydraulic

hi·dró·ge·no, m. hydrogen

hi·dro·pe·sía, f. dropsy

hie·dra, f. ivy

hie·lo, m. ice

hie·na, f. hyena

hier·ba, f. grass; herb. **ma·la hier·ba,** weed

hie·rro, m. iron; pl. irons. **hie·rro fun·di·do,** cast iron

hí·ga·do, m. liver

hi·gie·ne, f. hygiene

hi·go, m. fig

hi·ja, f. daughter

hi·jas·tra, f. stepdaughter

hi·jas·tro, m. stepson

hi·jo, m. son; pl. children

hi·la, f. lint; row

hi·la·za, f. yarn

hi·le·ra, f. row; file

hi·lo, m. thread

hil·va·nar, v. baste; tack

him·no, m. hymn. **him·no na·cio·nal,** anthem

hin·char(se), v. swell; bloat; stuff; billow

hin·cha·zón, f. bump

hip·no·sis, f. hypnosis

hip·nó·ti·co, a. hypnotic. **es·ta·do hip·nó·ti·co,** trance

hip·no·ti·zar, v. hypnotize

hi·po, m. hiccup, hiccough

hi·po·con·dría·co, m., **hi·po·con·dría·ca,** f. hypochondriac

hi·po·cre·sía, f. hypocrisy

hi·pó·cri·ta, m., f. hypocrite

hi·po·dér·mi·co, a. hypodermic

hi·po·pó·ta·mo, m. hippopotamus

hi·po·te·ca, f. mortgage

hi·po·te·car, v. mortgage

hi·po·te·nu·sa, f. hypotenuse

hi·pó·te·sis, f. hypothesis

his·té·ri·co, a. hysteric(al)

his·to·ria, f. history; story; record

his·to·ria·dor, m., **his·to·ria·do·ra,** f. historian

his·tó·ri·co, a. historic(al)

his·trió·ni·co, a. histrionic(al)

ho·ci·co, m. snout; muzzle

ho·gar, m. home; hearth; fireplace

ho·gue·ra, f. bonfire

ho·ja, f. sheet; leaf; blade

ho·jear, v. browse; skim; leaf through

ho·jue·la, f. pancake; pl. flakes

ho·la, int. hello

ho·lo·caus·to, m. holocaust

ho·llar, v. tread on

ho·llín, m. soot

hom·bre, m. man

hom·bro, m. shoulder

ho·me·na·je, m. homage; tribute

ho·mi·ci·dio, m. homicide

ho·mi·lía, f. homily

ho·mo·gé·neo, a. homogeneous

ho·mó·ni·mo, m. homonym

hon·do, a. deep

hon·go, m. mushroom; toadstool; fungus

ho·nor, m. honor; credit; pl. laurels

ho·no·ra·rio, a. honorary. m. pl. fees

hon·ra, f. honor; virtue

hon·ra·dez, f. honesty

hon·ra·do, a. honest; upstanding

hon·rar, v. honor; exalt; dignify

ho·ra, f. hour; time. **ho·ra de a·ta·que,** zero hour

ho·ra·rio, m. schedule; timetable

hor·ca, f. gallows

hor·da, f. horde

ho·ri·zon·tal, a. horizontal

ho·ri·zon·te, m. horizon

hor·mi·ga, f. ant

hor·mi·gón, m. concrete

hor·mo·na, f. hormone

hor·na·da, f. batch

hor·no, m. oven; kiln; furnace

ho·rós·co·po, m. horoscope

hor·qui·lla, f. barrette; hairpin

ho·rren·do, a. dire

ho·rri·ble, *a.* horrible; hideous; gruesome; ghastly; awful

ho·rror, *m.* horror

ho·rro·ri·zar(se), *v.* horrify

hor·ti·cul·tu·ra, *f.* horticulture

hos·co, *a.* surly; gloomy

hos·pe·dar(se), *v.* lodge; harbor

hos·pi·tal, *m.* hospital

hos·pi·ta·la·rio, *a.* hospitable

hos·pi·ta·li·dad, *f.* hospitality

hos·tia, *f.* wafer; host

hos·ti·ga·mien·to, *m.* harassment

hos·ti·gar, *v.* harry; scourge

hos·til, *a.* hostile

hos·ti·li·dad, *f.* hostility

ho·tel, *m.* hotel

hoy, *m.* today; present time. *adv.* today, to-day

ho·yo, *m.* hole; pit; cavity

ho·yue·lo, *m.* dimple

hu·cha, *f.* bin

hue·co, *m.* gap; hollow

huel·ga, *f.* strike; walkout

hue·lla, *f.* footprint; trace. hue·lla dac·ti·lar, fingerprint

huér·fa·no, *m.* orphan

huer·ta, *f.* garden

huer·to, *m.* orchard

hue·so, *m.* bone; pit

hués·ped, *m.* host; guest; boarder

hués·pe·da, *f.* hostess; guest

hue·vo, *m.* egg

hui·da, *f.* flight

huir(se), *v.* escape; flee

hu·ma·ni·dad, *f.* humanity

hu·ma·ni·ta·rio, *a.* humanitarian. *m.* humanitarian

hu·ma·no, *m.* human. *a.* human

hu·mear, *v.* smoke; fume

hu·me·dad, *f.* humidity; moisture

hu·me·de·cer(se), *v.* humidify; moisten

hú·me·do, *a.* humid; damp; wet; moist

hu·mil·dad, *f.* humility

hu·mil·de, *a.* humble; low

hu·mi·lla·ción, *f.* humiliation

hu·mi·llar(se), *v.* humble; humiliate

hu·mo, *m.* smoke

hu·mor, *m.* humor; mood

hun·di·do, *a.* sunken

hun·dir(se), *v.* sink; slump; cave in; collapse

hu·ra·cán, *m.* hurricane

hu·rón, *m.* ferret

hur·tar(se), *v.* rob; steal; steal away

hus·mear, *v.* sniff; scent

hu·so, *m.* spindle

I

i·bis, *f.* ibis

i·ce·berg, *m.* iceberg

i·co·no, *m.* icon

i·co·no·clas·ta, *m., f.* iconoclast

ic·te·ri·cia, *f.* jaundice

i·da, *f.* going

i·dea, *f.* idea; thought; notion

i·de·al, *a.* ideal. *m.* ideal

i·dea·li·zar, *v.* idealize

i·dear, *v.* design; invent

i·dén·ti·co, *a.* identical; same

i·den·ti·dad, *f.* identity

i·den·ti·fi·ca·ción, *f.* identification

i·deo·lo·gía, *f.* ideology

i·di·lio, *m.* idyll

i·dio·ma, *m.* tongue; language

i·dio·má·ti·co, *a.* idiomatic

i·dio·sin·cra·sia, *f.* idiosyncrasy

i·dio·ta, *m., f.* idiot

i·dio·tis·mo, *m.* idiom

i·do·la·trar, *v.* idolize

i·do·la·tría, *f.* idolatry

í·do·lo, *m.* idol

i·gle·sia, *f.* church

ig·no·ran·cia, *f.* ignorance

ig·no·ran·te, *a.* ignorant

i·gual, *a.* equal; even. *m.* equal; match

i·gua·lar(se), *v.* even; equal; match

i·gual·dad, *f.* equality

i·ja·da, *f.* loin; flank

i·le·gal, *a.* illegal; unlawful

i·le·gi·ble, *a.* illegible

i·le·gi·ti·mi·dad, *f.* illegitimacy

i·le·gí·ti·mo, *a.* illegitimate; bastard

i·le·so, *a.* unhurt; unscathed

i·lí·ci·to, *a.* illicit

i·lu·mi·nar, *v.* illuminate; light; enlighten

i·lu·sión, *f.* illusion

i·lu·sio·nis·ta, *m., f.* magician; conjurer, conjuror

i·lus·tra·ción, *f.* illustration; picture

i·lus·trar, *v.* illustrate

i·ma·gen, *f.* image

i·ma·gi·na·ción, *f.* imagination

i·ma·gi·nar(se), *v.* imagine; conceive; guess; fancy

i·mán, *m.* magnet

im·bé·cil, *m., f.* imbecile; half-wit. *a.* imbecile

i·mi·ta·ción, *f.* imitation

i·mi·tar, *v.* imitate; mimic

im·pa·cien·te, *a.* impatient; anxious; eager

im·pac·to, *m.* impact

im·par, *a.* odd

im·par·cial, *a.* impartial

im·pa·si·ble, *a.* stolid

im·pá·vi·do, *a.* dauntless

im·pe·ca·ble, *a.* impeccable

im·pe·di·men·to, *m.* impediment; check; obstacle

im·pe·dir, *v.* impede; hinder; prevent; deter

im·pe·ler, *v.* urge

im·pe·ne·tra·ble, *a.* impervious

im·per·di·ble, *m.* safety pin
im·per·fec·ción, *f.* flaw
im·pe·rio, *m.* empire
im·pe·rio·so, *a.* imperious; authoritative
im·per·mea·ble, *m.* waterproof; raincoat
im·per·so·nal, *a.* impersonal
im·per·ti·nen·te, *a.* impertinent
ím·pe·tu, *m.* impetus; momentum
im·pe·tuo·so, *a.* impetuous; brash
im·plo·rar, *v.* implore; invoke
im·po·ner, *v.* impose; charge
im·por·tan·cia, *f.* importance; value
im·por·tan·te, *a.* important; prominent; weighty
im·por·tar, *v.* matter; care; import
im·por·tu·nar, *v.* solicit; pester
im·po·si·ble, *a.* impossible
im·pos·tor, *m.,* im·pos·to·ra, *f.* impostor
im·pos·tu·ra, *f.* sham; fake
im·po·ten·te, *a.* impotent
im·pre·me·di·ta·do, *a.* impromptu; unpremeditated
im·pren·ta, *f.* press; printing
im·pres·cin·di·ble, *a.* indispensable
im·pre·sión, *f.* impression; print
im·pre·sio·nan·te, *a.* striking; stunning
im·pre·sio·nar(se), *v.* impress
im·pre·vis·to, *a.* sudden; unexpected; un-looked-for; extemporaneous
im·pri·mir, *v.* print; imprint; impress
im·pro·ba·ble, *a.* improbable
im·pro·pio, *a.* improper
im·pro·vi·sar, *v.* improvise
im·pru·den·te, *a.* rash
im·pú·di·co, *a.* immodest
im·pues·to, *m.* tax
im·pul·sar, *v.* impel
im·pul·so, *m.* impulse; urge
im·pu·re·za, *f.* impurity
in·a·bor·da·ble, *a.* unapproachable
in·ac·ti·vo, *a.* quiescent; inactive
in·a·de·cua·do, *a.* inadequate
in·a·ni·ma·do, *a.* inanimate
in·a·pli·ca·ble, *a.* irrelevant
in·a·pre·cia·ble, *a.* priceless
in·au·di·to, *a.* unheard-of
in·au·gu·rar, *v.* inaugurate
in·cal·cu·la·ble, *a.* untold
in·can·des·cen·te, *a.* incandescent
in·ca·pa·ci·dad, *f.* disability
in·ca·pa·ci·tar, *v.* incapacitate
in·ca·paz, *a.* incapable; unable; helpless
in·cau·to, *a.* unwary
in·cen·diar(se), *v.* burn; catch fire
in·cen·dio, *m.* fire. in·cen·dio pre·me·di·ta·do, arson
in·cen·ti·vo, *m.* incentive
in·cer·ti·dum·bre, *f.* uncertainty;

suspense
in·ce·san·te, *a.* ceaseless; incessant
in·ces·to, *m.* incest
in·ci·den·tal, *a.* incidental
in·ci·den·te, *m.* incident
in·cien·so, *m.* incense
in·cier·to, *a.* uncertain; vague; treacherous
in·ci·ne·ra·ción, *f.* cremation
in·ci·ne·rar, *v.* incinerate; cremate
in·ci·sión, *f.* incision
in·ci·tar, *v.* incite; spur; urge; prompt
in·cle·men·to, *a.* inclement
in·cli·na·ción, *f.* inclination; propensity; slant; slope; tilt
in·cli·nar(se), *v.* incline; lean; slant; slope; sway; bow
in·cluir, *v.* include; enclose
in·co·mo·dar(se), *v.* inconvenience
in·co·mo·di·dad, *f.* discomfort; inconvenience
in·có·mo·do, *a.* uncomfortable
in·com·pe·ten·te, *a.* incompetent
in·com·ple·to, *a.* incomplete; unfinished
in·con·di·cio·nal, *a.* unconditional
in·con·gruo, *a.* incongruous
in·cons·cien·te, *a.* unconscious; unwitting
in·con·se·cuen·te, *a.* inconsequential
in·con·si·de·ra·do, *a.* thoughtless; wanton
in·cons·tan·te, *a.* fickle
in·con·ve·nien·cia, *f.* inconvenience
in·co·rrec·to, *a.* incorrect
in·creí·ble, *a.* incredible
in·cri·mi·nar, *v.* incriminate
in·cu·ba·do·ra, *f.* incubator
in·cues·tio·na·ble, *a.* unquestionable
in·cul·to, *a.* crude
in·cu·rrir, *v.* incur; commit
in·da·ga·ción, *f.* inquiry
in·de·cen·cia, *f.* indecency
in·de·cen·te, *a.* indecent; unseemly
in·de·ci·sión, *f.* indecision; hesitation
in·de·ci·so, *a.* uncertain; undecided
in·de·co·ro·so, *a.* unseemly; unbecoming
in·dem·ni·za·ción, *f.* indemnity
in·dem·ni·zar, *v.* compensate
in·de·pen·den·cia, *f.* independence
in·de·pen·dien·te, *a.* independent; self-sufficient; strong-minded
in·des·truc·ti·ble, *a.* indestructible
in·di·ca·ción, *f.* indication; suggestion
in·di·ca·dor, *m.* gauge; register. *a.* telltale
in·di·car, *v.* indicate; show; suggest; insinuate
in·di·ce, *m.* index
in·di·cio, *m.* symptom; trace; clue

in·di·fe·ren·te, a. indifferent; apathetic
in·dí·ge·na, m., f. native, a. indigenous
in·di·gen·cia, f. destitution
in·di·gen·te, a. indigent
in·di·ges·tión, f. indigestion
in·dig·ni·dad, f. indignity
in·dig·no, a. unworthy
in·di·rec·ta, f. hint
in·di·rec·to, a. indirect; oblique; round
in·dis·cre·ción, f. indiscretion
in·dis·pues·to, a. out of sorts; unwell
in·dis·tin·to, a. vague; obscure
in·di·vi·dual, a. individual
in·di·vi·duo, a. individual
in·do·len·te, a. indolent
in·du·cir, v. induce
in·dul·gen·te, a. lenient
in·dul·to, m. pardon
in·dus·tria, f. industry
in·e·fi·caz, a. weak; inefficient
in·fa·li·ble, a. foolproof
in·fan·te·ría, f. infantry
in·fan·til, a. infant; baby; childish
in·fec·ción, f. infection
in·fec·tar(se), v. infect
in·fe·liz, a. unhappy; unfortunate
in·fe·rior, a. inferior; worse; under. m. inferior
in·fe·rir, v. infer
in·fer·nal, a. infernal; hellish
in·fes·tar, v. infest
in·fi·de·li·dad, f. infidelity
in·fiel, a. unfaithful. m. infidel
in·fier·no, m. hell
in·fil·trar(se), v. infiltrate
in·fi·ni·ti·vo, m. infinitive
in·fi·ni·to, a. infinite. m. infinity
in·fla·ma·ble, a. flammable
in·flar(se), v. blow up; puff up
in·fle·xi·ble, a. inflexible; unyielding; grim
in·fluen·cia, f. influence; sway
in·for·ma·ción, f. information; intelligence
in·for·mal, a. informal; unceremonious
in·for·mar(se), v. inform; report
in·for·me, m. report
in·for·tu·nio, m. misfortune
in·fre·cuen·te, a. infrequent; seldom
in·frin·gir, v. trespass
in·fun·dir, v. infuse
in·fu·sión, f. infusion
in·ge·nie·ría, f. engineering*
in·ge·nie·ro, m. engineer
in·ge·nio, m. device; wit
in·ge·nio·so, a. ingenious; clever; subtle; witty
in·ge·nuo, a. naive
in·gle, f. groin
in·glés, m., in·gle·sa, f. English. a.

English
in·gre·dien·te, m. ingredient
in·gre·sar, v. enter; deposit
in·gre·so, m. entry; pl. income; revenue
in·ha·bi·li·dad, f. inability
in·ha·lar, v. inhale
in·he·ren·te, a. inherent
in·hi·bi·ción, f. inhibition
in·hu·ma·no, a. inhuman
i·ni·cia·ción, f. initiation
i·ni·cial, a. initial. f. initial
i·ni·ciar, v. initiate
i·ni·cia·ti·va, f. initiative; enterprise
i·ni·qui·dad, f. iniquity
in·jer·tar, v. graft
in·ju·ria, f. injury; abuse
in·jus·ta·men·te, adv. unjustly; wrong
in·jus·ti·cia, f. injustice
in·jus·to, a. unjust
in·ma·du·ro, a. immature
in·me·dia·to, a. immediate; instant
in·men·so, a. immense; huge; vast
in·mer·sión, f. immersion
in·mi·gra·ción, f. immigration
in·mi·gran·te, m., f. immigrant
in·mi·grar, v. immigrate
in·mi·nen·te, a. imminent
in·mo·ral, a. immoral
in·mor·tal, a. immortal
in·mó·vil, a. immobile; still; stationary
in·mun·di·cia, f. filth
in·mu·ni·dad, f. immunity
in·na·to, a. inborn; innate
in·no·ble, a. ignoble
in·no·cuo, a. harmless
in·no·va·ción, f. innovation
in·nu·me·ra·ble, a. unnumbered; innumerable; countless
i·no·cen·cia, f. innocence
i·no·cen·te, a. innocent; clear
i·no·cu·la·ción, f. inoculation
in·o·por·tu·no, a. untimely; inopportune
in·quie·tar(se), v. worry; upset; trouble; harry; agitate
in·quie·to, a. anxious; concerned; fidgety
in·quie·tud, f. unrest; alarm; anxiety; inf. jitters
in·qui·li·no, m. inmate; tenant
in·qui·si·ción, f. inquisition
in·sa·lu·bre, a. unhealthy; unwholesome
ins·cri·bir(se), v. inscribe; enroll
ins·crip·ción, f. inscription
in·sec·to, m. insect
in·se·gu·ro, a. insecure; unsteady
in·sen·sa·to, a. insane; senseless
in·ser·tar, v. insert
in·sig·nias, f. pl. insignia
in·sig·ni·fi·can·cia, f. insignificance

in·sig·ni·fi·can·te, *a.* insignificant; negligible
in·si·nua·ción, *f.* insinuation
in·si·nuar, *v.* insinuate; hint
in·sí·pi·do, *a.* insipid; vapid; flat
in·sis·tir, *v.* insist
in·so·la·ción, *f.* sunstroke
in·so·len·cia, *f.* insolence
in·sol·ven·te, *a.* bankrupt
in·som·nio, *m.* insomnia
ins·pec·ción, *f.* inspection; survey
ins·pec·cio·nar, *v.* inspect; survey
ins·pi·ra·ción, *f.* inspiration
ins·pi·rar, *v.* inspire
ins·ta·la·ción, *f.* fixture; wiring. **ins·ta·la·ción de ca·ñe·rías,** plumbing
ins·ta·lar, *v.* install
ins·tan·tá·neo, *a.* instantaneous
ins·tan·te, *m.* instant; *inf.* jiffy
ins·ti·gar, *v.* instigate; abet
ins·tin·to, *m.* instinct; flair
ins·ti·tu·ción, *f.* institution
ins·ti·tuir, *v.* institute
ins·ti·tu·to, *m.* institution; institute
ins·ti·tu·triz, *f.* governess
ins·truc·ción, *f.* instruction
ins·truir(se), *v.* instruct; teach; enlighten; learn
ins·tru·men·to, *m.* instrument; tool
in·su·fi·cien·te, *a.* insufficient; short; deficient
in·su·li·na, *f.* insulin
in·sul·tar, *v.* insult
in·su·rrec·ción, *f.* insurrection; uprising
in·tac·to, *a.* intact
in·ta·cha·ble, *a.* blameless
in·te·gra·ción, *f.* integration
in·te·grar(se), *v.* integrate
in·te·gri·dad, *f.* integrity
in·te·lec·to, *m.* intellect
in·te·li·gen·cia, *f.* intelligence; mind; intellect
in·te·li·gen·te, *a.* intelligent; brainy
in·ten·ción, *f.* intention; meaning
in·ten·si·dad, *f.* intensity
in·ten·si·fi·car, *v.* intensify; deepen
in·ten·so, *a.* intense; strong; vivid; violent. *m.* intent
in·ten·tar, *v.* try; endeavor; attempt; essay; mean
in·ter·ac·ción, *f.* interplay
in·ter·cam·biar, *v.* interchange
in·ter·cam·bio, *m.* interchange
in·ter·ce·der, *v.* intercede
in·ter·ce·sión, *f.* intercession
in·te·rés, *m.* interest; stir; cause
in·te·re·sar(se), *v.* interest; concern
in·ter·fe·ren·cia, *f.* interference
in·te·rin, *m.* interim; meantime
in·te·rior, *m.* interior; inside. *a.* interior; internal; inner; indoor
in·ter·jec·ción, *f.* interjection
in·ter·me·dio, *a.* intermediate. *m.* interlude; medium

in·ter·mi·sión, *f.* intermission
in·ter·na·cio·nal, *a.* international
in·ter·no, *a.* internal; inside; inward(s). *m.* intern
in·ter·po·ner(se), *v.* interpose; intervene
in·ter·pre·ta·ción, *f.* translation; interpretation
in·ter·pre·tar, *v.* interpret
in·te·rro·ga·ción, *f.* interrogation. sig·no de in·te·rro·ga·ción, question mark
in·te·rro·gar, *v.* interrogate; examine; quiz; *inf.* grill
in·te·rrum·pir, *v.* interrupt
in·te·rrup·ción, *f.* interruption
in·ter·sec·ción, *f.* intersection
in·ter·ven·ción, *f.* interference
in·ter·ve·nir, *v.* intervene; interfere; mediate; audit
in·ter·ven·tor, *m.* comptroller; auditor
in·tes·ti·no, *m.* intestine; gut; *pl.* bowels
in·ti·mar, *v.* intimate
in·ti·mi·dad, *f.* closeness
in·ti·mi·dar(se), *v.* intimidate; browbeat; bully; cow
ín·ti·mo, *a.* intimate
in·to·le·ran·te, *a.* intolerant
in·tran·qui·lo, *a.* uneasy; restless
in·tran·si·ti·vo, *a.* intransitive
in·tra·ve·no·so, *a.* intravenous
in·tré·pi·do, *a.* intrepid; bold; fearless
in·tri·ga, *f.* intrigue
in·tri·gar, *v.* intrigue; scheme; plot
in·trín·se·co, *a.* intrinsic(al)
in·tro·duc·ción, *f.* introduction
in·tro·du·cir(se), *v.* introduce; broach; slip in
in·tui·ción, *f.* intuition
i·nun·da·ción, *f.* flood
i·nun·dar, *v.* deluge; flood; swamp
in·ú·til, *a.* useless; futile
in·va·dir, *v.* invade; overrun
in·va·li·dar, *v.* void; invalidate
in·va·sión, *f.* invasion
in·ven·ci·ble, *a.* invincible
in·ven·ción, *f.* invention; contrivance; figment
in·ven·tar, *v.* invent; fabricate; devise; contrive
in·ver·nal, *a.* winter; wintry
in·ver·nar, *v.* winter
in·ver·sión, *f.* inversion
in·ver·so, *a.* reverse
in·ver·te·bra·do, *m.* invertebrate. *a.* invertebrate
in·ver·tir, *v.* reverse; invert; invest
in·ves·ti·ga·ción, *f.* investigation; probe; *pl.* research

in.ves.ti.gar, v. investigate
in.ves.tir, v. invest
in.vic.ti.va, f. tirade
in.vier.no, m. winter
in.vi.si.ble, a. invisible
in.vi.ta.ción, f. invitation
in.vi.tar, v. invite; treat
in.vo.car, v. invoke
in.vo.lun.ta.rio, a. involuntary
in.yec.ción, f. injection; inf. shot
in.yec.tar, v. inject
ion, m. ion
ir(se), v. go; leave; depart; quit; move; ride
i.ra, f. ire; rage; anger
i.ri.des.cen.te, a. iridescent
i.ris, m. iris. ar.co i.ris, rainbow
i.ro.nía, f. irony
i.ró.ni.co, a. ironic(al); wry
i.rra.cio.nal, a. irrational
i.rra.diar, v. irradiate
i.rre.gu.lar, a. irregular
i.rre.sis.ti.ble, a. irresistible
i.rres.pon.sa.ble, a. irresponsible
i.rre.ve.ren.cia, f. irreverence
i.rri.sión, f. derision
i.rri.ta.ble, a. irritable; touchy; crusty
i.rri.ta.ción, f. irritation
i.rri.tar(se), v. irritate; chafe; anger; pique
is.la, f. island; isle
i.sós.ce.les, a. isosceles
ist.mo, m. isthmus
i.ti.ne.ra.rio, m. itinerary
iz.quier.da, f. left
iz.quier.do, a. left

J

ja.ba.lí, m. wild boar
ja.ba.li.na, f. javelin
ja.bón, m. soap
ja.bo.na.du.ras, f. pl. suds
ja.ca, f. pony; cob; nag
ja.cin.to, m. hyacinth
jac.tan.cia, f. bluster; bragging
jac.tar.se, v. brag; boast
ja.de, m. jade
ja.dear, v. pant
ja.deo, m. pant
ja.guar, m. jaguar
jal.be.gue, m. whitewash
ja.lea, f. jelly
ja.leo, m. fuss; racket
ja.más, adv. never; ever
jam.ba, f. jamb
ja.món, m. ham
ja.que, m. check in chess. dar ja.que ma.te, checkmate
ja.ra.be, m. syrup
ja.ra.near, v. carouse
jar.dín, m. garden; park. jar.dín bo.tá.ni.co, arboretum. jar.dín de la

in.fan.cia, kindergarten. jar.dín zoo.ló.gi.co, zoo
ja.rra, f. jug
ja.rro, m. jug; flagon
ja.rrón, m. vase
jau.la, f. cage; cell
jaz.mín, m. jasmine; jasmin
jazz, m. jazz
jeep, m. jeep
je.fe, m. boss; chief; head; leader
Je.ho.vá, m. Jehovah
je.jén, m. gnat
jen.gi.bre, m. ginger. cer.ve.za de jen.gi.bre, gingerale. pan de jen.gi.bre, gingerbread
je.que, m. sheik, sheikh
je.rar.quía, f. hierarchy
jer.ga, f. slang; jargon; gibberish
je.rin.ga, f. syringe
je.ro.glí.fi.co, a. hieroglyphic. m. hieroglyphic; hieroglyph
jer.sey, m. sweater; jersey
ji.ga, f. jig
ji.ne.ta, f. equestrienne
ji.ne.te, m. horseman; equestrian
ji.ra, f. picnic
ji.ra.fa, f. giraffe
ji.ro.nes, m. pl. tatters
jo.ckey, m. jockey
jo.co.so, a. jocose; jocular
jo.fai.na, f. basin
jor.nal, m. often pl. wage
jo.ro.ba, f. hump
jo.ro.ba.do, a. hunchback
jo.ro.bar, v. tease; annoy
jo.ta, f. iota; jot
jo.ven, a. young; juvenile. m., f. youth; pl. youth
jo.ven.ci.to, m., jo.ven.ci.ta, f. youngster
jo.vial, a. jovial
jo.ya, f. jewel; gem; pl. jewelry
jo.ye.ro, m. jeweler
jua.ne.te, m. bunion
ju.bi.lar(se), v. retire; pension
ju.bi.leo, m. jubilee
jú.bi.lo, m. jubilation; glee
ju.daís.mo, m. Judaism
ju.día, f. bean
ju.di.cial, a. judicial
ju.do, m. judo
jue.go, m. game; play; set; suite
juer.ga, f. spree
jue.ves, m. Thursday
juez, m. judge; justice
ju.ga.da, f. gamble; move
ju.gar, v. play; game; toy with; gamble
ju.go, m. juice
ju.gue.te, m. toy; plaything
ju.gue.tear, v. frolic; play
ju.gue.tón, a. playful
jui.cio, m. judgment; verdict; sense; wit. jui.cio sa.no, sanity

ju·lio, *m.* July
jun·co, *m.* junk; rush
ju·nio, *m.* June
jun·qui·llo, *m.* jonquil
jun·ta, *f.* union; board
jun·ta·men·te, *adv.* together
jun·tar(se), *v.* join; connect; band; assemble
jun·to, *a.* joined. *adv.* together. **jun·to a**, near; against
jun·tu·ra, *f.* junction; joint; splice
ju·ra·do, *m.* juror; jury
ju·ra·men·to, *m.* oath
ju·rar, *v.* swear; vow
ju·ris·dic·ción, *f.* jurisdiction
ju·ris·pru·den·cia, *f.* law; jurisprudence
ju·ris·ta, *m., f.* jurist
jus·ta, *f.* joust
jus·ta·men·te, *adv.* fairly
jus·tar, *v.* joust
jus·ti·cia, *f.* justice
jus·ti·fi·ca·ción, *f.* justification; substantiation
jus·ti·fi·car, *v.* justify; warrant
jus·ti·llo, *m.* jerkin
jus·to, *a.* just; fair
ju·ve·nil, *a.* juvenile; youth
ju·ven·tud, *f.* youth
juz·gar, *v.* judge; try; deem

K

ki·lo, *m.* kilogram
ki·lo·ci·clo, *m.* kilocycle
ki·lo·gra·mo, *m.* kilogram
ki·lo·mé·tri·co, *a.* kilometric
ki·ló·me·tro, *m.* kilometer
ki·lo·va·tio, *m.* kilowatt

L

la(s), *def. art.* the; *pl.* them
la·be·rin·to, *m.* labyrinth; maze
la·bial, *a.* labial
la·bio, *m.* lip
la·bor, *f.* labor; work; task
la·bo·ra·to·rio, *m.* laboratory; *inf.* lab
la·bo·rio·so, *a.* laborious; painstaking
la·bra·dor, *m.* farmer
la·bran·tío, *a.* arable
la·brar, *v.* till
la·ca, *f.* lacquer
la·ca·yo, *m.* lackey
la·ce·rar, *v.* lacerate
la·cio, *a.* lank; limp
la·có·ni·co, *a.* laconic
lac·tar, *v.* suckle
lác·ti·co, *a.* lactic
la·dear(se), *v.* lean; skirt; tip; heel
la·do, *m.* side; flank
la·drar, *v.* bark

la·dri·do, *m.* bark
la·drón, *m.* thief; burglar; *inf.* crook
la·gar, *m.* winery
la·gar·to, *m.* alligator; lizard
lá·gri·ma, *f.* tear
la·gu·na, *f.* lagoon; lacuna
lai·ca·do, *m.* laity
la·ma, *m.* lama. *f.* lamé
la·me·du·ra, *f.* lick
la·men·ta·ción, *f.* lamentation
la·men·tar(se), *v.* lament; mourn; regret; rue; wail
la·mer, *v.* lick; lap
lá·mi·na, *f.* sheet
la·mi·nar, *v.* laminate
lám·pa·ra, *f.* lamp; light
lam·prea, *f.* lamprey
la·na, *f.* wool
lan·ce, *m.* throw; stroke
lan·cha, *f.* launch
lan·gos·ta, *f.* lobster
lan·gui·de·cer, *v.* languish; pine
lán·gui·do, *a.* languid; listless
la·ni·lla, *f.* nap; bunting
la·no·li·na, *f.* lanolin
la·nu·do, *a.* fleecy
lan·za, *f.* spear; lance
lan·za·de·ra, *f.* shuttle
lan·zar(se), *v.* throw; hurl; launch
lá·pi·da, *f.* stone. **lá·pi·da se·pul·cral**, tombstone
lá·piz, *m.* pencil. **lá·piz de co·lor**, crayon
lap·so, *m.* lapse; span
lar·go, *m.* length. *a.* long. **a lo lar·go**, along
la·rin·ge, *f.* larynx
la·rin·gi·tis, *f.* laryngitis
lar·va, *f.* larva
las·ci·vo, *a.* lascivious; sensual; lewd; wanton
la·si·tud, *f.* lassitude
lás·ti·ma, *f.* pity
las·ti·mo·so, *a.* pitiful; sorry
las·tre, *m.* ballast
la·ta, *f.* can. **con·ser·var en la·tas**, can
la·ten·te, *a.* latent
la·te·ral, *a.* lateral; sidelong. *m.* side
la·te·ral·men·te, *adv.* sidelong
lá·tex, *m.* latex
la·ti·ga·zo, *m.* lash
lá·ti·go, *m.* whip; lash. **lá·ti·go mo·cho**, crop
la·ti·tud, *f.* latitude
la·tón, *m.* brass
la·tro·ci·nio, *m.* larceny
laúd, *m.* lute
lau·rel, *m.* laurel; bay
la·va, *f.* lava
la·va·bo, *m.* washstand; washroom
la·va·de·ro, *m.* laundry
la·va·do, *a.* washed. *m.* wash
la·va·do·ra, *f.* washer

la.va.ma.nos, *m.* washstand
la.var(se), *v.* wash. **la.var y plan-char,** launder
la.xan.te, *a.* laxative. *m.* laxative
la.xo, *a.* lax
la.zar, *v.* lasso
la.zo, *m.* lasso; lariat; bow; band. **la-zo co.rre.di.zo,** noose
le(s), *pron.* him; *pl.* them
leal, *a.* loyal
leal.men.te, *adv.* faithfully
leal.tad, *f.* loyalty; devotion
lec.ción, *f.* lesson; reading
lec.tu.ra, *f.* reading; lecture
le.che, *f.* milk. **le.che de man.te.ca,** buttermilk
le.che.ría, *f.* dairy
le.cho, *m.* watercourse; bed
le.chu.ga, *f.* lettuce; frill
le.chu.za, *f.* owl
leer, *v.* read
le.ga.ción, *f.* legation
le.ga.do, *m.* legacy; bequest
le.gal, *a.* legal; lawful
le.ga.li.dad, *f.* legality
lé.ga.mo, *m.* slime
le.ga.ño.so, *a.* bleary
le.gar, *v.* will; bequeath
le.gen.da.rio, *a.* legendary
le.gi.ble, *a.* legible
le.gión, *f.* legion
le.gio.na.rio, *m.* legionnaire
le.gis.la.ción, *f.* legislation
le.gis.lar, *v.* legislate
le.gi.ti.mar, *v.* legitimate
le.gí.ti.mo, *a.* legitimate; rightful
le.go, *a.* lay. *m.* layman
le.gum.bre, *f.* vegetable; legume
le.ja.no, *a.* far; distant; far off
le.jía, *f.* lye; bleach
le.jos, *adv.* far; away; wide. *prep.* off. **más le.jos,** further
le.ma, *m.* motto
len.gua, *f.* tongue; language
len.gua.je, *m.* language
len.güe.ta, *f.* tongue; reed
le.ni.dad, *f.* lenience; leniency
len.te, *m.* lens. **len.tes de con.tac.to,** contact lenses
len.te.jue.la, *f.* sequin
len.to, *a.* slow; sluggish
le.ño, *m.* log; lumber; kindling
león, *m.* lion
leo.na.do, *a.* tawny
leo.par.do, *m.* leopard
le.pra, *f.* leprosy
le.pro.so, *m.*, **le.pro.sa,** *f.* leper
le.tar.go, *m.* lethargy
le.tra, *f.* letter. **le.tra bas.tar.di.lla,** italic. **le.tra cur.si.va,** script. **le.tra de u.na can.ción,** lyric
le.tre.ro, *m.* sign
leu.ce.mia, *f.* leukemia
le.va, *f.* levy

le.va.du.ra, *f.* yeast; leaven; leavening
le.van.tar(se), *v.* rise; raise; erect; lift
lé.xi.co, *m.* lexicon
ley, *f.* law; act
le.yen.da, *f.* legend
liar(se), *v.* tie; bind; bundle
li.be.ral, *a.* liberal. *m., f.* liberal
li.be.ra.li.dad, *f.* liberality; bounty
li.ber.tad, *f.* freedom; liberty; release
li.ber.tar, *v.* liberate; free
li.ber.ti.no, *a.* promiscuous. *m.* rake
li.bi.do, *m.* libido
li.bra, *f.* pound
li.brar(se), *v.* rid; free
li.bre, *a.* free; vacant
li.bre.to, *m.* libretto
li.bro, *m.* book
li.cen.cia, *f.* license; furlough
li.cen.cia.do, *m.,* **li.cen.cia.da,** *f.* graduate; bachelor
li.cen.ciar, *v.* license
li.ci.ta.dor, *m.* auctioneer
li.cor, *m.* liquor; liqueur; spirits
lí.der, *m.* leader
lie.bre, *f.* hare
lien.zo, *m.* canvas; linen
li.ga, *f.* league; garter
li.ga.do, *a.* bound
li.ga.du.ra, *f.* ligature
li.ga.men.to, *m.* ligament
li.gar(se), *v.* tie; band together; alloy
li.ge.ra.men.te, *adv.* lightly
li.ge.re.za, *f.* levity
li.ge.ro, *a.* airy; light; mild; flippant
li.la, *f.* lilac
li.ma, *f.* file; lime
li.ma.du.ras, *f., pl.* filings
li.mar, *v.* file
lim.bo, *m.* limbo
li.mi.ta.ción, *f.* limitation
li.mi.tar(se), *v.* limit; confine; restrict; bound
lí.mi.te, *m.* limit; *pl.* bounds
li.món, *m.* lemon
li.mo.na.da, *f.* lemonade
li.mo.ne.ro, *a.* lemon
li.mos.na, *f.* alms; dole; charity
lim.piar(se), *v.* clean; cleanse; polish
lim.pie.za, *f.* cleanliness
lim.pio, *a.* clean
li.mu.si.na, *f.* limousine
li.na.je, *m.* lineage; ancestry; birth
lin.ce, *m.* lynx; bobcat
lin.char, *v.* lynch
lin.dar, *v.* flank; adjoin
lí.nea, *f.* line. **lí.nea aé.rea,** airline
li.neal, *a.* linear
lin.fa, *f.* lymph
lin.go.te, *m.* ingot
lin.güís.ta, *m., f.* linguist
li.ni.men.to, *m.* liniment
li.no, *m.* linen; flax
li.nó.leo, *m.* linoleum

lin·ter·na, *f.* lantern. **lin·ter·na e·léc·tri·ca,** flashlight
lío, *m.* bundle; liaison; row; *inf.* ruckus
li·quen, *m.* lichen
li·qui·dar(se), *v.* liquefy; liquidate
li·qui·do, *a.* liquid. *m.* liquid
li·ra, *f.* lyre
li·ri·co, *a.* lyric
li·rio, *m.* lily; iris
li·sia·do, *m.* cripple. *a.* lame
li·siar, *v.* lame; cripple
li·so, *a.* smooth; sleek
li·son·je·ro, *a.* complimentary
lis·ta, *f.* list; roll. **lis·ta de pla·tos,** menu. **lis·ta nó·mi·na,** roster
lis·tar, *v.* streak; list
lis·to, *a.* ready; nimble; quick; smart; clever
lis·tón, *m.* lath
li·te·ra, *f.* litter; berth
li·te·ral, *a.* literal
li·te·ra·rio, *a.* literary
li·te·ra·tu·ra, *f.* literature
li·to·ral, *m.* coastline
li·tur·gia, *f.* liturgy
lí·vi·do, *a.* livid
lo(s), *neuter def. art.* the; *m. pl of* **el**
loa·ble, *a.* laudable
lo·bo, *m.* wolf
ló·bre·go, *a.* gloomy
lo·cal, *a.* local. *m.* site
lo·ca·li·dad, *f.* locality
lo·ción, *f.* lotion
lo·co, *a.* insane; mad; crazy; wild. *m.* madman; lunatic
lo·co·mo·tor, *a.* locomotive
lo·co·mo·to·ra, *f.* engine; locomotive
lo·cu·ra, *f.* insanity; lunacy; folly
lo·do, *m.* mud
lo·gia, *f.* lodge
ló·gi·ca, *f.* logic
ló·gi·co, *a.* logical; coherent
lo·grar, *v.* succeed; achieve; win; carry; get; attain
lo·gro, *m.* attainment; success
lom·briz, *f.* angleworm
lo·mo, *m.* loin; *pl.* ribs
lon·ge·vi·dad, *f.* longevity
lon·gi·tud, *f.* longitude
lo·ro, *m.* parrot
lo·sa, *f.* flagstone
lo·te·ría, *f.* lottery
lo·za, *f.* crockery. **lo·za de ba·rro,** earthenware
lo·za·no, *a.* luxuriant
lu·bri·can·te, *m.* lubricant
lu·bri·car, *v.* lubricate
lu·bri·fi·car, *v.* oil; grease
lú·ci·do, *a.* lucid
lu·ciér·na·ga, *f.* firefly; glowworm
lu·cir(se), *v.* flaunt; show off; light up
lu·cra·ti·vo, *a.* lucrative
lu·cha, *f.* battle; fight; strife; struggle

lu·char, *v.* fight; battle; struggle
lue·go, *adv.* then
lu·gar, *m.* place; space; room
lu·jo, *m.* luxury. **de lu·jo,** deluxe; fancy
lu·jo·so, *a.* luxurious
lu·ju·ria, *f.* lust
lu·ju·riar, *v.* lust
lu·mi·no·so, *a.* luminous; illuminated
lu·na, *f.* moon. **lu·na de miel,** honeymoon
lu·nar, *a.* lunar. *m.* mole
lu·nes, *m.* Monday
lus·tre, *m.* luster; shine; sheen; gloss; brightness
lus·tro·so, *a.* glossy
lu·to, *m.* mourning
luz, *f.* light. **luz del día,** daylight. **luz de la lu·na,** moonlight

LL

lla·ga, *f.* sore; ulcer
lla·ma, *f.* flame; blaze; llama
lla·ma·da, *f.* call; knock
lla·ma·do, *a.* so-called
lla·mar(se), *v.* be named; name; call; ring; summon; rap
lla·ma·ti·vo, *a.* flamboyant; garish; showy
lla·no, *a.* even; flat. *m.* plain
llan·to, *m.* cry
lla·ve, *f.* key
lle·ga·da, *f.* arrival
lle·gar(se), *v.* arrive; come; land; approach. **lle·gar a ser,** become
lle·nar(se), *v.* fill; stuff; pack; occupy
lle·no, *a.* full. **lle·no de,** full of; fraught with
lle·var(se), *v.* carry; bear; convey; tote; lead; wear
llo·rar, *v.* cry; weep; bawl; mourn
llo·ri·quear, *v.* whimper
llo·ver, *v.* rain; shower
llo·viz·nar, *v.* drizzle; sprinkle
llu·via, *f.* rain; rainfall
llu·vio·so, *a.* rainy; wet

M

ma·ca·bro, *a.* macabre
ma·ca·rrón, *m.* macaroon
ma·ca·rro·nes, *m. pl.* macaroni
ma·ci·zo, *a.* massive; solid
ma·cha·do, *m.* hatchet
ma·che·te, *m.* machete
ma·cho, *a.* male; masculine. *m.* male
ma·de·ra, *f.* wood; timber; lumber
Ma·do·na, *f.* Madonna
ma·dras·tra, *f.* stepmother
ma·dre, *f.* mother
ma·dri·gue·ra, *f.* burrow
ma·dri·na, *f.* godmother

ma·dru·ga·da, *f.* morning
ma·du·rar(se), *v.* mature; ripen
ma·du·rez, *f.* maturity
ma·du·ro, *a.* mature; ripe
maes·tro, *m.* teacher; master; maestro. *a.* skilled
ma·gen·ta, *f.* magenta
ma·gia, *f.* magic. ma·gia ne·gra, black magic
má·gi·co, *a.* magic
ma·gis·tra·do, *m.* magistrate
mag·ná·ni·mo, *a.* magnanimous
mag·ne·si·o, *m.* magnesium
mag·ne·si·o, *m.* magnesium
mag·ne·tis·mo, *m.* magnetism
mag·ní·fi·co, *a.* magnificent; grand; splendid
mag·ni·tud, *f.* magnitude
ma·go, *m.* magician
ma·gro, *a.* lean
ma·gu·llar, *v.* bruise
ma·ha·ra·ja, *m.* maharajah, maharaja
maíz, *m.* corn; maize
ma·jes·tad, *f.* majesty
ma·jes·tuo·so, *a.* stately
mal, *a.* bad; ill. *adv.* wrongly. *m.* evil; mischief; harm
ma·la·men·te, *adv.* evil; badly
mal·dad, *f.* badness; evil; villainy
mal·de·cir, *v.* curse
mal·di·ción, *f.* curse
ma·lea·ble, *a.* malleable
ma·le·cón, *m.* jetty
ma·le·ta, *f.* suitcase; valise; bag
ma·lé·vo·lo, *a.* malignant
ma·le·za, *f.* underbrush; scrub
mal·gas·tar, *v.* waste; squander
mal·he·chor, *m.,* mal·he·cho·ra, *f.* evildoer; wrongdoer
mal·hu·mo·ra·do, *a.* cross; crabby; cantankerous
ma·li·cia, *f.* malice
ma·li·cio·so, *a.* malicious; wicked; mischievous
ma·lig·no, *a.* malignant
ma·lí·si·mo, *a.* wretched; very bad
ma·lo, *a.* bad; evil; wrong; poor; naughty
ma·lo·gro, *m.* miscarriage
mal·par·to, *m.* miscarriage
mal·ta, *f.* malt
mal·tra·tar, *v.* mistreat; misuse
mal·va·do, *m.* villain
mal·ver·sa·dor, *m.* embezzler
ma·lla, *f.* mesh; mail
ma·lle·ja, *f.* gizzard
ma·má, *f.* mama, mamma; *inf.* mom; ma
ma·mar, *v.* suck
ma·mí·fe·ro, *m.* mammal
ma·mut, *m.* mammoth
ma·ná, *f.* manna
man·co·mu·nar(se), *v.* pool; merge

man·cha, *f.* smudge; spot; soil; smear
man·char(se), *v.* blemish; soil; dirty; spot
man·chi·ta, *f.* speck
man·da·mien·to, *m.* commandment
man·dar, *v.* send; command; order; control; lead; tell
man·da·rín, *m.* mandarin
man·da·to, *m.* mandate; order
man·do, *m.* command; rule
man·do·li·na, *f.* mandolin
man·dril, *m.* baboon
ma·ne·jar(se), *v.* manage; handle; drive
ma·ne·ra, *f.* manner; way
man·ga, *f.* sleeve; beam; hose
man·ga·ne·so, *m.* manganese
man·go, *m.* handle; mango
man·gos·ta, *f.* mongoose
man·gui·to, *m.* muff
ma·nía, *f.* mania; rage; fad
ma·nia·co, *a.* maniac. *m.,* ma·nia·ca, *f.* maniac
ma·nia·tar, *v.* handcuff
ma·ni·co·mio, *m.* asylum; madhouse
ma·ni·cu·ra, *f.* manicure
ma·ni·fes·ta·ción, *f.* manifestation; demonstration
ma·ni·fes·tar(se), *v.* manifest; show
ma·ni·fies·to, *a.* manifest; evident. *m.* manifest; manifesto
ma·nio·bra, *f.* maneuver; handling
ma·nio·brar, *v.* maneuver; handle
ma·ni·pu·la·ción, *f.* manipulation
ma·ni·pu·lar, *v.* manipulate; maneuver
ma·ni·quí, *m.* mannequin; dummy
ma·no, *f.* hand. he·cho a ma·no, handmade. ma·no de o·bra, handicraft
ma·no·sear, *v.* handle; paw
ma·no·ta·da, *f.* smack
man·so, *a.* tame; mild
man·ta, *f.* blanket
man·te·ca, *f.* fat; butter. man·te·ca de cer·do, lard
man·te·co·so, *a.* a buttery
man·te·ner(se), *v.* maintain; support; hold; service
man·te·ni·mien·to, *m.* maintenance
man·te·que·ra, *f.* churn
man·te·qui·lla, *f.* butter
man·to, *m.* mantel; cloak
ma·nual, *a.* manual. *m.* manual; handbook
ma·nu·brio, *m.* crank; handle
ma·nu·fac·tu·ra, *f.* manufacture
ma·nus·cri·to, *m.* manuscript
ma·nu·ten·ción, *f.* upkeep
man·za·na, *f.* apple; block. man·za·na sil·ves·tre, crab apple
ma·ña, *f.* knack
ma·ña·na, *f.* morning; tomorrow. *adv.* tomorrow

ma·pa, *m.* map
ma·qui·lla·je, *f.* makeup
má·qui·na, *f.* machine
ma·qui·na·ria, *f.* machinery
mar, *m., f.* sea
ma·ra·vi·lla, *f.* wonder
ma·ra·vi·llar(se), *v.* marvel
mar·be·te, *m.* tag; label. **mar·be·te en·go·ma·do,** sticker
mar·ca, *f.* mark; brand; check; print; landmark. **mar·ca re·gis·tra·da,** trademark
mar·ca·do, *a.* pronounced
mar·car(se), *v.* mark; brand; dial
mar·cial, *a.* martial
mar·co, *m.* frame; setting
mar·cha, *f.* march; run
mar·char(se), *v.* go; travel; march; function
mar·chi·tar(se), *v.* wilt; wither; sear
ma·rea, *f.* tide
ma·rear(se), *v.* get seasick; feel dizzy; navigate
ma·reo, *m.* seasickness
mar·fil, *m.* ivory
mar·ga·ri·na, *f.* margarine
mar·gen, *m.* margin; fringe
ma·ri·cón, *f. inf.* queer
ma·ri·do, *m.* husband
ma·ri·jua·na, *f. inf.* pot
ma·ri·na, *f.* navigation. **ma·ri·na de gue·rra,** navy
ma·ri·ne·ro, *m.* sailor; seaman
ma·ri·no, *a.* marine
ma·rio·ne·ta, *f.* marionette
ma·ri·po·sa, *f.* butterfly
ma·ris·cal, *m.* marshal
ma·ris·co, *m.* shellfish
ma·ri·tal, *a.* marital
ma·rí·ti·mo, *a.* maritime; naval
már·mol, *m.* marble
mar·qués, *m.* marquis
mar·que·sa, *f.* marquise
mar·so·pa, *f.* porpoise
mar·su·pial, *a.* marsupial. *m.* marsupial
mar·tes, *m.* Tuesday
mar·ti·llar, *v.* hammer
mar·ti·lleo, *m.* hammering; clatter
már·tir, *m. f.* martyr
mar·ti·ri·zar, *v.* martyr
mar·zo, *m.* March
mas, *conj.* but
más, *a.* more; most; plus. *adv.* more. *m.* more. **más de,** over
ma·sa, *f.* mass; lump; dough. **en ma·sa,** wholesale
mas·car, *v.* chew
más·ca·ra, *f.* mask
mas·ca·ra·da, *f.* masquerade; masque, mask
mas·ca·rón de proa, figurehead
mas·co·ta, *f.* mascot
mas·cu·li·no, *a.* masculine; male. *m.* masculine

ma·si·lla, *f.* putty
ma·so·quis·mo, *m.* masochism
ma·so·quis·ta, *m., f.* masochist
mas·ti·car, *v.* masticate
más·til, *m.* mast
mas·to·don·te, *m.* mastodon
mas·tur·ba·ción, *f.* masturbation
ma·tan·za, *f.* slaughter
ma·tar(se), *v.* kill (oneself); slaughter; slay
ma·ta·se·llos, *m.* postmark
ma·te, *a.* mat, matt, matte. *m.* checkmate
ma·te·má·ti·cas, *f.* mathematics; *inf.* math
ma·te·ria, *f.* material; matter; substance; stuff
ma·te·rial, *a.* material. *m.* material
ma·ter·nal, *a.* maternal
ma·ter·ni·dad, *f.* motherhood; maternity
ma·ter·no, *a.* mother
ma·tiz, *f.* shade; hue
ma·ti·zar, *v.* tinge
ma·tón, *m.* hoodlum; bully
ma·trí·cu·la, *f.* enrollment
ma·tri·cu·lar(se), *v.* enroll; matriculate
ma·tri·mo·nio, *m.* marriage; matrimony; wedlock
ma·triz, *f.* womb; matrix
ma·tro·na, *f.* matron
mau·so·leo, *m.* mausoleum
má·xi·ma, *f.* maxim
má·xi·mo, *a.* maximum; greatest
má·xi·mum, *m.* maximum
ma·yo, *m.* May
ma·yo·ne·sa, *f.* mayonnaise
ma·yor, *a.* adult; utmost; main; major. *m.* elder; (*mus.*) major. **al por ma·yor,** wholesale
ma·yor·do·mo, *m.* butler
ma·yo·ría, *f.* majority
ma·yús·cu·la, *f.* capital letter
ma·za, *f.* wench; bat
maz·mo·rra, *f.* dungeon
ma·zo, *m.* mallet
me, *pron.* me
me·cá·ni·ca, *f.* mechanics
me·cá·ni·co, *a.* mechanical. *m.* mechanic
me·ca·nis·mo, *m.* mechanism
me·ca·nó·gra·fo, *m.,* **me·ca·nó·gra·fa,** *f.* typist
me·ce·nas, *m.* patron
me·cer, *v.* rock; cradle
me·cha, *f.* wick
me·da·lla, *f.* medal
me·da·llón, *m.* medallion
me·dia, *f.* stocking; *pl.* nylons; hose
me·dia·no, *a.* median; medium
me·dia·no·che, *f.* midnight
me·diar, *v.* mediate; intervene

me·di·ca·ción, *f.* medication
me·di·ca·men·to, *m.* medicine
me·di·ci·na, *f.* medicine
mé·di·co, *a.* medical. *m.* doctor;
physician
me·di·da, *f.* measure; measurement;
arrangement
me·die·val, *a.* medieval
me·dio, *a.* half; average; mean; middle. *adv.* mid; half. *m.* midst; middle; mean; medium; agency. **en
me·dio,** between. **en me·dio de,**
among
me·dio·día, *m.* noon; midday
me·dir, *v.* measure; gauge; span; survey
me·di·ta·ción, *f.* meditation
me·di·tar, *v.* meditate; ponder
mé·du·la, *f.* marrow
me·du·sa, *f.* jellyfish
me·ji·lla, *f.* cheek
me·jor, *a.* better; best. *adv.* better;
best
me·jo·ra, *f.* improvement
me·jo·ra·mien·to, *m.* betterment;
improvement
me·jo·rar(se), *v.* improve; better
me·lan·co·lía, *f.* dejection; melan-
choly; blues
me·lan·có·li·co, *a.* wistful; gloomy;
blue
me·la·za, *f.* molasses
me·lo·co·tón, *m.* peach
me·lo·día, *f.* melody
me·lo·dra·ma, *m.* melodrama
me·lón, *m.* melon
me·llar, *v.* indent; notch; dent
me·llo, *m.* indentation; notch
mem·bra·na, *f.* membrane; web
me·mo·ra·ble, *a.* memorable; eventful
me·mo·rán·dum, *m.* memorandum;
inf. memo
me·mo·ria, *f.* memory; memoir
me·mo·rial, *m.* memorial
me·na, *f.* ore
men·ción, *f.* mention
men·cio·nar, *v.* mention
men·di·gar, *v.* beg; *inf.* panhandle
men·di·go, *m.* beggar
me·near(se), *v.* wag; wiggle; flutter
men·guar, *v.* ebb; wane; lessen
me·no·pau·sia, *f.* menopause
me·nor, *a.* least; less; minor; junior.
m. junior. **me·nor de e·dad,** minor
me·nos, *a.* less. *adv.* least; less. *prep.*
less; minus. **a me·nos que,** except;
unless. **sig·no me·nos,** minus sign
me·nos·pre·ciar, *v.* disparage; despise; underrate
me·nos·pre·cio, *m.* contempt; scorn
men·sa·je·ro, *m.* messenger
mens·trua·ción, *f.* menstruation
men·sual, *a.* monthly

men·sual·men·te, *adv.* monthly
men·ta, *f.* mint; peppermint. **men·ta
ver·de,** spearmint
men·tal, *a.* mental
men·te, *f.* mind
men·tir, *v.* lie; fib
men·ti·ra, *f.* lie; falsehood
men·ti·ro·so, *m.,* **men·ti·ro·sa,** *f.*
liar. *a.* untruthful
men·tol, *m.* menthol
me·nú, *m.* menu; bill of fare
me·nu·di·llos, *m. pl.* giblets
me·nu·do, *a.* minute; insignificant. **a
me·nu·do,** often
mer·ca·de·ría, *f.* commodity
mer·ca·do, *m.* market; mart
mer·can·cías, *f. pl.* wares; goods
mer·ced, *f.* mercy
mer·ce·na·rio, *a.* mercenary. *m.*
mercenary; hireling
mer·cu·rio, *m.* mercury
me·re·cer, *v.* merit; deserve; earn
me·ren·gue, *m.* meringue
me·ri·dia·no, *m.* meridian
me·ri·dio·nal, *a.* southern
me·rien·da, *f.* snack
mé·ri·to, *m.* merit; worth
mer·me·la·da, *f.* marmalade; jam
me·ro, *a.* mere; very
mes, *m.* month
me·sa, *f.* table; plateau
mes·ti·zo, *m.,* **mes·ti·za,** *f.* half-
caste; mongrel. *a.* half-breed;
mongrel
me·ta, *f.* goal
me·ta·bo·lis·mo, *m.* metabolism
me·tá·fo·ra, *f.* metaphor
me·tal, *m.* metal
me·ta·mor·fo·sis, *f.* metamorphosis
me·teo·ri·to, *m.* meteorite
me·teo·ro·lo·gía, *f.* meteorology
me·ter(se), *v.* insert; put; interfere;
meddle
mé·to·do, *m.* method; system; way
me·tro, *m.* meter; metre; subway
me·tró·po·li, *f.* metropolis
me·tro·po·li·ta·no, *a.* metropolitan
mez·cla, *f.* mixture; mix; concoction
mez·clar(se), *v.* mix; blend; mingle;
jumble
mez·qui·no, *a.* petty
mi, *a.* my
mí, *pron.* me; myself
mía, *f. pron.* mine
mi·ca, *f.* mica
mi·cro·bio, *m.* microbe
mi·cro·cos·mo, *m.* microcosm
mi·cró·fo·no, *m.* microphone
mi·cros·co·pio, *m.* microscope
mie·do, *m.* fear. **te·ner mie·do,** fear;
be afraid
miel, *f.* honey
miem·bro, *m.* member; limb
mien·tras, *conj.* while. *adv.* mean-

while. **mien·tras tan·to,** meantime

miér·co·les, m. Wednesday

mi·ga, f. crumb

mi·gra·to·rio, a. migratory

mil, a. thousand. m. thousand

mi·la·gro, m. miracle; wonder

mi·la·gro·so, a. miraculous

mil·deu, m. mildew

mi·le·nio, m. millennium

mi·lé·si·mo, a. thousandth

mi·li·cia, f. militia

mi·lí·me·tro, m. millimeter

mi·li·tan·te, a. militant

mi·li·tar, a. military. m. soldier; serviceman

mi·lla, f. mile

mi·llón, m. million

mi·llo·na·rio, m., **mi·llo·na·ria,** f. millionaire

mi·mar, v. pamper; coddle

mi·meó·gra·fo, m. mimeograph

mi·mo, m. mime

mi·na, f. mine

mi·nar, v. mine

mi·ne·ral, a. mineral. m. mineral

mi·nia·tu·ra, f. miniature

mí·ni·mo, a. minimum; least. m. minimum

mi·nis·te·rio, m. ministry

mi·nis·tro, m. minister; (cap.) Secretary

mi·no·ría, f. minority

mi·nu·cio·so, a. exhaustive; meticulous

mi·nu·to, m. minute

mío, m. pron. mine

mio·pe, a. near-sighted; myopic

mi·ra·da, f. look; gaze; expression

mi·rar(se), v. watch; look; glance; gaze; regard

mi·ría·da, f. myriad

mir·lo, m. blackbird

mi·sa, f. mass

mi·sal, m. missal

mi·sán·tro·po, m. misanthrope

mis·ce·lá·neo, a. miscellaneous

mi·se·ra·ble, a. miserable; wretched; paltry. m. wretch

mi·se·ria, f. misery

mi·se·ri·cor·dia, f. mercy

mi·sión, f. mission

mi·sio·ne·ro, m., **mi·sio·ne·ra,** f. missionary

mis·mo, a. same; self-same; very

mis·te·rio, m. mystery

mis·te·rio·so, a. mysterious; uncanny

mís·ti·ca, f. mysticism

mis·ti·cis·mo, m. mysticism

mís·ti·co, m., **mís·ti·ca,** f. mystic. a. mystic

mi·tad, f. half

mí·ti·co, a. mythic(al)

mi·ti·gar, v. mitigate; alleviate; soften

mi·to, m. myth

mi·to·lo·gía, f. mythology

mi·tón, m. mitten

mi·tra, f. miter, mitre

mo·bi·lia·rio, m. furniture; pl. furnishings

mo·ca·sín, m. moccasin

mo·ción, f. motion

mo·co, m. mucus

mo·co·so, m. brat

mo·chi·la, f. knapsack; rucksack; haversack

mo·da, f. mode; fashion; vogue. **de mo·da,** fashionable

mo·de·lar, v. model; form

mo·de·lo, m. model; pattern; ideal; norm; mannequin

mo·de·ra·ción, f. moderation

mo·de·ra·do, a. moderate. m. moderate

mo·de·rar(se), v. moderate; temper

mo·der·ni·zar(se), v. modernize; update

mo·der·no, a. modern; new

mo·des·to, a. modest

mo·di·fi·ca·ción, f. modification

mo·di·fi·car, v. modify; alter

mo·dis·ta, f. dressmaker

mo·do, m. mode; manner; guise; sort; pl. means

mo·du·lar, v. modulate

mo·fa, f. mockery; taunt

mo·far(se), v. taunt; sneer; jeer; scoff; gibe

mo·fe·ta, f. skunk

mo·hí·no, a. sulky

mo·ho, m. mold, mould; mildew

mo·ho·so, a. rusty

mo·ja·do, a. wet

mo·jar(se), v. wet; dampen; drench

mo·jón, m. landmark

mol·de, m. mold, mould; cast

mol·dear, v. mold, mould; shape

mo·lé·cu·la, f. molecule

mo·ler, v. grind; mill

mo·les·tar(se), v. trouble; molest; pester; bother; annoy; vex

mo·les·tia, f. nuisance; bother; annoyance

mo·les·to, a. troublesome; tiresome; unpleasant

mo·li·no, m. mill. **mo·li·no de vien·to,** windmill

mo·lus·co, m. mollusk, mollusc

mo·lle·te, m. muffin

mo·men·tá·neo, a. momentary

mo·men·to, m. moment; minute; momentum

mo·mia, f. mummy

mo·nar·ca, m., f. monarch; sovereign

mo·nar·quía, f. monarchy

mo·nas·te·rio, m. monastery

mo·ne·da, f. coin; currency; silver

mo·ni·tor, *m.* monitor

mon·ja, *f.* nun

mon·je, *m.* monk

mo·no, *m.* monkey; ape; simian. *a.* pretty; cute

mo·no·ga·mia, *f.* monogamy

mo·no·gra·ma, *m.* monogram

mo·no·li·ta, *f.* monolith

mo·nó·lo·go, *m.* monologue, monolog

mo·no·po·lio, *m.* monopoly

mo·no·po·li·zar, *v.* monopolize; engross

mo·no·to·nía, *f.* monotony

mo·nó·to·no, *a.* monotonous

mo·nó·xi·do, *m.* monoxide. **mo·nó·xi·do de car·bo·no**, carbon monoxide

mons·truo, *m.* monster

mons·truo·si·dad, *f.* monstrosity; freak

mon·ta·car·gas, *m.* hoist

mon·ta·je, *m.* erection; hookup; montage

mon·ta·ña, *f.* mountain

mon·ta·ño·so, *a.* hilly; mountainous

mon·tar, *v.* ride; mount; put together

mon·te, *m.* woodland; mountain

mon·tón, *m.* mound; heap; pile; bank

mo·nu·men·to, *m.* monument

mo·ra·da, *f.* dwelling

mo·ra·dor, *m.*, **mo·ra·do·ra**, *f.* tenant; inhabitant

mo·ral, *a.* moral. *f.* morale

mo·ra·le·ja, *f.* moral

mo·ra·li·dad, *f.* morality

mo·ra·li·zar, *v.* moralize

mo·rar, *v.* live; dwell; reside; sojourn

mo·ra·to·ria, *f.* moratorium

mór·bi·do, *a.* morbid

mor·daz, *a.* trenchant; biting

mor·da·za, *f.* gag

mor·de·du·ra, *f.* bite

mo·re·na, *f.* brunette

mo·re·no, *a.* brown; dark

mor·fi·na, *f.* morphine

mo·rir(se), *v.* die; kill

mor·sa, *f.* walrus

mor·ta·ja, *f.* shroud

mor·tal, *a.* mortal; deadly; lethal; fatal. *m.*, *f.* mortal

mor·ta·li·dad, *f.* mortality

mor·tuo·rio, *a.* mortuary

mo·rue·co, *m.* ram

mo·sai·co, *m.* mosaic

mos·ca, *f.* fly

mos·que·te, *m.* musket

mos·qui·to, *m.* mosquito

mos·ta·za, *f.* mustard

mos·tra·dor, *m.* counter

mos·trar(se), *v.* show; exhibit; demonstrate; appear

mo·te, *m.* motto; slogan

mo·tín, *m.* mutiny; uprising; riot

mo·ti·vo, *m.* motive; sake; reason

mo·to·ci·cle·ta, *f.* motorcycle

mo·tor, *m.* motor; engine. *a.* motor

mo·ver(se), *v.* move; shift; power

mó·vil, *a.* mobile

mo·vi·mien·to, *m.* movement; motion; traffic

mo·za, *f.* lass; girl

mo·zo, *m.* lad; chap. **mo·zo de ca·ba·llos**, groom. **mo·zo de es·ta·ción**, porter

mu·co·so, *a.* mucous

mu·cha·cha, *f.* girl; lass

mu·cha·cho, *m.* boy; lad

mu·che·dum·bre, *f.* crowd; throng

mu·cho, *a.* many. *adv.* much. *m.* much; *pl.* many

mu·dar(se), *v.* move; change

mu·do, *a.* dumb; mute; silent

mue·ble, *m.* furniture

mue·la, *f.* tooth; molar; grindstone. **do·lor de mue·las**, toothache

mue·lle, *m.* pier; jetty; spring

muer·te, *f.* death

muer·to, *a.* dead; lifeless

mues·ca, *f.* notch; nick

mues·tra, *f.* sample; specimen

mu·gre, *f.* dirt; grime

mu·jer, *f.* woman; wife

mu·le·ta, *f.* crutch

mu·lo, *m.* mule

mul·ta, *f.* ticket; fine

mul·tar, *v.* fine

múl·ti·ple, *a.* multiple

mul·ti·pli·ca·ción, *f.* multiplication

mul·ti·pli·car(se), *v.* multiply; increase

múl·ti·plo, *m.* multiple

mul·ti·tud, *f.* multitude; crowd; army

mun·da·no, *a.* mundane; worldy

mun·dial, *a.* world; world-wide

mun·do, *m.* world

mu·ni·ción, *f.* ammunition; *pl.* munitions

mu·ni·ci·pal, *a.* municipal

mu·ñe·ca, *f.* doll; wrist

mu·ñón, *m.* stump

mu·ral, *m.* mural. *a.* mural

mu·ra·lla, *f.* wall; rampart

mur·cié·la·go, *m.* bat

mur·mu·llo, *m.* murmur; muttering

mur·mu·rar, *v.* murmur; mutter; gossip

mu·ro, *m.* wall

mu·sa, *f.* muse

mús·cu·lo, *m.* muscle

mu·se·li·na, *f.* muslin

mu·seo, *m.* museum

mus·go, *m.* moss

mú·si·ca, *f.* music

mu·si·cal, *a.* musical

mú·si·co, *a.* musical. *m.* musician

mus·lo, *m.* thigh

mu·ti·lar, v. mutilate; maim; cripple
mu·tuo, a. mutual; joint
muy, adv. very; much; too; greatly

N

na·bo, m. turnip
na·cer(se), v. be born; give birth; spring from; sprout
na·ci·do, a. born
na·cien·te, m. infant; recent
na·ci·mien·to, m. birth; origin. de·re·chos de na·ci·mien·to, birthright
na·ción, f. nation
na·cio·nal, m., f. national. a. national; native
na·cio·na·li·dad, f. nationality
na·cio·na·lis·mo, m. nationalism
na·da, pron. none. adv. by no means. f. nothing; naught
na·da·dor, m., na·da·do·ra, f. swimmer
na·dar, v. swim
na·die, pron. no one; one; nobody; none
naf·ta, f. naphtha
nai·lon, m. nylon
nai·pe, m. playing card; pl. cards
nal·gas, f. pl. buttocks
na·ran·ja, f. orange. na·ran·ja man·da·ri·na or tan·ge·ri·na, tangerine
na·ran·ja·da, f. orangeade
nar·ci·sis·mo, m. narcissism
nar·ci·so, m. narcissus
nar·có·ti·co, a. narcotic. m. narcotic; drug; dope
nar·co·ti·zar, v. dope; drug
na·ri·ces, f. pl. nostrils
na·riz, f. nose
na·rra·ción, f. narration; story
na·rrar, v. narrate; tell
na·rra·ti·va, f. narrative
na·rra·ti·vo, a. narrative
na·sal, a. nasal
na·ta, f. cream. na·ta ba·ti·da, whipped cream
na·ta·ción, f. swim; swimming
na·tal, a. natal
na·ti·llas, f. pl. custard
na·ti·vi·dad, f. nativity
na·ti·vo, m., na·ti·va, f. native. a. native
na·tu·ral, a. natural; native
na·tu·ra·le·za, f. nature
na·tu·ra·li·zar(se), v. naturalize
na·tu·ral·men·te, adv. naturally; by all means
nau·fra·gar, v. be shipwrecked; sink
nau·fra·gio, m. wreck; shipwreck
náu·sea, f. nausea; qualm; repulsion
nau·sear, v. nauseate
náu·ti·ca, f. navigation
náu·ti·co, a. nautical

na·va·ja, f. pocketknife; jackknife
na·val, a. naval
na·ve, f. nave; ship. na·ve la·te·ral, aisle
na·ve·ga·ble, a. navigable
na·ve·ga·ción, f. navigation
na·ve·gar, v. navigate; cruise; sail
Na·vi·dad, f. Christmas; nativity; yule
ne·bli·na, f. mist
ne·bu·lo·sa, f. nebula
ne·ce·sa·rio, a. necessary
ne·ce·si·dad, f. necessity; need
ne·ce·si·tar, v. require; need; necessitate; want; lack
ne·cio, a. foolish; vacuous. m. dolt
ne·cro·lo·gía, f. obituary
néc·tar, m. nectar
ne·fa·rio, a. nefarious
ne·gar, v. deny; disclaim; refuse
ne·ga·ti·va, f. denial; negative
ne·ga·ti·vo, a negative; minus. m. (photog.) negative
ne·gli·gen·te, a. negligent; slack
ne·go·cia·ción, f. negotiation
ne·go·ciar, v. negotiate; bargain
ne·go·cio, m. trade; transaction; business; affair
ne·gro, a. black
ne·na, f. baby; tot
ne·ne, m. baby; tot
ne·nú·far, m. water lily
ne·ón, m. neon
ner·vio, m. nerve
ner·vio·so, a. nervous; edgy; highstrung
nes·ga, f. gore
ne·to, a. net; clean; pure
neu·má·ti·co, m. tire. neu·má·ti·co de re·pues·to, spare tire
neu·ral·gia, f. neuralgia
neu·ro·sis, f. neurosis
neu·ró·ti·co, m., neu·ró·ti·ca, f. neurotic. a. neurotic
neu·tral, a. neutral. m., f. neutral
neu·tra·li·dad, f. neutrality
neu·tra·li·zar, v. neutralize
neu·tro, a. neuter
neu·trón, m. neutron
ne·var, v. snow
ni, a. neither. conj. neither; nor
nia·ra, f. stack
ni·co·ti·na, f. nicotine
ni·cho, m. recess
ni·do, m. nest
nie·bla, f. fog
nie·ta, f. granddaughter
nie·to, m. grandson
nie·ve, f. snow. bo·la de nie·ve, snowball. co·po de nie·ve, snowflake. fi·gu·ra de nie·ve, snowman
ni·lón, m. nylon
nin·fa, f. nymph
nin·gu·no (nin·gún), pron. none; nei-

ther; nobody. *a.* none; no. **en nin-gu·na par·te,** nowhere

ni·ña, *f.* girl; child; baby

ni·ñe·ra, *f.* nurse

ni·ñez, *f.* childhood

ni·ño, *m.* boy; child; baby. **ni·ño ex-pó·si·to,** foundling

ni·quel, *m.* nickel

ni·tra·to, *m.* nitrate

ni·tró·ge·no, *m.* nitrogen

ni·tro·gli·ce·ri·na, *f.* nitroglycerin

ni·vel, *m.* standard; level

ni·ve·la·do, *a.* flush

no, *adv.* no; not; nay. *m.* no

no·ble, *a.* noble. *m.* noble; nobleman

no·ble·za, *f.* nobility

no·ción, *f.* notion

noc·tur·no, *a.* nightly; nocturnal; right

no·che, *f.* night; nighttime. **es·ta no·che,** tonight

no·gal, *m.* walnut

nó·ma·da, *m., f.* nomad

nom·bra·mien·to, *m.* nomination; appointment; designation

nom·brar, *v.* name; call; nominate; appoint

nom·bre, *m.* name; title; reputation

nó·mi·na, *f.* payroll; list

no·mi·na·ción, *f.* nomination

no·mi·nal, *a.* nominal

nor·des·te, *m.* northeast

nor·ma, *f.* norm; standard. **nor·ma de me·di·das,** gauge

nor·mal, *a.* normal; standard; regular

nor·mal·men·te, *adv.* normally

no·roes·te, *m.* northwest. *a.* northwest

nor·te, *m.* north. *a.* north; northern

nos, *pron.* us

no·so·tras, *f. pron.* we; us; ourselves

no·so·tros, *m. pron.* we; us; ourselves

nos·tal·gia, *f.* nostalgia

nos·tál·gi·co, *a.* homesick; nostalgic

no·ta, *f.* mark; footnote; *often pl.* note

no·ta·ble, *a.* notable. *m., f.* notable

no·ta·ción, *f.* notation

no·tar, *v.* note; notice; remark

no·ta·rio, *m.* notary; notary public

no·ti·cia, *f.* notice; information; *pl.* news; tidings

no·ti·fi·car, *v.* notify

no·to·rio, *a.* notorious; flagrant

no·ve·dad, *f.* novelty; fad

no·ve·la, *f.* novel

no·ve·les·co, *a.* fictional; romantic

no·ve·no, *a.* ninth

no·ven·ta, *a.* ninety

no·via, *f.* fiancée; girl friend; bride

no·viaz·go, *m.* courtship

no·vi·cio, *m.,* **no·vi·cia,** *f.* novice

no·viem·bre, *m.* November

no·vi·lle·ro, *m.* novice; truant

no·vi·llo, *m.* steer; bullock

no·vio, *m.* fiancé; boyfriend; bridegroom

nu·be, *f.* cloud

nu·bla·do, *a.* cloudy. *m.* storm cloud

nu·blar(se), *v.* cloud over; darken

nu·bo·si·dad, *f.* cloudiness

nu·bo·so, *a.* cloudy

nu·ca, *f.* nape of the neck

nu·clear, *a.* nuclear

nú·cleo, *m.* nucleus; kernel

nu·di·llo, *m.* knuckle

nu·do, *m.* knot. **nu·do co·rre·di·zo,** slipknot

nue·ra, *f.* daughter-in-law

nues·tro, *a.* our; ours

nue·va·men·te, *adv.* newly; new

nue·vas, *f. pl.* news

nue·ve, *a.* nine. *m.* nine

nue·vo, *a.* new; novel; fresh; young. **de nue·vo,** again

nuez, *f.* nut

nu·lo, *a.* null; void

nu·me·ra·dor, *m.* numerator

nu·me·rar, *v.* number

nu·mé·ri·co, *a.* numerical

nú·me·ro, *m.* number. **nú·me·ros a·rá·bi·gos,** Arabic numerals. **nú·me·ros ro·ma·nos,** Roman numerals

nu·me·ro·so, *a.* numerous

nun·ca, *adv.* never; ever

nup·cial, *a.* nuptial; bridal

nup·cias, *f. pl.* nuptials

nu·tri·ción, *f.* nutrition

nu·trir, *v.* nourish; nurture; feed

nu·tri·ti·vo, *a.* nutritious

Ñ

ña·me, *m.* yam

ña·pa, *f.* tip

ña·que, *m.* junk

ñi·qui·ña·que, *m.* trash

ño·ñe·ría, *f.* timidity; bashfulness

ño·ñez, *f.* timidity; bashfulness

ño·ño, *a.* insipid; timid

O

o, *conj.* or

oa·sis, *m.* oasis

o·be·de·cer, *v.* obey; mind; comply

o·be·dien·cia, *f.* obedience

o·be·dien·te, *a.* dutiful; obedient

o·be·si·dad, *f.* obesity; corpulence; corpulency

o·be·so, *a.* obese

o·bis·pa·do, *m.* bishopric

o·bis·po, *m.* bishop

ob·jec·ción, *f.* objection

ob·je·tar, *v.* object

ob·je·ti·vo, *a.* objective; detached.

m. objective

ob·je·to, *m.* object; thing; article. **ob·je·to ex·pues·to,** exhibit

o·blea, *f.* wafer

o·bli·cua·men·te, *adv.* sideways; obliquely

o·bli·cuo, *a.* oblique

o·bli·ga·ción, *f.* obligation; liability; bond; trust

o·bli·ga·do, *a.* indebted; liable

o·bli·gar(se), *v.* obligate; make; compel; bind

o·bli·ga·to·rio, *a.* mandatory; compulsory

o·blon·go, *a.* oblong

o·boe, *m.* oboe

o·bra, *f.* work; handiwork; opus. **o·bras clá·si·cas,** classics. **o·bra dra·má·ti·ca,** play. **o·bra maes·tra,** masterpiece

o·brar, *v.* work; operate; proceed

o·bre·ro, *m.,* **o·bre·ra,** *f.* worker; workman. *a.* labor

obs·ce·ni·dad, *f.* obscenity

obs·ce·no, *a.* obscene; lewd

obs·cu·re·cer(se), *v.* obscure; shadow; darken

obs·cu·ri·dad, *f.* obscurity

obs·cu·ro, *a.* obscure; opaque; dark

ob·ser·va·ción, *f.* observation; remark; comment

ob·ser·van·cia, *f.* observance

ob·ser·var, *v.* observe; watch

ob·ser·va·to·rio, *m.* observatory

ob·se·sión, *f.* obsession

obs·tá·cu·lo, *m.* obstacle; hindrance; bar; clog; snag

obs·tan·te, *adv.* in the way. **no obs·tan·te,** notwithstanding; nevertheless

obs·ti·na·do, *a.* obstinate; stubborn

obs·truc·ción, *f.* obstruction; blockage

obs·truc·cio·nis·ta, *m., f.* obstructionist; filibuster

obs·truir, *v.* obstruct; block

ob·te·ner, *v.* obtain; get; procure

ob·vio, *a.* obvious; self-explanatory

o·ca·sión, *f.* occasion; cause

oc·ci·den·tal, *a.* western

oc·ci·den·te, *m.* west

o·céa·no, *m.* ocean

o·cio, *m.* leisure

o·cio·so, *a.* idle

oc·tá·go·no, *m.* octagon

oc·ta·va, *f.* octave

oc·ta·vo, *a.* eighth. *m.* eighth

oc·to·gé·si·mo, *a.* eightieth

oc·tu·bre, *m.* October

o·cu·lar, *a.* ocular. **tes·ti·go o·cu·lar,** eyewitness

o·cul·tar(se), *v.* hide; conceal; secrete; cache

o·cul·to, *a.* secret; occult

o·cu·pa·ción, *f.* occupation; profession; occupancy

o·cu·pa·do, *a.* busy; engaged; occupied

o·cu·par(se), *v.* occupy; fill; employ; busy

o·cu·rrir(se), *v.* occur; happen

o·chen·ta, *a.* eighty; fourscore

o·cho, *a.* eight. *m.* eight

o·da, *f.* ode

o·diar, *v.* hate

o·dio, *m.* hate. **o·dio de san·gre,** vendetta

o·dio·so, *a.* odious; hateful

oes·te, *m.* west. *a.* west; western

o·fen·der(se), *v.* offend; take offense; injure; insult

o·fen·sa, *f.* offense

o·fen·si·vo, *a.* offensive; obnoxious; repugnant

o·fer·ta, *f.* offer; bid

o·fi·cial, *a.* official. *m.* official; officer

o·fi·ci·na, *f.* office. **de o·fi·ci·na,** clerical

o·fi·ci·nes·co, *a.* white-collar

o·fi·ci·nis·ta, *m., f.* clerk

o·fi·cio, *m.* business; role; occupation

o·fre·cer(se), *v.* offer; present; extend; volunteer; bid

o·fre·ci·mien·to, *m.* offer; offering

o·gro, *m.* ogre

oí·ble, *a.* audible

oí·do, *m.* ear; hearing. **al·can·ce del oí·do,** earshot

oír, *v.* hear; listen. **oír por ca·sua·li·dad,** overhear

o·ja·lá, *int.* if only; if only it were so

o·jea·da, *f.* glance

o·jear, *v.* ogle; eye

o·je·ro·so, *a.* haggard

o·je·te, *m.* eyelet

o·jo, *m.* eye

o·la, *f.* wave

o·lé, *int.* bravo

o·lea·da, *f.* billow; surge

o·lea·je, *m.* surf

o·ler, *v.* smell; sniff; reek

ol·fa·to, *m.* sense of smell

o·li·va, *f.* olive

ol·mo, *m.* elm

o·lor, *m.* odor; smell; scent

o·lo·ro·so, *a.* fragrant

ol·vi·da·di·zo, *a.* forgetful

ol·vi·dar(se), forget; omit

ol·vi·do, *m.* oversight; oblivion

o·lla, *f.* pot; stew

om·bli·go, *m.* navel

o·mi·sión, *f.* omission

o·mi·tir, *v.* omit; leave out

om·ni·po·ten·cia, *f.* omnipotence

om·ni·po·ten·te, *a.* omnipotent; almighty

om·ni·pre·sen·cia, *f.* omnipresence;

ubiquity
om·nis·cien·cia, f. omniscience
om·ni·vo·ro, a. omnivorous
on·ce, a. eleven. m. eleven
on·da, f. wave
on·dear, v. wave; flap
on·du·la·ción, f. wave; undulation
on·du·la·do, a. wavy; undulating
on·du·lar(se), v. wave; undulate
ó·ni·ce, m. onyx
on·za, f. ounce
o·pa·ci·dad, f. opacity
o·pa·co, a. opaque
ó·pa·lo, m. opal
op·ción, f. option
ó·pe·ra, f. opera
o·pe·ra·ción, f. operation; deal
o·pe·rar(se), v. operate; work; bring
about
o·pe·re·ta, f. operetta
o·pi·nar, v. judge
o·pi·nión, f. opinion; view
o·pio, m. opium
o·po·ner(se), v. oppose; object; encounter
o·por·to, m. port
o·por·tu·ni·dad, f. opportunity;
chance
o·por·tu·no, a. opportune; timely;
due; happy
o·pri·mir, v. oppress; press; squeeze
óp·ti·co, a. optical
op·ti·mis·mo, m. optimism
o·pues·to, a. opposite
o·pu·len·to, a. opulent; affluent
o·ra·ción, f. oration; prayer
o·rá·cu·lo, m. oracle
o·ra·dor, m., o·ra·do·ra, f. speaker
o·ral, a. oral
o·rar, v. pray
or·be, m. orb
ór·bi·ta, f. orbit
or·den, m. order; arrangement; command. f. order; writ. or·den del
día, agenda
or·de·na·do, a. tidy
or·de·nar(se), v. ordain; arrange; bid
or·de·ñar, v. milk
or·di·na·rio, a. ordinary; common;
coarse
o·re·ja, f. ear; tab; lug
or·gan·dí, m. organdy; organdie
or·gá·ni·co, a. organic
or·ga·ni·llo, m. barrel organ
or·ga·nis·mo, m. organism
or·ga·ni·za·ción, f. organization
or·ga·ni·zar(se), v. organize
ór·ga·no, m. organ
or·gía, f. orgy
or·gu·llo, m. pride
or·gu·llo·so, a. proud; lofty; haughty
o·rien·tal, m., f. oriental. a. oriental;
eastern
o·rien·tar(se), v. orient oneself; di-

rect
o·rien·te, m. east; (cap.) the Orient
o·ri·fi·cio, m. vent; orifice
o·ri·gen, m. origin; source
o·ri·gi·nal, a. original; eccentric. m.
original
o·ri·gi·nar(se), v. originate
o·ri·lla, f. bank; shore. o·ri·lla del
mar, seashore
o·rín, m. rust
o·ri·na, f. urine
o·ri·nar(se), v. urinate
o·ri·nes, m. pl. urine
or·la, f. fringe; trimming
or·na·men·ta·ción, f. ornamentation
or·na·men·to, m. ornament
or·na·to, m. decoration
o·ro, m. gold; (cards) pl. diamonds
o·ro·pel, m. tinsel
or·ques·ta, f. orchestra
or·ques·tar, v. score; orchestrate
or·to·do·xia, f. orthodoxy
or·to·do·xo, a. orthodox
or·to·gra·fía, f. spelling; orthogra-
phy
o·ru·ga, f. caterpillar
or·zue·lo, m. (med.) sty
os·ci·la·ción, f. swing; oscillation
os·ci·lar, v. vibrate; waver; oscillate
os·cu·re·cer(se), v. darken; dim;
overshadow
os·cu·ri·dad, f. darkness; gloom
os·cu·ro, a. dark; dim; dusky
os·mo·sis, f. osmosis
o·so, m. bear. o·so hor·mi·gue·ro,
anteater
os·ten·ta·ción, f. ostentation; pomp
os·tra, f. oyster
os·tra·cis·mo, m. ostracism
o·te·ro, m. knoll
o·to·ño, m. autumn; fall
o·tor·gar, v. grant; confer; bestow;
award
o·tro, a. other; another; else. pron.
another. o·tra vez, again
o·va·ción, f. ovation
o·val, a. oval
ó·va·lo, m. oval
o·va·rio, m. ovary
o·ve·ja, f. sheep; ewe
ó·vu·lo, m. ovum
ox·i·dar(se), v. oxidize; rust
óx·i·do, m. oxide
ox·í·ge·no, m. oxygen
o·zo·no, m. ozone

P

pa·be·llón, m. pavilion
pa·cer, v. graze
pa·cien·cia, f. patience
pa·cien·te, a. patient
pa·ci·fi·car(se), v. pacify; calm
pa·cí·fi·co, a. pacific

pa·ci·fis·mo, *m.* pacifism
pac·to, *m.* pact; covenant; treaty; bargain
pa·de·cer, *v.* suffer
pa·dras·tro, *m.* stepfather
pa·dre, *m.* father; sire; parent
pa·dri·no, *m.* godfather; *pl.* godparents
pa·ga, *f.* pay; payment
pa·ga·no, *m.*, **-ga·na**, *f.* pagan. *a.* pagan; heathen
pa·gar, *v.* pay; repay; defray
pá·gi·na, *f.* page
pa·gi·nar, *v.* page
pa·go·da, *f.* pagoda
país, *m.* country; land; landscape
pai·sa·je, *m.* landscape; scenery
pa·ja, *f.* straw
pá·ja·ro, *m.* bird
pa·ji·lla, *f.* straw
pa·la, *f.* shovel; spade
pa·la·bra, *f.* word; speech
pa·la·bro·ta, *f.* swearword
pa·la·cio, *m.* palace
pa·la·dar, *m.* palate
pa·la·dín, *m.* paladin; champion
pa·lan·ca, *f.* crowbar; lever
pa·lan·que·ta, *f.* jimmy
pa·le·on·to·lo·gía, *f.* paleontology
pa·le·ta, *f.* palette; scoop
pa·li·de·cer(se), *v.* pale; blanch
pa·li·dez, *f.* pallor
pá·li·do, *a.* pale; pallid; wan; waxen
pa·li·za·da, *f.* palisade; stockade
pal·ma, *f.* palm
pal·ma·da, *f.* clap; slap; *pl.* applause
pal·mo·teo, *m.* clap
pa·lo, *m.* pole; staff; (*cards*) suit
pa·lo·ma, *f.* pigeon
pal·pa·ble, *a.* palpable
pal·par, *v.* touch; feel
pal·pi·ta·ción, *f.* palpitation; throb
pal·pi·tar, *v.* throb; palpitate
pa·lu·dis·mo, *m.* malaria
pan, *m.* bread; loaf. **pan tos·ta·do**, toast
pa·na, *f.* corduroy
pa·na·cea, *f.* panacea
pa·na·de·ría, *f.* bakery
pa·na·de·ro, *m.* baker
pa·nal, *m.* honeycomb
pán·creas, *m.* pancreas
pan·de·re·ta, *f.* tambourine
pan·di·lla, *f.* clique; gang
pa·ne·ci·llo, *m.* roll
pa·nel, *m.* panel
pa·no·ra·ma, *m.* panorama; view
pan·ta·lo·nes, *m. pl.* pants; trousers; slacks
pan·ta·lla, *f.* screen
pan·ta·no, *m.* swamp; bog; marsh; morass
pan·teís·mo, *m.* pantheism
pan·te·ra, *f.* panther

pan·to·mi·ma, *f.* pantomime; mime
pan·to·que, *m.* bilge
pa·ñal, *m.* diaper
pa·ñe·ría, *f.* drapery
pa·ñi·to, *m.* cloth. **pa·ñi·to de a·dor·no**, doily
pa·ño, *m.* cloth. **pa·ño pa·ra la·var·se**, washcloth
pa·ñue·lo, *m.* handkerchief; kerchief; babushka
pa·pa, *m.* (*cap.*) Pope; potato
pa·pá, *m.* papa; pa; dad; daddy
pa·pa·do, *m.* papacy
pa·pa·ga·yo, *m.* parrot
pa·pel, *m.* paper; role. **pa·pel pin·ta·do**, wallpaper. **pa·pel se·can·te**, blotter
pa·pe·le·ría, *f.* stationery
pa·pe·ras, *f. pl.* mumps
pa·pi·ro, *m.* papyrus
pa·que·te, *m.* package; parcel
par, *m.* pair; pair; couple; peer; even number. *a.* even
pa·ra, *prep.* for
pa·rá·bo·la, *f.* parable; parabola
pa·ra·bri·sas, *m.* windshield
pa·ra·caí·das, *m.* parachute
pa·ra·cai·dis·ta, *m.* paratrooper
pa·ra·cho·ques, *m.* bumper
pa·ra·da, *f.* stop; standstill; halt; breakdown; check; parade
pa·ra·de·ro, *m.* whereabouts; lodging
pa·ra·do·ja, *f.* paradox
pa·ra·fi·na, *f.* paraffin
pa·rá·fra·sis, *f.* paraphrase
pa·ra·guas, *m.* umbrella
pa·raí·so, *m.* paradise
pa·ra·le·lo, *a.* parallel. *m.* parallel
pa·rá·li·sis, *f.* paralysis
pa·ra·li·zar(se), *v.* paralyze
pa·rá·me·tro, *m.* parameter
pá·ra·mo, *m.* moor
pa·ra·noia, *f.* paranoia
pa·rar(se), *v.* stop; halt; stay; check; parry; rest
pa·ra·rra·yos, *m.* lightning rod
pa·rá·si·to, *m.* parasite; *pl.* static
par·ce·la, *f.* plot
par·cial, *a.* partial; part
par·cia·li·dad, *f.* partiality; faction
pa·re·cer(se), *v.* resemble; appear; look like; seem
pa·re·ci·do, *a.* like; similar; such. *m.* semblance
pa·red, *f.* wall
pa·re·ja, *f.* pair; couple. **sin pa·re·ja**, odd
pa·ren·tes·co, *m.* kinship
pa·rén·te·sis, *m.* parenthesis
pa·ria, *m., f.* pariah
pa·rien·te, *m.* relation; kinsman; *pl.* kin; kindred
pa·rir, *v.* give birth

par·la·men·to, *m. usu. cap.* parliament; parley
pa·ro·dia, *f.* parody; skit; travesty
pa·ro·diar, *v.* caricature; burlesque
pa·ró·ti·das, *f.* mumps
pa·rox·is·mo, *m.* paroxysm
par·pa·dear, *v.* blink; wink
par·pa·deo, *m.* winking; blinking
par·que, *m.* park
pá·rra·fo, *m.* paragraph
pa·rri·lla, *f.* grill; grating
pa·rro·quia, *f.* parish; customers
pa·rro·quial, *a.* parochial
par·te, *f.* part; portion; lot; share. **en to·das par·tes,** anywhere; everywhere
par·te·ra, *f.* midwife
par·ti·ción, *f.* partition
par·ti·ci·pa·ción, *f.* participation; share; notice
par·ti·ci·par, *v.* participate; notify
par·ti·ci·pe, *m., f.* participant
par·tí·cu·la, *f.* speck; particle
par·ti·cu·lar, *a.* particular; private; special
par·ti·cu·la·ri·dad, *f.* particularity; peculiarity
par·ti·da, *f.* departure; party; group; item; certificate
par·ti·da·rio, *m.,* **par·ti·da·ria,** *f.* partisan; follower; campaigner. *a.* partisan
par·ti·do, *m.* side; party; match; game. **de dos par·ti·dos,** bipartisan
par·tir(se), *v.* part; depart; cleave; share
par·to, *m.* labor
pa·sa, *f.* raisin
pa·sa·ble, *a.* respectable; passable
pa·sa·do, *m.* past. *adv.* ago. *a.* ago; past; bygone. **pa·sa·do de mo·da,** out-of-date
pa·sa·dor, *m.* bolt; *pl.* cufflinks
pa·sa·je, *m.* passage
pa·sa·je·ro, *m.,* **pa·sa·je·ra,** *f.* passenger. *a.* transient
pa·sa·ma·no, *m.* bannister; banister
pa·sa·por·te, *m.* passport
pa·sar(se), *v.* happen; pass; spend; elapse; while; live; fade. **pa·sar por al·to,** miss
pa·sa·tiem·po, *m.* pastime; amusement; hobby
pa·sear(se), *v.* walk; stroll
pa·se·o, *m.* walk; stroll; airing; run. **pa·seo en co·che,** drive
pa·si·llo, *m.* corridor; hallway; aisle; gangway
pa·sión, *f.* passion
pa·si·vo, *a.* passive
pas·mar(se), *v.* dumfound; dumbfound; amaze
pa·so, *m.* pace; step; footstep; tread; gateway. **pa·so a ni·vel,** crossing

pas·ta, *f.* paste; cardboard; pasta
pas·tel, *m.* cake; pie; *pl.* pastry
pas·te·li·llo, *m.* pat
pas·teu·ri·za·ción, *f.* pasteurization
pas·teu·ri·zar, *v.* pasteurize
pas·ti·lla, *f.* lozenge; cake
pas·to, *m.* pasture; grass
pas·tor, *m.* shepherd; herdsman; pastor; minister
pa·ta, *f.* leg of an animal; paw; foot. **pa·tas a·rri·ba,** topsy-turvy
pa·ta·da, *f.* kick
pa·tán, *m.* lout
pa·ta·ta, *f.* potato
pa·tear, *v.* stamp
pa·ten·te, *a.* patent. *a.* patent; self-evident
pa·ter·ni·dad, *f.* fatherhood; paternity
pa·ter·no, *a.* paternal
pa·té·ti·co, *a.* pathetic
pa·ti·llas, *f. pl.* sideburns
pa·tín, *m.* skate
pa·ti·nar, *v.* skate; skid
pa·ti·na·zo, *m.* skid
pa·tio, *m.* yard; patio. **pa·tio de re·creo,** playground
pa·to, *m.* duck
pa·to·lo·gía, *f.* pathology
pa·tria, *f.* fatherland; native land
pa·triar·ca·do, *m.* patriarchy
pa·tri·mo·nio, *m.* patrimony; inheritance
pa·trio·ta, *m., f.* patriot
pa·tro·ci·na·dor, *m.,* **pa·tro·ci·na·do·ra,** *f.* sponsor
pa·trón, *m.* employer; host; pattern
pa·tru·lla, *f.* patrol
pa·tru·llar, *v.* patrol
pau·sa, *f.* pause; interruption
pa·vi·men·tar, *v.* pave
pa·vi·men·to, *m.* pavement
pa·vo, *m.* turkey. **pa·vo real,** peacock
pa·vo·near(se), *v.* strut; swagger
pa·vor, *m.* dread
pa·ya·so, *m.* clown. **ha·cer el pa·ya·so,** clown
paz, *f.* peace; tranquility
pea·je, *m.* toll. **au·to·pis·ta de pea·je,** tollway; tollroad
pea·tón, *m.* pedestrian
pe·ca, *f.* freckle
pe·ca·di·llo, *m.* peccadillo
pe·ca·do, *m.* sin; transgression
pe·ca·dor, *m.,* **pe·ca·do·ra,** *f.* sinner. *a.* sinful
pe·car, *v.* sin; transgress; trespass
pe·ce·ra, *f.* fishbowl
pe·cio, *m.* flotsam
pe·cu·liar, *a.* peculiar; characteristic
pe·cu·lia·ri·dad, *f.* peculiarity; kink
pe·cho, *m.* breast; bust; chest
pe·dal, *m.* pedal
pe·da·zo, *m.* piece; patch; bit; mor-

scl. **ha·cer·se pe·da·zos**, shatter

pe·der·nal, *m.* flint

pe·des·tal, *m.* pedestal

pe·des·tre, *a.* pedestrian; walking

pe·día·tra, *m., f.* pediatrician

pe·di·cu·ro, *m.* chiropodist

pe·dir, *v.* charge; order; ask; beg; request; bid

pe·dre·go·so, *a.* stony, stoney

pe·dre·jón, *m.* boulder

pe·ga·jo·so, *a.* adhesive; catching

pe·gar(se), *v.* slap; strike; glue; paste; cleave; adhere; attach; hang

pe·go·te, *m.* hanger-on; sticking plaster

pei·na·do, *m.* coiffure; hairdo

pei·nar, *v.* comb; arrange the hair

pei·ne, *m.* comb

pe·la·do, *a.* bare; hairless

pe·lar(se), *v.* peel; shear

pel·da·ño, *m.* rung; stair

pe·lea, *f.* fight; scuffle; *inf.* hassle

pe·lear(se), *v.* fight; scuffle

pe·le·jo, *m.* pelt

pe·lí·cu·la, *f.* movie; picture; motion picture; film. **pe·lí·cu·la del oes·te**, western

pe·li·gro, *m.* danger; peril; jeopardy. **po·ner en pe·li·gro**, endanger

pe·li·gro·sa·men·te, *adv.* dangerously

pe·li·gro·so, *a.* dangerous

pe·li·rro·jo, *a.* red-headed

pe·lo, *m.* hair; coat; fur

pe·lo·ta, *f.* ball

pe·lo·tón, *m.* squad; platoon; tangle

pel·tre, *m.* pewter

pe·lu·ca, *f.* wig

pe·lu·do, *a.* a furry; hairy

pe·lu·que·ría, *f.* barber shop; beauty shop

pe·lu·que·ro, *m.* barber; hairdresser

pe·lu·sa, *f.* fuzz; fluff; down

pel·vis, *f.* pelvis

pe·lla, *f.* pellet

pe·lle·jo, *m.* hide; skin

pe·lliz·car, *v.* pinch; nip

pe·na, *f.* distress; anxiety; trouble; hardship; penalty

pe·na·do, *m.* convict

pe·nal, *a.* penal

pen·dien·te, *m.* pendant; pendent; earring; incline. *a* pending; hanging

pén·du·lo, *m.* pendulum

pe·ne·tran·te, *a.* sharp; penetrating

pe·ne·trar(se), *v.* penetrate; pierce; fathom

pe·ni·ci·li·na, *f.* penicillin

pe·nín·su·la, *f.* peninsula

pe·ni·ten·te, *a.* penitent; *m., f.* penitent

pe·no·so, *a.* painful; grueling; wearing; laborious; grievous; trying;

uphill

pen·sa·mien·to, *m.* thought; notion; pansy

pen·sar, *v.* think; ponder; think over; think up

pen·sa·ti·vo, *a.* pensive; wistful; thoughtful

pen·sión, *f.* pension; room and board; boarding house

pen·sio·nis·ta, *m., f.* boarder; pensioner

pen·tá·go·no, *m.* pentagon

pe·ñón, *m.* large rock; wall of rock

peón, *m.* laborer; peon

peo·nía, *f.* peony

peon·za, *f.* top

peor, *a.* worse; worst. *adv.* worse; worst

pe·pi·ni·llo, *m.* gherkin

pe·pi·no, *m.* cucumber

pe·que·ñi·to, *a.* a wee; tiny

pe·que·ño, *a.* small; little; slight; short

pe·ra, *f.* pear

per·ca, *f.* perch

per·ce·be, *m.* barnacle

per·cep·ción, *f.* perception

per·cep·ti·ble, *a.* discernible; perceptible

per·cep·ti·vo, *a.* perceptive

per·ci·bir, *v.* see; perceive; espy

per·cha, *f.* roost; perch; rack; hanger

per·der(se), *v.* lose; forfeit; waste; miss; get lost. **per·der su sa·bor**, pall

per·di·ción, *f.* perdition

pér·di·da, *f.* loss; forfeiture

per·di·do, *a.* lost; missing; inveterate

per·di·gón, *m.* buckshot

per·diz, *f.* partridge

per·dón, *m.* pardon; forgiveness

per·do·nar, *v.* pardon; remit; spare; forgive; excuse

per·du·ra·ble, *a.* enduring

per·du·rar, *v.* endure; last

pe·re·cer, *v.* perish

pe·re·gri·na·ción, *f.* peregrination

pe·re·gri·no, *m.*, **pe·re·gri·na**, *f.* pilgrim. *a* traveling

pe·re·jil, *m.* parsley

pe·ren·ne, *a.* perennial

pe·re·zo·so, *a.* lazy; sluggish

per·fec·ción, *f.* perfection

per·fec·cio·nar, *v.* perfect

per·fec·cio·nis·ta, *m., f.* perfectionist

per·fec·to, *a.* perfect. *m.* perfect tense

per·fil, *m.* profile; outline

per·fo·ra·ción, *f.* perforation

per·fo·rar, *v.* perforate; puncture

per·fu·mar, *v.* perfume

per·fu·me, *m.* perfume; scent; essence

per·ga·mi·no, *m.* parchment. **ro·llo de per·ga·mi·no**, scroll

pe·ri·cia, *f.* expertise; proficiency; skill; *inf.* know-how

pe·ri·crá·neo, *m.* scalp

pe·ri·fe·ria, *f.* periphery

pe·rí·me·tro, *m.* perimeter

pe·rió·di·co, *m.* periodical; newspaper; journal

pe·rio·dis·mo, *m.* journalism

pe·rio·dis·ta, *m., f.* journalist

pe·rio·do, *m.* period

pe·ris·co·pio, *m.* periscope

per·ju·di·cial, *v.* prejudice; handicap; damage

per·ju·di·cial, *a.* harmful

per·ju·rar(se), *v.* perjure

per·ju·rio, *m.* perjury

per·la, *f.* pearl

per·ma·ne·cer, *v.* remain

per·ma·nen·te, *a.* permanent

per·mi·si·vo, *a.* permissive

per·mi·so, *m.* permission; consent; permit; pass; leave

per·mi·tir(se), *v.* permit; let; admit; allow; tolerate; enable; give

per·mu·tar, *v.* barter; exchange

pe·ro, *conj.* but; yet

per·pen·di·cu·lar, *a.* perpendicular. *f.* perpendicular

per·pe·tra·ción, *f.* commission; perpetration

per·pe·trar, *v.* perpetrate

per·pe·tuo, *a.* perpetual

per·ple·jo, *a.* perplexed. *m.* puzzle

pe·rra, *f.* female dog; bitch; slut

pe·rre·ra, *f.* kennel

pe·rro, *m.* dog; canine

per·se·cu·ción, *f.* persecution; chase

per·se·gui·mien·to, *m.* pursuit

per·se·guir, *v.* pursue; follow; chase; hunt; hound; persecute

per·sis·tir, *v.* persist

per·so·na, *f.* person. **por per·so·na**, apiece

per·so·na·je, *m.* somebody; character; personality

per·so·nal, *a.* personal. *m.* personnel; staff

per·so·na·li·dad, *f.* personality

pers·pec·ti·va, *f.* perspective; outlook; prospect; insight

pers·pi·ca·cia, *f.* foresight; perspicacity

pers·pi·caz, *a.* keen; discerning

per·sua·dir(se), *v.* persuade

per·sua·sión, *f.* persuasion

per·te·ne·cer, *v.* pertain; appertain; concern; belong

per·te·nen·cias, *f. pl.* belongings; possessions

per·ti·nen·cia, *f.* relevance; relevancy

per·ti·nen·te, *a.* pertinent; relevant

per·tur·ba·ción, *f.* perturbation; upset

per·tur·ba·do, *a.* upset

per·tur·bar, *v.* disturb; upset; faze

per·ver·si·dad, *f.* perversity

per·ver·sión, *f.* perversion

per·ver·ti·do, *a.* perverted

per·ver·tir(se), *v.* pervert; warp

pe·sa·dez, *f.* heaviness; tediousness

pe·sa·di·lla, *f.* nightmare

pe·sa·do, *a.* heavy; weighty; tiresome; dull; boring; clumsy

pé·sa·me, *m.* condolence

pe·sar, *v.* weigh; sorrow; grieve; regret. **a pe·sar de**, in spite of; notwithstanding

pes·ca, *f.* fishing

pes·ca·do, *m.* fish. **so·pa de pes·ca·do**, chowder

pes·ca·dor, *m.* fisherman

pes·car, *v.* fish

pe·se·bre, *m.* manger; crib

pe·si·mis·mo, *m.* pessimism

pe·si·mis·ta, *a.* pessimistic; morbid. *m., f.* pessimist

pe·so, *m.* weight; load; burden

pes·que·ra, *f.* fishery

pes·qui·sa, *f.* investigation. **pes·qui·sa ju·di·cial**, inquest

pes·ta·ña, *f.* eyelash

pes·ta·ñear, *v.* wink

pes·te, *f.* plague

pes·ti·ci·da, *f.* pesticide

pé·ta·lo, *m.* petal

pe·tar·deo, *m.* backfire

pe·tar·dis·ta, *m., f.* cheat

pe·tar·do, *m.* firecracker

pe·ti·ción, *f.* petition; request; demand

pe·ti·me·tre, *m.* fop; dude

pe·ti·rro·jo, *m.* robin

pe·tró·leo, *m.* petroleum; oil

pez, *m.* fish. *f.* pitch

pe·zón, *m.* nipple; teat

pia·do·so, *a.* pious; clement; godly

pia·nis·ta, *m., f.* pianist

pia·no, *m.* piano

piar, *v.* chirp

pi·ca·di·llo, *m.* hash

pi·ca·do, *a.* choppy; minced

pi·ca·du·ra, *f.* sting

pi·ca·ma·de·ros, *m.* woodpecker

pi·car(se), *v.* stick; prick; sting; pink; pick; chop; chip; nibble; bite; itch

pí·ca·ra, *f.* hussy

pi·ca·res·co, *a.* picaresque

pí·ca·ro, *m.* rascal; rogue. *a.* naughty; villainous

pi·ca·zón, *m.* itch

pi·cea, *f.* spruce

pi·co, *m.* beak; bill; peak; pick

pi·chel, *m.* mug

pie, *m.* foot; bottom. **a pie**, on foot. **de·do del pie**, toe

pie·dad, *f.* pity; piety
pie·dra, *f.* stone. **pie·dra ca·li·za,** limestone. **pie·dra cla·ve,** keystone. **pie·dra de a·fi·lar,** hone. **pie·dra de gra·ni·zo,** hailstone. **pie·dra pó·mez,** pumice stone
piel, *f.* skin; rind; pelt; leather; fur. **piel de o·so,** bearskin
pier·na, *f.* leg
pie·za, *f.* piece; chessman
pig·men·to, *m.* pigment
pig·meo, *m.* **pig·mea,** *f.* pygmy; pigmy. *a.* pygmy; pigmy
pi·ja·ma, *m.* pyjamas
pi·la, *f.* battery; sink
pi·lar, *m.* pillar
pil·do·ra, *f.* pill
pi·lón, *m.* loaf; pylon
pi·lo·to, *m.* pilot
pi·llar, *v.* pillage; plunder
pi·llo, *m.* blackguard; rascal
pi·llue·lo, *m.* urchin
pi·men·tón, *m.* cayenne pepper
pi·mien·ta, *f.* pepper
pi·mien·to, *m.* pepper
pi·ná·cu·lo, *m.* pinnacle
pin·char(se), *v.* pierce; puncture; jab
pin·cha·zo, *m.* puncture; flat
pi·no, *m.* pine
pin·ta, *f.* pint; spot
pin·tar(se), *v.* paint; put on makeup
pin·ta·rra·jo, *m.* daub
pin·tor, *m.,* **pin·to·ra,** *f.* painter
pin·tu·ra, *f.* paint; painting
pin·za, *f.* tongs; clothespin
pin·zón, *m.* finch
pio·jo, *m.* louse; *pl.* lice
pi·pa, *f.* pipe
pi·que, *m.* pique
pi·ra, *f.* pyre
pi·rá·mi·de, *f.* pyramid
pi·ra·ta, *m.* pirate; freebooter
pi·ro·po, *m.* compliment
pi·ro·tec·nia, *f.* pyrotechnics
pi·rue·tear, *v.* pirouette; twirl
pi·ru·lí, *m.* lollipop; lollypop
pi·sar, *v.* step; tread; walk on; trample
pis·ci·na, *f.* swimming pool; *inf.* pool
pi·so, *m.* floor; story; apartment; flat
pi·so·tear, *v.* trample on
pis·ta, *f.* track; court; rink; clue; trail; scent. **pis·ta de a·te·rri·za·je,** runway. **pis·ta de ce·ni·za,** speedway
pis·to·la, *f.* pistol
pis·to·le·ra, *f.* holster
pis·to·le·ro, *m.* gangster
pis·tón, *m.* piston
pi·ti·llo, *m.* cigarette; cigaret
pi·to, *m.* whistle; woodpecker
pi·tón, *m.* spout; python
pi·vo·te, *m.* pivot
pi·za·rra, *f.* blackboard; slate

piz·ca, *f.* particle; pinch
pla·cen·ta, *f.* placenta
pla·cer, *v.* pleasure; enjoyment; treat; gratification
plá·ci·do, *a.* placid
pla·ga, *f.* plague
pla·gar(se), *v.* infest; plague
pla·gio, *m.* plagiarism
plan, *m.* plan; layout; scheme; contrivance
plan·cha, *f.* iron; slab; gangplank
plan·char, *v.* iron; press. **la·var y plan·char,** launder
pla·near, *v.* plan
pla·neo, *m.* glide
pla·ne·ta, *m.* planet
pla·no, *a.* flat; level. *m.* plan; plane. **pri·mer pla·no,** foreground
plan·ta, *f.* plant; floor; story; sole of the foot
plan·ta·ción, *f.* plantation
plan·tar, *v.* plant
plan·tear, *v.* pose; create
plan·tel, *m.* nursery
pla·ñi·de·ra, *f.* paid mourner
plas·ma, *m.* plasma
plás·ti·co, *m.* plastic. *a.* plastic
pla·ta, *f.* silver; money
pla·ta·for·ma, *f.* platform
plá·ta·no, *m.* banana
pla·te·ro, *m.* silversmith
pla·ti·llo, *m.* saucer; cymbal
pla·ti·no, *m.* platinum
pla·to, *m.* plate; dish; course
pla·tó·ni·co, *a.* platonic
plau·si·ble, *a.* plausible
pla·ya, *f.* beach; shore
pla·za, *f.* public square
pla·zo, *m.* installment; term
ple·bis·ci·to, *m.* plebiscite
ple·gar(se), *v.* fold; pleat; crease
ple·ga·ria, *f.* prayer
plei·to, *m.* lawsuit; suit; controversy
ple·ni·po·ten·cia·rio, *m.* plenipotentiary
ple·no, *a.* full
plé·to·ra, *f.* plethora
plie·gue, *m.* pleat; fold; wrinkle; crease
plo·mo, *m.* lead
plu·ma, *f.* feather; pen. **plu·ma de gan·so,** quill
plu·ma·da, *f.* stroke of the pen
plu·ma·je, *m.* plumage
plu·món, *m.* down
plu·mo·so, *a.* feathery; fluffy
plu·ral, *a.* plural. *m.* plural
plus, *m.* bonus
plus·cuam·per·fec·to, *m.* pluperfect
plu·to·cra·cia, *f.* plutocracy
po·bla·ción, *f.* population
po·blar, *v.* people; populate; inhabit
po·bre, *a.* poor. *m.,* *f.* indigent person; pauper

po·bre·za, *f.* poverty
po·cil·go, *m.* sty
po·ción, *f.* potion
po·co, *adv.* little; *pl.* few. *a.* little. **po·co a po·co**, gradually
po·dar, *v.* prune
po·den·co, *m.* hound
po·der, *v.* can; may; be able to. *m.* power; might; strength; proxy
po·de·ro·so, *a.* powerful; forceful
po·dio, *m.* podium
po·dri·do, *a.* rotten; putrid; bad
poe·ma, *m.* poem. **poe·ma lí·ri·co**, lyric
poe·sía, *f.* poem; poetry
poe·ta, *m.* poet; bard
poé·ti·co, *a.* poetic; poetical
poe·ti·sa, *f.* poetess
pó·ker, *m.* poker
po·lar, *a.* polar
po·la·ri·dad, *f.* polarity
po·la·ri·zar(se), *v.* polarize
pol·ca, *f.* polka
po·lea, *f.* pulley
po·lé·mi·ca, *f.* polemic
po·len, *m.* pollen
po·li·cía, *f.* police; constabulary; policeman; constable. **a·gen·te de po·li·cía**, policeman; cop
po·lie·ti·le·no, *m.* polyethylene
po·li·fa·cé·ti·co, *a.* versatile
po·li·ga·mia, *f.* polygamy
po·lí·go·no, *m.* polygon
po·li·lla, *f.* moth
pó·li·po, *m.* polyp
po·li·teís·mo, *m.* polytheism
po·lí·ti·ca, *f.* politics; policy
po·lí·ti·co, *m.* politician. *a.* political
pó·li·za, *f.* insurance policy
po·li·zón, *m.* bustle; stowaway
po·lo, *m.* polo; pole
po·lu·ción, *f.* pollution
pol·vo, *m.* dust; powder. **qui·tar el pol·vo**, dust
pól·vo·ra, *f.* gunpowder
pol·vo·rien·to, *a.* dusty
po·lla, *f.* (*cards*) kitty
po·llo, *m.* chicken; fowl
po·llue·lo, *m.* chick
pom·pa, *f.* pomp; ostentation
pom·po·so, *a.* pompous; grandiose; highfalutin, highfaluting
pon·che, *m.* punch
pon·de·rar, *v.* ponder; consider
pon·de·ro·so, *a.* ponderous
po·ner(se), *v.* put; place; lay; set; shelter; don. **po·ner·se a ha·cer**, set about. **po·ner en bas·tar·di·lla**, italicize. **po·ner cua·ren·te·na**, quarantine. **po·ner en ca·mi·no**, set out. **po·ner en du·da**, doubt. **po·ner·se pol·vos**, powder
pon·ti·fi·ca·do, *m.* papacy

pon·ti·fi·ce, *m.* pontiff; pope
pon·ti·fi·cial, *a.* pontifical
po·pa, *f.* stern. **a po·pa**, aft
po·pu·la·cho, *m.* populace
po·pu·lar, *a.* popular
po·pu·la·ri·dad, *f.* popularity
po·pu·la·ri·zar(se), *v.* popularize
pó·quer, *m.* poker
po·qui·tín, *m.* a little bit. *a.* very little
po·qui·to, *a.* very little
por, *prep.* for; by; from; per; along; through, thru; via. **por cien·to**, percent. **es·tar por**, feel like. **por la no·che**, nightly. **por más que**, notwithstanding; however much. **por me·dio de**, through; by means of. **por su·pues·to**, of course. **por qué**, why?
por·ce·la·na, *f.* porcelain; china
por·cen·ta·je, *m.* percentage
por·ción, *f.* portion; section; fraction; part
por·fía, *f.* stubbornness
por·fia·do, *a.* insistent; obstinate
por·no·gra·fía, *f.* pornography
por·no·grá·fi·co, *a.* pornographic
po·ro, *m.* pore
po·ro·si·dad, *f.* porosity
por·que, *conj.* because
por·qué, *m.* why; reason
por·que·ría, *f.* filth; nastiness
po·rra, *f.* club; cudgel
por·rón, *m.* wine jar with a long spout
por·ta·dor, *m.* carrier
por·tae·qui·pa·je, *m.* trunk of a car
por·tal, *m.* entrance
por·tar·se, *v.* behave; comport oneself
por·tá·til, *a.* portable
por·ta·voz, *m.* spokesman
por·te, *m.* bearing; demeanor; carriage; postage
por·te·ro, *m.* porter; concierge; janitor
por·te·zue·la, *f.* hatch
pór·ti·co, *m.* porch; portico
por·ve·nir, *m.* future
po·sa·da, *f.* inn
po·sa·de·ro, *m.* landlord; innkeeper
po·sar(se), *v.* perch; sit upon; alight
pos·da·ta, *f.* postscript
po·seer, *v.* own; possess; have
po·se·sión, *f.* possession; tenancy; dependency, dependancy; *pl.* possessions; lands
po·se·si·vo, *a.* possessive
po·si·bi·li·dad, *f.* possibility
po·si·bi·li·tar, *v.* facilitate
po·si·ble, *a.* possible
po·si·ble·men·te, *adv.* possibly
po·si·ción, *f.* position; place; place-

ment; standing; status
po·si·ti·vo, *a.* positive; certain; absolute
po·so, *m.* deposit; sediment; *pl.* grounds
pos·ta, *f.* slug
pos·tal, *f.* postcard
pos·te, *m.* post
pos·te·ri·dad, *f.* posterity
pos·te·rior, *a.* posterior; later; after
pos·ti·zo, *a.* artificial. *m.* toupé
post·me·ri·dia·no, *a.* postmeridian. *Abbr.* p.m., P.M.
pos·tra·ción, *f.* prostration. **pos·tra·ción ner·vio·sa,** shock
pos·trar(se), *v.* prostrate; exhaust
pos·tre, *m.* dessert
pos·tre·ro, *a.* hindmost
pos·tu·ra, *f.* posture; attitude; wager
po·ta·sio, *m.* potassium
po·ten·cial, *a.* potential
po·ten·te, *a.* potent; powerful
po·tra, *f.* filly
po·tran·ca, *f.* filly
po·tro, *m.* rack; foal; colt
po·zo, *m.* well; shaft. **po·zo de pe·tró·leo,** oilwell. **po·zo de vi·si·ta,** manhole
prác·ti·ca, *f.* practice; observance; custom
prac·ti·ca·ble, *a.* practicable
prac·ti·car, *v.* practice
prác·ti·co, *a.* practical
pra·de·ra, *f.* prairie; meadow; field; pasture
prag·má·ti·co, *a.* pragmatic
prag·ma·tis·mo, *m.* pragmatism
prag·ma·tis·ta, *m., f.* pragmatist
pre·ám·bu·lo, *m.* preamble
pre·ca·rio, *a.* insecure; precarious
pre·cau·ción, *f.* precaution
pre·ca·ver(se), *v.* beware; prevent
pre·ce·den·cia, *f.* precedence
pre·ce·den·te, *m.* precedent. *a.* precedent
pre·ce·der, *v.* precede; antedate; forego
pre·cep·to, *m.* precept; commandment
pre·cep·tor, *m.* teacher; tutor
pre·cio, *m.* price; cost; value; rate; fare. **a pre·cio re·du·ci·do,** cutrate
pre·cio·so, *a.* valuable; precious; rich
pre·ci·pi·cio, *m.* precipice
pre·ci·pi·ta·ción, *f.* precipitation
pre·ci·pi·ta·do, *a.* precipitate; hasty; headlong
pre·ci·pi·tar(se), *v.* rush; hasten; dash
pre·ci·sa·men·te, *adv.* precisely; just so
pre·ci·sar, *v.* obligate; compel
pre·ci·sión, *f.* precision; obligation

pre·ci·so, *a.* precise; mandatory
pre·co·ci·dad, *f.* precocity; earliness
pre·coz, *a.* precocious
pre·cur·sor, *m., f.* precursor; forerunner; herald
pre·de·ce·sor, *m.,* **pre·de·ce·so·ra,** *f.* predecessor
pre·de·cir, *v.* predict; foretell
pre·des·ti·na·ción, *f.* predestination
pre·de·ter·mi·na·do, *a.* foregone; predetermined
pre·di·ca·ción, *f.* sermon
pre·di·car, *v.* preach
pre·di·lec·ción, *f.* predilection
pre·dis·po·ner, *v.* prejudice; predispose
pre·do·mi·na·ción, *f.* predominance
pre·do·mi·nan·te, *a.* predominant
pre·do·mi·nar, *v.* prevail; predominate; compel
pre·fa·cio, *m.* preface; foreword
pre·fe·ren·cia, *f.* preference; choice
pre·fe·ri·ble, *a.* preferable
pre·fe·ri·do, *a.* chosen; preferred
pre·fe·rir, *v.* prefer
pre·fi·jo, *m.* prefix
pre·gun·ta, *f.* question; query; inquiry
pre·gun·tar, *v.* question; query; inquire; ask
pre·his·tó·ri·co, *a.* prehistoric
pre·jui·cio, *m.* prejudice; bias; detriment
pre·juz·gar, *v.* prejudge
pre·li·mi·nar, *a.* preliminary
pre·lu·dio, *m.* prelude
pre·me·di·ta·do, *a.* premeditated; deliberate; willful; wilful
pre·me·di·tar, *v.* premeditate
pre·miar, *v.* reward; prize
pre·mio, *m.* award; prize; premium; bounty
pren·da, *f.* pledge; token. **pren·da de ves·tir,** garment
pren·der, *v.* apprehend; catch; *inf.* nab
pren·sa, *f.* press
pre·o·cu·pa·ción, *f.* preoccupation; worry; concern
pre·o·cu·pa·do, *a.* preoccupied
pre·o·cu·par(se), *v.* preoccupy; absorb; worry; mind; fuss
pre·pa·ra·ción, *f.* preparation
pre·pa·ra·do, *a.* prepared
pre·pa·rar(se), *v.* prepare; ready; coach; fix
pre·pa·ra·ti·vo, *m.* preparation
pre·pon·de·ran·cia, *f.* preponderance
pre·po·si·ción, *f.* preposition
pre·pós·te·ro, *a.* preposterous
pre·pu·cio, *m.* foreskin
pre·rro·ga·ti·va, *f.* prerogative
pre·sa, *f.* prey; quarry; dam; booty

pre·sa·giar, v. forebode; forbode; presage; bode

pre·sa·gio, m. omen

pres·cri·bir, v. prescribe

pre·sen·cia, f. presence

pre·sen·ta·ción, f. presentation; debut; début

pre·sen·tar(se), v. present; introduce; exhibit; feature; submit

pre·sen·te, a. present; current. **te·ner pre·sen·te,** bear in mind

pre·sen·ti·mien·to, m. premonition; foreboding; *often pl.* misgiving

pre·ser·var, v. preserve; keep

pre·ser·va·ti·vo, a. preservative. m. preservative

pre·si·den·cia, f. presidency

pre·si·den·te, m. president (*often cap.*); chairman

pre·si·dio, m. penitentiary

pre·si·dir, v. preside

pre·sión, f. pressure

pre·so, m., **pre·sa,** f. prisoner

prés·ta·mo, m. loan

pres·tar, v. lend; loan; extend

pres·ti·di·gi·ta·ción, f. prestidigitation; sleight of hand

pres·ti·gio, m. prestige; status

pre·su·mir, v. presume

pre·sun·ción, f. presumption; conceit; self-importance

pre·su·po·ner, v. presuppose

pre·su·pues·to, m. pretext; budget

pre·ten·der, v. pretend; seek; attempt

pre·ten·dien·te, m., f. pretender; suitor

pre·té·ri·to, m. preterite. a. preterite; past

pre·tex·to, m. pretext; pretense

pre·va·le·cer, v. prevail

pre·ven·ción, f. prevention; preparation

pre·ve·nir(se), v. arrange; prepare; avert; prevent; bias

pre·ver, v. foresee

pre·vio, a. previous; prerequisite

pre·vi·sión, f. foresight; forecast

pri·ma, f. cousin; insurance premium

pri·ma·do, a. primary. m. primate

pri·mal, m. yearling

pri·ma·ria·men·te, adv. primarily; principally

pri·ma·rio, a. primarily; elementary

pri·ma·ve·ra, f. spring; springtime

pri·ma·ve·ral, a. spring

pri·maz·go, m. cousinship

pri·me·ra·men·te, adv. first; mainly

pri·me·ro (pri·mer), a. first; foremost; erstwhile; prime. adv. uppermost; first. **de pri·me·ra ma·no,** firsthand; first-hand. **de pri·me·ra cla·se,** first-class. **pri·me·ra cu·ra,** first aid

pri·mi·ti·vo, a. primitive; early;

original

pri·mo, m. cousin

pri·mo·ge·ni·tu·ra, f. primogeniture

pri·mor·dial, a. primordial

pri·mo·ro·so, a. neat; fine; delicate

prin·ce·sa, f. princess

prin·ci·pa·do, m. principality

prin·ci·pal, a. principal; main; chief; leading; prime; head; master. adv. uppermost. m. principal; capital

prin·ci·pal·men·te, adv. mostly; principally

prín·ci·pe, m. prince

prin·ci·pian·te, m., f. novice; beginner

prin·ci·pio, m. principle; beginning; outset. **al prin·ci·pio,** at the beginning; at first

prin·gar, v. baste, as meat

prior, a. prior. m. prior

prio·ra, f. prioress

prio·ra·to, m. priory

pri·sa, f. hurry; haste; promptness. **dar·se pri·sa,** hurry

pri·sión, f. confinement; imprisonment; prison

pri·sio·ne·ro, m. prisoner

pris·ma, m. prism

pris·má·ti·co, a. prismatic

pri·va·ción, f. hardship; privation; deprivation

pri·va·do, a. private; deprived

pri·var(se), v. deprive; prohibit

pri·vi·le·gio, m. privilege; concession

proa, f. prow; bow

pro·ba·bi·li·dad, f. probability; chance

pro·ba·ble, a. probable; likely

pro·ba·ble·men·te, adv. probably

pro·ba·do, a. tried

pro·ban·za, f. proof

pro·bar(se), v. try; taste; sample; fit; prove; give evidence; chance

pro·ble·ma, m. problem

pro·ble·má·ti·co, a. problematical

pro·ce·der, v. proceed; behave. **pro·ce·der de,** stem from

pro·ce·di·mien·to, m. procedure

pro·ce·sar, v. prosecute; indict

pro·ce·sión, f. procession; parade

pro·ce·so, m. process; trial; action

pro·cla·ma·ción, f. proclamation

pro·cla·mar, v. proclaim; announce; herald

pro·cli·vi·dad, f. proclivity

pro·cón·sul, m. proconsul

pro·cre·a·ción, f. procreation

pro·cre·ar, v. procreate; produce

pro·cu·rar, v. procure; obtain; endeavor

pró·di·ga·men·te, adv. richly; wastefully

pro·di·gar, v. lavish; waste; squander

pro·di·gio, *m.* prodigy
pro·di·gio·sa·men·te, *adv.* prodigiously
pro·di·gio·so, *a.* prodigious
pró·di·go, *a.* prodigal; lavish; extravagant; spendthrift. *m.* prodigal
pro·duc·ción, *f.* production; output; turnout; yield. **pro·duc·ción en serie,** mass production
pro·du·cir, *v.* produce; create; yield; bear; do; turn out
pro·duc·ti·vi·dad, *f.* productivity
pro·duc·ti·vo, *a.* productive
pro·duc·to, *m.* product; produce. **pro·duc·to se·cun·da·rio,** by-product
proe·mio, *m.* preface
proe·za, *f.* feat; prowess
pro·fa·ni·dad, *f.* profanity
pro·fa·no, *a.* profane; irreligious
pro·fe·cía, *f.* prophecy
pro·fe·rir, *v.* utter
pro·fe·sar, *v.* profess; sustain
pro·fe·sión, *f.* profession; occupation; vocation; trade
pro·fe·sio·nal, *a.* professional. *m., f.* professional
pro·fe·sio·nal·men·te, *adv.* professionally
pro·fe·sor, *m.,* **pro·fe·so·ra,** *f.* professor; teacher
pro·fe·ta, *m.* prophet; seer
pro·fé·ti·ca·men·te, *adv.* prophetically
pro·fé·ti·co, *a.* prophetic; prophetical
pro·fe·ti·za, *f.* prophetess
pro·fe·ti·zar, *v.* prophesy
pro·fi·cien·te, *a.* proficient
pro·fi·lá·ti·co, *a.* prophylactic. *m.* prophylactic
pro·fun·da·men·te, *adv.* profoundly
pro·fun·di·dad, *f.* depth; profundity
pro·fun·di·zar, *v.* deepen
pro·fun·do, *a.* profound; deep
pro·fu·sa·men·te, *adv.* profusely
pro·fu·sión, *f.* profusion
pro·fu·so, *a.* profuse
pro·ge·nie, *f.* progeny; offspring; brood
pro·ge·ni·tor, *m.* progenitor; ancestor
prog·no·sis, *f.* forecast
pro·gra·ma, *m.* program; plan; syllabus
pro·gre·sar, *v.* progress; advance
pro·gre·sión, *f.* progression; progress
pro·gre·si·va·men·te, *adv.* progressively
pro·gre·si·vo, *a.* progressive; onward
pro·gre·so, *m.* progress; headway; march
pro·hi·bi·ción, *f.* prohibition; ban
pro·hi·bi·do, *a.* prohibited; forbidden

pro·hi·bir, *v.* prohibit; forbid; debar; ban
pro·hi·bi·ti·vo, *a.* prohibitive
pro·hi·jar, *v.* adopt
pro·jec·tar, *v.* scheme
pró·ji·mo, *m.* fellow man
pro·le·ta·rio, *m.,* **pro·le·ta·ria,** *f.* proletarian. *a.* proletarian
pro·li·fe·ra·ción, *f.* proliferation
pro·li·fe·rar, *v.* proliferate
pro·lí·fi·co, *a.* prolific
pró·lo·go, *m.* prologue; preface
pro·lon·ga·ción, *f.* lengthening; extension
pro·lon·ga·do, *a.* prolonged; long
pro·lon·gar(se), *v.* prolong; lengthen; continue
pro·me·diar, *v.* find the average of
pro·me·dio, *m.* average; mean
pro·me·sa, *f.* promise; pledge; vow
pro·me·ter(se), *v.* promise; pledge
pro·me·ti·do, *a.* engaged. *m.* offer; promise
pro·mi·nen·cia, *f.* prominence; protuberance
pro·mi·nen·te, *a.* prominent
pro·mis·cuo, *a.* promiscuous
pro·mo·ción, *f.* promotion
pro·mon·to·rio, *m.* promontory; headland
pro·mo·ver, *v.* promote; advance; pioneer
pro·mul·ga·ción, *f.* promulgation
pro·mul·gar, *v.* promulgate; proclaim
pro·nom·bre, *m.* pronoun
pro·no·mial, *a.* pronomial
pro·nos·ti·ca·ción, *f.* prediction
pro·nos·ti·car, *v.* forecast; predict
pro·nós·ti·co, *m.* prognosis; prediction; forecast
pron·ta·men·te, *adv.* promptly
pron·ti·tud, *f.* swiftness; promptness
pron·to, *a.* ready; prompt. *adv.* soon. **de pron·to,** suddenly
pro·nun·cia·ción, *f.* pronunciation; utterance
pro·nun·cia·do, *a.* pronounced
pro·nun·ciar(se), *v.* pronounce; utter; enunciate; deliver
pro·pa·ga·ción, *f.* propagation
pro·pa·gan·da, *f.* propaganda
pro·pa·gan·dis·ta, *m., f.* propagandist
pro·pa·gar(se), *v.* spread; propagate
pro·pen·sión, *f.* propensity; bias; bent
pro·pen·so, *a.* subject to; inclined
pro·pia·men·te, *adv.* properly
pro·pi·cia·ción, *f.* propitiation
pro·pi·ciar, *v.* propitiate
pro·pi·cio, *a.* propitious; favorable
pro·pie·dad, *f.* property; estate;

copyright

pro·pie·ta·ria, f. proprietress; landlady

pro·pie·ta·rio, m. proprietor; landlord

pro·pi·na, f. tip; gratuity. **dar pro·pi·na a,** tip

pro·pi·nar, v. tip

pro·pio, a. own; proper; fitting; very

pro·po·ner(se), v. propose; intend; present

pro·por·ción, f. proportion

pro·por·cio·na·do, a. proportionate

pro·por·cio·nal, a. proportional

pro·por·cio·nal·men·te, adv. proportionally

pro·por·cio·nar, v. supply; provide; furnish

pro·po·si·ción, f. proposition

pro·pó·si·to, m. purpose; intention; aim; object. **a pro·pó·si·to,** pertinent. **a pro·pó·si·to de,** apropos of; about

pro·pues·ta, f. proposition; offer; proposal; view

pro·pul·sar, v. propel; push

pro·pul·sión, f. propulsion

pro·sa, f. prose

pro·sai·ca·men·te, adv. prosaically

pro·sai·co, a. prosaic

pros·cri·bir, v. proscribe; outlaw

pros·crip·ción, f. proscription

pros·cri·to, a. proscribed. m. outcast

pro·se·guir, v. prosecute; pursue

pro·sé·li·to, m. proselyte

pros·pec·to, m. prospectus

prós·pe·ra·men·te, adv. prosperously

pros·pe·rar, v. prosper; thrive

pros·pe·ri·dad, f. prosperity. **pros·pe·ri·dad re·pen·ti·na,** boom

prós·pe·ro, a. successful; prosperous

pros·ta·ta, f. prostate

pros·ti·tu·ción, f. prostitution; harlotry

pros·ti·tuir, v. prostitute oneself

pros·ti·tu·ta, f. prostitute; whore

pro·ta·go·nis·ta, m., f. protagonist

pro·tec·ción, f. protection; pl. auspices

pro·tec·tor, m., **pro·tec·to·ra,** f. patron. a. protective

pro·tec·to·ra·do, m. protectorate

pro·te·ger, v. protect; shield; defend

pro·teí·na, f. protein

pro·tes·ta, f. protest

pro·tes·ta·ción, f. solemn declaration; protestation

pro·tes·tan·te, m., f. Protestant. a. Protestant

pro·tes·tar, v. protest

pro·to·co·lo, m. protocol

pro·tón, m. proton

pro·to·plas·ma, m. protoplasm

pro·to·ti·po, m. prototype

pro·tu·be·ran·cia, f. protuberance

pro·ve·cho, m. usefulness; profit; advantage. **buen pro·ve·cho,** good appetite; enjoy your meal

pro·ve·cho·sa·men·te, adv. beneficially

pro·ve·cho·so, a. beneficial; profitable; fruitful

pro·veer, v. provide; furnish; supply; cater; equip; fit out; fill

pro·ver·bial, a. proverbial

pro·ver·bio, m. proverb

pro·vi·den·cia, f. providence; judgment

pro·vi·den·cial, a. providential

pro·vi·den·te, a. provident

pro·vin·cia, f. province

pro·vin·cial, m., **pro·vin·cia·la,** f. provincial. a. provincial

pro·vin·cia·nis·mo, m. provincialism

pro·vi·sión, f. provision; hoard; pl. supplies

pro·vi·sio·nal, a. temporary; tentative; provisional

pro·vi·sio·nal·men·te, adv. provisionally

pro·vo·ca·ción, f. provocation

pro·vo·ca·dor, a. provocative

pro·vo·car, v. provoke; excite; irritate; nettle; antagonize

pro·vo·ca·ti·vo, a. provocative; sexy; defiant

prox·i·mi·dad, f. vicinity; proximity; closeness

próx·i·mo, a. next; near; handy; forthcoming

pro·yec·ción, f. projection; slide

pro·yec·tar(se), v. project; map; contemplate; throw out

pro·yec·til, m. missile; projectile

pro·yec·to, m. project; plan

pru·den·cia, f. caution; prudence

pru·den·te, a. prudent; shrewd; canny

pru·den·te·men·te, adv. prudently; wisely

prue·ba, f. proof; evidence; test; trial

prú·ri·to, m. itch

psi·coa·ná·li·sis, m. psychoanalysis

psi·coa·na·li·zar, v. psychoanalyze

psi·co·lo·gía, f. psychology

psi·co·ló·gi·ca·men·te, adv. psychologically

psi·co·ló·gi·co, a. psychological

psi·có·lo·go, m., f. psychologist

psi·co·sis, f. psychosis

psi·co·te·ra·pia, f. psychotherapy

psi·có·ti·co, a. psychotic

psi·que·dé·li·co, a. psychedelic

psi·quia·tra, psi·quía·tra, m., f. psychiatrist

psi·quia·tría, f. psychiatry

psi·quiá·tri·co, a. psychiatric

pto·maí·na, f. ptomaine, ptomain

púa, f. barb; spine; tooth

pu·ber·tad, f. puberty

pu·bli·ca·ción, f. publication. pu·bli·ca·ción pe·rió·di·ca, periodical

pú·bli·ca·men·te, adv. publicly

pu·bli·car, v. publish; issue; advertise

pu·bli·ci·dad, f. publicity; advertising

pú·bli·co, a. public; overt. m. public; audience

pu·din, m. pudding

pu·drir(se), v. rot; decay; putrefy

pue·blo, m. town; village; people; populace; nation

puen·te, m. bridge, puen·te col·gan·te, suspension bridge. puen·te le·va·di·zo, drawbridge

puer·co, a. foul; rude. m. hog; swine.

puer·co es·pin, porcupine

puer·ta, f. door; entrance; gate. de puer·ta en puer·ta, from door to door. de puer·ta a·den·tro, indoor

puer·to, m. port; harbor; haven. puer·to de en·tra·da, port of entry

pues, conj. for; then; since. adv. well; exactly. int. well

pues·ta, f. (cards) bet; setting. pues·ta del sol, sunset

pues·to, m. position; post; station; booth; stall; stand

pues·to que, conj. inasmuch as; since

pug·na, f. conflict

pug·na·ci·dad, f. pugnacity

pug·nar, v. fight

pug·naz, a. pugnacious

pu·ja, f. bid; effort

pu·jar, v. push; bid

pul·cri·tud, f. pulchritude; neatness

pul·cro, a. sleek; graceful; neat

pul·ga, f. flea

pul·ga·da, f. inch

pul·gar, m. thumb

pu·li·do, a. polished; buffed; tidy

pu·li·mien·to, m. polish

pu·lir(se), v. polish; buff; shine

pul·món, m. lung

pul·mo·nar, a. pulmonary

pul·mo·ní·a, f. pneumonia

pul·pa, f. pulp; flesh

púl·pi·to, m. pulpit

pul·po, m. octopus

pul·po·so, a. pulpy

pul·que, m. pulque

pul·sa·ción, f. pulsation; beating

pul·sar, v. pulsate; beat

pul·se·ra, f. bracelet

pul·so, m. pulse; wrist

pu·lu·lar, v. swarm

pul·ve·ri·za·ción, f. pulverization

pul·ve·ri·zar, v. pulverize; grind; spray

pu·lla, f. wisecrack

pu·ni·ti·vo, a. punitive

pun·ta, f. tip; point. pun·ta del pie, toe

pun·ta·da, f. stitch

pun·ta·pié, m. kick. dar un pun·ta·pié, kick

pun·tea·do, a. dotted

pun·tear, v. dot; sew

pun·te·rí·a, f. aim

pun·tia·gu·do, a. sharp

pun·ti·lla, f. lace; tack

pun·ti·llo·so, a. punctilious

pun·to, m. point; period; state; spot; dot; stitch. dos pun·tos, colon. ha·cer pun·to, knit. pun·to de vis·ta, standpoint. pun·to fi·no, nicety. pun·to y co·ma, semicolon

pun·tua·ción, f. punctuation

pun·tual, a. punctual; prompt; reliable

pun·tua·li·dad, f. punctuality; promptness

pun·tual·men·te, adv. punctually; promptly

pun·tuar, v. punctuate

pun·za·da, f. pang; sharp pain; puncture

pun·zar, v. punch; prod; prick; puncture

pun·zón, m. punch

pu·ña·do, m. handful

pu·ñal, m. dagger

pu·ña·la·da, f. stab

pu·ñe·ta·zo, m. punch; pl. fisticuffs

pu·ño, m. fist; cuff; hilt of a sword

pu·pi·la, f. pupil of the eye

pu·pi·lo, m. ward

pu·pi·tre, m. desk

pu·ra·men·te, adv. purely; entirely

pu·ré, m. mash; purée

pu·re·za, f. purity; pureness

pur·gan·te, a. purgative; cathartic. m. purgative; cathartic

pur·gar(se), v. purge

pur·ga·ti·vo, a. purgative

pur·ga·to·rio, m. purgatory

pu·ri·fi·ca·ción, f. purification

pu·ri·fi·car(se), v. purify; cleanse

pu·ris·ta, m., f. purist

pu·ri·ta·nis·mo, m. puritanism

pu·ri·ta·no, m., pu·ri·ta·na, f. puritan. a. puritan

pu·ro, a. pure; genuine; simple; unblemished. m. cigar

púr·pu·ra, f. purple

pur·pú·reo, a. purple

pus, m. pus

pu·ta, f. whore; prostitute

pu·tre·fac·ción, f. rot; putrefaction

pu·tre·fac·to, a. rotten

Q

que, rel. pron. what; whom; which; when. conj. than; that

qué, *interrog. pron.* what?
que·bra·di·zo, *a.* brittle; easily broken
que·bra·do, *a.* broken; uneven; bankrupt
que·bra·du·ra, *f.* breaking; fissure; rupture
que·brar(se), *v.* break; fracture; hinder; bankrupt
que·che, *m.* ketch
que·da, *f.* curfew
que·dar(se), *v.* stay; remain; last. **que·dar mal**, come off badly
que·ha·cer, *m.* affairs; task
que·ja, *f.* complaint; resentment; groan
que·jar·se, *v.* complain; grumble; moan; *inf.* beef; bitch
que·ji·do, *m.* whine; moan
que·jo·so, *a.* complaining; querulous
que·ma, *f.* burn; conflagration; burning
que·ma·do, *a.* burnt; burned
que·ma·du·ra, *f.* burn
que·mar(se), *v.* burn; scald; scorch
que·re·lla, *f.* complaint
que·re·llar(se), *v.* lament; complain; scold
que·rer, *v.* want; desire; wish; love; like. *m.* desire; love. **co·mo quie·ra**, as you like. **que·rer de·cir**, mean
que·ri·da, *a.* dear; darling. *f.* dear; darling; beloved; *inf.* mistress
que·ri·do, *a.* dear; darling; beloved. *m.* dear; darling; beloved
que·ru·bín, *m.* cherub
que·se·ría, *f.* dairy
que·so, *m.* cheese
quie·bra, *f.* bankruptcy; fissure; break
quien, *rel. pron.* who. **a quien**, whom
quién, *interrog. pron.* who? **a quién**, to whom?
quien·quie·ra, *pron.* whoever. **a quien·quie·ra**, whomever
quie·ta·men·te, *adv.* quietly
quie·tar(se), *v.* quiet; quiet down; calm down
quie·to, *a.* quiet; quiescent; still
quie·tud, *f.* quiet; stillness; tranquility
qui·ja·da, *f.* jaw; chin; jowl
qui·jo·tes·co, *a.* quixotic
qui·la·te, *m.* carat; karet
qui·lla, *f.* keel
qui·me·ra, *f.* chimera, chimaera; fancy
qui·mé·ri·co, *a.* chimeric; chimerical
quí·mi·ca, *f.* chemistry
quí·mi·co, *a.* chemical. *m.* chemist
quin·ce, *a.* fifteen
quin·ce·na, *f.* fortnight
quin·ce·no, *a.* fifteenth

quin·cua·gé·si·mo, *a.* fiftieth
qui·nien·tos, *a.* five hundred
qui·ni·na, *f.* quinine
quin·ta, *f.* country house
quin·taes·cen·cia, *f.* quintessence
quin·to, *a.* a fifth. *m.* fifth
quin·tu·pli·car(se), *v.* quintuple
quín·tu·plo, *a.* quintuple. *m.* quintuple; quintuplet
quios·co, *m.* kiosk
qui·ro·man·cia, *f.* palmistry
qui·ro·pe·dia, *f.* chiropody
qui·rúr·gi·co, *a.* surgical
quis·qui·llo·so, *a.* oversensitive
quis·te, *m.* cyst
qui·ta·es·mal·te, *m.* nail polish remover
qui·ta·man·chas, *m.* stain remover
qui·tar(se), *v.* shed; take off; remove; get rid of
qui·ta·sol, *m.* parasol
qui·te, *m.* removal
qui·za(s), *adv.* maybe; perhaps
quó·rum, *m.* quorum

R

rá·ba·no, *m.* radish. **rá·ba·no pi·can·te**, horseradish
ra·bí, *m.* rabbi
ra·bia, *f.* rabies; rage
ra·bie·ta, *f.* tantrum
ra·bí·ni·co, *a.* rabbinical
ra·bi·no, *m.* rabbi
ra·bio·so, *a.* rabid; furious; violent
ra·bo, *m.* tail
ra·cial, *a.* racial
ra·ci·mo, *m.* cluster; bunch
ra·ción, *f.* ration; helping; allowance
ra·cio·nal, *a.* rational
ra·cio·na·li·dad, *f.* rationality
ra·cio·na·lis·mo, *m.* rationalism
ra·cio·nal·men·te, *adv.* rationally
ra·cis·mo, *m.* racism
ra·dar, *m.* radar
ra·dia·ción, *f.* radiation
ra·diac·ti·vi·dad, *f.* radioactivity
ra·diac·ti·vo, *a.* radioactive
ra·dian·te, *a.* radiant; shining
ra·diar, *v.* radiate; broadcast
ra·di·cal, *a.* radical. *m.* radical; root
ra·di·cal·men·te, *adv.* radically
ra·dio, *m.* radium; radius. *f.* radio
ra·dio·gra·fía, *f.* X-ray
ra·dio·gra·fiar, *v.* X-ray
ra·dio·so, *a.* radiant
raer, *v.* scrape; remove the bark of
rá·fa·ga, *f.* squall; gust; blast; flurry
raí·do, *a.* shabby; worn; threadbare
raíz, *f. pl.* **raí·ces**. root; origin. **bie·nes raí·ces**, property
ra·ja, *f.* slit; sliver
ra·já, *m.* rajah
ra·jar(se), *v.* crack; split; sliver; slice

ra·ma, *f.* limb; branch; bough
ra·ma·da, *f.* branches
ra·mal, *m.* strand; branch
ra·me·ra, *f.* prostitute; harlot; strumpet
ra·mi·fi·ca·ción, *f.* ramification
ra·mi·fi·car·se, *v.* branch; ramify
ra·mi·ta, *f.* sprig; twig
ra·mo, *m.* bouquet; branch
ram·pa, *f.* ramp
ra·na, *f.* frog
ran·cio, *a.* rancid; mellow. *m.* rankness
ran·cho, *m.* ranch
ran·go, *m.* rank; degree; position
ra·nu·ra, *f.* slot; groove
ra·paz, *a.* rapacious. *f.* bird of prey
ra·pé, *m.* snuff
rá·pi·da·men·te, *adv.* rapidly; fast; zippy
ra·pi·dez, *f.* rapidity; speediness
rá·pi·do, *a.* rapid; fast; quick; express; cursory
ra·pi·ña, *f.* rapine. **a·ve de ra·pi·ña,** bird of prey
ra·pi·ñar, *v.* steal
ra·po·so, *m.* fox
rap·so·dia, *f.* rhapsody
rap·só·di·co, *a.* rhapsodic
rap·to, *m.* rapture; ravishment; rape
rap·tor, *m.* kidnapper
ra·que·ta, *f.* racket
ra·ra·men·te, *adv.* seldom; rarely
ra·re·fac·ción, *f.* rarefaction
ra·re·za, *f.* oddity; rarity; infrequency
ra·ri·dad, *f.* rarity
ra·ri·fi·car(se), *v.* dilute
ra·ro, *a.* odd; rare; strange; unusual; bizarre; queer
ras·ca·cie·los, *m.* skyscraper
ras·ca·du·ra, *f.* rasping; scraping
ras·ca·mo·ño, *m.* zinnia; hatpin
ras·car, *v.* scratch; scrape; rasp
ras·ga·du·ra, *f.* rip; rent
ras·gar(se), *v.* tear; rend; rip
ras·go, *m.* trait; feature; flourish; stroke
ras·gón, *m.* tear; snag
ras·guear, *v.* strum a guitar
ras·gu·ñar, *v.* scratch
ras·gu·ño, *m.* scratch; outline drawing
ra·so, *a.* flat; clear. *m.* satin. **sol·da·do ra·so,** private
ras·pa, *f.* rasp
ras·pa·dor, *m.* scraper
ras·pa·du·ra, *f.* abrasion; rasping; scraping
ras·par, *v.* scrape; erase; scratch
ras·tra, *f.* dredge; sledge
ras·trear, *v.* track; trail; investigate
ras·tri·llar, *v.* rake
ras·tri·llo, *m.* rake

ras·tro, *m.* trace; trail; vestige; rake
ras·tro·jo, *m.* stubble
ra·su·ra, *f.* levelness; shaving
ra·su·rar(se), *v.* shave
ra·ta, *f.* rat. **ra·ta al·miz·cle·ra,** muskrat
ra·tear, *v.* filch; pilfer; creep
ra·te·ro, *m.* pickpocket
ra·ti·fi·ca·ción, *f.* ratification
ra·ti·fi·car, *v.* ratify
ra·ti·to, *m.* little while
ra·to, *m.* while; time. **pa·sar el ra·to,** pass the time
ra·tón, *m.* mouse
ra·to·ne·ra, *f.* mousetrap; mousehole
rau·do, *a.* rushing
ra·ya, *f.* line; stripe; streak; dash
ra·ya·do, *a.* striped; ruled; variegated
ra·yar(se), *v.* stripe; streak; rule; line; scratch
ra·yo, *m.* ray; beam; bolt; thunderbolt; spoke
ra·yón, *m.* rayon
ra·za, *f.* race; lineage; strain
ra·zón, *f.* reason; cause; *sometimes pl.* grounds; rate; ratio
ra·zo·na·ble, *a.* reasonable; rational; sensible
ra·zo·na·ble·men·te, *adv.* reasonably
ra·zo·na·mien·to, *m.* reasoning
ra·zo·nar, *v.* argue; reason
re, *m.* (*mus.*) re
rea·bas·te·cer, *v.* refuel
reac·ción, *f.* reaction; response; backlash
reac·cio·nar, *v.* react
reac·cio·na·rio, *m.,* **reac·cio·na·ria,** *f.* reactionary. *a.* reactionary
reac·tor, *m.* reactor
re·a·fir·ma·ción, *f.* reaffirmation
re·a·gru·par(se), *v.* regroup
re·a·jus·tar(se), *v.* readjust
re·a·jus·te, *m.* readjustment
real, *a.* real; actual; true; veritable; royal; regal
rea·le·za, *f.* royalty
rea·li·dad, *f.* reality. **en rea·li·dad,** really
rea·lis·mo, *m.* realism
rea·lis·ta, *m., f.* realist. *a.* realistic
rea·li·za·ción, *f.* fruition; realization
rea·li·zar, *v.* realize; fulfill; fulfil; sell
real·men·te, *adv.* really; truly
real·zar, *v.* heighten; emboss
re·a·ni·mar(se), *v.* reanimate; revive; rally
re·a·nu·dar, *v.* resume
re·a·pa·re·cer, *v.* reappear
re·a·pa·ri·ción, *f.* reappearance
rea·ta, *f.* rope
re·ba·ja, *f.* reduction; discount
re·ba·jar(se), *v.* stoop; abase; reduce;

lessen; depress
re·bal·sar, v. dam up
re·ba·na·da, f. slice, as of bread
re·ba·nar, v. slice
re·ba·ño, m. herd; flock
re·ba·tir, v. ward off; refute
re·be·ca, f. cardigan
re·be·lar·se, v. revolt; rebel; balk
re·bel·de, a. rebel; rebellious. m., f. rebel
re·bel·día, f. default; disobedience
re·be·lión, f. rebellion; revolt
re·be·lón, a. fractious; stubborn; restive
re·bor·de, m. border
re·bo·sar, v. overflow
re·bo·tar, v. bounce; glance off
re·bo·te, m. ricochet; rebound; bounce
re·bo·zo, m. muffler
re·bu·far, v. recoil
re·bus·car, v. search through
re·buz·nar, v. bray
re·buz·no, m. bray
re·ca·do, m. errand; message; pl. provisions
re·caer, v. relapse
re·caí·da, f. relapse
re·cal·car, v. emphasize; squeeze
re·cal·ci·tran·te, a. recalcitrant
re·ca·len·tar(se), v. reheat; overheat
re·ca·ma·do, m. embroidery
re·ca·mar, v. embroider
re·cá·ma·ra, f. chamber; small room; breech
re·ca·pi·tu·la·ción, f. recapitulation
re·ca·pi·tu·lar, v. recapitulate
re·car·gar, v. reload; overload
re·car·go, m. increase
re·ca·to, m. caution; modesty
re·cau·da·ción, f. collection
re·cau·dar, v. collect
re·cau·do, m. precaution; collection
re·ce·lar, v. apprehend; fear
re·ce·lo, m. mistrust; jealousy; distrust
re·ce·lo·so, a. mistrustful; suspicious
re·cep·ción, f. reception; welcome
re·cep·tá·cu·lo, m. receptacle
re·cep·ti·vi·dad, f. receptivity
re·cep·ti·vo, a. receptive
re·cep·tor, m. receiver
re·ce·sión, f. recession
re·ce·ta, f. recipe; prescription
re·ci·bi·mien·to, m. reception; receiving; lobby
re·ci·bir, v. receive; accept; welcome
re·ci·bo, m. usu. pl. receipt
re·cién, adv. recently. **re·cién ca·sa·dos**, newlyweds
re·cien·te, a. recent; new
re·cien·te·men·te, adv. lately; recently
re·cin·to, m. campus; precinct; en-

closure
re·cio, a. strong
re·ci·pien·te, m. recipient
re·ci·pro·ca·ción, f. reciprocation
re·ci·pro·ca·men·te, adv. reciprocally
re·ci·pro·car(se), v. reciprocate
re·ci·pro·ci·dad, f. reciprocity
re·cí·pro·co, a. reciprocal
re·ci·ta·ción, f. recitation
re·ci·tar, v. recite
re·cla·ma·ción, f. reclamation; claim
re·cla·mar, v. claim; reclaim
re·cli·nar(se), v. recline
re·clu·so, m. recluse
re·clu·ta, m. recruit
re·clu·tar, v. recruit
re·clu·ta·mien·to, m. recruitment
re·co·brar(se), v. recover; regain; retrieve; recuperate
re·co·bro, m. recovery; recuperation
re·co·ger(se), v. gather; collect; harvest; shorten; shelter
re·co·gi·da, f. withdrawal
re·co·gi·mien·to, m. withdrawal; collection
re·co·men·da·ción, f. recommendation; testimonial
re·co·men·dar, v. recommend; advocate
re·com·pen·sa, f. recompense; reward
re·com·pen·sar, v. recompense; repay
re·con·ci·lia·ble, a. reconcilable
re·con·ci·lia·ción, f. reconciliation
re·con·ci·liar(se), v. reconcile
re·cón·di·to, a. concealed
re·con·for·tar, v. strengthen
re·co·no·cer, v. recognize; acknowledge; own up to; avow; reconnoiter
re·co·no·ci·ble, a. recognizable
re·co·no·ci·mien·to, m. recognition; gratitude; inspection; reconnaissance
re·con·quis·ta, f. reconquest
re·con·quis·tar, v. reconquest; recapture
re·con·si·de·rar, v. reconsider
re·cons·truc·ción, f. reconstruction
re·cons·truir, v. reconstruct
re·con·tar, v. retell; recount
re·con·ver·tir, v. reconvert
re·cor·dar(se), v. remind; remember
re·co·rrer, v. scour; run over; travel; traverse
re·co·rri·do, m. round; course; reconnaissance
re·cor·tar, v. trim; shorten
re·cor·te, m. snip; cutting
re·co·si·do, v. darn
re·cos·tar(se), v. recline; lean back; lie down

re·crear(se), v. recreate; entertain
re·crea·ti·vo, a. recreational
re·creo, m. recreation
re·cri·mi·na·ción, f. recrimination
re·cri·mi·nar, v. recriminate
re·cru·de·cer, v. worsen
re·cru·des·cen·cia, f. recrudescence
rec·tal, a. rectal
rec·ta·men·te, adv. honestly; justly
rec·tan·gu·lar, a. rectangular
rec·tán·gu·lo, m. rectangle. a. rectangular
rec·ti·fi·car, v. rectify
rec·ti·tud, f. rectitude; rightness
rec·to, a. upright; right; straight. m. rectum
re·cuer·do, m. souvenir; remembrance; memento; memory; often pl. remembrances
re·cu·pe·ra·ción, f. recuperation; recovery
re·cu·pe·rar(se), v. recuperate; recover; retrieve
re·cu·rrir, v. resort to
re·cur·so, m. recourse; remedy; expedient; resource; resort
re·cu·sa·ción, f. challenge
re·cu·sar, v. challenge
re·cha·za·do, m. outcast; repulsed
re·cha·zar, v. rebuff; repel; reject; turn out; fend off
re·cha·zo, m. rejection
re·chi·na·mien·to, m. grating; gnashing
re·chi·nar, v. gnash; grate
re·chon·cho, a. squat; stocky; chubby
red, f. net; network; mesh; trap
re·dac·ción, f. editing; writing
re·dac·tar, v. compose; edit
re·dac·tor, m., **re·dac·to·ra,** f. editor; writer
re·da·da, f. catch, as of fish
re·den·ción, f. redemption
re·den·tor, m. redeemer. a. redeeming
re·di·mir, v. redeem; pay off
ré·di·to, m. yield; rent
re·don·do, a. round(ed); spherical
re·dro·jo, m. runt
re·duc·ción, f. reduction; lessening
re·du·ci·do, a. reduced; narrow; low
re·du·cir(se), v. reduce; abate; shorten; condense; confine
re·dun·dan·te, a. redundant
re·e·di·fi·car, v. rebuild
re·e·lec·ción, f. re-election
re·e·le·gir, v. re-elect
re·em·bol·sar, v. repay; reimburse
re·em·bol·so, m. refund; repayment
re·em·pla·za·ble, a. replaceable
re·em·pla·zar, v. replace; substitute
re·em·pla·zo, m. replacement; substitution

re·en·car·na·ción, f. reincarnation
re·fe·ren·cia, f. reference
re·fe·ren·dum, m. referendum
re·fe·ren·te, a. referring
re·fe·rir(se), v. refer; recite; relate
re·fi·na·ción, f. refinement
re·fi·na·do, a. refined; polished
re·fi·na·mien·to, m. refinement
re·fi·nar, v. refine; polish
re·fi·ne·ría, f. refinery
re·fle·ja, f. reflection. a. reflected
re·fle·jar(se), v. reflect; consider
re·fle·jo, a. reflex; reflexive
re·flex·io·nar, v. reflect; speculate
re·flex·i·va·men·te, adv. reflectively
re·flex·i·vo, a. reflexive
re·flu·jo, m. ebb
re·for·ma, f. reform; (usu. cap.) Reformation
re·for·ma·ción, f. reformation
re·for·ma·do, a. reformed
re·for·mar(se), v. reform; mend; reconstruct
re·for·za·do, a. reinforced
re·for·zar, v. reinforce; brace; strengthen
re·frac·ción, f. refraction
re·frac·tar(se), v. refract
re·frán, m. proverb
re·fre·nar, v. refrain; restrain; curb
re·fren·dar, v. countersign
re·fres·ca·mien·to, m. refreshment
re·fres·car(se), v. refresh; freshen
re·fres·co, m. refreshment
re·fri·ge·ra·ción, f. refrigeration
re·fri·ge·ra·dor, m. refrigerator
re·fri·ge·rar, v. refrigerate; cool
re·fu·gia·do, m., **re·fu·gia·da,** f. refugee. a. refugee
re·fu·giar(se), v. take refuge
re·fu·gio, m. refuge; shelter; asylum
re·fun·fu·ñar, v. grumble; inf. grouch
re·fun·fu·ño, m. grumbling
re·fu·ta·ción, f. rebuttal; refutation
re·fu·tar, v. refute
re·ga·du·ra, f. irrigation
re·ga·la, f. gunwale, gunnel
re·ga·lar(se), v. make a present of; regale
re·ga·liz, m. licorice, liquorice
re·ga·lo, m. gift; present
re·ga·ñar, v. nag; scold; berate
re·gar, v. water; irrigate
re·ga·tear, v. bargain; dicker; haggle
re·ga·tón, m. tip
re·ga·zo, m. lap
re·ge·ne·ra·ción, f. regeneration
re·ge·ne·rar, v. regenerate
re·gen·te, m. regent
re·gi·ci·dio, m. regicide
ré·gi·men, m. regime; regimen; diet
re·gi·mien·to, m. regiment; administration

re·gión, *f.* region; district; area

re·gio·nal, *a.* regional

re·gio·na·lis·mo, *m.* regionalism

re·gir, *v.* govern; conduct; obtain

re·gis·trar(se), *v.* register; log; record; search

re·gis·tro, *m.* register; record; search

re·gla, *f.* law; rule; ruler

re·gla·men·ta·ción, *f.* regulations

re·gla·men·tar, *v.* regulate

re·gla·men·to, *m.* regulation; bylaw

re·glar, *v.* rule off

re·go·ci·ja·da·men·te, *adv.* merrily

re·go·ci·ja·do, *a.* merry; festive; joyous

re·go·ci·jar(se), *v.* rejoice; gladden; exult

re·go·ci·jo, *m.* joy; elation; festivity

re·gor·de·te, *a.* chubby

re·gre·sar, *v.* return

re·gre·si·vo, *a.* regressive

re·gu·la·ción, *f.* regulation

re·gu·la·dor, *m.* throttle. *a.* regulating

re·gu·lar, *a.* regular; common; tolerable. *v.* regulate

re·gu·la·ri·dad, *f.* regularity; custom

re·gu·lar·men·te, *adv.* regularly; generally

re·ha·bi·li·ta·ción, *f.* rehabilitation

re·ha·bi·li·tar, *v.* rehabilitate

re·ha·cer, *v.* redo; remake

re·hén, *m.* hostage

re·hi·lar, *v.* whiz, whizz; reel

re·huir, *v.* refuse

re·hu·sar, *v.* refuse; decline; deny

re·im·pri·mir, *v.* reprint

rei·na, *f.* queen

rei·na·do, *m.* reign

rei·nar, *v.* reign; command

re·in·ci·dir, *v.* backslide

rei·no, *m.* realm; kingdom

reír(se), *v.* laugh; scoff. reír en·tre dien·tes, chuckle; chortle

rei·te·ra·ción, *f.* reiteration

rei·te·rar, *v.* reiterate

re·ja, *f.* grating; grid

re·ju·ve·ne·cer(se), *v.* rejuvenate

re·la·ción, *f.* relation; recital; correspondence; bearing; account

re·la·cio·nar(se), *v.* relate; connect

re·la·ja·ción, *f.* relaxation

re·la·jar(se), *v.* relax; loosen; weaken

re·la·tar, *v.* relate; report; impart

re·la·ti·va·men·te, *adv.* relatively

re·la·ti·vi·dad, *f.* relativity

re·la·ti·vo, *a.* relative; comparative; germane

re·la·to, *m.* report; account; narration

re·le·ga·ción, *f.* relegation

re·le·gar, *v.* relegate

re·le·var, *v.* pardon; relieve

re·li·ca·rio, *m.* shrine

re·lie·ve, *m.* relief

re·li·gión, *f.* religion; creed; piety

re·li·gio·sa·men·te, *adv.* religiously

re·li·gio·so, *a.* religious; pious; godly

re·lin·char, *v.* whinny

re·lin·cho, *m.* whinny

re·li·quia, *f.* relic; vestige

re·loj, *m.* clock; watch; timepiece. re·loj des·per·ta·dor, alarm clock

re·lu·cien·te, *a.* glittering; shining

re·lu·cir, *v.* glitter; shine; glisten

re·lum·brar, *v.* glare; sparkle; glisten

re·lum·bre, *m.* luster

re·lle·nar(se), *v.* refill; stuff; cram

re·lle·no, *m.* filling; stuffing. *a.* stuffed

re·ma·che, *m.* rivet

re·mar, *v.* row

re·ma·te, *m.* conclusion; end; auction

re·me·da·dor, *m.*, re·me·da·do·ra, *f.* mimic

re·me·dar, *v.* mimic

re·me·diar, *v.* remedy; cure; repair

re·me·dio, *m.* remedy; recourse; help

re·men·da·do, *a.* repaired

re·men·dar, *v.* repair; patch; mend; blotch

re·me·sa, *f.* remittance

re·mien·do, *m.* patch

re·mil·ga·do, *a.* squeamish; prudish

re·mil·gar·se, *v.* be squeamish

re·mil·go, *m.* squeamishness; prudery

re·mi·nis·cen·cia, *f.* reminiscence; memory

re·mi·sión, *f.* remission; remitment

re·mi·so, *a.* remiss

re·mi·tir(se), *v.* remit; refer to; defer; postpone

re·mo, *m.* oar

re·mo·de·lar, *v.* remodel

re·mo·jar, *v.* soak

re·mo·la·cha, *f.* beet

re·mol·ca·dor, *m.* tugboat

re·mol·car, *v.* tug; tow

re·mo·ler, *v.* grind up

re·mo·li·nar(se), *v.* swirl; whirl

re·mo·li·no, *m.* swirl; whirlpool; eddy

re·mol·que, *m.* tow; caravan; trailer

re·mon·tar(se), *v.* soar; remount; resole

re·mor·di·mien·to, *m.* remorse; regret; compunction

re·mo·ta·men·te, *adv.* remotely

re·mo·to, *a.* remote; faraway; unlikely

re·mo·ver, *v.* remove; transfer; shift

re·mo·zar(se), *v.* rejuvenate

re·mu·ne·ra·ción, *f.* remuneration

re·mu·ne·ra·dor, *a.* remunerative

re·mu·ne·rar, *v.* remunerate

re·na·cer, *v.* be reborn; grow again;

revive

re·na·ci·mien·to, *m.* rebirth; (*usu. cap.*) Renaissance

re·na·cua·jo, *m.* tadpole

ren·ci·lla, *f.* grudge; feud

ren·ci·llo·so, *a.* quarrelsome

ren·cor, *m.* rancor; grudge; spite; spleen; bitterness; venom

ren·co·ro·sa·men·te, *adv.* resentfully

ren·co·ro·so, *a.* rancorous; bitter; catty

ren·di·ción, *f.* surrender; yielding

ren·di·do, *a.* worn-out; submissive

ren·di·mien·to, *m.* submission; rent; exhaustion

ren·dir(se), *v.* surrender; yield; overcome

re·ne·ga·do, *m.,* **re·ne·ga·da,** *f.* renegade. *a.* renegade

re·nom·bra·do, *a.* renowned

re·nom·bre, *m.* renown

re·no·va·ble, *a.* renewable

re·no·va·ción, *f.* renovation

re·no·va·do, *a.* renovated; renewed

re·no·var(se), *v.* renew; renovate; repair; reform

ren·ta, *f.* revenue; income; rent. **ren·ta vi·ta·li·cia,** *f.* annuity

re·nun·cia, *f.* renunciation; disclaimer; waiver

re·nun·ciar, *v.* renounce; surrender; resign; waive; forego; abnegate

re·ñir, *v.* quarrel; argue; feud; bicker

reo, *m., f.* criminal; defendant

re·or·ga·ni·za·ción, *f.* reorganization

re·or·ga·ni·zar, *v.* reorganize

re·pa·ra·ción, *f.* repair; amends; reparation

re·pa·ra·dor, *m.* serviceman

re·pa·rar, *v.* repair; mend; make amends

re·pa·ro, *m.* recovery; repair; doubt

re·par·ti·dor, *m.* deliveryman

re·par·ti·mien·to, *m.* division; apportionment; distribution

re·par·tir(se), *v.* apportion; distribute; mete out; share; dole; cast

re·par·to, *m.* allocation; delivery; deal; theatrical cast

re·pa·sar, *v.* revise; review; glance over

re·pa·so, *m.* revision; review

re·pa·tria·ción, *f.* repatriation

re·pa·triar(se), *v.* repatriate

re·pe·ler, *v.* repel

re·pen·ti·na·men·te, *adv.* suddenly

re·pen·ti·no, *a.* sudden; abrupt; snap

re·per·cu·sión, *f.* repercussion

re·per·to·rio, *m.* repertory; repertoire

re·pe·ti·ción, *f.* repetition; recurrence; encore

re·pe·ti·da·men·te, *adv.* repeatedly

re·pe·tir(se), *v.* repeat; recur; rehearse

re·pi·car, *v.* peal; chime

re·pi·que, *m.* chime

re·ple·gar, *v.* refold

re·po·blar, *v.* repopulate

re·po·ner(se), *v.* replace; replenish; recuperate

re·por·ta·je, *m.* report; reporting

re·po·sa·da·men·te, *adv.* restfully

re·po·sa·do, *a.* restful; quiet

re·po·sar, *v.* repose; rest

re·po·si·ción, *f.* reposition

re·po·si·to·rio, *m.* repository

re·po·so, *m.* repose

re·pre·gun·tar, *v.* cross-examine

re·pren·der, *v.* reprimand; rebuke; berate; chide

re·pren·si·ble, *a.* reprehensible

re·pre·sar, *v.* dam; stem

re·pre·sen·ta·ción, *f.* representation; performance; authority

re·pre·sen·tan·te, *m., f.* representative; agent

re·pre·sen·tar, *v.* represent; depict; perform; act; stage

re·pre·sen·ta·ti·vo, *a.* representative

re·pre·si·vo, *a.* a repressive

re·pri·men·da, *f.* reprimand; rebuke

re·pri·mir, *v.* repress; quell; curb

re·pro·bar, *v.* chide; condemn

re·pro·char, *v.* reproach

re·pro·che, *m.* reproach; rebuke

re·pro·duc·ción, *f.* reproduction

re·pro·du·cir(se), *v.* reproduce; breed

rep·til, *a.* reptile. *m.* reptile

re·pú·bli·ca, *f.* republic

re·pu·dia·ción, *f.* repudiation

re·pu·diar, *v.* repudiate; disown; divorce

re·pues·to, *m.* store. **de re·pues·to,** spare

re·pug·nan·cia, *f.* repugnance; disgust

re·pug·nan·te, *a.* repugnant; revolting; ugly

re·pul·sa, *f.* repulse; snub; rebuff

re·pul·sar, *v.* repulse; reject; refuse

re·pul·si·vo, *a.* repulsive; unsightly

re·pu·ta·ción, *f.* reputation; credit

re·que·rir, *v.* require; need; want; investigate

re·qui·sar, *v.* commandeer; requisition

re·qui·si·ción, *f.* requisition

re·qui·si·to, *m.* prerequisite; requirement; necessity

res, *m.* beast. **res muer·ta,** carcass

re·sa·ca, *f.* hangover

re·sal·tar, *v.* stand out; stick out

re·sar·ci·mien·to, *m.* compensation

re·sar·cir, *v.* compensate
res·ba·la·di·zo, *a.* slippery
res·ba·la·mien·to, *m.* slip
res·ba·lar, *v.* slip; glide; slip up; err
res·ba·lón, *m.* slide; offense
res·ca·tar, *v.* ransom; rescue; recover
res·ca·te, *m.* ransom; rescue; deliverance
re·sen·ti·do, *a.* resentful; sullen
re·sen·ti·mien·to, *m.* resentment; umbrage
re·sen·tir·se, *v.* resent
re·se·ña, *f.* review
re·ser·va, *f.* reserve; reservation; closeness. **con re·ser·va**, in confidence
re·ser·va·ción, *f.* reservation
re·ser·va·da·men·te, *adv.* privately
re·ser·va·do, *a.* reserved; shy; aloof
re·ser·var, *v.* reserve; set aside; bespeak; book
res·fria·do, *a.* cold
res·friar(se), *v.* catch cold; cool
res·guar·dar(se), *v.* shelter; protect
res·guar·do, *m.* shelter; guard; collateral
re·si·den·cia, *f.* residence
re·si·den·cial, *a.* residential
re·si·den·te, *a.* resident. *m., f.* resident
re·si·dir, *v.* reside; dwell; live
re·si·dual, *a.* residual
re·sig·na·ción, *f.* resignation; submission
re·sig·na·da·men·te, *adv.* resignedly
re·sig·nar(se), *v.* resign; give up
re·si·na, *f.* resin
re·sis·ten·cia, *f.* resistance; stamina; strength; endurance
re·sis·ten·te, *a.* tough; resistant
re·sis·tir(se), *v.* resist; withstand; oppose; contend
res·ma, *f.* ream
re·so·lu·ción, *f.* resolve; resolution; decision; purpose; steadfastness. **con re·so·lu·ción**, decisively
re·so·lu·to, *a.* resolute; determined
re·sol·ver(se), *v.* resolve; settle; determine; solve; figure out
re·so·llar, *v.* wheeze
re·so·nan·cia, *f.* resonance
re·so·nan·te, *a.* resonant
re·so·nar, *v.* echo; resound
res·pal·do, *m.* back
res·pec·ti·va·men·te, *adv.* respectively
res·pec·ti·vo, *a.* respective
res·pec·to, *m.* respect. **res·pec·to a**, re; with regard to
res·pe·ta·bi·li·dad, *f.* respectability
res·pe·ta·ble, *a.* respectable
res·pe·tar, *v.* respect
res·pe·to, *m.* respect; consideration
res·pe·tuo·sa·men·te, *adv.* respect-

fully
res·pe·tuo·so, *a.* respectful
res·pin·gar, *v.* wince; balk
res·pi·ra·ción, *f.* breathing; respiration
res·pi·rar, *v.* breathe; inhale. **res·pi·rar as·má·ti·ca·men·te**, wheeze
res·pi·ra·to·rio, *a.* respiratory
res·pi·ro, *m.* respite; breathing
res·plan·de·cer, *v.* glitter; glow; shine
res·plan·de·cien·te, *adv.* gleaming
res·plan·dor, *m.* glitter; blaze
res·pon·der, *v.* respond; answer; reply
res·pon·sa·bi·li·dad, *f.* responsibility
res·pon·sa·ble, *a.* responsible; accountable; amenable
res·pues·ta, *f.* reply; response; answer
res·ta, *f.* remainder; subtraction
res·ta·ble·cer(se), *v.* revive; re-establish
res·ta·ble·ci·mien·to, *m.* re-establishment; recovery
res·tan·te, *a.* remaining
res·ta·ñar, *v.* stanch, staunch
res·tar, *v.* deduct; subtract
res·tau·ra·ción, *f.* restoration
res·tau·ran·te, res·tau·rán, *m.* restaurant
res·tau·rar, *v.* restore; renew
res·ti·tu·ción, *f.* restitution
res·to, *m.* rest; remainder; balance; *pl.* wreckage
res·tric·ción, *f.* restriction
res·tric·ti·va·men·te, *adv.* restrictively
res·tric·ti·vo, *a.* restrictive
res·trin·gir, *v.* restrict; restrain; cramp
re·su·ci·ta·ción, *f.* resuscitation
re·su·ci·tar, *v.* resuscitate; resurrect; revive
re·suel·ta·men·te, *adv.* resolutely
re·suel·to, *a.* resolute; determined; unflinching; strong-minded; stout
re·sul·ta·do, *m.* result; outcome; product; issue; sequel; upshot
re·sul·tan·te, *a.* resultant
re·sul·tar, *v.* result; follow; prove to be
re·su·men, *m.* resume, résumé; syllabus; summary; abstract; rundown. **en re·su·men**, in short
re·su·mir, *v.* summarize; condense; abridge
re·sur·gi·mien·to, *m.* resurgence
re·su·rrec·ción, *f.* resurrection
re·ta·guar·dia, *f.* rearguard
re·tar·da·ción, *f.* retardation
re·tar·da·do, *a.* belated; held up; delayed
re·tar·dar, *v.* retard; slow down;

delay

re·ten·ción, f. retention

re·te·ner, v. retain; withhold; keep; detain

re·ti·na, f. retina

re·tin·tín, m. jingle; tinkling

re·ti·ñir, v. jingle; tinkle

re·ti·ra·da, f. retreat; withdrawal

re·ti·ra·do, a. retired; pensioned

re·ti·rar(se), v. retire; withdraw; recall

re·ti·ro, m. retreat; seclusion

re·to·ñar, v. sprout

re·to·ño, m. sprout

re·tor·cer(se), v. contort; twist; wring; writhe; squirm

re·tor·ci·do, a. twisted

re·tor·ci·mien·to, m. twisting; writhing

re·tó·ri·ca, f. rhetoric

re·tó·ri·ca·men·te, adv. rhetorically

re·tó·ri·co, a. rhetorical

re·tor·nar, v. restore; return

re·tor·no, m. return

re·to·zar, v. frisk about; romp; frolic

re·to·zón, a. frolicsome

re·trac·ción, f. retraction

re·trac·tar(se), v. retract; take back; recant

re·tra·sa·do, a. late; delayed

re·tra·sar, v. delay

re·tra·tar, v. portray

re·tra·to, m. picture; portrait; description

re·tre·te, m. toilet; water-closet

re·tri·bu·ción, f. payment; vengeance; retribution

re·tro·ac·ti·vo, a. retroactive

re·tro·ce·der, v. recede; fall back

re·tro·ce·so, m. recession; retrocession

re·tros·pec·ti·va·men·te, adv. retrospectively

re·tros·pec·ti·vo, a. retrospective

re·tum·bar, v. rumble; boom; clink

re·tum·bo, m. rumble; boom

reu·má·ti·co, a. rheumatic

reu·ma·tis·mo, m. rheumatism

reu·nión, f. reunion; assembly; rally; meeting

reu·nir(se), v. meet; gather; combine; collect; mass; rally; herd

re·ve·la·ción, f. revelation; exposure; disclosure

re·ve·la·dor, a. revealing

re·ve·lar, v. reveal; manifest; unbosom; betray; disclose

re·ven·tar, v. burst

re·ven·tón, m. burst; explosion; difficulty

re·ve·ren·cia, f. reverence; homage; bow; curtsy

re·ve·ren·cial, a. reverential

re·ve·ren·do, m. reverend. a. revered

re·ve·ren·te, a. reverent

re·ve·ren·te·men·te, adv. reverently

re·ver·so, m. reverse

re·ver·tir, v. revert to

re·vés, m. reverse; back side; setback. **al re·vés**, backward

re·ves·tir(se), v. put on

re·vi·sar, v. revise; review; go over; overhaul

re·vi·sión, f. revision; review; audit

re·vis·ta, f. magazine; journal; review

re·vi·vir, v. revive

re·vo·ca·ción, f. revocation; repeal

re·vo·car, v. revoke; annul; repeal

re·vol·car(se), v. welter; wallow in; knock over

re·vo·lo·tear, v. flutter; flit

re·vo·lu·ción, f. revolution; revolt

re·vo·lu·cio·na·rio, m., a. revolucionaria, a. revolutionary. a. revolutionary

re·vól·ver, m. revolver; pistol

re·vol·ver(se), v. revolve; revert; scramble; rummage

re·vuel·to, a. scrambled; confused. **hue·vos re·vuel·tos**, scrambled eggs

rey, m. king

re·za·ga·do, m. straggler

re·za·gar(se), v. lag; straggle behind

re·zar, v. pray

re·zu·mar(se), v. exude; leak; seep

ria·chue·lo, m. creek

ri·bal·de·ría, f. ribaldry

ri·be·ra, f. shore

ri·be·te, m. trimming

ri·be·tear, v. edge; hem

ri·ca·men·te, adv. richly; lavishly

ri·co, a. rich; wealthy; affluent

ri·dí·cu·la·men·te, adv. ridiculously

ri·di·cu·li·zar, v. ridicule; deride

ri·dí·cu·lo, m. ridicule. a. ridiculous; ludicrous; farcical

rie·go, m. irrigation. **bo·ca de rie·go**, hydrant

rie·lar, v. shimmer

rien·da, f. usu. pl. rein

ries·go, m. risk; chance; danger; hazard; liability

ri·fa, f. raffle

ri·fle, m. rifle

ri·gi·da·men·te, adv. rigidly; sternly

ri·gi·dez, f. rigidity

rí·gi·do, a. rigid; stiff; set; stern

ri·gor, m. rigor; strictness; severity; inflexibility

ri·go·ris·ta, m., f. stickler

ri·gu·ro·sa·men·te, adv. rigorously

ri·gu·ro·so, a. rigorous; strict; stringent; severe

ri·ma, f. rhyme

ri·mar, v. rhyme

ri·me·ro, m. stack; pile

rin·cón, m. corner
ri·no·ce·ron·te, m. rhinoceros
ri·ña, f. quarrel; dispute; fracas
ri·ñón, m. kidney
río, m. river
ri·pio, m. rubble
ri·que·za, f. wealth; affluence; riches
ri·sa, f. laugh; laughter. ri·sa so·fo·ca·da, giggle
ris·co, m. bluff; cliff; crag
ri·si·ta, f. chortle; titter
rít·mi·co, a. rhythmic; rhythmical
rit·mo, m. rhythm; cadence; beat
ri·to, m. rite
ri·tual, a. ritual. m. ritual
ri·tua·lis·mo, m. ritualism
ri·val, a. rival. m. rival
ri·va·li·dad, f. rivalry
ri·va·li·zar, v. rival; compete with
ri·za·do, a. curly
ri·zar(se), v. curl; ruffle
ri·zo, m. curl; ringlet
ro·ba·do, a. robbed
ró·ba·lo, m. bass
ro·bar, v. rob; steal; burglarize; inf. snitch; rustle
ro·ble, m. oak
ro·bo, m. theft; robbery
ro·bus·ta·men·te, adv. robustly
ro·bus·tez, f. robustness; hardiness
ro·bus·to, a. robust; strong; hale; hardy; lusty
ro·ca, f. rock
ro·cia·da, f. spray
ro·ciar, v. spray; sprinkle; scatter
ro·cín, m. hack; jade
ro·cío, m. dew
ro·da·do, a. dappled; rounded
ro·da·ja, f. castor
ro·dar, v. roll; wheel along
ro·dear, v. encircle; circle; surround; ring; loop
ro·deo, m. detour
ro·de·ra, f. rut
ro·di·lla, f. knee
ro·do·den·dro, m. rhododendron
roe·dor, m. rodent
roer, v. gnaw; gnaw at; eat away
ro·gar, v. pray; plead with; entreat; request; ask
ro·jear, v. turn red
ro·ji·zo, a. reddish
ro·jo, a. red. m. red
ro·llo, m. roll; coil; bolt
ro·man·ce, m. tale of chivalry. a. (cap.) Romance
ro·mán·ti·ca·men·te, adv. romantically
ro·man·ti·cis·mo, m. romanticism
ro·mán·ti·co, a. romantic
ro·me·ría, f. pilgrimage
rom·pe·ca·be·zas, m. jigsaw puzzle; puzzle
rom·peo·las, m. breakwater

rom·per(se), v. break; crush; smash; burst; dash; breach; tear
rom·pi·mien·to, m. break; rupture
ron, m. rum
ron·car, v. snore
ron·co, a. husky; hoarse
ron·da, f. round; patrol; beat, as of a policeman
ron·dar, v. do the rounds
ron·que·dad, f. hoarseness
ron·qui·do, m. snore
ron·ro·near, v. purr
ron·ro·neo, m. purr
ro·pa, f. clothes; clothing; dress; apparel; wear. ro·pa blan·ca, lingerie. ro·pa de ca·ma, bedclothes; bedding. ro·pa in·te·rior, underclothes; underwear. ro·pa la·va·da, laundry
ro·pe·ro, m. wardrobe
ro·sa, f. rose
ro·sa·do, a. pink; rosy
ro·sa·rio, m. rosary
ros·ca, f. thread, as of a screw; ring
ros·tro, m. face
ro·ta·ción, f. rotation
ro·to, a. broken; shattered; smashed
ro·tu·lar, v. label; ticket; letter
ró·tu·lo, m. label
ro·tun·da·men·te, adv. roundly
ro·tun·do, a. rotund; round
ro·tu·ra, f. breakage; rupture; crack
ro·za·mien·to, m. chafing
ro·zar(se), v. graze; rub; chafe; browse
ru·bí, m. ruby
ru·bia, f. blonde
ru·bio, a. blond, blonde; fair; red
ru·bor, m. flush
ru·bo·ri·za·do, a. flushed
ru·bo·ri·zar(se), v. make blush; flush
ru·di·men·tal, a. rudimentary
ru·di·men·to, m. rudiment
ru·do, a. rude; uncouth; churlish
rue·da, f. wheel. rue·da vo·lan·te, flywheel
rue·go, m. request; plea; entreaty
ru·fián, m. ruffian
ru·gi·do, m. roar; bellow
ru·gir, v. roar; bellow
ru·i·bar·bo, m. rhubarb
rui·do, m. noise; sound; clatter; noisiness; rattle; row; commotion
rui·do·sa·men·te, adv. noisily
rui·do·so, a. noisy; loud; blatant; rowdy; boisterous
ruin, a. mean; weak
rui·na, f. ruin; downfall; bane; wreck
rui·nar, v. ruin
rui·no·so, a. ruinous
rui·se·ñor, m. nightingale
ru·le·ta, f. roulette
rum·bo, m. route; direction; course; way

ru·mia, *f.* cud; rumination

ru·mi·nar, *v.* chew cud; brood over

ru·mor, *m.* murmur; rumor; hearsay

rup·tu·ra, *f.* break; rupture

ru·ral, *a.* rural

ru·ral·men·te, *adv.* rurally

rús·ti·co, *m.*, rús·ti·ca, *f.* rustic. *a.* rustic; countrified

ru·ti·na, *f.* routine; route; rut

ru·ti·na·rio, *a.* routine

S

sá·ba·do, *m.* Saturday

sá·ba·na, *f.* sheet

sa·ban·di·jas, *f.* insect; bug; *pl.* vermin

sa·ba·ni·lla, *f.* small piece of cloth

sa·ba·ñón, *f.* chilblain

sa·ber, *m.* knowledge; ken; learning. *v.* know; learn; ken. **a sa·ber**, namely; that is to say

sa·bia·men·te, *adv.* wisely; sagely

sa·bi·du·ría, *f.* learning; wisdom

sa·bio, *a.* wise; sage; learned; sapient. *m.* sage

sa·bor, *m.* flavor; taste; savor

sa·bo·rear, *v.* taste; savor

sa·bo·ta·je, *m.* sabotage

sa·bo·tear, *v.* sabotage

sa·bro·sa·men·te, *adv.* deliciously

sa·bro·so, *a.* tasty; delicious

sa·bue·so, *m.* bloodhound; hound

sa·ca, *f.* extraction; export

sa·ca·cor·chos, *m.* corkscrew

sa·car, *v.* take out; elicit; extract; draw out; withdraw. **sa·car u·na fo·to**, photograph; take a picture

sa·ca·ri·na, *f.* saccharine

sa·cer·do·cio, *m.* priesthood

sa·cer·do·te, *m.* priest

sa·ciar, *v.* sate; satiate

sa·cie·dad, *f.* satiety

sa·co, *m.* sack; bagful. **sa·co de ma·no**, grip

sa·cra·men·tal, *a.* sacramental

sa·cra·men·to, *m.* sacrament

sa·cri·fi·car(se), *v.* sacrifice; sacrifice oneself

sa·cri·fi·cio, *m.* sacrifice; offering

sa·cri·le·gio, *m.* sacrilege

sa·cri·le·go, *a.* sacrilegious

sa·cris·tía, *f.* vestry; sacristy

sa·cro·san·to, *a.* sacrosanct

sa·cu·di·da, *f.* jolt; shaking

sa·cu·di·mien·to, *m.* shock

sa·cu·dir(se), *v.* shake; jar; jerk; jolt; thrash; flap

sa·dis·mo, *m.* sadism

sae·ta, *f.* dart; religious song

sa·fa·ri, *m.* safari

sa·ga, *f.* saga

sa·ga·ci·dad, *f.* sagacity

sa·gaz, *a.* wise; shrewd; discerning

sa·gaz·men·te, *adv.* sagaciously

sa·gra·do, *a.* holy; sacred. **Sa·gra·da Es·cri·tu·ra**, Holy Scriptures

sai·ne·te, *m.* farce

sal, *f.* salt (sodium chloride); wit

sa·la, *f.* hall. **sa·la de es·tar**, lounge; drawing room. **sa·la de re·ci·bo**, parlor, parlour

sa·la·do, *a.* salt; salty; witty

sa·la·man·dra, *f.* salamander

sa·lar, *v.* salt

sa·la·rio, *m.* salary; *often pl.* wage

sa·laz, *a.* salacious

sal·chi·cha, *f.* frankfurter; sausage

sal·do, *m.* balance

sa·li·da, *f.* departure; emergence; exit; outlet; vent; sally

sa·lien·te, *a.* projecting

sa·li·no, *a.* saline

sa·lir, *v.* emerge; come out; issue; leave; escape. **sa·lir bien**, succeed. **sa·lir fue·ra**, protrude

sa·li·va, *f.* saliva; spit; spittle

sa·li·va·ción, *f.* salivation

sal·mo, *m.* psalm

sal·món, *m.* salmon

sa·lo·bre, *a.* brackish

sa·lón, *m.* salon; assembly room. **sa·lón de bai·le**, ballroom

sal·pi·ca·du·ra, *f.* splash; splatter; spatter

sal·pi·car, *v.* splash; spatter; dabble

sal·sa, *f.* sauce; gravy. **sal·sa pi·can·te de to·ma·te**, ketchup, catsup

sal·ta·dor, *m.* jumper

sal·ta·mon·tes, *m.* grasshopper

sal·tar, *v.* jump; leap; hop; spring; skip; vault; bound

sal·tear, *v.* hold up

sal·te·rio, *m.* psalter

sal·to, *m.* jump; hop; leap; *usu. m.* bound; dive. **sal·to mor·tal**, somersault

sa·lu·bre, *a.* healthy

sa·lu·bri·dad, *f.* salubrity

sa·lud, *f.* health

sa·lu·da·ble, *a.* salutary; healthy; wholesome

sa·lu·dar, *v.* greet; salute; hail

sa·lu·do, *m.* greeting; salutation; salute; hail

sa·lu·ta·ción, *f.* salutation

sal·va, *m.* salvo; salute

sal·va·ción, *f.* salvation

sal·va·do, *m.* bran

sal·va·dor, *m.* savior; (*cap.*) Savior, Saviour

sal·va·guar·dia, *f.* safeguard

sal·va·ja·da, *f.* savage act

sal·va·je, *a.* savage; wild. *m.*, *f.* savage

sal·va·men·to, *m.* salvage; salvation

sal·var(se), *v.* save; rescue; escape from danger

sal·va·vi·das, *m.* life preserver
sal·ve, *int.* hail
sal·via, *f.* sage
sal·vo, *prep.* saving. *a.* safe; except
San (San·to), *m.* Saint
sa·na·ble, *a.* curable
sa·na·men·te, *adv.* sanely; wholesomely
sa·nar, *v.* heal; recover
sa·na·to·rio, *m.* sanatorium. Also sanitarium
san·ción, *f.* sanction
san·cio·nar, *v.* sanction
san·da·lia, *f.* sandal
san·día, *f.* watermelon
sa·nea·mien·to, *m.* indemnification; drainage
sa·near, *v.* indemnify; drain
san·grar, *v.* bleed; tap; drain; indent
san·gre, *f.* blood; gore. **de san·gre fría,** cold-blooded. **in·yec·ta·do de san·gre,** bloodshot. **pu·ra san·gre,** thoroughbred
san·grí·a, *f.* drink made of red wine and fruit; drainage
san·grien·ta·men·te, *adv.* bloodily
san·grien·to, *a.* bloody
san·gui·jue·la, *f.* leech
san·gui·na·rio, *a.* sanguinary; bloodthirsty
san·guí·neo, *a.* sanguine; of blood
sa·ni·dad, *f.* health
sa·ni·ta·rio, *a.* sanitary; healthy
sa·no, *a.* healthy; healthful; sane; sound; fit; hearty
san·ta, *f.* (female) saint
san·ti·dad, *f.* sanctity; holiness
san·ti·fi·ca·ción, *f.* sanctification
san·ti·fi·car, *v.* sanctify; consecrate
san·to, *m.* saint. *a.* holy; saintly. **san·to y se·ña,** password; watchword
san·tua·rio, *m.* sanctuary
sa·ñu·da·men·te, *adv.* furiously
sa·po, *m.* toad
sa·quea·dor, *m.* ransacker; looter
sa·quear, *v.* loot; plunder; ransack; sack
sa·queo, *m.* plunder; ransacking
sa·ram·pión, *m.* measles
sa·ra·pe, *m.* blanket
sar·cas·mo, *m.* sarcasm; taunt
sar·cás·ti·ca·men·te, *adv.* sarcastically
sar·cás·ti·co, *a.* sarcastic
sar·có·fa·go, *m.* sarcophagus
sar·di·na, *f.* sardine
sar·dó·ni·ca·men·te, *adv.* sardonically
sar·dó·ni·co, *a.* sardonic
sar·gen·to, *m.* sergeant
sa·ri, *m.* sari, saree
sar·na, *f.* itch
sar·tén, *m.* skillet; frying pan
sas·tre, *m.* tailor

sas·tre·ría, *f.* tailoring
Sa·ta·nás, *m.* Satan
sa·tá·ni·ca·men·te, *adv.* satanically
sa·tá·ni·co, *a.* satanic. Also satanical
sa·té·li·te, *m.* satellite
sá·ti·ra, *f.* satire
sa·tí·ri·ca·men·te, *adv.* satirically
sa·tí·ri·co, *a.* satirical
sa·ti·ri·zar, *v.* satirize; lampoon
sá·ti·ro, *m.* satyr
sa·tis·fac·ción, *f.* satisfaction; content; amends; apology
sa·tis·fa·cer, *v.* satisfy; gratify; quench; indulge; sate
sa·tis·fac·to·ria·men·te, *adv.* satisfactorily
sa·tis·fac·to·rio, *a.* satisfactory
sa·tis·fe·cho, *a.* satisfied
sa·tu·ra·ción, *f.* saturation
sa·tu·rar, *v.* saturate; steep
sa·tur·ni·no, *a.* morose; saturnine
sau·ce, *m.* willow
sa·via, *f.* sap
sa·xo·fón, *m.* saxophone
sa·zón, *f.* ripeness; flavoring
sa·zo·na·do, *a.* seasoned
sa·zo·nar, *v.* flavor; season
se, *pron. m., f., neuter.* himself; herself; yourself; itself; *pl.* themselves; yourselves; one; one another
se·bo, *m.* suet; tallow
se·bo·so, *a.* greasy
se·ca·men·te, *adv.* drily
se·car(se), *v.* dry; wipe; blot; wither; shrivel; parch
sec·ción, *f.* section; segment; department; branch
se·ce·sión, *f.* secession; sequence
se·ce·sio·nis·ta, *m., f.* secessionist
se·co, *a.* dry; withered; unvarnished
se·cre·ción, *f.* secretion
se·cre·ta·men·te, *adv.* secretly
se·cre·tar, *v.* secrete
se·cre·ta·rio, *m.,* **se·cre·ta·ria,** *f.* secretary
se·cre·tear, *v.* whisper (secrets)
se·cre·to, *a.* secret; confidential; covert; cryptic; classified; undercover; underhanded. *m.* secret; secrecy
sec·ta, *f.* sect
sec·tor, *m.* sector
se·cues·tra·ción, *f.* sequestration; kidnapping
se·cues·tra·dor, *m.,* **se·cues·tra·do·ra,** *f.* kidnapper
se·cues·trar, *v.* kidnap; abduct; sequester
se·cues·tro, *m.* kidnapping
se·cu·lar, *a.* secular
se·cu·la·ri·za·ción, *f.* secularization
se·cu·la·ri·zar, *v.* secularize
se·cun·dar, *v.* second
se·cun·da·rio, *a.* secondary; circumstantial; subordinate; minor

se·cun·di·nas, *f. pl.* afterbirth

sed, *f.* thirst. te·ner sed, be thirsty

se·da, *f.* silk. se·da flo·ja, floss

se·da·ti·vo, *m.* sedative

se·de, *f.* see

se·den·ta·rio, *a.* sedentary

se·di·ción, *f.* sedition

se·di·cio·sa·men·te, *adv.* seditiously

se·di·cio·so, *a.* seditious

se·di·men·ta·ción, *f.* sedimentation

se·di·men·ta·rio, *a.* sedimentary

se·di·men·to, *m.* sediment; silt

se·do·so, *a.* silky

se·duc·ción, *f.* seduction; seducement; allure

se·du·cir, *v.* seduce; lead astray; captivate

se·duc·tor, *m.* seducer

se·ga·dor, *m.* harvester

se·gar, *v.* mow; reap; harvest

se·glar, *m.* layman

seg·men·to, *m.* segment

se·gre·ga·ción, *f.* segregation

se·gre·gar, *v.* segregate

se·gui·da, *f.* continuation. en se·gui·da, at once; immediately

se·gui·da·men·te, *adv.* continuously

se·gui·do, *a.* continuous

se·gui·dor, *m.*, se·gui·do·ra, *f.* follower

se·gui·mien·to, *m.* continuation; pursuit

se·guir, *v.* follow; continue; ensue; pursue; shadow

se·gún, *prep.* according to; by; as

se·gun·do, *a.* second. *m.* second

se·gu·ra·men·te, *adv.* surely; certainly

se·gu·ri·dad, *f.* security; certainty; safety

se·gu·ro, *a.* sure; certain; secure; safe; sound; confident; reliable; watertight; trusty. *m.* insurance

seis, *a.* six. *m.* six

seis·cien·tos, *a.* six hundred

seís·mo, *m.* earthquake

se·lec·ción, *f.* selection; choice

se·lec·cio·nar, *v.* select; choose

se·lec·ti·vi·dad, *f.* selectivity

se·lec·ti·vo, *a.* selective

se·lec·to, *a.* select; choice

sel·va, *a.* jungle; forest

sel·vá·ti·co, *a.* wild; rustic

sel·vo·so, *a.* wooded; of the jungle

se·lla·du·ra, *f.* sealing

se·llar, *v.* stamp; seal

se·llo, *m.* stamp; seal. se·llo de co·rreo, postage stamp

se·má·fo·ro, *m.* stoplight; semaphore

se·ma·na, *f.* week. Se·ma·na San·ta, Holy Week

se·ma·nal, *a.* weekly

se·mán·ti·ca, *f.* semantics

se·mán·ti·co, *a.* semantic

sem·blan·te, *m.* countenance; aspect

sem·brar, *v.* sow; seed; plant

se·me·jan·te, *a.* similar; alike; akin

se·me·jan·za, *f.* similarity; likeness; resemblance

se·men, *m.* semen

se·mes·tral, *a.* half-yearly

se·mes·tre, *m.* semester; six months

se·mi·cir·cu·lar, *a.* semicircular

se·mi·cir·cu·lo, *m.* semicircle

se·mi·con·so·nan·te, *a.* semiconsonant. *f.* semiconsonant

se·mi·fi·nal, *a.* semifinal. *m. usu. pl.* semifinal

se·mi·fi·na·lis·ta, *a.* semifinalist. *m.*, *f.* semifinalist

se·mi·lla, *f.* seed

se·mi·nal, *a.* seminal

se·mi·na·rio, *m.* seminar; seminary

se·mi·vi·vo, *a.* half-alive

se·na·do, *m.* senate; (*cap.*) Senate

se·na·dor, *m.* senator

se·na·to·rial, *a.* senatorial

sen·ci·lla, *a.* simple; plain; unassuming; naive; single

sen·ci·lla·men·te, *adv.* simply; plainly

sen·ci·llez, *f.* simplicity

sen·da, *f.* track; lane; footpath

se·nil, *a.* senile

se·no, *m.* breast; bosom; sinus

sen·sa·ción, *f.* sensation; sense; feeling

sen·sa·cio·nal, *a.* sensational; lurid

sen·sa·tez, *f.* sensibleness

sen·sa·to, *a.* sensible; lucid

sen·si·bi·li·dad, *f.* sensibility

sen·si·ble, *a.* sensitive; alive; lamentable

sen·si·ble·men·te, *adv.* sensitively; markedly

sen·si·ti·vo, *a.* sensitive

sen·so·rio, *a.* sensory. Also sensorial

sen·sual, *a.* sensual

sen·sua·li·dad, *f.* sensuality

sen·sual·men·te, *adv.* sensually

sen·ta·da, *f.* sitting

sen·tar(se), *v.* sit down; sit; seat

sen·ten·cia, *f.* sentence; judgment; conviction

sen·ten·ciar, *v.* adjudge; sentence

sen·ten·cio·sa·men·te, *adv.* sententiously

sen·ten·cio·so, *a.* sententious

sen·ti·do, *m.* meaning; sense; construction

sen·ti·men·tal, *a.* sentimental

sen·ti·men·tal·men·te, *adv.* sentimentally

sen·ti·mien·to, *m.* sentiment; regret

sen·tir(se), *v.* feel; sense; regret

se·ña, *f.* sign; mark. ha·cer se·ñas, motion; signal

se·ñal, *f.* signal; sign; token; (*often pl.*) note

se·ña·la·da·men·te, *adv.* signally; plainly

se·ña·la·do, *a.* signal; noted

se·ña·lar(se), *v.* mark; appoint; designate; distinguish

se·ñor, *m.* mister, abbr. Mr.; sir; gentleman; master; lord

se·ño·ra, *f.* lady; madam; mistress; Mrs.; wife; *inf.* ma'am

se·ño·rear, *v.* domineer; rule

se·ño·ril, *a.* lordly

se·ño·río, *m.* manor; lordliness; lordship

se·ño·ri·ta, *f.* miss; young lady

se·ñue·lo, *m.* bait; lure; decoy

sé·pa·lo, *m.* sepal

se·pa·ra·ción, *f.* separation; segregation; isolation

se·pa·ra·da·men·te, *adv.* separately

se·pa·ra·do, *a.* separate; detached; isolated

se·pa·rar(se), *v.* separate; part; detach; split; sever; sequester

se·pa·ra·tis·mo, *m.* separatism

sep·ten·trio·nal, *a.* northern

sép·ti·co, *a.* septic

sep·tiem·bre, *m.* September

sép·ti·mo, *a.* seventh. *m.* seventh

se·pul·cro, *m.* tomb; sepulcher

se·pul·tar, *v.* bury

se·pul·tu·ra, *f.* vault; grave; tomb

se·que·dad, *f.* dryness; gruffness

se·quía, *f.* drought

sé·qui·to, *m.* following; entourage

ser, *v.* be; belong. **ser de,** be of; be made of

ser, *m.* being; life. **ser hu·ma·no,** *m.* human being

se·rá·fi·co, *a.* seraphic

se·ra·fín, *m.* seraph

se·re·na·men·te, *adv.* serenely; quietly

se·re·na·ta, *f.* serenade

se·re·ni·dad, *f.* serenity; calmness; composure

se·re·no, *a.* serene; calm; fair; sober. *m.* night watchman

se·ria·men·te, *adv.* seriously

se·rie, *f.* series; sequence; string; run; suite; train. **en se·rie,** mass

se·rie·dad, *f.* seriousness; gravity. **con se·rie·dad,** earnestly

se·rio, *a.* serious; grave; sober; earnest

ser·món, *m.* sermon

ser·pen·tear, *v.* wind; meander

ser·pen·ti·no, *a.* snakelike; winding

ser·pien·te, *f.* serpent; snake. **serpien·te de cas·ca·bel,** rattlesnake

se·rra·nía, *f.* mountain range

se·rrar, *v.* saw

ser·vi·cio, *m.* service. **ser·vi·cio do·**

més·ti·co, domestic service

ser·vi·dor, *m.,* **ser·vi·do·ra,** *f.* servant

ser·vi·dum·bre, *f.* servitude; servants

ser·vil, *a.* servile; menial; subservient

ser·vi·lle·ta, *f.* napkin

ser·vir(se), *v.* serve; wait on; do; answer

se·sen·ta, *a.* sixty; threescore. *m., f.* sixty

ses·ga·da·men·te, *adv.* slanting; sloping

ses·ga·do, *a.* slanting; bias; awry

ses·gar(se), *v.* slant; slope

ses·go, *a.* slope; slant; bias. **al ses·go,** aslant

se·sión, *f.* session; meeting

se·so, *m.* brain; understanding

se·te·cien·tos, *a.* seven hundred

se·ten·ta, *a.* seventy. *m., f.* seventy

se·to, *m.* hedge; fence

seu·dó·ni·mo, *m.* pseudonym

se·ve·ra·men·te, *adv.* severely; harshly

se·ve·ri·dad, *f.* severity; sternness; harshness

se·ve·ro, *a.* severe; harsh; stern; strict; forbidding; grim; rough; rugged

sex·o, *m.* sex. **sex·o fe·me·ni·no,** womankind

sex·te·to, *m.* sextet

sex·to, *a.* sixth

se·xual, *a.* sexual

se·xua·li·dad, *f.* sexuality

se·xual·men·te, *adv.* sexually

si, *conj.* if; whether

sí, *reflexive pron.* *sí mis·mo,* himself; yourself; itself; oneself; also one's self. **sí mis·ma,** herself; yourself; itself

sí, *adv.* yes. *int.* aye; ay; yea

si·co·mo·ro, *m.* sycamore

si·dra, *f.* cider

siem·pre, *adv.* always; forever; ever. **siem·pre que,** whenever

sien, *f.* temple

sie·rra, *f.* saw. **sie·rra de vai·vén,** jigsaw

sier·vo, *m.,* **sier·va,** *f.* serf; slave

sies·ta, *f.* nap

sie·te, *a.* seven. *m., f.* seven

sí·fi·lis, *f.* syphilis

si·fón, *m.* siphon; syphon

si·gi·lo, *m.* secrecy; secret

si·gi·lo·sa·men·te, *adv.* secretly

si·glo, *m.* century

sig·ni·fi·ca·ción, *f.* significance

sig·ni·fi·ca·do, *m.* significance

sig·ni·fi·can·te, *a.* significant

sig·ni·fi·car(se), *v.* signify; mean; imply; make known

sig·ni·fi·ca·ti·va·men·te, *adv.* significantly

sig·no, *m.* sign
si·guien·te, *a.* next; following
sí·la·ba, *f.* syllable
si·la·bear, *v.* syllabicate; syllabify
si·la·beo, *m.* syllabication; syllabification
sil·bar, *v.* whistle; hiss; whiz; whizz
sil·bi·do, *m.* whistle; hiss; whiz; whizz
si·len·cio, *m.* silence; hush; quiet
si·len·cio·sa·men·te, *adv.* silently
si·len·cio·so, *a.* silent; quiet
sí·li·ce, *f.* silica
si·li·cio, *m.* silicon
si·lo, *m.* silo
si·lue·ta, *f.* silhouette
sil·ves·tre, *a.* wild; sylvan, silvan
sil·vi·cul·tu·ra, *f.* forestry
si·lla, *f.* chair. **si·lla de mon·tar,** saddle. **si·lla de rue·das,** wheelchair
si·ma, *f.* chasm
sim·bó·li·ca·men·te, *adv.* symbolically
sim·bó·li·co, *a.* symbolic; symbolical
sim·bo·lis·mo, *m.* symbolism
sim·bo·li·zar, *v.* symbolize; typify
sím·bo·lo, *m.* symbol
si·me·tría, *f.* symmetry
si·mé·tri·ca·men·te, *adv.* symmetrically
si·mé·tri·co, *a.* symmetrical
si·mi·co, *a.* simian
si·mien·te, *m.* seed
si·mi·lar, *a.* similar
sim·pa·tía, *f.* sympathy; friendliness
sim·pá·ti·co, *a.* nice; congenial; likeable; sympathetic
sim·ple, *a.* simple; plain
sim·ple·men·te, *adv.* simply; barely; plainly
sim·pli·ci·dad, *f.* simplicity
sim·pli·fi·ca·ción, *f.* simplification
sim·pli·fi·car, *v.* simplify
si·mu·lar, *v.* simulate
si·mul·tá·nea·men·te, *adv.* simultaneously; together
si·mul·tá·neo, *a.* simultaneous
sin, *prep.* without; wanting. **sin em·bar·go,** however; yet. **sin ton ni son,** without rhyme or reason. **sin va·lor,** worthless. **sin vo·lun·tad,** weak-minded
si·na·go·ga, *f.* synagogue, synagog
sin·ce·ra·men·te, *adv.* sincerely
sin·ce·ri·dad, *f.* sincerity; cordiality
sin·ce·ro, *a.* sincere; genuine; wholehearted; heartfelt
sin·cro·ni·zar(se), *v.* synchronize
sin·di·car, *v.* syndicate; unionize
sin·di·ca·to, *m.* union; trade union; syndicate
si·ne·cu·ra, *f.* sinecure
sin·fo·nía, *f.* symphony
sin·gu·lar, *a.* singular; quaint. *m.* singular

sin·gu·la·ri·dad, *f.* singularity; oddity
sin·gu·lar·men·te, *a.* singularly
si·nies·tro, *a.* sinister; baleful
si·no, *conj.* but; except
si·no·do, *m.* synod
si·nó·ni·mo, *m.* synonym. *a.* synonymous
si·nop·sis, *f.* synopsis
sín·te·sis, *f.* synthesis
sin·té·ti·ca·men·te, *adv.* synthetically
sin·té·ti·co, *a.* synthetic
sín·to·ma, *m.* symptom
sin·to·ni·zar, *v.* tune
sin·ver·güen·za, *m., f.* person without shame
sio·nis·mo, *m.* Zionism
si·quie·ra, *adv.* although; at least. **ni si·quie·ra,** not even
si·re·na, *f.* mermaid; siren
sir·vien·te, *m.,* **sir·vien·ta,** *f.* servant
sis·mó·gra·fo, *m.* seismograph
sis·te·ma, *m.* system
sis·te·má·ti·ca·men·te, *adv.* systematically
sis·te·má·ti·co, *a.* systematic
sis·te·ma·ti·zar, *v.* systematize
si·tiar, *v.* besiege; surround; beleaguer; beset; invest
si·tio, *m.* place; space; site; spot; room; siege
si·tua·ción, *f.* situation; location; plight. **si·tua·ción e·co·nó·mi·ca,** circumstances
si·tuar, *v.* situate; post; station
smo·king, *m.* tuxedo
so·ba·co, *m.* armpit
so·be·ra·nía, *f.* sovereignty
so·be·ra·no, *a.* sovereign. *a.* sovereign
so·ber·bia, *f.* haughtiness; anger
so·ber·bio, *a.* haughty
so·bor·nar, *v.* bribe
so·bor·no, *m.* bribe; graft
so·bra, *f.* surplus; *pl.* scraps
so·bran·te, *a.* spare; remaining; odd; waste. *m.* margin
so·brar, *v.* remain; surpass
so·bre, *prep.* on; upon; atop; onto; over; above; about. *m.* envelope. **so·bre to·do,** above all
so·bre·car·ga, *f.* surcharge; overload
so·bre·car·gar, *v.* overload
so·bre·co·ger(se), *v.* surprise
so·bre·hu·ma·no, *a.* superhuman
so·bre·na·dar, *v.* buoy; float
so·bre·po·ner(se), *v.* superimpose; overcome
so·bre·sa·lien·te, *a.* outstanding. *m., f.* understudy
so·bre·sa·lir, *v.* project; jut; excel; transcend

so·bre·sal·tar(se), v. start; startle
so·bre·sal·to, m. scare; surprise
so·bres·cri·to, m. superscription
so·bre·to·do, m. topcoat
so·bre·vi·vien·te, m., f. survivor
so·bre·vi·vir, v. survive
so·brie·dad, f. sobriety; restraint
so·bri·na, f. niece
so·bri·no, m. nephew
so·brio, a. sober
so·ca·var, v. undermine
so·cia·bi·li·dad, f. sociability
so·cia·ble, a. sociable
so·cia·ble·men·te, adv. sociably
so·cial, a. social
so·cia·lis·mo, m. socialism
so·cia·li·zar, v. socialize; fraternize
so·cie·dad, f. society; association; corporation; league. **so·cie·dad a·nó·ni·ma**, incorporated company
so·cio, m. associate; partner
so·cio·lo·gia, f. sociology
so·cio·ló·gi·co, a. sociological
so·co·rrer, v. succor; help; aid
so·co·rro, m. help; succor. int. help!
so·dio, m. sodium
so·do·mía, f. sodomy
so·fá, m. sofa; couch
so·fis·ma, f. sophism; chicanery
so·fis·te·ría, f. sophistry; chicanery
so·fo·ca·ción, f. suffocation
so·fo·can·te, a. suffocating; stifling; close
so·fo·car(se), v. suffocate; smother; choke; swelter; quell
so·ga, f. rope
so·juz·ga·ción, f. subjugation
so·juz·gar, v. subjugate; conquer; subdue
sol, m. sun; sunlight; sunshine. **luz del sol**, sunlight; sunshine. **pues·ta del sol**, sundown; sunset. **sa·li·da del sol**, sunrise. **to·mar el sol**, sun; sunbathe
so·la·men·te, adv. only; alone; solely
so·la·pa, f. lapel; flap
so·la·par, v. overlap
so·lar, a. solar. m. site; floor
so·laz, m. solace; relaxation
sol·da·do, m. soldier; GI, also G.I.; pl. military. **sol·da·do de ca·ba·lle·ría**, trooper; cavalryman. **sol·da·do ra·so**, private
sol·dar, v. soldar; weld
so·le·dad, f. privacy; solitude
so·lem·ne, a. solemn; impressive
so·lem·ne·men·te, adv. solemnly
so·lem·ni·dad, f. solemnity; ceremony
so·lem·ni·zar, v. celebrate
so·li·ci·ta·ción, f. solicitation
so·li·ci·tar, v. solicit; request; seek; apply for; canvass
so·li·ci·tud, f. care; application

só·li·da·men·te, adv. solidly
so·li·da·ri·dad, f. solidarity
so·li·di·fi·ca·ción, f. solidification
só·li·do, a. solid. m. solid
so·li·lo·quio, m. soliloquy
so·li·ta·ria·men·te, adv. solitarily
so·li·ta·rio, a. solitary; lonely; lone; lonesome. m. recluse
so·lo, a. sole; solitary; one; alone; lonely; lonesome. m. (mus.) solo
só·lo, adv. only; solely. conj. but
sol·tar(se), v. release; loose; undo
sol·te·ra, f. maiden; spinster
sol·te·ría, f. bachelorhood
sol·te·ro, a. unattached; single. m. bachelor
sol·te·ro·na, f. spinster
so·lu·ble, a. soluble
so·lu·ción, f. solution; answer
so·lu·cio·nar, v. solve
sol·ven·te, m. solvent
llo·rar, v. sob; wail
llo·ro, m. sob
som·bra, f. shadow; shade; suspicion
som·brea·do, a. shady
som·brear, v. shade
som·bre·ro, m. hat
som·brío, a. somber; dismal; overcast
so·me·ter(se), v. submit; subject; yield
so·me·ti·mien·to, m. submission
som·no·len·cia, f. drowsiness; sleepiness
som·no·len·te, a. drowsy; sleepy
so·mor·gu·jo, m. loon
son, m. sound. **sin ton ni son**, without rhyme or reason
so·na·je·ro, m. rattle
so·nar(se), v. sound; ring; rattle; chink; blow the nose
son·da, f. probe
son·deo, m. poll; canvass
so·ne·to, m. sonnet
so·ni·do, m. sound
so·no·ro, a. sonorous
son·reir(se), v. smile; grin
son·ri·sa, f. smile. **son·ri·sa bur·lo·na**, sneer
son·ro·jar·se, v. flush; blush
son·ro·jo, m. blush
so·ña·dor, m., **so·ña·do·ra**, f. dreamer. a. dreamy
so·ñar, v. dream
so·ño·lien·ta·men·te, adv. sleepily
so·ño·lien·to, a. sleepy; drowsy
so·pa, f. soup. **so·pa de pes·ca·do**, chowder
so·pe·ra, f. tureen
so·plar, v. blow; puff; inf. snitch
so·plo, m. blow; puff; blast; tip
so·por·ta·ble, a. bearable
so·por·tar, v. endure; bear; tolerate; abide; bracket; support

so.pra.no, *m., f.* soprano
sor.ber, *v.* sip; soak up
sor.be.te, *m.* sherbet
sor.bo, *m.* sip; swallow; taste
sor.de.ra, *f.* deafness
sór.di.do, *a.* sordid; dirty; nasty
sor.di.na, *f.* (*mus.*) mute
sor.do, *a.* deaf
sor.do.mu.do, *m.,* **sor.do.mu.da,** *f.* deaf-mute
sor.pren.den.te, *a.* surprising; astonishing; startling
sor.pren.der(se), *v.* surprise; amaze; startle
sor.pre.sa, *f.* surprise; amazement
sor.te.o, *m.* raffle
so.sa, *f.* soda
so.se.ga.da.men.te, *adv.* quietly
so.se.ga.do, *a.* quiet; sedate; gentle
so.se.gar(se), *v.* pacify; calm; rest
so.sie.go, *m.* peace; calmness
so.so, *a.* insipid; tame; shy
sos.pe.cha, *f.* suspicion; inkling
sos.pe.char, *v.* suspect; be suspicious of
sos.pe.cho.sa.men.te, *adv.* suspiciously
sos.pe.cho.so, *a.* suspect; suspicious; doubtful; fishy
sos.tén, *m.* support; stand; brassiere; *inf.* bra
sos.te.ner, *v.* support; sustain; maintain; uphold
sos.te.ni.do, *a.* sustained. *m.* (*mus.*) sharp
sos.te.ni.mien.to, *m.* maintenance
so.ta, *f.* (cards) jack
so.ta.na, *f.* cassock
só.ta.no, *m.* cellar; basement
so.ta.ven.to, *m.* lee
su, *a.* his; her; its; your; *pl.* your; their
sua.ve, *a.* soft; smooth; mild; bland; gentle; balmy; mellow
sua.ve.men.te, *adv.* gently; softly; mildly; smoothly
sua.vi.dad, *f.* gentleness; smoothness; softness
sua.vi.za.dor, *m.* strop
sua.vi.zar, *v.* soften; smooth; mellow; subdue
su.ba.rren.dar, *v.* sublease; sublet
su.bas.ta, *f.* sale; auction
su.bas.ta.dor, *m.* auctioneer
su.bas.tar, *v.* auction
sub.cons.cien.cia, *f.* subconscious
sub.cons.cien.te, *a.* subconscious
sub.cons.cien.te.men.te, *adv.* subconsciously
sub.cu.tá.neo, *a.* subcutaneous
súb.di.to, *m.* subject
sub.di.vi.dir, *v.* subdivide
sub.di.vi.sión, *f.* subdivision
su.bes.ti.mar, *v.* underestimate
su.bi.da, *f.* ascent; rise; increase

su.bir(se), *v.* raise; lift up; rise; ascend; increase; accede
sú.bi.ta.men.te, *adv.* suddenly
sú.bi.to, *a.* sudden
sub.je.ti.va.men.te, *adv.* subjectively
sub.je.ti.vi.dad, *f.* subjectivity
sub.je.ti.vo, *a.* subjective
sub.jun.ti.vo, *m.* subjunctive
su.ble.va.ción, *f.* uprising; revolt
su.bli.ma.ción, *f.* sublimation
su.bli.mar, *v.* sublimate
su.bli.me, *a.* sublime; majestic
su.bli.me.men.te, *adv.* sublimely
su.bli.mi.dad, *f.* sublimity
sub.ma.ri.no, *a.* submarine; *inf.* sub
su.bor.di.na.ción, *f.* subordination
su.bor.di.na.do, *a.* subordinate. *m.* underling; minor
su.bor.di.nar, *v.* subordinate
sub.ra.yar, *v.* underscore; underline; emphasize
subs.cri.bir(se), *v.* subscribe to
subs.crip.ción, *f.* subscription
sub.si.dia.rio, *a.* subsidiary
sub.si.dio, *m.* subsidy; benefit
sub.si.guien.te, *a.* subsequent
sub.sis.ten.cia, *f.* subsistence
sub.sis.tir, *v.* subsist; live; endure
subs.tan.cia, *f.* substance; meaning
subs.tan.cia.ción, *f.* substantiation
subs.tan.cial, *a.* substantial; material
subs.tan.cial.men.te, *adv.* substantially
subs.tan.ti.vo, *m.* noun; substantive. *a.* substantive
subs.ti.tu.ción, *f.* substitution
subs.ti.tuir, *v.* substitute
subs.ti.tu.to, *m.* substitute; surrogate. *a.* substitute; vicarious
subs.trac.ción, *f.* subtraction
sub.traer, *v.* subtract
sub.ter.fu.gio, *m.* subterfuge
sub.te.rrá.neo, *a.* subterranean; underground
sub.tí.tu.lo, *m.* subheading; subtitle
su.bur.ba.no, *a.* suburban
su.bur.bio, *m.* suburb, *often pl.*
sub.ven.ción, *f.* subsidy
sub.ven.cio.nar, *v.* subsidize
sub.ver.sión, *f.* subversion
sub.ver.si.vo, *a.* subversive. *m.* subversive
sub.ver.tir, *v.* subvert
su.byu.ga.ción, *f.* subjugation
su.byu.gar, *v.* subjugate; overcome
suc.ción, *f.* suction
su.ce.der, *v.* happen; occur; transpire; succeed; make out
su.ce.sión, *f.* succession; issue; estate
su.ce.si.vo, *a.* successive; consecutive
su.ce.so, *m.* event; incident; result
su.ce.sor, *m.,* **su.ce.so.ra,** *f.* succes-

sor
su·cie·dad, *f.* dirtiness
su·cin·to, *a.* succinct; brief
su·cio, *a.* dirty; unclean; filthy; foul; nasty; grubby; dingy
su·cu·len·to, *a.* succulent
su·cum·bir, *v.* succumb
su·dar, *v.* perspire; sweat
sud·es·te, *m.* southeast
sud·oes·te, *m.* southwest
su·dor, *m.* perspiration; sweat
su·do·ro·so, *a.* sweaty
sue·gra, *f.* mother-in-law
sue·gro, *m.* father-in-law
sue·la, *f.* sole
suel·do, *m.* pay; salary
sue·lo, *m.* ground; land; floor
suel·to, *a.* unattached; loose; free
sue·ño, *m.* sleep; dream
sue·ro, *m.* serum
suer·te, *f.* luck; chance; fate; doom; fortune; lot
sué·ter, *m.* sweater
su·fi·cien·cia, *f.* sufficiency; complacency
su·fi·cien·te, *a.* sufficient; adequate
su·fi·cien·te·men·te, *adv.* sufficiently
su·fi·jo, *m.* suffix
su·fra·gio, *m.* suffrage; vote
su·fri·mien·to, *m.* suffering; misery; patience
su·frir, *v.* suffer; sustain; undergo
su·ge·rir, *v.* suggest; hint
su·ges·tión, *f.* suggestion; hint
su·ges·ti·vo, *a.* suggestive
sui·ci·da, *m., f.* suicide
sui·ci·dar·se, *v.* commit suicide
sui·ci·dio, *m.* suicide
su·je·ción, *f.* subjection; control
su·je·tar(se), *v.* attach; clamp; cramp; subject
su·je·to, *m.* subject; matter. *a.* subject; attached
sul·fa·to, *m.* sulphate
sul·fú·ri·co, *a.* sulphuric
sul·tán, *m.* sultan
sul·ta·na·to, *m.* length of a sultan's reign
sul·ta·nía, *f.* sultanate
su·ma, *f.* sum; amount; total
su·ma·men·te, *adv.* exceedingly; very
su·mar, *v.* add; sum up
su·ma·rio, *a.* summary
su·mer·gi·mien·to, *m.* submergence
su·mer·gir(se), *v.* submerge; submerse; dive
su·mer·sión, *f.* submergence; submersion
su·mi·nis·trar, *v.* supply; provide
su·mi·sión, *f.* submission; compliance
su·mi·so, *a.* submissive; compliant; obedient

su·mo, *a.* utmost; highest; supreme.
su·mo sa·cer·do·te, high priest
sun·tuo·sa·men·te, *adv.* sumptuously
sun·tuo·so, *a.* sumptuous
su·pe·rar, *v.* surmount; surpass; exceed; cap
su·pe·ren·ten·der, *v.* superintend; supervise
su·per·fi·cial, *a.* superficial
su·per·fi·cial·men·te, *adv.* superficially
su·per·fi·cie, *f.* surface
su·per·flua·men·te, *adv.* superfluously
su·per·flui·dad, *f.* superfluity
su·per·fluo, *a.* superfluous; needless
su·pe·rin·ten·den·cia, *f.* superintendence
su·pe·rin·ten·den·te, *m., f.* superintendent; supervisor
su·pe·rior, *a.* superior; better; senior; upper. *m. usu. pl.* superior; better
su·pe·rio·ri·dad, *f.* superiority
su·per·la·ti·vo, *a.* superlative
su·per·mer·ca·do, *m.* supermarket
su·per·nu·me·ra·rio, *m.,* su·per·nu·me·ra·ria, *f.* supernumerary. *a.* supernumerary
su·per·só·ni·co, *a.* supersonic
su·pers·ti·ción, *f.* superstition
su·pers·ti·cio·sa·men·te, *adv.* superstitiously
su·pers·ti·cio·so, *a.* superstitious
su·per·vi·sor, *m.,* su·per·vi·so·ra, *f.* supervisor
su·per·vi·ven·cia, *f.* survival
su·pi·no, *a.* supine
su·plan·tar, *v.* supplant; supersede
su·ple·men·ta·rio, *a.* supplementary
su·ple·men·to, *m.* supplement
sú·pli·ca, *f.* supplication; plea; appeal
su·pli·can·te, *m., f.* supplicant; applicant
su·pli·car, *v.* supplicate; plead; beseech; appeal; crave
su·plir, *v.* supplement
su·po·ner, *v.* suppose; presume; *inf.* reckon
su·po·si·ción, *f.* supposition; assumption
su·pre·ma·cia, *f.* supremacy
su·pre·ma·men·te, *adv.* supremely
su·pre·mo, *a.* supreme; final
su·pre·sión, *f.* suppression; deletion
su·pri·mir, *v.* suppress; remove
su·pues·to, *a.* alleged; so-called; would-be. **por su·pues·to**, of course
su·pu·ra·ción, *f.* suppuration
su·pu·rar, *v.* suppurate
sur, *m.* south
sur·car, *v.* furrow

sur·co, *m.* furrow

sur·gir, *v.* emerge; originate; arise

sur·ti·da, *f.* sally

sur·ti·do, *m.* stock; assortment

sur·ti·dor, *m.* jet of water

sur·tir, *v.* stock; supply

sus·cep·ti·bi·li·dad, *f.* susceptibility

sus·cep·ti·ble, *a.* susceptible

sus·pen·der, *v.* hang; sling; suspend; stop; cease; adjourn; knock off

sus·pen·sión, *f.* suspension; recess; reprieve

sus·pi·rar, *v.* sigh; yearn for

sus·pi·ro, *m.* sigh

sus·ten·tan·te, *a.* sustaining

sus·ten·tar, *v.* sustain; support

sus·ten·to, *m.* sustenance

sus·to, *m.* fright; shock; surprise

su·su·rrar, *v.* whisper; rustle

su·su·rro, *m.* whisper; rustle

su·til, *a.* subtle; keen; thin

su·ti·le·za, *f.* subtlety; finesse; cunning; fineness

su·ti·li·zar, *v.* refine

su·til·men·te, *adv.* subtly; finely

su·yo, *pron.* his; hers; yours; its; one's; *pl.* theirs; yours

T

ta·ba·co, *m.* tobacco

tá·ba·no, *m.* gadfly

ta·ber·na, *f.* tavern; barroom; *inf.* pub

ta·ber·ná·cu·lo, *m.* tabernacle

ta·bi·que, *m.* partition

ta·bla, *f.* board; slab

ta·ble·ro, *m.* panel; board. **ta·ble·ro de ins·tru·men·tos,** dashboard

ta·ble·ta, *f.* tablet

ta·bli·lla, *f.* slat; splint

ta·blón, *m.* plank

ta·bú, *a.* taboo. *m.* taboo, tabu

ta·bu·lar, *v.* tabulate. *a.* tabular

ta·bu·re·te, *m.* stool

ta·ca·ño, *a.* stingy; mean; parsimonious

tá·ci·ta·men·te, *adv.* tacitly

tá·ci·to, *a.* tacit

ta·ci·tur·no, *a.* taciturn; reserved; sullen

ta·co, *m.* tablet; wad; cue

ta·cón, *m.* heel

tác·ti·ca, *f.* tactics

tác·ti·co, *a.* tactical

tac·to, *m.* tact; feel; touch

ta·cha, *f.* blemish

ta·char, *v.* delete; find fault with

ta·chón, *m.* trimming

ta·chue·la, *f.* tack

ta·fe·tán, *m.* taffeta

ta·ja·da, *f.* slice

ta·jar, *v.* hew; chop; slice

tal, *a.* such. *adv.* so. *pron.* such; such

a thing. **tal vez,** maybe; perhaps

ta·la·drar, *v.* bore; drill

ta·la·dro, *m.* bore; drill

ta·lar, *v.* fell

tal·co, *m.* talc. **pol·vo de tal·co,** talcum powder

ta·len·to, *m.* talent

ta·len·to·so, *a.* talented

ta·lis·mán, *m.* talisman

ta·lón, *m.* heel

ta·lla, *f.* size; sculpture

ta·llar, *v.* (cards) deal; carve

ta·lla·rín, *m.* noodle

ta·lle, *m.* shape; figure; waistline

ta·ller, *m.* studio; atelier; shop; workshop

ta·llo, *m.* stalk; stem

ta·ma·ño, *m.* size; bulk. **de ta·ma·ño na·tu·ral,** life size, also life-sized

tam·ba·lean·te, *a.* rickety

tam·ba·lear·se, *v.* stagger; reel

tam·bién, *adv.* also; besides; too; likewise

tam·bor, *m.* drum

tam·bo·ri·lear, *v.* drum

ta·miz, *f.* sieve

ta·mi·zar, *v.* sift; sieve

tam·po·co, *adv.* neither

tan, *adv.* so; such

tan·da, *f.* shift; batch

tan·gen·te, *a.* tangent. *f.* tangent

tan·gi·ble, *a.* tangible

tan·go, *m.* tango

tan·que, *m.* tank; cistern

tan·tear, *v.* score; calculate; size up

tan·teo, *m.* score

tan·to, *adv.* so much; as many. **por lo tan·to,** therefore. **tan·to me·jor,** so much the better

ta·ñer, *v.* toll; ring

ta·ñi·do, *m.* twang; ring

ta·pa, *f.* cap; lid; top

ta·pa·gu·je·ros, *m.* stopgap

ta·par, *v.* plug; stop up; cover up

ta·pi·ce·ría, *f.* tapestry; upholstery

ta·pio·ca, *f.* tapioca

ta·pir, *m.* tapir

ta·piz, *m.*, *pl.* **ta·pi·ces.** tapestry

ta·pi·zar, *v.* upholster; hang with tapestries

ta·pón, *m.* stopper; plug

ta·qui·gra·fía, *f.* stenography; shorthand

ta·qui·gra·fo, *m.*, **ta·quí·gra·fa,** *f.* stenographer

ta·rán·tu·la, *f.* tarantula

tar·dan·za, *f.* delay

tar·dar, *v.* delay; tarry; linger

tar·de, *adv.* late. *f.* afternoon; evening. **bue·nas tar·des,** good afternoon; good evening

tar·dío, *a.* late; belated; tardy

ta·rea, *f.* task; job; homework

ta·ri·fa, *f.* tariff

ta·ri·ma, *f.* bunk; platform

tar·je·ta, *f.* card. **tar·je·ta pos·tal,** postcard

tar·ta, *f.* tart; cake

tar·ta·mu·dear, *v.* stammer; stutter

tar·ta·mu·deo, *m.* stammer; stutter

tar·tán, *m.* plaid; tartan

tár·ta·ro, *m.* tartar

ta·sa, *f.* estimate; price

ta·sa·ción, *f.* valuation

ta·sar, *v.* rate; appraise; assess; tax

ta·tua·je, *m.* tatoo

ta·tuar, *v.* tatoo

ta·xi, *m.* taxi; taxicab; cab

ta·xis·ta, *m.* cabdriver; *inf.* cabby

ta·za, *f.* cup. **ta·za pa·ra té,** teacup

ta·zón, *m.* basin

te, *pron.* you; thee

té, *m.* tea. **mu·ñe·ca de té,** teabag. **so·bre de té,** teabag. **ta·za pa·ra té,** teacup

tea·tral, *a.* theatrical

tea·tral·men·te, *adv.* theatrically

tea·tro, *m.* theater; drama

te·beo, *m.* comic strip

te·cla, *f.* key, as of a typewriter

te·cla·do, *m.* keyboard

téc·ni·ca, *f.* technique

téc·ni·ca·men·te, *adv.* technically

téc·ni·co, *a.* technical. *m.* technician

tec·no·lo·gía, *f.* technology

tec·no·ló·gi·co, *a.* technological

te·char, *v.* roof

te·cho, *m.* roof; ceiling

te·dio, *m.* tedium; tediousness

te·dio·so, *a.* tedious; wearisome; loathsome

te·ja, *f.* tile

te·ja·do, *m.* tiled roof

te·ja·ma·nil, *m.* shingle

te·je·dor, *m.,* **te·je·do·ra,** *f.* weaver

te·jer, *v.* weave; knit

te·ji·do, *m.* textile; weave; tissue; *pl.* yardgoods

te·jo, *m.* yew

te·jón, *m.* badger

te·la, *f.* material; fabric; cloth; web. **te·la de a·ra·ña,** spiderweb; cobweb

te·lar, *v.* loom

te·la·ra·ña, *f.* spiderweb; cobweb

te·le·co·mu·ni·ca·ción, *f.* telecommunication

te·le·fo·near, *v.* telephone; *inf.* phone

te·lé·fo·no, *m.* telephone; *inf.* phone

te·le·gra·fía, *f.* telegraphy

te·le·gra·fiar, *v.* telegraphy; wire

te·lé·gra·fo, *m.* telegraph

te·le·gra·ma, *m.* telegram; *inf.* wire

te·le·pa·tía, *f.* telepathy

te·les·có·pi·co, *a.* telescopic

te·les·co·pio, *m.* telescope

te·le·vi·sar, *v.* televise

te·le·vi·sión, *f.* television. Abbr. T.V.

te·le·vi·sor, *m.* television. Abbr. T.V.

te·lón, *m.* curtain. **te·lón de fo·ro,** backdrop

te·ma, *m.* theme; text; topic

te·má·ti·co, *a.* thematic

tem·blar, *v.* tremble; shake; quiver; shiver

tem·blor, *m.* quiver; tremor; trembling

te·mer, *v.* dread; be afraid

te·me·ra·ria·men·te, *adv.* recklessly

te·me·ra·rio, *a.* foolhardy; reckless; rash

te·me·ri·dad, *f.* temerity; boldness

te·me·ro·so, *a.* fearful; timid

te·mi·ble, *a.* fearsome; awful

te·mor, *m.* fear

tém·pa·no, *m.* ice floe; kettledrum

tem·pe·ra·men·tal, *a.* temperamental

tem·pe·ra·men·to, *m.* temperament

tem·pe·ra·tu·ra, *f.* body or atmospheric temperature

tem·pes·tad, *f.* storm; tempest

tem·pes·tuo·sa·men·te, *adv.* tempestuously

tem·pes·tuo·so, *a.* stormy; tempestuous

tem·pla, *f. usu. pl.* temple

tem·pla·da·men·te, *adv.* temperately

tem·pla·do, *a.* temperate; lukewarm

tem·plan·za, *f.* temperance; mildness

tem·plar, *v.* temper; anneal; warm up

tem·plo, *m.* temple; church

tem·po·ra·da, *f.* spell; season

tem·po·ral, *a.* temporary; temporal

tem·po·rá·neo, *a.* temporary

tem·pra·no, *a.* early. *adv.* early (in the day)

te·naz, *a.* tenacious; dogged; tough

te·na·zas, *f. pl.* tongs

ten·den·cia, *f.* tendency; trend; tone

ten·der(se), *v.* tend; trend; stretch out

ten·de·ro, *m.* shopkeeper

ten·dón, *m.* tendon; sinew

te·ne·bro·so, *a.* dark; gloomy

te·ne·dor, *m.* fork. **te·ne·dor de li·bros,** bookkeeper

te·nen·cia, *f.* lieutenancy; tenure; holding; occupation

te·ner, *v.* have; possess; hold; keep; include. **te·ner deu·das,** owe. **te·ner ham·bre,** be hungry. **te·ner hi·po,** hiccup, also hiccough. **te·ner mie·do,** be afraid. **te·ner que,** ought; must. **te·ner vein·te a·ños,** be twenty years old

te·nia, *f.* tapeworm

te·nien·te, *m.* lieutenant

te·nis, *m.* tennis

te·nor, *m.* tenor

ten·sión, *f.* tension; stress; strain

ten·so, *a.* tense

ten·ta·ción, *f.* temptation; enticement

ten·tá·cu·lo, *m.* tentacle

ten·tar, *v.* attempt; try; tempt; lure; entice; allure

ten·ta·ti·va, *f.* try; attempt

te·nue, *a.* tenuous; thin; faint

te·ñir, *v.* dye; stain; tinge

teo·lo·gía, *f.* theology

teo·ló·gi·ca·men·te, *adv.* theologically

teo·ló·gi·co, *a.* theological

teó·lo·go, *m.* theologian

teo·re·ma, *m.* theorem

teo·ría, *f.* theory

teó·ri·ca·men·te, *adv.* theoretically

teó·ri·co, *a.* theoretical

teo·ri·zar, *v.* theorize

te·ra·péu·ti·ca, *f.* therapy

ter·ce·ra, *f.* third. *a* third

ter·ce·ro, *m.* third person. *a.* third

ter·cio, *m.* third

ter·cio·pe·lo, *m.* velvet

ter·co, *a.* unyielding; obstinate; headstrong; willful, wilful

ter·mal, *a.* thermal

ter·mi·nal, *a.* terminal; final. *m.* terminal

ter·mi·nar, *v.* terminate; end; finish; complete; stop; close; culminate; expire

tér·mi·no, *m.* end; term; terminus; territory; boundary

ter·mi·no·lo·gía, *f.* terminology

ter·mó·me·tro, *m.* thermometer

ter·mo·nu·clear, *a.* thermonuclear

ter·mos·ta·to, *m.* thermostat

ter·ne·ra, *f.* veal

ter·que·dad, *f.* stubbornness; self-will

te·rra·plén, *m.* mound; embankment

te·rra·za, *f.* terrace

te·rre·mo·to, *m.* earthquake; quake

te·rre·no, *m.* terrain; *sometimes pl.* ground. **te·rre·no de pas·to,** range.

te·rre·no ri·be·re·ño, waterfront

te·rres·tre, *a.* terrestrial; earthly

te·rri·ble, *a.* terrible; dreadful

te·rri·ble·men·te, *adv.* terribly

te·rri·fi·co, *a.* terrific

te·rri·to·ria·li·dad, *f.* territoriality

te·rri·to·rio, *m.* territory; region

te·rrón, *m.* lump

te·rror, *m.* terror; panic

te·rro·ris·mo, *m.* terrorism

te·rro·ris·ta, *m., f.* terrorist

te·rro·so, *a.* earthy

te·sau·ro, *m.* thesaurus

te·sis, *f.* thesis

te·so·re·ría, *f.* treasury

te·so·re·ro, *m.* treasurer

te·so·ro, *m.* treasure; treasury

tes·ta·men·to, *m.* testament; will

tes·ti·fi·car, *v.* testify; attest

tes·ti·go, *m.* witness. **tes·ti·go de vis·ta,** eyewitness

tes·ti·mo·nio, *m.* testimony; certificate; witness; evidence

te·ta, *f.* teat

te·te·ra, *f.* teakettle; teapot; kettle

tex·til, *a.* textile

tex·to, *m.* text; textbook

tex·tual, *a.* textual

tex·tu·ra, *f.* texture

ti, *pron.* you; thee

tía, *f.* aunt

ti·bia, *f.* tibia

ti·bio, *a.* tepid; lukewarm

ti·bu·rón, *m.* shark

tic, *m.* tic

tic·tac, *m.* tick

tiem·po, *m.* time; movement; tempo; weather. **de tiem·po en tiem·po,** from time to time. **ha·ce mal tiem·po,** the weather is bad. **ha·ce mu·cho tiem·po,** a long time ago. **per·der el tiem·po,** dawdle; dally

tien·da, *f.* store; shop. **tien·da de cam·pa·ña,** tent

tier·na·men·te, *adv.* tenderly; affectionately

tier·no, *a.* tender; soft; affectionate

tie·rra, *f.* earth; land; soil; *sometimes pl* ground

tie·so, *a.* taut; rigid

ties·to, *m.* pot

tie·su·ra, *f.* tautness; rigidity

ti·fón, *m.* typhoon

ti·fus, *m.* typhus

ti·gre, *m.* tiger

ti·je·ras, *f. pl.* scissors. **ti·je·ras gran·des,** shears

ti·je·re·ta·da, *f.* clip; snip

ti·je·re·tear, *v.* snip

ti·mar, *v.* chisel; cheat; gull

tim·bre, *m.* timbre

tí·mi·da·men·te, *adv.* timidly; shyly

ti·mi·dez, *f.* timidity; bashfulness; coyness

tí·mi·do, *a.* timid; shy; coy; self-conscious; sheepish

ti·món, *m.* helm; rudder. **ca·ña del ti·món,** tiller

ti·mo·nel, *m.* helmsman

tím·pa·no, *m.* kettledrum. **tím·pa·no del oí·do,** eardrum

ti·na, *f.* tub; vat

ti·nie·bla, *f. usu. pl.* darkness

tin·ta, *f.* ink

tin·tar, *v.* dye; tinge

tin·te, *m.* dye; tinge

tin·tu·ra, *f.* tincture; dyeing

tío, *m.* uncle; chap; *inf.* guy

tio·vi·vo, *m.* merry-go-round

tí·pi·ca·men·te, *adv.* typically

tí·pi·co, *a.* typical; characteristic

ti·ple, *m.* (*mus.*) treble. *m., f.* so-

prano
ti·po, *m.* type; figure; pattern
ti·po·gra·fía, *f.* typography; printing
ti·ra, *f.* band; strip
ti·ra·da, *f.* throw
ti·ra·dor, *m.* knob; shot; marksman
ti·ra·ní·a, *f.* tyranny; oppression
ti·rá·ni·ca·men·te, *adv.* tyrannically
ti·rá·ni·co, *a.* tyrannical; *inf.* bossy
ti·ra·ni·zar, *v.* tyrannize; domineer
ti·ra·no, *m., f.* tyrant
ti·ran·te, *a.* taut. *m.* strap
ti·rar, *v.* throw; cast; pitch; sling; pull; haul
ti·ro, *m.* shot
ti·roi·des, *m.* thyroid gland
ti·rón, *m.* pull; jerk; tug; haul
ti·tá·ni·co, *a.* titanic
ti·te·re, *m.* puppet
ti·tu·bear, *v.* falter; stagger
ti·tu·lar, *v.* title; entitle; name
tí·tu·lo, *m.* title; heading; caption
ti·za, *f.* chalk
tiz·nar, *v.* smudge; brand
ti·zón, *m.* brand; blight
toa·lla, *f.* towel
to·bi·llo, *m.* ankle
to·bo·gán, *m.* toboggan
to·ca·dis·cos, *m.* phonograph; record player
to·ca·do, *m.* coiffure
to·car(se), *v.* touch; handle; finger; (*mus.*) play
to·ca·yo, *m.* namesake
to·ci·no, *m.* bacon
to·cón, *m.* stump
to·da·vía, *adv.* yet; still
to·do, *a.* all; whole; every. *adv.* entirely. *m.* whole; all. **a pe·sar de to·do,** all the same. **so·bre to·do,** above all. **to·do el día,** all day long. **to·do lo po·si·ble,** *inf.* the works. **to·do lo que,** whatever
to·do·po·de·ro·so, *a.* almighty
to·ga, *f.* toga
tol·do, *m.* awning
to·le·ra·ble, *a.* tolerable; bearable
to·le·ran·cia, *f.* tolerance; sufferance
to·le·ran·te, *a.* tolerant; broad-minded
to·le·rar, *v.* tolerate; permit; endure
tol·va, *f.* chute
to·ma, *f.* taking
to·mar, *v.* take; assume; accept; eat. **to·mar el a pa·pel de,** portray. **to·mar el pe·lo,** tease; *inf.* kid. **to·mar el sol,** bask in the sun. **to·mar par·te,** partake in
to·ma·te, *m.* tomato
to·mo, *m.* volume
to·nel, *m.* cask
to·ne·la·da, *f.* ton
to·ne·la·je, *m.* tonnage
tó·ni·co, *a.* tonic. *a.* bracing

to·no, *m.* tone; manner; pitch; key
ton·si·la, *f.* tonsil
ton·ta·men·te, *adv.* foolishly; dumbly
ton·te·ría, *f.* nonsense; foolishness; folly; balderdash
ton·to, *a.* silly; foolish; witless. *m.* fool; half-wit; idiot; chump
to·pa·cio, *m.* topaz
to·pe·tar, *v.* butt
tó·pi·co, *a.* topical
to·po, *m.* mole
to·po·gra·fía, *f.* topography
to·po·grá·fi·co, *a.* topographical
to·que, *m.* touch. **to·que de trom·pe·ta,** fanfare
tó·rax, *m.* thorax
tor·be·lli·no, *m.* whirlwind
tor·ce·du·ra, *f.* sprain; wrench
tor·cer(se), *v.* twist; distort; sprain; strain; swerve; wring; buckle; gnarl
tor·ci·do, *a.* twisted; wry
to·rear, *v.* fight bulls
to·re·ro, *m.* bullfighter
tor·men·ta, *f.* storm
tor·men·to, *m.* torment; affliction
tor·na·do, *m.* tornado
tor·na·pun·ta, *f.* strut
tor·neo, *m.* tournament
tor·ni·llo, *m.* vise; screw
tor·ni·que·te, *m.* tourniquet; turnstile
tor·no, *m.* lathe; winch
to·ro, *m.* bull
to·ron·ja, *f.* grapefruit
tor·pe, *a.* slow; dull; dumb; rusty; clumsy; awkward; gauche; crass
tor·pe·do, *m.* torpedo
tor·pe·men·te, *adv.* slowly; awkwardly
tor·pe·za, *f.* clumsiness; dullness; awkwardness
to·rre, *f.* tower; (*chess*) castel; rook
to·rre·ci·lla, *f.* turret
to·rren·cial, *a.* torrential
to·rren·te, *m.* torrent; stream
tó·rri·do, *a.* torrid
tor·sión, *f.* twist; torsion
tor·so, *m.* torso
tor·ta, *f.* tart
tor·te·ra, *f.* griddle
tor·ti·lla, *f.* omelet
tor·tu·ga, *f.* turtle; tortoise
tor·tuo·so, *a.* tortuous; winding; sinuous; devious
tor·tu·ra, *f.* torture
tor·tu·rar, *v.* torture; worry
to·run·da, *f.* swab
tos, *f.* cough. **tos se·ca,** hack
tos·ca·men·te, *adv.* coarsely; roughly
tos·co, *a.* rough; coarse; rude
to·ser, *v.* cough

tos·ta·da, *f.* toast

tos·ta·do, *a.* crisp; toasted; tanned

tos·tar, *v.* toast; tan

to·tal, *a.* total; whole; utter; aggregate. *m.* total; count

to·ta·li·dad, *f.* whole; entirety; all

to·ta·li·ta·rio, *a.* totalitarian

to·ta·li·zar, *v.* total

to·tal·men·te, *adv.* totally; entirely

tóx·i·co, *a.* toxic. *m.* poison

tox·i·co·lo·gia, *f.* toxicology

tox·i·na, *f.* toxin

tra·ba, *f.* tether; bond

tra·ba·ja·dor, *m.,* **tra·ba·ja·do·ra,** *f.* worker

tra·ba·jar, *v.* work; toil; labor. **tra·ba·jar de·ma·sia·do,** overwork

tra·ba·jo, *m.* work; toil; labor; job; avocation; occupation. **tra·ba·jo a des·ta·jo,** piecework

tra·ba·jo·sa·men·te, *adv.* laboriously

tra·ba·jo·so, *a.* laborious

tra·bar, *v.* fetter; fasten; tie; join

trac·tor, *m.* tractor

tra·di·ción, *f.* tradition

tra·di·cio·nal, *a.* traditional

tra·di·cio·nal·men·te, *adv.* traditionally

tra·duc·ción, *f.* translation

tra·du·cir, *v.* translate

tra·duc·tor, *m.,* **tra·duc·to·ra,** *f.* translator

traer, *v.* bring; carry

tra·fi·car, *v.* traffic in; trade

trá·fi·co, *m.* traffic; trade

tra·gar, *v.* swallow; gulp

tra·ge·dia, *f.* tragedy

trá·gi·ca·men·te, *adv.* tragically

trá·gi·co, *a.* tragic

tra·go, *m.* gulp; swallow; drink (*usu.* alcoholic)

trai·ción, *f.* treason; betrayal; treachery

trai·cio·nar, *v.* betray

trai·cio·ne·ro, *a.* treacherous

trai·dor, *m.,* **trai·do·ra,** *f.* traitor; turncoat. *a.* treacherous

traí·lla, *f.* leash

tra·je, *m.* suit; dress; outfit; robe. **tra·je de ba·ño,** bathing suit. **tra·je de no·che,** evening dress

tra·mar, *v.* plot; concoct; cabal

trá·mi·te, *m.* stage; procedure

tra·mo, *m.* flight of stairs

tram·pa, *f.* trap; snare; catch; trick; cheat. **tram·pa ca·mu·fla·da,** booby trap

tran·qui·la·men·te, *adv.* tranquilly; quietly

tran·qui·li·dad, *f.* tranquility; calmness; ease. **tran·qui·li·dad an·tes de u·na tor·men·ta,** lull before the storm

tran·qui·li·zar, *v.* tranquilize; calm;

quiet; reassure

tran·qui·lo, *a.* tranquil; still; quiet; calm; peaceful

tran·sac·ción, *f.* transaction

trans·at·lán·ti·co, *a.* transatlantic

trans·bor·da·dor, *m.* ferry

trans·bor·do, *m.* transfer

trans·cri·bir, *v.* transcribe; copy

trans·crip·ción, *f.* transcription; copy

tran·seún·te, *m., f.* transient

trans·fe·ren·cia, *f.* transference; transfer

trans·fe·rir, *v.* transfer

trans·for·ma·ción, *f.* transformation; change

trans·for·ma·dor, *m.* transformer

trans·for·mar(se), *v.* transform; change

trans·fu·sión, *f.* transfusion

trans·gre·sión, *f.* sin; transgression

tran·si·ción, *f.* transition

tran·si·gir, *v.* compromise

tran·sis·tor, *m.* transistor

tran·si·ti·vo, *a.* transitive

trán·si·to, *m.* transit; movement; transition

tran·si·to·rio, *a.* transitory; transient

trans·lu·ci·dez, *f.* translucence

trans·lú·ci·do, *a.* translucent

trans·mi·sión, *f.* transmission

trans·mi·sor, *m.* transmitter

trans·mi·tir, *v.* transmit; transfer

trans·mu·ta·ción, *f.* transmutation

trans·pa·ren·cia, *f.* transparency

trans·pa·ren·te, *a.* transparent; sheer; clear

trans·pi·rar, *v.* perspire; transpire

trans·po·ner, *v.* transpose; transfer

trans·por·ta·ción, *f.* transportation

trans·por·tar, *v.* transport; convey; ship; carry; (*mus.*) transpose

trans·por·te, *m.* transport; transportation; conveyance

trans·ver·sal, *a.* transverse

trans·ver·sal·men·te, *adv.* transversally

tran·vía, *f.* trolley; streetcar

tra·pe·cio, *m.* trapeze

tra·pe·zoi·de, *m.* trapezoid

tra·po, *m.* rag; tatter

trá·quea, *f.* trachea; windpipe

tras, *prep.* after; behind. **u·no tras o·tro,** one after the other

tra·se·ra, *f.* backside

tra·se·ro, *a.* back; hind. *m.* backside

tras·go, *m.* goblin

tras·la·dar(se), *v.* move; transfer; postpone

tras·la·par, *v.* overlap; lap

tras·pa·sar, *v.* transgress; cross; penetrate

tras·pié, *m.* stumble; trip

tras·plan·tar, *v.* transplant

tras·to, *m.* furniture. **tras·tos vie·jos,** junk

tras·tor·nar, *v.* upset; overturn; daze

tras·tor·no, *m.* upset; disturbance

tra·sun·to, *m.* transcript

tra·ta·ble, *a.* amenable; sociable

tra·ta·do, *m.* treaty; treatise; tract

tra·ta·mien·to, *m.* treatment

tra·tan·te, *m.* dealer

tra·tar(se), *v.* treat; discuss. **tra·tar de,** try to; deal with

tra·to, *m.* treatment; intercourse; deal

trau·ma, *m.* trauma

trau·má·ti·co, *a.* traumatic

tra·vés, *m.* slant; misfortune. **a través de,** aslant; across; through, thru. **al tra·vés,** crosswise. **de través,** across; crosswise; awry

tra·ve·sa·ño, *m.* transom; crosspiece

tra·ve·se·ro, *m.* bolster

tra·ve·sía, *f.* crossing; passage; voyage

tra·ve·su·ra, *f.* mischief; antic; prank; caper; frolic

tra·vie·so, *a.* naughty; wayward; mischievous

tra·yec·to·ria, *f.* trajectory

tra·za, *f.* appearance; design; sketch

tra·zar, *v.* trace; map; sketch

tré·bol, *m.* clover

tre·ce, *a.* thirteen. *m.* thirteen; baker's dozen

tre·gua, *f.* truce; cease-fire; respite

trein·ta, *a.* thirty

tre·me·dal, *m.* quagmire

tre·men·do, *a.* terrific; *inf.* tremendous

tre·men·ti·na, *f.* turpentine

tren, *m.* train. **tren rá·pi·do,** express train

tren·za, *f.* tress of hair; braid

tren·zar, *v.* braid

tre·par, *v.* climb; drill

tres, *a.* three. *m.* three

tre·ta, *f.* feint, as in swordplay

trian·gu·lar, *a.* triangular

trian·gu·lar·men·te, *adv.* triangularly

trián·gu·lo, *m.* triangle

tri·bu, *f.* tribe

tri·bu·la·ción, *f.* tribulation; affliction; persecution; adversity

tri·bu·na, *f.* rostrum

tri·bu·nal, *m.* court; tribunal

tri·bu·ta·rio, *m.* tributary. *a.* tributary

tri·bu·to, *m.* tribute

tri·ci·clo, *m.* tricycle

tri·go, *m.* wheat

tri·go·no·me·tría, *f.* trigonometry

tri·lo·gía, *f.* trilogy

tri·lla·do, *a.* hackneyed; beaten

tri·mes·tral, *a.* quarterly

tri·mes·tre, *m.* term

tri·nar, *v.* warble; trill

trin·char, *v.* carve

trin·che·ra, *f.* trench; entrenchment

tri·neo, *m.* sled; sleigh

tri·no, *m.* warble; trill

trío, *m.* trio

tri·pa, *f.* gut; intestine; tripe

tri·ple, *a.* triple; treble; threefold

tri·pli·ca·do, *a.* triplicate

tri·pli·car(se), *v.* triplicate; triple

trí·po·de, *m.* tripod

tri·pu·la·ción, *f.* crew

tris·te, *a.* sad; sorry; dreary; bleak; cheerless; dismal

tris·te·men·te, *adv.* sadly; sorrowfully; drearily; bleakly; dismally

tris·te·za, *f.* sadness; gloom; bleakness

triun·fal, *a.* triumphal; victorious

triun·fal·men·te, *adv.* triumphantly

triun·fan·te, *a.* triumphant; victorious

triun·far, *v.* triumph; win; be victorious

triun·fo, *m.* triumph; victory; win; (*cards*) trump. **triun·fo fá·cil,** *inf.* walkover

triun·vi·ra·to, *m.* triumvirate

tri·vial, *a.* trivial; common; of little importance

tri·via·li·dad, *f.* triviality; banality

tri·vial·men·te, *adv.* trivially; commonly

tri·za, *f.* shred; fragment

tro·car, *v.* change; trade; barter

tro·ci·to, *m.* snatch; little bit

tro·feo, *m.* trophy

trom·ba ma·ri·na, *f.* waterspout

trom·bón, *m.* trombone

trom·bo·sis, *f.* coronary thrombosis

trom·pa, *f.* elephant's trunk

trom·pe·ta, *f.* trumpet. *m.* bugler

tro·nar, *v.* boom; thunder; fulminate

tron·co, *m.* trunk of a tree; trunk line; team of horses

tro·no, *m.* throne

tro·pa, *f.* troop

tro·pel, *m.* throng; mob; confusion

tro·pe·zar, *v.* stumble; slip; trip; flounder. **tro·pe·zar con,** bump into; meet

tro·pe·zón, *m.* stumble

tro·pi·cal, *a.* tropical

tró·pi·co, *m.* tropic

tro·pie·zo, *m.* trip; difficulty; setback

tro·quel, *m.* die

tro·te, *m.* trot

tro·va·dor, *m.* troubadour

tro·zo, *m.* piece; bit

tru·co, *m.* trick; gimmick; pool

tru·cha, *f.* trout

true·no, *m.* thunder; thunderclap

trun·car, *v.* truncate; cut short

tu, *poss. a.* your; thy; *pl.* yours

tú, *pron.* you (familiar); thou. tú mis·mo, yourself

tu·ba, *f.* tuba

tu·ber·cu·lo·sis, *f.* tuberculosis

tu·ber·cu·lo·so, *a.* tuberculose

tu·bo, *m.* tube; pipe. tu·bo de en·sa·yo, test tube

tu·fo, *m.* stench; exhalation

tu·li·pán, *m.* tulip

tu·lli·do, *m.,* tu·lli·da, *f.* cripple. *a.* paralyzed

tu·llir(se), *v.* cripple

tum·ba, *f.* tomb

tu·mor, *m.* tumor; growth

tu·mul·to, *m.* tumult; turmoil; riot

tu·mul·tua·rio, *a.* tumultuous; uproarious

tu·mul·tuo·sa·men·te, *adv.* tumultuously

tu·mul·tuo·so, *a.* tumultuous; uproarious

tun·dra, *f.* tundra

tú·nel, *m.* tunnel

tú·ni·ca, *f.* tunic

tur·ba, *f.* multitude; mob

tur·ba·ción, *f.* perturbation; embarrassment

tur·ba·do, *a.* distraught; embarrassed

tur·ban·te, *m.* turban

tur·bi·na, *f.* turbine

tur·bu·len·cia, *f.* turbulence; disorder

tur·bu·len·ta·men·te, *adv.* turbulently

tur·bu·len·to, *a.* turbulent; unsettled; muddy

tu·ris·mo, *m.* tourism

tu·ris·ta, *m., f.* tourist; sightseer

tur·no, *m.* turn; say

tur·que·sa, *f.* turquoise

tu·te·la, *f.* tutelage; protection

tu·yo, *pron.* yours; thine

U

u, *conj.* or (before a word beginning with *o* or *ho)*

u·bi·cui·dad, *f.* ubiquity

u·bi·cuo, *a.* ubiquitous. Also ubiquitary

u·bre, *f.* udder

úl·ce·ra, *f.* ulcer

ul·te·rior, *a.* ulterior; farther

ul·te·rior·men·te, *adv.* subsequently

úl·ti·ma·men·te, *adv.* finally; ultimately

ul·ti·má·tum, *m.* ultimatum

úl·ti·mo, *a.* ultimate; last; final

ul·tra, *a.* ultra; beyond

ul·tra·jar, *v.* insult

ul·tra·je, *m.* insult

ul·tra·jo·so, *a.* outrageous

ul·tra·só·ni·co, *a.* ultrasonic

ul·tra·vio·le·ta, *a.* ultraviolet

u·lu·lar, *v.* hoot

um·bi·li·cal, *a.* umbilical

um·bral, *m.* threshold

un, *indef. art.* a; an. *a.* one

u·na, *indef. art.* a; an. *a.* one. u·na vez, once

u·ná·ni·me, *a.* unanimous

u·ná·ni·me·men·te, *adv.* unanimously

un·ción, *f.* unction

un·dé·ci·mo, *a.* eleventh

un·gir, *v.* anoint

un·güen·to, *m.* ointment; salve; unguent

ú·ni·ca·men·te, *adv.* solely; only

ú·ni·co, *a.* only; sole; single; unique

u·ni·cor·nio, *m.* unicorn

u·ni·dad, *f.* unity; unit

u·ni·do, *a.* united

u·ni·fi·ca·ción, *f.* unification

u·ni·fi·car, *v.* unify

u·ni·for·mar, *v.* standardize; make uniform

a·ni·for·me, *a.* uniform; even; steady. *m.* uniform

u·ni·for·me·men·te, *adv.* uniformly

u·ni·for·mi·dad, *f.* uniformity

u·ni·la·te·ral, *a.* unilateral

u·ni·la·te·ral·men·te, *adv.* unilaterally

u·nión, *f.* union; unity; joint; connection

u·nir(se), *v.* join; unite; couple; attach; link

u·ní·so·no, *a.* sounding alike; in harmony. al u·ní·so·no, in unison

u·ni·ver·sal, *a.* universal; general; world-wide

u·ni·ver·sa·li·zar, *v.* universalize

u·ni·ver·sal·men·te, *adv.* universally

u·ni·ver·si·dad, *f.* university

u·ni·ver·si·ta·rio, *a.* university

u·no, *indef. art.* a; an. *a.* one. *pron.* one; *pl.* some. u·no a u·no, one by one. u·no u o·tro, either

un·tar, *v.* anoint; smear

un·tuo·so, *a.* greasy

u·ña, *f.* fingernail; nail; claw

u·ra·nio, *m.* uranium

U·ra·no, *m.* Uranus

ur·ba·ni·dad, *f.* urbanity; politeness

ur·ba·no, *a.* urban; urbane; courteous

ur·dir, *v.* plot; brew

ur·gen·cia, *f.* urgency; exigence; pressure

ur·gen·te, *a.* urgent

ur·gen·te·men·te, *adv.* urgently

ur·na, *f.* urn

ur·ti·ca·ria, *f.* hive

u·sa·do, *a.* used; worn; well-worn

u·san·za, *f.* usage

u·sar(se), v. use; make use of; wear
u·so, m. use; usage; wear; custom; mode
us·ted, pron. m., f., pl. us·te·des. you. Abbr. Vd., Ud. us·ted mis·mo, yourself
u·sual, a. usual; customary; general
u·sual·men·te, adv. usually; regularly
u·su·ra, f. usury
u·sur·pa·ción, f. usurpation; encroachment
u·sur·par, v. usurp; encroach
u·ten·si·lio, m. utensil; pl. tools
ú·te·ro, m. uterus; womb
ú·til, a. useful; helpful; serviceable
u·ti·li·dad, f. utility; usefulness; profit
u·ti·li·ta·rio, a. utilitarian
u·ti·li·za·ble, a. usable
u·ti·li·zar, v. utilize; use; make use of; profit from
u·to·pia, u·to·pía, f. utopia
u·va, f. grape. u·va es·pi·na, gooseberry. u·va pa·sa, raisin

V

va·ca, f. cow
va·ca·ción, f. usu. pl. vacation; holiday
va·can·te, f. vacancy. a. vacant; unoccupied
va·ciar(se), v. empty; void; hollow out
va·cie·dad, f. emptiness
va·ci·la·ción, f. vacillation; hesitation
va·ci·lan·te, a. vacillating; hesitant; halting
va·ci·lar, v. vacillate; hesitate; falter; waver
va·cío, a. void; vacant; empty; hollow. m. void; vacuum
va·cui·dad, f. vacuity; emptiness
va·cu·na, f. vaccine
va·cu·na·ción, f. vaccination
va·cu·nar, v. vaccinate
va·dear, v. wade; ford
va·do, m. ford
va·ga·bun·dear, v. rove; wander
va·ga·bun·do, a. vagabond; vagrant. m. vagabond; tramp; bum; hobo
va·ga·men·te, adv. vaguely
va·gan·cia, f. vagrancy
va·gar, v. wander; roam; rove; stray; stroll
va·gi·na, f. vagina
va·go, a. vague; indistinct; hazy; vacant; wandering
va·gón, m. wagon; coach; carriage
va·gue·dad, f. vagueness
va·ho, m. fume; vapor
vai·na, f. pod; sheath

vai·ni·lla, f. vanilla
va·ji·lla, f. service. va·ji·lla de pla·ta, silverware
va·le, m. IOU
va·le·de·ro, a. valid
va·len·tía, f. valor; bravery; courage; feat
va·ler, v. be worth; be valid; make use of. m. value
va·le·ro·sa·men·te, adv. valiantly
va·le·ro·so, a. valorous; valiant
va·li·dar, v. validate
va·li·dez, f. validity; soundness
vá·li·do, a. valid; good; sound; strong
va·lien·te, a. valiant; brave; courageous
va·lien·te·men·te, adv. valiantly; courageously
va·lio·so, a. valuable; wealthy
va·lor, m. bravery; valor; courage; value; worth; pl. securities; stocks
va·lo·ra·ción, f. appraisal; assessment
va·lo·rar, v. appraise; value; price
va·lua·ción, f. valuation
va·luar, v. price
vál·vu·la, f. valve. vál·vu·la de se·gu·ri·dad, safety valve
va·lla, f. hurdle; barricade
va·lle, m. valley; dale; vale
vam·pi·ro, m. vampire
va·na·glo·riar·se, v. boast
van·da·lis·mo, m. vandalism
ván·da·lo, m. vandal
van·guar·dia, f. vanguard; van
va·ni·dad, f. vanity; nonsense; shallowness
va·ni·do·so, a. vain; conceited; haughty
va·no, a. vain; useless; empty. en va·no, in vain
va·por, m. vapor; steam; steamship. bu·que de va·por, steamer; steamboat
va·po·ri·zar(se), v. vaporize
va·po·ro·so, a. vaporous; steamy; cloudy
va·que·ro, m. cowboy
va·qui·lla, f. heifer
va·ra, f. rod; wand. va·ra de me·dir, yardstick
va·ria·bi·li·dad, f. variability; variableness
va·ria·ble, a. variable
va·ria·ble·men·te, adv. variably
va·ria·ción, f. variation; variance; change
va·ria·do, a. varied; various; assorted
va·rian·te, a. variant. f. variant
va·riar, v. vary; change; alternate
va·ri·co·so, a. varicose
va·rie·dad, f. variety
va·rio, a. various; variable; pl. sev-

eral
va·rón, a. male. m. male; man
va·ro·nil, a. manly; masculine
va·sa·llo, m. vassal
vas·cu·lar, a. vascular
va·se·li·na, f. vaseline
va·si·ja, f. vessel; receptacle
va·so, m. glass; tumbler; vessel. va·so
ca·pi·lar, capillary. va·so de a·
gua, glass of water
vás·ta·go, m. shout; offspring
vas·te·dad, f. vastness
vas·to, a. vast
va·ti·ci·nar, v. foretell; predict
va·ti·ci·nio, m. prediction
va·tio, m. watt
va·ya, int. well!
ve·ci·nal, a. local; neighboring
ve·ci·na·men·te, adv. next
ve·cin·dad, f. vicinity; neighborhood
ve·cin·da·rio, m. neighborhood
ve·ci·no, m., ve·ci·na, f. neighbor. a.
next; neighboring
vec·tor, m. vector
ve·da, f. prohibition
ve·dar, v. prohibit; impede; suspend
ve·ge·ta·bi·li·dad, f. vegetability
ve·ge·ta·ción, f. vegetation
ve·ge·tal, a. vegetable. m. vegetable
ve·ge·tar, v. vegetate
ve·ge·ta·ria·nis·mo, m. vegetarian-
ism
ve·ge·ta·ria·no, m., ve·ge·ta·ria·na,
f. vegetarian. a. vegetarian
ve·he·men·cia, f. vehemence; vehe-
mency; impetuosity
ve·he·men·te, a. vehement; violent;
impetuous
ve·he·men·te·men·te, adv. vehe-
mently
ve·hí·cu·lo, m. vehicle
vein·te, a. twenty. m. twenty; score
vein·te·na, f. score
ve·ja·ción, f. vexation; oppression
ve·jar, v. vex; harass; persecute; condemn
ve·je·to·rio, a. vexatious
ve·jez, f. old age
ve·ji·ga, f. bladder
ve·la, f. candle; sail; watchfulness;
vigil
ve·la·da, f. social gathering
ve·la·dor, m. watchman
ve·lar, v. watch; guard; sit up at
night watching a sick person
ve·lei·do·so, a. fickle
ve·le·ta, f. vane
ve·lo, m. veil; pretext
ve·lo·ci·dad, f. velocity; rate; speed.
a to·da ve·lo·ci·dad, at full speed
ve·loz, a. swift; fleet; fast
ve·loz·men·te, adv. swiftly; rapidly
ve·llón, m. fleece
ve·llo·so, a. fuzzy

ve·llu·di·llo, m. velour
ve·llu·do, a. shaggy; fuzzy; downy
ve·na, f. vein; strain
ve·na·do, m. stag. car·ne de ve·na·
do, venison
ve·nal, a. venal; commercial
ve·na·li·dad, f. venality
ven·ce·dor, m., ven·ce·do·ra, f. vic-
tor; conqueror
ven·cer, v. vanquish; conquer; defeat;
beat
ven·ci·do, a. defeated; conquered
ven·da, f. bandage
ven·da·je, m. bandaging
ven·dar, v. bandage; bind
ven·de·dor, m., ven·de·do·ra, f. ven-
dor
ven·der, v. sell; market; trade. se
ven·de, for sale
ven·di·ble, a. vendible; marketable
ven·di·mia, f. vintage; grape harvest
ven·di·miar, v. harvest grapes
ve·ne·no, m. venom; poison
ve·ne·no·si·dad, f. poisonousness
ve·ne·no·so, a. venomous; poisonous
ve·ne·ra, f. scallop
ve·ne·ra·ble, a. venerable
ve·ne·ra·ción, f. veneration
ve·ne·rar, v. venerate; worship;
revere
ve·né·reo, a. venereal. m. venereal
disease
ven·ga·dor, m., ven·ga·do·ra, f.
avenger
ven·gan·za, f. vengeance; revenge
ven·gar(se), v. revenge; avenge
ven·ga·ti·vo, a. vindictive
ve·nia, f. forgiveness
ve·nial, a. venial
ve·nir, v. come; happen. el a·ño que
vie·ne, next year. ve·nir·se a·ba·
jo, topple
ven·ta, f. sale; market. de ven·ta, on
sale. ven·ta a pla·zos, sell on credit
ven·ta·ja, f. advantage; blessing;
vantage
ven·ta·jo·sa·men·te, adv. advanta-
geously
ven·ta·jo·so, a. advantageous
ven·ta·na, f. window. ven·ta·na de la
na·riz, nostril
ven·ta·rrón, m. gale; gust of wind
ven·ti·la·ción, f. ventilation; airing
ven·ti·la·dor, m. ventilator
ven·ti·lar, v. ventilate; air; discuss
ven·tis·ca, f. blizzard
ven·to·le·ra, f. vanity
ven·to·so, a. windy
ven·tral, a. ventral
ven·trí·cu·lo, m. ventricle
ven·trí·lo·cuo, m., ven·trí·lo·cua, f.
ventriloquist
ven·tri·lo·quia, f. ventriloquism
ven·tu·ra, f. fortune; happiness

ven·tu·ro·so, *a.* lucky; fortunate

Ve·nus, *m.* Venus

ver(se), *v.* see; view; sight; meet. **te·ner que ver con,** pertain to; concern. **va·mos a ver,** let's see

ve·ra, *f.* border

ve·ra·ci·dad, *f.* veracity; truthfulness

ve·ra·nie·go, *a.* summer; summery

ve·ra·no, *m.* summer

ve·ras, *f. pl.* truth. **de ve·ras,** indeed; really

ve·raz, *a.* veracious; truthful

ver·bal, *a.* verbal; oral

ver·bal·men·te, *adv.* verbally

ver·bo, *m.* verb. **e·char ver·bos,** swear

ver·bo·si·dad, *f.* verbosity; verbiage

ver·bo·so, *a.* verbose; wordy

ver·dad, *f.* truth; veracity. **ver·dad de Pe·ro Gru·llo,** truism

ver·da·de·ra·men·te, *adv.* truly; indeed

ver·da·de·ro, *a.* veritable; true; real

ver·de, *a.* green; verdant; dirty; obscene. *m.* green

ver·du·go, *m.* lash

ver·du·gón, *m.* welt

ver·du·ra, *f.* greenery

ve·re·da, *f.* path

ve·re·dic·to, *m.* verdict

ver·gon·zan·te, *a.* shamefaced

ver·gon·zo·sa·men·te, *adv.* shamefully

ver·gon·zo·so, *a.* disgraceful; shameful; bashful

ver·güen·za, *f.* shame; disgrace; bashfulness

ve·ri·fi·ca·ción, *f.* verification; confirmation

ve·ri·fi·car(se), *v.* verify; confirm; carry out

ver·ja, *f.* grille, grill

ver·mi·no·so, *a.* full of vermin

ver·mut, *m.* vermouth

ver·ná·cu·lo, *a.* vernacular

ver·nal, *a.* vernal

ve·ro·sí·mil, *a.* probable

ve·ro·si·mi·li·tud, *f.* verisimilitude

ve·rra·co, *m.* boar

ve·rru·ga, *f.* wart

ver·sa·do, *a.* versed. **ver·sa·do en,** conversant with

ver·sal, *f.* capital letter

ver·sá·til, *a.* changeable

ver·sa·ti·li·dad, *f.* fickleness; versatility

ver·sí·cu·lo, *m.* verse

ver·si·fi·ca·ción, *f.* versification

ver·si·fi·car, *v.* versify

ver·sión, *f.* version

ver·so, *m.* verse. **ver·so suel·to,** blank verse

vér·te·bra, *f.* vertebra

ver·te·bra·do, *a.* vertebrate. *m.*

vertebrate

ver·ter(se), *v.* spill; slop; pour; shed

ver·ti·cal, *a.* vertical; upright. *m.* vertical

ver·ti·cal·men·te, *adv.* vertically

vér·ti·ce, *m.* vertex

ver·ti·gi·no·sa·men·te, *adv.* dizzily

ver·ti·gi·no·so, *a.* dizzy; vertiginous

vér·ti·go, *m.* vertigo; dizziness; giddiness

ves·tí·bu·lo, *m.* vestibule; hall; foyer

ves·ti·do, *m.* dress; frock; garb; clothing. *a.* clad; dressed

ves·ti·gio, *m.* vestige; *pl.* remains

ves·tir(se), *v.* dress; clothe; attire. **en vez de,** instead of. **ha·bía u·na vez,** once upon a time. **tal vez,** perhaps

ves·tir·se bien, dress well

ves·tua·rio, *m.* wardrobe; dressing room

ve·ta, *f.* vein; lode

ve·tar, *v.* veto

ve·tea·do, *a.* veined; striped

ve·te·ra·no, *a.* veteran. *m.* veteran

ve·te·ri·na·ria, *f.* veterinary science

ve·te·ri·na·rio, *m.* veterinarian; *inf.* vet. *a.* veterinary

vez, *f. pl.* **ve·ces.** time. **a ve·ces,** sometimes; at times. **de vez en cuan·do,** from time to time; off and on.

vi·a, *f.* way; route; line; means. **por vía aé·rea,** by airmail. **por vía de,** by way of

via·bi·li·dad, *f.* viability; feasibility

via·ble, *a.* viable; feasible

via·duc·to, *m.* viaduct

via·jan·te, *m.; f.* traveler. *a.* traveling

via·jar, *v.* travel; take a trip; voyage; journey. **via·jar por,** tour

via·je, *m.* trip; excursion; voyage; journey; ride; *pl.* travels

via·je·ro, *m.; via·je·ra,* *f.* traveler; passenger; wayfarer

vi·bo·ra, *f.* viper

vi·bra·ción, *f.* vibration; shaking

vi·bran·te, *a.* vibrant

vi·brar, *v.* vibrate; quaver; shake

vi·ca·rio, *m.* vicar

vi·ce·pre·si·den·cia, *f.* vice-presidency

vi·ce·pre·si·den·te, *m.* vice-president

vi·ce·ver·sa, *adv.* vice versa

vi·ciar(se), *v.* vitiate; corrupt; invalidate

vi·cio, *m.* vice; bad habit; forwardness

vi·cio·sa·men·te, *adv.* viciously

vi·cio·so, *a.* vicious; defective

víc·ti·ma, *m.; f.* victim; casualty

vic·to·ria, *f.* victory; win; triumph

vic·to·rio·sa·men·te, *adv.* victoriously

vic·to·rio·so, a. victorious; winning
vid, f. vine
vi·da, f. life; livelihood. en mi vi·da, never in my life
vi·den·te, m., f. seer; clairvoyant
vi·driar, v. glaze
vi·drio, m. glass. ho·ja de vi·drio, pane
vi·drio·so, a. glassy
vie·jo, a. old; aged; antiquated. m. old man
vien·to, m. wind. ha·ce vien·to, it's windy
vien·tre, m. abdomen; belly. do·lor de vien·tre, bellyache
vier·nes, m. Friday
vi·ga, f. beam; girder
vi·gen·te, a. in force; valid
vi·gí·a, f. lookout
vi·gi·lan·cia, f. vigilance; surveillance
vi·gi·lan·te, a. vigilant; watchful; alert; heedful. m. watchman; caretaker; guard
vi·gi·lan·te·men·te, adv. vigilantly
vi·gi·lar, v. watch; guard; oversee
vi·gi·lia, f. vigil; watchfulness
vi·gor, m. vigor; force; vim; strength
vi·go·ri·zar, v. invigorate; exhilarate
vi·go·ro·sa·men·te, adv. vigorously
vi·go·ro·so, a. vigorous; robust; forceful; strong
vil, a. vile; low; mean; miserable; sordid; sorry
vi·li·pen·dio·so, a. contemptible
vil·men·te, adv. vilely; meanly; sordidly
vi·lla, f. villa
vi·llan·ci·co, m. Christmas carol
vi·lla·ní·a, f. villainy
vi·na·gre, m. vinegar
vi·na·gro·so, a. vinegary
vin·cu·la·ción, f. entail
vin·cu·lar, v. entail
vin·di·ca·ción, f. vindication
vin·di·car, v. vindicate; avenge
vin·di·ca·ti·vo, a. vindictive
vi·no, m. wine vi·no blan·co, white wine. vi·no se·co, dry wine. vi·no tin·to, red wine
vi·ña, f. vineyard
vi·ñe·ta, f. vignette
vio·la, f viol; viola
vio·la·ción, f. violation; rape
vio·la·do, a. violet
vio·lar, v. violate; rape; ravish
vio·len·cia, f. violence
vio·len·tar(se), v. force
vio·len·te·men·te, adv. violently
vio·len·to, a. violent
vio·le·ta, f. violet
vio·lín, m. violin; fiddle; violinist
vio·lon·ce·lis·ta, vio·lon·che·lis·ta, m., f. cellist; violoncellist

vio·lon·ce·lo, vio·lon·che·lo, m. violoncello
vi·ra·da, f. tack
vi·rar, v. veer; change direction
vir·gen, a. virgin; maiden. f. virgin
vir·gi·nal, a. virginal
vir·gi·ni·dad, f. virginity
vi·ril, a. virile
vi·ri·li·dad, f. virility; manhood
vi·rrey, m. viceroy
vir·tual, a. virtual
vir·tual·men·te, adv. virtually
vir·tud, f. virtue
vir·tuo·sa·men·te, adv. virtuously
vir·tuo·sis·mo, m. virtuosity
vir·tuo·so, a. virtuous. m. virtuoso
vi·rue·la, f. smallpox
vi·ru·len·cia, f. venom; virulence
vi·ru·len·to, a. virulent
vi·rus, m. virus
vi·sa·je, m. grimace
vi·sar, v. grant a visa; endorse
vis·co·si·dad, f. viscosity
vis·co·so, a. viscous; sticky
vi·se·ra, f. visor
vi·si·bi·li·dad, f. visibility
vi·si·ble, a. visible; conspicuous
vi·si·ble·men·te, adv. visibly; conspicuously
vi·sión, f. vision; sight; view
vi·sio·na·rio, m., vi·sio·na·ria, f. visionary
vi·si·ta, f. visit; call; visitor. ha·cer u·na vi·si·ta, pay a visit
vi·si·ta·ción, f. visitation
vi·si·tar, v. visit; see; call upon
vis·lum·brar, v. sight; catch sight of; glimpse
vis·lum·bre, f. glimpse; glimmer
vi·so, m. viewpoint; outlook; aspect
vi·són, m. mink
vis·ta, f. view; vision; sight; scenery. a vis·ta de, in view of. has·ta la vis·ta, good-bye; so long; until we meet again. pun·to de vis·ta, viewpoint
vis·ta·zo, m. glance; inf. gander
vis·to·so, a. gorgeous; gay; showy
vi·sual, a. visual
vi·tal, a. vital; essential
vi·ta·li·dad, f. vitality
vi·ta·mi·na, f. vitamin
vi·te·la, f. vellum
ví·treo, a. vitreous; glassy
vi·tri·na, f. showcase; cabinet
vi·trio·lo, m. vitriol
vi·tu·pe·ra·ción, f. vituperation; censure
vi·tu·pe·rar, v. vituperate; censure
vi·tu·pe·rio·sa·men·te, adv. reproachfully
viu·da, f. widow
viu·dez, f. widowhood

viu·do, *m.* widower

vi·va·ci·dad, *f.* vivacity; liveliness

vi·va·men·te, *adv.* vividly; acutely; deeply

vi·va·que, *m.* bivouac

vi·va·quear, *v.* bivouac

vi·va·ra·cho, *a.* vivacious; sprightly

vi·vaz, *a.* vivacious; lively

ví·ve·res, *m. pl.* victuals; provisions

ví·vi·do, *a.* vivid

vi·vien·da, *f.* dwelling; place where one lives

vi·vien·te, *a.* living

vi·vir, *v.* live; have life; reside

vi·vo, *a.* live; lively; vivid; smart; sharp

viz·con·de, *m.* viscount

viz·con·de·sa, *f.* viscountess

vo·ca·blo, *m.* word

vo·ca·bu·la·rio, *m.* vocabulary

vo·ca·ción, *f.* vocation; calling; occupation

vo·cal, *a.* vocal. *f.* vowel

vo·ca·li·za·ción, *f.* vocalization

vo·ca·li·zar, *v.* vocalize

vo·ci·fe·ra·ción, *f.* vociferation

vo·ci·fe·rar, *v.* clamor; blare; shout

vod·ka, *f.* vodka

vo·lan·te, *a.* flying. *m.* flywheel

vo·lar, *v.* fly; explode; blast

vo·lá·til, *a.* volatile

vo·la·ti·li·dad, *f.* volatility

vo·la·ti·li·zar, *v.* vaporize

vol·cán, *m.* volcano

vol·cá·ni·co, *a.* volcanic

vol·car(se), *v.* upset; overturn; capsize

vo·lea, *f.* volley

vo·lear, *v.* volley

vo·leo, *m.* volley

vo·li·ción, *f.* volition

vol·ta·je, *m.* voltage

vol·tea·dor, *m.*, **vol·tea·do·ra**, *f.* tumbler

vol·tear, *v.* tumble; roll over; upset

vol·te·re·ta, *f.* somersault

vol·tio, *m.* volt

vo·lu·bi·li·dad, *f.* volubility; fickleness

vo·lu·ble, *a.* voluble; fickle

vo·lu·men, *m.* volume; bulkiness

vo·lu·mi·no·so, *a.* voluminous; bulky

vo·lun·tad, *f.* will; volition; determination. **a vo·lun·tad**, at will. **ma·la vo·lun·tad**, ill will

vo·lun·ta·ria·men·te, *adv.* voluntarily

vo·lun·ta·rio, *a.* voluntary; unconstrained. *m.* volunteer

vo·lun·ta·rio·sa·men·te, *adv.* willfully

vo·lun·ta·rio·so, *a.* willful; wilful; wayward

vo·lup·tuo·sa·men·te, *adv.* voluptuously

vo·lup·tuo·so, *a.* voluptuous. *m.* voluptuary

vol·ver(se), *v.* return; turn back; recur; revert; turn; render. **vol·ver en sí**, come to one's senses

vo·mi·tar, *v.* vomit; puke; spew; spue

vó·mi·to, *m.* vomit

vo·raz, *a.* voracious; greedy

vo·raz·men·te, *adv.* voraciously; greedily

vór·ti·ce, *m.* vortex; hurricane

vos, *pron. m., f.* you

vo·so·tras, *pron. f.* you; ye

vo·so·tros, *pron. m.* you; ye

vo·ta·ción, *f.* vote; balloting

vo·tan·te, *a.* voter

vo·tar, *v.* vote

vo·to, *m.* vote; vow

voz, *f.* voice; report. **en voz al·ta**, aloud; loudly. **dar vo·ces**, shout

vue·lco, *m.* spill

vue·lo, *m.* flight

vuel·ta, *f.* return; spin; turn. **dar u·na vuel·ta**, take a ride. **de i·da y vuel·ta**, round trip

vues·tra, *a.* your. *poss. pron. f.* yours

vues·tro, *a.* your. *poss. pron. m.* yours

vul·ca·ni·za·ción, *f.* vulcanization

vul·ca·ni·zar, *v.* vulcanize

vul·gar, *a.* vulgar; common; coarse

vul·ga·ri·dad, *f.* vulgarity

vul·ga·ri·zar, *v.* vulgarize; popularize

vul·gar·men·te, *adv.* vulgarly; commonly

vul·ne·ra·bi·li·dad, *f.* vulnerability

vul·ne·ra·ble, *a.* vulnerable

vul·va, *f.* vulva

W-X-Y

wá·ter, *m.* lavatory; toilet; watercloset

whis·key, *m.* whiskey, whisky

xe·no·fo·bia, *f.* xenophobia

xe·nón, *m.* xenon

xe·ro·co·pia, *f.* xerox copy

xe·ro·co·piar, *v.* xerox

xi·ló·fo·no, *m.* xylophone

xi·lo·gra·fía, *f.* xylography

y, *conj.* and; plus

ya, *adv.* already; now

yac, **yak**, *m.* yak

yan·qui, *m., f.* Yankee. *a.* Yankee

yar·da, *f.* yard

ya·te, *m.* yacht

ye·gua, *f.* mare

ye·gua·da, *f.* stud

ye·ma, *f.* yolk of an egg. **ye·ma del de·do**, fingertip

yer·mo, *m.* wilderness; wasteland; *often pl.* wilds

yer·no, *m.* son-in-law

yes·ca, *f.* tinder

ye·so, *m.* gypsum; plaster

yo, *pron.* I. *m.* ego. **yo mis·mo**, myself

yo·do, *m.* iodine

yo·ga, *m.* yoga

yo·gui, *m.* yogi

yo·gur, *v.* yogurt

yo·quéy, yo·qui, *m.* jockey

yu·ca, *f.* yucca

yu·go, *m.* yoke

yu·gu·lar, *a.* jugular

yun·que, *m.* anvil

yun·ta, *f.* yoke of oxen; team

yu·te, *m.* jute

yux·ta·po·ner, *v.* juxtapose

yux·ta·po·si·ción, *f.* juxtaposition

Z

za·far(se), *v.* run away; loosen; embellish

za·fi·ro, *m.* sapphire

za·gal, *m.* lad

za·ga·la, *f.* lass

za·ho·rí, *m.* seer; soothsayer

za·la·gar·da, *f.* ambush; ambuscade

za·la·me·ro, *a.* unctuous. *m.* flatterer

za·ma·rra, *f.* sheepskin jacket

za·ma·rro, *m.* sheepskin

zam·bu·lli·da, *f.* dive; submersion

zam·bu·llir, *v.* douse; plunge; dive

za·na·ho·ria, *f.* carrot

zan·ca·da, *f.* stride

zan·ca·jo, *m.* heel, as of a shoe or stocking

zan·co, *m.* stilt

zán·ga·no, *m.* drone

zan·ja, *f.* ditch; trench; conduit

zan·jar, *v.* dig ditches

zan·qui·va·no, *m.* spindlelegs. *a.* spindle-legged

za·par, *v.* sap

za·pa·te·ría, *f.* shoeshop

za·pa·te·ro, *m.* cobbler; shoemaker

za·pa·ti·lla, *f.* slipper

za·pa·to, *m.* shoe

zar, *m.* czar

za·ran·dear, *v.* sift

zar·ci·lla, *f.* tendril

za·ri·na, *f.* czarina

zar·par, *v.* weigh anchor

zar·za, *f.* bramble

zar·za·mo·ra, *f.* blackberry

zar·zo, *m.* hurdle

zig·zag, *m.* zigzag

zig·za·guear, *v.* zigzag

zo·co, *a.* left-handed

zo·día·co, *m.* zodiac

zo·na, *f.* zone

zoo·lo·gía, *f.* zoology

zoo·ló·gi·co, *a.* zoological. *m.* zoo. **jar·dín zoo·ló·gi·co**, zoo

zoó·lo·go, *m.* zoologist

zo·pen·co, *m.* dunce. *a.* stupid; doltish

zo·que·te, *m.* oaf; chunk of wood

zo·rra, *f.* fox; vixen

zo·rro, *m.* fox

zo·te, *m.* booby; dunce. *a.* dense

zo·zo·bra, *f.* foundering; overturning

zo·zo·brar, *v.* keel over; overturn; capsize

zue·co, *m.* wooden shoe; clog

zu·ma·que, *m.* sumac; sumach

zum·ba, *f.* banter; raillery

zum·ba·dor, *m.* electrical buzzer

zum·bar, *v.* buzz; whir, whirr; hum; drone; zoom; tease

zum·bi·do, *m.* buzz; hum; zoom; whir, whirr

zu·mo, *m.* juice

zu·mo·so, *a.* juicy

zur·ci·do, *m.* mending; darn; stitch

zur·cir, *v.* darn; mend; stitch

zu·rrar, *v.* spank; thrash; *inf.* wallop; dress leather

zu·rria·go, *m.* whip

zu·ta·no, *m.*, **zu·ta·na**, *f.* so-and-so

A

a, *indef. art.* un, una
a.back, *adv.* detrás; atrás
a.ba.cus, *n.* ábaco
a.ban.don, *v.* abandonar
a.base, *v.* humillar; rebajar
a.bash, *v.* avergonzar
a.bate, *v.* disminuir; reducir
ab.bey, *n. pl.* -beys. abadía; monasterio; convento
ab.bre.vi.a.tion, *n.* abreviación
ab.di.cate, *v.* abdicar
ab.do.men, *n.* abdomen; vientre
ab.duct, *v.* secuestrar
ab.er.ra.tion, *n.* aberración
a.bet, *v.* instigar; ayudar
ab.hor, *v.* aborrecer
a.bide, *v.* habitar; soportar
a.bil.i.ty, *n.* habilidad; aptitud
ab.ject, *a.* abyecto
ab.jure, *v.* abjurar
a.ble, *a.* capaz; competente
ab.ne.gate, *v.* renunciar; negar
ab.nor.mal, *a.* anormal
a.board, *adv., prep.* a bordo
a.bode, *n.* domicilio
a.bol.ish, *v.* abolir
a.bom.i.nate, *v.* abominar
ab.o.rig.i.nes, *n.* aborígenes
a.bor.tion, *n.* aborto
a.bound, *v.* abundar
a.bout, *prep.* alrededor de; sobre. *adv.* casi; cerca de
a.bove, *prep.* encima de; sobre. *a.* anterior. *adv.* encima; arriba
a.bra.sion, *n.* abrasión; raspadura
a.breast, *adv.* de frente; al lado
a.bridge, *v.* abreviar; resumir
a.broad, *adv.* fuera (de casa); en el extranjero
ab.ro.gate, *v.* abrogar
ab.rupt, *a.* repentino; brusco; escarpado
ab.scess, *n.* absceso
ab.scond, *v.* fugarse
ab.sent, *a.* ausente
ab.so.lute, *a.* absoluto; positivo; completo
ab.solve, *v.* absolver
ab.sorb, *v.* absorber; preocupar
ab.stain, *v.* abstenerse
ab.ste.mi.ous, *a.* abstemio
ab.stract, *v.* abstraer. *a.* abstracto. *n.* resumen
ab.surd, *a.* absurdo
a.bun.dant, *a.* abundante
a.buse, *v.* abusar. *n.* abuso; injuria
a.but, *v.* confinar
a.byss, *n.* abismo
ac.a.dem.ic, *a.* académico
a.cad.e.my, *n. pl.,* -mies. academia; colegio
ac.cede, *v.* acceder; consentir; subir

ac.cel.er.ate, *v.* acelerar
ac.cent, *n.* acento. *v.* acentuar
ac.cept, *v.* aceptar; recibir
ac.cess, *n.* acceso
ac.ces.si.ble, *a.* accesible
ac.ces.so.ry, *n. pl.,* -ries. accesorios; cómplice. *a.* accesorio
ac.ci.dent, *n.* accidente
ac.claim, *v.* aclamar. *n.* aclamación
ac.cli.mate, *v.* aclimatar
ac.co.lade, *n.* acolada
ac.com.mo.date, *v.* acomodar
ac.com.pa.ny, *v.* acompañar
ac.com.plice, *n.* cómplice
ac.com.plish, *v.* acabar; efectuar; cumplir
ac.cord, *n.* acuerdo; armonía. *v.* conceder; convenir
ac.cor.di.on, *n.* acordeón
ac.count, *v.* considerar; explicar. *n.* cuenta; relato; consideración
ac.count.a.ble, *a.* responsable
ac.cu.mu.late, *v.* acumular
ac.cu.ra.cy, *n.* exactitud
ac.cu.rate, *a.* exacto; fiel
ac.cuse, *v.* acusar; culpar
ac.cus.tom, *v.* acostumbrar
ace, *n.* as
a.ce.tic, *a.* acético
ac.e.tone, *n.* acetona
ache, *n.* dolor. *v.* doler
a.chieve, *v.* lograr; acabar
ac.id, *a.* agrio. *n.* ácido
ac.knowl.edge, *v.* reconocer; confesar; agradecer
ac.me, *n.* cima
ac.ne, *n.* acné
ac.o.lyte, *n.* acólito
a.corn, *n.* bellota
a.cous.tics, *n.* acústica
ac.quaint, *v.* dar a conocer; informar; enterar
ac.quaint.ance, *n.* conocido
ac.qui.esce, *v.* consentir
ac.quire, *v.* adquirir
ac.quit, *v.* absolver
a.cre, *n.* acre
ac.rid, *a.* acre
ac.ri.mo.ny, *n.* acrimonia
ac.ro.bat, *n.* acróbata
a.cross, *adv.* de través. *prep.* a través de
act, *v.* hacer; actuar; representar; fingir. *n.* acto; hecho; obra; ley
ac.tion, *n.* acción; proceso
ac.ti.vate, *v.* activar
ac.tive, *a.* activo; ágil
ac.tor, *n.* actor
ac.tress, *n.* actriz
ac.tu.al, *a.* real; efectivo; actual
a.cu.i.ty, *n.* agudeza
a.cu.men, *n.* agudeza
a.cute, *a.* agudo; fino
ad.age, *n.* adagio
ad.a.mant, *a.* firme

a.dapt, v. adaptar

add, v. añadir; aumentar; sumar

ad.di.tion, n. adición; añadidura

ad.dress, v. dirigir(se a). n. dirección; discurso

a.dept, n., a. experto

ad.e.quate, a. adecuado; suficiente

ad.here, v. adherirse; pegarse; cumplir

ad.he.sive, a., n. adhesivo

ad.ja.cent, a. adyacente; contiguo

ad.jec.tive, n. adjetivo

ad.join, v. juntar; estar contiguo

ad.journ, v. suspender

ad.judge, v. juzgar; sentenciar

ad.just, v. ajustar; adaptar

ad.ju.tant, n. ayudante

ad.lib, v. improvisar

ad.min.is.ter, v. administrar

ad.min.is.tra.tion, n. administración

ad.mire, v. admirar

ad.mis.si.ble, a. admisible

ad.mis.sion, n. entrada; confesión

ad.mit, v. dar entrada; admitir; confesar; permitir

ad.mon.ish, v. amonestar

a.do.be, n. adobe

ad.o.les.cence, n. adolescencia

a.dopt, v. adoptar; aceptar

a.dore, v. adorar

a.dorn, v. adornar

a.dren.a.line, n. adrenalina

a.droit, a. hábil; diestro

ad.u.la.tion, n. adulación

a.dult, a. mayor. n. adulto

a.dul.ter.y, n. adulterio

ad.vance, v. avanzar; ascender; adelantado. n. avance; adelanto

ad.van.tage, n. ventaja

ad.ven.ture, n. aventura

ad.ven.ture.some, a. aventurado

ad.verb, n. adverbio

ad.ver.sar.y, n., pl. -ies. adversario

ad.verse, a. adverso; contrario

ad.ver.si.ty, n., pl. -ties. adversidad

ad.ver.tise, v. anunciar; publicar; poner un anuncio

ad.vice, n. consejo

ad.vise, v. aconsejar; avisar

ad.vo.cate, v. abogar; recomendar. n. abogado; defenso

adz, adze, n. azuela

ae.gis, n. égido

aer.ate, v. ventilar; airear

aer.i.al, a. aéreo. n. antena

aer.o.naut.ics, n. pl. aeronáutica

aes.thete, n. esteta, m., f.

aes.thet.ic, a. estético

a.far, adv. lejos

af.fa.ble, a. afable; cortés

af.fair, n. asunto; acción; aventura amorosa

af.fect, v. afectar

af.fec.ta.tion, n. afectación

af.fec.tion, n. afección; afecto

af.fec.tion.ate, a. cariñoso

af.fi.ance, v. desposarse

af.fi.da.vit, n. declaración jurada

af.fil.i.ate, v. afiliar

af.fin.i.ty, n., pl. -ties. afinidad

af.firm, v. afirmar

af.firm.a.tion, n. aserción. a. afirmativo

af.firm.a.tive, n. aserción. a. afirmativo

af.fix, v. añadir; fijar. n. afijo

af.flict, v. afligir

af.flic.tion, n. aflicción

af.flu.ence, n. afluencia; riqueza

af.flu.ent, a. rico; opulento

af.ford, v. tener medios para; dar

af.front, v. afrentar. n. afrenta

a.fire, a., adv. ardiendo

a.flame, a., adv. en llamas

a.float, a., adv. a flote

a.foul, a., adv. enredado

a.fraid, a. atemorizado

a.fresh, adv. de nuevo; otra vez

aft, a., adv. en (a) popa

af.ter, a. posterior. adv. después. prep. después de; detrás de

af.ter.birth, n. secundinas, f. pl.

af.ter.noon, n. tarde, f.

af.ter.ward, af.ter.wards, adv. después

a.gain, adv. otra vez; de nuevo

a.gainst, prep. contra; junto

a.gape, a., adv. boquiabierto

age, n. edad; época; vejez. v. envejecer

a.ged, a. viejo

a.gen.cy, n., pl. -cies. agencia; acción; medio

a.gen.da, n. pl. orden del día

a.gent, n. agente; representante

ag.glom.er.ate, v. aglomerar. a. aglomerado

ag.gran.dize, v. engrandecer

ag.gra.vate, v. agravar

ag.gre.gate, v. agregar; juntar. n. masa. a. total

ag.gres.sion, n. agresión

ag.gres.sive, a. agresivo

a.ghast, a. horrorizado

ag.ile, a. ágil

a.gil.i.ty, n. agilidad

ag.i.tate, v. agitar; inquietar

a.glow, a. ardiente

ag.nos.tic, n. agnóstico

a.go, a., adv. hace; pasado

ag.o.ny, n. pl. -nies. agonía; angustia

a.grar.i.an, a. agrario

a.gree, v. concordar; acordar; ponerse de acuerdo

a.gree.a.ble, a. agradable; conforme

a.gree.ment, n. acuerdo; contrato

ag.ri.cul.ture, n. agricultura

a.gron.o.my, n. agronomía

a.ground, *a., adv.* encallado

a.head, *adv.* delante; al frente

aid, *v.* ayudar. *n.* ayuda; auxilio

ail.ment, *n.* enfermedad; dolencia

aim, *v.* apuntar; aspirar. *n.* puntería; blanco; propósito

air, *n.* aire. *v.* airear; ventilar

air con.di.tion.er, *n.* acondicionador de aire

air.craft, *n. pl.,* **air.craft,** avión

air.field, *n.* campo de aviación

air.ing, *n.* ventilación; paseo

air.lift, *n.* puente aéreo

air.line, *n.* línea aérea

air.mail, air.mail, *n.* correo aéreo

air.plane, *n.* avión

air.port, *n.* aeropuerto

air.raid, *n.* ataque aéreo

air.y, *a.* ligero; alegre

aisle, *n.* nave lateral; pasillo

a.jar, *a., adv.* entreabierto

a.kin, *a.* semejante; consanguíneo

al.a.bas.ter, *n.* alabastro

a.lac.ri.ty, *n.* alacridad

a.larm, *n.* alarma; inquietud. *v.* alarmar

a.larm.ist, *n.* alarmista, *m., f.*

al.ba.tross, *n.* albatros

al.bi.no, *n. pl.,* **-nos.** albino

al.bum, *n.* álbum

al.bu.men, *n.* albumen

al.bu.min, *n.* albúmina

al.che.my, *n.* alquimia

al.co.hol, *n.* alcohol

ale, *n.* cerveza

a.lee, *adv.* a sotavento

a.lert, *a.* alerta; vigilante. *n.* alarma. *v.* alertar

al.fal.fa, *n.* alfalfa

al.ga, *n. pl.,* **al.gae.** alga

al.ge.bra, *n.* álgebra

a.li.as, *n. pl.,* **a.li.as.es.** alias

al.i.bi, *n.* coartada; excusa

al.ien, *a.* ajeno. *n.* extranjero

al.ien.ate, *v.* enajenar

a.light, *v.* bajar; posarse

a.lign, *v.* alinear; aliar

a.like, *a.* semejante. *adv.* igualmente; del mismo modo

al.i.ment, *n.* alimento

al.i.men.ta.ry, *a.* alimenticio

al.i.mo.ny, *n.* alimentos, *m. pl.*

a.live, *a.* vivo; activo; sensible

al.ka.li, *n. pl.,* **-lies, -lis.** álcali

al.ka.lize, *v.* alcalizar

all, *a.* todo(s). *n.* totalidad. *adv.* completamente. **above all,** sobre todo. **all but,** casi

al.lay, *v.* aliviar; aquietar

al.le.ga.tion, *n.* alegación

al.lege, *v.* alegar; declarar

al.leged, *a.* supuesto; alegado

al.le.giance, *n.* lealtad

al.le.go.ry, *n. pl.,* **-ries.** alegoría

al.ler.gy, *n. pl.,* **-gies.** alergia

al.le.vi.ate, *v.* aliviar; calmar; mitigar

al.le.vi.a.tion, *n.* aligeramiento

al.ley, *n. pl.,* **-leys.** callejuela

al.li.ance, *n.* alianza

al.li.ga.tor, *n.* caimán; lagarto

al.lo.cate, *v.* asignar

al.lo.ca.tion, *n.* reparto; cupo

al.lot, *v.* asignar; distribuir; adjudicar

al.low, *v.* permitir; aceptar; dar; conceder

al.low.ance, *n.* permisión; concesión; ración

al.loy, *n.* aleación. *v.* ligar

al.lude, *v.* aludir

al.lure, *v.* atraer; tentar. *n.* encanto

al.lu.sion, *n.* alusión

al.lu.vi.um, *n. pl.,* **-vi.ums, -vi.a.** derrubio

al.ly, *n. pl.* **-lies.** aliado; confederado

al.ly, *v.* aliarse; hacer alianza

al.ma.nac, *n.* almanaque

al.might.y, *a.* omnipotente; todopoderoso

al.mond, *n.* almendra; almendro

al.most, *adv.* casi

alms, *n. pl., alms.* limosna

a.loft, *adv.* en alto

a.lone, *a.* solo. *adv.* sólo; solamente

a.long, *adv.* con. *prep.* por; a lo largo

a.loof, *adv.* lejos. *a.* reservado

a.loof.ness, *n.* frialdad

a.loud, *adv.* en voz alta; alto

al.pha.bet, *n.* alfabeto

al.read.y, *adv.* ya

al.so, *adv.* también; además

al.tar, *n.* altar

al.ter, *v.* cambiar; alterar; modificar

al.ter.a.tion, *n.* alteración; cambio

al.ter.ca.tion, *n.* altercación; altercado

al.ter e.go, *n.* álter ego

al.ter.nate, *v.* alternar; variar. *a.* alterno

al.ter.na.tive, *n.* alternativa

al.though, *conj.* aunque

al.tim.e.ter, *n.* altímetro

al.ti.tude, *n.* altura; altitud

al.to, *n.* alto; contralto

al.to.geth.er, *adv.* enteramente; en total

al.tru.ism, *n.* altruismo

a.lu.mi.num, *n.* aluminio

a.lum.na, *n. f. pl.,* **-nae.** graduada

a.lum.nus, *n. pl.,* **-ni.** graduado

al.ways, *adv.* siempre

a.m., antemeridiano

a.mal.gam, *n.* amalgama

a.mal.gam.ate, *v.* amalgamar

a.mass, *v.* acumular; amontonar

am.a.teur, *n.* aficionado

am·a·to·ry, a. amatorio
a·maze, v. asombrar
a·maze·ment, n. asombro; sorpresa
am·a·zon, n. amazona
am·bas·sa·dor, n. embajador
am·ber, n. ámbar. a ambarino
am·bi·dex·trous, a. ambidextro
am·bi·gu·i·ty, n. ambigüedad; doble sentido
am·big·u·ous, a. ambiguo
am·bi·tion, n. ambición
am·bi·tious, a. ambicioso
am·biv·a·lence, n. ambivalencia
am·ble, v. amblar; andar lentamente. n. paso de andadura
am·bu·late, v. andar
am·bu·la·to·ry, a. ambulante. n. claustro
am·bus·cade, n. emboscada
am·bush, n. emboscada. v. emboscar
a·me·ba, n. amiba
a·me·lio·rate, v. mejorar
a·me·lio·ra·tion, n. mejora; mejoramiento
a·men, int. amén
a·me·na·ble, a. tratable; dócil; responsable
a·mend, v. enmendar; corregir
a·mends, n. pl. compensación
a·men·i·ty, n. pl., -ties. amenidad; pl. conveniencias
A·mer·i·can, a. americano
am·e·thyst, n. amatista
a·mi·a·ble, a. amable
am·i·ca·ble, a. amistoso
a·mid, prep. en medio de; entre. Also a·midst
a·mid·ships, adv. en medio del navío
a·miss, adv., a. impropiamente; mal
am·mo·nia, n. amoníaco
am·mu·ni·tion, n. munición
am·ne·sia, n. amnesia
am·nes·ty, n. pl., -ties. amnistía. v. amnistiar
a·moe·ba, n. pl., -bae, -bas. amiba
a·mong, prep. entre; en medio de. Also a·mongst
a·mor·al, a. amoral
am·o·rous, a. amoroso
a·mor·phous, a. amorfo
am·or·tize, v. amortizar
a·mount, n. cantidad; suma. v. importar; ascender
am·pere, n. amperio
am·phib·i·an, a., n. anfibio
am·phib·i·ous, a. anfibio
am·phi·the·a·ter, n. anfiteatro
am·ple, a. amplio; abundante
am·pli·fy, v. amplificar; extender
am·pli·tude, n. amplitud; abundancia
am·pu·tate, v. amputar
am·pu·ta·tion, n. amputación
a·muck, adv. furiosamente

am·u·let, n. amuleto
a·muse, v. divertir; entretener
a·muse·ment, n. diversión; pasatiempo
an, a., indef. art. un; uno; una
a·nach·ro·nism, n. anacronismo
an·a·con·da, n. anaconda
a·nae·mi·a, n. anemia
an·a·gram, n. anagrama, m.
a·nal, a. anal
an·al·ge·sic, a., n. analgésico
a·nal·o·gize, v. analogizar
a·nal·o·gy, n. pl., -gies. analogía
a·nal·y·sis, n. pl., -ses. análisis
an·a·lyst, n. analizador
an·a·lyze, v. analizar
an·ar·chism, n. anarquismo
an·ar·chist, n. anarquista, m., f.
an·ar·chy, n. anarquía
a·nath·e·ma, n. pl., -mas. anatema, m.
a·nat·o·my, n. pl., -mies. anatomía
an·ces·tor, n. antepasado
an·ces·try, n. pl., -tries. linaje; abolengo
an·chor, n. ancla; áncora. v. asegurar
an·cho·vy, n. pl., -vies. anchoa
an·cient, a. antiguo
and, conj. y (e before i-, hi-)
an·ec·dote, n. anécdota
a·ne·mi·a, n. anemia
an·e·mom·e·ter, n. anemómetro
an·es·the·sia, n. anestesia
an·es·thet·ic, n., a. anestésico
a·new, adv. de nuevo; otra vez
an·gel, n. ángel
an·gel·ic, a. angélico
an·ger, n. ira; cólera. v. enojar
an·gle, n. ángulo. v. pescar con caña
an·gle·worm, n. lombriz, f.
An·gli·cize, v. inglesar
an·gling, n. pesca con caña
An·glo-Sax·on, n., a. anglosajón
an·go·ra, n. angora
an·gry, a. colérico; enfadado
an·guish, n. angustia; ansia. v. atormentar
an·gu·lar, a. angular; anguloso
an·hy·drous, a. anhidro
an·i·mad·ver·sion, n. animadversión
an·i·mad·vert, v. censurar
an·i·mal, n. animal; bestia. a. animal
an·i·mal·ize, v. animalizar
an·i·mate, v. animar; dar vida. a. vivo; animado
an·i·ma·tion, n. animación
an·i·mos·i·ty, n. animosidad
an·ise, n. anís, m.
an·kle, n. tobillo
an·nals, n. pl anales, m. pl
an·neal, v. templar
an·nex, v. anexar; adjuntar. n. adición
an·nex·a·tion, n. anexión

an·ni·hi·late, v. aniquilar
an·ni·hi·la·tion, n. aniquilación
an·ni·ver·sa·ry, n. pl., -ries. aniversario
an·no·tate, v. anotar
an·nounce, v. anunciar; proclamar
an·nounce·ment, n. anuncio; aviso
an·noy, v. molestar
an·noy·ance, n. molestia; fastidio
an·nu·al, a. anual. n. planta anual
an·nu·i·ty, n. pl., -ties. renta vitalicia
an·nul, v. anular
an·nul·ment, n. anulación
an·nun·ci·ate, v. anunciar
an·nun·ci·a·tion, n. anunciación
an·ode, n. ánodo
a·noint, v. untar; ungir
a·nom·a·lous, a. anómalo
a·nom·a·ly, n. anomalía
a·non·y·mous, a. anónimo
an·oth·er, a., pron. otro
an·swer, v. responder; contestar; servir. n. respuesta; contestación; solución
ant, n. hormiga
ant·ac·id, n. antiácido
an·tag·o·nist, n. antagonista, m., f.
an·tag·o·nize, v. provocar; contender
ant·arc·tic, a. antártico
ant·eat·er, n. oso hormiguero
an·te·cede, v. anteceder
an·te·ced·ent, n. antecedente
an·te·date, v. antedatar; preceder
an·te·di·lu·vi·an, a. antediluviano
an·te·lope, n. pl., -lopes, -lope. antílope
an·ten·na, n. pl., -nae, -nas. antena
an·te·ri·or, a. anterior
an·te·room, n. antecámara
an·them, n. antífona. na·tion·al an·them, himno nacional
an·ther, n. antera
an·thol·o·gy, n. pl., -gies. antología
an·thra·cite, n. antracita
an·thrax, n. pl., -thra·ces. ántrax
an·thro·poid, a. antropoide
an·thro·pol·o·gist, n. antropólogo
an·thro·pol·o·gy, n. antropología
an·ti-, prefix anti; contra
an·ti·bi·ot·ic, n., a. antibiótico
an·ti·bod·y, n. pl., -bod·ies. anticuerpo
an·tic, n. travesura; cabriola
an·tic·i·pate, v. anticipar; esperar
an·tic·i·pa·tion, n. anticipación; expectación
an·ti·cli·max, n. anticlímax
an·ti·dote, n. antídoto
an·ti·pa·thy, n. pl., -thies. antipatía
an·ti·po·des, n. pl. antípoda
an·ti·quate, v. anticuar
an·ti·quat·ed, a. viejo; anticuado
an·tique, a. antiguo. n.

an·tiq·ui·ty, n. pl., -ties. antigüedad
an·ti·Sem·i·tism, n. antisemitismo
an·ti·sep·tic, a., n. antiséptico
an·ti·so·cial, a. antisocial
an·tith·e·sis, n. pl., -ses. antítesis, f.
an·ti·tox·in, n. antitoxina
ant·ler, n. cuerna; asta
an·to·nym, n. antónimo
a·nus, n. ano
an·vil, n. yunque
anx·i·e·ty, n. pl., -ties. inquietud; ansia
anx·ious, a. inquieto; impaciente
an·y, a., pron. algún; cualquier; alguno
an·y·bod·y, pron. alguno; alguien; cualquiera
an·y·how, adv. de cualquier modo; de todas formas
an·y·one, pron. alguno; alguien; cualquiera
an·y·thing, pron. algo; cualquier cosa
an·y·way, adv. de cualquier modo; de todas formas
an·y·where, adv. en todas partes; dondequiera
a·or·ta, n. pl., -tas, -tae. aorta
a·part, adv. aparte. a·part from, aparte de
a·part·ment, n. piso; apartamento
ap·a·thet·ic, a. indiferente
ap·a·thy, n. pl., -thies. apatía
ape, n. mono. v. imitar
ap·er·ture, n. abertura
a·pex, n. pl., -pex·es, -pi·ces. ápice, m.
aph·o·rism, n. aforismo
aph·ro·dis·i·ac, n. afrodisíaco
a·pi·a·rist, n. colmenero
a·pi·ar·y, n. pl., -ies. colmenar
a·piece, adv. cada uno; por persona
a·plomb, n. aplomo
a·poc·a·lypse, n. apocalipsis, m.
a·pol·o·gize, v. disculparse; excusar
a·pol·o·gy, n. pl., -gies. apología; disculpa
ap·o·plec·tic, a. apoplético
ap·o·plex·y, n. apoplejía
a·port, adv. a babor
a·pos·tate, n. apóstata, m., f.
a·pos·ta·tize, v. apostatar
a·pos·tle, n. apóstol
a·pos·tol·ic, a. apostólico
a·pos·tro·phe, n. apóstrofo
a·poth·e·car·y, n. pl., -ies. boticario
ap·pall, ap·pal, v. aterrar
ap·pa·rat·us, n. pl., -rat·us, -us·es. aparato
ap·par·el, n. ropa v. vestir
ap·par·ent, a. claro; aparente
ap·pa·ri·tion, n. fantasma, m.
ap·peal, v. apelar; suplicar; atraer. n. súplica; apelación

ap·pear, v. aparecer; parecer
ap·pear·ance, n. aparición; apariencia
ap·pease, v. apaciguar
ap·pel·lant, n. apelante, m., f.
ap·pel·la·tion, n. nombre
ap·pend, v. anexar
ap·pen·dage, n. apéndice
ap·pen·dec·to·my, n. pl., -mies. apendectomía
ap·pen·di·ci·tis, n. apendicitis, f.
ap·pen·dix, n. pl., -dix·es, -di·ces. apéndice
ap·per·tain, v. pertenecer
ap·pe·tite, n. apetito; gana
ap·pe·tiz·ing, a. apetitoso; apetitivo
ap·plaud, v. aplaudir
ap·plause, n. aplauso
ap·ple, n. manzana
ap·pli·cant, n. suplicante, m., f.
ap·pli·ca·tion, n. aplicación; solicitud
ap·ply, v. aplicar; solicitar
ap·point, v. señalar; nombrar
ap·point·ment, n. cita; nombramiento
ap·por·tion, v. repartir
ap·po·si·tion, n. aposición
ap·prais·al, n. valoración
ap·praise, v. valorar
ap·pre·ci·ate, v. apreciar; valorar; agradecer
ap·pre·ci·a·tion, n. aprecio; aumento en valor
ap·pre·hend, v. prender; entender; recelar
ap·pre·hen·sion, n. aprehensión
ap·pren·tice, n. aprendiz, m. v. poner de aprendiz
ap·prise, ap·prize, v. informar
ap·proach, v. acercarse; aproximarse. n. acceso; aproximación
ap·pro·ba·tion, n. aprobación
ap·pro·pri·ate, v. apropiar; destinar. a. apropiado
ap·prov·al, n. aprobación
ap·prove, v. aprobar
ap·prox·i·mate, a. aproximado. v. aproximar
ap·ri·cot, n. albaricoque
A·pril, n. abril
a·pron, n. delantal, m.
ap·ro·pos of, prep. a propósito de
apt, a. apto; listo
ap·ti·tude, n. aptitud
a·quar·i·um, n. pl., -i·ums, -i·a. acuario
a·quat·ic, a. acuático. n. pl. deportes acuáticos
aq·ue·duct, n. acueducto
a·que·ous, a. ácueo
aq·ui·line, a. aguileño
Ar·ab, n., a. árabe, m., f.
Ar·a·bic nu·mer·als, n. números

arábigos
ar·a·ble, a. labrantío; cultivable
ar·bi·ter, n. árbitro
ar·bi·trar·y, a. arbitrario
ar·bi·trate, v. arbitrar
ar·bi·tra·tion, n. arbitraje
ar·bo·re·al, a. arbóreo
ar·bo·re·tum, n. pl., -tums, -ta. jardín botánico
arc, n. arco. v. formar un arco voltaico
ar·cade, n. arcada; galería
arch, n. arco. v. arquear
arch-, prefix. principal
ar·chae·ol·o·gy, ar·che·ol·o·gy, n. arqueología
ar·cha·ic, a. arcaico
arch·an·gel, n. arcángel
arch·bish·op, n. arzobispo
arch·duch·ess, n. archiduquesa
arch·duke, n. archiduque
arch·er, n. arquero
ar·cher·y, n. ballestería
ar·che·type, n. arquetipo
ar·chi·pel·a·go, n. pl., -goes, -gos. archipiélago
ar·chi·tect, n. arquitecto
ar·chi·tec·tur·al, a. arquitectónico
ar·chi·tec·ture, n. arquitectura
ar·chive, n. archivo
arch·priest, n. arcipreste
arc·tic, a. ártico; glacial
ar·dent, a. ardiente; fervoroso
ar·dor, n. ardor
ar·du·ous, a. arduo; difícil
ar·e·a, n. área; región
a·re·na, n. arena
ar·gon, n. argo
ar·got, n. jerga
ar·gue, v. discutir; razonar
ar·gu·ment, n. argumento; disputa
ar·gu·men·ta·tive, a. argumentador
a·ri·a, n. aria
ar·id, a. árido
a·rid·i·ty, n. aridez
a·rise, v. alzarse; surgir
ar·is·toc·ra·cy, n. pl., -cies. aristocracia
a·ris·to·crat, n. aristócrata, m., f.
a·ris·to·crat·ic, a. aristocrático
a·rith·me·tic, n. aritmética
a·rith·me·ti·cian, n. aritmético
ark, n. arca
arm, n. brazo; arma. v. armar
ar·ma·da, n. armada
ar·ma·dil·lo, n. pl., -los. armadillo
ar·ma·ment, n. armamento
arm·ful, n. pl., -fuls. brazado
ar·mi·stice, n. armisticio
ar·moire, n. armario
ar·mor, n. armadura
ar·mored, a. blindado
ar·mor·y, n. pl., -ies. armería
arm·pit, n. sobaco

ar.my, n. pl. -mies. ejército; multitud
a.ro.ma, n. aroma, m.
a.o.mat.ic, a. aromático
a.round, adv. alrededor; a la vuelta. prep. alrededor de
a.rouse, v. despertar; excitar
ar.range, v. arreglar; prevenir
ar.range.ment n. arreglo; orden; medida
ar.rant, a. consumado
ar.ray, n. orden; formación; adorno. v. colocar; ataviar
ar.rest, v. detener. n. detención
ar.ri.val, n. llegada
ar.rive, v. llegar
ar.ro.gance, n. arrogancia
ar.ro.gant, a. arrogante
ar.row, n. flecha
ar.row.head, n. punta de flecha
ar.se.nal, n. arsenal
ar.se.nic, n. arsénico
ar.son, n. incendio premeditado
art, n. arte, m.; destreza; pl. artes, f.
ar.te.ri.al, a. arterial
ar.ter.y, n. pl. -ies. arteria
art.ful, a. ingenioso; astuto
ar.thrit.ic, a. artrítico
ar.thri.tis, n. artritis, f.
ar.ti.cle, n. artículo; objeto
ar.tic.u.late, a. articulado; claro. v. articular
ar.tic.u.la.tion, n. articulación
ar.ti.fi.cial, a. artificial
ar.til.ler.y, n. artillería
art.ist, n. artista, m., f.
ar.tis.tic, a. artístico
as, adv., conj., prep. como
as.bes.tos, as.bes.tus, n. asbesto
as.cend, v. subir; ascender
as.cen.sion, n. ascensión
as.cent, n. subida; cuesta
as.cer.tain, v. averiguar
as.cet.ic, a. ascético. n. asceta, m., f.
as.cet.i.cism, n. ascetismo
as.cribe, v. adscribir; atribuir
a.sex.u.al, a. asexual
ash, n. ceniza; fresno
a.shamed, a. avergonzado
a.side, adv. a un lado. n. aparte
as.i.nine, a. asnal
ask, v. preguntar; pedir; rogar
a.skance, adv. con recelo. Also a.skant
a.slant, adv. al sesgo. prep. a través de
a.sleep, a., adv. dormido
asp, n. áspid, m.
as.par.a.gus, n. espárrago
as.pect, n. aspecto; aire
as.per.i.ty, n. pl. -ties. aspereza
as.per.sion, n. calumnia
as.phalt, n. asfalto
as.phyx.i.ate, v. asfixiar

as.phyx.i.a.tion, n. asfixia
as.pi.ra.tion, n. aspiración; anhelo
as.pire, v. aspirar
as.pi.rin, n. aspirina
ass, n. burro; tonto
as.sail, v. acometer
as.sail.ant, n. asaltador
as.sas.sin, n. asesino
as.sas.si.nate, v. asesinar
as.sas.si.na.tion, n. asesinato
as.sault, n. asalto. v. atacar
as.sem.ble, v. congregar; juntar
as.sem.bly, n. pl. -blies. reunión; asamblea
as.sent, n. asentimiento. v. asentir
as.sert, v. afirmar
as.sess, v. fijar; tasar
as.sess.ment, n. valoración; imposición
as.set, n. haber; pl. activo
as.sev.er.ate, v. aseverar
as.sid.u.ous, a. asiduo
as.sign, v. asignar
as.sig.na.tion, n. cita
as.sign.ment, n. asignación
as.sim.i.late, v. asimilar
as.sim.i.la.tion, n. asimilación
as.sist, v. ayudar
as.sist.ance, n. ayuda
as.sist.ant, a. auxiliar. n. asistente; ayudante
as.so.ci.ate, v. asociar(se). a. asociado. n. socio; compañero
as.so.ci.a.tion, n. asociación; sociedad
as.so.nance, n. asonancia
as.sort.ed, a. variado
as.sort.ment, n. surtido
as.suage, v. mitigar
as.sume, v. asumir; tomar
as.sump.tion, n. asunción; suposición
as.sure, v. asegurar
as.ter, n. aster, m.
as.ter.isk, n. asterisco
a.stern, adv. por la popa; a popa
asth.ma, n. asma
asth.mat.ic, a. asmático
a.stir, adv. activo
as.ton.ish, v. asombrar
as.ton.ish.ment, n. asombro
as.tound, v. asombrar
a.stray, adv. descarriado
a.stride, adv., prep. a horcajadas
as.trol.o.ger, n. astrólogo
as.trol.o.gy, n. astrología
as.tro.naut, n. astronauta, m., f.
as.tron.o.mer, n. astrónomo
as.tron.o.my, n. astronomía
as.tute, a. astuto
a.sun.der, adv. aparte
a.sy.lum, n. asilo; manicomio
at, prep. en; a
at.el.ier, n. taller

a·the·ism, *n.* ateísmo

a·the·ist, *n.* ateo

ath·lete, *n.* atleta, *m., f.*

ath·let·ic, *a.* atlético

a·thwart, *adv.* contrariamente. *prep.* al través

at·las, *n. pl.*, -las·es. atlas

at·mos·phere, *n.* atmósfera; ambiente

at·mos·pher·ic, *a.* atmosférico

at·oll, *n.* atolón

at·om, *n.* átomo

a·tom·ic, *a.* atómico

at·om·ize, *v.* atomizar

a·tone, *v.* expiar

a·tone·ment, *n.* expiación

a·top, *adv.* encima. *prep.* sobre

a·tro·cious, *a.* atroz

a·troc·i·ty, *n. pl.*, -ties. atrocidad

at·ro·phy, *n. pl.*, -phies. atrofia

at·tach, *v.* sujetar; unir; pegar

at·tack, *v.* atacar. *n.* ataque

at·tain, *v.* lograr; alcanzar

at·tain·ment, *n.* logro

at·tempt, *v.* intentar. *n.* tentativa; esfuerzo

at·tend, *v.* acompañar; asistir

at·ten·tion, *n.* atención

at·test, *v.* atestiguar

at·tic, *n.* desván

at·tire, *v.* vestir

at·ti·tude, *n.* actitud; postura

at·tor·ney, *n. pl.*, -neys. abogado

at·tract, *v.* atraer

at·trac·tion, *n.* atracción

at·trib·ute, *v.* atribuir

at·tri·bu·tion, *n.* atribución

a·typ·i·cal, *a.* atípico

auc·tion, *n.* subasta. *v.* subastar

auc·tion·eer, *n.* subastador; licitador

au·da·cious, *a.* audaz

au·dac·i·ty, *n.* atrevimiento

au·di·ble, *a.* oíble

au·di·ence, *n.* audiencia; público

au·dit, *n.* revisión. *v.* intervenir

au·di·tion, *n.* audición

au·di·tor, *n.* interventor

au·di·to·ri·um, *n.* auditorio

au·di·to·ry, *a.* auditivo

aught, *n.* algo

aug·ment, *v.* aumentar

Au·gust, *n.* agosto

aunt, *n.* tía

au·re·ate, *a.* áureo

au·ri·cle, *n.* aurícula

au·ro·ra, *n.* aurora

aus·pice, *n. pl.*, -pic·es. auspicio; *usu. pl.* protección

aus·pi·cious, *a.* favorable

aus·tere, *a.* austero

aus·ter·i·ty, *n.* austeridad

au·then·tic, *a.* auténtico

au·then·ti·cate, *v.* autenticar

au·then·tic·i·ty, *n.* autenticidad

au·thor, *n.* autor

au·thor·i·ta·tive, *a.* autorizado; imperioso

au·thor·i·ty, *n. pl.*, -ties. autoridad

au·thor·i·za·tion, *n.* autorización

au·thor·ize, *v.* autorizar

au·to, *n. inf.* automóvil

au·to·bi·og·ra·pher, *n.* autobiógrafo

au·to·bi·og·ra·phy, *n. pl.*, -phies. autobiografía

au·toc·ra·cy, *n. pl.*, -cies. autocracia

au·to·crat, *n.* autócrata, *m., f.*

au·to·graph, *n.* autógrafo. *v.* firmar

au·to·mat·ic, *a.* automático

au·to·ma·tion, *n.* automatización

au·tom·a·ton, *n. pl.*, -tons, -ta. autómata

au·to·mo·bile, *n.* automóvil; coche

au·ton·o·mous, *a.* autónomo

au·ton·o·my, *n. pl.*, -mies. autonomía

au·top·sy, *n. pl.*, -sies. autopsia

au·tumn, *n.* otoño

aux·il·ia·ry, *a.* auxiliar

a·vail, *v.* aprovechar(se); ser útil. *n.* utilidad

a·vail·a·ble, *a.* disponible

av·a·lanche, *n.* alud, *m.*

av·a·rice, *n.* avaricia

av·a·ri·cious, *a.* avaro

a·venge, *v.* vengar

a·veng·er, *n.* vengador

av·e·nue, *n.* avenida

a·ver, *v.* afirmar

av·er·age, *n.* promedio. *a.* medio. *v.* calcular el término medio

a·verse, *a.* adverso

a·ver·sion, *n.* aversión

a·vert, *v.* desviar; apartar; prevenir

a·vi·a·tion, *n.* aviación

a·vi·a·tor, *n.* aviador

av·id, *a.* ávido

av·o·ca·do, *n. pl.*, -dos. aguacate

av·o·ca·tion, *n.* diversión; trabajo

a·void, *v.* evitar

a·void·a·ble, *a.* evitable; eludible

a·vow, *v.* reconocer

a·vow·al, *n.* confesión

a·wait, *v.* esperar

a·wake, *a.* despierto. *v.* despertar(se)

a·wak·en, *v.* despertar(se)

a·ward, *v.* adjudicar; otorgar. *n.* adjudicación; premio

a·ware, *a.* enterado

a·way, *adv.* lejos. *a.* fuera

awe, *n.* temor reverencial. *v.* infundir miedo

aw·ful, *a.* imponente; horrible

a·while, *adv.* un rato

awk·ward, *a.* torpe; difícil; embarazoso

awn·ing, *n.* toldo

a·wry, *a.* sesgado. *adv.* de través

ax, axe, *n. pl.*, ax·es. hacha

ax·i·om, n. axioma, m.
ax·i·o·mat·ic, a. axiomático
ax·is, n. pl., **ax·es.** axis; eje
ax·le, n. eje
aye, ay, int., n. sí
az·ure, a., n. azul celeste

B

baa, n. balido. v. balar
bab·ble, n. murmullo. v. parlotear; balbucear
babe, n. criatura
ba·bel, n. babel. Also **Ba·bel**
ba·boon, n. mandril
ba·bush·ka, n. pañuelo
ba·by, n. pl., **-bies.** nene; niño. a. infantil. v. tratar como niño
bac·ca·lau·re·ate, n. bachillerato
bac·cha·na·li·an, a. bacanal
bach·e·lor, n. soltero
bach·e·lor·hood, n. soltería
ba·cil·lus, n. pl., **-li.** bacilo
back, n. espalda; fondo. v. apoyar; retroceder. a. trasero. adv. atrás
back·bone, n. espinazo; firmeza
back·drop, n. telón de foro
back·fire, n. petardeo. v. salir el tiro por la culata
back·gam·mon, n. juego de chaquete
back·ground, n. fondo; antecedentes
back·hand·ed, a. dado con el revés de la mano
back·lash, n. reacción
back·side, n. trasero
back·slide, v. apostatar; reincidir
back·ward, adv. atrás; al revés. a. atrasado. Also **back·wards**
ba·con, n. tocino
bac·te·ri·ol·o·gist, n. bacteriólogo
bac·te·ri·ol·o·gy, n. bacteriología
bac·ter·i·um, n. pl., **-i·a.** bacteria
bad, a. malo; podrido. n. lo malo
badge, n. divisa
badg·er, n. tejón. v. molestar
bad·min·ton, n. juego de volante
bad·ness, n. maldad
baf·fle, v. confundir; desconcertar
bag, n. saco; maleta; bolso. v. ensacar; cazar
bag·gage, n. equipaje
bagn·io, n. pl., **-ios.** burdel
bag·pipe, n. usu. pl. gaita
bail, v. achicar; afianzar. n. caución
bail·iff, n. alguacil
bait, n. cebo. v. cebar; atormentar
bake, v. cocer en horno; endurecer
bak·er, n. panadero
bak·er's doz·en, n. trece
bak·er·y, n. pl., **-ies.** panadería
bal·ance, n. balanza; equilibrio; resto. v. equilibrar(se)
bal·co·ny, n. pl., **-nies.** balcón
bald, a. calvo

bal·der·dash, n. tonterías
bald·ness, n. calvicie, f.
bale, n. bala. v. embalar; empacar
ba·leen, n. ballena
bale·ful, a. calamitoso; siniestro
balk, n. viga; obstáculo. v. impedir; rebelarse
ball, n. bola; pelota; baile
bal·lad, n. balada
bal·last, n. lastre. v. lastrar
bal·le·ri·na, n. bailarina
bal·let, n. ballet
bal·lis·tic, a. balístico
bal·lis·tics, n. pl. balística
bal·loon, n. globo
bal·lot, n. balota; votación
ball·room, n. salón de baile
balm, n. bálsamo
balm·y, a. balsámico; suave
ba·lo·ney, n. inf. disparates
bal·sa, n. balsa
bal·sam, n. bálsamo
bal·us·trade, n. balaustrada
bam·boo, n. bambú, m.
ban, v. prohibir. n. prohibición
ba·nal, a. vulgar
ba·nal·i·ty, n. trivialidad
ba·nan·a, n. plátano; banana
band, n. grupo; faja; banda. v. juntar
band·age, n. venda. v. vendar
ban·dit, n. pl., **-dits, -dit·ti.** bandido
ban·dy, v. cambiar. a. arqueado
ban·dy-leg·ged, a. estevado
bane, n. ruina; daño
bane·ful, a. funesto
bang, v. golpear; hacer estrépito. n. golpe
ban·ish, v. desterrar
ban·ish·ment, n. destierro
ban·is·ter, n. pasamano
ban·jo, n. banjo
bank, n. orilla; montón; banco. v. amontonar; cubrir; depositar
bank·er, n. banquero
bank·rupt, a. insolvente. v. quebrar
bank·rupt·cy, n. pl., **-cies.** bancarrota; quiebra
ban·nis·ter, n. pasamano
ban·quet, n. banquete. v. banquetear
ban·ter, n. zumba; burla. v. zumbar; chancearse con
bap·tism, n. bautismo; bautizo
bar, n. barra; obstáculo; bar. v. impedir; excluir
barb, n. púa
bar·bar·i·an, n. bárbaro
bar·bar·ic, a. bárbaro
bar·bar·i·ty, n. pl., **-ties.** barbaridad
bar·be·cue, n. barbacoa. v. asar entero
barbed wire, n. alambre de púas (de espino). Also **barb·wire**
bar·ber, n. peluquero; barbero
bar·ber·shop, n. peluquería

bar·bi·tu·rate, n. barbiturato

bard, n. poeta, m.; bardo

bare, a. desnudo; pelado. v. desnudar; descubrir

bare·faced, a. descarado

bare·ly, adv. simplemente; apenas

bar·gain, n. pacto; ganga. v. negociar; regatear

barge, n. gabarra

bar·i·tone, n. barítono

bar·i·um, n. bario

bark, n. corteza; ladrido. v. descortezar; raer; ladrar

bar·ley, n. pl., -leys. cebada

bar·maid, n. camarera

barn, n. granero

barn·yard, n. corral, m.

ba·rom·et·er, n. barómetro

bar·o·met·ric, a. barométrico

bar·on, n. barón

bar·on·ess, n. baronesa

ba·roque, a. barroco

bar·rack, n. usu. pl. cuartel, m.

bar·rage, n. cortina de fuego

bar·rel, n. barril, m.; cañón

bar·rel or·gan, n. organillo

bar·ren, a. estéril

bar·rette, n. horquilla

bar·ri·cade, n. barricada

bar·ri·er, n. barrera

bar·room, n. taberna; cantina

bar·ter, v. trocar; permutar

ba·sal, a. básico

ba·salt, n. basalto

base, n. base. f. a. bajo; vil

base·ball, n. béisbol

base·born, a. de nacimiento humilde

base·less, a. infundado

base·ment, n. sótano

bash, v. inf. golpear

bash·ful, a. vergonzoso

bash·ful·ness, n. timidez, f.

ba·sic, a. básico

ba·sil, n. albahaca

ba·sil·i·ca, n. basílica

ba·sin, n. tazón; jofaina; cuenca

ba·sis, n. pl., -ses. base, f.

bask, v. tomar el sol

bas·ket, n. cesta; canasta

bas·ket·ball, n. baloncesto; básquetbol

bass, n. bajo; contrabajo. a. bajo

bass, n. pl., bass, bass·es. róbalo

bas·si·net, n. cuna

bas·soon, n. bajón

bas·tard, n. bastardo. a. ilegítimo

bas·tard·ize, v. bastardear

baste, v. hilvanar; pringar

bas·tion, n. baluarte

bat, n. murciélago; maza. v. golpear

batch, n. hornada; colección

bath, n. pl. **baths**. baño

bathe, v. bañar(se)

bath·er, n. bañista, m., f.

bat·on, n. bastón; batuta

bat·tal·ion, n. batallón

bat·ter, v. apalear; desgastar. n. batido

bat·ter·y, n. pl., -ies. violencia; batería; pila

bat·tle, n. batalla; lucha. v. luchar

bat·ty, a. inf. loco

bau·ble, n. chuchería

bawd, n. alcahueta

bawd·y, a. obsceno

bawl, v. gritar; llorar

bay, n. bahía; laurel; aullido. a. bayo. v. aullar; encerrar

bay·o·net, n. bayoneta

ba·zaar, n. bazar

ba·zoo·ka, n. bazuca

be, v. ser; estar

beach, n. playa

bea·con, n. faro; almenara

bead, n. cuenta; gota

beak, n. pico

beam, n. viga; manga; rayo. v. emitir; brillar

bean, n. judía; haba

bear, n. pl., **bears**, **bear**. oso. v. llevar; soportar; producir

bear·a·ble, a. soportable

beard, n. barba

beard·ed, a. barbado

bear·ing, n. cojinete; porte; relación

bear·skin, n. piel de oso

beast, n. bestia; bruto

beast·li·ness, n. bestialidad

beat, v. golpear; batir; vencer. n. ritmo; ronda

beat·en, a. batido; derrotado

be·a·tif·ic, a. beatífico

be·at·i·tude, n. beatitud

beau·te·ous, a. bello

beau·ti·ful, a. hermoso

beau·ty, n. pl., -ties. belleza

bea·ver, n. castor

be·cause, conj. porque; a causa de

beck·on, v. llamar con señas

be·come, v. llegar a ser; hacerse; favorecer

be·com·ing, a. conveniente; que va bien

bed, n. cama; lecho; estrato

bed·clothes, n. pl. ropa de cama

bed·ding, n. ropa de cama

be·deck, v. adornar

be·dev·il, v. endiablar

bed·lam, n. confusión; manicomio

be·drag·gle, v. ensuciar

bed·rid·den, a. postrado en cama

bed·room, n. alcoba

bed·stead, n. armazón

bee, n. abeja

beech, n. haya

beef, n. pl., **beefs**, **beeves**. carne de vaca; buey; inf. fuerza muscular. v.

inf. quejarse
bee‧hive, *n.* colmena
beer, *n.* cerveza
bees‧wax, *n.* cera de abejas
beet, *n.* remolacha
bee‧tle, *n.* escarabajo
be‧fall, *v.* suceder (a)
be‧fit, *v.* convenir
be‧fit‧ting, *a.* conveniente
be‧fore, *adv.* delante; antes. *prep.* delante de; antes de. *conj.* antes que
be‧fore‧hand, *adv.* de antemano
be‧friend, *v.* amistar; favorecer
beg, *v.* mendigar; pedir
beg‧gar, *n.* mendigo
be‧gin, *v.* empezar; comenzar; iniciar
be‧gin‧ning, *n.* comienzo; principio
be‧guile, *v.* engañar; distraer
be‧half, *n.* favor; beneficio
be‧have, *v.* comportarse; portarse
be‧hav‧ior, *n.* conducta; comportamiento
be‧head, *v.* decapitar
be‧hind, *prep.* detrás de. *adv.* detrás; atrás; en retardo
be‧hind‧hand, *adv.* atrasada; con atraso
beige, *n.* beige
be‧ing, *n.* existencia; ser
be‧lat‧ed, *a.* retardado; tardío
belch, *v.* eructar. *n.* eructo
be‧lea‧guer, *v.* sitiar
bel‧fry, *n. pl.* **-fries.** campanario
be‧lief, *n.* creencia; fe, *f.*
be‧liev‧a‧ble, *a.* creíble
be‧lieve, *v.* creer
bell, *n.* campana; cascabel, *m.*
bell‧boy, *n.* botones. Also **bell‧hop**
bel‧li‧cose, *a.* belicoso
bel‧lig‧er‧en‧cy, *n.* beligerancia
bel‧lig‧er‧ent, *a.* beligerante
bel‧low, *n.* bramido. *v.* bramar; rugir
bel‧lows, *n. pl.* fuelle
bel‧ly, *n. pl.* **-lies.** vientre; barriga
bel‧ly‧ache, *n.* dolor de vientre. *v. inf.* quejarse
be‧long, *v.* pertenecer
be‧long‧ings, *n. pl.* pertenencias
be‧loved, *a.* querido. *n.* amado
be‧low, *prep.* debajo de. *adv.* abajo
belt, *n.* cinturón. *v. inf.* golpear
be‧moan, *v.* lamentar
be‧muse, *v.* confundir
bench, *n.* banco; tribunal de justicia
bend, *v.* doblar; encorvar; inclinar. *n.* comba; curva
be‧neath, *adv.* abajo. *prep.* debajo de
ben‧e‧dic‧tion, *n.* bendición
ben‧e‧fac‧tion, *n.* beneficio
ben‧e‧fac‧tor, *n.* bienhechor
ben‧e‧fi‧cent, *a.* benéfico
ben‧e‧fi‧cial, *a.* provechoso; beneficioso

ben‧e‧fi‧ci‧ar‧y, *n. pl.* **-ar‧ies.** beneficiario
ben‧e‧fit, *n.* beneficio. *v.* beneficiar; aprovechar(se)
be‧nev‧o‧lence, *n.* benevolencia
be‧nev‧o‧lent, *a.* benévolo
be‧nign, *a.* benigno
be‧nig‧nant, *a.* benigno
be‧nig‧ni‧ty, *n. pl.* **-ties.** benignidad
bent, *a.* encorvado; determinado. *n.* inclinación
be‧queath, *v.* legar
be‧quest, *n.* legado
be‧rate, *v.* reprender; regañar
be‧reave‧ment, *n.* aflicción
be‧ret, *n.* boina
ber‧ga‧mot, *n.* bergamota
ber‧ry, *n. pl.* **-ries.** baya
ber‧serk, *a.* enloquecido
berth, *n.* amarradero; litera
be‧seech, *v.* suplicar
be‧set, *v.* sitiar; acosar
be‧side, *prep.* cerca; junto a
be‧sides, *adv.* además, *prep.* además de
be‧siege, *v.* sitiar; asediar
be‧smirch, *v.* manchar
be‧speak, *v.* reservar; apalabrar
best, *a., irreg. superl. of good.* mejor. *adv.* mejor; más bien. *n.* lo mejor. *v.* vencer
bes‧tial, *a.* bestial
bes‧ti‧al‧i‧ty, *n. pl.* **-ties.** bestialidad
be‧stow, *v.* dar; otorgar; conferir
bet, *n.* apuesta. *v.* apostar
be‧tray, *v.* traicionar; revelar
be‧tray‧al, *n.* traición
be‧troth, *v.* prometer en matrimonio
bet‧ter, *a., compar. of good.* mejor; superior. *adv. compar. of well.* mejor. *n. usu. pl.* superiores. *v.* mejorar
bet‧ter‧ment, *n.* mejoramiento
be‧tween, *prep.* entre. *adv.* en medio
bev‧er‧age, *n.* bebida
bev‧y, *n. pl.* **-ies.** bandada; grupo
be‧wail, *v.* lamentar
be‧ware, *v.* guardarse; precaverse
be‧wil‧der, *v.* aturdir
be‧wil‧der‧ment, *n.* aturdimiento
be‧witch, *v.* hechizar; encantar
be‧yond, *adv.* más allá. *prep.* después de
bi‧as, *n.* sesgo; propensión; prejuicio. *a.* sesgado. *v.* prevenir
bib, *n.* babero
Bi‧ble, *n.* Biblia
Bib‧li‧cal, *a.* bíblico
bib‧li‧og‧ra‧pher, *n.* bibliógrafo
bib‧li‧og‧ra‧phy, *n. pl.* **-phies.** bibliografía
bi‧ceps, *n. pl.* bíceps, *m.*
bick‧er, *v.* reñir
bi‧cy‧cle, *n.* bicicleta. *v.* ir en bici-

cleta
bi·cy·clist, n. biciclista, m., f.
bid, v. pedir; ordenar; ofrecer. n. oferta; puja
bid·dy, n. pl., **-dies.** gallina
bide, v. esperar
bi·en·ni·al, a. bienal
bier, n. féretro
big, a. grande; importante
big·a·mist, n. bígamo
big·a·my, n. pl., **-mies.** bigamia
bight, n. caleta
big·ot, n. fanático
big·ot·ry, n. pl., **-ries.** fanatismo; intolerancia
bike, n. inf. bicicleta
bi·lat·er·al, a. bilateral
bile, n. bilis, f.; mal genio
bilge, n. pantoque
bil·ious, a. bilioso
bilk, v. defraudar
bill, n. cuenta; billete; propuesta de ley; pico. v. facturar
bill·board, n. cartelera
bil·let, n. alojamiento. v. alojar
bill·fold, n. cartera
bil·liards, n. pl. billar
bil·lion, n. billón
bill of fare, n. menú, m.
bil·low, n. oleada. v. hincharse
bil·low·y, a. hinchado
bil·ly goat, n. macho cabrío
bi·month·ly, a., adv. bimestral(mente); bimensual(mente)
bin, n. hucha
bi·na·ry, a. binario
bind, v. atar; vendar; encuadernar; obligar
bind·er, n. encuadernador
bind·er·y, n. pl., **-ies.** taller de encuadernar
bi·noc·u·lar, n. usu. pl. gemelos
bi·og·ra·pher, n. biógrafo
bi·o·graph·ic, a. biográfico
bi·og·ra·phy, n. pl., **-phies.** biografía
bi·o·log·i·cal, a. biológico
bi·ol·o·gist, n. biólogo
bi·ol·o·gy, n. biología
bi·op·sy, n. pl., **-sies.** biopsia
bi·par·ti·san, a. de dos partidos
bi·ped, n. bípedo
birch, n. abedul, m.
bird, n. ave, f.; pájaro
bird's-eye, a. vista de pájaro
birth, n. nacimiento; linaje
birth·day, n. cumpleaños
birth·mark, n. marca de nacimiento
birth·right, n. derechos de nacimiento
bis·cuit, n. galleta
bi·sect, v. bisecar
bi·sec·tion, n. bisección
bi·sex·u·al, a. bisexual
bish·op, n. obispo

bish·op·ric, n. obispado
bis·muth, n. bismuto
bi·son, n. bisonte
bis·tro, n. pl., **-tros.** cabaret, m.
bit, n. trozo; pedazo; bocado del freno
bitch, n. perra. v. inf. quejarse
bite, v. morder; picar. n. mordedura; bocado
bit·ter, a. amargo
bit·ter·ness, n. amargura; rencor
bi·tu·mi·nous, a. bituminoso
bi·valve, n. molusco bivalvo
biv·ou·ac, n. vivaque. v. vivaquear
bi·zarre, a. fantástico; raro
blab, v. divulgar; chismear
black, a. n. negro. v. ennegrecer
black·ber·ry, n. pl., **-ries.** zarzamora
black·bird, n. mirlo
black·board, n. pizarra
black·en, v. ennegrecer; difamar
black·guard, n. pillo
black·head, n. espinilla
black·heart·ed, a. malvado
black·jack, n. cachiporra; juego de naipes
black magic, n. magia negra
black·mail, n. chantaje
black·smith, n. herrero
blad·der, n. vejiga
blade, n. brizna; hoja
blame, v. culpar; censurar. n. censura
blame·less, a. intachable
blame·wor·thy, a. culpable
blanch, v. blanquear; palidecer
bland, a. suave
blan·dish, v. engatusar
blank, a. blanco. n. blanco
blan·ket, n. manta. a. general
blare, v. vociferar
blar·ney, n. adulación
blas·pheme, v. blasfemar
blas·phem·y, n. pl., **-ies.** blasfemia
blast, n. ráfaga; explosión. v. destruir; volar
bla·tant, a. ruidoso; poco sutil
blaze, n. llama; resplandor. v. arder; brillar
bleach, v. blanquear. n. lejía
bleach·ers, n. pl. gradas
bleak, a. desierto; triste
blear·y, a. legañoso
bleat, v. balar. n. balido
bleed, v. sangrar
blem·ish, n. desfigurar; manchar. n. tacha
blend, v. mezclar. n. combinación
bless, v. bendecir
bless·ing, n. bendición; ventaja
blight, n. tizón. v. añublar
blind, a. ciego. v. cegar; deslumbrar
blind·fold, n. venda. v. vendar los ojos
blind·ness, n. ceguera

blink, v. parpadear. n. destello
bliss, n. felicidad
bliss·ful, a. bienaventurado
blis·ter, n. ampolla. v. ampollar(se)
blithe, a. alegre
bliz·zard, n. ventisca
bloat, v. hinchar
block, n. bloque; manzana; obstáculo. v. obstruir
block·ade, a. bloqueo. v. bloquear
block·age, n. obstrucción
blond, blonde, a. rubio
blood, n. sangre, f.
blood·hound, n. sabueso
blood·shed, n. efusión de sangre; carnicería
blood·shot, a. inyectado de sangre
blood·thirst·y, a. sanguinario
blood·y, a. sangriento; ensangrentado. v. ensangrentar
bloom, n. flor, f. v. florecer
bloom·ing, a. floreciente
blos·som, n. flor, f. v. florecer
blot, n. borrón. v. manchar; secar
blotch, n. erupción
blot·ter, n. papel secante
blouse, n. blusa
blow, v. soplar; sonar; inflar. n. soplo; golpe
blow·up, n. explosión
blub·ber, n. grasa de ballena. v. llorar a lágrima viva
bludg·eon, n. cachiporra
blue, a. azul; melancólico. n. azul. v. azular
blue·print, n. ferroprusiato
blues, n. pl. melancolía
bluff, a. escarpado; francote. n. risco. v. engañar; similar
blu·ing, n. añil, m.
blun·der, v. disparatar. n. desatino
blunt, a. embotado; abrupto. v. embotar
blur, v. borrar; hacer borroso. n. borrón
blurt, v. decir sin pensar
blush, v. ruborizarse. n. sonrojo
blus·ter, v. bramar. n. jactancia
blus·ter·ous, a. tempestuoso
boar, n. verraco
board, n. tabla; pensión; consejo. v. entablar; abordar
board·er, n. pensionista; huésped
boast, v. jactarse. n. baladronada; alarde
boast·ful, a. jactancioso
boat, n. barco; bote
boat·swain, n. contramaestre
bob, v. fluctuar; desmochar
bob·by pin, n. horquilla
bob·cat, n. lince
bob·white, n. codorniz, f.
bode, v. presagiar
bod·ice, n. corpiño

bod·i·ly, a. corpóreo. adv. enteramente
bod·y, n. pl. -ies. cuerpo; cadáver; grupo
bod·y·guard, n. guardaespaldas
bog, n. pantano
bog·gy, a. pantanoso
bo·gus, a. falso
bo·gy, bo·gey, bog·ie, n. duende
boil, v. hervir. n. furúnculo
boil·er, n. caldera
bois·ter·ous, a. borrascoso; ruidoso
bold, a. intrépido; descarado
bold·ly, adv. audazmente
bol·ster, n. travesero. v. apoyar
bolt, n. rayo; cerrojo; rollo. v. empernar; engullir
bomb, n. bomba. v. bombardear
bom·bard, v. bombardear
bom·bar·dier, n. bombardero
bom·bard·ment, n. bombardeo
bom·bast, n. ampulosidad
bom·bas·tic, a. altisonante
bomb·er, n. bombardero
bond, n. lazo; obligación. v. dar fianza
bond·age, n. esclavitud
bone, n. hueso. v. deshuesar
bon·fire, n. hoguera
bon·net, n. gorra
bo·nus, n. pl. -nus·es. adehala; plus
bon·y, a. huesudo
boo·boo, n. inf. desatino
boo·by, n. pl. -bies. zote
boo·by trap, n. trampa camuflada
book, n. libro. v. reservar
book·bind·er, n. encuadernador de libros
book·keep·er, n. tenedor de libros
book·keep·ing, n. teneduría de libros
book·let, n. folleto
boom, n. estampido; prosperidad repentina. v. tronar; desarrollar rápidamente
boo·me·rang, n. bumerang, m.
boon, n. beneficio
boor, n. persona grosera
boost, v. empujar. n. empuje
boot, n. bota. v. da una patada a
booth, n. puesto
boo·ty, n. pl. -ties. botín
booze, n. bebida alcohólica. v. emborracharse
borax, n. bórax, m.
bor·der, n. borde; frontera
bore, v. taladrar; aburrir. n. pesado; taladro
bore·dom, n. aburrimiento
bo·ric ac·id, n. ácido bórico
born, a. nacido
bor·row, v. pedir prestado; apropiarse
bos·om, n. seno. a. íntimo
boss, n. jefe. v. dominar

boss·y, a. inf. tiránico

bo·sun, n. contramaestre. Also bos'n, bo's'n, bo'sun

bo·tan·ic, bo·tan·i·cal, a. botánico

bot·a·nist, n. botánico

bot·a·ny, n. botánica

botch, n. chapucería. v. remendar

both, a., pron. ambos; los dos. conj. a la vez

both·er, n. molestia. v. molestar

both·er·some, a. fastidioso

bot·tle, n. botella. v. embotellar

bot·tler, n. embotellador

bot·tom, n. fondo; pie. a. último

bou·doir, n. tocador de señora

bough, n. rama

bought, pt. and pp. of buy

bouil·lon, n. caldo

boul·der, n. pedrejón

boul·e·vard, n. avenida; bulevar

bounce, v. rebotar. n. bote; rebote

bounc·ing, a. fuerte

bound, n. usu. pl. límite; confín; salto. v. limitar; saltar. a. ligado; obligado

bound·a·ry, n. pl. -ries. término; frontera

boun·te·ous, a. abundante

boun·te·ous·ness, n. generosidad

boun·ty, n. pl., -ties. liberalidad; premio

bou·quet, n. ramo; aroma distinto

bour·geois, n. pl., -geois. burgués. a. burgués

bour·geoi·sie, n. pl., -sie. burguesía

bout, n. vez, f.; lucha

bo·vine, a. bovino

bow, n. arco; lazo. v. encorvar

bow, v. inclinar. n. reverencia; proa

bow·el, n. usu. pl. intestino

bow·er, n. enramada

bowl, n. escudilla. v. jugar a las bochas

bow·leg·ged, a. patiestevado

bowl·ing, n. juego de bolos

box, n. pl., box·es. caja. v. encajonar; boxear

box·er, n. boxeador

box·ing, n. boxeo

boy, n. niño; chico; muchacho

boy·cott, v. boicotear. n. boicoteo

boy·hood, n. muchachez, f.

boy·ish, a. juvenil

bra, n. inf. sostén

brace, n. abrazadera. v. atar; reforzar

brace·let, n. pulsera

brac·ing, a. tónico

brack·et, n. soporte; corchete. v. poner entre corchetes

brack·ish, a. salobre

brad, n. punta

brag, v. jactarse. n. bravata

brag·gart, n. jactancioso

braid, v. trenzar. n. trenza

brain, n. cerebro; pl. sesos

brain·less, a. estúpido

brain·y, a. listo; inteligente

braise, v. dorar (carne) y cocer a fuego lento

brake, n. freno. v. frenar

bram·ble, n. zarza

bran, n. salvado

branch, n. rama; sección. v. ramificar

brand, n. tizón; marca. v. marcar

bran·dish, v. blandir

bran·dy, n. pl., -dies. coñac

brash, a. impetuoso

brass, n. latón. a. de latón

bras·siere, n. sostén

brass·y, a. descarado

brat, n. mocoso

bra·va·do, n. bravata

brave, a. valiente. v. desafiar

brav·er·y, n. pl., -ies. valor

bra·vo, int. ¡bravo!

brawl, v. alborotar. n. alboroto

brawn, n. fuerza muscular

brawn·y, a. musculoso

bray, v. rebuznar. n. rebuzno

bra·zen, a. descarado

breach, n. brecha; abertura. v. romper

bread, n. pan

breadth, n. anchura

break, v. romper; quebrar; domar. n. rompimiento; ruptura; interrupción

break·a·ble, a. frágil

break·age, n. fractura; rotura

break·down, n. parada; avería; crisis, f.; análisis, m.

break·fast, n. desayuno. v. desayunar(se)

break·wa·ter, n. rompeolas

breast, n. pecho; seno

breast·bone, n. esternón

breath, n. aliento

breathe, v. respirar

breath·ing, n. respiración

breath·less, a. sin aliento

breech, n. trasero; recámara

breech·es, n. pl. calzones

breed, v. criar; engendrar. n. casta

breeze, n. brisa

breth·ren, n. pl. of broth·er

brev·i·ty, n. brevedad

brew, v. hacer; urdir

brew·er·y, n. pl., -ies. cervecería

bribe, v. soborno. v. cohechar

brib·er·y, n. pl., -ies. cohecho

brick, n. ladrillo

brid·al, a. nupcial

bride, n. novia

bride·groom, n. novio

brides·maid, n. dama de honor

bridge, n. puente; juego de naipes. v. cruzar

bri·dle, n. brida. v. enfrenar

brief, *a.* breve. *n.* escrito. *v.* dar órdenes a
brief·ly, *adv.* en pocas palabras
bri·gade, *n.* brigada
bright, *a.* claro; brillante; listo
bright·en, *v.* abrillantar
bright·ness, *n.* lustre; agudeza
bril·liance, *n.* brillantez, *f.*
bril·liant, *a.* brillante
brim, *n.* borde
brim·stone, *n.* azufre
bring, *v.* traer
brink, *n.* borde; extremo
brisk, *a.* activo; vigoroso
bris·tle, *n.* cerda. *v.* erizar(se)
bris·tly, *a.* cerdoso
brit·tle, *a.* quebradizo
broach, *v.* introducir
broad, *a.* ancho; amplia; comprensivo
broad·cast, *v.* emitir. *n.* emisión
broad-mind·ed, *a.* tolerante
broad·side, *n.* andanada
bro·cade, *n.* brocado
broc·co·li, *n.* brécol, *m.*
bro·chure, *n.* folleto
broil, *v.* asar a la parrilla
bro·ken, *a.* quebrado; roto; accidentado
bro·ker, *n.* corredor
bro·ker·age, *n.* corretaje
bro·mide, *n.* bromuro
bron·chi·al, *a.* bronquial
bronze, *n.* bronce. *v.* broncear
brooch, *n.* broche; alfiler de pecho
brood, *n.* camada; progenie, *f. v.* empollar; ruminar
brook, *n.* arroyo
broom, *n.* escoba
broth, *n.* caldo
broth·el, *n.* burdel, *m.*
broth·er, *n. pl.,* broth·ers, breth·ren. hermano
broth·er·hood, *n.* hermandad; fraternidad
broth·er-in-law, *n. pl.,* broth·ers-in-law. cuñado
brow, *n.* ceja; frente, *f.*
brow·beat, *v.* intimidar
brown, *a.* moreno. *n.* color pardo
browse, *v.* rozar; hojear
bru·in, *n.* oso
bruise, *v.* magullar. *n.* contusión
bru·net, bru·nette, *a.* moreno. *n.* morena
brush, *n.* cepillo; brocha; maleza. *v.* (a)cepillar
brusque, brusk, *a.* áspero; brusco
bru·tal, *a.* brutal
bru·tal·i·ty, *n. pl.,* -ties. brutalidad
bru·tal·ize, *v.* embrutecer(se)
brute, *a., n.* bruto
bub·ble, *n.* burbuja. *v.* burbujear
buc·ca·neer, *n.* bucanero

buck, *n.* macho de algunos animales. *v.* corcovear
buck·et, *n.* cubo
buck·le, *n.* hebilla. *v.* hebillar; torcer
buck·shot, *n.* perdigón
buck·skin, *n.* piel de ante
buck·wheat, *n.* alforfón
bud, *n.* brote. *v.* brotar
bud·dy, bud·die, *n. pl.,* -dies. compañero
budge, *v.* mover(se)
budg·et, *n.* presupuesto. *v.* presupuestar
buff, *n.* ante. *v.* pulir
buf·fa·lo, *n. pl.,* -loes, -los. búfalo
buf·fet, *n.* bofetada. *v.* golpear
buf·fet, *n.* armario; aparador
buf·foon, *n.* bufón
bug, *n.* bicho. *v. inf.* fastidiar
bug·gy, *n. pl.,* -gies. calesín
bu·gle, *n.* clarín
bu·gler, *n.* corneta, *m.*
build, *v.* construir; hacer. *n.* forma
build·ing, *n.* construcción
bulb, *n.* bulbo; bombilla
bul·bous, *a.* bulboso
bulge, *n.* pandeo. *v.* pandearse
bulk, *n.* bulto
bulk·y, *a.* voluminoso
bull, *n.* toro
bul·let, *n.* bala
bul·le·tin, *n.* anuncio; boletín
bul·lion, *n.* oro o plata en barras
bull·ock, *n.* novillo
bull's-eye, *n.* centro del blanco
bul·ly, *n. pl.,* -lies. matón. *v.* intimidar
bul·rush, *n.* anea
bul·wark, *n.* baluarte
bum, *n.* vagabundo. *v.* holgazanear
bum·ble·bee, *n.* abejorro
bump, *v.* chocar; tropezar con. *n.* hinchazón; bollo; choque
bump·er, *n.* parachoques
bun, *n.* bollo
bunch, *n.* grupo; racimo. *v.* agrupar
bun·dle, *n.* lío. *v.* liar
bun·ga·low, *n.* casa de un solo piso
bun·gle, *v.* chapucear
bun·gler, *n.* chapucero
bun·ion, *n.* juanete
bunk, *n.* tarima
bun·ny, *n. pl.,* -nies. conejito
bun·ting, *n.* lanilla
bu·oy, *n.* boya. *v.* sobrenadar
buoy·ant, *a.* boyante
bur·den, *n.* carga; peso. *v.* cargar
bur·den·some, *a.* gravoso
bu·reau, *n. pl.,* bu·reaus, bu·reaux. escritorio; agencia
bu·reauc·ra·cy, *n. pl.,* -cies. burocracia
bu·reau·crat, *n.* burócrata, *m., f.*
bur·glar, *n.* ladrón

bur·glar·ize, v. robar

bur·gla·ry, n. pl., -ries. robo en una casa

bur·i·al, n. entierro

bur·lap, n. arpillera

bur·lesque, n. parodia. a. cómico. v. parodiar

bur·ly, a. membrudo

burn, v. quemar; incendiar. n. quemadura

burn·ing, a. ardiente

bur·nish, n. brillo. v. bruñir

burnt, a. quemado

bur·ro, n. pl., -ros. burro

bur·row, n. madriguera. v. amadrigar

burst, v. reventar; romper. n. reventón; estallido

bur·y, v. enterrar

bus, n. pl., bus·es, bus·ses. autobús

bush, n. arbusto

bush·el, n. medida de áridos

bush·y, a. espeso

busi·ness, n. comercio; oficio; asunto; empresa

bust, n. pecho; busto

bus·tle, v. apresurarse. n. bullicio; polizón

bus·y, a. ocupado; lleno de movimiento. v. ocupar(se)

bus·y·bod·y, n. pl., -ies. entrometido

but, conj. pero; sino; sólo. prep. excepto

butch·er, n. carnicero. v. matar

but·ler, n. mayordomo

butt, n. cabo; blanco. v. topetar

but·ter, n. mantequilla. v. untar con mantequilla

but·ter·fly, n. pl., -flies. mariposa

but·ter·milk, n. leche de manteca

but·ter·y, a. mantecoso

but·tocks, n. pl. nalgas

but·ton, n. botón. v. abotonar

but·tress, n. contrafuerte. v. apoyar

bux·om, a. frescachón

buy, v. comprar. n. compra

buy·er, n. comprador

buzz, v. zumbar; llamar. n. zumbido

buzz·er, n. zumbador

by, prep. por; cerca de; según. adv. cerca

by·gone, a. pasado. n. pl. lo pasado

by·law, n. reglamento

by·prod·uct, n. derivado; producto secundario

by·stand·er, n. espectador

by·way, n. camino apartado

by·word, n. dicho

C

cab, n. taxi, m.; casilla

ca·bal, n. cábala. v. tramar

cab·a·ret, n. cabaret, m.

cab·bage, n. col, f.

cab·by, n. pl., -bies. inf. taxista, m. f.

cab·in, n. cabaña; camarote

cab·i·net, n. vitrina; gabinete

ca·ble, n. cable; cablegrama, m. v. cablegrafiar

ca·ble·gram, n. cablegrama, m.

ca·boose, n. furgón de cola

cache, n. escondite. v. ocultar

cack·le, v. cacarear. n. cacareo

ca·coph·o·ny, n. pl., -nies. cacofonía

cac·tus, n. pl., -tus·es, -ti. cacto

cad, n. persona mal educada

ca·dav·er, n. cadáver

ca·dav·er·ous, a. cadavérico

cad·dish, a. desvergonzado

ca·dence, n. cadencia; ritmo

ca·det, n. cadete

ca·fe, ca·fé, n. café

caf·e·te·ri·a, n. cafetería

caf·feine, n. cafeína

cage, n. jaula. v. enjaular

ca·jole, v. halagar

ca·jol·er·y, n. pl., -ries. halago

cake, n. tarta; pastel, m.; pastilla. v. endurecer

ca·la·boose, n. inf. cárcel, f.

ca·lam·i·tous, a. calamitoso

ca·lam·i·ty, n. pl., -ties. calamidad

cal·ci·fi·ca·tion, n. calcificación

cal·ci·fy, v. calcificar

cal·ci·um, n. calcio

cal·cu·late, v. calcular

cal·cu·lat·ed, a. calculado; intencionado

cal·cu·lat·ing, a. intrigante

cal·cu·la·tion, n. cálculo

cal·cu·lus, n. pl., -li, -lus·es. cálculo

cal·dron, n. caldera

cal·en·dar, n. calendario

calf, n. pl., calves. becerro; ternero pantorrilla

cal·i·ber, cal·i·bre, n. calibre; capacidad

cal·i·brate, v. calibrar

cal·i·bra·tion, n. calibración

cal·i·co, n. pl., -coes, -cos. calicó

ca·liph, ca·lif, n. califa, m.

cal·i·phate, cal·if·ate, n. califato

cal·is·then·ics, n. calistenia

call, v. llamar; nombrar; dar voces. n. llamada; visita

call·ing, n. vocación

cal·lous, a. insensible

cal·low, a. inexperto

cal·lus, n. pl., -lus·es. callo

calm, n. calma. a. tranquilo. v. calmar(se)

ca·lor·ic, a. calórico

cal·o·rie, n. pl., -ries. caloría

ca·lum·ni·ate, v. calumniar

cal·um·ny, n. pl., -nies. calumnia

ca·lyp·so, n. pl., -sos. calipso

ca·lyx, *n. pl.* **ca·lyx·es, cal·y·ces.**
cáliz

cam, *n.* leva

cam·el, *n.* camello

ca·mel·lia, *n.* camelia

cam·e·o, *n.* camafeo

cam·er·a, *n.* máquina fotográfica; cámara

cam·ou·flage, *n.* camuflaje. *v.* camuflar

camp, *n.* campamento. *v.* acampar

cam·paign, *n.* campaña. *v.* servir en campaña

cam·paign·er, *n.* veterano; partidario

camp·er, *n.* campista, *m., f.*

cam·pus, *n. pl.* **-pus·es.** recinto

can, *aux. v.* **could.** poder

can, *n.* lata. *v.* conservar en latas

ca·nal, *n.* canal, *m.*

ca·nar·y, *n.* canario

can·cel, *v.* cancelar; anular

can·cel·la·tion, *n.* cancelación

can·cer, *n.* cáncer

can·de·la·brum, *n. pl.* **-bra, -brums.**
candelabro

can·did, *a.* franco

can·di·da·cy, *n. pl.* **-cies.** candidato

can·di·date, *n.* aspirante; candidato

can·dle, *n.* candela; vela

can·dor, *n.* franqueza

can·dy, *n. pl.* **-dies.** dulce; azúcar cande o candi. *v.* garapiñar

cane, *n.* caña; bastón

ca·nine, *a.* canino. *n.* perro

can·is·ter, *n.* bote

can·ker, *n.* llaga gangrenosa

can·na·bis, *n.* marijuana

can·ner·y, *n. pl.* **-ies.** fábrica de conservas

can·ni·bal, *n.* caníbal, *m., f.*

can·ni·bal·ism, *n.* canibalismo

can·non, *n. pl.* **can·nons, can·non.**
cañón

can·ny, *a.* prudente; astuto

ca·noe, *n.* canoa. *v.* ir en canoa

can·on, *n.* canon

ca·non·i·za·tion, *n.* canonización

can·on·ize, *v.* canonizar

can·o·py, *n. pl.* **-pies.** dosel; baldaquín

cant, *n.* hipocresía; jerga; sesgo

can·ta·loup, can·ta·loupe, can·ta·lope, *n.* cantalupo

can·tan·ker·ous, *a.* malhumorado

can·teen, *n.* cantina; cantimplora

can·ter, *n.* medio galope

can·vas, *n.* lona; tela; lienzo

can·vass, *v.* solicitar; discutir. *n.* sondeo

can·vass·er, *n.* solicitador

can·yon, *n.* cañón

cap, *n.* gorra; tapa. *v.* poner tapa; superar

ca·pa·bil·i·ty, *n. pl.* **-ties.** capacidad

ca·pa·ble, *a.* capaz

ca·pac·i·ty, *n. pl.* **-ties.** capacidad

cape, *n.* cabo; capa

ca·per, *n.* cabriola; travesura. *v.* brincar

cap·il·lar·y, *n. pl.* **-ies.** vaso capilar.
a. capilar

cap·i·tal, *a.* capital; principal. *n.*
capital, *m., f.;* mayúscula

cap·i·tal·ism, *n.* capitalismo

cap·i·tal·ist, *n.* capitalista, *m., f.*

cap·i·tal·is·tic, *a.* capitalista

cap·i·tal·ize, *v.* capitalizar

cap·i·tol, *n.* capitolio

ca·pit·u·late, *v.* capitular

ca·price, *n.* capricho

ca·pri·cious, *a.* caprichoso

cap·size, *v.* volcar

cap·sule, *n.* cápsula

cap·tain, *n.* capitán. *v.* capitanear

cap·tion, *n.* encabezamiento; título

cap·ti·vate, *v.* cautivar

cap·ti·va·tion, *n.* encanto

cap·tive, *a., n.* cautivo

cap·tiv·i·ty, *n. pl.* **-ties.** cautiverio

cap·tor, *n.* apresador

cap·ture, *v.* apresar; capturar

car, *n.* automóvil; coche

car·a·mel, *n.* caramelo

car·at, *n.* quilate

car·a·van, *n.* caravana; remolque

car·a·way, *n.* alcaravea

car·bine, *n.* carabina. Also **car·a·bine**

car·bon, *n.* carbono

car·bo·nate, *n.* carbonato

car·bon di·ox·ide, *n.* bióxido de carbono

car·bon mon·ox·ide, *n.* monóxido de carbono

car·bon pa·per, *n.* papel carbón

car·bun·cle, *n.* carbunco

car·bu·re·tor, *n.* carburador

car·cass, car·case, *n.* res muerta

car·ci·no·ma, *n. pl.* **-mas, -ma·ta.**
carcinoma, *m.*

card, *n.* tarjeta; carta; *pl.* naipes

card·board, *n.* cartón

car·di·ac, *a.* cardiaco, cardíaco

car·di·gan, *n.* jersey; rebeca

car·di·nal, *n.* cardenal, *m. a.* cardinal

care, *v.* cuidar; importar. *n.* cuidado; solicitud; cargo

ca·reer, *n.* carrera

care·free, *a.* despreocupado

care·ful, *a.* cuidadoso; vigilante

care·less, *a.* descuidado

care·tak·er, *n.* vigilante; guardián

car·go, *n. pl.* **-goes, -gos.** cargamento

car·i·bou, *n. pl.* **-bous, -bou.** caribú, *m.*

car·i·ca·ture, *n.* caricatura. *v.*

parodiar

car·il·lon, *n.* carillón

car·nage, *n.* carnicería

car·nal, *a.* carnal

car·nal·i·ty, *n.* carnalidad

car·na·tion, *n.* clavel, *m.*

car·ni·val, *n.* carnaval, *m.*

car·niv·o·rous, *a.* carnívoro

car·ol, *n.* villancico

ca·rouse, *n.* jarana. *v.* jaranear

ca·rous·er, *n.* jaranero

carp, *n. pl.,* **carp, carps.** carpa. *v.* criticar

car·pen·ter, *n.* carpintero

car·pen·try, *n.* carpintería

car·pet, *n.* alfombra. *v.* alfombrar

car·riage, *n.* porte; carruaje; vagón

car·ri·er, *n.* portador; carrero

car·ri·on, *n.* carroña

car·rot, *n.* zanahoria

car·ry, *v.* llevar; tener consigo; transportar; lograr

cart, *n.* carro. *v.* acarrear

cart·age, *n.* carretaje; acarreo

car·ti·lage, *n.* cartílago

car·tog·ra·pher, *n.* cartógrafo

car·tog·ra·phy, *n.* cartografía

car·ton, *n.* caja de cartón

car·toon, *n.* dibujo cómico

car·toon·ist, *n.* dibujante, *m., f.*

car·tridge, *n.* cartucho

carve, *v.* esculpir; trinchar

cas·cade, *n.* cascada

case, *n.* caso; caja; estuche. *v.* encajonar

cash, *n.* dinero contante. *v.* cobrar

cash·ew, *n.* anacardo

cash·ier, *n.* cajero

cash·mere, *n.* casimir

cas·ing, *n.* cubierta; envoltura

ca·si·no, *n. pl.,* **-nos.** casino

cask, *n.* barril, *m.;* tonel, *m.*

cas·ket, *n.* cajita; ataúd, *m.*

cas·se·role, *n.* cacerola

cas·sock, *n.* sotana

cast, *v.* echar; tirar; repartir; fundir. *n.* reparto; molde; echada; casta

cas·ta·nets, *n. pl.* castañuelas

caste, *n.* casta

cast·er, *n.* rodaja

cas·ti·gate, *v.* castigar

cas·ti·ga·tion, *n.* castigo

cas·ti·ga·tor, *n.* castigador

cast i·ron, *n.* hierro fundido

cast-i·ron, *a.* de hierro fundido; inflexible

cas·tle, *n.* castillo; (*chess*) torre, *f.*

cast-off, *a.* de desecho. *n.* cosa desechada

cas·tor, *n.* castóreo

cas·trate, *v.* castrar

cas·tra·tion, *n.* castración

cas·u·al, *a.* fortuito; despreocupado

cas·u·al·ly, *adv.* casualmente

cas·u·al·ty, *n. pl.,* **-ties.** accidente; víctima; baja

cat, *n.* gato

cat·a·clysm, *n.* cataclismo

cat·a·comb, *n. usu. pl* catacumbas

cat·a·log, cat·a·logue, *n.* catálogo. *v.* catalogar

cat·a·lyst, *n.* catalizador

cat·a·pult, *n.* catapulta. *v.* catapultar

cat·a·ract, *n.* catarata

ca·tarrh, *n.* catarro

ca·tas·tro·phe, *n.* catástrofe, *f.*

cat·as·troph·ic, *a.* catastrófico

catch, *v.* coger; prender; enganchar. *n.* cogida; captura; trampa

catch·ing, *n.* contagioso

cat·e·chism, *n.* catequismo

cat·e·gor·i·cal, *a.* categórico

cat·e·gor·i·cal·ly, *adv.* categóricamente

cat·e·gor·ize, *v.* clasificar

cat·e·go·ry, *n. pl.,* **-ries.** categoría

ca·ter, *v.* atender; proveer

ca·ter·er, *n.* abastecedor

cat·er·pil·lar, *n.* oruga

cat·gut, *n.* cuerda de tripa

ca·thar·sis, *n. pl.,* **-ses.** catarsis, *f.*

ca·thar·tic, *a., n.* catártico; purgante

ca·the·dral, *n.* catedral, *f.*

cath·o·lic, *a.* católico. *n.* (*cap.*) católico

ca·thol·i·cism, *n.* catolicismo

cat·kin, *n.* amento

cat·nap, *n.* duermevela. *v.* dormitar

cat·sup, *n.* salsa picante de tomate

cat·tle, *n.* ganado

cat·tle·man, *n. pl.,* **-men.** ganadero

cat·ty, *a.* rencoroso

cau·cus, *n. pl.,* **-cus·es.** reunión de partido

caul·dron, cal·dron, *n.* caldera

cau·li·flow·er, *n.* coliflor, *f.*

caulk, calk, *v.* calafatear

cause, *n.* causa; razón; interés, *m. v.* causar

cause·way, *n.* calzada

caus·tic, *a., n.* cáustico

cau·ter·ize, *v.* cauterizar

cau·tion, *n.* cautela; prudencia. *v.* advertir; amonestar

cau·tious, *a.* cauteloso

cav·al·cade, *n.* cabalgata

cav·a·lier, *n.* caballero. *a.* desdeñoso

cav·al·ry, *n. pl.,* **-ries.** caballería

cav·al·ry·man, *n. pl.,* **-men.** soldado de caballería

cave, *n.* cueva. *v.* hundirse

cav·ern, *n.* caverna

cav·ern·ous, *a.* cavernoso

cav·i·ar, cav·i·are, *n.* caviar

cav·il, *v.* sutilizar

cav·i·ty, *n. pl.,* **-ties.** cavidad; hoyo

ca·vort, *v. inf.* hacer cabriolas

cay·enne, *n.* pimentón

cease, *v.* cesar; dejar de; suspender

cease-fire, *n.* alto el fuego; tregua

cease·less, *a.* incesante

ce·dar, *n.* cedro

cede, *v.* ceder

ceil·ing, *n.* techo; límite

cel·e·brate, *v.* celebrar; solemnizar

cel·e·brat·ed, *a.* célebre

cel·e·bra·tion, *n.* celebración; fiesta

ce·leb·ri·ty, *n. pl.,* -ties. celebridad

ce·ler·i·ty, *n.* celeridad

cel·er·y, *n.* apio

ce·les·tial, *a.* celestial

cel·i·ba·cy, *n.* celibato

cel·i·bate, *n., a.* celibato; célibe

cell, *n.* celda; célula

cel·lar, *n.* sótano

cel·list, *n.* violoncelista, violon-chelista, *m., f.*

cel·lo, 'cel·lo, *n. pl.,* -los. violoncelo, violonchelo

cel·lo·phane, *n.* celofán

cel·lu·lar, *a.* celular

cel·lu·lose, *n.* celulosa

ce·ment, *n.* cemento. *v.* cementar

cem·e·ter·y, *n. pl.,* -ies. cementerio

cen·sor, *n.* censor. *v.* censurar

cen·sor·ship, *n.* censura

cen·sur·a·ble, *a.* censurable

cen·sure, *n.* censura; crítica. *v.* censurar; culpar

cen·sus, *n. pl.,* -sus·es. censo

cent, *n.* centavo

cen·taur, *n.* centauro

cen·ten·ni·al, *a., n.* centenario

cen·ter, *n.* centro. *v.* centrar; concentrar

cen·ti·grade, *a.* centígrado. Also Cel·sius

cen·ti·me·ter, *n.* centímetro

cen·tral, *a.* central; céntrico

cen·tral·ize, *v.* centralizar

cen·tu·ri·on, *n.* centurión

cen·tu·ry, *n. pl.,* -ries. siglo

ce·ram·ic, *a.* cerámico

ce·ram·ics, *n.* cerámica

ce·re·al, *n.* cereal, *m.;* grano

cer·e·bral, *a.* cerebral

cer·e·mo·ni·al, *a., n.* ceremonial

cer·e·mo·ni·ous, *a.* ceremonioso

cer·e·mo·ny, *n. pl.,* -nies. ceremonia

ce·rise, *n., a.* color de cereza

cer·tain, *a.* cierto; seguro

cer·tain·ly, *adv.* ciertamente; desde luego

cer·tain·ty, *n. pl.,* -ties. certidumbre, *f.*

cer·ti·fi·a·ble, *a.* certificable

cer·tif·i·cate, *n.* certificado; testimonio; partida

cer·ti·fy, *v.* certificar

cer·ti·tude, *n.* certidumbre, *f.;* certeza

ces·sa·tion, *n.* cesación; cese

ces·sion, *n.* cesión

chafe, *v.* frotar; rozar; irritar

chaff, *n.* ahechadura. *v.* tomar el pelo a

cha·grin, *n.* mortificación. *v.* disgustar

chain, *n.* cadena. *v.* encadenar

chair, *n.* silla

chair·man, *n. pl.,* -men. presidente

chal·et, *n.* chalet, *m.*

chal·ice, *n.* cáliz, *m.*

chalk, *n.* tiza; creta

chal·lenge, *n.* desafío; demanda; recusación. *v.* desafiar; recusar

cham·ber, *n.* cuarto; cámara; recámara

cham·ber·maid, *n.* camarera

cha·me·le·on, *n.* camaleón

cham·ois, *n. pl.,* cham·ois. gamuza

cham·pagne, *n.* champán, champaña

cham·pi·on, *n.* campeón; paladín

chance, *n.* suerte; casualidad; riesgo. *v.* acontecer; probar

chan·cel·lor, *n.* canciller

chan·de·lier, *n.* araña de luces

change, *v.* cambiar; trocar; transformar. *n.* cambio

chan·nel, *n.* canal, *m.;* cauce

chant, *v.* cantar. *n.* canto llano

chan·ti·cleer, *n.* gallo

cha·os, *n.* caos, *m.*

cha·ot·ic, *a.* caótico

chap, *v.* agrietar(se). *n.* grieta

chap, *n.* tio; mozo

chap·el, *n.* capilla

chap·er·on, chap·er·one, *n.* carabina; dueña

chap·lain, *n.* capellán

chap·ter, *n.* capítulo

char, *v.* carbonizar

char·ac·ter, *n.* carácter; personaje

char·ac·ter·is·tic, *a.* característico. *n.* característica

char·ac·ter·i·za·tion, *n.* caracterización

char·ac·ter·ize, *v.* caracterizar

cha·rade, *n.* charada

char·coal, *n.* carbón vegetal

charge, *v.* cargar; imponer; acusar; pedir; atacar. *n.* carga; cargo; acusación

char·i·ot, *n.* carroza; carro

char·i·ot·eer, *n.* auriga, *m.*

char·i·ta·ble, *a.* caritativo

char·i·ty, *n. pl.,* -ties. caridad

char·la·tan, *n.* charlatán

charm, *n.* encanto; hechizo; amuleto. *v.* encantar; hechizar

chart, *n.* gráfico; carta de navegar. *v.* poner en una carta

char·ter, *n.* cédula; carta. *v.* estatuir; alquilar

chase, *v.* cazar; perseguir. *n.* persecución

chasm, *n.* sima
chas·sis, *n.* chasis
chaste, *a.* casto
chaste·ly, *adv.* castamente
chas·tise, *v.* castigar
chas·tise·ment, *n.* castigo
chas·ti·ty, *n.* castidad
chat, *v.* charlar. *n.* charla
chat·tel, *n.* enseres, *m.*
chat·ter, *v.* charlar; castañetear. *v.* cháchara
chauf·feur, *n.* chófer
cheap, *a.* barato; cursi. *adv.* barato
cheap·en, *v.* abaratar
cheap·ly, *adv.* barato
cheat, *v.* defraudar; engañar. *n.* trampa; petardista, *m., f.*
check, *n.* parada; impedimento; cheque; cuenta; marca; cuadro. *v.* parar; examinar
check·mate, *n.* mate; derrota. *v.* dar jaque mate
cheek, *n.* mejilla
cheek·y, *a.* descarado
cheer, *n.* alegría; aplauso. *v.* alegrar; aplaudir
cheer·ful, *a.* alegre
cheer·less, *a.* triste
cheese, *n.* queso
chef, *n.* cocinero
chem·i·cal, *n.* químico
chem·ist, *n.* químico
chem·is·try, *n.* química
cher·ish, *v.* querer; cuidar
cher·ry, *n. pl.,* **-ries.** cereza; cerezo
cher·ub, *n. pl.,* **-ubs, -u·bim.** querubín
chess, *n.* ajedrez, *m.*
chess·man, *n. pl.,* **-men.** pieza
chest, *n.* pecho; cofre
chew, *v.* mascar
chic, *a.* elegante
chi·can·er·y, *n. pl.,* **-ies.** sofistería; sofismas, *m. pl.*
chick, *n.* polluelo
chick·en, *n.* pollo; gallina
chic·o·ry, *n. pl.,* **-ries.** achicoria
chide, *v.* reprobar; reprender
chief, *a.* principal. *n.* jefe; cacique
chief·tain, *n.* cacique
chif·fon, *n.* gasa
chil·blain, *n.* sabañón
child, *n. pl.,* **chil·dren.** niño; hijo
child·hood, *n.* niñez
child·ish, *a.* infantil; aniñado
chil·i, *chil·li, chil·e,** *n. pl.,* **-ies, -lies, -es.** chile
chill, *n.* frío; escalofrío. *v.* enfriar
chill·y, *a.* frío
chime, *n.* juego de campanas. *v.* repicar
chi·me·ra, chi·mae·ra, *n.* quimera
chi·mer·ic, *a.* quimérico

chim·ney, *n.* chimenea
chim·pan·zee, *n.* chimpancé. Also **chimp**
chin, *n.* barba
chi·na, *n.* porcelana; china
chin·chil·la, *n.* chinchilla
chink, *n.* grieta. *v.* hender(se); sonar
chintz·y, *a.* barato
chip, *v.* picar; astillar. *n.* astilla
chi·rop·o·dist, *n.* pedicuro
chirp, *n.* gorjeo. *v.* piar; chirriar
chis·el, *n.* cincel, *m.;* formón. *v.* escoplear; timar
chiv·al·rous, *a.* caballeroso
chiv·al·ry, *n. pl.,* **-ries.** caballerosidad
chlo·rine, *n.* cloro
chlo·ro·phyll, chlo·ro·phyl, *n.* clorofila
choc·o·late, *n.* chocolate
choice, *n.* selección; preferencia. *a.* selecto
choir, *n.* coro
choke, *v.* estrangular; sofocar; obstruir
chol·er, *n.* cólera
chol·er·a, *n.* cólera
chol·er·ic, *a.* colérico
choose, *v.* escoger; elegir
chop, *v.* cortar; picar. *n.* chuleta
chop·py, *a.* picado
cho·ral, *a.* coral
cho·rale, *n.* coral, *m.*
chord, *n.* acorde
cho·re·og·ra·pher, *n.* coreógrafo
cho·re·og·ra·phy, *n.* coreografía
chor·is·ter, *n.* corista, *m., f.*
chor·tle, *v.* reírse entre dientes. *n.* risita
cho·rus, *n. pl.,* **-rus·es.** coro; estribillo
cho·sen, *a.* escogido; preferido
chow·der, *n.* sopa de pescado
Christ, *n.* Cristo
chris·ten, *v.* bautizar
Chris·ten·dom, *n.* cristiandad
chris·ten·ing, *n.* bautismo
Chris·tian, *n., a.* cristiano
Chris·ti·an·i·ty, *n. pl.,* **-ties.** cristianismo
Christ·mas, *n.* Navidad
chro·mat·ic, *a.* cromático
chrome, *n.* cromo
chro·mo·some, *n.* cromosoma, *m.*
chron·ic, *a.* crónico
chron·i·cle, *n.* crónica. *v.* historiar
chron·i·cler, *n.* cronista, *m., f.*
chron·o·log·i·cal, *a.* cronológico
chro·nol·o·gy, *n. pl.,* **-gies.** cronología
chro·nom·e·ter, *n.* cronómetro
chrys·a·lis, *n. pl.,* **-lis·es, chry·sal·i·des.** crisálida
chry·san·the·mum, *n.* crisantemo

chub·by, a. regordete; rechoncho
chuck, v. dar la mamola; arrojar
chuck·le, v. reír entre dientes
chum, n. compinche
chum·my, a. íntimo
chump, n. tonto
chunk, n. pedazo grueso
church, n. iglesia
churl·ish, a. grosero; rudo
churn, n. mantequera. v. batir; agitar
chute, n. tolva
ci·der, n. sidra
ci·gar, n. puro
cig·a·rette, cig·a·ret, n. cigarrillo; pitillo
cinch, n. cincha
cin·der, n. carbonilla; pl. cenizas
cin·e·ma, n. pl., -mas. cine
cin·na·mon, n. canela
ci·pher, n. cero; cifra. v. cifrar
cir·cle, n. círculo; ciclo. v. rodear; dar vueltas
cir·cuit, n. gira; circuito
cir·cu·lar, a., n. circular
cir·cu·late, v. hacer circular; divulgar; esparcir; circular
cir·cu·la·tion, n. circulación
cir·cum·cise, v. circuncidar
cir·cum·ci·sion, n. circuncisión
cir·cum·fer·ence, n. circunferencia
cir·cum·lo·cu·tion, n. circunlocución
cir·cum·nav·i·gate, v. circunnavegar
cir·cum·scribe, v. circunscribir; limitar
cir·cum·spect, a. circunspecto
cir·cum·stance, n. circunstancia; pl. situación económica
cir·cum·stan·tial, a. circunstanciado; secundario
cir·cus, n. pl., -cus·es. circo
cir·rho·sis, n. cirrosis, f.
cir·rus, n. pl., -ri. cirro
cis·tern, n. tanque; cisterna
cit·a·del, n. ciudadela
ci·ta·tion, n. cita; citación
cite, v. citar
cit·i·zen, n. ciudadano
cit·i·zen·ry, n. pl., -ries. ciudadanos
cit·ric ac·id, n. ácido cítrico
cit·y, n. pl., -ties. ciudad
civ·ic, a. cívico
civ·il, a. civil; cortés
ci·vil·ian, a. civil. n. civil, m., f.
ci·vil·i·ty, n. pl., -ties. cortesía; civilidad
civ·i·li·za·tion, n. civilización
civ·i·lize, v. civilizar
civ·il war, n. guerra civil
clad, a. vestido
claim, v. reclamar; demandar. n. demanda; reclamación
claim·ant, n. demandante, m., f.
clair·voy·ance, n. clarividencia

clair·voy·ant, a. vidente, m., f.
clam, n. almeja
clam·or, n. clamor. v. vociferar
clam·or·ous, a. clamoroso
clamp, n. abrazadera; grapa. v. sujetar; juntar
clan, n. clan
clan·des·tine, a. clandestino
clang, n. sonido metálico. v. hacer sonar
clap, v. aplaudir; batir. n. palmada; palmoteo
clar·et, n. clarete
clar·i·fi·ca·tion, n. clarificación; aclaración
clar·i·fy, v. clarificar; aclarar
clar·i·net, n. clarinete
clar·i·ty, n. claridad
clash, n. choque; batir. n. fragor; choque; conflicto
clasp, n. broche; corchete; abrazo. v. abrochar; abrazar
class, n. clase, f. v. clasificar
clas·sic, a. clásico. n. autor clásico; pl. obras clásicas
clas·si·cal, a. clásico
clas·si·fi·ca·tion, n. clasificación
clas·si·fied, a. secreto
clas·si·fy, v. clasificar
clat·ter, v. hacer ruido. n. ruido; martilleo
clause, n. cláusula
claw, n. garra; uña. v. desgarrar
clay, n. arcilla; barro
clean, a. limpio; neto. v. limpiar
clean·li·ness, n. limpieza
clean·ly, a. aseado
cleanse, v. limpiar; purificar
clear, a. claro; transparente; inocente; despejado. v. aclarar; despejar; absolver
clear·ance, n. despacho de aduana; espacio muerto
clear·ing, n. claro
clear·ly, adv. claramente
clear·ness, n. claridad
cleave, v. hender; partir; pegarse; adherir
clef, n. clave, f.
cleft, n. hendedura
clem·en·cy, n. clemencia
clem·ent, a. clemente; piadoso
clench, v. apretar
cler·gy, n. pl., -gies. clero
cler·i·cal, a. clerical; de oficina
clerk, n. oficinista, m., f.; dependiente
clev·er, a. listo; ingenioso
clev·er·ness, n. destreza
click, n. golpe seco. v. chasquear
cli·ent, n. cliente, m., f.
cliff, n. risco
cli·mate, n. clima, m.
cli·max, n. clímax, m.; colmo

climb, v. trepar

clinch, v. afianzar; agarrar

cling, v. adherirse

clin·ic, n. clínica

clin·i·cal, a. clínico

clip, v. cortar; acortar. n. tijeretada; golpe

clique, n. pandilla

cloak, n. capa; manto. v. encapotar; encubrir

clock, n. reloj, m.

clock·wise, adv., a. en la dirección de las agujas o manecillas del reloj

clog, v. impedir; atascar. n. obstáculo; zueco

clois·ter, n. claustro. v. enclaustrar

close, v. cerrar; terminar. n. fin

close, a. sofocante; cercano; denso. adv. cerca

close·ness, n. proximidad; reserva; intimidad

clos·et, n. armario. v. estar encerrado con; deliberar en secreto

clot, n. grumo. v. cuajarse

cloth, n. pl., cloths. tela; paño

clothe, v. vestir

clothes, n. pl. ropa

cloth·ing, n. vestidos; ropa

cloud, n. nube, f. v. anublar(se); nublar

cloud·i·ness, n. nubosidad

cloud·y, a. nuboso

clove, n. clavo de especia; diente (de ajo)

clo·ver, n. trébol, m.

clown, n. payaso. v. hacer el payaso

cloy, v. empalagar

club, n. porra; club; pl. bastos. v. aporrear

cluck, v. cloquear

clue, n. pista; indicio

clum·si·ness, n. torpeza

clum·sy, a. torpe; pesado

clus·ter, n. racimo. v. agruparse

clutch, v. agarrar; apretar. n. agarro; embrague

clut·ter, n. desorden. v. atestar

coach, n. coche; carroza; vagón; entrenador. v. preparar

co·ag·u·late, v. coagular(se)

co·ag·u·la·tion, n. coagulación

coal, n. carbón

co·a·lesce, v. unir(se)

co·a·les·cence, n. fusión

co·a·li·tion, n. coalición; alianza

coarse, a. basto; tosco; grosero

coars·en, v. curtir(se)

coast, n. costa. v. ir en punto muerto

coast·line, n. litoral, m.

coat, n. abrigo; pelo; mano, f. v. cubrir

coat·ing, n. capa

coax, v. engatusar

cob, n. mazorca de maíz; jaca

co·balt, n. cobalto

cob·ble, v. remendar

cob·bler, n. zapatero

co·bra, n. cobra

cob·web, n. telaraña

co·caine, n. cocaína

cock, n. gallo; grifo. v. amartillar

cock·a·too, n. pl., -toos. cacatúa

cock·roach, n. cucaracha

cock·tail, n. coctel, m.

cock·y, a. engreído

co·coa, n. cacao; chocolate

co·co·nut, co·coa·nut, n. coco

co·coon, n. capullo

cod, n. pl. cod, cods. bacalao

cod·dle, v. mimar

code, n. código; cifra. v. cifrar

cod·fish, n. bacalao

cod·i·fy, v. codificar

co·ed, n. alumna de una escuela coeducacional

co·ed·u·ca·tion, n. coeducación

co·erce, v. forzar; coercer

co·er·cion, n. coerción; compulsión

co·er·cive, a. coactivo

cof·fee, n. café

cof·fin, n. ataúd, m.

cog, n. diente de rueda

co·gen·cy, n. fuerza

co·gent, a. convincente

cog·i·tate, v. meditar

cog·nac, n. coñac, m.

cog·ni·zance, n. conocimiento

co·here, v. adherirse

co·her·ence, n. coherencia

co·her·ent, a. coherente; lógico

co·he·sive, a. cohesivo

co·hort, n. cohorte, f.

coif·fure, n. peinado

coil, n. carrete; rollo; adujada. v. arrollar

coin, n. moneda. v. acuñar

coin·age, n. acuñación; invención

co·in·cide, v. coincidir

co·in·ci·dence, n. coincidencia; casualidad

co·in·ci·den·tal, a. coincidente

co·i·tus, n. coito

coke, n. coque

cold, a. frío. n. frío; resfriado

cold-blood·ed, a. de sangre fría

cold·ness, n. frialdad

cole·slaw, n. ensalada de col

col·ic, n. cólico

col·i·se·um, n. coliseo

col·lab·o·rate, v. colaborar

col·lab·o·ra·tion, n. colaboración

col·lapse, v. hundirse. n. derrumbamiento; colapso

col·lar, n. cuello

col·lat·er·al, a. colateral. n. resguardo

col·league, n. colega, m., f.

col·lect, v. recaudar; reunir; colec-

cionar; recoger
col·lec·tion, *n.* colección; cobro
col·lec·tive, *a.* colectivo
col·lege, *n.* colegio
col·le·gi·ate, *a.* colegiado
col·lide, *v.* chocar
col·li·sion, *n.* choque
col·lo·qui·al, *a.* familiar
col·lo·qui·al·ism, *n.* expresión familiar
col·lu·sion, *n.* colusión; confabulación
co·lon, *n. pl.,* -lons, -la. colon; dos puntos
colo·nel, *n.* coronel
co·lo·ni·al, *a.* colonial
col·o·nist, *n.* colonizador
col·o·ni·za·tion, *n.* colonización
col·on·nade, *n.* columnata
col·o·ny, *n. pl.,* -nies. colonia
col·or, *n.* color; *usu. pl* bandera. *v.* colorear; teñir
col·or·ful, *a.* lleno de color
co·los·sal, *a.* colosal
co·los·sus, *n. pl.,* -si, -sus·es. coloso
colt, *n.* potro
col·umn, *n.* columna
col·umn·ist, *n.* columnista, *m., f.*
co·ma, *n. pl.,* -mas. coma, *m.*
co·ma·tose, *a.* comatoso
comb, *n.* peine. *v.* peinar
com·bat, *v.* combatir. *n.* combate
com·bat·ant, *a., n.* combatiente
com·bi·na·tion, *n.* combinación
com·bine, *v.* combinar; reunir. *n.* asociación
com·bus·ti·ble, *a.* combustible
com·bus·tion, *n.* combustión
come, *v.* venir; aparecer; llegar
co·me·di·an, *n.* cómico
co·me·di·enne, *n.* cómica
com·e·dy, *n. pl.,* -dies. comedia
come·ly, *a.* gentil
com·et, *n.* cometa, *m.*
com·fort, *v.* confortar; consolar. *n.* consuelo
com·fort·a·ble, *a.* cómodo
com·fort·er, *n.* colcha
com·fy, *a. inf.* cómodo
com·ic, *a., n.* cómico
com·i·cal, *a.* cómico
com·ic strip, *n.* tebeo
com·ma, *n. pl.,* -mas. coma
com·mand, *v.* mandar; comandar. *n.* mando; orden
com·man·deer, *v.* requisar
com·mand·er, *n.* comandante
com·mand·ment, *n.* mandamiento; mandato
com·mem·o·rate, *v.* conmemorar
com·mem·o·ra·tion, *n.* conmemoración
com·mence, *v.* comenzar
com·mence·ment, *n.* comienzo;

graduación
com·mend, *v.* alabar; encomendar
com·men·da·tion, *n.* encomio
com·ment, *v.* comentar. *n.* observación
com·men·tar·y, *n. pl.,* -ies. comentario
com·men·ta·tor, *n.* comentador
com·merce, *n.* comercio
com·mer·cial, *a.* comercial
com·mis·sar·y, *n. pl.,* -ies. comisario
com·mis·sion, *n.* comisión; perpetración. *v.* nombrar; encargar
com·mis·sion·er, *n.* comisario; apoderado
com·mit, *v.* cometer; entregar
com·mit·ment, *n.* compromiso
com·mit·tee, *n.* comité
com·mod·i·ty, *n. pl.,* -ties. mercadería
com·mon, *a.* común; corriente; vulgar
com·mon·place, *n.* lugar común. *a.* trivial
com·mon·wealth, *n.* república; estado
com·mo·tion, *n.* tumulto
com·mune, *v.* conversar
com·mu·ni·ca·ble, *a.* comunicable
com·mu·ni·cate, *v.* comunicar(se)
com·mu·ni·ca·tion, *n.* comunicación
com·mun·ion, *n.* comunión
com·mun·ism, *n.* comunismo
com·mun·ist, *n.* comunista, *m., f.*
com·mu·ni·ty, *n. pl.,* -ties. comunidad
com·mute, *v.* conmutar
com·pact, *n.* pacto. *a.* compacto; breve
com·pan·ion, *n.* compañero
com·pa·ny, *n. pl.,* -nies. compañía; sociedad
com·pa·ra·ble, *a.* comparable
com·par·a·tive, *a.* relativo
com·pare, *v.* comparar
com·par·i·son, *n.* comparación
com·part·ment, *n.* compartimiento
com·pass, *n.* brújula; compás, *m.*; extensión
com·pas·sion, *n.* compasión
com·pas·sion·ate, *a.* compasivo
com·pat·i·ble, *a.* compatible
com·pa·tri·ot, *n.* compatriota, *m., f.*
com·pel, *v.* obligar; forzar
com·pen·sate, *v.* compensar; indemnizar
com·pen·sa·tion, *n.* compensación
com·pete, *v.* competir
com·pe·tence, *n.* competencia; capacidad
com·pe·tent, *a.* competente
com·pe·ti·tion, *n.* competencia
com·pet·i·tive, *a.* de competencia
com·pet·i·tor, *n.* competidor

com·pi·la·tion, *n.* compilación
com·pile, *v.* compilar
com·pla·cence, *n.* suficiencia. Also com·pla·cen·cy
com·plain, *v.* quejarse
com·plaint, *n.* queja
com·ple·ment, *n.* complemento
com·plete, *a.* completo; acabado. *v.* completar; terminar
com·ple·tion, *n.* terminación
com·plex, *a., n.* complejo
com·plex·ion, *n.* cutis, *m.*
com·plex·i·ty, *n. pl.*, -ties. complejidad
com·pli·ance, *n.* sumisión
com·pli·ant, *a.* condescendiente
com·pli·cate, *v.* complicar
com·pli·cat·ed, *a.* complicado
com·pli·ca·tion, *n.* complicación
com·pli·ment, *n.* cumplido; piropo. *v.* cumplimentar
com·pli·men·ta·ry, *a.* lisonjero; gratuito
com·ply, *v.* cumplir; obedecer
com·po·nent, *a.* componente
com·pose, *v.* componer; redactar; calmar
com·pos·ite, *a., n.* compuesto
com·po·si·tion, *n.* composición
com·po·sure, *n.* serenidad
com·pound, *v.* componer. *a.* compuesto. *n.* compuesto; mezcla
com·pre·hend, *v.* comprender
com·pre·hen·sion, *n.* comprensión
com·pre·hen·sive, *a.* extenso
com·press, *v.* comprimir, *n.* compresa
com·pres·sion, *n.* compresión
com·prise, *v.* comprender; abarcar
com·pro·mise, *n.* arreglo. *v.* comprometer; transigir
comp·trol·ler, *n.* interventor
com·pul·sion, *n.* fuerza; coacción
com·pul·so·ry, *a.* obligatorio
com·punc·tion, *n.* remordimiento
com·pu·ta·tion, *n.* cómputo
com·pute, *v.* computar
com·put·er, *n.* computador
com·rade, *n.* camarada, *m., f.*
con, *adv.* contra
con·cave, *a.* cóncavo
con·ceal, *v.* ocultar
con·cede, *v.* conceder
con·ceit, *n.* presunción; amor propio
con·ceit·ed, *a.* vanidoso
con·ceiv·a·ble, *a.* concebible
con·ceive, *v.* concebir; imaginar
con·cen·trate, *v.* concentrar(se)
con·cen·tra·tion, *n.* concentración
con·cept, *n.* concepto
con·cep·tion, *n.* concepción; idea
con·cep·tu·al, *a.* conceptual
con·cern, *v.* interesar; concernir. *n.* preocupación; asunto

con·cerned, *a.* inquieto
con·cern·ing, *prep.* acerca de
con·cert, *n.* concierto
con·ces·sion, *n.* concesión
con·cil·i·ate, *v.* conciliar
con·cil·i·a·tion, *n.* conciliación
con·cise, *a.* conciso
con·clude, *v.* concluir
con·clu·sion, *n.* conclusión
con·coct, *v.* tramar; confeccionar
con·coc·tion, *n.* mezcla
con·cord, *n.* concordia
con·course, *n.* concurso
con·crete, *a.* concreto; de hormigon. *n.* hormigón
con·cu·bine, *n.* concubina
con·cur, *v.* estar de acuerdo; concurrir
con·cur·rent, *a.* concurrente
con·cus·sion, *n.* conmoción
con·demn, *v.* condenar
con·dem·na·tion, *n.* condenación
con·den·sa·tion, *n.* condensación
con·dense, *v.* condensar; abreviar
con·de·scend, *v.* dignarse
con·di·ment, *n.* condimento
con·di·tion, *n.* condición. *v.* condicionar
con·di·tion·al, *a.* condicional
con·do·lence, *n.* pésame; condolencia
con·done, *v.* condonar
con·du·cive, *a.* conducente
con·duct, *v.* conducir; dirigir. *n.* conducta
con·duc·tor, *n.* director; cobrador
con·duit, *n.* conducto
cone, *n.* cono
con·fec·tion, *n.* dulce; confección
con·fed·er·a·cy, *n. pl.*, -cies. confederación
con·fed·er·ate, *a., n.* confederado
con·fed·er·a·tion, *n.* confederación
con·fer, *v.* otorgar; conferenciar
con·fer·ence, *n.* conferencia
con·fess, *v.* confesar
con·fes·sion, *n.* confesión
con·fes·sion·al, *n.* confesonario
con·fes·sor, *n.* confesor
con·fet·ti, *n.* confeti, *m.*
con·fide, *v.* confiar
con·fi·dence, *n.* confianza
con·fi·dent, *a.* seguro
con·fi·den·tial, *a.* confidencial
con·fig·u·ra·tion, *n.* configuración; aspecto
con·fine, *n. usu. pl.* confín. *v.* limitar; encerrar
con·fine·ment, *n.* prisión
con·firm, *v.* confirmar; verificar
con·fir·ma·tion, *n.* confirmación
con·firmed, *a.* inveterado; fijo
con·fis·cate, *v.* confiscar
con·fis·ca·tion, *n.* confiscación

con·fla·gra·tion, *n.* conflagración
con·flict, *n.* conflicto. *v.* chocar
con·form, *v.* conformar(se)
con·form·i·ty, *n. pl.,* -ties. conformidad
con·found, *v.* confundir
con·found·ed, *a. inf.* maldito; condenado
con·front, *v.* confrontar; hacer frente a
con·fron·ta·tion, *n.* confrontación
con·fuse, *v.* confundir
con·fu·sion, *n.* confusión
con·fute, *v.* confutar
con·geal, *v.* congelar
con·gen·ial, *a.* simpático
con·gen·i·tal, *a.* congénito
con·gest, *v.* acumular
con·ges·tion, *n.* congestión
con·glom·er·ate, *n.* conglomerado
con·glom·er·a·tion, *n.* conglomeración
con·grat·u·late, *v.* felicitar
con·grat·u·la·tion, *n. usu. pl.* felicitación
con·gre·gate, *v.* congregar(se)
con·gre·ga·tion, *n.* fieles
con·gress, *n.* congreso
con·gres·sion·al, *a.* del congreso
con·gress·man, *n. pl.,* -men. diputado
con·ic, *a.* cónico
con·i·cal, *a.* cónico
co·ni·fer, *n.* conífera
con·jec·ture, *n.* conjetura. *v.* conjeturar
con·ju·gate, *v.* conjugar
con·junc·tion, *n.* conjunción
con·jure, *v.* conjurar; hacer juegos de manos
con·jur·er, con·jur·or, *n.* ilusionista, *m., f.*
con·nect, *v.* juntar; conectar
con·nec·tion, *n.* unión, *f.;* conexión
con·nive, *v.* hacer la vista gorda
con·no·ta·tion, *n.* connotación
con·note, *v.* connotar
con·quer, *v.* vencer; conquistar
con·quer·or, *n.* conquistador
con·quest, *n.* conquista
con·science, *n.* conciencia
con·sci·en·tious, *a.* concienzudo
con·scious, *a.* consciente; intencional
con·se·crate, *v.* consagrar
con·se·cra·tion, *n.* consagración
con·sec·u·tive, *a.* consecutivo; sucesivo
con·sen·sus, *n.* consenso
con·sent, *v.* consentir. *n.* consentimiento; permiso
con·se·quence, *n.* consecuencia
con·se·quent, *a.* consiguiente
con·ser·va·tion, *n.* conservación
con·serv·a·tive, *a.* moderado. *n.* conservador
con·serv·a·to·ry, *n. pl.,* -ries. invernadero; conservatorio
con·serve, *v.* conservar; cuidar
con·sid·er, *v.* considerar; tomar en cuenta
con·sid·er·a·ble, *a.* considerable
con·sid·er·ate, *a.* considerado; atento
con·sid·er·a·tion, *n.* consideración
con·sid·er·ing, *prep.* en consideración a
con·sign, *v.* consignar
con·sign·ment, *n.* consignación; envío
con·sist, *v.* consistir; constar
con·sist·en·cy, *n. pl.,* -cies. consistencia; consecuencia
con·sist·ent, *a.* consecuente
con·so·la·tion, *n.* consuelo
con·sol·i·date, *v.* consolidar
con·sol·i·da·tion, *n.* consolidación
con·so·nant, *n.* consonante, *f.*
con·sort, *n.* consorte. *v.* asociarse
con·spic·u·ous, *a.* visible
con·spir·a·cy, *n. pl.,* -cies. conspiración
con·spir·a·tor, *n.* conspirador
con·spire, *v.* conspirar
con·sta·ble, *n.* policía
con·stab·u·lar·y, *n. pl.,* -ies. policía
con·stan·cy, *n.* constancia
con·stant, *a.* constante; continuo
con·stant·ly, *adv.* constantemente
con·stel·la·tion, *n.* constelación
con·ster·na·tion, *n.* consternación
con·sti·pate, *v.* estreñir
con·sti·pa·tion, *n.* estreñimiento
con·sti·tute, *v.* componer; constituir
con·sti·tu·tion, *n.* constitución
con·strain, *v.* obligar; forzar
con·straint, *n.* encierro; coacción
con·struct, *v.* construir
con·struc·tion, *n.* construcción; sentido
con·struc·tive, *a.* constructivo
con·strue, *v.* interpretar
con·sul, *n.* cónsul, *m.*
con·su·late, *n.* consulado
con·sult, *v.* consultar
con·sul·ta·tion, *n.* consulta
con·sume, *v.* consumir; comerse
con·sum·er, *n.* consumidor
con·sum·mate, *v.* consumar
con·sum·ma·tion, *n.* consumación
con·sump·tion, *n.* consumo; consunción
con·tact, *n.* contacto
con·ta·gion, *n.* contagio
con·ta·gious, *a.* contagioso
con·tain, *v.* contener
con·tain·er, *n.* continente
con·tam·i·nate, *v.* contaminar

con·tam·i·na·tion, *n.* contaminación
con·tem·plate, *v.* contemplar; proyectar
con·tem·pla·tion, *n.* contemplación
con·tem·po·rar·y, *n. pl.* -ies. coetáneos. *a.* contemporáneo
con·tempt, *n.* desprecio
con·tempt·i·ble, *a.* vil
con·temp·tu·ous, *a.* desdeñoso
con·tend, *v.* contender; disputar; afirmar
con·tent, *a.* contento. *n.* satisfacción; *usu. pl.* contenido
con·test, *v.* defender; contender. *n.* contienda; concurso
con·test·ant, *n.* contendiente, *m., f.*
con·ti·nent, *n.* continente
con·ti·nen·tal, *a.* continental
con·tin·gen·cy, *n. pl.* -cies. contingencia
con·tin·gent, *a.* contingente
con·tin·u·a·tion, *n.* continuación
con·tin·ue, *v.* continuar; prolongar; seguir
con·tin·u·ous, *a.* continuo
con·tort, *v.* retorcer
con·tour, *n.* contorno
con·tra·band, *n.* contrabando
con·tra·cep·tion, *n.* anticoncepcionismo
con·tra·cep·tive, *a.* anticoncepcional
con·tract, *v.* contraer. *n.* contrato
con·trac·tion, *n.* contracción
con·tra·dict, *v.* contradecir
con·tra·dic·tion, *n.* contradicción
con·tra·dic·to·ry, *a.* contradictorio
con·tral·to, *n. pl.* -tos, -ti. contralto
con·tra·ry, *n. pl.* -ries. contrario. *a.* contrario
con·trast, *v.* comparar; contrastar. *n.* contraste
con·trib·ute, *v.* contribuir
con·tri·bu·tion, *n.* contribución
con·trite, *a.* arrepentido
con·tri·tion, *n.* arrepentimiento
con·triv·ance, *n.* plan; invención
con·trive, *v.* inventar; efectuar
con·trol, *v.* controlar; mandar; dirigir. *n.* dirección; control
con·tro·ver·sy, *n. pl.* -sies. controversia
con·tu·sion, *n.* contusión
con·va·lesce, *v.* convalecer
con·va·les·cence, *n.* convalecencia
con·va·les·cent, *a., n.* convaleciente, *m., f.*
con·vene, *v.* convocar
con·ven·ience, *n.* comodidad
con·ven·ient, *a.* conveniente; cómodo
con·vent, *n.* convento
con·ven·tion, *n.* convención; congreso
con·ven·tion·al, *a.* convencional

con·verge, *v.* convergir
con·ver·gence, *n.* convergencia
con·ver·sant, *a.* familiar; versado e:
con·ver·sa·tion, *n.* conversación
con·verse, *v.* conversar. *n.* conversación; inversa
con·ver·sion, *n.* conversión
con·vert, *v.* convertir. *n.* converso
con·vex, *a.* convexo
con·vey, *v.* transportar; llevar
con·vey·ance, *n.* transporte; vehículo
con·vict, *v.* condenar. *n.* penado
con·vic·tion, *n.* sentencia; convicción
con·vince, *v.* convencer
con·viv·i·al, *a.* alegre
con·vo·ca·tion, *n.* convocación
con·voy, *v.* convoyar. *n.* convoy, *m.*
con·vulse, *v.* convulsionar
con·vul·sion, *n.* convulsión
coo, *v.* arrullar
cook, *v.* cocer; cocinar. *n.* cocinero
cook·ie, cook·y, *n. pl.* cook·ies. galleta; dulce
cool, *a.* frío; fresco. *v.* enfriar
cool·ness, *n.* frescura; frío
coop, *n.* gallinero. *v.* encerrar
co·op·er·ate, *v.* cooperar
co·op·er·a·tion, *n.* cooperación
co·or·di·nate, *v.* coordinar
co·or·di·na·tion, *n.* coordinación
cop, *v., inf.* coger. *n.* agente de policía
cope, *v.* contender con
co·pi·ous, *a.* copioso
cop·per, *n.* cobre
cop·u·late, *v.* copularse
cop·u·la·tion, *n.* cópula
cop·y, *n. pl.* -ies. copia. *v.* copiar
cop·y·right, *n.* propiedad literaria
co·quette, *n.* coqueta
cor·al, *n.* coral, *m.*
cord, *n.* cuerda
cor·dial, *a.* cordial
cor·dial·i·ty, *n.* cordialidad
cor·do·van, *a.* cordobán
cor·du·roy, *n.* pana
core, *n.* corazón; centro
cork, *n.* corcho. *v.* tapar con corcho
cork·screw, *n.* sacacorchos
corn, *n.* maíz, *m.;* callo
cor·ner, *n.* rincón; ángulo; esquina. *v.* arrinconar
cor·net, *n.* corneta
cor·nice, *n.* cornisa
cor·nu·co·pi·a, *n.* cornucopia
co·rol·la, *n.* corola
cor·ol·lar·y, *n. pl.* -ies. corolario
co·ro·na, *n. pl.* -nas, -nae. corona
cor·o·nar·y, *n.* trombosis coronaria
cor·o·na·tion, *n.* coronación
cor·po·ral, *a.* corporal. *n.* cabo
cor·po·rate, *a.* corporativo
cor·po·ra·tion, *n.* corporación; socie-

dad anónima

orps, *n. pl.,* **corps.** cuerpo

orpse, *n.* cadáver

or·pu·lence, cor·pu·len·cy, *n.* obesidad

or·pu·lent, *a.* gordo

or·pus·cle, *n.* corpúsculo; glóbulo

or·pus·cu·lar, *a.* corpuscular

or·ral, *n.* corral, *m. v.* acorralar

:or·rect, *v.* corregir, *a.* correcto

cor·rec·tion, *n.* corrección

cor·re·la·tion, *n.* correlación

cor·re·spond, *v.* corresponder; escribir

cor·re·spond·ence, *n.* correspondencia

cor·ri·dor, *n.* pasillo

cor·rob·o·rate, *v.* corroborar

cor·rob·o·ra·tion, *n.* confirmación

cor·rode, *v.* corroer

cor·ro·sion, *n.* corrosión

cor·ro·sive, *a.* corrosivo

cor·rupt, *v.* corromper. *a.* corrompido

cor·rup·tion, *n.* corrupción

cor·sage, *n.* corpiño

cor·set, *n.* corsé

cos·met·ic, *a., n.* cosmético

cos·mic, *a.* cósmico

cos·mo·pol·i·tan, *a.* cosmopolita. *n.* cosmopolita, *m., f.*

cos·mos, *n.* cosmos, *m.*

cost, *n.* precio; coste. *v.* costar

cost·ly, *a.* costoso

cos·tume, *n.* disfraz, *m.*

cot, *n.* catre

cot·tage, *n.* casita de campo

cot·ton, *n.* algodón. *a.* de algodón

couch, *n.* sofá, *m.*

cough, *n.* tos, *f. v.* toser

coun·cil, *n.* concejo

coun·cil·or, coun·cil·man, *n.* concejal

coun·sel, *n.* consejo; abogado. *v.* avisar

coun·se·lor, *n.* consejero

count, *v.* contar; considerar. *n.* cuenta; total; conde

coun·te·nance, *n.* cara; semblante

count·er, *n.* mostrador. *a.; adv.* contrario. *v.* oponerse

coun·ter·feit, *a.* falso. *n.* falsificación; imitación. *v.* contrahacer

coun·ter·sign, *v.* refrendar

count·ess, *n.* condesa

count·less, *a.* innumerable

coun·tri·fied, *a.* rústico

coun·try, *n. pl.,* **-tries.** país; campo. *a.* campesino

coun·ty, *n. pl.,* **-ties.** condado

coup, *n. pl.,* **coups.** golpe

cou·ple, *n.* par; pareja. *v.* unir

cou·pon, *n.* cupón

cour·age, *n.* valor

cou·ra·geous, *a.* valiente

cour·i·er, *n.* estafeta

course, *n.* curso; dirección; rumbo; plato

court, *n.* corte; tribunal, *m.;* pista. *v.* cortejar

cour·te·ous, *a.* cortés

cour·te·sy, *n. pl.,* **-sies.** cortesía

court·ly, *a.* cortés

court-mar·tial, *n. pl.,* **courts-mar·tial.** consejo de guerra

court·ship, *n.* noviazgo

cous·in, *n.* primo

cove, *n.* cala

cov·e·nant, *n.* pacto; alianza

cov·er, *v.* cubrir; tapar. *n.* cubierta

cov·er·let, *n.* colcha

cov·ert, *a.* secreto

cov·et, *v.* codiciar

cov·et·ous, *a.* codicioso

cov·et·ous·ness, *n.* codicia

cow, *n. pl.,* **cows.** vaca. *v.* intimidar

cow·ard, *n.* cobarde

cow·ard·ice, *n.* cobardía

cow·boy, *n.* vaquero

cowl, *n.* cogulla

coy, *a.* tímido

coy·ness, *n.* timidez, *f.*

coy·o·te, *n.* coyote

co·zi·ness, *n.* comodidad

co·zy, *a.* cómodo

crab, *n.* cangrejo. *v.* quejarse

crab ap·ple, *n.* manzana silvestre

crab·by, *a.* malhumorado

crack, *v.* hender; chasquear. *n.* crujido; grieta

crack·er, *n.* galleta

cra·dle, *n.* cuna. *v.* mecer

craft, *n.* arte, *m.;* habilidad; embarcación

craft·i·ness, *n.* astucia

crafts·man, *n. pl.* **-men.** artesano

craft·y, *a.* astuto

crag, *n.* risco

crag·gy, *a.* escarpado

cramp, *v.* restringir; sujetar. *n.* calambre

cran·ber·ry, *n. pl.,* **-ries,** arándano

crane, *n.* grulla; grúa

crank, *n.* manubrio; *inf.* chiflado

crank·y, *a.* chiflado

crash, *v.* estrellar; romperse. *n.* estrépito; estallido; choque

crass, *a.* craso; torpe

crate, *n.* caja de embalaje

cra·ter, *n.* cráter

cra·vat, *n.* corbata

crave, *v.* anhelar; suplicar

cra·ven, *a, n.* cobarde ·

crav·ing, *n.* deseo ardiente

crawl, *v.* arrastrar(se). *n.* arrastramiento

cray·fish, *n. pl.,* **-fish·es, -fish.** ástaco

cray·on, *n.* lápiz de color

cra·zy, *a.* loco
creak, *v.* crujir. *n.* crujido
cream, *n.* nata; crema
crease, *n.* pliegue. *v.* doblar
cre·ate, *v.* crear; producir
cre·a·tion, *n.* creación
cre·a·tor, *n.* creador
crea·ture, *n.* criatura
cre·den·tial, *n.* credencial; *pl.* credenciales
cred·it, *v.* creer; abonar. *n.* crédito; honor
cred·i·tor, *n.* acreedor
cre·do, *n. pl.*, **-dos.** credo
cred·u·lous, *a.* crédulo
creed, *n.* credo
creek, *n.* riachuelo
creep, *v.* arrastrar(se)
cre·mate, *v.* incinerar
cre·ma·tion, *n.* incineración
cres·cent, *a.* creciente
crest, *n.* cresta; cima
crew, *n.* tripulación
crib, *n.* pesebre
crick·et, *n.* grillo
crime, *n.* crimen
crim·i·nal, *a., n.* criminal
crim·son, *a., n.* carmesí
cringe, *v.* acobardarse
crin·kle, *v.* arrugar
crip·ple, *n.* tullido; lisiado. *v.* mutilar
cri·sis, *n. pl.*, **cri·ses.** crisis, *f.*
crisp, *a.* tostado; crespo
cri·te·ri·on, *n. pl.*, **-ri·a, -ons.** criterio
crit·ic, *n.* crítico
crit·i·cal, *a.* crítico
crit·i·cism, *n.* crítica
crit·i·cize, *v.* criticar
croak, *v.* croar. *n.* canto
cro·chet, *v.* hacer croché
crock·er·y, *n.* loza
croc·o·dile, *n.* cocodrilo
cro·cus, *n. pl.*, **-cus·es, -ci.** azafrán
crook, *n.* curva; *inf.* ladrón
crook·ed, *a.* encorvado
croon, *v.* canturrear
crop, *n.* cosecha; látigo mocho. *v.* cortar
cro·quet, *n.* croquet, *m.*
cro·quette, *n.* croqueta
cross, *n.* cruz, *f. a.* malhumorado. *v.* cruzar
cross-ex·am·ine, *v.* repreguntar
cross·ing, *n.* cruce; paso a nivel
cross·roads, *n.* encrucijada
cross·wise, *adv.* de través; al través
crotch, *n.* horcajadura
crouch, *v.* agacharse
crow, *n.* cuervo; canto del gallo. *v.* cacarear
crow·bar, *n.* palanca
crowd, *n.* muchedumbre, *f. v.* apretar
crown, *n.* corona; cumbre, *f. v.* coronar

cru·cial, *a.* decisivo
cru·ci·ble, *n.* crisol, *m.*
cru·ci·fix, *n.* crucifijo
cru·ci·fix·ion, *n.* crucifixión
cru·ci·fy, *v.* crucificar
crude, *a.* crudo; inculto
cru·el, *a.* cruel
cru·el·ty, *n. pl.*, **-ties.** crueldad; atrocidad
cruise, *v.* navegar
cruis·er, *n.* crucero
crumb, *n.* miga
crum·ble, *v.* desmigajar(se); desmenuzar(se)
crum·ple, *v.* ajar
crunch, *v.* crujir
cru·sade, *n.* cruzada. *v.* ir en una cruzada
cru·sad·er, *n.* cruzado
crush, *v.* aplastar
crush·ing, *a.* aplastante; abrumador
crust, *n.* corteza
crus·ta·cean, *n.* crustáceo
crust·y, *a.* costroso; irritable
crutch, *n.* muleta
cry, *v.* gritar; llorar. *n. pl.*, **cries.** grito; llanto
crypt, *n.* cripta
cryp·tic, *a.* secreto
crys·tal, *n.* cristal, *m. a.* cristalino
crys·tal·li·za·tion, *n.* cristalización
crys·tal·lize, *v.* cristalizar(se)
cub, *n.* cachorro
cube, *n.* cubo. *v.* cubicar
cu·bic, *a.* cúbico
cuck·oo, *n. pl.*, **-oos.** cuco
cu·cum·ber, *n.* pepino
cud, *n.* rumia
cud·dle, *v.* abrazarse
cudg·el, *n.* garrote; porra. *v.* aporrear
cue, *n.* apunte; taco
cuff, *n.* puño. *v.* abofetear
cu·li·nar·y, *a.* culinario
cull, *v.* coger
cul·mi·nate, *v.* culminar; terminar
cul·mi·na·tion, *n.* culminación; colmo
cul·prit, *n.* delincuente
cult, *n.* culto
cul·ti·vate, *v.* cultivar
cul·ti·va·tion, *n.* cultivo
cul·tur·al, *a.* cultural
cul·ture, *n.* cultura. *v.* cultivar
cul·vert, *n.* alcantarilla
cum·ber·some, *a.* incómodo
cu·mu·late, *v.* acumular
cun·ning, *n.* astucia; sutileza. *a.* astuto; artificioso
cup, *n.* taza
cup·ful, *n. pl.*, **-fuls.** contenido de una taza
cu·pid·i·ty, *n.* codicia; avaricia
cur, *n.* perro de mala raza
curb, *n.* freno; bordillo. *v.* refrenar

curd, *n.* (*often pl.*) cuajada
cur·dle, *v.* cuajar(se)
cure, *v.* curar. *n.* cura
cur·few, *n.* queda
cu·ri·os·i·ty, *n. pl.*, **-ties.** curiosidad
cu·ri·ous, *a.* curioso
curl, *v.* rizar(se); arrollar(se). *n.* rizo; bucle
curl·y, *a.* rizado
cur·rant, *n.* grosella
cur·ren·cy, *n. pl.*, **-cies.** circulación; moneda
cur·rent, *a.* corriente. *n.* corriente, *f.*
cur·ric·u·lum, *n. pl.*, **-lums**, **-la.** curso de estudios
curse, *v.* maldecir; blasfemar. *n.* maldición
cur·so·ry, *a.* rápido
curt, *a.* brusco
cur·tail, *v.* abreviar
cur·tain, *n.* cortina; telón
curt·sy, *n. pl.* **-ies.** reverencia. *v.* hacer una reverencia
curve, *n.* curva. *v.* encorvar(se)
cush·ion, *n.* cojín
cus·tard, *n.* natillas
cus·to·di·an, *n.* custodio
cus·to·dy, *n. pl.*, **-dies.** custodia; encierro
cus·tom, *n.* costumbre, *f.*; *pl.* aduana
cus·tom·ar·y, *a.* usual
cus·tom·er, *n.* cliente
cut, *v.* cortar; dividir. *n.* corte; cortadura. *a.* cortado
ute, *a.* mono
u·ti·cle, *n.* cutícula
ut·ler·y, *n.* cuchillería
ut·let, *n.* chuleta
cut-rate, *a.* a precio reducido
cut·throat, *n.* asesino. *a.* despiadado
cy·a·nide, *n.* cianuro
cyc·la·men, *n.* ciclamino
cy·cle, *n.* ciclo. *v.* ir en bicicleta
cy·clic, *a.* cíclico
cy·clist, *n.* ciclista, *m., f.*
cy·clone, *n.* ciclón
cy·clo·tron, *n.* ciclotrón
cyg·net, *n.* pollo del cisne
cyl·in·der, *n.* cilindro
cy·lin·dric, **cy·lin·dri·cal**, *a.* cilíndrico
cym·bal, *n.* platillo
cyn·ic, *n.* cínico
cyn·i·cal, *a.* cínico
cyn·i·cism, *n.* cinismo
cy·press, *n.* ciprés, *f.*
cyst, *n.* quiste
czar, *n.* zar
cza·ri·na, *n.* zarina

D

dab, *v.* tocar ligeramente. *n.* golpecito

dab·ble, *v.* salpicar
dad, *n. inf.* papá, *m.* Also **dad·dy**, *pl.* **dad·dies**
daft, *a.* loco
dag·ger, *n.* puñal, *m.*
dai·ly, *a.* diario; cotidiano. *adv.* cada día
dain·ti·ness, *n.* delicadeza
dain·ty, *a.* delicado. *n. pl.*, **-ties.** golosina
dair·y, *n. pl.*, **-ies.** lechería; quesería
dair·y·man, *n. pl.*, **-men.** lechero
da·is, *n.* estrado
dale, *n.* valle
dal·li·ance, *n.* diversión
dal·ly, *v.* perder tiempo; entretenerse
dam, *n.* presa. *v.* represar
dam·age, *n.* daño; avería. *v.* perjudicar; dañar
damn, *v.* condenar. *a.* maldito
dam·na·ble, *a.* detestable
dam·na·tion, *n.* condenación
damned, *a.* condenado
damp, *a.* húmedo
damp·en, *v.* mojar
dance, *v.* bailar; danzar. *n.* baile; danza
dan·cer, *n.* bailador
dan·der, *n.* ira
dan·druff, *n.* caspa
dan·ger, *n.* peligro; riesgo
dan·ger·ous, *a.* peligroso
dan·gle, *v.* colgar
dank, *a.* liento
dap·pled, *a.* rodado
dare, *v.* atreverse; arriesgarse
dar·ing, *n.* atrevimiento
dark, *a.* oscuro; moreno. *n.* oscuridad
dark·en, *v.* oscurecer
dark·ness, *n.* oscuridad
darl·ing, *n.* querido
darn, *v.* zurcir
dash, *v.* romper; golpear; precipitarse. *n.* guión; raya
dash·board, *n.* tablero de instrumentos
das·tard, *n.* cobarde
das·tard·ly, *a.* vil
date, *n.* fecha; cita; dátil. *v.* fechar
daub, *v.* pintarrajar
daugh·ter, *n.* hija
daugh·ter-in-law, *n. pl.*, **daugh·ters-in-law.** nuera
daunt·less, *a.* impávido
daw·dle, *v.* perder el tiempo
dawn, *v.* amanecer. *n.* alba
day, *n.* día, *m.*
day·break, *n.* amanecer
day·dream, *n.* ensueño
day·light, *n.* luz del día
day·time, *n.* día
daze, *v.* aturdir. *n.* deslumbramiento
daz·zle, *v.* deslumbrar

daz·zling, a. deslumbrante

dea·con, n. diácono

dea·con·ess, n. f. diaconisa

dea·con·ry, n. diaconía

dead, a. muerto

dead·en, v. amortiguar

dead-end, a. calle sin salida

dead end, n. callejón sin salida

dead·ly, a. mortal

deaf, a. sordo

deaf·en, v. ensordecer

deaf-mute, n. sordomudo

deaf·ness, n. sordera

deal, n. cantidad; trato; reparto. v. tratar de; dar

deal·er, n. tratante

dean, n. decano; deán

dear, a. querido; caro

dear·ness, n. carestía

death, n. muerte, f.

death·less, a. inmortal

death·ly, a. mortal

de·ba·cle, n. fracaso

de·bar, v. prohibir

de·bat·a·ble, a. discutible

de·bate, v. debatir. n. debate; discusión

de·bat·er, n. polemista, m., f.

de·bauch, v. corromper

de·bauch·er·y, n. pl. -ies. libertinaje

de·bil·i·tate, v. debilitar

de·bil·i·ta·tion, n. debilitación

de·bil·i·ty, n. pl. -ties. debilidad

deb·it, n. debe

deb·o·nair, a. cortés; elegante. Also deb·o·naire, deb·on·naire

de·bris, n. escombros, m.

debt, n. deuda

debt·or, n. deudor

de·but, dé·but, n. presentación; estreno

deb·u·tant, deb·u·tante, n. debutante

dec·ade, n. decenio

dec·a·dence, n. decadencia

dec·a·dent, a. decadente

dec·ant·er, n. garrafa

de·cay, v. decaer; cariarse; deteriorar

de·cease, v. morir; fallecer

de·ceased, a. muerto; difunto

de·ceit, n. engaño

de·ceit·ful, a. engañoso

de·ceive, v. engañar

De·cem·ber, n. diciembre

de·cen·cy, n. pl. -cies. decencia

de·cent, a. decente

de·cep·tion, n. fraude

de·cep·tive, a. engañoso

de·cide, v. decidir

de·cid·ed, a. decidido

de·cid·ed·ly, adv. decididamente

dec·i·mal, a., n. decimal, f.

de·ci·pher, v. descifrar

de·ci·sion, n. decisión; firmeza

de·ci·sive, a. decisivo

de·ci·sive·ly, adv. con resolución

deck, v. adornar. n. cubierta; baraja

dec·la·ra·tion, n. declaración

de·clare, v. declarar

de·cline, v. declinar; rehusar. n. descenso

de·com·pose, v. descomponer(se)

de·com·po·si·tion, n. descomposición

dec·o·rate, v. adornar; condecorar

dec·o·ra·tion, n. decoración; ornato

dec·o·ra·tor, n. decorador

de·coy, n. señuelo

de·crease, v. disminuir(se)

de·creas·ing·ly, adv. en disminución

de·cree, n. decreto. v. decretar; mandar

de·crep·it, a. decrépito

de·cry, v. rebajar

de·duce, v. deducir

de·duct, v. restar

de·duc·tion, n. deducción; descuento

deed, n. hecho

deem, v. juzgar

deep, a. hondo; profundo

deep·en, v. profundizar; intensificar

de·face, v. desfigurar

def·a·ma·tion, n. difamación

de·fame, v. difamar

de·fault, n. a falta de

de·feat, n. derrota. v. vencer; frustrar

de·fect, n. defecto. v. desertar

de·fec·tion, n. defección

de·fec·tive, a. defectuoso

de·fend, v. defender

de·fend·ant, n. demandado

de·fense, de·fence, n. defensa

de·fen·sive, a. defensivo

de·fer, v. diferir; aplazar

def·er·ence, n. deferencia

de·fer·ment, n. aplazamiento

de·fi·ance, n. desafío

de·fi·ant, a. provocativo

de·fi·cien·cy, n. pl., -cies. deficiencia; falta

de·fi·cient, a. insuficiente

def·i·cit, n. déficit, m.

de·file, v. manchar

de·fine, v. definir

def·i·nite, a. concreto; definido

def·i·ni·tion, n. definición

de·fin·i·tive, a. definitivo

de·flate, v. desinflar

de·fla·tion, n. desinflación

de·flect, v. desviar

de·form, v. deformar; desfigurar

de·form·i·ty, n. pl., -ties. deformidad

de·fraud, v. defraudar; estafar

de·fray, v. pagar

deft, a. diestro

deft·ness, n. habilidad

de·funct, a. difunto

de·fy, v. desafiar; contravenir

de·gen·er·ate, v. degenerar
deg·ra·da·tion, n. degradación
de·grade, v. degradar
de·gree, n. grado; rango
de·hy·drate, v. deshidratar
de·hy·dra·tion, n. deshidratación
de·i·fy, v. deificar
deign, v. dignarse
de·i·ty, n. pl. -ties. deidad
de·ject·ed, a. abatido
de·jec·tion, n. melancolía; abatimiento
de·lay, v. aplazar; demorar
de·lec·ta·ble, a. deleitable
del·e·gate, v. delegar. n. delegado
del·e·ga·tion, n. diputación
de·lete, v. tachar
de·le·tion, n. supresión; borradura
de·lib·er·ate, v. deliberar. a. premeditado
del·i·ca·cy, n. pl. -cies. delicadeza
del·i·cate, a. delicado; fino
de·li·cious, a. delicioso
de·light, v. deleitar
de·light·ful, a. agradable; encantador
de·lin·e·ate, v. delinear
de·lin·e·a·tion, n. bosquejo
de·lin·quen·cy, n. pl. -cies. delincuencia
de·lin·quent, a. n. delincuente, m., f.
de·lir·i·ous, a. delirante
de·lir·i·um, n. pl. -i·ums, -ia. delirio
de·liv·er, v. entregar; pronunciar
de·liv·er·ance, n. rescate
de·liv·er·y, n. entrega; reparto
del·ta, n. delta
de·lude, v. engañar
del·uge, n. diluvio. v. inundar
de·lu·sion, n. engaño; ilusión
de·luxe, a. de lujo
delve, v. cavar
dem·a·gogue, dem·a·gog, n. demagogo
dem·a·gogu·er·y, n. demagogismo
de·mand, v. exigir; demandar. n. petición
de·mar·ca·tion, n. demarcación. Also de·mar·ka·tion
de·mean, v. degradarse
de·mean·or, n. porte
de·ment·ed, a. demente
de·mer·it, n. demérito
de·mise, n. fallecimiento; cesión
de·moc·ra·cy, n. pl. -cies. democracia
dem·o·crat, n. demócrata, m., f.
dem·o·crat·ic, a. democrático
de·mol·ish, v. demoler
dem·o·li·tion, n. derribo
de·mon, n. demonio
dem·on·strate, v. demostrar
dem·on·stra·tion, n. demostración; manifestación

de·mor·al·ize, v. desmoralizar
de·mote, v. degradar
de·mo·tion, n. degradación
den, n. guarida; estudio
de·ni·al, n. negativa
den·im, n. dril de algodón
de·nom·i·na·tion, n. denominación
de·nom·i·na·tor, n. denominador
de·note, v. denotar
de·nounce, v. denunciar
dense, a. denso; compacto
den·si·ty, n. pl. -ties. densidad
dent, n. abolladura. v. mellar
den·tal, a. dental
den·tist, n. dentista, m., f.
den·ture, n. dentadura
de·nude, v. desnudar
de·nun·ci·ate, v. denunciar
de·nun·ci·a·tion, n. denuncia
de·ny, v. negar; rehusar
de·o·dor·ant, n. desodorante
de·o·dor·ize, v. desodorizar
de·part, v. irse; partir
de·part·ment, n. departamento; sección
de·part·men·tal, a. departamental
de·par·ture, n. partida; salida
de·pend, v. depender; contar con
de·pend·ence, de·pend·ance, n. confianza
de·pend·en·cy, de·pend·an·cy, n. pl. -cies. dependencia; posesión
de·pend·ent, de·pend·ant, n. dependiente
de·pict, v. representar
de·plete, v. agotar
de·ple·tion, n. agotamiento
de·plor·a·ble, a. deplorable
de·plore, v. lamentar
de·port, v. deportar
de·por·ta·tion, n. deportación
de·port·ment, n. comportamiento
de·pose, v. deponer
de·pos·it, v. depositar. n. depósito; poso
de·pot, n. estación; depósito
de·prave, v. depravar
de·praved, a. depravado
de·prav·i·ty, n. pl. -ties. depravación
de·pre·ci·a·tion, n. depreciación
de·press, v. deprimir; rebajar
de·pressed, a. deprimido; desalentado
de·pres·sion, n. depresión; desaliento
dep·ri·va·tion, n. privación
de·prive, v. privar
depth, n. fondo; profundidad
dep·u·ty, n. pl. -ties. suplente
de·range, v. desarreglar
de·range·ment, n. desarreglo
der·e·lict, a. abandonado
der·e·lic·tion, n. abandono

de·ride, v. mofar
de·ri·sion, n. irrisión
der·i·va·tion, n. derivación
de·riv·a·tive, a. derivado
de·rive, v. derivar(se)
der·rick, n. grúa
de·scend, v. descender; bajar
de·scend·ant, n. descendiente, m., f.
de·scribe, v. describir
de·scrip·tion, n. descripción
de·scrip·tive, a. descriptivo
des·ert, n. desierto. v. abandonar
de·sert·er, n. desertor
de·serve, v. merecer
de·sign, v. idear; diseñar
des·ig·nate, v. señalar; nombrar
des·ig·na·tion, n. nombramiento
de·sign·er, n. diseñador; dibujante, m., f.
de·sire, v. desear
de·sist, v. desistir
desk, n. pupitre
des·o·la·tion, n. desolación
de·spair, v. desesperar
des·per·ate, a. desesperado; arriesgado
des·per·a·tion, n. desesperación
des·pi·ca·ble, a. despreciable
de·spise, v. despreciar
de·spite, prep. a pesar de
de·spoil, v. despojar
de·spond·en·cy, n. desaliento
des·pot, n. déspota, m.
des·pot·ism, n. despotismo
des·sert, n. postre
des·ti·na·tion, n. destino
des·tine, v. destinar
des·ti·ny, n. pl., -nies. destino
des·ti·tute, a. desamparado
des·ti·tu·tion, n. indigencia
de·stroy, v. destruir
de·struct·i·ble, a. destructible
de·struc·tion, n. destrucción
de·tach, v. separar
de·tached, a. separado; objetivo
de·tail, v. detallar. n. detalle
de·tain, v. detener; retener
de·tect, v. descubrir
de·tec·tive, n. detective
dé·tente, n. detente
de·ter, v. disuadir; impedir
de·ter·gent, n.; a. detergente
de·te·ri·o·rate, v. deteriorar(se)
de·te·ri·o·ra·tion, n. empeoramiento
de·ter·mi·na·tion, n. determinación
de·ter·mine, v. determinar; fijar; resolver
de·ter·mined, a. resuelto
de·test, v. detestar
de·test·a·ble, a. detestable
de·tour, n. rodeo
det·ri·ment, n. prejuicio
de·val·u·ate, v. desvalorizar
de·val·u·a·tion, n. devaluación

dev·as·tate, v. devastar
dev·as·ta·tion, n. devastación
de·vel·op, v. desarrollar; desenvolver
de·vel·op·ment, n. desarrollo; explotación
de·vi·ate, v. desviarse
de·vi·a·tion, n. desviación; divergencia
de·vice, n. ingenio; estratagema
dev·il, n. diablo; demonio
dev·il·ish, a. diabólico
de·vi·ous, a. tortuoso
de·vise, v. inventar
de·void, a. desprovisto
de·vote, v. dedicar
de·vot·ed, a. fiel
de·vo·tee, n. devoto
de·vo·tion, n. devoción; lealtad
de·vour, v. devorar
de·vout, a. devoto
dew, n. rocío
dex·ter·i·ty, n. destreza
dex·ter·ous, a. diestro; hábil
di·a·be·tes, n. diabetes, f.
di·a·bet·ic, a., n. diabético
di·a·bol·ic, a. diabólico. Also di·a·bol·i·cal
di·a·dem, n. diadema
di·ag·nose, v. diagnosticar
di·ag·no·sis, n. pl., -ses. diagnóstico
di·ag·o·nal, a., n. diagonal, f.
di·a·gram, n. diagrama, m.
di·al, n. cuadrante; disco. v. marcar
di·a·lect, n. dialecto
di·a·logue, n. diálogo
di·am·e·ter, n. diámetro
di·a·met·ric, a. diametral. Also di·a·met·ri·cal
dia·mond, n. diamante; oros
dia·per, n. pañal
di·a·phragm, n. diafragma, m.
di·ar·rhe·a, n. diarrea. Also di·ar·rhoe·a
di·a·ry, n. pl., -ries. diario
dice, n. pl.; sing. die. dados. v. jugar a los dados; cortar en cuadritos
dick·er, v. regatear
dic·tate, v. mandar; dictar. n. orden
dic·ta·tion, n. dictado
dic·ta·tor, n. dictador
dic·ta·tor·ship, n. dictadura
dic·tion, n. dicción
dic·tion·ar·y, n. pl., -ies. diccionario
did, v. past tense of do
die, v. morir. n. dado; troquel, m.
di·et, n. régimen. v. estar a dieta
di·e·tar·y, a. dietético
dif·fer, v. diferenciarse; discrepar
dif·fer·ence, n. diferencia
dif·fer·ent, a. diferente
dif·fi·cult, a. difícil
dif·fi·cul·ty, n. pl., -ties. dificultad
dif·fuse, v. difundir. a. difuso

dif·fu·sion, n. difusión
dig, v. cavar; extraer. n. excavación
di·gest, v. digerir. n. digesto
di·ges·tion, n. digestión
dig·it, n. dígito; dedo
dig·ni·fied, a. grave
dig·ni·fy, v. dignificar; honrar
dig·ni·ty, n. pl. -ties. dignidad
di·gres·sion, n. digresión
dike, n. dique
di·lap·i·dat·ed, a. desmoronado
di·late, v. dilatar(se)
di·lem·ma, n. dilema, m.
dil·i·gence, n. diligencia
dil·i·gent, a. diligente; asiduo
dill, n. eneldo
di·lute, v. diluir
di·lu·tion, n. dilución
dim, a. débil; oscuro. v. oscurecer
dime, n. diez centavos
di·men·sion, n. dimensión
di·min·ish, v. disminuir(se)
di·min·u·tive, a. diminuto
dim·ple, n. hoyuelo
din, n. estruendo
dine, v. cenar
din·er, n. coche-comedor
din·gy, a. sucio; deslucido
din·ner, n. cena
di·no·saur, n. dinosaurio
dint, n. fuerza
di·oc·e·san, a. diocesano
di·o·cese, n. diócesis, f.
dip, v. mojar; meter
diph·the·ri·a, n. difteria
diph·thong, n. diptongo
di·plo·ma, n. diploma, m.
di·plo·ma·cy, n. pl. -cies. diplomacia
dip·lo·mat, n. diplomático
dip·lo·mat·ic, a. diplomático
dire, a. horrendo
di·rect, a. directo; franco. v. dirigir
di·rec·tion, n. dirección
di·rect·ly, adv. directamente
di·rec·tor, n. director
dirge, n. endecha
dirt, n. mugre, f.; tierra; porquería
dirt·y, a. sucio; verde. v. ensuciar
dis·a·bil·i·ty, n. pl. -ties. incapacidad
dis·a·ble, v. mutilar; inutilizar
dis·ad·van·tage, n. desventaja
dis·ad·van·ta·geous, a. desventajoso
dis·a·gree, v. discrepar
dis·a·gree·a·ble, a. desagradable
dis·a·gree·ment, n. desacuerdo
dis·ap·pear, v. desaparecer
dis·ap·pear·ance, n. desaparición
dis·ap·point, v. desilusionar
dis·ap·point·ment, n. contratiempo
dis·ap·prov·al, n. desaprobación
dis·ap·prove, v. desaprobar
dis·arm, v. desarmar

dis·ar·ray, n. desorden
dis·as·ter, n. desastre
dis·as·trous, a. desastroso
dis·a·vow, v. desconocer
dis·band, v. licenciar
dis·bar, v. expulsar
dis·burse, v. desembolsar
dis·burse·ment, n. desembolso
disc, disk, n. disco
dis·card, v. descartar
dis·cern, v. discernir
dis·cern·i·ble, a. perceptible
dis·cern·ing, a. perspicaz
dis·cern·ment, n. discernimiento
dis·charge, v. descargar; despedir; cumplir
dis·ci·ple, n. discípulo
dis·ci·pli·nar·y, a. disciplinario
dis·ci·pline, n. disciplina; castigo. v. disciplinar
dis·claim, v. negar
dis·claim·er, n. renuncia
dis·clo·sure, n. revelación
dis·com·fort, n. incomodidad
dis·con·cert, v. desconcertar
dis·con·nect, v. desacoplar; desconectar
dis·con·tent, n. descontento
dis·con·tin·ue, v. descontinuar
dis·con·tin·u·ous, a. discontinuo
dis·cord, n. discordia
dis·count, n. descuento
dis·cour·age, v. desanimar
dis·cour·age·ment, n. desaliento
dis·cour·te·ous, a. descortés
dis·cov·er, v. descubrir; encontrar
dis·cov·er·y, n. pl. -ies. descubrimiento; hallazgo
dis·cred·it, v. desacreditar
dis·creet, a. discreto
dis·crep·an·cy, n. pl. -cies. discrepancia
dis·cre·tion, n. discreción
dis·crim·i·nate, v. distinguir
dis·crim·i·na·tion, n. discriminación; discernimiento
dis·cuss, v. discutir
dis·cus·sion, n. discusión
dis·dain, v. desdeñar
dis·dain·ful, a. desdeñoso
dis·ease, n. enfermedad
dis·en·chant, v. desencantar
dis·en·chant·ment, n. desencanto
dis·fig·ure, v. desfigurar
dis·grace, n. deshonra; vergüenza. v. deshonrar
dis·grace·ful, a. vergonzoso
dis·guise, v. disfrazar. n. disfraz, m.
dis·gust, n. asco; repugnancia. v. disgustar
dis·gust·ing, a. asqueroso
dish, n. plato
dis·heart·en, v. desalentar; descorazonar

dis·hon·est, *a.* fraudulento; falso
dis·hon·es·ty, *n. pl.,* **-ties.** fraude
dis·hon·or, *n.* deshonra. *v.* deshonrar
dis·hon·or·a·ble, *a.* deshonroso
dis·il·lu·sion, *v.* desilusionar
dis·in·fect·ant, *n.* desinfectante
dis·in·her·it, *v.* desheredar
dis·in·te·grate, *v.* disgregar(se)
dis·in·te·gra·tion, *n.* desagregación
dis·in·ter·est, *n.* desinterés
disk, disc, *n.* disco
dis·like, *n.* antipatía
dis·lo·cate, *v.* dislocar
dis·lo·ca·tion, *n.* dislocación
dis·loy·al, *a.* desleal
dis·loy·al·ty, *n.* deslealtad
dis·mal, *a.* triste; sombrío
dis·man·tle, *v.* desmontar
dis·may, *v.* consternar; desanimar
dis·mem·ber, *v.* desmembrar
dis·miss, *v.* despedir
dis·o·be·di·ence, *n.* desobediencia
dis·o·bey, *v.* desobedecer
dis·or·der, *n.* desorden, *m.*
dis·or·gan·i·za·tion, *n.* desorganiza-
ción
dis·own, *v.* desconocer
dis·par·age, *v.* menospreciar
dis·par·i·ty, *n.* disparidad
dis·patch, *v.* enviar; despachar
dis·pel, *v.* dispersar
dis·pen·sa·tion, *n.* dispensa
dis·pense, *v.* dispensar
dis·perse, *v.* dispersar(se)
dis·play, *v.* exponer; demostrar
dis·please, *v.* desagradar
dis·pleas·ure, *n.* disgusto
dis·pose, *v.* disponer
dis·prove, *v.* confutar
dis·pute, *v.* disputar. *n.* disputa
dis·qual·i·fi·ca·tion, *n.* inhabilita-
ción
dis·qual·i·fy, *v.* descalificar
dis·re·gard, *n.* descuido. *v.* desaten-
der
dis·rep·u·ta·ble, *a.* de mala fama
dis·re·spect, *n.* desacato
dis·re·spect·ful, *a.* irrespetuoso
dis·rupt, *v.* desorganizar
dis·sat·is·fac·tion, *n.* descontento
dis·sect, *v.* disecar
dis·sen·sion, *n.* disensión
dis·sent, *v.* disentir
dis·si·pate, *v.* disipar
dis·solve, *v.* disolver(se)
dis·so·nance, *n.* disonancia
dis·suade, *v.* disuadir
dis·sua·sion, *n.* disuasión
dis·tance, *n.* distancia
dis·tant, *a.* lejano; distante
dis·taste, *n.* aversión
dis·till, *v.* destilar
dis·till·er·y, *n.* destilería
dis·tinct, *a.* distinto

dis·tinc·tion, *n.* distinción
dis·tin·guish, *v.* distinguir
dis·tin·guish·a·ble, *a.* distinguible
dis·tin·guished, *a.* distinguido
dis·tort, *v.* torcer
dis·tract, *v.* distraer
dis·tract·ed, *a.* distraído
dis·trac·tion, *n.* distracción; diversión
dis·traught, *a.* turbado
dis·tress, *n.* dolor; pena
dis·trib·ute, *v.* distribuir
dis·tri·bu·tion, *n.* distribución
dis·trict, *n.* distrito; región
dis·trust, *v.* desconfiar. *n.* recelo
dis·turb, *v.* perturbar
dis·turb·ance, *n.* alboroto; disturbio
dis·u·nite, *v.* desunir
ditch, *n.* zanja
dive, *v.* sumergirse. *n.* salto; zambu-
llida
div·er, *n.* buzo
di·verge, *v.* divergir
di·ver·gence, *n.* divergencia
di·verse, *a.* diverso
di·ver·sion, *n.* diversión
di·ver·si·ty, *n.* diversidad
di·vert, *v.* desviar; divertir
di·vide, *v.* dividir(se)
div·i·dend, *n.* dividendo
di·vine, *a.* divino. *v.* adivinar
di·vin·i·ty, *n. pl.,* **-ties.** divinidad
di·vi·sion, *n.* división; repartimiento
di·vorce, *n.* divorcio. *v.* divorciarse
di·vulge, *v.* divulgar
diz·zi·ness, *n.* vértigo
diz·zy, *a.* mareado; vertiginoso
do, *v.,* **did, done, do·ing.** hacer;
producir; cumplir; representar;
servir
doc·ile, *a.* dócil
dock, *n.* dársena; dique
doc·tor, *n.* médico; doctor
doc·trine, *n.* doctrina
doc·u·ment, *n.* documento. *v.* docu-
mentar
doc·u·men·ta·ry, *a.* documental
dodge, *v.* evadir
doe, *n. pl.,* **does, doe.** gama
doff, *v.* quitar(se)
dog, *n.* perro
dog·ged, *a.* tenaz
dog·ma, *n. pl.,* **-mas.** dogma, *m.*
dog·mat·ic, *a.* dogmático
dog·ma·tize, *v.* dogmatizar
doi·ly, *n. pl.,* **-lies.** pañito de adorno
dol·drums, *n. pl.* desánimo
dole, *n.* limosna. *v.* repartir
doll, *n.* muñeca
dol·lar, *n.* dólar
dol·or·ous, *a.* doloroso
dolt, *n.* imbécil; necio
do·main, *n.* dominio; heredad
dome, *n.* cúpula

do·mes·tic, a., n. doméstico

do·mes·ti·cate, v. domesticar

dom·i·nant, a. dominante

dom·i·nate, v. dominar

dom·i·na·tion, n. dominación

dom·i·neer, v. tiranizar

dom·i·neer·ing, a. dominante

do·min·ion, n. dominio

don, v. ponerse; asumir

do·nate, v. donar

done, a. hecho

do·nor, n. donante

doom, n. juicio; suerte, f. v. condenar

door, n. puerta; entrada

dope, n. narcótico. v. narcotizar

dor·mi·to·ry, n. pl. -ries. dormitorio

dor·sal, a. dorsal

dos·age, n. dosificación

dose, n. dosis, f.

dot, n. punto. v. puntear

dot·age, n. chochez, f.

dou·ble, a. doble. v. doblar(se)

doubt, v. dudar. n. duda

doubt·ful, a. dudoso; sospechoso

doubt·less, adv. sin duda

dough, n. masa

dough·nut, n. buñuelo

dour, a. austero

douse, v. mojar; zambullir

dow·a·ger, n. viuda de un titulado

dow·dy, a. desaliñado; poco elegante

down, adv. abajo; por tierra. prep. abajo. a. descendente. n. plumón

down·cast, a. abatido

down·fall, n. caída

down·heart·ed, a. desanimado

down·ward, adv. hacia abajo. Also down·wards

doze, v. dormitar

doz·en, n. pl. -ens. docena

drab, a. monótono

draft, n. destacamento; giro; borrador

drag, v. arrastrar

drag·on, n. dragón

drain, v. agotar; desaguar. n. desagüe; desaguadero

drain·age, n. desagüe; drenaje

dra·ma, n. drama, m.

dra·mat·ic, a. dramático

dram·a·tist, n. dramaturgo

dram·a·tize, v. dramatizar

drape, v. poner colgaduras. n. colgadura

dra·per·y, n. pl. -ies. pañería

dras·tic, a. drástico; enérgico

draw, v. arrastrar; girar; sacar; atraer; dibujar

draw·back, n. desventaja

draw·bridge, n. puente levadizo

draw·er, n. cajón

draw·ing, n. dibujo

drawl, v. arrastrar las palabras

drawn, a. ojeroso

dread, v. temer. n. pavor

dread·ful, a. terrible

dream, n. sueño. v. soñar

dream·er, n. soñador

dream·y, a. soñador

drear·y, a. triste

dredge, n. rastra. v. dragar

dreg, n. usu. pl. heces, f. pl.

drench, v. empapar

dress, v. vestir(se). n. ropa; vestido

dress·er, n. aparador

drib·ble, v. caer gota a gota

drift, n. impulso de la corriente; montón. v. amontonar(se); derivar

drift·wood, n. madera llevada por el agua

drill, v. taladrar. n. taladro; ejercicios

drink, v. drank, drunk, drink·ing. beber. n. bebida

drip, v. gotear. n. gota

drive, v. conducir; manejar; empujar. n. paseo en coche; energía; calzada

driz·zle, v. lloviznar

droll, a. gracioso

droll·er·y, n. pl. -ies. chuscada

drone, n. zángano. v. zumbar

drool, v. babear

droop, v. inclinar

drop, n. gota; declive. v. dejar caer

drop·sy, n. hidropesía

dross, n. escoria

drought, n. sequía

drown, v. ahogar; anegar

drowse, v. adormecer(se)

drow·si·ness, n. somnolencia

drow·sy, a. soñoliento

drudg·er·y, n. pl. -ies. faena penosa

drug, n. droga; narcótico. v. administrar drogas

drug·gist, n. farmacéutico; boticario

drum, n. tambor. v. tamborilear

drum·stick, n. baqueta

drunk, a. borracho; ebrio

drunk·ard, n. borracho

drunk·en, a. borracho

drunk·en·ness, n. embriaguez, f.

dry, a. seco; árido. v. secar(se)

dry·ness, n. sequedad

du·al, a. dual

du·al·i·ty, n. dualidad

dub, v. armar caballero

du·bi·ous, a. dudoso

duch·ess, n. duquesa

duck, v. chapuzar(se). n. pato

duct, n. conducto

dude, n. petimetre

due, a. debido; oportuno. n. derecho

du·el, n. duelo. v. batirse en duelo

du·el·ist, n. duelista, m.

du·et, n. dúo

duke, n. duque

duke·dom, n. ducado

dull, a. torpe; pesado; embotado. v. embotar; deslustrar

dull·ness, dul·ness, n. torpeza

du·ly, adv. debidamente

dumb, a. torpe; mudo

dum·found, v. pasmar. Also **dumb·found**

dum·my, n. pl., **-mies.** maniquí, m.; muerto

dump, v. descargar. n. basurero

dump·ling, n. bola de masa

dunce, n. zopenco

dune, n. duna

dung, n. estiércol, m.

dun·geon, n. mazmorra

dupe, v. embaucar

du·pli·cate, v. duplicar. a. duplicado. n. copia

du·pli·ca·tion, n. duplicación

du·plic·i·ty, n. pl., **-ties.** duplicidad

du·ra·ble, a. duradero

du·ra·tion, n. duración

du·ress, n. compulsión

dur·ing, prep. durante

dusk, n. crepúsculo

dusk·y, a. oscuro

dust, n. polvo. v. quitar el polvo

dust·y, a. polvoriento

du·ti·ful, a. obediente

du·ty, n. pl., **-ties.** deber; derechos

dwarf, n. enano

dwell, v. morar; habitar

dwell·ing, n. morada

dwin·dle, v. disminuir

dye, n. tinte. v. teñir

dye·ing, n. tintura

dy·nam·ic, a. dinámico

dy·nam·i·cal, a. dinámico

dy·na·mite, n. dinamita

dy·na·mo, n. pl., **-mos.** dinamo, dínamo, f.

dy·nas·ty, n. pl., **-ties.** dinastía

dys·en·ter·y, n. disentería

E

each, a. cada. pron. cada uno. adv. para cada uno

ea·ger, a. ansioso; impaciente

ea·ger·ly, adv. con ansia

ea·ger·ness, n. ansia

ea·gle, n. águila

ea·glet, n. aguilucho

ear, n. oreja; oído; espiga

ear·drum, n. tímpano del oído

earl, n. conde

earl·dom, n. condado

ear·li·ness, n. precocidad

ear·ly, adv. temprano. a. avanzado; temprano; primitivo

earn, v. ganar; merecer

ear·nest, a. fervoroso; serio

ear·nest·ly, adv. con seriedad

earn·ings, n. pl. ganancias; sueldo

ear·ring, n. pendiente

ear·shot, n. alcance del oído

earth, n. tierra; mundo

earth·en·ware, n. loza de barro

earth·ly, a. terrestre; mundano

earth·quake, n. terremoto

earth·y, a. terroso

ease, n. tranquilidad; facilidad. v. aliviar; facilitar

ea·sel, n. caballete

eas·i·ly, adv. fácilmente

eas·i·ness, n. facilidad

east, n. este; oriente. a. oriental. adv. al este

east·ern, a. del este

east·ward, adv. hacia el este. Also **east·wards**

eas·y, a. cómodo; fácil

eas·y·go·ing, a. acomodadizo; de manga ancha

eat, v. comer; gastar

eat·a·ble, a. comestible. n. pl. comestibles

eaves, n. pl. alero

eaves·drop, v. escuchar a escondidas; espiar

ebb, v. menguar; decaer. n. reflujo

eb·on·y, n. pl., **-ies.** ébano. a. de ébano

ec·cen·tric, a. n. excéntrico

ec·cen·tric·i·ty, n. pl., **-ties.** excentricidad

ec·cle·si·as·tic, a., n. eclesiástico

ec·cle·si·as·ti·cal, a. eclesiástico

ech·o, n. pl., **-oes.** eco. v. resonar

e·clipse, n. eclipse. v. eclipsar

e·clip·tic, a. eclíptico

ec·o·log·ic, a. ecológico

ec·o·log·i·cal, a. ecológico

e·col·o·gist, n. ecólogo

e·col·o·gy, n. ecología

ec·o·nom·ic, a. económico

ec·o·nom·i·cal, a. económico

ec·o·nom·ics, n. pl. economía

e·con·o·mist, n. economista, m., f.

e·con·o·mize, v. economizar

e·con·o·my, n. pl., **-mies.** economía

ec·sta·sy, n. pl., **-sies.** éxtasis, m.

ec·stat·ic, a. extático

ec·u·men·i·cal, a. ecuménico

ec·ze·ma, n. eczema, eccema, m.

ed·dy, n. pl., **-dies.** remolino

e·den·tate, a. desdentado

edge, n. filo; agudeza; borde. v. ribetear

edged, a. cortante

edg·y, a. nervioso

ed·i·ble, a. comestible. n. usu. pl. comestibles

e·dict, n. edicto

ed·i·fi·ca·tion, n. edificación

ed·i·fice, n. edificio

ed·i·fy, v. edificar

ed·it, v. editar; dirigir

e·di·tion, n. edición

ed·i·tor, n. director; editor

ed·i·to·ri·al, a. editorial. n. artículo

de fondo

ed·i·to·ri·al·ist, n. editorialista, m., f.

ed·u·cate, v. educar

ed·u·ca·tion, n. educación

eel, n. pl., eels, eel. anguila

ee·rie, a. espantoso; fantástico

ef·face, v. borrar

ef·fect, n. efecto; resultado; pl. efectos. v. efectuar

ef·fec·tive, a. efectivo; eficaz

ef·fec·tu·al, a. eficaz

ef·fem·i·nate, a. afeminado

ef·fer·vesce, v. estar en efervescencia

ef·fer·ves·cence, n. efervescencia

ef·fer·ves·cent, a. efervescente

ef·fi·ca·cious, a. eficaz

ef·fi·cien·cy, n. pl., -cies. eficiencia

ef·fi·cient, a. eficiente

ef·fi·gy, n. pl., -gies. efigie, f.

ef·fort, n. esfuerzo

ef·fort·less, a. sin esfuerzo

ef·fuse, v. derramar

ef·fu·sion, n. efusión

ef·fu·sive, a. expansivo; efusivo

egg, n. huevo. v. incitar

e·go, n. pl., -gos. el yo

e·go·tist, n. egotista, m., f.

e·gress, n. salida

eight, a., n. ocho

eight·een, a., n. dieciocho

eight·eenth, a., n. decimoctavo

eighth, a., n. octavo

eight·i·eth, a., n. octogésimo

eight·y, a., n. pl., -ies. ochenta

ei·ther, a. cualquier. pron. uno u otro. adv. también; tampoco

e·ject, v. aumentar. eke out, ganar a duras penas

e·lab·o·rate, v. elaborar. a. detallado

e·lab·o·ra·tion, n. elaboración

e·lapse, v. pasar

e·las·tic, a. elástico

e·las·tic·i·ty, n. elasticidad

e·late, v. exaltar; alegrar

e·la·tion, n. regocijo

el·bow, n. codo

eld·er, a. mayor. n. mayor; anciano

eld·er·ly, a. de edad

eld·est, a. el mayor

e·lect, v. elegir. a. elegido; electo

e·lec·tion, n. elección

e·lec·tive, a. electivo

e·lec·tor, n. elector

e·lec·tor·ate, n. electorado

e·lec·tric, a. eléctrico; vivo. Also e·lec·tri·cal

e·lec·tri·cian, n. electricista, m., f.

e·lec·tric·i·ty, n. electricidad

e·lec·tri·fy, v. electrizar

e·lec·tro·cute, v. electrocutar

e·lec·tro·cu·tion, n. electrocución

e·lec·trode, n. electrodo

e·lec·tron, n. electrón

e·lec·tron·ic, a. electrónico

e·lec·tron·ics, n. pl. electrónica

el·e·gance, n. el·e·gan·cy, n. elegancia

el·e·gant, a. elegante

el·e·gize, v. hacer una elegía

el·e·gy, n. pl., -gies. elegía

el·e·ment, n. elemento

el·e·men·ta·ry, a. elemental; primario

el·e·phant, n. elefante

el·e·phan·tine, a. elefantino

el·e·vate, v. elevar; exaltar

el·e·va·tion, n. elevación; altura

el·e·va·tor, n. ascensor

el·ev·en, a., n. once

el·ev·enth, a., n. undécimo

elf, n. pl. elves. duende

elf·in, a. de elfo

e·lic·it, v. sacar

el·i·gi·bil·i·ty, n. elegibilidad

el·i·gi·ble, a. elegible; deseable

e·lim·i·nate, v. eliminar

e·lim·i·na·tion, n. eliminación

e·lite, n. lo mejor

e·lix·ir, n. elixir

elk, n. pl., elks, elk. alce

e·lipse, n. elipse, f.

e·lip·ti·cal, a. elíptico

elm, n. olmo

el·o·cu·tion, n. elocución

e·lon·gate, v. alargar

e·lope, v. fugarse con su amante para casarse

e·lope·ment, n. fuga

el·o·quence, n. elocuencia

el·o·quent, a. elocuente

else, a. otro; más. adv. en otro caso

else·where, adv. en (a) otra parte

e·lu·ci·date, v. elucidar

e·lude, v. eludir; escapar de

e·lu·sive, a. esquivo

e·ma·ci·ate, v. enflaquecer(se)

e·ma·ci·a·tion, n. demacración

em·a·nate, v. emanar

e·man·ci·pate, v. emancipar

e·man·ci·pa·tion, n. emancipación

em·balm, v. embalsamar

em·balm·er, n. embalsamador

em·bar·go, n. pl., -goes. embargo

em·bark, v. embarcar(se)

em·bar·rass, v. desconcertar

em·bas·sy, n. pl., -sies. embajada

em·bel·lish, v. embellecer

em·ber, n. ascua

em·bez·zle, v. desfalcar

em·bez·zler, n. malversador

em·blem, n. emblema, m.

em·boss, v. realzar

em·brace, v. abrazar; aceptar; abarcar. n. abrazo

em·broi·der, v. recamar

em·broi·der·y, n. pl., -ies. bordado

em·bry·o, *n. pl.,* -os. embrión

em·er·ald, *n.* esmeralda. *a.* de color de esmeralda

e·merge, *v.* surgir; salir

e·mer·gence, *n.* salida

e·mer·gen·cy, *n. pl.,* -cies. crisis, *f.;* necesidad

em·er·y, *n.* esmeril, *m.*

em·i·grant, *n.* emigrante, *m., f.*

em·i·grate, *v.* emigrar

em·i·gra·tion, *n.* emigración

em·i·nence, *n.* eminencia

em·i·nent, *a.* eminente

em·is·sar·y, *n. pl.,* -ies. emisario

e·mis·sion, *n.* emisión

e·mit, *v.* emitir; arrojar

e·mo·tion, *n.* emoción

em·per·or, *n.* emperador

em·pha·sis, *n. pl.,* -ses. énfasis, *m.*

em·pha·size, *v.* acentuar; recalcar

em·phat·ic, *a.* enfático

em·pire, *n.* imperio

em·ploy, *v.* emplear; ocupar

em·ploy·ee, em·ploy·e, *n.* empleado

em·ploy·er, *n.* amo; patrón

em·ploy·ment, *n.* empleo; colocación

em·pow·er, *v.* autorizar

em·press, *n. f.* emperatriz

emp·ti·ness, *n.* vacuidad; vacío

emp·ty, *a.* vacío; desocupado; vano. *v.* vaciar(se)

em·u·late, *v.* emular

e·mul·sion, *n.* emulsión

e·mul·sive, *a.* emulsivo

en·a·ble, *v.* hacer que; permitir

en·act, *v.* decretar; hacer el papel de

en·am·el, *n.* esmalte. *v.* esmaltar

en·am·or, *v.* enamorar

en·case, *v.* encerrar; encajar

en·chant, *v.* encantar

en·chant·ing, *a.* encantador

en·chant·ment, *n.* encanto

en·cir·cle, *v.* ceñir; rodear

en·close, *v.* cercar; encerrar; incluir

en·clo·sure, *n.* cercamiento; carta adjunta

en·com·pass, *v.* cercar; abarcar

en·core, *n.* repetición

en·coun·ter, *n.* encuentro. *v.* encontrar; oponerse

en·cour·age, *v.* animar; fomentar

en·cour·ag·ing, *a.* alentador

en·croach, *v.* usurpar; pasar los límites

en·croach·ment, *n.* usurpación; abuso

en·cum·ber, *v.* estorbar; gravar

en·cy·clo·pe·di·a, *n.* enciclopedia. Also en·cy·clo·pae·di·a

end, *n.* fin; conclusión; extremo; final, *m.;* desenlace. *v.* terminar; acabar

en·dan·ger, *v.* poner en peligro

en·dear, *v.* hacer querer

en·deav·or, *n.* esfuerzo. *v.* esforzarse; intentar

end·ing, *n.* fin, *m.;* desenlace

en·dorse, *v.* endosar

en·dorse·ment, *n.* endoso

en·dow, *v.* dotar

en·dur·ance, *n.* resistencia

en·dure, *v.* soportar; aguantar; durar

en·dur·ing, *a.* perdurable

en·e·my, *n. pl.,* -mies. enemigo

en·er·get·ic, *a.* enérgico

en·er·gy, *n. pl.,* -gies. energía

en·force, *v.* hacer cumplir; exigir

en·gage, *v.* emplear; apalabrar; atraer; engranar

en·gaged, *a.* ocupado; prometido

en·gage·ment, *n.* compromiso; obligación

en·gag·ing, *a.* atractivo

en·gen·der, *v.* engendrar

en·gine, *n.* motor; locomotora

en·gi·neer, *n.* ingeniero

en·gi·neer·ing, *n.* ingeniería

Eng·lish, *a., n.* inglés

en·grave, *v.* grabar

en·grav·er, *n.* grabador

en·grav·ing, *n.* grabado

en·gross, *v.* absorber; monopolizar

en·hance, *v.* aumentar

e·nig·ma, *n.* enigma, *m.*

en·ig·mat·ic, en·ig·mat·i·cal, *a.* enigmático

en·join, *v.* imponer

en·joy, *v.* gozar de; disfrutar

en·joy·ment, *n.* placer; disfrute

en·large, *v.* extender(se)

en·large·ment, *n.* aumento; ampliación

en·light·en, *v.* iluminar; instruir

en·list, *v.* alistar(se)

en·list·ment, *n.* alistamiento

en·liv·en, *v.* avivar

en·mi·ty, *n. pl.,* -ties. enemistad

en·no·ble, *v.* ennoblecer

e·nor·mi·ty, *n. pl.,* -ties. enormidad; atrocidad

e·nor·mous, *a.* enorme

e·nough, *a., adv.* bastante. *n.* lo suficiente

en·rage, *v.* enfurecer

en·rich, *v.* enriquecer

en·roll, *v.* matricular(se); inscribir(se)

en·roll·ment, *n.* matrícula

en·sem·ble, *n.* conjunto

en·sign, *n.* bandera. *milit.* alférez, *m.*

en·slave, *v.* esclavizar

en·sue, *v.* seguir

en·tail, *v.* vincular

en·tan·gle, *v.* enredar

en·ter, *v.* entrar (en); ingresar; anotar

en·ter·prise, *n.* empresa; iniciativa

en·ter·pris·ing, *a.* emprendedor

en·ter·tain, *v.* festejar; entretener;

considerar

en·ter·tain·ment, n. diversión; espectáculo
en·thrall, v. encantar. Also en·thral
en·thu·si·asm, n. entusiasmo
en·thu·si·ast, n. entusiasta, m., f.
en·tice, v. tentar
en·tice·ment, n. tentación
en·tire, a. entero
en·tire·ly, adv. totalmente
en·tire·ty, n. totalidad
en·ti·tle, v. dar derecho; titular
en·ti·ty, n. pl., -ties. entidad
en·trails, n. pl. entrañas
en·trance, n. entrada. Also en·trance·way
en·trance, v. hechizar
en·treat, v. rogar
en·treat·y, n. ruego
en·tree, n. entrada
en·trench, v. atrincherar
en·trench·ment, n. trinchera
en·trust, v. entregar; confiar
en·try, n. pl., -ties. entrada; ingreso; partida
e·nu·mer·ate, v. enumerar
e·nu·mer·a·tion, n. enumeración
e·nun·ci·ate, v. enunciar; pronunciar
en·vel·op, v. envolver
en·ve·lope, n. sobre
en·vi·ous, a. envidioso
en·vi·ron·ment, n. ambiente
en·voy, n. enviado
en·vy, n. pl., -vies. envidia. v. envidiar
en·zyme, n. enzima
e·phem·er·al, a. efímero
ep·ic, a. épico. n. epopeya
ep·i·dem·ic, a. epidémico. n. epidemia
ep·i·der·mis, n. epidermis, f.
ep·i·lep·sy, n. epilepsia
ep·i·lep·tic, a., n. epiléptico
ep·i·logue, ep·i·log, n. epílogo
e·pis·co·pal, a. episcopal
ep·i·sode, n. episodio
e·pis·tle, n. epístola
ep·i·taph, n. epitafio
ep·i·thet, n. epíteto
ep·it·o·me, n. resumen; epítome
e·pit·o·mize, v. epitomar
ep·och, n. época
e·qua·bil·i·ty, n. uniformidad
e·qua·ble, a. uniforme
e·qual, a., n. igual. v. igualar
e·qual·i·ty, n. pl., -ties. igualdad
e·qual·ize, v. igualar
e·qual·ly, adv. igualmente
e·qua·nim·i·ty, n. ecuanimidad
e·quate, v. comparar
e·qua·tion, n. ecuación
e·qua·tor, n. ecuador
e·ques·tri·an, a. ecuestre. n. jinete
e·ques·tri·enne, n. f. jineta

e·qui·lib·ri·um, n. pl., -ums, -a. equilibrio
e·qui·nox, n. equinoccio
e·quip, v. proveer; equipar
e·quip·ment, n. equipo
e·qui·ta·ble, a. equitativo
eq·ui·ty, n. pl., -ties. equidad
e·quiv·a·lent, a., n. equivalente
e·quiv·o·cal, a. equívoco
e·ra, n. era
e·rad·i·cate, v. desarraigar
e·rad·i·ca·tion, n. extirpación
e·rase, v. borrar
e·ras·er, n. borrador
ere, conj. antes de que. prep. antes de
e·rect, v. levantar; erigir. a. erguido
e·rec·tion, n. erección; montaje
er·mine, n. pl., -mine, -mines. armiño
e·rode, v. corroer
e·ro·sion, n. erosión
e·rot·ic, a. erótico
e·rot·i·cism, n. erotomanía
err, v. vagar; errar
er·rand, n. recado
er·rant, a. errante
er·rat·ic, a. errático; excéntrico
er·ro·ne·ous, a. erróneo
er·ror, n. error
erst·while, a. antiguo; primero
er·u·dite, a. erudito
er·u·di·tion, n. erudición
e·rupt, v. estar en erupción
e·rup·tion, n. erupción
es·ca·la·tor, n. escalera móvil
es·ca·pade, n. aventura
es·cape, v. escapar; huir. n. fuga; escape
es·chew, v. evitar
es·cort, n. acompañante; escolta: v. acompañar; escoltar
e·soph·a·gus, oe·soph·a·gus, n. pl., -gi, -ji. esófago
es·o·ter·ic, a. esotérico
es·pe·cial, a. especial
es·pe·cial·ly, adv. especialmente
es·pi·o·nage, n. espionaje
es·pouse, v. adherirse a; casarse
es·py, v. divisar; percebir
es·say, n. ensayo. v. intentar
es·say·ist, n. ensayista, m., f.
es·sence, n. esencia; perfume
es·sen·tial, a., n. esencial
es·tab·lish, v. establecer; probar; fundar
es·tab·lish·ment, n. establecimiento
es·tate, n. finca; propiedad
es·teem, v. estimar. n. estima
es·thet·ic, a. estético
es·ti·ma·ble, a. estimable
es·ti·mate, v. calcular; estimar. n. tasa
es·ti·ma·tion, n. juicio; aprecio
es·trange, v. apartar
es·tu·ar·y, n. pl., -ies. estuario

et cet·er·a, n. etcétera

etch, v. grabar al agua fuerte

etch·ing, n. aguafuerte, f.

e·ter·nal, a. eterno

e·ter·nal·ly, adv. eternamente

e·ter·ni·ty, n. pl., -ties. eternidad

e·ther, n. éter

e·the·re·al, a. etéreo

eth·i·cal, a. ético

eth·ics, n. pl. ética

eth·nic, a. étnico. Also eth·ni·cal

eth·nol·o·gy, n. etnología

et·i·quette, n. etiqueta

é·tude, n. estudio

et·y·mol·o·gist, n. etimologista, m., f.

et·y·mol·o·gy, n. pl., -gies. etimología

eu·gen·ics, n. pl. eugenismo

eu·lo·gize, v. elogiar

eu·lo·gy, n. pl., -gies. elogio

eu·nuch, n. eunuco

eu·phe·mism, n. eufemismo

eu·phon·ic, a. eufónico

eu·pho·ny, n. eufonia

eu·pho·ri·a, n. euforia

eu·phor·ic, a. eufórico

eu·tha·na·sia, n. eutanasia

e·vac·u·ate, v. evacuar

e·vac·u·a·tion, n. evacuación

e·vade, v. evadir

e·val·u·ate, v. evaluar

e·val·u·a·tion, n. evaluación

e·van·gel·i·cal, a. evangélico

e·van·ge·lism, n. evangelismo

e·van·ge·list, n. evangelista, m.; evangelizador

e·vap·o·rate, v. evaporar(se)

e·vap·o·ra·tion, n. evaporación

e·va·sion, n. evasión; evasiva

e·va·sive, a. evasivo

eve, n. víspera

e·ven, a. llano; uniforme; par. adv. aun. v. igualar; allanar

eve·ning, n. tarde, f. de noche

e·vent, n. suceso

e·vent·ful, a. memorable

e·ven·tu·al·i·ty, n. pl., -ties. eventualidad

ev·er, adv. siempre; nunca; jamás

eve·ry, a. cada; todo

e·vict, v. expulsar; desahuciar

e·vic·tion, n. desahucio

ev·i·dence, n. prueba; testimonio; evidencia. v. probar

ev·i·dent, a. evidente

e·vil, a. malo. adv. malamente. n. mal, m.

e·vil·do·er, n. malhechor

e·voke, v. evocar

ev·o·lu·tion, n. desarrollo; evolución

e·volve, v. desarrollar

ewe, n. oveja

ew·er, n. aguamanil, m.

ex·act, v. exigir. a. exacto

ex·act·ing, a. exigente

ex·ag·ger·ate, v. exagerar

ex·ag·ger·a·tion, n. exageración

ex·alt, v. exaltar; honrar

ex·al·ta·tion, n. exaltación

ex·am·in·a·tion, n. examen

ex·am·ine, v. examinar; interrogar

ex·am·in·er, n. examinador

ex·am·ple, n. ejemplo

ex·as·per·ate, v. exasperar

ex·as·per·a·tion, n. exasperación

ex·ca·vate, v. excavar

ex·ca·va·tion, n. excavación

ex·ceed, v. exceder; superar

ex·ceed·ing·ly, adv. sumamente

ex·cel, v. sobresalir; aventajar

ex·cel·lence, n. excelencia

ex·cel·lent, a. excelente

ex·cept, v. exceptuar. prep. excepto. conj. a. menos que

ex·cep·tion, n. excepción

ex·cep·tion·al, a. excepcional

ex·cerpt, v. citar un texto. n. extracto

ex·cess, n. exceso

ex·ces·sive, a. excesivo

ex·change, v. cambiar. n. cambio; canje

ex·cise, n. impuestos sobre ciertos artículos. Also ex·cise tax

ex·cit·a·ble, a. excitable

ex·cite, v. excitar; provocar

ex·cite·ment, n. agitación; emoción

ex·cit·ing, a. emocionante

ex·claim, v. exclamar

ex·cla·ma·tion, n. exclamación

ex·clude, v. excluir

ex·clu·sion, n. exclusión

ex·clu·sive, a. exclusivo

ex·com·mu·ni·cate, v. excomulgar

ex·com·mu·ni·ca·tion, n. excomunión

ex·cre·ment, n. excremento

ex·cur·sion, n. viaje; excursión

ex·cuse, v. perdonar; disculpar; excusar. n. excusa; disculpa

ex·e·cute, v. ejecutar; llevar a cabo

ex·e·cu·tion, n. ejecución

ex·ec·u·tive, a. ejecutivo. n. poder ejecutivo

ex·ec·u·tor, n. albacea, m.

ex·em·pla·ry, a. ejemplar

ex·empt, v. exentar. a. exento

ex·emp·tion, n. exención

ex·er·cise, n. ejercicio. v. ejercitar(se); ejercer

ex·ert, v. ejercer

ex·er·tion, n. esfuerzo

ex·hale, v. exhalar; espirar

ex·haust, v. agotar

ex·haus·tion, n. agotamiento

ex·haus·tive, a. minucioso

ex·hib·it, v. mostrar; presentar. n. objeto expuesto

ex·hi·bi·tion, *n.* exposición
ex·hib·i·tor, *n.* expositor
ex·hil·a·rate, *v.* vigorizar; alegrar
ex·hort, *v.* exhortar
ex·hor·ta·tion, *n.* exhortación
ex·i·gent, *a.* exigente
ex·ile, *n.* destierro; desterrado; exilado. *v.* desterrar
ex·ist, *v.* existir
ex·ist·ence, *n.* existencia
ex·it, *n.* salida
ex·o·dus, *n.* éxodo
ex·or·bi·tant, *a.* excesivo
ex·o·tic, *a.* exótico
ex·pand, *v.* extender; ensanchar
ex·panse, *n.* extensión
ex·pan·sion, *n.* expansión
ex·pan·sive, *a.* expansivo
ex·pect, *v.* esperar; contar con
ex·pect·an·cy, *n. pl.* -cies. expectación
ex·pect·ant, *a.* expectante
ex·pec·ta·tion, *n.* esperanza; expectación
ex·pe·di·en·cy, *n.* conveniencia
ex·pe·di·ent, *a.* conveniente. *n.* recurso
ex·pe·dite, *v.* facilitar; acelerar
ex·pe·di·tion, *n.* expedición
ex·pel, *v.* arrojar; expulsar
ex·pend, *v.* expender
ex·pend·i·ture, *n.* gasto
ex·pense, *n.* gasto; *pl.* gastos
ex·pen·sive, *a.* caro
ex·pe·ri·ence, *n.* experiencia. *v.* experimentar
ex·per·i·ment, *n.* experimento
ex·per·i·men·tal, *a.* experimental
ex·pert, *a., n.* experto
ex·pire, *v.* exhalar; morir; terminar
ex·plain, *v.* explicar
ex·pla·na·tion, *n.* explicación
ex·plic·it, *a.* explícito
ex·plic·it·ly, *adv.* explícitamente
ex·plode, *v.* estallar; volar
ex·ploit, *n.* hazaña. *v.* explotar
ex·ploi·ta·tion, *n.* explotación
ex·plo·ra·tion, *n.* exploración
ex·plore, *v.* explorar; examinar
ex·plor·er, *n.* explorador
ex·plo·sion, *n.* explosión
ex·po·nent, *n.* exponente
ex·port, *v.* exportar. *n.* exportación. *a.* de exportación
ex·por·ta·tion, *n.* exportación
ex·pose, *v.* exponer; desenmascarar
ex·po·si·tion, *n.* exposición
ex·po·sure, *n.* exposición, revelación
ex·pound, *v.* exponer
ex·press, *v.* expresar. *a.* explícito; rápido
ex·pres·sion, *n.* expresión; gesto
ex·pres·sive, *a.* expresivo
ex·pul·sion, *n.* expulsión

ex·pul·sive, *a.* expulsivo
ex·qui·site, *a.* exquisito; agudo
ex·tant, *a.* existente
ex·tem·po·ra·ne·ous, *a.* improviso
ex·tend, *v.* extender; ofrecer
ex·ten·sion, *n.* extensión; prolongación
ex·ten·sive, *a.* extenso
ex·tent, *n.* extensión; alcance
ex·te·ri·or, *a., n.* exterior
ex·ter·mi·nate, *v.* exterminar
ex·ter·mi·na·tion, *n.* exterminación; exterminio
ex·ter·nal, *a.* externo
ex·tinct, *a.* extinto
ex·tinc·tion, *n.* extinción
ex·tin·guish, *v.* extinguir
ex·tol, *v.* alabar
ex·tort, *v.* obtener por fuerza
ex·tor·tion, *n.* exacción
ex·tra, *a.* adicional. *n.* extra. *adv.* extraordinariamente
ex·tract, *v.* extraer; sacar. *n.* cita
ex·trac·tion, *n.* extracción
ex·tra·or·di·nar·y, *a.* extraordinario
ex·trav·a·gance, *n.* exorbitancia
ex·trav·a·gant, *a.* pródigo
ex·treme, *a., n.* extremo
ex·trem·i·ty, *n. pl.* -ties. necesidad; *usu. pl.* extremidades
ex·tri·cate, *v.* desenredar
ex·tro·vert, *n.* extrovertido
ex·u·ber·ant, *a.* exuberante
ex·ude, *v.* rezumar
ex·ult, *v.* regocijarse
ex·ul·ta·tion, *n.* exultación
eye, *n.* ojo. *v.* ojear
eye·let, *n.* ojete
eye·sight, *n.* vista
eye·tooth, *n. pl.* -teeth. colmillo
eye·wit·ness, *n.* testigo ocular

F

fa·ble, *n.* fábula
fab·ric, *n.* tela
fab·ri·cate, *v.* inventar
fab·u·lous, *a.* fabuloso
fa·cade, *n.* fachada
face, *n.* cara; rostro. *v.* encararse
fac·et, *n.* faceta
fa·ce·tious, *a.* chistoso
fa·cial, *a.* facial
fac·ile, *a.* fácil
fa·cil·i·tate, *v.* facilitar
fa·cil·i·ty, *n. pl.* -ties. facilidad; *often pl.* facilidades
fac·sim·i·le, *n.* facsímile
fact, *n.* hecho
fac·tion, *n.* facción
fac·tor, *n.* factor
fac·to·ry, *n. pl.* -ries. fábrica
fac·tu·al, *a.* basado en datos
fac·ul·ty, *n.* facultad

fad, n. novedad

fade, v. descolorar(se)

fag, v. fatigar

fag·ot, n. haz de leña

Fahr·en·heit, a. de Fahrenheit

fail, v. faltar; acabar; fracasar

fail·ure, n. fracaso

faint, v. desmayarse. n. desmayo. a. débil

faint·ness, n. debilidad

fair, a. rubio; sereno; justo. n. feria

fair·ly, adv. justamente

fair·y, n. pl. -ies. hada

faith, n. fe, f.; creencia; confianza

faith·ful, a. fiel

faith·ful·ly, adv. lealmente

faith·less, a. desleal

fake, v. fingir. n. impostura

fal·con, n. halcón

fall, v., fell, fall·en, fall·ing. caer(se). n. caída; otoño; usu. pl. cascada. fall back, retroceder. fall off, disminuir. fall out, reñir. fall to, empezar

fal·la·cious, a. engañoso

fal·la·cy, n. error; falacia

fal·li·ble, a. falible

fal·low, a. en barbecho

false, a. falso

false·hood, n. mentira

false·ly, adv. falsamente

fal·si·fy, v. falsificar

fal·si·ty, n. falsedad

fal·ter, v. vacilar; titubear

fame, n. fama

fa·mil·iar, a. conocido; familiar

fa·mil·i·ar·i·ty, n. familiaridad

fam·i·ly, n. pl. -lies. familia

fam·ine, n. hambre, f.

fam·ish, v. morirse de hambre

fa·mous, a. famoso

fan, n. abanico; aficionado. v. abanicar

fa·nat·ic, n., a. fanático. Also fa·nat·i·cal.

fa·nat·i·cism, n. fanatismo

fan·ci·er, n. aficionado

fan·ci·ful, a. fantástico

fan·cy, n. pl. -cies. fantasía; capricho; inclinación. a. de lujo. v. imaginarse

fan·fare, n. toque de trompetas

fang, n. colmillo

fan·tas·tic, a. fantástico

fan·ta·sy, n. pl. -sies. fantasía

far, a. lejano. adv. lejos

far·a·way, a. remoto

farce, n. farsa

far·ci·cal, a. ridículo

fare, v. pasarlo. n. precio; comida

fare·well, int. adiós. n. despedida

far·fetched, a. improbable

farm, n. granja; estancia. v. cultivar

farm·er, n. labrador; agricultor

farm·house, n. alquería

farm·ing, n. agricultura

far·off, a. lejano

fas·ci·nate, v. fascinar

fas·cism, n. fascismo

fas·cist, n. fascista, m., f.

fash·ion, n. estilo; moda; uso. v. formar

fash·ion·a·ble, a. de moda

fast, a. rápido; fijo; firme. adv. rápidamente. v. ayunar. n. ayuno

fas·ten, v. abrochar; asegurar

fas·tid·i·ous, a. fino; esquilimoso

fat, a. gordo; graso. n. grasa

fa·tal, a. fatal

fa·tal·ism, n. fatalismo

fa·tal·ist, n. fatalista, m., f.

fa·tal·i·ty, n. pl. -ties. fatalidad

fate, n. destino; hado; suerte, f.

fate·ful, a. fatal

fa·ther, n. padre. v. engendrar

fa·ther·hood, n. paternidad

fa·ther·in·law, n. pl. fa·thers·in·law, suegro

fath·om, n. pl. -oms, -om. braza. v. penetrar

fa·tigue, n. fatiga. v. fatigar

fat·ten, v. engordar

fau·cet, n. grifo

fault, n. defecto; falta; culpa. v. tachar

fault·y, a. defectuoso

fa·vor, n. favor. v. favorecer

fa·vor·a·ble, a. favorable

fa·vored, a. favorecido

fa·vor·ite, a., n. favorito

fa·vor·it·ism, n. favoritismo

fawn, n. cervato

faze, v. perturbar

fear, n. miedo; temor. v. tener miedo

fear·ful, a. temeroso

fear·less, a. intrépido

fear·some, a. temible

fea·si·bil·i·ty, n. viabilidad

fea·si·ble, a. factible

feast, n. banquete; fiesta. v. banquetear

feat, n. proeza

feath·er, n. pluma

feath·er·y, a. plumoso

fea·ture, n. facción; rasgo. v. presentar

Feb·ru·ar·y, n. febrero

fe·ces, n. pl. excrementos

fe·cund, a. fecundo

fed·er·al, a. federal

fed·er·a·tion, n. federación

fee, n. honorario

fee·ble, a. débil

fee·bly, adv. flojamente

feed, v. dar de comer; alimentar

feel, v. sentir(se). n. tacto

feel·er, n. antena

feel·ing, n. sensación; emoción

feign, *v.* fingir
feint, *n.* treta
fe·lic·i·tate, *v.* felicitar
fe·lic·i·tous, *a.* oportuno; feliz
fe·lic·i·ty, *n.* felicidad
fe·line, *a., n.* felino
fell, *v.* derribar; talar
fel·low, *n.* compañero. *a.* asociado
fel·low·ship, *n.* compañerismo
fel·on, *n.* criminal, *m., f.*
fel·o·ny, *n.* crimen
felt, *n.* fieltro
fe·male, *a.* femenino. *n.* hembra
fem·i·nine, *a.* femenino
fem·i·nism, *n.* feminismo
fe·mur, *n.* fémur
fence, *n.* cerca. *v.* cercar; esgrimir
fenc·ing, *n.* esgrima
fend, *v.* rechazar
fen·der, *n.* guardafango
fer·ment, *v.* fermentar
fer·men·ta·tion, *n.* fermentación
fern, *n.* helecho
fe·ro·cious, *a.* feroz
fe·ro·ci·ty, *n.* ferocidad
fer·ret, *n.* hurón
fer·ry, *n.* transbordador
fer·tile, *a.* fértil; fecundo
fer·til·i·ty, *n.* fecundidad
fer·ti·lize, *v.* fertilizar; abonar
fer·ti·liz·er, *n.* abono
fer·vid, *a.* férvido
fer·vor, *n.* fervor
fes·ter, *v.* enconarse
fes·ti·val, *n.* fiesta
fes·tive, *a.* festivo
fes·tiv·i·ty, *n. pl.* -ties. regocijo; fiesta
fes·toon, *n.* festón
fetch, *v.* ir por
fetch·ing, *a.* atractivo
fete, fête, *n.* fiesta. *v.* festejar
fet·id, *a.* fétido
fet·ish, *n.* fetiche
fet·ter, *n.* grillos, *pl. v.* trabar
fet·tle, *n.* condición
fe·tus, *n.* feto
feud, *n.* enemistad. *v.* reñir
feu·dal, *a.* feudal
feu·dal·ism, *n.* feudalismo
fe·ver, *n.* fiebre, *f.*
fe·ver·ish, *a.* febril
few, *a.* pocos
fi·an·ce, *n.* novio
fi·an·cee, *n.* novia
fi·as·co, *n. pl.* -cos, -coes. fiasco
fi·at, *n.* fiat, *m.*
fib, *n.* bola. *v.* mentir
fi·ber, fi·bre, *n.* fibra
fi·brous, *a.* fibroso
fick·le, *a.* inconstante
fic·tion, *n.* ficción
fic·tion·al, *a.* novelesco
fic·ti·tious, *a.* ficticio

fid·dle, *n.* violín. *v.* tocar el violín
fi·del·i·ty, *n.* fidelidad
fidg·et, *v.* inquietar
fidg·et·y, *a.* inquieto; azogado
field, *n.* campo; esfera; prado
fiend, *n.* demonio
fiend·ish, *a.* diabólico
fierce, *a.* feroz
fier·y, *a.* ardiente; apasionado
fif·teen, *a., n.* quince
fifth, *a.* quinto. *n.* quinta
fif·teenth, *a.* decimoquinto
fif·ti·eth, *a.* quincuagésimo
fif·ty, *a., n.* cincuenta
fig, *n.* higo
fight, *n.* combate; lucha; pelea. *v.* luchar; pelear
fight·er, *n.* guerrero
fig·ment, *n.* invención
fig·ur·a·tive, *a.* figurado
fig·ure, *n.* figura; cifra; tipo. *v.* figurar(se). figure out, resolver
fig·ure·head, *n.* mascarón de proa
fig·ur·ine, *n.* figurín
fil·a·ment, *n.* filamento
filch, *v.* ratear
file, *n.* lima; archivo; fila. *v.* limar; archivar
fi·let, *n.* filete. Also fil·let
fil·i·bus·ter, *n.* obstruccionista
fil·i·gree, *n.* filigrana
fil·ings, *n. pl.* limaduras
fill, *v.* llenar; ocupar. fill out, llenar
fill·ing, *n.* empaste; relleno
fil·ly, *n. pl.,* -lies. potra
film, *n.* película. *v.* filmar; empañarse
fil·ter, *n.* filtro. *v.* filtrar
filth, *n.* inmundicia
filth·y, *a.* sucio
fin, *n.* aleta
fi·nal, *a.* final; último
fi·na·le, *n.* final, *m.*
fi·nal·ist, *n.* finalista, *m., f.*
fi·nal·i·ty, *n.* finalidad
fi·nal·ly, *adv.* finalmente; por fin
fi·nance, *n.* finanzas; *pl.* fondos. *v.* financiar
fi·nan·cial, *a.* financiero
fin·an·cier, *n.* financiero
finch, *n.* pinzón
find, *v.* encontrar; descubrir; hallar
fine, *a.* fino; admirable; multa. *v.* multar
fin·er·y, *n.* adornos
fi·nesse, *n.* sutileza; diplomacia
fin·ger, *n.* dedo. *v.* tocar
fin·ger·nail, *n.* uña
fin·ger·print, *n.* huella dactilar
fin·ish, *v.* terminar; acabar. *n.* fin, *m.;* acabado
fi·nite, *a.* finito
fir, *n.* abeto
fire, *n.* fuego; ardor. *v.* encender; disparar; despedir

fire·arm, n. arma de fuego
fire·crack·er, n. petardo
fire en·gine, n. bomba de incendios
fire·fly, n. luciérnaga
fire·man, n. pl., **-men.** bombero
fire·place, n. hogar
fire·works, n. pl. fuegos artificiales
firm, n. firma. a. firme
fir·ma·ment, n. firmamento
firm·ly, adv. firmemente
firm·ness, n. firmeza
first, a., n. primero
first·class, a. de primera clase
first·hand, first-hand, a. de primera mano
first·rate, a. de primera clase
fis·cal, a. fiscal
fish, n. pl., **fish, fish·es.** pez, m.; pescado. v. pescar
fish·er·man, n. pl., **-men.** pescador
fish·er·y, n. pesquera
fish·y, a. sospechoso
fis·sion, n. fisión
fis·sure, n. grieta
fist, n. puño
fist·i·cuffs, n. pl. puñetazos
fit, n. acceso; ajuste. a. adecuado; sano. v. acomodar; proveer; probar
fit·ful, a. espasmódico
fit·ting, n. ajuste; pl. guarniciones. a. propio; conveniente
five, a., n. cinco
fix, v. fijar; preparar; arreglar. n. aprieto
fix·a·tion, n. fijación
fixed, a. fijo
fix·ture, n. cosa o instalación fija
flab·by, a. flojo; débil
flag, n. bandera. v. flaquear
flag·on, n. jarro; frasco
fla·grant, a. notorio
flag·stone, n. losa
flail, n. mayal, m. v. golpear
flair, n. instinto
flake, n. escama. v. formar hojuelas
flak·y, a. escamoso
flam·boy·ant, a. llamativo
flame, v. flamear. n. llama
flam·ma·ble, a. inflamable
flank, n. ijada; lado. v. lindar; flanquear
flap, v. sacudir; ondear. n. cartera; solapa
flare, v. brillar; fulgurar. n. bengala
flash, n. relámpago; ráfaga. v. lanzar
flash·light, n. linterna eléctrica
flash·y, a. charro
flask, n. frasco
flat, a. llano; plano; insípido. n. piso; pinchazo; bemol, m.
flat·ter, v. adular
flat·ter·y, n. adulación
flaunt, v. lucir

fla·vor, n. sabor. v. sazonar
fla·vor·ing, n. condimento
flaw, n. imperfección. v. estropear
flax, n. lino
flay, v. desollar
flea, n. pulga
fleck, n. mancha
flee, v. huir; fugarse; escapar de
fleece, n. vellón
fleec·y, a. lanudo
fleet, a. veloz. n. flota
fleet·ing, a. fugaz
flesh, n. carne, f.; pulpa
flex, v. doblar
flex·i·ble, a. flexible
flick, n. golpecito. v. dar un golpecito a
fli·er, n. aviador
flight, n. vuelo; huida; tramo
flim·sy, a. endeble
flinch, v. acobardarse
fling, v. arrojar
flint, n. pedernal, m.
flip, v. mover de un tirón
flip·pant, a. ligero
flirt, v. flirtear; coquetear. n. coqueta
flit, v. revolotear
float, v. flotar; hacer flotar. n. carroza
flock, n. rebaño. v. congregarse
floe, n. témpano
flog, v. azotar
flood, n. diluvio; inundación. v. inundar
floor, n. suelo; piso. v. solar; derribar
flop, v. caer pesadamente; fracasar
flo·ra, n. pl., **-ras, -rae.** flora
flo·ral, a. floral
flor·id, a. florido
flo·rist, n. florista, m.; f.
floss, n. seda floja
flo·til·la, n. flotilla
flot·sam, n. pecio
flounce, v. moverse airadamente. n. volante
floun·der, v. tropezar
flour, n. harina
flour·ish, v. florecer; blandir. n. rasgo; floreo
flout, v. mofarse
flow, v. fluir. n. corriente, f.; flujo
flow·er, n. flor, f. v. florecer
flu, n. inf. gripe, f.
fluc·tu·ate, v. fluctuar
flue, n. cañón de chimenea
flu·en·cy, n. fluidez, f.
flu·ent, a. facundo
fluff·y, a. plumosa
flu·id, a., n. fluido
fluke, n. chiripa
flunk, v. inf. no aprobar
flu·o·res·cent, a. fluorescente
fluor·i·da·tion, n. fluorización
flur·ry, n. pl., **-ries.** ráfaga; agitación
flush, v. sonrojarse; brotar. n. rubor.

a. nivelado

flus·ter, *v.* aturdir

flute, *n.* flauta

flut·ter, *v.* menear; revolotear. *n.* agitación; aleteo

flux, *n.* mudanza; flujo. *v.* fundir

fly, *n. pl.,* **flies.** mosca; bragueta. *v.* volar; ir en avión

fly·er, *n.* aviador

fly·wheel, *n.* rueda volante

foal, *n.* potro

foam, *n.* espuma

fo·cus, *n. pl.,* **-cus·es, fo·ci.** foco. *v.* enfocar; concentrar

fod·der, *n.* forraje

foe, *n.* enemigo

fog, *n.* niebla

fo·gy, fo·gey, *n. pl.,* **-gies, -geys.** persona de ideas anticuadas

foi·ble, *n.* flaco

foil, *n.* hoja; florete. *n.* frustrar

foist, *v.* encajar

fold, *v* doblar; plegar. *n.* pliegue

fold·er, *n.* carpeta

fo·li·age, *n.* follaje

folk, *n. pl.,* **folk, folks.** gente, *f.; pl.* parientes

folk·lore, *n.* folklore

fol·li·cle, *n.* folículo

fol·low, *v.* seguir; resultar; perseguir

fol·low·er, *n.* seguidor; partidario

fol·low·ing, *n.* séquito. *a.* siguiente

fol·ly, *n. pl.,* **-lies.** locura; tontería

fo·ment, *v.* fomentar

fond, *a.* cariñoso

fon·dle, *v.* acariciar

fond·ly, *adv.* afectuosamente

food, *n.* alimento

fool, *n.* tonto. *v.* embaucar; engañar

fool·har·dy, *a.* temerario

fool·ish, *a.* necio

fool·proof, *a.* infalible

foot, *n. pl.,* **feet.** pie; pata

foot·ball, *n.* fútbol, *m.*

foot·note, *n.* nota

foot·print, *n.* huella

foot·step, *n.* paso

fop, *n.* petimetre

for, *prep. for; para. conj.* pues

for·age, *n.* forraje. *v.* forrajear

for·ay, *n.* correría

for·bear, *v.* contenerse

for·bid, *v.* prohibir

for·bid·den, *a.* prohibido

for·bid·ding, *a.* severo

force, *n.* fuerza; vigor; cuerpo. *v.* forzar

force·ful, *a.* vigoroso; poderoso

for·ceps, *n.* fórceps, *m.*

for·ci·ble, *a.* enérgico; eficaz

ford, *n.* vado. *v.* vadear

fore, *a.* anterior

fore·arm, *n.* antebrazo

fore·bode, for·bode, *v.* presagiar

fore·bod·ing, *n.* presentimiento

fore·cast, *v.* pronosticar. *n.* pronóstico

fore·fa·ther, *n.* antepasado

fore·fin·ger, *n.* dedo índice

fore·go, *v.* preceder; renunciar

fore·gone, *a.* predeterminado

fore·ground, *n.* primer plano

fore·head, *n.* frente, *f.*

for·eign, *a.* extranjero; exterior

for·eign·er, *n.* extranjero

fore·man, *n. pl.,* **-men.** capataz, *m.*

fore·most, *a.* primero

fore·run·ner, *n.* precursor

fore·see, *v.* prever

fore·sight, *n.* previsión; perspicacia

fore·skin, *n.* prepucio

for·est, *n.* bosque

for·est·ry, *n.* silvicultura

fore·tell, *v.* predecir

for·ev·er, *adv.* siempre

fore·word, *n.* prefacio

for·feit, *v.* perder

for·fei·ture, *n.* pérdida; multa

forge, *n.* fragua. *v.* forjar; falsear

for·ger·y, *n.* falsificación

for·get, *v.* olvidar(se)

for·get·ful, *a.* olvidadizo

for·give, *v.* perdonar

for·give·ness, *n.* perdón

fork, *n.* tenedor. *v.* bifurcarse

for·lorn, *a.* abandonado

form, *n.* forma. *v.* formar; establecer

for·mal, *a.* ceremonioso

for·mal·i·ty, *n. pl.,* **-ties.** formalidad; ceremonia

for·mat, *n.* formato

for·ma·tion, *n.* formación

for·mer, *a.* anterior

for·mer·ly, *adv.* antiguamente

for·mi·da·ble, *a.* formidable

for·mu·la, *n. pl.,* **-las, -lae.** fórmula

for·ni·cate, *v.* fornicar

for·ni·ca·tion, *n.* fornicación

for·sake, *v.* abandonar

fort, *n.* fuerte

forth, *adv.* en adelante

forth·com·ing, *a.* próximo

forth·right, *a.* directo

forth·with, *adv.* sin dilación

for·ti·eth, *a.* cuadragésimo

for·ti·fi·ca·tion, *n.* fortificación

for·ti·fy, *v.* fortalecer

for·ti·tude, *n.* fortaleza

for·tress, *n.* fortaleza

for·tu·i·tous, *a.* fortuito

for·tu·nate, *a.* afortunado

for·tune, *n.* fortuna; suerte, *f.*

for·ty, *n. pl.,* **-ties.** cuarenta

fo·rum, *n.* foro

for·ward, *adv.* adelante. Also **for·wards.** *a.* delantero; atrevido. *v.* enviar

fos·sil, *n.* fósil, *m.*

fos·ter, v. alentar; criar

foul, a. sucio; vil. n. falta. v. ensuciar

found, v.: pt. and pp. of **find.** fundar

foun·da·tion, n. fundación; base, f.

found·er, v. irse a pique. n. fundador

found·ling, n. niño expósito

found·ry, n. pl. **-ries.** fundición

fount, n. fuente, f.

foun·tain, n. fuente, f.

four, a., n. cuatro

four·score, a., n. ochenta

four·teen, a., n. catorce

four·teenth, a. decimocuarto

fourth, a., n. cuarto

fowl, n. ave, f.; pollo

fox, n. pl. **fox·es.** zorra. v. confundir

fox·y, a. astuto

foy·er, n. vestíbulo

fra·cas, n. riña

frac·tion, n. fracción; porción

frac·tious, a. rebelón

frac·ture, n. fractura. v. fracturar; quebrar

frag·ile, a. frágil

frag·ment, n. fragmento

fra·grance, n. fragancia

fra·grant, a. oloroso

frail, a. débil; frágil

frail·ty, n. pl., **-ties.** fragilidad

frame, n. estructura; marco. v. poner un marco a

frame·work, n. esqueleto

franc, n. franco

fran·chise, n. derecho de sufragio

frank, a. franco. v. franquear

frank·furt·er, n. salchicha

frank·in·cense, n. incienso

frank·ly, adv. francamente

frank·ness, n. franqueza

fran·tic, a. frenético

fra·ter·nal, a. fraternal

fra·ter·ni·ty, n. pl., **-ties.** fraternidad

fraud, n. fraude

fraud·u·lent, a. fraudulento

fraught, a. lleno de

fray, v. deshilacharse

freak, n. monstruosidad; fenómeno

freck·le, n. peca

free, a. libre; gratis. v. libertar

free·boot·er, n. pirata, m.

free·dom, n. libertad

free·way, n. autopista

freeze, v. helar(se); congelar

freight, n. flete

freight·er, n. buque de carga

French, a., n. francés

fre·net·ic, a. frenético

fren·zy, n. pl., **-zies.** frenesí, m.

fre·quen·cy, n. pl., **-cies.** frecuencia

fre·quent, a. frecuente. v. frecuentar

fres·co, n. pl., **-coes, -cos.** fresco

fresh, a. fresco; nuevo

fresh·en, v. refrescar(se)

fresh·man, n. pl., **-men.** estudiante de primer año

fret, v. apurarse

fret·ful, a. displicente

fri·ar, n. fraile

fric·tion, n. fricción; frote

Fri·day, n. viernes, m.

friend, n. amigo

friend·ly, a. amistoso

friend·ship, n. amistad

frieze, n. friso

fright, n. susto

fright·en, v. asustar

fright·ful, a. espantoso

frig·id, a. frío

frill, n. lechuga

fringe, n. orla; margen

frisk, v. retozar

frisk·y, a. juguetón

frit·ter, v. desperdiciar. n. buñuelo

friv·o·lous, a. frívolo

fro, adv. atrás

frock, n. vestido

frog, n. rana

frol·ic, n. travesura. v. juguetear

frol·ic·some, a. retozón

from, prep. de; desde; por

front, n. frente. a. delantero. v. dar a

fron·tal, a. frontal

fron·tier, n. frontera

frost, n. helada; escarcha

frost·bit·ten, a. congelado

froth, n. espuma

fro·ward, a. indócil

frown, v. mirar con ceño. n. ceño

frow·zy, a. desaliñado

fru·gal, a. frugal

fruit, n. fruta

fruit·ful, a. provechoso

fru·i·tion, n. realización

fruit·less, a. infructuoso

frus·trate, v. frustrar

frus·tra·tion, n. frustración

fry, v. freír(se)

fudge, v. contrahacer. n. dulce

fu·el, n. combustible

fu·gi·tive, a., n. fugitivo

ful·crum, n. pl., **-crums, -cra.** fulcro

ful·fill, ful·fil, v. cumplir; realizar

ful·fill·ment, ful·fil·ment, n. cumplimiento

full, a. lleno; completo. adv. en pleno

full·blown, a. maduro

full·ness, n. amplitud

ful·ly, adv. completamente

ful·mi·nate, v. volar; tronar

ful·some, a. insincero

fum·ble, v. manosear

fume, n. vaho. v. humear; enojarse

fu·mi·gate, v. fumigar

fun, n. diversión

func·tion, n. función. v. funcionar

func·tion·al, a. funcional

fund, n. fondo; pl. fondos. v. acumular; consolidar

fun·da·men·tal, *a.* fundamental. *n.* esencial

fu·ner·al, *n.* entierro

fu·ne·re·al, *a.* fúnebre

fun·gus, *n. pl.* **-gi**, **-gus·es**. hongo

fun·nel, *n.* embudo

fun·ny, *a.* gracioso; cómico

fur, *n.* piel, *f.*

fu·ri·ous, *a.* furioso

furl, *v.* aferrar

fur·long, *n.* estadio

fur·lough, *n.* licencia

fur·nace, *n.* horno

fur·nish, *v.* proveer; proporcionar

fur·nish·ings, *n. pl.* mobiliario

fur·ni·ture, *n.* mueblaje

fu·ror, *n.* furor

fur·row, *n.* surco. *v.* surcar

fur·ry, *a.* peludo

fur·ther, *adv.* más lejos; además. *a.* más lejos; nuevo. *v.* adelantar

fur·ther·more, *adv.* además

fur·thest, *a.. adv.* más lejos

fur·tive, *a.* furtivo

fu·ry, *n. pl.*, **-ries**. furia

fuse, *n.* fusible; espoleta. *v.* fundir

fuss, *n.* bulla. *v.* preocuparse

fuss·y, *a.* exigente

fu·tile, *a.* inútil

fu·ture, *a., n.* futuro

fuzz, *n.* pelusa

fuzz·y, *a.* velloso

G

gab·ar·dine, *n.* gabardina

ga·ble, *n.* aguilón; faldón

gad, *v.* andorrear

gad·fly, *n.* tábano

gad·get, *n.* aparato

gaff, *n.* arpón

gag, *v.* amordazar. *n.* mordaza; *inf.* chiste

gai·e·ty, *n.* alegría

gai·ly, *adv.* alegremente

gain, *v.* ganar; alcanzar. *n.* ganancia

gain·say, *v.* contradecir

gait, *n.* modo de andar

ga·la, *n.* fiesta

gal·ax·y, *n. pl.*, **-ies**. galaxia

gale, *n.* ventarrón

gall, *n.* bilis, *f.*; descaro. *v.* irritar

gal·lant, *a.* valeroso

gal·lant·ry, *n.* galantería

gal·ler·y, *n. pl.*, **-ies**. galería

gal·ley, *n.* galera; fogón

gal·lon, *n.* galón

gal·lop, *n.* galope. *v.* galopar

gal·lows, *n.* horca

gal·va·nize, *v.* galvanizar

gam·bit, *n.* gambito

gam·ble, *v.* jugar. *n.* jugada

gam·bol, *v.* brincar

game, *n.* juego; partido; caza. *a.* cojo.

v. jugar

gam·ut, *n.* gama

gan·der, *n.* ganso; *inf.* vistazo

gang, *n.* pandilla

gang·plank, *n.* plancha

gan·grene, *n.* gangrena

gang·ster, *n.* gángster; pistolero

gang·way, *n.* pasillo

gap, *n.* abertura; hueco

ga·rage, *n.* garaje

garb, *n.* vestido

gar·bage, *n.* basura

gar·den, *n.* jardín

gar·gan·tu·an, *a.* colosal

gar·gle, *v.* gargarizar. *n.* gárgaras

gar·ish, *v.* llamativo

gar·land, *n.* guirnalda

gar·ment, *n.* prenda de vestir

gar·ner, *n.* granero. *v.* entrojar

gar·net, *n.* granate

gar·nish, *v.* aderezar; adornar. *n.* aderezo

gar·ret, *n.* guardilla

gar·ri·son, *n.* guarnición

gar·ru·lous, *a.* gárrulo

gar·ter, *n.* liga

gas, *n.* gas; gasolina. *v.* asfixiar con gas

gas·e·ous, *a.* gaseoso

gash, *n.* cuchillada. *v.* hender

gas·o·line, *n.* gasolina

gasp, *v.* boquear. *n.* boqueada

gas·tric, *a.* gástrico

gas·tron·o·my, *n.* gastronomía

gate, *n.* puerta

gate·way, *n.* paso

gath·er, *v.* reunir; recoger; fruncir. *n.* frunce

gauche, *a.* torpe

gaud·y, *a.* chillón

gauge, *n.* norma de medida; indicador, *v.* medir

gaunt, *a.* flaco

gaunt·let, *n.* guantelete

gauze, *n.* gasa

gauz·y, *a.* de gasa

gawk·y, *a.* desgarbado

gay, *a.* alegre; vistoso

gaze, *v.* mirar. *n.* mirada

ga·zelle, *n.* gacela

ga·zette, *n.* gaceta

gaz·et·teer, *n.* diccionario geográfico

gear, *n.* engranaje; herramientas. *v.* engranar

gel·a·tin, *n.* gelatina

ge·lat·i·nous, *a.* gelatinoso

geld, *v.* castrar

gem, *n.* joya; gema

gen·der, *n.* género

gene, *n.* gen

ge·ne·al·o·gy, *n.* genealogía

gen·er·al, *a.* general; usual. **in gen·er·al**, en general gen·er·al·i·ty, n. generalidad

gen·er·al·ize, v. generalizar

gen·er·ate, v. generar

gen·er·a·tion, n. generación

gen·er·a·tor, n. generador

ge·ner·ic, a. genérico

gen·er·os·i·ty, n. generosidad

gen·er·ous, a. generoso

gen·e·sis, n. génesis, f.; (cap.) Génesis

ge·net·ic, a. genésico

ge·net·ics, n. pl. genética

gen·ial, a. afable

gen·i·tal, a. genital

gen·i·tals, n. pl. órganos genitales

gen·ius, n. genio

gen·o·cide, n. genocidio

gen·til·i·ty, n. gentileza

gen·tle, a. suave; apacible

gen·tle·man, n. pl., -men. caballero; señor

gen·tly, adv. suavemente

gen·u·ine, a. genuino; sincero

ge·nus, n. género

ge·o·gra·pher, n. geógrafo

ge·o·gra·phic, ge·o·graph·i·cal, a. geográfico

ge·o·gra·phy, n. geografía

ge·o·log·ic, ge·o·log·i·cal, a. geológico

ge·ol·o·gist, n. geólogo

ge·ol·o·gy, n. geología

ge·o·met·ric, a. geométrico

ge·om·e·try, n. geometría

ge·o·phys·i·cal, a. geofísico

ge·o·phys·ics, n. pl. geofísica

ger·i·at·rics, n. pl. geriatría

germ, n. germen

ger·mane, a. relativo

ger·mi·nate, v. germinar

ger·mi·na·tion, n. germinación

ger·und, n. gerundio

ges·tic·u·late, v. gesticular

ges·ture, n. ademán; gesto. v. hacer gestos

get, v. got, got or got·ten, get·ting. obtener; lograr; comprender. get a·way, quitar. get at, llegar a. get e·ven with, desquitarse con. get o·ver, vencer. get up, levantarse

gey·ser, n. géiser

ghast·ly, a. horrible

gher·kin, n. pepinillo

ghost, n. fantasma, m.

ghost·ly, a. espectral

ghoul, n. demonio

GI, n. pl., GI's, GIs. soldado. Also G.I.

gi·ant, n. gigante, a. gigantesco

gib·ber·ish, n. galimatías; jerga

gib·bon, n. gibón

gibe, jibe, v. mofarse; burlarse

gib·let, n. usu. pl. menudillos

gid·di·ness, n. vértigo

gid·dy, a. mareado; ligero

gift, n. regalo; don

gi·gan·tic, a. gigantesco

gig·gle, n. risa sofocada

gild, v. dorar

gill, n. agalla

gilt, a. dorado

gim·mick, n. truco

gin, n. desmotadera de algodón; ginebra

gin·ger, n. jengibre

gin·ger ale, n. cerveza de jengibre

gin·ger·bread, n. pan de jengibre

gin·ger·ly, a. cauteloso

gip·sy, gyp·sy, n. pl., -sies. gitano

gi·raffe, n. jirafa

gird, v. ceñir

gird·er, n. viga

gir·dle, n. cinto; faja

girl, n. niña; chica; muchacha

girl·ish, a. de niña

girth, n. cincha

gist, n. esencial; clave, f.

give, v., gave, giv·en, giv·ing. dar; conceder; entregar; permitir; ceder. give in, ceder. give off, emitir. give out, estar agotado; distribuir. give up, entregar; renunciar

giv·en, a. citado

giz·zard, n. molleja

gla·cial, a. glacial

gla·cier, n. glaciar

glad, a. alegre

glad·den, v. regocijar

glade, n. claro

glad·ly, adv. con mucho gusto

glad·ness, n. alegría

glad·i·o·lus, n. gladíolo, gladiolo. Also glad·i·o·la

glam·our, glam·or, n. encanto

glam·our·ous, a. encantador

glance, v. mirar; lanzar miradas; rebotar. n. vistazo; ojeada

gland, n. glándula

glan·du·lar, a. glandular

glare, v. relumbrar. n. brillo; mirada feroz

glar·ing, a. evidente

glass, n. vidrio; vaso; pl. gafas

glass·y, a. vítreo

glau·co·ma, n. glaucoma, m.

glaze, v. vidriar. n. barniz, m.

gleam, n. destello. v. brillar

glean, v. espigar

glee, n. júbilo

glen, n. cañada

glide, v. deslizarse. n. planeo

glim·mer, v. brillar débilmente

glimpse, n. vislumbre, f.

glint, v. destellar

glis·ten, v. relucir

glit·ter, v. relucir. n. resplandor

gloat, v. manifestar satisfacción

maligna
globe, *n.* globo; esfera
glob·ule, *n.* glóbulo
gloom, *n.* oscuridad; tristeza
gloom·y, *a.* lóbrego; melancólico
glo·ri·fy, *v.* glorificar
glo·ri·ous, *a.* glorioso
glo·ry, *n.* gloria. *v.* gloriarse
gloss, *n.* lustre
glos·sa·ry, *n. pl.,* **-ries.** glosario
gloss·y, *a.* lustroso
glot·tis, *n.* glotis, *f.*
glove, *n.* guante
glow, *v.* brillar. *n.* calor vivo
glow·er, *v.* mirar con ceño
glow·worm, *n.* luciérnaga
glue, *v.* pegar; encolar. *n.* cola
glum, *a.* abatido
glut, *v.* hartar
glut·ton, *n.* glotón
glut·ton·y, *n.* gula
gnarl, *v.* torcer
gnash, *v.* rechinar
gnat, *n.* jején
gnaw, *v.* roer
gnome, *n.* gnomo
go, *v.* **went, gone, go·ing.** ir(se); marchar(se); convenir. *n.* energía. **go af·ter,** seguir. **go off,** dispararse. **go over,** revisar. **go with,** acompañar
goad, *n.* aguijada; incitar
goal, *n.* meta; gol, *m.*
goat, *n.* cabra
gob·ble, *v.* engullir
gob·let, *n.* copa
gob·lin, *n.* trasgo
God, *n.* Dios
god, *n.* dios
god·child, *n. pl.,* **-chil·dren.** ahijado
god·daugh·ter, *n.* ahijada
god·dess, *n.* diosa
god·fa·ther, *n.* padrino
god·ly, *a.* piadoso
god·moth·er, *n.* madrina
god·par·ent, *n.* padrino; madrina
god·send, *n.* buena suerte
god·son, *n.* ahijado
gog·gles, *n. pl.* anteojos
go·ing, *n.* ida; estado del camino
gold, *n.* oro; dinero. *a.* de oro
golf, *n.* golf, *m.*
gon·do·la, *n.* góndola
gon·do·lier, *n.* gondolero
gong, *n.* gong, *m.*
gon·or·rhe·a, *n.* gonorrea
good, *n.* bien; *pl.* mercancías; efectos. *a.* **bet·ter, best.** bueno; bondadoso; genuino; válido
good·by, good·bye, *int., n.* adiós
good·heart·ed, *a.* amable
good·look·ing, *a.* guapo
good·ly, *a.* agradable; considerable
good·ness, *n.* bondad

good·y, *n. pl.,* **-ies,** *inf.* golosina
goose, *n. pl.* **geese.** ganso
goose·ber·ry, *n. pl.,* **-ries.** uva espina
gore, *n.* sangre, *f.;* nesga. *v.* acornear
gorge, *n.* barranco. *v.* hartarse
gor·geous, *a.* magnífico; vistoso
gos·pel, *n.* evangelio
gos·sa·mer, *n.* gasa sutil
gos·sip, *n.* chisme; comadre, *f. v.* charlar
gouge, *n.* gubia. *v.* excavar
gourd, *n.* calabaza
gour·met, *n.* gastrónomo
gout, *n.* gota
gov·ern, *v.* gobernar
gov·ern·ess, *n.* institutriz, *f.*
gov·ern·ment, *n.* gobierno
gov·er·nor, *n.* gobernador; director
gown, *n.* vestido
grab, *v.* asir; arrebatar. *n.* agarro
grace, *n.* elegancia; gracia; bendición de la mesa. *v.* adornar
grace·ful, *a.* gracioso
gra·cious, *a.* agradable; cortés
gra·da·tion, *n.* gradación
grade, *n.* grado; clase, *f. v.* clasificar
grad·u·al, *a.* gradual
grad·u·al·ly, *adv.* poco a poco
grad·u·ate, *v.* graduar(se). *n.* licenciado
grad·u·a·tion, *n.* graduación
graft, *n.* injerto; soborno. *v.* injertar
grain, *n.* grano; fibra
gram, *n.* gramo
gram·mar, *n.* gramática
gram·mat·i·cal, *a.* gramatical
gra·na·ry, *n. pl.,* **-ries.** granero
grand, *a.* grandioso; augusto; magnífico
grand·child, *n. pl.,* **-chil·dren.** nieto
grand·daugh·ter, *n.* nieta
grand·fa·ther, *n.* abuelo
gran·di·ose, *a.* grandioso; pomposo
grand·moth·er, *n.* abuela
grand·par·ent, *n.* abuelo
grand·son, *n.* nieto
grange, *n.* cortijo
gran·ite, *n.* granito
grant, *v.* otorgar; conceder; conferir. *n.* cesión; concesión
gran·u·late, *v.* granular
gran·ule, *n.* gránulo
grape, *n.* uva
grape·fruit, *n.* toronja
graph, *n.* gráfica
graph·ic, *a.* gráfico
graph·ite, *n.* grafito
grap·nel, *n.* arpeo
grap·ple, *n.* arpeo. *v.* agarrar
grasp, *v.* agarrar; comprender. *n.* asimiento; garras
grasp·ing, *a.* codicioso
grass, *n.* pasto; hierba; césped, *m.*
grass·hop·per, *n.* saltamontes

grass·y, a. herboso

grate, n. parrilla de hogar. v. rechinar

grate·ful, a. agradecido

grat·i·fi·ca·tion, n. gratificación; placer

grat·i·fy, v. complacer; satisfacer

grat·ing, n. reja

gra·tis, a., adv. gratis

grat·i·tude, n. reconocimiento

gra·tu·i·tous, a. gratuito; injustificado

gra·tu·i·ty, n. pl. -ties. propina

grave, n. sepultura. a. grave

grav·el, n. cascajo

grav·en, a. grabado

grave·yard, n. cementerio

grav·i·tate, v. gravitar

grav·i·ta·tion, n. gravitación

grav·i·ty, n. pl. -ties. seriedad; gravedad

gra·vy, n. salsa

gray, grey, a., n. gris

graze, v. pacer; rozar

grease, n. grasa. v. engrasar

greas·y, a. grasiento

great, a. grande; gran

greed, n. avaricia; codicia

greed·y, a. avaro; codicioso; goloso

green, a., n. verde

green·er·y, n. verdura

greet, v. saludar

greet·ing, n. saludo

gre·gar·i·ous, a. gregario

gre·nade, n. granada de mano

grid, n. reja; parrilla

grid·dle, n. tortera

grid·i·ron, n. campo de fútbol; parrilla

grief, n. pesar

griev·ance, n. agravio

grieve, v. afligirse

griev·ous, a. grave; penoso

grif·fin, griff·fon, n. grifo

grill, v. asar a la parrilla; inf. interrogar

grille, grill, n. verja

grim, a. inflexible; severo

grim·ace, n. visaje. v. hacer muecas

grime, n. mugre, f.

grim·y, a. mugriento

grin, v. sonreír. n. sonrisa burlona

grind, v. moler; pulverizar

grind·stone, n. muela

grip, n. agarro; apretón; saco de mano. v. asir

grippe, n. gripe, f.

gris·ly, a. horroroso

gris·tle, n. cartílago

grit, n. arena; firmeza

grit·ty, a. arenoso

griz·zled, griz·zly, a. gris

groan, v. gemir. n. gemido

gro·cer, n. abacero

gro·cer·y, n. pl. -ies. abacería; pl. comestibles

groin, n. ingle, f.

groom, n. novio; mozo de caballos. v. cuidar

groove, n. estría

grope, v. buscar a tientas

gross, a. bruto; grosero; grueso. n. gruesa

gro·tesque, a. grotesco

grot·to, n. pl. -toes, -tos. gruta

grouch, v. inf. refunfuñar

ground, n. sometimes pl. tierra; terreno; razón; poso. a. molido

ground·work, n. fundamento

group, n. grupo. v. agrupar

grouse, v. quejarse

grove, n. arboleda

grov·el, v. arrastrarse

grow, v. grew, grown, grow·ing. crecer; cultivar; aumentar

growl, v. gruñir

grown-up, a. adulto

grown-up, n. adulto

growth, n. crecimiento; tumor

grub·by, a. sucio

grudge, v. dar de mala gana. n. rencor

gru·el·ing, a. penoso

grue·some, a. horrible

gruff, a. malhumorado

grum·ble, v. quejarse

grump·y, a. gruñón

grunt, v. gruñir. n. gruñido

guar·an·tee, v. garantizar. n. garantía. Also guar·an·ty

guard, v. guardar; vigilar. n. guardia

guard·house, n. cárcel militar

guard·i·an, n. guardián

gu·ber·na·to·ri·al, a. del gobernador

guer·ril·la, n. guerrillero

guess, v. adivinar; imaginar. n. conjetura

guest, n. huésped; convidado

guf·faw, n. carcajada

guid·ance, n. gobierno

guide, v. guiar. n guía, m., f.

guild, n. gremio

guile, n. astucia

guil·lo·tine, n. guillotina

guilt, n. culpabilidad

guilt·y, a. culpable

guise, n. modo; apariencia

gui·tar, n. guitarra

gulf, n. golfo

gull, n. gaviota. v. timar

gul·let, n. esófago

gul·li·ble, a. crédulo

gul·ly, n. pl. -lies. barranca

gulp, v. tragar. n. trago

gum, n. encía; goma; chicle. v. engomar

gun, n. arma de fuego

gun·pow·der, n. pólvora

gun·wale, gun·nel, *n.* regala
gur·gle, *v.* gorgotear. *n.* gorgoteo
gush, *v.* chorrear
gust, *n.* ráfaga
gus·to, *n.* gusto; entusiasmo
gut, *n.* intestino; cuerda de tripa; *pl. inf.* valor. *v.* destripar
gut·ter, *n.* arroyo; gotera
gut·tur·al, *a.* gutural
guy, *n.* viento; *inf.* individuo; tío
guz·zle, *v.* engullir
gym, *n. inf.* gimnasio
gym·na·si·um, *n.* gimnasio
gym·nast, *n.* gimnasta, *m., f.*
gym·nas·tic, *a.* gimnástico
gym·nas·tics, *n. pl.* gimnasia
gy·ne·col·o·gy, *n.* ginecología
gyp, *v. inf.* estafar. *n.* estafa
gyp·sum, *n.* yeso
gyp·sy, *n. pl.,* **-sies.** gitano
gy·rate, *v.* girar
gy·ro·scope, *n.* giroscopio

H

ha, hah, *int.* ah
hab·it, *n.* hábito; costumbre, *f.*
hab·it·a·ble, *a.* habitable
hab·i·tat, *n.* habitación
hab·i·ta·tion, *n.* habitación
ha·bit·u·al, *a.* habitual
ha·bit·u·ate, *v.* acostumbrarse
hack, *v.* acuchillar. *n.* tos seca; rocín
hack·neyed, *a.* trillado
had, *v. pt. and pp. of* have
hag, *n.* bruja
hag·gard, *a.* ojeroso
hag·gle, *v.* regatear
hail, *v.* saludar; granizar. *int.* salve. *n.* saludo; granizo
hail·stone, *n.* piedra de granizo
hair, *n.* pelo; cabello
hair·breadth, *n.* ancho de un pelo. Also **hair's·breadth, hairs·breadth**
hair·dress·er, *n.* peluquero
hair·pin, *n.* horquilla
hale, *a.* robusto
half, *n. pl.,* **halves.** mitad. *a.* medio. *adv.* medio
half·heart·ed, *a.* indiferente
half·way, *adv.* a medio camino
half·wit, *n.* imbécil; tonto
hall, *n.* sala; vestíbulo
hal·le·lu·jah, *int.* aleluya
hal·low, *v.* consagrar
hal·lu·ci·na·tion, *n.* alucinación
hall·way, *n.* pasillo
ha·lo, *n. pl.,* **-los, -loes.** halo; aureola
halt, *n.* parada. *v.* parar; hacer alto
hal·ter, *n.* cabestro
halt·ing, *a.* vacilante
halve, *v.* partir por mitad
ham, *n.* jamón
ham·burg·er, *n.* hamburguesa

ham·let, *n.* aldehuela
ham·mer, *n.* martillo. *v.* martillar
ham·mock, *n.* hamaca
ham·per, *v.* impedir. *n.* canasta
hand, *n.* mano, *f.;* obrero; aplauso. *v.* dar; alargar
hand·bag, *n.* bolso
hand·book, *n.* manual
hand·cuff, *n. usu. pl.* esposas. *v.* maniatar
hand·ful, *n. pl.,* **-fuls,** puñado
hand·i·cap, *n.* desventaja. *v.* perjudicar
hand·i·craft, *n.* mano de obra; artesanía
hand·i·ly, *adv.* con destreza
hand·i·work, *n.* obra
hand·ker·chief, *n.* pañuelo
han·dle, *n.* mango; manubrio. *v.* manosear; tocar; manejar
hand·maid·en, *n.* criada. Also **hand·maid**
hand·some, *a.* hermoso; generoso
hand·y, *a.* conveniente; próximo; hábil
hand·y·man, *n. pl.,* **-men.** factótum
hang, *v.,* **hung** or **hanged.** colgar; ahorcar; pegar
hang·er·on, *n. pl.,* **-ers·on.** pegote
hank·er, *v.* anhelar
hank·er·ing, *n.* anhelo; añoranza
hap·haz·ard, *a.* fortuito
hap·less, *a.* desventurado
hap·pen, *v.* ocurrir; pasar; acontecer
hap·pen·ing, *n.* acontecimiento
hap·pi·ly, *adv.* alegremente
hap·pi·ness, *n.* felicidad; alegría
hap·py, *a.* feliz; oportuno
ha·rangue, *n.* arenga. *v.* arengar
har·ass, *v.* atormentar; acosar
har·ass·ment, *n.* hostigamiento
har·bor, *n.* puerto. *v.* hospedar; abrigar
hard, *a.* duro; firme; difícil. *adv.* diligentemente; mucho
hard·core, *a.* inflexible
hard·en, *v.* endurecer
hard·heart·ed, *a.* cruel
har·di·ness, *n.* robustez, *f.*
hard·ly, *adv.* apenas; difícilmente
hard·ness, *n.* dureza
hard·ship, *n.* privación; pena
hard·ware, *n.* ferretería
har·dy, *a.* robusto
hare, *n. pl.,* **hares, hare.** liebre, *f.*
har·em, *n.* harén
hark, *v.* escuchar
har·lot, *n.* ramera
har·lot·ry, *n.* prostitución
harm, *n.* daño. *v.* dañar; hacer daño a
harm·ful, *a.* dañino; perjudicial
harm·less, *a.* innocuo
har·mon·i·ca, *n.* armónica

har·mo·ni·ous, *a.* armonioso
har·mo·nize, *v.* armonizar
har·mo·ny, *n. pl.,* -nies. armonía
har·ness, *n.* arreos. *v.* enjaezar; *fig.* utilizar
harp, *n.* arpa. *v. inf.* machacar
harp·ist, *n.* arpista, *m., f.*
har·poon, *n.* arpón. *v.* arponear
har·ri·dan, *n.* bruja
har·row·ing, *a.* angustioso
har·ry, *v.* hostigar; inquietar
harsh, *a.* áspero; severo
harsh·ness, *n.* severidad
hart, *n. pl.,* harts, hart. ciervo
har·vest, *n.* cosecha. *v.* cosechar
har·ves·ter, *n.* segador
hash, *n.* picadillo
has·sle, *n. inf.* pelea. *v.* fastidiar
has·sock, *n.* escabel, *m.*
haste, *n.* prisa
has·ten, *v.* darse prisa
hast·y, *a.* apresurado; precipitado
hat, *n.* sombrero
hatch, *n.* escotilla; portezuela. *v.* empollar
hatch·et, *n.* machado
hatch·way, *n.* escotilla
hate, *v.* odiar; detestar. *n.* odio
hate·ful, *a.* odioso
ha·tred, *n.* aborrecimiento
haugh·ti·ness, *n.* arrogancia
haugh·ty, *a.* altanero
haul, *v.* tirar. *n.* tirón
haunch, *n.* anca
haunt, *v.* frecuentar; aparecer
hau·teur, *n.* arrogancia
have, *v.,* have, has; had; hav·ing. tener; poseer
ha·ven, *n.* puerto; asilo
hav·er·sack, *n.* mochila
hav·oc, *n.* estrago
hawk, *n.* halcón
hay, *n.* heno
hay·stack, *n.* almiar
haz·ard, *n.* riesgo; azar. *v.* arriesgar
haz·ard·ous, *a.* arriesgado
haze, *n.* calina
ha·zel, *n.* avellano
ha·zy, *a.* brumoso; vago
he, *pron., sing. nom.* he; *poss.* his; *obj.* him; *intens. and refl.* himself; *pl. nom.* they; *poss.* their or theirs; *obj.* them. él
head, *n.* cabeza; jefe; crisis, *f. a.* principal
head·ache, *n.* dolor de cabeza
head·ing, *n.* título
head·land, *n.* promontorio
head·light, *n.* faro
head·long, *adv.* de cabeza. *a.* precipitado
head·quar·ters, *n. pl.* cuartel general
head·strong, *a.* terco
head·way, *n.* progreso

head·y, *a.* cabezudo
heal, *v.* sanar; curar
health, *n.* salud, *f.;* sanidad
health·ful, *a.* sano
health·y, *a.* salubre; sano
heap, *n.* montón. *v.* amontonar
hear, *v.,* heard, hear·ing. oír; hacer caso
hear·ing, *n.* oído
heark·en, *v.* escuchar
hear·say, *n.* rumor
hearse, *n.* coche fúnebre
heart, *n.* corazón; (*cards*) coros
heart·ache, *n.* angustia
heart·break, *n.* angustia
heart·en, *v.* alentar
heart·felt, *a.* sincero
hearth, *n.* hogar
heart·less, *a.* cruel
heart·sick, *a.* desconsolado
heart·y, *a.* cordial; sano
heat, *n.* calor. *v.* calentar(se)
heat·er, *n.* calentador
heath, *n.* brezal, *m.*
hea·then, *a., n.* pagano
heave, *v.,* heaved or hove, heav·ing. levantar
heav·en, *n.* cielo; *usu. pl.* cielos
heav·en·ly, *a.* celestial
heav·i·ness, *n.* pesadez, *f.*
heav·y, *a.* pesado; fuerte
heck·le, *v.* interrumpir
hec·tic, *a.* febril
hedge, *n.* seto
heed, *v.* escuchar; hacer caso. *n.* cuidado
heel, *v.* ladearse; poner tacón. *n.* talón; tacón
heft, *n.* bulto
heft·y, *a.* fuerte
heif·er, *n.* vaquilla
height, *n.* estatura; altura
height·en, *v.* elevar; realzar
hei·nous, *a.* atroz
heir, *n.* heredero
heir·ess, *n.* heredera
heir·loom, *n.* herencia; reliquia de familia
hel·i·cop·ter, *n.* helicóptero
he·li·um, *n.* helio
he·lix, *n. pl.,* hel·i·ces, he·lix·es. hélice, *f.*
hell, *n.* infierno
hell·ish, *a.* infernal
hel·lo, *int.* hola
helm, *n.* timón
hel·met, *n.* casco
helms·man, *n. pl.,* -men. timonel, *m.*
help, *v.* ayudar; auxiliar. *n.* ayuda; criada
help·er, *n.* asistente
help·ful, *a.* útil
help·ing, *n.* ración
help·less, *a.* incapaz

hem, n. dobladillo. v. dobladillar; encerrar

hem·i·sphere, n. hemisferio

hem·i·spher·ic, hem·i·spher·i·cal, a. hemisférico

hem·lock, n. cicuta

hem·or·rhage, n. hemorragia

hem·or·rhoid, haem·or·rhoid, n. usu. pl. hemorroides, f. pl.

hemp, n. cáñamo

hen, n. gallina

hence, adv. de aquí; por lo tanto

hence·forth, adv. de aquí en adelante. Also hence·for·ward

her, pron. obj. and poss. case of she

her·ald, n. heraldo; precursor. v. proclamar

he·ral·dic, a. heráldico

her·ald·ry, n. pl., -ries. heráldica

herb, n. hierba

her·ba·ceous, a. herbáceo

her·cu·le·an, a. hercúleo

herd, n. rebaño. v. reunir

herds·man, n. pl., -men. pastor

here, adv. aquí; acá

here·af·ter, adv. en el futuro

he·red·i·tar·y, a. hereditario

he·red·i·ty, n. pl., -ties. herencia

here·in, adv. incluso

her·e·sy, n. pl., -sies. herejía

her·e·tic, n. hereje; m. pl.

he·ret·i·cal, a. herético

here·to·fore, adv. hasta ahora

her·it·age, n. herencia

her·met·ic, a. hermético. Also her·met·i·cal

her·mit, n. ermitaño

her·mit·age, n. ermita

her·ni·a, n. hernia

he·ro, n. pl., -roes. héroe

he·ro·ic, a. heroico

her·o·in, n. heroína

her·o·ine, n. heroína

her·o·ism, n. heroísmo

her·on, n. garza

hers, pron. poss. case of she

her·self, pron. ella misma; sí misma

hes·i·tan·cy, n. pl., -cies. indecisión

hes·i·tant, a. vacilante

hes·i·tate, v. vacilar

hes·i·ta·tion, n. indecisión

het·er·o·ge·ne·ous, a. heterogéneo

hew, v., hewed, hewed or hewn, hew·ing. tajar

hex·a·gon, n. hexágono

hex·ag·o·nal, a. hexagonal

hey·day, hey·dey, n. apogeo

hi·ber·nate, v. invernar

hic·cup, n. hipo. v. tener hipo. Also hic·cough

hide, v., hid, hid·den or hid, hid·ing. esconder(se); ocultar(se). n. pellejo

hid·e·ous, a. horrible; feo

hi·er·ar·chy, n. pl., -chies. jerarquía

hi·er·o·glyph·ic, a., n. jeroglífico. Also hi·er·o·glyph

high, a. alto; elevado. adv. arriba

high·fa·lu·tin, a. pomposo. Also high·fa·lu·ting

high·way, n. carretera

hike, v. ir a pie. n. caminata

hi·lar·i·ous, a. alegre

hi·lar·i·ty, n. alegría

hill, n. colina

hill·y, a. montañoso

hilt, n. puño

him, pron. obj. case of he

him·self, pron. él mismo; sí mismo

hind, a. trasero

hin·der, v. impedir

hind·most, a. postrero

hin·drance, n. obstáculo

hinge, n. gozne. Also hinge joint. v. engoznar

hint, n. indirecta. v. insinuar

hip, n. cadera

hip·po·pot·a·mus, n. pl., -mus·es, -mi. hipopótamo

hire, v. alquilar

hire·ling, n. mercenario

his, pron. suyo. a su

hiss, v. silbar. n. silbido

his·to·ri·an, n. historiador

his·tor·ic, his·tor·i·cal, a. histórico

his·to·ry, n. pl., -ries. historia

his·tri·on·ic, a. histriónico. Also his·tri·on·i·cal

hit, v. golpear; chocar. n. golpe; éxito

hitch, n. tirón. n. obstáculo

hitch·hike, v. hacer autostop

hith·er, adv. acá

hith·er·to, adv. hasta ahora

hive, n. colmena; pl. urticaria

hoard, n. provisión. v. amontonar

hoarse, a. ronco

hoax, n. engaño. v. engañar

hob·ble, v. cojear

hob·by, n. pl., -bies. pasatiempo

ho·bo, n. pl., -boes, -bos. vagabundo

hoe, n. azadón. v. azadonar

hog, n. puerco

hoist, v. alzar. n. montacargas; cabria

hold, v., held, hold·ing. tener; mantener; contener. n. bodega

hold·ing, n. tenencia

hole, n. hoyo; agujero

hol·i·day, n. día de fiesta; pl. vacaciones

ho·li·ness, n. santidad

hol·ler, v. inf. gritar

hol·low, a. hueco; vacío. n. concavidad

hol·ly, n. pl., -lies. acebo

hol·o·caust, n. holocausto

hol·ster, n. pistolera

ho·ly, a. santo; sagrada

hom·age, n. homenaje

home, n. casa; hogar. a. doméstico

adv. a casa

home·ly, *a.* feo

home·sick, *a.* nostálgico

home·ward, *adv.* hacia casa. Also **home·wards**

home·y, hom·y, *a. inf.* cómodo

hom·i·cide, *n.* homicidio

hom·i·ly, *n. pl.*, **-lies.** homilía

ho·mo·gen·e·ous, *a.* homogéneo

hone, *n.* piedra de afilar. *v.* afilar

hon·est, *a.* honrado

hon·es·ty, *n. pl.*, **-ties.** honradez

hon·ey, *n. pl.*, **-eys.** miel, *f.*

hon·ey·comb, *n.* panal, *m.*

hon·ey·moon, *n.* luna de miel

hon·ey·suck·le, *n.* madreselva

hon·or, *n.* honor; honra. *v.* honrar

hon·or·a·ble, *a.* honorable

hon·or·ar·y, *a.* honorario

hood, *n.* capucha

hood·lum, *n.* matón

hood·wink, *v.* engañar

hoof, *n.*, **hoofs, hooves.** casco

hook, *n.* gancho. *v.* enganchar; encorvar

hoop, *n.* aro

hoot, *v.* ulular. *n.* grito

hop, *v.* saltar. *n.* salto

hope, *n.* esperanza. *v.* esperar; desear

hope·less, *a.* desesperado

horde, *n.* horda

ho·ri·zon, *n.* horizonte

hor·i·zon·tal, *a.* horizontal

hor·mone, *n.* hormona

horn, *n.* cuerno

hor·o·scope, *n.* horóscopo

hor·ri·ble, *a.* horrible

hor·ri·fy, *v.* horrorizar

hor·ror, *n.* horror

horse, *n. pl.*, **hors·es, horse.** caballo

horse·man, *n. pl.*, **-men.** jinete

horse·pow·er, *n.* caballo de fuerza

horse·rad·ish, *n.* rábano picante

horse·shoe, *n.* herradura

hor·ti·cul·ture, *n.* horticultura

hose, *n. pl.*, **hose.** *pl.* medias

hose, *n. pl.*, **hos·es.** manga

ho·sier·y, *n.* calcetería

hos·pi·ta·ble, *a.* hospitalario

hos·pi·tal, *n.* hospital, *m.*

hos·pi·tal·i·ty, *n. pl.*, **-ties.** hospitalidad

host, *n.* anfitrión; patrón; multitud

hos·tage, *n.* rehén

hos·tile, *a.* hostil; enemigo

hos·til·i·ty, *n. pl.*, **-ties.** hostilidad

hot, *a.* caliente; cálido

ho·tel, *n.* hotel, *m.*

hot·house, *n.* invernáculo

hound, *n.* podenco. *v.* perseguir

hour, *n.* hora

house, *n. pl.*, **hous·es.** casa; cámara

house·keep·er, *n.* ama de llaves

hous·ing, *n.* alojamiento

how, *adv.* cómo; hasta qué punto

how·ev·er, *adv.* en todo caso. *conj.* sin embargo

howl, *v.* aullar. *n.* aullido

hub, *n.* cubo

hud·dle, *v.* amontonar(se)

hue, *n.* color; matiz, *m.*

hug, *v.* abrazar. *n.* abrazo

huge, *a.* inmenso; enorme

hulk, *n.* casco

hull, *n.* cáscara; casco

hum, *v.* zumbar; canturrear. *n.* zumbido

hu·man, *a.*, *n.* humano

hu·man·i·tar·i·an, *a.*, *n.* humanitario

hu·man·i·ty, *n. pl.*, **-ties.** humanidad

hum·ble, *a.* humilde. *v.* humillar

hu·mid, *a.* húmedo

hu·mid·i·fy, *v.* humedecer

hu·mid·i·ty, *n.* humedad

hu·mil·i·ate, *v.* humillar

hu·mil·i·a·tion, *n.* humillación

hu·mil·i·ty, *n.* humildad

hum·ming·bird, *n.* colibrí, *m.*

hu·mor, *n.* humor. *v.* complacer

hump, *n.* giba; joroba

hunch, *v.* corazonada

hunch·back, *n.* jorobado

hun·dred, *a.*, *n. pl.*, **-dred, -dreds.** ciento (cien)

hun·dredth, *a.* centésimo

hun·ger, *n.* hambre, *f.*

hun·gry, *a.* hambriento

hunt, *v.* cazar; perseguir. *n.* caza

hunt·er, *n.* cazador

hur·dle, *n.* valla; zarzo

hurl, *v.* lanzar

hur·ri·cane, *n.* huracán

hur·ry, *v.* apresurar; darse prisa. *n.* prisa

hurt, *v.* hacer daño; doler; dañar. *n.* herida

hus·band, *n.* marido; esposo

hush, *v.* callar. *n.* silencio

husk, *n.* cáscara

husk·y, *a.* ronco

hus·sy, *n. pl.*, **huss·ies.** pícara

hus·tle, *v.* empujar

hut, *n.* barraca

hy·a·cinth, *n.* jacinto

hy·brid, *n.* híbrido

hy·drant, *n.* boca de riego

hy·drau·lic, *a.* hidráulico

hy·dro·gen, *n.* hidrógeno

hy·e·na, *n.* hiena. Also **hy·ae·na**

hy·giene, *n.* higiene, *f.*

hymn, *n.* himno

hy·phen, *n.* guión

hyp·no·sis, *n. pl.*, **-ses.** hipnosis, *f.*

hyp·no·tize, *v.* hipnotizar

hy·po·chon·dri·ac, *n.* hipocondríaco

hy·poc·ri·sy, *n. pl.*, **-sies.** hipocresía**

hyp·o·crite, n. hipócrita, m., f.
hy·po·der·mic, a. hipodérmico
hy·pot·e·nuse, n. hipotenusa
hy·poth·e·sis, n. pl., -ses. hipótesis, f.
hy·po·thet·i·cal, a. hipotético
hys·te·ri·a, n. histerismo
hys·ter·ic, hys·ter·i·cal, a. histérico
hys·ter·ics, n. pl. histerismo

I

I, pron. yo
i·bis, n. pl., i·bis·es, i·bis. ibis, f.
ice, n. hielo. v. helar
ice·berg, n. iceberg, m.
ice cream, n. helado
i·ci·cle, n. carámbano
ic·ing, n. garapiña
i·con, n. icono
i·con·o·clast, n. iconoclasta, m., f.
i·cy, a. helado; glacial
i·de·a, n. idea
i·de·al, a. ideal. n. ideal; modelo
i·de·al·ize, v. idealizar
i·den·ti·cal, a. idéntico
i·den·ti·fi·ca·tion, n. identificación
i·den·ti·fy, v. identificar
i·den·ti·ty, n. pl., -ties. identidad
i·de·ol·o·gy, n. pl., -gies. ideología
id·i·om, n. gram. idiotismo
id·i·o·mat·ic, a. idiomático
id·i·o·syn·cra·sy, n. pl., -sies. idiosincrasia
id·i·ot, n. idiota, m., f.; tonto
i·dle, a. ocioso. v. haraganear
i·dol, n. ídolo
i·dol·a·trous, a. idólatra
i·dol·a·try, n. pl., -tries. idolatría
i·dol·ize, v. idolatrar
i·dyll, i·dyl, n. idilio
i·dyl·lic, a. idílico
if, conj. si
ig·nite, v. encender(se)
ig·no·ble, a. innoble
ig·no·min·y, n. pl., -ies. ignominia
ig·no·rance, n. ignorancia
ig·no·rant, a. ignorante
ig·nore, v. no hacer caso de
ill, a., worse, worst. enfermo; mal
il·le·gal, a. ilegal
il·leg·i·ble, a. ilegible
il·le·git·i·ma·cy, n. pl., -cies. ilegitimidad
il·le·git·i·mate, a. ilegítimo
il·lic·it, a. ilícito
il·lit·er·a·cy, n. pl., -cies. analfabetismo
il·lit·er·ate, a., n. analfabeto
ill·ness, n. enfermedad
il·lu·mi·nate, v. iluminar
il·lu·sion, n. ilusión
il·lus·trate, v. ilustrar
il·lus·tra·tion, n. ilustración; ejemplo

im·age, n. imagen, f.
im·ag·i·nar·y, a. imaginario
im·ag·i·na·tion, n. imaginación
im·ag·ine, v. imaginar(se)
im·be·cile, n., a. imbécil
im·i·tate, v. imitar
im·i·ta·tion, n. imitación; copia
im·ma·ture, a. inmaturo
im·meas·ur·a·ble, a. inmensurable
im·me·di·ate, a. inmediato
im·mense, a. inmenso
im·mer·sion, n. inmersión
im·mi·grant, n. inmigrante
im·mi·grate, v. inmigrar
im·mi·gra·tion, n. inmigración
im·mi·nent, a. inminente
im·mo·bile, a. inmóvil
im·mod·est, a. impúdico
im·mor·al, a. inmoral
im·mor·tal, a. inmortal
im·mune, a. inmune
im·mu·ni·ty, n. pl., -ties. inmunidad
imp, n. diablillo
im·pact, n. impacto
im·pair, v. deteriorar
im·part, v. comunicar; relatar; dar
im·par·tial, a. imparcial
im·pa·tient, a. impaciente
im·peach, v. acusar
im·pec·ca·ble, a. impecable
im·pede, v. impedir; estorbar
im·ped·i·ment, n. impedimento; estorbo
im·pel, v. impulsar
im·pe·ri·al, a. imperial
im·pe·ri·ous, a. imperioso
im·per·son·al, a. impersonal
im·per·ti·nent, a. impertinente
im·per·vi·ous, a. impenetrable
im·pet·u·ous, a. impetuoso
im·pe·tus, n. pl., -tus·es. ímpetu, m.
im·pi·e·ty, n. pl., -ties. impiedad
im·ple·ment, n. herramienta
im·pli·cate, v. enredar
im·plore, v. implorar
im·ply, v. dar a entender; significar
im·po·lite, a. descortés
im·port, v. importar
im·por·tance, n. importancia
im·por·tant, a. importante
im·pose, v. imponer
im·pos·si·bil·i·ty, n. pl., -ties. imposibilidad
im·pos·si·ble, a. imposible
im·pos·tor, n. impostor
im·po·tence, im·po·ten·cy, n. impotencia
im·po·tent, a. impotente
im·pov·er·ish, v. empobrecer
im·prac·ti·cal, a. impracticable
im·preg·na·ble, a. inexpugnable
im·press, v. estampar; imprimir; impresionar
im·pres·sion, n. impresión

im·print, *v.* imprimir
im·prob·a·ble, *a.* improbable
im·promp·tu, *a.* impremeditado. *adv.* de improviso
im·prop·er, *a.* impropio
im·prove, *v.* mejorar
im·prove·ment, *n.* mejora
im·prov·i·sa·tion, *n.* improvisación
im·pro·vise, *v.* improvisar
im·pulse, *n.* impulso; estímulo
im·pu·ri·ty, *n. pl.* **-ties.** impureza
in, *prep.* en; durante; dentro de. *adv.* dentro
in·a·bil·i·ty, *n.* inhabilidad
in·ad·e·quate, *a.* inadecuado
in·an·i·mate, *a.* inanimado
in·as·much as, *conj.* puesto que
in·au·gu·rate, *v.* inaugurar
in·born, *a.* innato
in·can·des·cent, *a.* incandescente
in·ca·pa·ble, *a.* incapaz
in·ca·pac·i·tate, *v.* incapacitar
in·car·na·tion, *n.* encarnación
in·cen·di·ar·y, *a.* incendiario
in·cense, *n.* incienso. *v.* encolerizar
in·cen·tive, *n.* incentivo
in·ces·sant, *a.* incesante
in·cest, *n.* incesto
in·ces·tu·ous, *a.* incestuoso
inch, *n.* pulgada
in·ci·dent, *n.* incidente; suceso
in·ci·den·tal, *a.* incidental; casual
in·cin·er·ate, *v.* incinerar
in·cip·i·ent, *a.* incipiente
in·ci·sion, *n.* incisión
in·cite, *v.* incitar
in·clem·ent, *a.* inclemente
in·cli·na·tion, *n.* inclinación
in·cline, *v.* inclinar(se)
in·clude, *v.* incluir; contener; tener
in·clu·sion, *n.* inclusión
in·cog·ni·to, *a., adv.* de incógnito
in·come, *n.* renta; ingresos
in·com·pa·ra·ble, *a.* incomparable
in·com·pe·tent, *a.* incompetente
in·com·plete, *a.* incompleto
in·com·pre·hen·si·ble, *a.* incomprensible
in·con·gru·ous, *a.* incongruo
in·con·se·quen·tial, *a.* inconsecuente
in·con·ven·ience, *n.* inconveniencia; incomodidad. *v.* incomodar
in·cor·rect, *a.* incorrecto
in·cor·ri·gi·ble, *a.* incorregible
in·crease, *v.* acrecentar; crecer; aumentar. *n.* aumento
in·cred·i·ble, *a.* increíble
in·crim·i·nate, *v.* incriminar
in·cu·ba·tor, *n.* incubadora
in·cur, *v.* incurrir
in·cur·a·ble, *a.* incurable
in·debt·ed, *a.* obligado
in·de·cen·cy, *n. pl.,* **-cies.** indecencia
in·de·cent, *a.* indecente

in·deed, *adv.* de veras
in·def·i·nite, *a.* indefinido
in·dem·ni·ty, *n. pl.* **-ties.** indemnización
in·dent, *v.* sangrar; mellar
in·den·ta·tion, *n.* mella
in·de·pend·ence, *n.* independencia
in·de·pend·ent, *a.* independiente
in·de·struct·i·ble, *a.* indestructible
in·dex, *n. pl.* **-dex·es, -di·ces.** índice
in·di·cate, *v.* indicar
in·di·ca·tion, *n.* indicación
in·dict, *v.* acusar
in·dif·fer·ent, *a.* indiferente
in·dig·e·nous, *a.* indígena
in·di·gent, *a.* indigente. *n.* pobre
in·di·ges·tion, *n.* indigestión
in·dig·nant, *a.* indignado
in·dig·ni·ty, *n. pl.* **-ties.** indignidad
in·di·go, *n. pl.,* **-gos, -goes.** añil, *m.*
in·di·rect, *a.* indirecto
in·dis·creet, *a.* indiscreto
in·dis·cre·tion, *n.* indiscreción
in·dis·pen·sa·ble, *a.* imprescindible
in·di·vid·u·al, *a.* individual. *n.* individuo
in·di·vid·u·al·i·ty, *n. pl.,* **-ties.** individualidad
in·doc·tri·nate, *v.* doctrinar
in·do·lent, *a.* indolente
in·door, *a.* interior; de puertas adentro
in·doors, *adv.* dentro
in·duce, *v.* inducir
in·duct, *v.* iniciar
in·dulge, *v.* satisfacer; consentir
in·dus·tri·al, *a.* industrial
in·dus·tri·ous, *a.* laborioso
in·dus·try, *n. pl.,* **-tries.** industria; diligencia
in·e·bri·ate, *v.* embriagar
in·el·i·gi·ble, *a.* inelegible
in·ept, *a.* inepto
in·ert, *a.* inerte
in·er·tia, *n.* inercia
in·ev·i·ta·ble, *a.* inevitable
in·ex·pli·ca·ble, *a.* inexplicable
in·fal·li·ble, *a.* infalible
in·fa·mous, *a.* infame
in·fa·my, *n. pl.,* **-mies.** infamia
in·fan·cy, *n. pl.,* **-cies.** infancia
in·fant, *n.* criatura. *a.* infantil; naciente
in·fan·try, *n. pl.,* **-tries.** infantería
in·fect, *v.* infectar; contagiar
in·fec·tion, *n.* infección
in·fer, *v.* inferir
in·fe·ri·or, *a., n.* inferior
in·fer·nal, *a.* infernal
in·fest, *v.* infestar
in·fi·del, *n.* infiel, *m., f.*
in·fi·del·i·ty, *n. pl.,* **-ties.** infidelidad
in·fil·trate, *v.* infiltrarse
in·fi·nite, *a.* infinito

in·fin·i·tive, *n.* infinitivo
in·fin·i·ty, *n. pl.,* -ties. infinito; infinidad
in·fir·ma·ry, *n. pl.,* -ries. enfermería
in·flame, *v.* inflamar; provocar
in·flam·ma·ble, *a.* inflamable
in·flate, *v.* hinchar; inflar
in·fla·tion, *n.* inflación
in·flec·tion, *n.* inflexión
in·flict, *v.* infligir; imponer
in·flu·ence, *n.* influencia. *v.* influir
in·flu·en·za, *n.* gripe, *f.*
in·form, *v.* informar; avisar
in·for·mal, *a.* sin ceremonia
in·for·ma·tion, *n.* información; conocimientos
in·for·ma·tive, *a.* informativo
in·fre·quent, *a.* infrecuente
in·fu·ri·ate, *v.* enfurecer
in·fuse, *v.* infundir
in·fu·sion, *n.* infusión
in·gen·ious, *a.* ingenioso
in·ge·nu·i·ty, *n.* ingeniosidad
in·got, *n.* lingote
in·gre·di·ent, *n.* ingrediente
in·hab·it, *v.* habitar
in·hab·it·ant, *n.* habitante
in·hale, *v.* inhalar; aspirar
in·her·ent, *a.* inmanente; inherente
in·her·it, *v.* heredar
in·her·it·ance, *n.* herencia
in·hib·it, *v.* inhibir
in·hi·bi·tion, *n.* inhibición
in·hu·man, *a.* inhumano; cruel
in·iq·ui·ty, *n. pl.,* -ties. iniquidad
in·i·tial, *a.* inicial. *f.*
in·i·ti·ate, *v.* iniciar
in·i·ti·a·tion, *n.* iniciación
in·i·ti·a·tive, *n.* iniciativa
in·ject, *v.* inyectar; introducir
in·jec·tion, *n.* inyección
in·jure, *v.* hacer daño a; ofender
in·ju·ry, *n. pl.,* -ries. daño; injuria
in·jus·tice, *n.* injusticia
ink, *n.* tinta
ink·ling, *n.* sospecha
in·let, *n.* entrada; ensenada
in·mate, *n.* inquilino
inn, *n.* posada
in·nate, *a.* innato
in·ner, *a.* interior
in·no·cence, *n.* inocencia
in·no·cent, *a.* inocente
in·no·va·tion, *n.* innovación
in·nu·en·do, *n. pl.,* -dos, -does. indirecta
in·nu·mer·a·ble, *a.* innumerable
in·oc·u·late, *v.* inocular
in·oc·u·la·tion, *n.* inoculación
in·quest, *n.* pesquisa judicial
in·quire, *v.* preguntar
in·quir·y, *n. pl.,* -ies. indagación; pregunta
in·qui·si·tion, *n.* inquisición

in·quis·i·tive, *a.* curioso
in·sane, *a.* insensato; loco
in·san·i·ty, *n. pl.,* -ties. locura
in·scribe, *v.* inscribir
in·scrip·tion, *n.* inscripción
in·sect, *n.* insecto
in·se·cure, *a.* inseguro; precario
in·sert, *v.* insertar; meter
in·ser·tion, *n.* inserción
in·side, *n.* interior. *a.* interno. *adv.* dentro. *prep.* dentro de
in·sight, *n.* perspicacia
in·sig·ni·a, *n. pl.* insignias
in·sig·nif·i·cance, *n.* insignificancia
in·sig·nif·i·cant, *a.* insignificante
in·sin·u·ate, *v.* insinuar
in·sin·u·a·tion, *n.* insinuación; indirecta
in·sip·id, *a.* insípido
in·sist, *v.* insistir
in·sist·ent, *a.* insistente; porfiado
in·so·lence, *n.* insolencia
in·so·lent, *a.* insolente; descarado
in·som·ni·a, *n.* insomnio
in·spect, *v.* examinar; inspeccionar
in·spec·tion, *n.* inspección; reconocimiento
in·spi·ra·tion, *n.* inspiración
in·spire, *v.* inspirar; estimular
in·stall, *v.* instalar
in·stall·ment, *n.* plazo; entrega
in·stance, *n.* ejemplo
in·stant, *a.* inmediato. *n.* instante
in·stan·ta·ne·ous, *a.* instantáneo
in·stead, *adv.* en lugar; en vez de
in·step, *n.* empeine
in·sti·gate, *v.* instigar
in·stinct, *n.* instinto
in·stinc·tive, *a.* instintivo. Also in·stinc·tu·al
in·sti·tute, *v.* instituir; empezar. *n.* instituto
in·sti·tu·tion, *n.* instituto; institución
in·struct, *v.* instruir; enseñar
in·struc·tion, *n.* instrucción
in·stru·ment, *n.* instrumento
in·suf·fi·cient, *a.* insuficiente
in·su·late, *v.* aislar
in·su·la·tion, *n.* aislamiento
in·su·lin, *n.* insulina
in·sult, *n.* insulto; ultraje. *v.* insultar
in·sur·ance, *n.* seguro
in·sure, *v.* asegurar
in·sur·rec·tion, *n.* insurrección
in·tact, *a.* intacto
in·te·ger, *n.* número entero
in·te·grate, *v.* integrar(se)
in·te·gra·tion, *n.* integración
in·teg·ri·ty, *n.* integridad
in·tel·lect, *n.* intelecto; inteligencia
in·tel·lec·tu·al, *a.* intelectual
in·tel·li·gence, *n.* inteligencia; información

in·tel·li·gent, *a.* inteligente
in·tend, *v.* proponerse; querer decir
in·tense, *a.* intenso
in·ten·si·ty, *n. pl.,* -ties. intensidad
in·tent, *a.* atento; absorto. *n.* intento
in·ten·tion, *n.* intención; propósito
in·ter, *v.* enterrar
in·ter·cede, *v.* interceder
in·ter·cept, *v.* interceptar
in·ter·ces·sion, *n.* intercesión
in·ter·change, *v.* intercambiar. *n.* intercambio
in·ter·course, *n.* comercio; trato; coito
in·ter·est, *n.* interés, *m.;* beneficio. *v.* interesar(se)
in·ter·fere, *v.* intervenir; meterse
in·ter·fer·ence, *n.* intervención; interferencia
in·ter·im, *n.* interín. *a.* interino
in·te·ri·or, *a., n.* interior
in·ter·jec·tion, *n.* interjección
in·ter·lude, *n.* intermedio; (*mus.*) interludio
in·ter·me·di·ate, *a.* intermedio. *v.* intervenir
in·ter·mis·sion, *n.* intermisión
in·tern, *n.* interno. *v.* encerrar
in·ter·nal, *a.* interno; interior
in·ter·na·tion·al, *a.* internacional
in·ter·play, *n.* interacción
in·ter·pose, *v.* interponer
in·ter·pret, *v.* explicar; interpretar; entender
in·ter·pre·ta·tion, *n.* interpretación
in·ter·ro·gate, *v.* interrogar
in·ter·ro·ga·tion, *n.* interrogación
in·ter·rupt, *v.* interrumpir; estorbar
in·ter·rup·tion, *n.* interrupción
in·ter·sect, *v.* cruzarse; intersecarse
in·ter·sec·tion, *n.* intersección; cruce
in·ter·twine, *v.* entretejer(se)
in·ter·val, *n.* intervalo
in·ter·vene, *v.* intervenir; interponerse
in·ter·view, *n.* entrevista. *v.* entrevistarse con
in·tes·tine, *n. often pl.* intestino
in·ti·mate, *a.* íntimo. *v.* intimar; dar a entender
in·tim·i·date, *v.* intimidar
in·to, *prep.* en; hacia el interior
in·tol·er·ant, *a.* intolerante
in·to·na·tion, *n.* entonación
in·tox·i·cate, *v.* embriagar; excitar
in·tran·si·tive, *a.* intransitivo
in·tra·ve·nous, *a.* intravenoso
in·trep·id, *a.* intrépido
in·tri·ca·cy, *n. pl.,* -cies. complejidad; enredo
in·tri·cate, *a.* intrincado
in·trigue, *v.* intrigar; fascinar. *n.* intriga
in·trin·sic, *a.* intrínseco. Also in-

trin·si·cal
in·tro·duce, *v.* introducir; presentar
in·tro·duc·tion, *n.* introducción; prólogo
in·trude, *v.* entremeterse
in·tu·i·tion, *n.* intuición
in·ure, *v.* habituar
in·vade, *v.* invadir
in·va·lid, *n., a.* inválido
in·var·i·a·ble, *a.* invariable
in·va·sion, *n.* invasión
in·vent, *v.* inventar
in·ven·tion, *n.* invención; inventiva
in·ven·to·ry, *n. pl.,* -ries. inventario
in·ver·sion, *n.* inversión
in·vert, *v.* invertir
in·ver·te·brate, *a., n.* invertebrado
in·vest, *v.* vestir; sitiar; invertir; vestir
in·ves·ti·gate, *v.* investigar
in·ves·ti·ga·tion, *n.* investigación; pesquisa
in·vig·or·ate, *v.* vigorizar
in·vin·ci·ble, *a.* invencible
in·vis·i·ble, *a.* invisible
in·vi·ta·tion, *n.* invitación; convite
in·vite, *v.* invitar; convidar
in·vo·ca·tion, *n.* invocación
in·voice, *n.* factura
in·voke, *v.* invocar; implorar
in·vol·un·tar·y, *a.* involuntario
in·volve, *v.* complicar; comprometer; enredar
in·ward, *adv.* hacia dentro. *a.* interno. Also in·wards
i·o·dine, *n.* yodo
i·on, *n.* ion
i·o·ta, *n.* jota
i·rate, *a.* colérico; enfurecido
ire, *n.* ira
ir·i·des·cent, *a.* iridiscente
i·ris, *n. pl.,* i·ris·es, ir·i·ses. iris; lirio
irk, *v.* molestar
i·ron, *n.* hierro; plancha; *pl.* hierros. *a.* de hierro. *v.* planchar
i·ron·ic, *a.* irónico. Also i·ron·i·cal
i·ro·ny, *n. pl.,* -nies. ironía
ir·ra·di·ate, *v.* irradiar
ir·ra·tion·al, *a.* irracional
ir·rec·on·cil·a·ble, *a.* irreconciliable
ir·ref·u·ta·ble, *a.* irrefutable
ir·reg·u·lar, *a.* irregular; desigual
ir·rel·e·vant, *a.* inaplicable
ir·re·sist·i·ble, *a.* irresistible
ir·re·spon·si·ble, *a.* irresponsable
ir·rev·er·ence, *n.* irreverencia
ir·ri·gate, *v.* regar
ir·ri·ga·tion, *n.* riego
ir·ri·ta·ble, *a.* irritable
ir·ri·tate, *v.* irritar; provocar; molestar
ir·ri·ta·tion, *n.* irritación
is, *v., third person pres. sing. of* be
is·land, *n.* isla

isle, *n.* isla

i·so·late, *v.* aislar

i·so·la·tion, *n.* aislamiento; separación

i·sos·ce·les, *a.* isósceles

is·sue, *n.* emisión; sucesión; resultado; asunto; edición. *v.* emitir; salir; distribuir; publicar

isth·mus, *n. pl.,* **-mus·es, -mi.** istmo

it, *pron., third person sing. neuter.* él, ella, ello, lo, la, le

i·tal·ic, *n. usu. pl.* letra bastardilla

i·tal·i·cize, *v.* poner en bastardilla

itch, *v.* picar. *n.* picazón; prurito

i·tem, *n.* artículo; partida

i·tem·ize, *v.* detallar

i·tin·er·ar·y, *n. pl.,* **-ies.** itinerario

its, *pron., a. poss. case of it*

it·self, *pron.* él, ella, ello o sí mismo

i·vo·ry, *n. pl.,* **-ries.** marfil, *m.; a.* de marfil

i·vy, *n. pl.,* **-vies.** hiedra

J

jab, *v.* golpear. *n.* pinchazo

jab·ber, *v.* farfullar. *n.* chapurreo; farfulla

jack, *n.* mozo; marinero; gato; sota

jack·al, *n.* chacal, *m.*

jack·ass, *n.* burro; tonto

jack·et, *n.* chaqueta

jack·knife, *n. pl.,* **-knives.** navaja. *v.* doblar

jack·pot, *n.* bote

jade, *n.* jade; rocín. *v.* cansar

jag·uar, *n.* jaguar

jail, *n.* cárcel, *f.;* calabozo. *v.* encarcelar

jal·ou·sie, *n.* celosía

jam, *v.* apiñar; atascar. *n.* agolpamiento; mermelada; *inf.* apuro

jamb, *n.* jamba

jam·bo·ree, *n. inf.* francachela

jan·gle, *n.* sonido discordante

jan·i·tor, *n.* portero

Jan·u·ar·y, *n.* enero

jar, *n.* jarra. *v.* sacudir

jar·gon, *n.* jerga

jas·mine, jas·min, *n.* jazmín

jaun·dice, *n.* ictericia

jaunt, *n.* excursión

jaun·ty, *a.* airoso

jave·lin, *n.* jabalina

jaw, *n.* quijada. *v.* charlar

jay, *n.* arrendajo

jazz, *n.* jazz, *m.*

jeal·ous, *a.* celoso; envidioso

jeal·ous·y, *n. pl.,* **-ies.** celos; recelo; envidia

Jeep, *n. trademark.* jeep

jeer, *v.* mofarse; befar

Je·ho·vah, *n.* Jehová

jell, *v.* cuajar(se)

jel·ly, *n. pl.,* **-lies.** jalea

jel·ly·fish, *n. pl.,* **-fish, -fish·es.** medusa

jeop·ar·dize, *v.* arriesgar

jeop·ar·dy, *n.* peligro

jerk, *v.* arrojar; sacudir. *n.* tirón

jer·kin, *n.* justillo

jer·sey, *n.* jersey, *m.*

jest, *n.* chanza

jet, *n.* chorro; surtidor; avión a reacción; azabache. *v.* chorrear

jet·sam, *n.* echazón, *f.*

jet·ti·son, *n.* echazón, *f. v.* echar

jet·ty, *n. pl.,* **-ties.** malecón; muelle

jew·el, *n.* joya

jew·el·er, *n.* joyero

jew·el·ry, *n.* joyas

jif·fy, *n. pl.,* **-fies.** *inf.* instante

jig, *n.* jiga

jig·saw, *n.* sierra de vaivén

jig·saw puz·zle, *n.* rompecabezas

jilt, *v.* dar calabazas

jim·my, *n. pl.,* **-mies.** palanqueta

jin·gle, *v.* retiñir; tintinear. *n.* retintín

jinx, *n. inf.* gafe

jit·ters, *n. pl. inf.* inquietud

job, *n.* trabajo; tarea

jock·ey, *n. pl.,* **-eys.** jockey, *m.*

jo·cose, *a.* jocoso

joc·u·lar, *a.* jocoso

joc·und, *a.* alegre

jog, *v.* empujar; correr despacio

join, *v.* juntar(se); unir(se). *n.* costura

joint, *n.* juntura; unión. *f. a.* combinado. *v.* juntar

joist, *n.* viga

joke, *n.* chiste; broma. *v.* bromear

jok·er, *n.* bromista, *m., f.; (cards)* comodín

jol·ly, *a.* alegre

jolt, *v.* sacudir. *n.* sacudida

jon·quil, *n.* junquillo

jos·tle, *v.* empujar. *n.* empellón

jot, *n.* jota. *v.* apuntar

jour·nal, *n.* diario; periódico; revista

jour·nal·ism, *n.* periodismo

jour·nal·ist, *n.* periodista, *m., f.*

jour·ney, *n.* viaje. *v.* viajar

jour·ney·man, *n. pl.,* **-men.** oficial, *m.*

joust, *n.* justa. *v.* justar

jo·vi·al, *a.* jovial

jowl, *n.* quijada; carrillo

joy, *n.* alegría; regocijo; deleite

joy·ous, *a.* alegre

ju·bi·la·tion, *n.* júbilo

ju·bi·lee, *n.* jubileo

Ju·da·ism, *n.* judaísmo

judge, *v.* juzgar; opinar; considerar. *n.* juez, *m.*

judg·ment, *n.* juicio; sentencia; discernimiento

ju·di·cial, *a.* judicial

ju·di·cious, *a.* juicioso

jug, *n.* jarro

jug·gle, v. hacer juegos malabares
jug·u·lar, a. yugular
juice, n. zumo; jugo
Ju·ly, n. julio
jum·ble, v. mezclar. n. confusión
jump, v. saltar; brincar. n. salto. **jump at,** apresurarse a aceptar
jump·er, n. saltador
junc·tion, n. juntura; empalme
junc·ture, n. juntura; coyuntura
June, n. junio
jun·gle, n. selva
jun·ior, a. más joven; menor. n. menor
ju·ni·per, n. enebro
junk, n. trastos viejos; junco
ju·ris·dic·tion, n. jurisdicción
ju·ris·pru·dence, n. jurisprudencia
ju·rist, n. jurista, m., f.
ju·ror, n. jurado
ju·ry, n. pl. -ries. jurado
just, a. justo; imparcial. adv. precisamente; apenas
jus·tice, n. justicia; juez, m.
jus·ti·fi·ca·tion, n. justificación
jus·ti·fy, v. justificar
jut, v. sobresalir
jute, n. yute
ju·ve·nile, a. juvenil. n. joven

K

kale, n. col rizada
ka·lei·do·scope, n. calidoscopio
kan·ga·roo, n. pl. -roos, roo. canguro
kar·at, n. quilate
keel, n. quilla. **keel o·ver,** zozobrar; volcar
keen, a. agudo; perspicaz; entusiasta; afilado
keep, v., kept, keep·ing. tener; retener; cumplir; guardar; detener; mantener; continuar. n. comida; cuidado
keep·ing, n. custodia
keg, n. cuñete
ken, v. saber. n. conocimientos
ken·nel, n. perrera
ker·chief, n. pañuelo
ker·nel, n. almendra; núcleo
ker·o·sene, ker·o·sine, n. querosene
ketch, n. queche
ketch·up, n. salsa picante de tomate
ket·tle, n. tetera
key, n. llave, f.; tecla; tono. a. clave. **key up,** excitar
key·board, n. teclado
key·stone, n. piedra clave
khak·i, n. caqui, m. a. de caqui
kick, v. dar patadas; dar un puntapié; inf. quejarse. n. patada
kid, n. cabrito; inf. niño. v. inf. tomar

el pelo
kid·nap, v. secuestrar
kid·ney, n. riñón
kill, v. matar; destruir. n. matanza
kiln, n. horno
kil·o·cy·cle, n. kilociclo
kil·o·gram, n. kilo; kilogramo
kil·o·me·ter, n. kilómetro
kil·o·watt, n. kilovatio
kin, n. parientes
kind, n. género. a. bueno; benigno; afable
kin·der·gar·ten, n. jardín de la infancia
kin·dle, v. encender
kind·ly, a. amable; bondadoso
kind·ness, n. benevolencia; atención
kin·dred, n. parientes. a. emparentado
king, n. rey, m.
king·dom, n. reino
kink, n. coca; peculiaridad
kin·ship, n. parentesco
kins·man, n. pl. -men. pariente
kiss, v. besar. n. beso
kit, n. equipo; avíos
kitch·en, n. cocina
kite, n. cometa
kith, n. archaic. amigos
kit·ten, n. gatito. Also **kit·ty**
knack, n. maña
knap·sack, n. mochila
knave, n. bribón
knead, v. amasar
knee, n. rodilla
kneel, v., knelt or kneeled, kneel·ing. arrodillarse
knell, n. doble
knick·knack, n. chuchería
knife, n. pl., knives. cuchillo. v. acuchillar
knight, n. caballero. v. armar caballero
knit, v., knit·ted or knit, knit·ting. hacer punto; juntar
knob, n. tirador; bulto
knock, v. chocar; golpear; dar golpes; inf. criticar. n. llamada; golpe. **knock down,** derribar. **knock off,** suspender
knoll, n. otero
knot, n. nudo. v. anudar
know, v., knew, known, know·ing. saber; conocer
know-how, n. inf. pericia
know·ing, a. astuto; hábil
knowl·edge, n. conocimiento; saber
knowl·edge·a·ble, a. erudito
knuck·le, n. nudillo
Ko·ran, n. Alcorán, Corán
ko·sher, a. autorizado por la ley judía

L

lab, *n. inf.* laboratorio
la·bel, *n.* marbete; etiqueta. *v.* rotular
la·bi·al, *a.* labial
la·bor, *n.* trabajo; labor, *f.;* parto. *v.* trabajar
lab·o·ra·to·ry, *n. pl.* -ries. laboratorio
la·bor·er, *n.* peón
la·bo·ri·ous, *a.* laborioso; penoso
lab·y·rinth, *n.* laberinto
lace, *n.* cordón; puntilla. *v.* atar
lac·er·ate, *v.* lacerar
lack, *n.* falta. *v.* faltar; necesitar
lack·ey, *n.* lacayo
la·con·ic, *a.* lacónico
lac·quer, *n.* laca
lac·tic, *a.* láctico
la·cu·na, *n. pl.* -nas, -nae. laguna; hoyo
lac·y, *a.* de encaje
lad, *n.* mozo; chico; muchacho
lad·der, *n.* escala; escalera
la·dle, *n.* cucharón
la·dy, *n.* señora; dama
lag, *v.* rezagarse
la·goon, *n.* laguna. Also **la·gune**
lair, *n.* cubil, *m.*
la·i·ty, *n. pl.* -ties. laicado
lake, *n.* lago
la·ma, *n.* lama, *m.*
lamb, *n.* cordero
lame, *a.* cojo; débil. *v.* lisiar
la·ment, *v.* lamentar(se). *n.* elegía
lam·en·ta·tion, *n.* lamentación
lam·i·nate, *v.* laminar
lamp, *n.* lámpara
lam·poon, *n.* pasquín. *v.* satirizar
lam·prey, *n. pl.* -preys. lamprea
lance, *n.* lanza. *v.* abrir con lanceta
lan·cet, *n.* lanceta
land, *n.* tierra; suelo; país, *v.* desembocar; llegar; aterrizar
land·la·dy, *n. pl.* -dies. propietaria
land·locked, *a.* cercado de tierra
land·lord, *n.* propietario; posadero
land·mark, *n.* mojón; marca
land·scape, *n.* paisaje
land·slide, *n.* desprendimiento de tierras
lane, *n.* vereda; senda
lan·guage, *n.* lenguaje
lan·guid, *a.* lánguido; flojo
lank, *a.* flaco, alto y descarnado; lacio
lan·o·lin, *n.* lanolina
lan·tern, *n.* linterna
lap, *v.* doblar; traslapar; lamer. *n.* regazo
la·pel, *n.* solapa
lapse, *n.* lapso; error. *v.* caer en un desliz
lar·ce·ny, *n. pl.* -nies. latrocinio

lard, *n.* manteca de cerdo
lar·der, *n.* despensa
large, *a.* grande; extenso
lar·gess, lar·gesse, *n.* dadivosidad
lar·i·at, *n.* lazo
lar·va, *n. pl.* -vae. larva
lar·yn·gi·tis, *n.* laringitis, *f.*
lar·ynx, *n. pl.* **lar·ynx·es, la·ryn·ges.** laringe, *f.*
las·civ·i·ous, *a.* lascivo
lash, *n.* látigo; latigazo; injuria. *v.* azotar; atar
lass, *n.* moza; chica; muchacha
las·si·tude, *n.* lasitud
las·so, *n. pl.* -sos, -soes. lazo. *v.* lazar
last, *a.* último; final. *adv.* finalmente. *v.* durar
last·ing, *a.* duradero
last·ly, *adv.* finalmente
latch, *n.* picaporte
late, *a.* tardío; atrasado; difunto. *adv.* tarde
late·ly, *adv.* recientemente
la·tent, *a.* latente
lat·er, *a.* posterior. *adv.* después; más tarde
lat·er·al, *a.* lateral
la·tex, *n. pl.* **la·tex·es, lat·i·ces.** látex, *m.*
lath, *n.* listón
lathe, *n.* torno
lath·er, *n.* espuma. *v.* enjabonar
lat·i·tude, *n.* latitud
lat·ter, *a.* más reciente
laud·a·ble, *a.* loable
laugh, *v.* reír(se). *n.* risa
laugh·ter, *n.* risa
launch, *v.* lanzar; echar al agua; crear. *n.* lancha
laun·der, *v.* lavar; lavar y planchar
laun·dry, *n. pl.* -dries. lavadero; ropa lavada
lau·rel, *n.* laurel, *m.; pl.* honor
la·va, *n.* lava
lav·a·to·ry, *n. pl.* -ries. wáter, *m.*
lav·en·der, *n.* espliego
lav·ish, *a.* pródigo. *v.* prodigar
law, *n.* ley, *f.;* regla; derecho; jurisprudencia
law·ful, *a.* legal; lícito
law·less, *a.* desordenado
lawn, *n.* césped
law·suit, *n.* pleito
law·yer, *n.* abogado
lax, *a.* descuidado; laxo
lax·a·tive, *a., n.* laxante
lay, *v., laid, lay·ing.* poner; colocar; dejar. *a.* lego
lay·er, *n.* capa; estrato
lay·ette, *n.* canastilla
lay·man, *n. pl.* -men. lego
lay·out, *n.* plan; disposición
la·zy, *a.* perezoso
lead, *n.* plomo

lead, v., **led, lead·ing.** llevar; conducir; dirigir; mandar; guiar. n. delantera
lead·er, n. líder; jefe
lead·er·ship, n. dirección
lead·ing, a. principal
leaf, n. pl., **leaves.** hoja. v. hojear
leaf·age, n. follaje
leaf·let, n. folleto
league, n. liga; sociedad
leak, v. rezumar(se); escaparse. n. gotera; escape
lean, v., **leaned** or **leant, lean·ing.** ladearse; inclinar(se). a. flaco; magro
leap, v. **leaped** or **leapt, leap·ing.** saltar; brincar. n. salto
learn, v., **learned** or **learnt, learn·ing.** aprender; enterarse de
learn·ed, a. docto
lease, n. arriendo. v. arrendar
leash, n. trailla
least, a. menor. n. lo menos. adv. menos
leath·er, n. cuero; piel, f. a. de cuero
leave, v., **left, leav·ing.** irse; salir; dejar. n. permiso
leav·en, n. levadura. Also **leav·en·ing**
lec·ture, n. conferencia. v. dar una conferencia
ledge, n. anaquel, m.
ledg·er, n. libro mayor
lee, n. sotavento
leech, n. sanguijuela
leer, v. mirar con malicia. n. mirada maliciosa o impúdica
left, a. izquierdo. n. izquierda. adv. a la izquierda
leg, n. pierna; pata. v. inf. correr
leg·a·cy, n. pl., **-cies.** legado
le·gal, a. legal; lícito
le·gal·i·ty, n. pl., **-ties.** legalidad
leg·end, n. leyenda
leg·end·ar·y, a. legendario
leg·i·ble, a. legible
le·gion, n. legión, f.; multitud
le·gion·naire, n. legionario
leg·is·late, v. legislar
leg·is·la·tion, n. legislación
leg·is·la·ture, n. cuerpo legislativo
le·git·i·mate, a. lícito; legítimo. v. legitimar
leg·ume, n. legumbre, f.
lei·sure, n. ocio
lem·on, n. limón. a. limonado
lem·on·ade, n. limonada
lend, v. **lent, lend·ing.** prestar
length, n. largo; duración
le·ni·ence, le·ni·en·cy, n. lenidad
le·ni·ent, a. indulgente
lens, n. pl., **lens·es.** lente, m., f.
leop·ard, n. leopardo

lep·er, n. leproso
lep·ro·sy, n. lepra
less, a. menos; menor. adv., prep. menos
less·en, v. disminuir(se); rebajar
les·son, n. lección
lest, conj. de miedo que
let, v., **let, let·ting.** permitir; dejar; alquilar
le·thal, a. mortal
leth·ar·gy, n. pl., **-gies.** letargo; estupor
let·ter, n. letra; carta; pl. letras. v. rotular
let·tuce, n. lechuga
leu·ke·mi·a, n. leucemia
lev·el, n. nivel, m.; llano. a. plano. v. nivelar
lev·er, n. palanca
lev·i·ty, n. ligereza
lev·y, n. pl., **-ies.** leva; exacción. v. exigir
lewd, a. lascivo; obsceno
lex·i·con, n. léxico
li·a·bil·i·ty, n. pl., **-ties.** responsabilidad; riesgo; obligación
li·a·ble, a. obligado; inclinado
li·ai·son, n. enlace; lío
li·ar, n. mentiroso
li·bel, n. difamación. v. calumniar
lib·er·al, a., n. liberal
lib·er·ate, v. libertar
lib·er·ty, n. pl., **-ties.** libertad
li·bi·do, n. libido
li·brar·i·an, n. bibliotecario
li·brar·y, n. pl., **-ies.** biblioteca
li·bret·to, n. pl., **-tos, -ti.** libreto
lice, n. pl. of **louse.** piojos
li·cense, n. licencia; desenfreno. v. licenciar
li·chen, n. liquen
lick, v. lamer; inf. vencer. n. lamedura
lic·o·rice, li·quo·rice, n. regaliz, m.
lid, n. tapa
lie, v., **lay, lain, ly·ing.** echarse; acostarse; estar tendido
lie, v., **lied, ly·ing.** mentir. n. mentira
lieu, n. archaic. lugar. **in lieu of,** en lugar de
lieu·ten·an·cy, n. pl., **-cies.** tenencia
lieu·ten·ant, n. teniente
life, n. pl., **lives.** vida; existencia; animación
life·boat, n. bote salvavidas
life·less, a. muerto; flojo
life·long, a. de toda la vida
life·size, a. de tamaño natural. Also **life·sized**
lift, v. alzar; elevar; levantar(se). n. alzamiento
lig·a·ment, n. ligamento
lig·a·ture, n. ligadura
light, n. luz, f.; lámpara. a. claro;

ligero. v. **light·ed** or **lit, light·ing.** encender(se); iluminar

light·en, v. iluminar; aligerar

light·heart·ed, light·heart·ed, a. alegre

light·house, n. faro

light·ly, adv. ligeramente

light·ning, n. relámpago

light·ning rod, n. pararrayos

light-year, n. año de luz

like, a. parecido. prep. como. conj. nonstandard. igual que. v. gustar; querer. n. gusto

lik·en, v. comparar

like·ness, n. semejanza

like·wise, adv. asimismo; también

li·lac, n. lila. a. de color de lila

lil·y, n. pl., **-ies.** lirio

limb, n. miembro; rama

lim·ber, a. flexible

lim·bo, n. limbo

lime, n. cal, f.; lima

lime·stone, n. piedra caliza

lim·it, n. límite; frontera. v. limitar

lim·i·ta·tion, n. limitación

lim·ou·sine, n. limusina

limp, v. cojear. n. cojera. a. flojo

line, n. línea; raya; fila; vía. v. rayar; alinear; forrar

lin·e·age, n. linaje

lin·e·ar, a. lineal

lin·en, n. lino. a. de lino

line-up, n. formación

lin·ger, v. tardar

lin·ge·rie, n. ropa blanca

lin·go, n. pl., **-goes.** inf. jerga

lin·guist, n. lingüista, m., f.

lin·guis·tics, n. pl. lingüística

lin·i·ment, n. linimento

link, n. eslabón. v. enlazar; unirse

li·no·le·um, n. linóleo

lint, n. hila

li·on, n. león

lip, n. labio; borde

liq·ue·fy, v. liquidar(se)

li·queur, n. licor

liq·uid, a., n. líquido

liq·ui·date, v. liquidar

liq·uor, n. licor; bebida alcohólica

lisp, v. cecear. n. ceceo

list, n. lista. v. poner en una lista; escorar

lis·ten, v. escuchar; oír

list·less, a. lánguido

lit·er·al, a. literal

lit·er·ar·y, a. literario

lit·er·a·ture, n. literatura

lithe, a. flexible; ágil. Also **lithe·some**

lit·ter, n. desorden; camada; litera. v. esparcir

lit·tle, a., **lit·tler** or **less** or **less·er;** **lit·tlest** or **least,** pequeño; poco. n. poco. adv., **less, least.** poco

lit·ur·gy, n. pl., **-gies.** liturgia

live, v. vivir; existir; pasar; morar

live, a. vivo; ardiente

live·li·hood, n. vida

live·ly, a. vivo; animado

liv·en, v. animar

liv·er, n. hígado

live·stock, n. ganado

liv·id, a. lívido

liz·ard, n. lagarto

lla·ma, n. llama

load, n. carga; peso. v. cargar

loaf, n. pl., **loaves.** pan; pilón. v. haraganear

loan, n. préstamo; empréstito. v. prestar

loath, loth, a. poco dispuesto

loathe, v. abominar

lob·by, n. pl., **-bies.** vestíbulo usado como una sala de espera; camarilla de cabilderos. v. cabildear

lob·ster, n. langosta

lo·cal, a. local; de la región; limitado

lo·cal·i·ty, n. pl., **-ties.** localidad

lo·cate, v. colocar; encontrar

lo·ca·tion, n. situación; colocación

lock, n. bucle; cerradura. v. cerrar(se) con llave; unirse

lo·co·mo·tive, a. locomotor. n. locomotora

lode, n. filón

lodge, v. alojar(se); albergar(se); hospedar(se); colocar. n. casa de guarda; logia

lodg·ing, n. habitación; alojamiento

loft, n. henil, m.; desván

loft·y, a. elevado; orgulloso

log, n. leño; diario de navegación. v. registrar

log·ic, n. lógica

log·i·cal, a. lógico

loin, n. usu. pl. ijada; lomo

loi·ter, v. holgazanear; perder el tiempo

lo·li·pop, lol·ly·pop, n. pirulí, m.; inf. chupechup

lone, a. solitario

lone·ly, a. solitario; solo

lone·some, a. solitario; solo

long, a. largo; prolongado. adv. mucho tiempo. v. anhelar

lon·gev·i·ty, n. longevidad

long, n. anhelo

lon·gi·tude, n. longitud

long·shore·man, n. pl., **-men.** estibador

long·wise, adv. a lo largo. Also **long·ways**

look, v. mirar; buscar; parecer. n. mirada; usu. pl. aspecto; apariencia

look·ing glass, n. espejo

look·out, n. vigilancia; vigía

loom, n. telar. v. asomar; amenazar

loon, n. somorgujo

loop, n. gaza. v. hacer gazas; rodear

loop-hole, n. escapatoria

loose, a. suelto; flojo; disoluto; vago. v. soltar; desatar

loot, n. botín; *inf.* dinero. v. saquear

lop-sid-ed, a. desequilibrado

lord, n. señor; (*cap.*) Dios; (*cap.*) British lord. v. dominar

lore, n. conocimientos

lose, v., lost, los-ing. perder(se)

loss, n. pérdida

lost, a. perdido; extraviado

lot, n. suerte, *f.*; parte, *f.*

lo-tion, n. loción

lot-ter-y, n. pl., -ies. lotería

loud, a. ruidoso; alto

loud-speak-er, n. altavoz, *m.*

lounge, v. gandulear. n. sala de estar

louse, n. pl., lice. piojo

lout, n. patán

lov-a-ble, love-a-ble, a. amabel

love, n. amor; cariño. v. querer; amar

love-ly, a. hermoso

lov-er, n. amante, *m., f.*

lov-ing, a. cariñoso

low, a. bajo; reducido; humilde; vil. *adv.* bajo; abajo

low-er, a. más bajo. v. bajar; rebajar

low-ly, a. humilde, *adv.* bajo

loy-al, a. leal; fiel

loy-al-ty, n. pl., -ties. lealtad; fidelidad

loz-enge, n. pastilla

lu-bri-cant, n. lubricante

lu-bri-cate, v. lubricar

lu-cid, a. lúcido; claro; sensato

luck, n. suerte, *f.*; azar

luck-y, a. afortunado; de buena sombra

lu-cra-tive, a. lucrativo

lu-di-crous, a. ridículo

lug, v. tirar de. n. oreja

lug-gage, n. equipaje

luke-warm, a. tibio; indiferente

lull, v. aquietar; calmar. n. tranquilidad antes o después de una tormenta

lull-a-by, n. pl., -bies. canción de cuna

lum-ber, v. andar pesadamente. n. maderas; leño

lu-mi-nous, a. luminoso

lump, n. masa; terrón; bulto. v. amontonar

lu-na-cy, n. pl., -cies. locura

lu-nar, a. lunar

lu-na-tic, n., a. loco

lunch, n. almuerzo. v. almorzar

lunch-eon, n. almuerzo

lung, n. pulmón

lure, n. señuelo. v. atraer; tentar

lu-rid, a. sensacional; cárdeno

lurk, v. acechar

lus-cious, a. delicioso

lust, n. lujuria. v. lujuriar

lus-ter, n. lustre

lus-ty, a. robusto

lute, n. laúd, *m.*

lux-u-ri-ant, a. lozano

lux-u-ri-ous, a. lujoso

lux-u-ry, n. pl., -ries. lujo

lye, n. lejía

lymph, n. linfa

lynch, v. linchar

lynx, n. pl., lynx, lynx-es. lince

lyre, n. lira

lyr-ic, a. lírico. n. poema lírico; *usu. pl.* letra de una canción

M

ma, n. *inf.* mamá

ma'am, n. *inf.* señora

ma-ca-bre, a. macabro

mac-a-ro-ni, n. macarrones

mac-a-roon, n. macarrón

ma-chet-e, n. machete

ma-chine, n. máquina

ma-chin-er-y, n. maquinaria

mack-er-el, n. escombro

mack-in-tosh, mac-in-tosh, n. impermeable

mad, a. loco; furioso; enfadado

mad-am, n. señora

mad-e-moi-selle, n. señorita

mad-house, n. casa de locos; manicomio

mad-man, n. loco

Ma-don-na, n. Madona

maes-tro, n. maestro

mag-a-zine, n. revista

ma-gen-ta, n. magenta

mag-got, n. cresa

mag-ic, n. magia. a. mágico

ma-gi-cian, n. mago; ilusionista, *m., f.*

mag-is-trate, n. magistrado

mag-nan-i-mous, a. magnánimo

mag-ne-si-um, n. magnesio

mag-net, n. imán

mag-net-ism, n. magnetismo

mag-nif-i-cent, a. magnífico; grandioso

mag-ni-fy, v. magnificar; aumentar

mag-ni-tude, n. magnitud

ma-ha-ra-jah, ma-ha-ra-ja, n. maharajá

ma-hog-a-ny, n. caoba

maid, n. criada; doncella

maid-en, n. doncella. a. soltera; virgen

mail, n. correo; cota de malla. v. echar al correo

mail-man, n. pl., -men. cartero

maim, v. mutilar

main, a. principal. n. cañería maestra; océano

main-land, n. continente

main·tain, *v.* mantener; sostener
main·te·nance, *n.* mantenimiento
maize, *n.* maíz, *m.*
maj·es·ty, *n.* majestad
ma·jor, *a.* mayor; (*mus.*) mayor. *n.* especialización; comandante. *v.* especializarse
ma·jor·i·ty, *n. pl.,* **-ties.** mayoría
make, *v.,* **made, mak·ing.** hacer; formar; crear; causar; fabricar; ganar; obligar; cometer. *n.* marca; forma. **make be·lieve,** fingir. **make out,** suceder; entender. **make sure,** asegurarse. **make up,** componer; pintarse. **make way,** hacer lugar
make·up, *n.* maquillaje; modo de ser
mal·a·dy, *n. pl.,* **-dies.** enfermedad
ma·lar·i·a, *n.* paludismo
male, *a., n.* macho; masculino; varón
mal·e·dic·tion, *n.* malévolo
mal·fea·sance, *n.* conducta ilegal
mal·ice, *n.* malicia; mala voluntad
ma·lig·nant, *a.* malévolo; maligno
mal·le·a·ble, *a.* maleable
mal·let, *n.* mazo
mal·nu·tri·tion, *n.* desnutrición
mal·prac·tice, *n.* tratamiento erróneo; mala conducta
malt, *n.* malta
mam·ma, ma·ma, *n.* mamá
mam·mal, *n.* mamífero
mam·moth, *n.* mamut, *m. a.* enorme
man, *n. pl.,* **men.** hombre; el género humano. *v.* guarnecer
man·a·cle, *n. often pl.* esposas
man·age, *v.* manejar; dirigir
man·ag·er, *n.* administrador; gerente
man·da·rin, *n.* mandarín
man·date, *n.* mandato
man·da·to·ry, *a.* obligatorio; preciso
man·do·lin, *n.* mandolina
mane, *n.* crin, *f.*
ma·neu·ver, *n.* maniobra. *v.* maniobrar; manipular
man·ga·nese, *n.* manganeso
man·ger, *n.* pesebre
man·go, *n.* mango
man·hole, *n.* pozo de visita
man·hood, *n.* virilidad
ma·ni·a, *n.* manía
ma·ni·ac, *n.* maníaco
man·i·cure, *n.* manicura
man·i·fest, *a.* manifiesto. *v.* manifestar; revelar. *n.* manifiesto
man·i·fes·to, *n.* manifiesto
man·i·fold, *a.* múltiple; vario
ma·nip·u·late, *v.* manipular
ma·nip·u·la·tion, *n.* manipulación
man·kind, *n.* el género humano
man·na, *n.* maná, *m.*
man·ne·quin, *n.* maniquí, *m.;* modelo
man·ner, *n.* manera; modo; aire; especie, *f.; pl.* modales

man·ner·ly, *a., adv.* bien criado
man·or, *n.* señorío; casa solariega
man·pow·er, *n.* mano de obra
man·sion, *n.* casa solariega
man·slaugh·ter, *n.* homicidio impremeditado
man·tel, *n.* manto
man·u·al, *a., n.* manual, *m.*
man·u·fac·ture, *n.* manufactura. *v.* fabricar
ma·nure, *n.* estiércol, *m.*
man·u·script, *n.* manuscrito
man·y, *a.,* **more, most.** muchos. *n., pron.* gran número
map, *n.* mapa, *m. v.* trazar; proyectar
ma·ple, *n.* arce
mar, *v.* estropear
mar·ble, *n.* mármol, *m.;* canica. *a.* marmóreo
March, *n.* marzo
march, *v.* marchar; desfilar. *n.* marcha; progreso
mare, *n.* yegua
mar·ga·rine, *n.* margarina
mar·gin, *n.* margen; sobrante
mar·i·jua·na, *n.* marijuana
mar·i·nate, *v.* escabechar
ma·rine, *a.* marino. *n.* soldado de marina
mar·i·on·ette, *n.* marioneta
mar·i·tal, *a.* marital
mar·i·time, *a.* marítimo
mark, *n.* marca; señal, *f.;* huella; nota; blanco. *v.* marcar; señalar
mar·ket, *n.* mercado; venta. *v.* vender
marks·man, *n. pl.,* **-men.** tirador
mar·ma·lade, *n.* mermelada
ma·roon, *v.* abandonar
mar·quis, *n. pl.,* **-quis·es, -quis.** marqués, *m.*
mar·quise, *n. f., pl.,* **-quis·es.** marquesa
mar·riage, *n.* matrimonio; boda
mar·row, *n.* médula
mar·ry, *v.* casar(se)
marsh, *n.* pantano
mar·shal, *n.* mariscal, *m.;* alguacil, *m. v.* arreglar
marsh·mal·low, *n.* bombón de merengue
mar·su·pi·al, *a., n.* marsupial, *m.*
mart, *n.* mercado
mar·tial, *a.* marcial
mar·tyr, *n.* mártir. *v.* martirizar
mar·vel, *n.* maravilla. *v.* maravillar(se)
mas·cot, *n.* mascota
mas·cu·line, *a.* masculino
mash, *v.* amasar. *n.* mezcla; puré
mask, *n.* máscara; disfraz, *m. v.* enmascarar
mas·och·ism, *n.* masoquismo
mas·och·ist, *n.* masoquista, *m., f.*

ma·son, n. albañil, m.

ma·son·ry, n. albañilería

masque, mask, n. mascarada

mas·quer·ade, n. mascarada

mass, n. masa; bulto; montón; misa.
a. en serie. v. reunir

mas·sa·cre, n. carnicería. v. hacer
una carnicería

mas·sage, n. masaje

mas·sive, a. macizo

mass pro·duc·tion, n. fabricación en
serie

mast, n. mástil, m.

mas·ter, n. dueño; señor; maestro. v.
dominar. a. principal

mas·ter·piece, n. obra maestra

mas·ti·cate, v. masticar

mas·to·don, n. mastodonte

mas·tur·ba·tion, n. masturbación

mat, n. felpudo; estera. v. enredar

mat, matt, matte, a. mate

match, n. cerilla; partido; igual, m., f.
v. igualar; hacer juego con

match·mak·er, n. casamentero

mate, n. compañero. v. casar; aparear

ma·te·ri·al, n. materia; material, m.;
tela. a. material

ma·ter·nal, a. maternal

ma·ter·ni·ty, n. maternidad

math, n. inf. matemáticas

math·e·mat·ics, n., pl. matemáticas

mat·i·nee, n. función de tarde

ma·tric·u·late, v. matricular(se)

mat·ri·mo·ny, n. matrimonio

ma·trix, n. pl., -tri·ces, -trix·es. matriz, f.

ma·tron, n. matrona

mat·ter, n. materia; asunto. v. importar

mat·tress, n. colchón

ma·ture, a. maduro. v. madurar

ma·tu·ri·ty, n. madurez, f.

maul, mall, v. maltratar

mau·so·le·um, n. mausoleo

max·im, n. máxima

max·i·mum, n. máximum. a. máx-
imo

May, n. mayo

may, v. pt. might. poder; ser posible

may·be, adv. quizá(s); tal vez

may·on·naise, n. mayonesa

may·or, n. alcalde

maze, n. laberinto

me, pron. me; mí

mead·ow, n. prado

mea·ger, a. exiguo

meal, n. comida; harina

mean, v., meant, mean·ing. intentar;
querer decir; significar. a. inferior;
tacaño; vil; medio. n. medio; pl.
modo; medios. by all means, natu-
ralmente. by no means, de ningún
modo

mean·ing, n. intención; sentido

mean·time, n. ínterin. adv. mientras
tanto

mea·sles, n. sarampión

meas·ure, n. medida; compás. v.
medir

meas·ure·ment, n. medida

meat, n. carne, f.

me·chan·ic, n. mecánico

me·chan·i·cal, a. mecánico

me·chan·ics, n. mecánica

mech·an·ism, n. mecanismo

med·al, n. medalla

me·dal·lion, n. medallón

med·dle, v. entrometerse; meterse

me·di·an, a. mediano

me·di·ate, v. mediar; intervenir

med·i·cal, a. médico

med·i·ca·tion, n. medicación

med·i·cine, n. medicamento; medici-
na

me·di·e·val, a. medieval

me·di·o·cre, a. mediocre

med·i·tate, v. meditar; contemplar

med·i·ta·tion, n. meditación

me·di·um, n. pl., -di·a, -di·ums. medio; intermedio. a. mediano

meek, a. dócil

meet, v., met, meet·ing. encon-
trar(se); tropezar con; reunirse;
honrar. n. reunión

meet·ing, n. reunión; encuentro; cita

mel·an·chol·y, n. melancolía

mel·low, v. suavizar. a. suave; maduro

mel·o·dra·ma, n. melodrama, m.

mel·o·dy, n. melodía

mel·on, n. melón

melt, v. derretir(se); fundir(se)

mem·ber, n. miembro

mem·brane, n. membrana

me·men·to, n. pl., -tos, -toes. recuerdo

mem·o, n. inf. memorándum, m.

mem·oir, n. memoria

mem·o·ra·ble, a. memorable

mem·o·ran·dum, n. pl., -dums, -da.
apunte; memorándum, m.

me·mo·ri·al, n. memorial. a. con-
memorativo

mem·o·rize, v. aprender de memoria

mem·o·ry, n. pl., -ries. memoria; recuerdo

men·ace, v. amenazar. n. amenaza

mend, v. reparar; reformar

me·ni·al, a. servil. n. doméstico

men·o·pause, n. menopausia

men·stru·a·tion, n. menstruación

men·tal, a. mental

men·thol, n. mentol, m.

men·tion, n. mención. v. mencionar

men·u, n. menú, m.; lista de platos

mer·ce·nar·y, n., a. mercenario

mer·chan·dise, n. mercancía

mer·chant, n. comerciante

mer·cu·ry, *n.* mercurio

mer·cy, *n.* misericordia; merced; clemencia

mere, *a.* mero

me·rid·i·an, *n.* meridiano

me·ringue, *n.* merengue

mer·it, *n.* mérito. *v.* merecer

mer·maid, *n.* sirena

mer·ry, *a.* regocijado; divertido; festivo

mer·ry-go-round, *n.* tiovivo

mesh, *n.* malla; *pl.* red. *v.* enredarse

mess, *n.* desorden; confusión. *v.* desordenar

mes·sage, *n.* comunicación; recado

mes·sen·ger, *n.* mensajero

me·tab·o·lism, *n.* metabolismo

met·al, *n.* metal, *m.*

met·a·mor·pho·sis, *n. pl.*, -ses. metamorfosis, *f.*

met·a·phor, *n.* metáfora

mete, *v.* repartir

me·te·or·ite, *n.* meteorito

me·te·or·ol·o·gy, *n.* meteorología

me·ter, me·tre, *n.* metro

meth·od, *n.* método

me·trop·o·lis, *n.* metrópoli, *f.*

met·ro·pol·i·tan, *a.* metropolitano

mez·za·nine, *n.* entresuelo

mi·ca, *n.* mica

mi·crobe, *n.* microbio

mi·cro·cosm, *n.* microcosmo

mi·cro·phone, *n.* micrófono

mi·cro·scope, *n.* microscopio

mid, *a., adv.* medio. *prep.* entre

mid·day, *n.* mediodía

mid·dle, *a.* medio. *n.* medio; centro

midg·et, *n.* enano

mid·night, *n.* medianoche

mid·ship·man, *n. pl.*, -men. guardia marina

midst, *n.* medio. *prep.* entre

mid·wife, *n. pl.*, -wives. partera

might, *n.* fuerza; poder

mi·grate, *v.* emigrar

mi·gra·to·ry, *a.* migratorio

mild, *a.* suave; manso; ligero

mil·dew, *n.* mildeu, *m.*; maho

mile, *n.* milla

mi·lieu, *n. pl.*, -lieus. medio ambiente

mil·i·tant, *a.* militante

mil·i·tar·y, *a.* militar. *n.* los militares; soldados

mi·li·tia, *n.* milicia

milk, *n.* leche, *f.* *v.* ordeñar

mill, *n.* molino; fábrica. *v.* moler

mil·len·ni·um, *n. pl.*, -ni·a, -ni·ums. milenio

mil·li·me·ter, *n.* milímetro

mil·lion, *n.* millón

mil·lion·aire, *n.* millonario

mime, *n.* mimo; pantomima

mim·e·o·graph, *n.* mimeógrafo

mim·ic, *v.* imitar. *n.* remedador

mince, *v.* desmenuzar

mind, *n.* mente, *f.*; inteligencia. *v.* obedecer; cuidar; preocuparse

mine, *pron.* mío; mía. *n.* mina. *v.* minar

min·er·al, *a., n.* mineral, *m.*

min·gle, *v.* mezclar(se)

min·i·a·ture, *n.* miniatura. *a.* en miniatura

min·i·mum, *a.* mínimo. *n.* mínimo

min·is·ter, *n.* pastor; eclesiástico; ministro

min·is·try, *n.* ministerio; clero

mink, *n.* visón

mi·nor, *a.* menor; secundario; menor de edad. *n.* subordinado; menor de edad

mi·nor·i·ty, *n.* minoría

mint, *n.* casa de moneda; menta. *v.* acuñar

mi·nus, *prep.* menos; falto de. *n.* signo menos. *a.* negativo

min·ute, *n.* minuto; momento; *pl.* acta

mi·nute, *a.* menudo

mir·a·cle, *n.* milagro

mi·rac·u·lous, *a.* milagroso

mi·rage, *n.* espejismo

mir·ror, *n.* espejo

mirth, *n.* alegría

mis·an·thrope, *n.* misántropo

mis·ap·pre·hend, *v.* entender mal

mis·car·riage, *n.* malparto; malogro

mis·cel·la·ne·ous, *a.* misceláneo; diverso

mis·chief, *n.* travesura; mal, *m.*

mis·chie·vous, *a.* malicioso

mis·con·cep·tion, *n.* equivocación

mis·de·mean·or, *n.* delito

mi·ser, *n.* avaro

mis·er·a·ble, *a.* desgraciado; infeliz; vil

mis·er·y, *n.* sufrimiento; miseria

mis·for·tune, *n.* infortunio

mis·giv·ing, *n. often pl.* presentimiento

mis·hap, *n.* contratiempo

mis·lay, *v.*, -laid, -lay·ing. extraviar

mis·lead, *v.*, -led, -lead·ing. despistar; engañar

mis·print, *n.* error de imprenta

mis·rep·re·sent, *v.* falsificar

miss, *v.* errar; perder; no acertar; pasar por alto. *n.* error; señorita

mis·sal, *n.* misal, *m.*

mis·sile, *n.* proyectil, *m.*

miss·ing, *a.* ausente; perdido

mis·sion, *n.* misión

mis·sion·ar·y, *n.* misionero

mist, *n.* neblina

mis·take, *v.*, -took, -tak·en, -tak·ing. equivocar(se)

mis·ter, *n.* señor. Abbr. *Mr.*

mis·tle·toe, *n.* muérdago

mis·treat, v. maltratar

mis·tress, n. señora; querida

mis·trust, n. recelo. v. desconfiar de

mis·un·der·stand, v., -stood, -stand·ing. entender mal

mis·use, v. maltratar; abusar

mit·i·gate, v. mitigar

mit·ten, n. mitón

mix, v. mezclar(se); confundir. n. mezcla

mix·ture, n. mezcla

moan, v. gemir; quejarse. n. quejido

moat, n. foso

mob, n. tropel, m.; turba. v. festejar tumultuosamente

mo·bile, a. móvil; ambulante

moc·ca·sin, n. mocasín

mock, v. burlarse de. a. falso

mock·er·y, n. mofa

mode, n. modo; moda

mod·el, n. modelo. v. modelar

mod·er·ate, a., n. moderado. v. moderar(se)

mod·ern, n., a. moderno

mod·est, a. modesto

mod·i·fi·ca·tion, n. modificación

mod·i·fy, v. modificar

mod·u·late, v. modular

moist, a. húmedo

mois·ten, v. humedecer

mois·ture, n. humedad

mo·lar, n. muela

mo·las·ses, n. melaza

mold, mould, n. molde; moho. v. moldear; amoldar

mold·ing, mould·ing, n. moldura

mole, n. lunar; topo

mol·e·cule, n. molécula

mo·lest, v. molestar; asaltar sexualmente

mol·lusk, mol·lusc, n. molusco

mol·ten, a. fundido

mom, n. inf. mamá

mo·ment, n. momento

mo·men·tar·y, a. momentáneo

mo·men·tum, n. ímpetu, m.

mon·arch, n. monarca, m.

mon·ar·chy, n. monarquía

mon·as·ter·y, n. pl., -ies. monasterio

Mon·day, n. lunes, m.

mon·e·tar·y, a. monetario

mon·ey, n. dinero

mon·goose, n. mangosta

mon·grel, n., a. mestizo

mon·i·tor, n. monitor

monk, n. monje

mon·key, n. pl., -keys. mono. v. imitar

mo·nog·a·my, n. monogamia

mon·o·gram, n. monograma, m.

mon·o·lith, n. monolito

mon·o·logue, mon·o·log, n. monólogo

mo·nop·o·lize, v. monopolizar

mo·nop·o·ly, n. monopolio

mon·o·tone, n. monotonía

mo·not·o·nous, a. monótono

mo·not·o·ny, n. monotonía

mon·ox·ide, n. monóxido

mon·sieur, n. pl., mes·sieurs. Fr. señor

mon·soon, n. monzón, m., f.

mon·ster, n. monstruo

mon·stros·i·ty, n. monstruosidad

month, n. mes, m.

month·ly, a. mensual. adv. mensualmente

mon·u·ment, n. monumento

mood, n. humor

moon, n. luna

moon·light, n. luz de la luna

moor, n. páramo. v. amarrar

moose, n. pl., moose. alce

mop, n. estropajo

mor·al, a. moral. n. moraleja; pl. moralidad

mo·rale, n. moral, f.

mor·al·ize, v. moralizar

mo·rass, n. pantano

mor·a·to·ri·um, n. pl., -ums, -a. moratoria

mor·bid, a. mórbido; pesimista

more, a. más; adicional. adv., n. más

more·o·ver, adv. además

morgue, n. depósito de cadáveres

morn·ing, n. mañana; madrugada

mo·rose, a. malhumorado; saturnino

mor·phine, n. morfina

mor·sel, n. pedazo; bocado

mor·tal, a. mortal; fatal. n. mortal, m., f.

mor·tal·i·ty, n. mortalidad

mort·gage, n. hipoteca. v. hipotecar

mor·tu·ar·y, n. mortuorio

mo·sa·ic, n. mosaico

mos·qui·to, n. pl., -toes, -tos. mosquito

moss, n. musgo

most, a. más; la mayor parte de. adv. lo más; muy

most·ly, adv. principalmente

moth, n. polilla

moth·er, n. madre. a. materno. v. servir de madre a

moth·er·hood, n. maternidad

moth·er·in·law, n. pl., moth·ers·in·law. suegra

mo·tion, n. movimiento; moción. v. hacer señas

mo·tion pic·ture, n. película

mo·tive, n. motivo

mot·ley, a. abigarrado

mo·tor, n., a. motor. v. ir en coche

mo·tor·cy·cle, n. motocicleta

mot·to, n. pl., -toes, -tos. mote; lema, m.

mound, n. terraplén; montón. v.

amontonar
moun·tain, *n.* montaña
mourn, *v.* lamentarse; llorar
mourn·ing, *n.* luto
mouse, *n. pl.,* **mice.** ratón
mouth, *n.* boca; embocadero
move, *v.* mover(se); trasladar(se); ir(se); mudar(se); conmover. *n.* acción; jugada
move·ment, *n.* movimiento; actividad; tiempo
mov·ie, *n.* película
mow, *v.,* **mowed, mowed** or **mown, mow·ing.** segar
Mr., *n. pl.,* **Messrs.** señor
Mrs., *n. pl.,* **Mmes.** señora
Ms., *n.* señorita; señora
much, *adv., a.* **more, most.** mucho; muy. *n.* mucho
mu·cous, *a.* mucoso
mu·cus, *n.* moco
mud, *n.* barro; lodo
mud·dle, *v.* aturdir. *n.* embrollo
muff, *n.* manguito
muf·fin, *n.* mollete
muf·fle, *v.* embozar; apagar
muf·fler, *n.* bufanda
mug, *n.* pichel, *m.; inf.* jeta. *v. inf.* asaltar
mule, *n.* mulo
mul·ti·ple, *a.* múltiple. *n.* múltiplo
mul·ti·pli·ca·tion, *n.* multiplicación
mul·ti·ply, *v.* multiplicar(se)
mul·ti·tude, *n.* multitud
mum·ble, *v.* hablar entre dientes
mum·my, *n.* momia
mumps, *n.* paperas; parótidas
mun·dane, *a.* mundano
mu·nic·i·pal, *a.* municipal
mu·ni·tion, *n. usu. pl.* municiones
mu·ral, *n., a.* mural, *m.*
mur·der, *v.* asesinar. *n.* asesinato
mur·mur, *n.* murmullo. *v.* murmurar
mus·cle, *n.* músculo
mus·cu·lar, *a.* muscular; musculoso
muse, *v.* meditar. *n.* musa
mu·se·um, *n.* museo
mush·room, *n.* champiñón; hongo
mu·sic, *n.* música
mu·si·cal, *a.* musical; músico
mu·si·cian, *n.* músico
mus·ket, *n.* mosquete
musk·rat, *n. pl.,* **-rat, -rats.** rata almizclera
mus·lin, *n.* muselina
must, *v.* deber; tener que
mus·tache, *n.* bigote
mus·tard, *n.* mostaza
mute, *a.* mudo. *n.* mudo; (*mus.*) sordina
mu·ti·late, *v.* mutilar
mu·ti·ny, *n.* motín. *v.* amotinarse
mut·ter, *v.* murmurar. *n.* rumor
mu·tu·al, *a.* mutuo

muz·zle, *n.* hocico; boca; bozal, *m. v.* abozalar
my, *a.* mi
myr·i·ad, *n.* miríada
my·self, *pron. pl.,* **our·selves.** yo mismo
mys·te·ri·ous, *a.* misterioso
mys·ter·y, *n. pl.,* **-ies.** misterio
mys·tic, *a., n.* místico
mys·ti·cism, *n.* misticismo; mística
myth, *n.* mito
myth·ic, myth·i·cal, *a.* mítico
my·thol·o·gy, *n.* mitología

N

nab, *v. inf.* coger; prender
nag, *v.* regañar. *n.* jaca
nail, *n.* clavo; uña. *v.* clavar
na·ive, na·ïve, *a.* ingenuo; sencillo
na·ive·té, na·ive·te, *n.* ingenuidad
na·ked, *a.* desnudo
name, *n.* nombre; apellido; fama. *v.* llamar; nombrar
name·sake, *n.* tocayo
nap, *v.* dormitar. *n.* siesta; lanilla
nape, *n.* nuca
naph·tha, *n.* nafta
nap·kin, *n.* servilleta
nar·cis·sism, *n.* narcisismo
nar·cis·sus, *n. pl.,* **-cis·sus·es, -cis·si.** narciso
nar·cot·ic, *n., a.* narcótico
nar·rate, *v.* narrar
nar·ra·tion, *n.* narración; relato
nar·ra·tive, *n.* narrativa. *a.* narrativo
nar·row, *a.* estrecho; angosto; reducido. *v.* estrechar(se)
na·sal, *a.* nasal. (*phon.*) sonido nasal
nas·ty, *a.* sucio; asqueroso; rencoroso
na·tal, *a.* natal
na·tion, *n.* nación; pueblo
na·tion·al, *a.* nacional. *n.* nacional, *m., f.*
na·tion·al·ism, *n.* nacionalismo
na·tion·al·i·ty, *n. pl.,* **-ties.** nacionalidad
na·tive, *a.* nativo; natural. *n.* natural, *m., f.;* indígena, *m., f.*
na·tiv·i·ty, *n. pl.,* **-ties.** natividad; (*cap.*) Navidad
nat·u·ral, *a.* natural; genuino
nat·u·ral·ize, *v.* naturalizar(se)
na·ture, *n.* naturaleza; carácter; género
naught, *n.* nada; (*arith.*) cero
naugh·ty, *a.* travieso; pícaro
nau·se·a, *n.* náusea
nau·se·ate, *v.* nausear; dar asco
nau·ti·cal, *a.* náutico
na·val, *a.* naval; marítimo
nave, *n.* nave, *f.*
na·vel, *n.* ombligo

nav·i·ga·ble, a. navegable
nav·i·gate, v. navegar; marear
nav·i·ga·tion, n. navegación; náutica
na·vy, n. pl., **-vies.** marina de guerra; azul marino o de mar. Also **na·vy blue**
nay, adv. no. n. voto negativo
near, a. cercano; próximo. adv. cerca. prep. cerca de; junto a. v. acercarse a
near·by, a., adv. cerca
near·sight·ed, a. miope
neat, a. esmerado; primoroso
neb·u·la, n. pl., **-las, -lae.** nebulosa
nec·es·sar·y, a. necesario; esencial. n. pl., **-ies.** lo necesario
ne·ces·si·tate, v. necesitar
ne·ces·si·ty, n. pl., **-ties.** necesidad; requisito
neck, n. cuello
nec·tar, n. néctar
need, n. carencia; necesidad. v. necesitar; requerir
nee·dle, n. aguja
need·less, a. superfluo
ne·far·i·ous, a. nefario
neg·a·tive, a. negativo. n. negativa; (photog.) negativo. v. negar; poner veto a
ne·glect, v. descuidar; faltar a. n. descuido; dejadez, f.
neg·li·gee, n. bata
neg·li·gi·ble, a. insignificante; sin importancia
ne·go·ti·ate, v. negociar; gestionar
ne·go·ti·a·tion, n. negociación
neigh·bor, n., a. vecino. v. estar contiguo a
neigh·bor·hood, n. vecindad; barrio
nei·ther, a., conj. ni; tampoco. pron. ninguno
ne·on, n. neón
neph·ew, n. sobrino
nerve, n. nervio; valor; inf. descaro
nerv·ous, a. nervioso
nest, n. nido. v. anidar
nes·tle, v. arrimarse
net, n. red, f. v. coger. a. neto
net·work, n. red, f.
neu·ral·gia, n. neuralgia
neu·ro·sis, n. pl., **-ses.** neurosis, f.
neu·rot·ic, a. neurótico. n. neurótico
neu·ter, a. neutro
neu·tral, a. neutral. n. neutral, m., f.
neu·tral·i·ty, n. neutralidad
neu·tral·ize, v. neutralizar
neu·tron, n. neutrón
nev·er, adv. nunca; jamás
nev·er·the·less, adv. sin embargo; a pesar de todo
new, a. nuevo; reciente; moderno. adv. nuevamente
new·ly, adv. nuevamente
new·ly·wed, n. recién casados

news, n. pl. noticias; nuevas
next, a. próximo; siguiente. adv. inmediatamente después. prep. contiguo
nib·ble, v. picar; mordiscar
nice, a. simpático; amable; agradable; fino
ni·ce·ty, n. pl., **-ties.** usu. pl. punto fino
nick, n. muesca
nick·el, n. níquel, m.; moneda de cinco centavos
nick·name, n. apodo. v. apodar
nic·o·tine, n. nicotina. Also **nic·o·tin**
niece, n. sobrina
night, n. noche, f. a. nocturno
night·in·gale, n. ruiseñor
night·ly, a. nocturno. adv. por la noche
night·mare, n. pesadilla
night·time, n. noche, f.
nim·ble, a. ágil; listo
nine, n., a. nueve
nine·teen, n., a. diecinueve
nine·ty, a., n. pl., **-ties.** noventa
nin·ny, n. pl., **-nies.** bobo
ninth, a. noveno
nip, v. pellizcar; cortar
nip·ple, n. pezón
ni·trate, n. nitrato
ni·tro·gen, n. nitrógeno
ni·tro·glyc·er·in, n. nitroglicerina
no, adv. no. n. pl., noes, nos. no. a. ninguno
no·bil·i·ty, n. pl., **-ties.** nobleza
no·ble, a. noble. n. noble
no·ble·man, n. pl., **-men.** noble; hidalgo
no·bod·y, pron. nadie. n. pl., **-ies.** nadie
noc·tur·nal, a. nocturno
nod, v. cabecear; inclinar (la cabeza). n. señal hecha con la cabeza
noise, n. ruido; clamor
nois·y, a. ruidoso; estrepitoso
no·mad, n. nómada, m., f.
nom·i·nal, a. nominal
nom·i·nate, v. nombrar
nom·i·na·tion, n. nombramiento; nominación
non·cha·lant, a. indiferente
non·con·form·i·ty, n. disidencia
non·de·script, a. inclasificable; indefinible
none, pron. nada; nadie; ninguno. adv. de ninguna manera
non·pa·reil, n. persona o cosa sin par. a. sin igual
non·prof·it, a. no comercial
non·sense, n. tontería
noo·dle, n. tallarín
noon, n. mediodía, m.
no one, pron. nadie. Also **no-one**
noose, n. lazo corredizo

nor, *conj.* ni

norm, *n.* norma; modelo

nor·mal, *a.* normal

nor·mal·ly, *adv.* normalmente

north, *a.* del norte. *adv.* al norte. *n.* norte

north·east, *n.* nordeste

north·ern, *a.* del norte; al norte

north·ward, *adv.* hacia el norte

north·west, *n.* noroeste

nose, *n.* nariz, *f.*

nos·tal·gia, *n.* nostalgia

nos·tril, *n.* ventana de la nariz; *pl.* narices, *f. pl.*

nos·y, *a. inf.* curioso

not, *adv.* no; de ningún modo

no·ta·ble, *a., n.* notable

no·ta·ry, *n. pl.,* **-ries.** notario. Also **no·ta·ry pub·lic**

no·ta·tion, *n.* notación

notch, *n.* mella; muesca. *v.* mellar

note, *n. often pl.* nota; apunte; señal, *f. v.* notar; apuntar

noth·ing, *n.* nada. *adv.* de ninguna manera

no·tice, *n.* aviso; anuncio; atención. *v.* notar; fijarse en

no·ti·fy, *v.* notificar

no·tion, *n.* noción; concepto; idea

no·to·ri·ous, *a.* notorio

not·with·stand·ing, *prep.* a pesar de. *adv.* no obstante. *conj.* por más que

noun, *n.* substantivo

nour·ish, *v.* nutrir; alimentar

nov·el, *n.* novela. *a.* nuevo

nov·el·ty, *n. pl.,* **-ties.** novedad

No·vem·ber, *n.* noviembre

nov·ice, *n.* principiante, *m., f.*

now, *adv.* ahora; actualmente

no·where, *adv.* en ninguna parte

noz·zle, *n.* boquilla

nu·cle·ar, *a.* nuclear

nu·cle·us, *n. pl.,* **-us·es, -i.** núcleo

nude, *a.* desnudo. *n.* desnudo

nu·di·ty, *n.* desnudez, *f.*

nui·sance, *n.* molestia; incomodidad

null, *a.* nulo

numb, *a.* entumecido; entorpecido. *v.* entumecer

num·ber, *n.* número. *v.* numerar; contar

nu·mer·a·tor, *n.* numerador

nu·mer·i·cal, *a.* numérico

nu·mer·ous, *a.* numeroso

nun, *n.* monja

nun·ner·y, *n. pl.,* **-ies.** convento de monjas

nup·tial, *a.* nupcial. *n. usu. pl.* nupcias

nurse, *n.* enfermera; niñera. *v.* criar; cuidar

nurs·er·y, *n. pl.,* **-ies.** cuarto de los niños; plantel, *m.*

nur·ture, *v.* nutrir; criar

nut, *n.* nuez, *f.*

nu·tri·tion, *n.* nutrición

nu·tri·tious, *a.* nutritivo

ny·lon, *n.* nailon; nilón; *pl.* medias

nymph, *n.* ninfa

O

oaf, *n.* zoquete

oak, *n.* roble. *a.* de roble

oar, *n.* remo

o·a·sis, *n. pl.,* **-ses.** oasis, *m.*

oat, *n. usu. pl.* avena

oath, *n. pl.,* **oaths.** juramento; blasfemia

o·be·di·ence, *n.* obediencia

o·bese, *a.* obeso

o·bey, *v.* obedecer; cumplir

o·bit·u·a·ry, *n. pl.,* **-ries.** necrología

ob·ject, *n.* objeto; propósito; fin. *v.* oponerse; objetar

ob·jec·tion, *n.* objeción; inconveniente

ob·jec·tive, *a.* objetivo. *n.* objetivo

ob·li·gate, *v.* obligar; precisar

ob·li·ga·tion, *n.* obligación; compromiso

o·blige, *v.* obligar; hacer un favor a

ob·lique, *a.* oblicuo; indirecto

ob·long, *a.* oblongo. *n.* cuadrilongo

ob·nox·ious, *a.* detestable; ofensivo

o·boe, *n.* oboe

ob·scene, *a.* obsceno

ob·scen·i·ty, *n. pl.,* **-ties.** obscenidad

ob·scure, *a.* oscuro; indistinto. *v.* oscurecer

ob·scu·ri·ty, *n. pl.,* **-ties.** oscuridad

ob·serv·ance, *n.* observancia; práctica

ob·ser·va·tion, *n.* observación

ob·ser·va·to·ry, *n. pl.,* **-ries.** observatorio

ob·serve, *v.* observar; cumplir

ob·ses·sion, *n.* obsesión

ob·so·lete, *a.* anticuado

ob·sta·cle, *n.* obstáculo; impedimento

ob·sti·nate, *a.* obstinado; terco

ob·struct, *v.* obstruir; estorbar

ob·tain, *v.* obtener; adquirir; regir

ob·vi·ous, *a.* obvio; evidente

oc·ca·sion, *n.* ocasión; acontecimiento

oc·cult, *a.* oculto

oc·cu·pan·cy, *n. pl.,* **-cies.** ocupación

oc·cu·pa·tion, *n.* empleo; tenencia; ocupación

oc·cu·py, *v.* ocupar

oc·cur, *v.,* **-curred, -cur·ring.** ocurrir; suceder

o·cean, *n.* océano

oc·ta·gon, *n.* octágono

oc·tave, *n.* octava

Oc·to·ber, *n.* octubre

oc·to·pus, *n.* pulpo

odd, *a.* raro; sobrante; sin pareja; impar. *n. pl.* ventaja

odd·i·ty, *n. pl.*, **-ties.** rareza

ode, *n.* oda

o·di·ous, *a.* odioso

o·dor, *n.* olor

of, *prep.* de; sobre

off, *adv.* fuera. *a.* desenchufado. *prep.* lejos. *int.* fuera de aquí. **be off,** irse; estar parado. **off and on,** de vez en cuando. **turn off,** cerrar; apagar

of·fend, *v.* ofender

of·fense, *n.* ofensa; crimen

of·fer, *v.* ofrecer(se); deparar. *n.* oferta; ofrecimiento

of·fice, *n.* oficina; cargo; departamento

of·fic·er, *n.* oficial, *m.;* agente

of·fi·cial, *a.* oficial. *n.* oficial, *m.*

off·spring, *n. pl.*, **-spring, -springs.** descendiente; descendencia

of·ten, *adv.* a menudo; muchas veces

of·ten·times, *adv.* a menudo. Also **oft·times**

o·gle, *v.* ojear

o·gre, *n.* ogro

oil, *n.* aceite; petróleo. *v.* lubrificar

oil·y, *a.* aceitoso; grasiento

oint·ment, *n.* ungüento

O.K., *a.* muy bien; vale; aprobado. *v.*, **O.K.'d, O.K.'ing.** aprobar. Also **OK, o·kay**

old, *a.* viejo o **eld·er** o **eld·er,** *a.* **old·er** o **eld·est.** viejo; antique; anciano

old-fash·ioned, *a.* pasado de moda

ol·ive, *n.* aceituna; olivo

om·e·let, **om·e·lette**, *n.* tortilla

o·men, *n.* agüero; presagio

o·mis·sion, *n.* omisión; descuido

o·mit, *v.*, **o·mit·ted, o·mit·ting.** omitir; olvidar

om·ni·bus, *n. pl.*, **-bus·es.** autobús, *m.*

om·nip·o·tence, *n.* omnipotencia

om·nis·cience, *n.* omnisciencia

om·niv·or·ous, *a.* omnívoro

on, *prep.* sobre; en. *adv.* sin cesar. **on foot**, a pie. **on sale**, de venta

once, *adv.* una vez; en otro tiempo. *n.* una vez

one, *a.* uno; un; una; solo. *n., pron.* uno

one·self, *pron.* sí mismo; sí. Also **one's self**

on·ion, *n.* cebolla

on·ly, *adv.* sólo; solamente. *a.* solo; único

on·slaught, *n.* ataque furioso

on·to, *prep.* en; sobre

on·ward, *a.* progresivo. *adv.* hacia adelante. Also **on·wards**

on·yx, *n.* ónice

o·pac·i·ty, *n. pl.*, **-ties.** opacidad

o·pal, *n.* ópalo

o·paque, *a.* opaco; oscuro

o·pen, *a.* abierto; franco. *v.* abrir(se); empezar

o·pen·hand·ed, *a.* generoso

o·pen·ing, *n.* abertura; oportunidad

o·per·a, *n.* ópera

op·er·ate, *v.* hacer funcionar; obrar; operar; dirigir

op·er·a·tion, *n.* operación

op·er·et·ta, *n.* opereta

o·pin·ion, *n.* opinión; juicio

o·pi·um, *n.* opio

op·po·nent, *n.* adversario. *a.* opuesto

op·por·tune, *a.* oportuno

op·por·tu·ni·ty, *n. pl.*, **-ties.** oportunidad

op·pose, *v.* oponerse; resistir

op·po·site, *a.* opuesto. *n.* lo contrario. *adv.* en frente. *prep.* en frente de

op·press, *v.* oprimir

opt, *v.* escoger

op·ti·cal, *a.* óptico

op·ti·mism, *n.* optimismo

op·tion, *n.* opción

op·u·lent, *a.* opulento

o·pus, *n. pl.*, **o·pe·ra, o·pus·es.** obra

or, *conj.* o; u

or·a·cle, *n.* oráculo

o·ral, *a.* oral; verbal

or·ange, *n.* naranja. *a.* anaranjado

or·ange·ade, *n.* naranjada

o·ra·tion, *n.* oración

orb, *n.* orbe

or·bit, *n.* órbita. *v.* girar

or·chard, *n.* huerto

or·ches·tra, *n.* orquesta

or·dain, *v.* ordenar

or·der, *n.* orden, *m., f.;* clase, *f.;* mandato. *v.* arreglar; mandar; encargar

or·der·ly, *a.* ordenado, *n. pl.*, **-lies.** asistente

or·di·nar·y, *a.* corriente; ordinario

ore, *n.* mena

or·gan, *n.* órgano

or·gan·dy, or·gan·die, *n.* organdí, *m.*

or·gan·ic, *a.* orgánico

or·gan·ism, *n.* organismo

or·gan·i·za·tion, *n.* organización

or·gan·ize, *v.* organizar(se)

or·gy, *n. pl.*, **-gies.** orgia

o·ri·ent, *n.* este; *(cap.)* oriente. *v.* orientar

or·i·gin, *n.* origen

o·rig·i·nal, *a., n.* original, *m.*

o·rig·i·nate, *v.* originar(se); surgir

or·na·ment, *n.* ornamento; adorno

or·phan, *n.* huérfano

or·phan·age, *n.* orfanato

or·tho·dox, *a.* ortodoxo

or·tho·dox·y, *n. pl.*, **-ies.** ortodoxia

os·mo·sis, *n.* ósmosis, osmosis, *f.*

os·ten·si·ble, *a.* aparente

os·ten·ta·tion, n. ostentación; fausto

os·tra·cism, n. ostracismo

os·trich, n. avestruz; m.

oth·er, a. otro. prep. el otro. adv. de otra manera

oth·er·wise, adv. de otra manera; si no

ought, aux. v. deber; tener que

ounce, n. onza

our, a. nuestro

ours, pron. el nuestro

our·selves, pron. pl. nosotros (mismos)

oust, v. expulsar

out, adv. fuera (de casa); afuera; apagado. prep. fuera de. a. sin sentido

out·break, n. erupción

out·cast, n. proscrito. a. rechazado

out·come, n. resultado

out·cry, n. pl. -cries. grito; clamor

out·dat·ed, a. fuera de moda

out·door, a. al aire libre

out·er, a. externo

out·fit, n. equipo; traje

out·grow, v., -grew, -grown, grow·ing. ser ya viejo para

out·ing, n. excursión

out·law, n. forajido. v. proscribir

out·let, n. salida

out·line, n. contorno; bosquejo. v. bosquejar

out·live, v. sobrevivir a

out·look, n. perspectiva

out-of-date, a. pasado de moda

out·put, n. producción

out·rage, n. atrocidad

out·right, adv. completamente; abiertamente. a. entero

out·set, n. principio

out·side, n. exterior. a. externo. adv. fuera

out·sid·er, n. forastero

out·spo·ken, a. franco

out·stand·ing, a. sobresaliente

out·ward, a. exterior; obvio. adv. hacia fuera. Also out·wards

out·wear, v., -wore, -worn, -wear·ing. durar más tiempo que

out·wit, v. ser más listo que

o·val, a. oval. n. óvalo

o·va·ry, n. pl., -ries. ovario

o·va·tion, n. ovación

ov·en, n. horno

o·ver, prep. encima de; sobre; más de. adv. de arriba abajo. a. otra vez

o·ver·all, a. en total

o·ver·bear·ing, a. imperioso

o·ver·board, adv. al agua

o·ver·coat, n. abrigo

o·ver·come, v., -came, -come, -com·ing. superar

o·ver·do, v., -did, -done, -do·ing. exagerar

o·ver·dose, n. dosis excesiva

o·ver·due, a. vencido y no pagado

o·ver·flow, v., -flowed, -flown, -flow·ing. rebosar; derramarse. n. inundación

o·ver·haul, v. revisar

o·ver·head, a. elevado. adv. encima

o·ver·hear, v., -heard, -hear·ing. oír por casualidad

o·ver·lap, v. traslapar; solapar. n. solape

o·ver·look, v. no hacer caso de; tener vista a

o·ver·night, adv. durante la noche. a. de noche

o·ver·pow·er, v. dominar

o·ver·run, v., -ran, -run, -run·ing. invadir

o·ver·seas, adv., a. en el extranjero. Also over·sea

o·ver·see, v., -saw, -seen, -see·ing. vigilar

o·ver·shoe, n. chanclo

o·ver·sight, n. descuido; olvido

o·ver·sleep, v., -slept, -sleep·ing. dormir demasiado

o·vert, a. público

o·ver·take, v., -took, -ta·ken, -tak·ing. alcanzar

o·ver·throw, v., -threw, -thrown, -throw·ing. echar abajo

o·ver·ture, n. (mus.) obertura; propuesta

o·ver·turn, v. volcar

o·ver·weight, a. exceso; gordo

o·ver·work, v. trabajar demasiado

o·vum, n. pl., o·va. óvulo

owe, v. tener deudas

owl, n. búho; lechuza

own, a. propio. v. poseer; reconocer

ox, n. pl., ox·en, buey, m.

ox·ide, n. óxido

ox·y·gen, n. oxígeno

oys·ter, n. ostra

o·zone, n. ozono

P

pa, n. inf. papá, m.

pace, n. paso. v. medir a pasos

pa·cif·ic, a. pacífico

pac·i·fism, n. pacifismo

pac·i·fy, v. pacificar; calmar

pack, n. fardo. v. llenar; empaquetar

pack·age, n. paquete

pact, n. pacto

pad, n. almohadilla. v. acolchar

pad·dle, n. canalete

pad·lock, n. candado

pa·gan, n. pagano

page, n. página. v. paginar

pag·eant, n. espectáculo

pa·go·da, n. pagoda

pail, n. cubo. Also pail·ful

pain, *n.* dolor. *v.* doler; apenar

pain·ful, *a.* doloroso; penoso

pains·tak·ing, *a.* laborioso; esmerado

paint, *v.* pintar. *n.* pintura

paint·ing, *n.* pintura; cuadro

pair, *n. pl.,* pairs, pair. pareja; par. *v.* aparear

pa·jam·as, *n. pl.* pijama, *m.*

pal·ace, *n.* palacio

pal·ate, *n.* paladar

pale, *a.* pálido; claro. *v.* palidecer(se)

pa·le·on·tol·o·gy, *n.* paleontología

pal·ette, *n.* paleta

pal·i·sade, *n.* palizada

pall, *v.* perder su sabor

pal·lid, *a.* pálido

pal·lor, *n.* palidez, *f.*

palm, *n.* palma

palm·is·try, *n.* quiromancia

pal·pa·ble, *a.* palpable

pal·pi·ta·tion, *n.* palpitación

pal·try, *a.* miserable

pam·per, *v.* mimar

pam·phlet, *n.* folleto

pan, *n.* cacerola; cazuela. *v.* separar en una gamella

pan·a·ce·a, *n.* panacea

pan·cake, *n.* hojuela

pan·cre·as, *n.* páncreas, *m.*

pan·de·mo·ni·um, *n.* pandemónium

pane, *n.* hoja de vidrio

pan·el, *n.* panel, *m.;* entrepaño; tablero; jurado

pang, *n.* punzada; dolor

pan·han·dle, *v. inf.* mendigar

pan·ic, *n.* terror

pan·o·ram·a, *n.* panorama, *m.*

pan·sy, *n. pl.,* -sies, pensamiento; *inf.* maricón

pant, *v.* jadear. *n.* jadeo; *pl.* pantalones

pan·the·ism, *n.* panteísmo

pan·ther, *n.* pantera

pan·to·mime, *n.* pantomima

pan·try, *n. pl.,* -tries, despensa

pa·pa, *n.* papá, *m.*

pa·pa·cy, *n. pl.,* -cies, papado; pontificado

pa·per, *n.* papel, *m.* v. empapelar

pa·pier-mâ·ché, *n.* cartón piedra

pa·poose, pap·poose, *n.* crio

pa·py·rus, *n. pl.,* -rus·es, -ri. papiro

par, *n.* par

par·a·ble, *n.* parábola

par·a·chute, *n.* paracaídas, *m.*

pa·rade, *n.* cabalgata; desfile; parada. *v.* formar en parada

par·a·dise, *n.* paraiso

par·a·dox, *n.* paradoja

par·af·fin, *n.* parafina

par·a·graph, *n.* párrafo

par·al·lel, *a.* paralelo. *n.* paralelo

pa·ral·y·sis, *n. pl.,* -ses. parálisis, *f.*

par·a·lyze, *v.* paralizar

pa·ram·e·ter, *n.* parámetro; límite

par·a·noi·a, *n.* paranoia

par·a·pher·nal·ia, *n. pl., sing. or pl. in constr.* arreos

par·a·phrase, *n.* paráfrasis, *f.*

par·a·site, *n.* parásito

par·a·troop·er, *n.* paracaidista, *m.*

par·cel, *n.* paquete; bulto

parch, *v.* secar

parch·ment, *n.* pergamino

par·don, *v.* perdonar. *n.* perdón; indulto

pare, *v.* cortar

par·ent, *n.* padre; madre, *f.*

pa·ren·the·sis, *n. pl.,* -ses, paréntesis, *m.*

pa·ri·ah, *n.* paria, *m., f.*

par·ish, *n.* parroquia

park, *n.* parque; jardín. *v.* estacionar; aparcar

par·ley, *v.* parlamentar. *n.* parlamento

par·lia·ment, *n.* (*usu. cap.*) parlamento

par·lor, par·lour, *n.* sala de recibo

pa·ro·chi·al, *a.* parroquial; estrecho

par·o·dy, *n. pl.,* -dies. parodia

pa·role, *n.* libertad bajo palabra

par·ox·ysm, *n.* paroxismo

par·rot, *n.* papagayo; loro

par·ry, *v.* parar

pars·ley, *n.* perejil, *m.*

par·son, *n.* clérigo

part, *n.* parte, *f.;* porción. *v.* partir(se); separar(se). *a.* parcial

par·take, *v.,* -took, -ta·ken, tak·ing. tomar parte

par·tial, *a.* parcial

par·tial·i·ty, *n. pl.,* -ties. parcialidad

par·tic·i·pant, *a.* participe. *n.* concursante, *m., f.*

par·tic·i·pate, *v.* participar

par·tic·i·pa·tion, *n.* participación

par·ti·ci·ple, *n.* participio

par·ti·cle, *n.* partículo; pizca

par·tic·u·lar, *a.* particular; exigente. *n. usu. pl.* detalle

par·tic·u·lar·i·ty, *n. pl.,* -ties. particularidad

part·ing, *a.* despedida

par·ti·san, *n.* partidario

par·ti·tion, *n.* partición; tabique

part·ner, *n.* socio

par·tridge, *n. pl.,* -tridg·es, -tridge. perdiz, *f.*

par·ty, *n. pl.,* -ties. partido; grupo; fiesta

pass, *v.* pasar; cruzar; aprobar. *n.* permiso

pas·sage, *n.* pasaje; travesía; pasadizo

pas·sen·ger, *n.* pasajero; viajero

pas·sion, *n.* pasión

pas·sion·ate, *a.* apasionado

pas·sive, a. pasivo

pass·port, n. pasaporte

pass·word, n. santo y seña

past, a. pasado. prep. después de. n. pasado

paste, n. engrudo; pasta. v. pegar

paste·board, n. cartón

pas·teur·i·za·tion, n. pasteurización

pas·teur·ize, v. pasteurizar

pas·time, n. pasatiempo

pas·tor, n. pastor

pas·try, n. pl. -tries. pasteles. m. pl.

pas·ture, n. pasto. v. pastar

pat, n. golpecito; pastelillo. v. dar una palmadita; acariciar

patch, n. pedazo. v. remendar

pat·ent, n. patente; a. f. a. patente

pa·ter·nal, a. paternal; paterno

pa·ter·ni·ty, n. paternidad

path, n. senda

pa·thet·ic, a. patético

pa·thol·o·gy, n. pl. -gies. patología

pa·tience, n. paciencia

pa·tient, a. paciente. n. enfermo

pa·ti·o, n. pl. -os. patio

pa·tri·ar·chy, n. pl. -chies. patriarcado

pat·ri·mo·ny, n. pl. -nies. patrimonio

pa·tri·ot, n. patriota, m., f.

pa·trol, v. patrullar. n. patrulla

pa·tron, n. cliente, m., f.; patrocinador

pat·tern, n. modelo; patrón

pau·per, n. pobre, m., f.

pause, n. pausa. v. detenerse

pave, v. empedrar; pavimentar

pave·ment, n. pavimento

pa·vil·ion, n. pabellón

paw, n. pata. v. manosear

pawn, v. empeñar

pay, v., paid, pay·ing. pagar; ser provechoso. n. paga; sueldo

pay·roll, n. nómina

pea, n. pl., peas, pease. guisante

peace, n. paz, f.; sosiego

peace·ful, a. tranquilo

peach, n. melocotón

pea·cock, n. pl., -cocks, -cock. pavo real; pavón

peak, n. pico; cumbre, f.

peal, v. repicar

pea·nut, n. cacahuete

pear, n. pera

pearl, n. perla

peas·ant, n. campesino. a. campesino

peb·ble, n. guijarro

pec·ca·dil·lo, n. pl., -loes, -los. pecadillo

pe·cu·liar, a. peculiar; raro

pe·cu·li·ar·i·ty, n. pl., -ties. particularidad; peculiaridad

ped·al, n. pedal, m.

ped·dle, v. vender por las calles

ped·dler, ped·ler, ped·lar, n. buhonero

ped·es·tal, n. pedestal, m.

pe·des·tri·an, n. peatón. a. pedestre

ped·i·gree, n. genealogía

peel, v. pelar. n. corteza

peer, n. par

peg, n. clavija; estaca

pel·let, n. bolita; pella

pelt, n. pellejo; piel, f. v. arrojar

pel·vis, n. pl., -vis·es, -ves. pelvis, f.

pen, n. pluma; corral, m.

pe·nal, a. penal

pen·al·ty, n. pl., -ties. pena; castigo

pen·cil, n. lápiz, m.

pend·ant, pend·ent, n. pendiente

pend·ing, a. pendiente

pen·du·lum, n. péndulo

pen·e·trate, v. penetrar; comprender

pen·i·cil·lin, n. penicilina

pen·in·su·la, n. península

pen·i·tent, a. penitente, m., f. a. penitente

pen·i·ten·tia·ry, n. pl., -ries. presidio

pen·ny, n. pl., -nies. centavo

pen·sion, n. pensión. v. jubilar

pen·sive, a. pensativo

pen·ta·gon, n. pentágono

pe·on, n. peón

pe·o·ny, n. pl., -nies. peonía

peo·ple, n. pl., -ple, -ples. pueblo; gente, f. v. poblar

pep·per, n. pimienta; pimiento

pep·per·mint, n. menta

per, prep. por

per·ceive, v. percibir; darse cuenta de

per·cent, per cent, n. pl., per·cent, per·cents. por ciento

per·cent·age, n. porcentaje

per·cep·tion, n. percepción

perch, n. percha; perca. v. posar(se)

per·di·tion, n. perdición

per·en·ni·al, a. perenne

per·fect, a. perfecto. v. perfeccionar

per·fec·tion, n. perfección

per·fo·rate, v. perforar

per·form, v. efectuar; hacer; representar

per·for·mance, n. representación; función

per·fume, n. perfume. v. perfumar

per·il, n. peligro

per·im·e·ter, n. perímetro

pe·ri·od, n. período; época; punto

pe·ri·od·i·cal, n. publicación periódica

pe·riph·er·y, n. pl., -ies. periferia

per·i·scope, n. periscopio

per·ish, v. perecer

per·jure, v. perjurar(se)

per·ju·ry, n. pl., -ries. perjurio

per·ma·nent, a. permanente

per·mis·sion, n. permiso

per·mit, v., -mit·ted, -mit·ting. permitir; tolerar. n. permiso

per·pen·dic·u·lar, a. perpendicular

per·pet·u·al, a. perpetuo; continuo

per·plex, v. confundir

per·se·cute, v. perseguir; molestar

per·se·cu·tion, n. persecución

per·sist, v. persistir

per·son, n. persona

per·son·al·i·ty, n. pl., -ties. personalidad; personaje

per·son·nel, n. personal

per·spec·tive, n. perspectiva

per·spi·ra·tion, n. sudor

per·spire, v. sudar; transpirar

per·suade, v. persuadir

per·sua·sion, n. persuasión

per·tain, v. pertenecer; tener que ver con

per·ti·nent, a. pertinente; a propósito

per·ver·sion, n. perversión

per·vert, v. pervertir; estropear; alterar

pes·si·mism, n. pesimismo

pest, n. plaga

pes·ter, v. importunar; molestar; fastidiar

pet, n. animal doméstico; favorito. a. favorito. v. acariciar

pet·al, n. pétalo

pe·ti·tion, n. petición. v. solicitar

pe·tro·le·um, n. petróleo

pet·ty, a. mezquino

pew, n. banco

pew·ter, n. peltre

phal·lus, n. pl., -li, -lus·es. falo

phan·tom, n. fantasma, m.

phar·aoh, n. faraón

phar·ma·ceu·ti·cal, a. farmacéutico

phar·ma·cy, n. pl., -cies. farmacia

phase, n. fase, f.

pheas·ant, n. pl., -ant, -ants. faisán

phe·nom·e·non, n. pl., -na, -nons. fenómeno

phi·lan·thro·py, n. pl., -pies. filantropía

phi·los·o·pher, n. filósofo

phi·los·o·phy, n. pl., -phies. filosofía

phlegm, n. flema

pho·bi·a, n. fobia

phone, n. inf. teléfono

pho·no·graph, n. tocadiscos

phos·phate, n. fosfato

phos·pho·res·cence, n. fosforescencia

phos·pho·rus, n. fósforo

pho·to·cop·y, n. fotocopia

pho·to·gen·ic, a. fotogénico

pho·to·graph, n. fotografía; foto, f. v. sacar una foto

pho·tog·ra·phy, n. fotografía

phrase, n. frase, f.

phys·i·cal, a. físico

phy·si·cian, n. médico

phys·ics, n. física

pi·an·ist, n. pianista, m., f.

pi·an·o, n. piano

pic·a·resque, a. picaresco

pick, v. escoger; elegir; coger; picar. n. pico

pick·le, n. encurtido

pick·pock·et, n. ratero

pic·nic, n. excursión al campo; jira

pic·ture, n. cuadro; retrato; ilustración; película; foto, f.

pie, n. pastel, m.

piece, n. pieza; pedazo; trozo

piece·work, n. trabajo a destajo

pier, n. embarcadero; muelle

pierce, v. penetrar; agujerear; pinchar

pi·e·ty, n. piedad

pig, n. cerdo

pi·geon, n. paloma

pig·ment, n. pigmento

pig·tail, n. coleta

pile, n. montón; rimero

pil·grim, n. peregrino

pill, n. píldora

pil·lage, v. pillar

pil·lar, n. pilar; columna

pil·low, n. almohada

pil·low·case, n. funda de almohada

pi·lot, n. piloto

pimp, n. alcahuete

pim·ple, n. grano

pin, n. alfiler

pinch, v. pellizcar; apretar

pin·cush·ion, n. acerico

pine, n. pino. v. languidecer

pink, v. picar. a. rosado

pin·na·cle, n. pináculo

pint, n. pinta

pi·o·neer, n. explorador. v. explorar; promover

pi·ous, a. piadoso

pipe, n. tubo; pipa

pique, n. pique. v. ofender; irritar

pi·rate, n. pirata, m.

pis·tol, n. pistola; revólver

pis·ton, n. pistón

pit, n. hoyo; hueso

pitch, n. pez, f.; tono. v. tirar

pitch·er, n. cántaro

pit·i·ful, a. lastimoso

pit·i·less, a. despiadado

pit·y, n. piedad; lástima. v. compadecer

piv·ot, n. pivote

pix·y, n. duende, f.

plac·ard, n. cartel, m.

pla·cate, v. apaciguar

place, n. sitio; lugar; posición. v. poner

pla·cen·ta, n. placenta

plac·id, a. plácido

pla·gia·rism, n. plagio

plague, n. peste, f.; plaga

plaid, n. tartán

plain, *n.* llano. *a.* llano; sencillo; evidente

plan, *n.* plan; plano; proyecto. *v.* planear

plane, *n.* cepillo; plano; *inf.* avión

plan·et, *n.* planeta, *m.*

plank, *n.* tablón

plant, *n.* planta. *v.* plantar; sembrar

plan·ta·tion, *n.* plantación

plas·ma, *n.* plasma, *m.*

plas·ter, *n.* argamasa

plas·tic, *a.* plástico. *n.* plástico

plate, *n.* plato

plat·form, *n.* plataforma; andén

plat·i·num, *n.* platino

pla·toon, *n.* pelotón

plau·si·ble, *a.* plausible; creíble

play, *n.* obra dramática; juego. *v.* jugar; (*mus.*) tocar

play·ful, *a.* juguetón

play·ground, *n.* patio de recreo

play·ing card, *n.* naipe

play-off, *n.* partido de desempate

play·thing, *n.* juguete

play·wright, *n.* dramaturgo

plea, *n.* súplica; defensa

plead, *v.* defender; suplicar; rogar

pleas·ant, *a.* agradable

please, *v.* dar gusto; contentar; gustar

pleas·ure, *n.* placer; gusto

pleat, *n.* pliegue. *v.* plegar

pleb·i·scite, *n.* plebiscito

pledge, *n.* prenda; promesa. *v.* empeñar; garantizar; prometer

plen·i·po·ten·ti·ar·y, *n.* plenipotenciario

plen·ti·ful, *a.* abundante

plen·ty, *n.* abundancia

pleth·o·ra, *n.* plétora

pli·ant, *a.* flexible

pli·ers, *n. pl.* alicates

plight, *n.* situación; apuro

plot, *n.* parcela; conspiración. *v.* intrigar

plow, *n.* arado

pluck, *v.* coger

plug, *n.* tapón; enchufe. *v.* tapar

plum, *n.* ciruela

plum·age, *n.* plumaje

plumb·er, *n.* fontanero

plumb·ing, *n.* instalación de cañerías

plun·der, *v.* saquear. *n.* saqueo; botín

plunge, *v.* hundir

plu·ral, *a.* plural. *n.* plural

plus, *a.* más; y

pneu·mo·nia, *n.* pulmonía

poach, *v.* escalfar; cazar o pescar en vedado

pock·et, *n.* bolsillo; bolsa

pock·et·knife, *n. pl.* -knives. navaja

pod, *n.* vaina

po·di·um, *n. pl.* -a, -ums. podio; estrado

po·em, *n.* poema, *m.,* poesía

po·et, *n.* poeta, *m.*

po·et·ic, po·et·i·cal, *a.* poético

po·et·ry, *n.* poesía

point, *n.* punto; punta; fin. *v.* apuntar

poise, *n.* equilibrio; aplomo

poi·son, *n.* veneno. *v.* envenenar

poke, *v.* atizar; empujar

pok·er, *n.* póquer

po·lar, *a.* polar

po·lar·i·ty, *n. pl.* -ties. polaridad

pole, *n.* palo; polo

po·lice, *n.* policía. *v.* mantener orden

pol·i·cy, *n. pl.* -cies. política; póliza

pol·ish, *v.* pulir; limpiar. *n.* bruñido; brillo; urbanidad

po·lite, *a.* cortés; fino

po·lit·i·cal, *a.* político

pol·i·ti·cian, *n.* político

pol·i·tics, *n. pl., sing. or pl. in constr.* política

pol·ka, *n.* polca

poll, *n.* elección; sondeo

pol·len, *n.* polen

pol·lute, *v.* ensuciar

pol·lu·tion, *n.* polución; contaminación

po·lyg·a·my, *n.* poligamia

pol·y·gon, *n.* polígono

pol·yp, *n.* pólipo

pol·y·the·ism, *n.* politeísmo

pomp, *n.* pompa

pomp·ous, *a.* pomposo

pond, *n.* charca; estanque

pon·der, *v.* ponderar; pensar; meditar

pon·tiff, *n.* pontífice

po·ny, *n. pl.* -nies. jaca

pool, *n.* estanque; polla; truco; *inf.* piscina. *v.* mancomunar

poor, *a.* pobre; malo

pope, *n.* (*often cap.*) papa, *m.*

pop·py, *n. pl.* -pies. adormidera

pop·u·lace, *n.* pueblo; populacho

pop·u·lar, *a.* popular

pop·u·late, *v.* poblar

pop·u·la·tion, *n.* población

por·ce·lain, *n.* porcelana

porch, *n.* pórtico

por·cu·pine, *n.* puerco espín

pore, *v.* examinar. *n.* poro

pork, *n.* carne de cerdo

por·nog·ra·phy, *n.* pornografía

por·poise, *n. pl.* -pois·es, -poise. marsopa

port, *n.* puerto; babor; oporto

port·a·ble, *a.* portátil

por·ter, *n.* portero; mozo de estación

port·fo·li·o, *n. pl.* -os. cartera

por·ti·co, *n. pl.* -coes, -cos. pórtico

por·tion, *n.* porción; parte, *f. v.* dividir

por·trait, *n.* retrato

por·tray, *v.* retratar; tomar el papel de

pose, v. colocarse; plantear. n. actitud

po·si·tion, n. posición; actitud; puesto

pos·i·tive, a. positivo; enfático

pos·sess, v. poseer

pos·ses·sion, n. posesión

pos·si·bil·i·ty, n. pl., -ties. posibilidad

pos·si·ble, a. posible

post, n. poste; puesto; correo. v. echar al correo; situar

post·age, n. porte; franqueo

post card, n. tarjeta (postal)

post·er, n. cartel, m.

pos·te·ri·or, a. posterior

post·man, n. pl., -men. cartero

post·mark, n. matasellos

post me·rid·i·em, a. postmeridiano. Abbr. p.m., P.M.

post·mor·tem, n. autopsia

post·pone, v. aplazar

post·script, v. posdata

pos·ture, n. postura

pot, n. olla; tiesto; inf. marijuana

po·tas·si·um, n. potasio

po·ta·to, n. pl., -toes. patata; papa

po·tent, a. potente; fuerte

po·ten·tial, a. potencial

po·tion, n. poción

pot·ter·y, n. pl., -ies. alfarería

pouch, n. bolsa

poul·try, n. aves de corral

pound, n. libra

pour, v. verter; diluviar

pout, v. hacer pucheros

pov·er·ty, n. pobreza

pow·der, n. polvo. v. ponerse polvos

pow·er, n. poder; fuerza; facultad

pow·er·ful, a. potente; poderoso

prac·ti·cal, a. práctico

prac·tice, v. practicar; ejercer. n. práctica; costumbre, f.

prag·mat·ic, a. pragmático

prai·rie, n. pradera

praise, n. alabanza. v. alabar

prank, n. travesura

pray, v. rezar; orar; rogar

prayer, n. oración

preach, v. predicar

pre·am·ble, n. preámbulo

pre·cau·tion, n. precaución

pre·cede, v. preceder

prec·e·dent, n. precedente

pre·cinct, n. recinto; distrito electoral

pre·cious, a. precioso; de gran valor

prec·i·pice, n. precipicio

pre·cip·i·ta·tion, n. precipitación

pre·cise, a. preciso; exacto

pre·co·cious, a. precoz

pre·cur·sor, n. precursor

pred·e·ces·sor, n. predecesor

pre·des·ti·na·tion, n. predestinación

pre·dic·a·ment, n. apuro

pre·dict, v. predecir; pronosticar

pre·dic·tion, n. pronóstico

pre·dom·i·nant, a. predominante

pref·ace, n. prólogo; prefacio

pre·fer, v. -ferred, -fer·ring. preferir

pref·er·ence, n. preferencia

pre·fix, n. prefijo

preg·nan·cy, n. pl., -cies. embarazo

preg·nant, a. encinta; embarazada

pre·his·tor·ic, a. prehistórico

prej·u·dice, n. prejuicio. v. perjudicar; predisponer

pre·lim·i·nar·y, n. pl., -ies. preliminar. a. preliminar

prel·ude, n. preludio

pre·med·i·tate, v. premeditar

pre·miere, n. estreno

pre·mi·um, n. premio; prima

pre·mo·ni·tion, n. presentimiento

pre·oc·cu·pied, a. preocupado

prep·a·ra·tion, n. preparación; preparativo

pre·pare, v. preparar(se); aparejar

prep·o·si·tion, n. preposición

pre·pos·ter·ous, a. absurdo

pre·req·ui·site, a. requisito previo

pre·rog·a·tive, n. prerrogativa

pre·scribe, v. prescribir; recetar

pre·scrip·tion, n. receta

pres·ence, n. presencia

pres·ent, v. presentar; ofrecer. n. regalo. a. presente

pres·en·ta·tion, n. presentación

pre·serv·a·tive, a. preservativo. n. preservativo

pre·serve, v. preservar; conservar. n. usu. pl. conserva

pre·side, v. presidir

pres·i·dent, n. (often cap.) presidente

press, n. prensa; imprenta. v. apretar; planchar

pres·sure, n. presión; urgencia

pres·ti·dig·i·ta·tion, n. prestidigitación

pres·tige, n. prestigio

pre·sume, v. presumir; suponer

pre·tend, v. fingir; pretender

pre·tense, n. pretexto

pret·ty, a. guapo; bonito; mono, adv. bastante

pre·vail, v. prevalecer; predominar

pre·vent, v. impedir

pre·vi·ous, a. previo

prey, n. presa

price, n. precio. v. valuar; fijar un precio

price·less, a. inapreciable

prick, v. punzar

pride, n. orgullo

priest, n. sacerdote; cura, m.

prim, a. estirado

pri·ma·ry, a. primario

prime, a. primero; principal. v. cebar

prim·i·tive, *a.* primitivo
pri·mo·gen·i·ture, *n.* primogenitura
prince, *n.* príncipe
prin·cess, *n.* princesa
prin·ci·pal, *a.* principal. *n.* principal
prin·ci·pal·i·ty, *n. pl.,* **-ties.** principado
prin·ci·ple, *n.* principio
print, *n.* marca; impresión; grabado. *v.* imprimir
print·ing, *n.* tipografía; imprenta
pri·or, *a.* anterior
pri·or·i·ty, *n. pl.,* **-ties.** prioridad
pri·or·y, *n. pl.,* **-ries.** priorato
prism, *n.* prisma, *m.*
pris·on, *n.* cárcel, *f.;* prisión
pri·va·cy, *n.* soledad
pri·vate, *a.* privado; confidencial; particular. *n.* soldado raso
priv·i·lege, *n.* privilegio
prize, *n.* premio
prob·a·bil·i·ty, *n. pl.,* **-ties.** probabilidad
prob·a·ble, *a.* probable
probe, *n.* sonda; investigación. *v.* explorar
prob·lem, *n.* problema, *m.*
pro·ce·dure, *n.* procedimiento
pro·ceed, *v.* proceder; adelantar
proc·ess, *n.* proceso
pro·claim, *v.* proclamar
pro·cliv·i·ty, *n. pl.,* **-ties.** proclividad; inclinación
pro·cras·ti·nate, *v.* dilatar; aplazar
pro·cure, *v.* obtener; alcahuetear
prod, *v.* punzar
prod·i·gal, *a.* pródigo. *n.* pródigo
prod·i·gy, *n. pl.,* **-gies.** prodigio
pro·duce, *v.* producir; causar. *n.* producto
prod·uct, *n.* producto; resultado
pro·fane, *a.* profano
pro·fan·i·ty, *n. pl.,* **-ties.** profanidad; blasfemia
pro·fes·sion, *n.* profesión; ocupación
pro·fes·sor, *n.* profesor; profesora; catedrático
pro·fi·cien·cy, *n.* pericia
pro·file, *n.* perfil, *m.*
prof·it, *n.* ganancia; beneficio. *v.* ganar; aprovechar
pro·found, *a.* profundo
pro·fuse, *a.* profuso
pro·fu·sion, *n.* profusión
prog·e·ny, *n. pl.,* **-nies.** progenie, *f.*
prog·no·sis, *n. pl.,* **-ses.** pronóstico
pro·gram, *n.* programa, *m.*
prog·ress, *n.* progreso; desarrollo
pro·gres·sive, *a.* progresivo
pro·hib·it, *v.* prohibir
pro·hi·bi·tion, *n.* prohibición
pro·ject, *v.* proyectar; sobresalir. *n.* proyecto
pro·jec·tile, *n.* proyectil, *m.*

pro·lif·ic, *a.* prolífico
pro·logue, *n.* prólogo
pro·long, *v.* prolongar; alargar
prom·i·nent, *a.* prominente; importante
pro·mis·cu·ous, *a.* promiscuo; libertino
prom·ise, *n.* promesa. *v.* prometer
prom·on·to·ry, *n. pl.,* **-ries.** promontorio
pro·mote, *v.* promover; fomentar; ascender
pro·mo·tion, *n.* promoción
prompt, *a.* puntual; pronto. *v.* incitar
pro·noun, *n.* pronombre
pro·nounce, *v.* pronunciar(se); declarar
pro·nounced, *a.* marcado
pro·nun·ci·a·tion, *n.* pronunciación
proof, *n.* prueba
proof·read·er, *n.* corrector de pruebas
prop, *n.* apoyo. *v.* apoyar
prop·a·gan·da, *n.* propaganda
pro·pel, *v.,* **-pelled, -pel·ling.** propulsar
pro·pel·ler, *n.* hélice, *f.*
pro·pen·si·ty, *n. pl.,* **-ties.** propensión; inclinación
prop·er, *a.* propio; apropiado; decente
prop·er·ty, *n. pl.,* **-ties.** propiedad
proph·e·cy, *n. pl.,* **-cies.** profecía
proph·e·sy, *v.* profetizar
proph·et, *n.* profeta, *m.*
pro·phy·lac·tic, *a.* profilático. *n.* profiláctico
pro·pi·tious, *a.* propicio
pro·por·tion, *n.* proporción
pro·pose, *v.* proponer(se); declararse
prop·o·si·tion, *n.* proposición; propuesta
pro·pri·e·tor, *n.* propietario
pro·pri·e·ty, *n. pl.,* **-ties.** corrección; decoro
pro·scribe, *v.* proscribir
prose, *n.* prosa
pros·e·cute, *v.* proseguir; procesar
pros·pect, *n.* perspectiva
pros·per, *v.* prosperar; florecer
pros·per·i·ty, *n.* prosperidad
pros·ti·tute, *n.* prostituta; ramera
pros·trate, *v.* postrar(se); derribar
pro·tag·o·nist, *n.* protagonista, *m., f.*
pro·tect, *v.* proteger
pro·tein, *n.* proteína
pro·test, *v.* protestar. *n.* protesta
pro·to·col, *n.* protocolo
pro·ton, *n.* protón
pro·to·plasm, *n.* protoplasma, *m.*
pro·trude, *v.* salir fuera
proud, *a.* orgulloso; arrogante
prove, *v.,* **proved, proved** or **prov·en, prov·ing.** probar; comprobar

prov·erb, *n.* proverbio; refrán

pro·vide, *v.* proporcionar; proveer

prov·ince, *n.* provincia

pro·vi·sion, *n.* provisión; abastecimiento

pro·voc·a·tive, *a.* provocativa; provocadora

pro·voke, *v.* provocar

prow, *n.* proa

prox·y, *n. pl.* -ies. poder; apoderado

prude, *n.* gazmoña

prune, *n.* ciruela pasa. *v.* podar

pry, *v.*, pried, pry·ing. meterse; fisgonear

psalm, *n.* salmo

pseu·do·nym, *n.* seudónimo

psych·e·del·ic, *a.* psiquedélico

psy·chi·a·trist, *n.* psiquiatra, psiquiatra, *m., f.*

psy·chi·a·try, *n.* psiquiatría

psy·cho·a·nal·y·sis, *n.* psicoanálisis, *m.*

psy·cho·an·a·lyze, *v.* psicoanalizar

psy·cho·log·i·cal, *a.* psicológico

psy·chol·o·gy, *n.* psicología

psy·cho·sis, *n. pl.* -ses. psicosis, *f.*

pto·maine, pto·main, *n.* ptomaína

pub, *n. inf.* taberna

pu·ber·ty, *n.* pubertad

pub·lic, *a.* público. *n.* público

pub·li·ca·tion, *n.* publicación

pub·lic·i·ty, *n.* publicidad

pub·lish, *v.* publicar

pub·lish·er, *n.* editor

puck·er, *v.* arrugar

pud·ding, *n.* pudín

pud·dle, *n.* charco

puff, *v.* soplar; inflar. *n.* soplo

pug·na·cious, *a.* pugnaz

puke, *v.* vomitar

pull, *v.* tirar; arrastrar. *n.* tirón; *inf.* influencia

pul·ley, *n.* polea

pul·mo·nar·y, *a.* pulmonar

pulp, *n.* pulpa; carne, *f.*

pul·pit, *n.* púlpito

pulse, *n.* pulso

pul·ver·ize, *v.* pulverizar

pum·ice, *n.* piedra pómez

pump, *n.* bomba. *v.* bombear; sacar por bomba

pump·kin, *n.* calabaza

pun, *n.* juego de palabras o vocablos

punch, *v.* punzar, *n.* punzón; puñetazo; ponche

punc·tu·al, *a.* puntual

punc·tu·a·tion, *n.* puntuación

punc·ture, *n.* pinchazo. *v.* pinchar; perforar

pun·ish, *v.* castigar

pu·ny, *a.* encanijado

pu·pa, *n. pl.* -pae, -pas. crisálida

pu·pil, *n.* alumno; pupila; estudiante, *m., f.*

pup·pet, *n.* títere

pur·chase, *v.* comprar. *n.* compra

pure, *a.* puro

pur·ga·to·ry, *n. pl.* -ries. purgatorio

pu·ri·fy, *v.* purificar; depurar

pu·ri·tan, *n.* puritano. *a.* puritano

pur·ple, *a.* purpúreo

pur·pose, *n.* fin; propósito; resolución

purr, pur, *n.* ronroneo

purse, *n.* bolso; bolsa. *v.* fruncir

pur·sue, *v.*, -sued, -su·ing. perseguir; seguir; acosar

pur·suit, *n.* perseguimiento; busca; ocupación

pus, *n.* pus, *m.*

push, *v.* empujar; apretar. *n.* empuje

puss·y, *n. pl.* -ies. gatito

put, *v.*, put, put·ting. poner(se); colocar; meter

pu·tre·fy, *v.* pudrir

pu·trid, *a.* podrido

put·ty, *n.* masilla

puz·zle, *v.* confundir; estar perplejo. *n.* rompecabezas, *m.*

pyg·my, pig·my, *n. pl.* -mies. pigmeo. *a.* pigmeo

pyr·a·mid, *n.* pirámide, *f.*

pyre, *n.* pira

py·ro·tech·nics, *n. pl., sing. or pl. in constr.* pirotecnia

py·thon, *n.* pitón

Q

quack, *n.* graznido del pato; charlatán

quad·ran·gle, *n.* cuadrángulo

quad·rant, *n.* cuadrante

quad·ri·lat·er·al, *a.* cuadrilátero. *n.* cuadrilátero

quad·ru·ped, *n.* cuadrúpedo

quad·ru·ple, *v.* cuadruplicar

quag·mire, *n.* tremedal, *m.*

quail, *n.* codorniz, *f.* *v.* acobardarse; desanimarse

quaint, *a.* singular

quake, *v.* estremecerse. *n.* terremoto

qual·i·fy, *v.* habilitar; modificar

qual·i·ty, *n. pl.* -ties. cualidad; calidad

qualm, *n.* náusea; escrúpulo

quan·da·ry, *n. pl.*, -ries. apuro

quan·ti·ty, *n. pl.* -ties. cantidad

quar·an·tine, *v.* poner en cuarentena

quar·rel, *n.* riña. *v.* reñir; disputar

quar·ry, *n. pl.*, -ries. presa; cantera

quart, *n.* cuarto de galón

quar·ter, *n.* cuarto; alojamiento

quartz, *n.* cuarzo

qua·si, *a.* cuasi

qua·ver, *v.* vibrar

queen, *n.* reina

queer, *a.* raro; *inf.* maricón

quell, v. sofocar; reprimir

quench, v. apagar; satisfacer

que·ry, n. pl., **-ries.** pregunta. v. preguntar; dudar

quest, n. búsqueda

ques·tion, n. pregunta; cuestión

ques·tion mark, n. signo de interrogación

ques·tion·naire, n. cuestionario

queue, n. cola

quib·ble, v. sutilizar

quick, a. rápido; listo

quick·en, v. apresurar(se)

quick·sand, n. arena movediza

quick·sil·ver, n. mercurio

quick·wit·ted, a. agudo

qui·es·cent, a. inactivo; quieto

qui·et, a. callado; silencioso; quieto

quill, n. pluma de ganso

quilt, n. colcha

qui·nine, n. quinina

quin·tu·plet, n. quíntuplo

quip, n. chiste

quirk, n. capricho

quit, v. quit or quit·ted, quit·ing. irse; dejar; abandonar

quite, adv. completamente

quiv·er, n. carcaj, m.; temblor. v. temblar

quix·ot·ic, a. quijotesco

quiz, n. pl., **quiz·zes.** examen corto. v. interrogar

quiz·zi·cal, a. burlón; cómico

quo·rum, n. quórum

quo·ta, n. cuota; cupo

quo·ta·tion, n. cita; cotización

quo·ta·tion mark, n. comillas

quote, v. citar

quo·tient, n. cociente

R

rab·bi, n. pl., **-bis.** rabino; rabí

rab·bit, n. conejo

ra·bies, n. rabia

race, n. carrera; raza. v. correr de prisa

ra·cial, a. racial

rac·ism, n. racismo

rack, n. percha; potro. v. atormentar

rack·et, n. raqueta; estrépito; inf. estafa

ra·dar, n. radar

ra·di·ant, a. radiante

ra·di·a·tion, n. radiación

rad·i·cal, a. radical; extremo. n. radical, m., f.

ra·di·o, n. pl., **-os.** radio, f.

ra·di·o·ac·tiv·i·ty, n. radiactividad

rad·ish, n. rábano

ra·di·um, n. radio

ra·di·us, n. pl., **di·i, -us·es.** radio

raf·fle, n. rifa

raft, n. balsa

raft·er, n. cabrio

rag, n. trapo

rage, n. rabia; ira; manía. v. enfurecerse

rag·ged, a. harapiento; desigual

raid, n. incursión. v. invadir; atacar

rail, n. barandilla; carril, m.

rail·ing, n. baranda

rail·road, n. ferrocarril, m.

rain, n. lluvia. v. llover

rain·bow, n. arco iris

rain·coat, n. impermeable

rain·fall, n. cantidad de lluvia

raise, v. levantar; elevar; criar; subir. n. aumento

rai·sin, n. pasa

rake, n. rastro; libertino. v. rastrillar

ral·ly, v. reunir(se); reanimar. n. pl., **-lies.** reunión

ram, n. morueco; carnero

ramp, n. rampa

ram·pant, a. desenfrenado

ram·shack·le, a. destartalado

ranch, n. rancho; hacienda

ran·cid, a. rancio

ran·cor, n. rencor

ran·dom, a. fortuito. **at ran·dom,** al azar

range, v. alinear; ordenar; colocar. n. terreno de pasto; alcance; extensión

rank, n. fila; rango; graduación

ran·sack, v. saquear

ran·som, n. rescate. v. rescatar

rant, v. vociferar

rap, v., **rapped, rap·ping.** golpear; llamar; inf. discutir. n. golpe seco; inf. culpa

rape, n. violación. v. violar

rap·id, a. rápido

rapt, a. extático; absorto

rap·ture, n. rapto; éxtasis, m.

rare, a. raro; poco asado

rar·i·ty, n. pl., **-ties.** rareza

ras·cal, n. pícaro; bribón

rash, a. imprudente. n. erupción

rasp·ber·ry, n. pl., **-ries.** frambuesa

rat, n. rata

rate, n. razón, f.; precio; velocidad. v. tasar

rath·er, adv. más bien; un poco

rat·i·fy, v. ratificar; confirmar

ra·tio, n. pl., **-tios.** razón

ra·tion, n. ración

ra·tion·al, a. racional; razonable

rat·tle, v. sonar; inf. confundir. n. ruido; sonajero

rat·tle·snake, n. serpiente de cascabel

rau·cous, a. ronco

rav·age, n. estrago. v. destruir

rave, v. delirar

rav·el, v. deshilar

ra·ven, n. cuervo

rav·en·ous, a. hambriento
ra·vine, n. barranca
rav·ish, v. violar; encantar
raw, a. crudo; bruto; inf. desnudo
ray, n. rayo
ray·on, n. rayón
ra·zor, n. navaja de afeitar
re, n. (mus.) re. prep. respecto a
reach, v. alargar; extenderse; alcanzar. n. alcance
re·act, v. reaccionar
re·ac·tion, n. reacción
re·ac·tion·ar·y, n. reaccionario
re·ac·tor, n. reactor
read, v. read, read·ing, leer; interpretar; decir. a. instruido
read·ing, n. lectura; lección
re·ad·just, v. reajustar
read·y, a. listo; pronto; dispuesto
read·y-made, a. hecho
re·al, a. real; verdadero
re·al·i·ty, n. pl., -ties. realidad
re·al·ize, v. darse cuenta de; realizar
re·al·ly, adv. en realidad; realmente
realm, n. reino
re·al·ty, n. bienes raíces
ream, n. resma
reap, v. segar
rear, v. criar. n. parte posterior
re·ar·range, v. arreglar de nuevo
rea·son, n. razón, f. v. razonar
rea·son·a·ble, a. razonable
re·as·sure, v. tranquilizar
reb·el, n. rebelde. a. rebelde
re·bel·lion, n. rebelión
re·buff, n. repulsa. v. rechazar
re·buke, v. reprender. n. reprimenda
re·but·tal, n. refutación
re·call, v. hacer volver; retirar
re·cant, v. retractar(se)
re·ca·pit·u·late, v. recapitular
re·cede, v. retroceder; alejarse
re·ceipt, n. usu. pl. recibo; pl. ingresos
re·ceive, v. recibir; cobrar; acoger
re·cent, a. reciente
re·cep·ta·cle, n. receptáculo
re·cep·tion, n. recepción; acogida
re·cess, n. suspensión; nicho
re·ces·sion, n. retroceso
rec·i·pe, n. receta
re·cip·ro·cal, a. recíproco
re·cit·al, n. relación; (mus.) recital,
m.
rec·i·ta·tion, n. recitación
re·cite, v. referir; recitar
reck·less, a. temerario; descuidado;
atolondrado
reck·on, v. calcular; considerar; inf.
suponer
re·claim, v. reclamar
re·cline, v. reclinar(se); recostar(se)
re·cluse, n. recluso. a. solitario
rec·og·ni·tion, n. reconocimiento

rec·og·nize, v. reconocer
rec·om·mend, v. recomendar
rec·om·men·da·tion, n. recomendación
rec·om·pense, v. recompensar. n.
recompensa
rec·on·cile, v. reconciliar
re·con·nais·sance, n. reconocimiento
re·con·noi·ter, v. reconocer
re·con·struct, v. reconstruir
re·cord, v. registrar; grabar. n. registro; historia; disco
re·course, n. recurso
re·cov·er, v. recuperar; recobrar
re·cov·er·y, n. pl., -ies. resta-
blecimiento
rec·re·a·tion, n. recreo
re·cruit, v. recluta, m. v. reclutar
rec·tan·gle, n. rectángulo
rec·ti·fy, v. rectificar
rec·tum, n. pl., -tums, -ta, recto
re·cu·per·ate, v. recuperar; repo-
nerse
re·cu·per·a·tion, n. recuperación
re·cur, v. -curred, -cur·ring, repe-
tirse; volver
re·cur·rence, n. repetición
red, a. rojo. n. color rojo
red·den, v. ponerse rojo
red·dish, a. rojizo
re·deem, v. redimir
re·demp·tion, n. amortización; re-
dención
re·do, v. -did, -done, -do·ing, rehacer
re·duce, v. reducir; rebajar; disminuir
re·duc·tion, n. reducción; rebaja
reed, n. caña; (mus.) lengüeta
reef, n. escollo
reek, v. oler. n. olor
reel, n. carrete. v. tambalear
re·fer, v. -ferred, -fer·ring, refe-
rir(se); remitir
ref·er·ee, n. árbitro
ref·er·ence, n. referencia
ref·er·en·dum, n. pl., -dums, -da.
referéndum, m.
re·fill, v. rellenar
re·fine, v. refinar
re·fin·er·y, n. pl., -ies. refinería
re·flect, v. reflejar; reflexionar
re·flec·tion, n. reflejo
re·flex, a. reflejo
re·flex·ive, a. reflexivo
re·form, v. reformarse. n. reforma
re·form·a·to·ry, n. pl., -ies. reforma-
torio
re·fract, v. refractar
re·frain, v. abstenerse; refrenar. n. estribillo
re·fresh, v. refrescar
re·fresh·ment, n. usu. pl. refresco
re·frig·er·ate, v. refrigerar

ref·uge, n. refugio
ref·u·gee, n. refugiado
re·fund, v. devolver. n. reembolso
re·fuse, v. rehusar; negar
re·gain, v. recobrar
re·gal, a. real
re·gard, v. mirar; considerar; apreciar. n. consideración
re·gard·ing, prep. en cuanto a
re·gen·er·ate, v. regenerar
re·gent, n. regente
re·gime, n. régimen
reg·i·men, n. régimen
reg·i·ment, n. regimiento
re·gion, n. región
reg·is·ter, n. registro; indicador. v. registrar
re·gret, v. lamentar. n. pesar; sentimiento
reg·u·lar, a. regular; corriente
reg·u·la·tion, n. regulación; reglamento
re·ha·bil·i·tate, v. rehabilitar
re·ha·bil·i·ta·tion, n. rehabilitación
re·hearse, v. ensayar
reign, n. reinado. v. reinar
re·im·burse, v. reembolsar
rein, n. usu. pl. rienda
re·in·car·na·tion, n. reencarnación
re·in·force, v. reforzar
re·it·er·ate, v. reiterar
re·ject, v. rechazar; desechar
re·joice, v. regocijar(se)
re·lapse, v. reincidir. n. recaída
re·late, v. relatar; contar
re·lat·ed, a. emparentado; afín
re·la·tion, n. relación; pariente
re·lax, v. relajar
re·lease, v. soltar. n. libertad; descargo
re·lent, v. ceder
rel·e·vance, rel·e·van·cy, n. pertinencia
re·li·a·ble, a. seguro; confiable
rel·ic, n. reliquia
re·lief, n. alivio
re·lieve, v. aliviar
re·li·gion, n. religión
re·li·gious, a. religioso
rel·ish, v. gustar. n. apetencia; condimento
re·luc·tant, a. poco dispuesto
re·ly, v., -lied, -ly·ing. confiar; contar con
re·main, v. quedar(se)
re·mark, n. observación. v. notar
rem·e·dy, n. pl., -dies. remedio; recurso. v. remediar
re·mem·ber, v. recordar; acordarse de
re·mem·brance, n. recuerdo; often pl. recuerdos
re·mind, v. recordar
rem·i·nis·cence, n. reminiscencia

re·miss, a. descuidado
re·mit, v., -mit·ted, -mit·ting. remitir; perdonar
re·mit·tance, n. remesa
re·morse, n. remordimiento
re·mote, a. remoto
re·move, v. quitar(se); suprimir; apartar(se)
re·nais·sance, n. renacimiento
rend, v., rent or rend·ed, rend·ing. rasgar; hender
ren·der, v. devolver; volver
ren·dez·vous, n. pl., -vous. cita. v. reunirse
ren·e·gade, n. renegado
re·new, v. renovar(se)
re·nounce, v. renunciar
re·nown, n. renombre
rent, n. alquiler. v. alquilar
re·pair, v. reparar; renovar; remendar. n. reparación
re·pay, v., -paid, -pay·ing. reembolsar; recompensar; pagar
re·peal, v. abrogar. n. revocación
re·peat, v. repetir(se)
re·pel, v., -pelled, -pel·ling. rechazar; repeler
re·pent, v. arrepentirse
re·per·cus·sion, n. repercusión
rep·er·toire, n. repertorio
rep·e·ti·tion, n. repetición
re·place, v. reponer; reemplazar
re·ply, v. contestar. n. pl., -plies. respuesta
re·port, v. informar; relatar. n. informe; voz, f.
re·pose, v. poner confianza; reposar
rep·re·hen·si·ble, a. reprensible
rep·re·sent, v. representar; describir
rep·re·sen·ta·tion, n. representación
rep·re·sent·a·tive, a. representativo. n. representante, m., f.
re·press, v. reprimir
re·prieve, n. suspensión
rep·ri·mand, n. reprimenda. v. reprender
re·proach, v. reprochar. n. reproche
re·pro·duce, v. reproducir
rep·tile, n. reptil, m.
re·pub·lic, n. república
re·pug·nant, a. repugnante; ofensivo
re·pulse, v. repulsar. n. repulsa
rep·u·ta·tion, n. reputación; nombre
re·quest, n. petición; ruego. v. rogar; solicitar
re·quire, v. exigir; requerir; necesitar
req·ui·si·tion, n. requisición
res·cue, v. rescatar; salvar. n. rescate
re·search, n. investigaciones, f. pl. v. investigar
re·sem·ble, v. parecerse a; asemejarse a
re·sent, v. resentirse de
res·er·va·tion, n. reservación; reser-

va

re·serve, v. reservar. n. reserva

re·side, v. residir; morar; vivir

res·i·dent, a. residente. n. residente, m., f.

re·sign, v. renunciar; resignarse

res·ig·na·tion, n. resignación

res·in, n. resina

re·sist, v. resistir

re·sist·ance, n. resistencia

res·o·lu·tion, n. resolución

re·solve, v. resolver(se); decidir. n. resolución

res·o·nance, n. resonancia

re·sort, v. recurrir. n. recurso

re·source, n. recurso; pl. recursos

re·spect, n. respeto

re·spect·a·ble, a. respetable; pasable

res·pi·ra·tion, n. respiración

res·pite, n. respiro; tregua

re·spond, v. responder

re·sponse, n. respuesta; reacción

re·spon·si·bil·i·ty, n. pl. -ties. responsabilidad

rest, n. descanso; resto. v. descansar; pararse

res·tau·rant, n. restaurante

rest·less, a. intranquilo

res·to·ra·tion, n. restauración

re·store, v. restaurar; devolver

re·strain, v. refrenar

re·strict, v. restringir

re·stric·tion, n. restricción

re·sult, v. resultar. n. resultado; consecuencia

re·sume, v. reanudar

ré·su·mé, re·su·me, n. resumen

res·ur·rect, v. resucitar

res·ur·rec·tion, n. resurrección

res·us·ci·tate, v. resucitar

re·tail, n. venta al por menor

re·tain, v. retener

re·take, v., -took, -tak·en, -tak·ing. volver a tomar

re·tal·i·ate, v. vengarse

re·tard, v. retardar

ret·i·na, n. pl., -nas, -nae. retina

re·tire, v. retirarse; jubilarse

re·tract, v. retractar(se)

re·treat, n. retirada; retiro

ret·ri·bu·tion, n. justo castigo

re·trieve, v. recuperar; recobrar

ret·ro·ac·tive, a. retroactivo

re·turn, v. devolver; volver. n. vuelta

re·un·ion, n. reunión

re·veal, v. revelar

rev·e·la·tion, n. revelación

re·venge, v. vengar(se). n. venganza

re·ve·nue, n. renta; ingresos

re·vere, v. venerar

rev·er·ie, rev·er·y, n. pl., -ies. ensueño

re·verse, v. volver al revés; invertir. a. inverso. n. lo contrario; revés,

m.

re·vert, v. volver

re·view, v. examinar; pasar revista. n. revista; reseña

re·vise, v. revisar; corregir; repasar

re·vi·sion, n. revisión

re·vive, v. restablecer; resucitar; revivir

re·voke, v. revocar

re·volt, v. rebelar(se). n. sublevación

rev·o·lu·tion, n. revolución

rev·o·lu·tion·ar·y, a. revolucionario. n. revolucionario

re·volve, v. revolverse; girar

re·volv·er, n. revólver

re·ward, v. premiar. n. recompensa

rhap·so·dy, n. pl., -dies. rapsodia

rhe·tor·i·cal, a. retórico

rheu·mat·ic, a. reumático

rheu·ma·tism, n. reumatismo

rhi·noc·er·os, n. pl., -os·es, -os. rinoceronte

rho·do·den·dron, n. rododendro

rhu·barb, n. ruibarbo

rhyme, n. rima. v. rimar

rhythm, n. ritmo

rib, n. costilla

rib·bon, n. cinta

rice, n. arroz, m.

rich, a. rico; precioso; fértil

rich·es, n. pl. riqueza

rick·et·y, a. tambaleante

ric·o·chet, n. rebote

rid, v., rid or rid·ded, rid·ding. librar(se)

rid·dle, n. acertijo

ride, v., rode, rid·den, rid·ing. montar; ir. n. viaje

ridge, n. caballón; cadena de colinas

rid·i·cule, n. burla; ridículo. v. ridiculizar

ri·dic·u·lous, a. ridículo

ri·fle, n. rifle

rift, n. grieta

rig, v. equipar; manipular

right, a. derecho; justo; correcto; exacto. n. derecho. adv. exactamente

right·ful, a. legítimo

rig·id, a. rígido; inflexible

rig·or·ous, a. riguroso

rile, v. inf. sulfurar

rim, n. aro; canto

rind, n. piel, f.; corteza

ring, n. anillo; argolla; repique de campana. v., rang, rung, ring·ing. rodear; sonar; llamar

ring·lead·er, n. cabecilla, m.

rink, n. pista

rinse, v. aclarar; enjuagar

ri·ot, n. motín; tumulto

rip, v., ripped, rip·ping. rasgar; descoser; arrancar. n. rasgadura

ripe, a. maduro

rise, v., rose, ris·en, ris·ing. levantarse; elevarse; subir. *n.* subida; desarrollo

risk, *n.* riesgo. *v.* arriesgar

rite, *n.* rito

rit·u·al, *a.* ritual. *n.* ritual, *m.*

ri·val, *n.* competidor. *a.* rival. *v.* rivalizar

ri·val·ry, *n. pl.,* **-ries.** rivalidad

riv·er, *n.* río

riv·et, *n.* remache

roach, *n. pl.,* **roach, roach·es.** cucaracha

road, *n.* camino; carretera

roam, *v.* vagar

roar, *n.* rugir. *n.* rugido; estruendo

roast, *v.* asar; *inf.* burlarse. *n.* carne asada

rob, *v.,* **robbed, rob·bing.** robar; hurtar

robe, *n.* traje talar; bata

rob·in, *n.* petirrojo

ro·bot, *n.* autómata, *m.*

ro·bust, *a.* robusto; vigoroso

rock, *n.* roca; *inf.* joya. *v.* mecer

rock·et, *n.* cohete

rock·y, *a.* inestable; escabroso

rod, *n.* vara; caña de pescar

ro·dent, *n.* roedor

roe, *n.* corzo

rogue, *n.* pícaro; bribón

role, *n.* papel, *m.*

roll, *v.* hacer rodar; rodar. *n.* lista; rollo; panecillo

ro·mance, *n.* cuenta de aventuras; amorío

Ro·man nu·mer·als, *n.* números romanos

ro·man·tic, *a.* romántico

ro·man·ti·cism, *n.* romanticismo

romp, *v.* retozar

roof, *n.* tejado. *v.* techar

rook, *n.* torre. *f. v.* estafar

room, *n.* cuarto; habitación; sitio; lugar

room·mate, *n.* compañero de cuarto

room·y, *a.* espacioso

roost, *n.* percha

roost·er, *n.* gallo

root, *n.* raíz, *f.;* esencia. *v.* echar raíces

rope, *n.* cuerda; soga. *v.* atar

ro·sa·ry, *n. pl.,* **-ries.** rosario

rose, *n.* rosa. *a.* de color de rosa

ros·ter, *n.* lista; nómina

ros·trum, *n. pl.,* **-tra, -trums.** tribuna

ros·y, *a.* rosado

rot, *v.,* **rot·ted, rot·ting.** pudrir(se). *n.* putrefacción

ro·tate, *v.* girar; alternar

rot·ten, *a.* podrido; malísimo

ro·tund, *a.* rotundo

rouge, *n.* colorete

rough, *a.* áspero; fragoso; tosco; severo

rou·lette, *n.* ruleta

round, *a.* redondo; esférico; de ida y vuelta. *adv.* alrededor. *prep.* alrededor de. *n.* ronda

round·a·bout, *a.* indirecto

rouse, *v.* despertar(se); animar

rout, *v.* derrotar

route, *n.* ruta; rumbo

rou·tine, *n.* rutina. *a.* de costumbre

rove, *v.* vagar

row, *v.* remar. *n.* fila; hilera; lío

row·dy, *a.* ruidoso

roy·al, *a.* real

roy·al·ty, *n. pl.,* **-ties.** realeza; derecho de autor

rub, *v.,* **rubbed, rub·bing.** frotar; fregar; borrar; rozar

rub·ber, *n.* caucho; goma; *pl.* chanclos

rub·bish, *n.* basura

rub·ble, *n.* cascote

ru·by, *n. pl.,* **-bies.** rubí, *m.*

ruck·sack, *n.* mochila

ruck·us, *n. inf.* lío; alboroto

rud·der, *n.* timón

rud·dy, *a.* frescote

rude, *a.* rudo; descortés; tosco

ru·di·ment, *n.* rudimento; *usu. pl.* rudimentos

rue, *v.,* **rued, ru·ing.** lamentar

ruf·fle, *v.* rizar(se); fruncir. *n.* volante fruncido

rug, *n.* alfombra

rug·ged, *a.* escabroso; severo

ru·in, *n.* ruina. *v.* derrotar; estropear; arruinar

rule, *n.* regla; mando. *v.* gobernar; rayar

rul·er, *n.* gobernador; regla

rum, *n.* ron

rum·ble, *v.* retumbar

rum·mage, *v.* revolver

ru·mor, *n.* rumor

rum·ple, *v.* arrugar

run, *v.,* **ran, run, run·ning.** correr; dirigir; funcionar. *n.* paseo; marcha; serie, *f.*

run·a·way, *a.* fugitivo

run·down, *n.* resumen. *a.* cansado; en decadencia

rung, *n.* peldaño

run·ning, *a.* corriente

runt, *n.* redrojo

run·way, *n.* pista de aterrizaje

rup·ture, *n.* hernia; rompimiento

ru·ral, *a.* rural

ruse, *n.* ardid

rush, *v.* ir de prisa; precipitarse. *n.* ímpetu, *m.;* junco

rus·set, *n.* color bermejo

rust, *n.* orín. *v.* aherrumbrar(se)

rus·tic, *a.* rústico

rus·tle, *v.* susurrar; *inf.* robar

rust·y, *a.* herrumbroso; mohoso;

torpe
rut, *n.* rodera; rutina
ruth·less, *a.* cruel; despiadado
rye, *n.* centeno

S

Sab·bath, *n.* (*cristiano*) domingo; (*judío*) sábado
sa·ber, *n.* sable
sa·ble, *n.* cebellina. *a.* negro
sab·o·tage, *n.* sabotaje. *v.* sabotear
sac·cha·rin, *n.* sacarina
sack, *n.* saco; costal, *m.*
sac·ra·ment, *n.* sacramento; (*often cap.*) Eucaristía
sa·cred, *a.* sagrado
sac·ri·fice, *n.* sacrificio. *v.* sacrificar
sac·ri·lege, *n.* sacrilegio
sad, *a.* triste
sad·den, *v.* entristecer
sad·dle, *n.* silla de montar. *v.* ensillar
sad·ism, *n.* sadismo
sa·fa·ri, *n. pl.* -ris. safari, *m.*
safe, *a.* seguro; salvo. *n.* caja de caudales
safe·ty, *n. pl.* -ties. seguridad
safe·ty pin, *n.* imperdible
sag, *v.*, sagged, sag·ging. combar(se). *n.* comba
sa·ga, *n.* saga
sage, *a.* sabio. *n.* sabio; salvia
sail, *n.* vela. *v.* navegar
sail·or, *n.* marinero
saint, *n.* santo. *n.* santo
sake, *n.* motivo; consideración
sal·ad, *n.* ensalada
sal·a·man·der, *n.* salamandra
sal·a·ry, *n. pl.* -ries. sueldo; salario
sale, *n.* venta; subasta
sa·line, *a.* salino
sa·li·va, *n.* saliva
sal·low, *a.* cetrino
sal·ly, *n. pl.* -lies. salida
salm·on, *n. pl.* -ons, -on. salmón
sa·lon, *n.* salón
sa·loon, *n.* taberna; salón
salt, *n.* sal, *f. a.* salado
sal·u·tar·y, *a.* saludable
sal·u·ta·tion, *n.* saludo
sa·lute, *v.* saludar. *n.* saludo; salva
sal·vage, *n.* salvamento
sal·va·tion, *n.* salvación
salve, *n.* ungüento
sal·vo, *n. pl.*, -vos, -voes. salva
same, *a.* idéntico; mismo
sam·ple, *n.* muestra. *v.* probar
san·a·to·ri·um, *n. pl.*, -ums, -a. sanatorio. Also san·i·tar·i·um
sanc·ti·fy, *v.* santificar
sanc·tion, *n.* sanción. *v.* sancionar; autorizar
sanc·ti·ty, *n. pl.*, -ties. santidad
sanc·tu·ar·y, *n. pl.*, -ies. santuario;

asilo
sand, *n.* arena. *v.* enarenar
san·dal, *n.* sandalia
sand·stone, *n.* arenisca
sand·wich, *n.* bocadillo
sand·y, *a.* arenoso
sane, *a.* cuerdo; sano
san·gui·nar·y, *a.* sanguinario
san·i·tar·i·um, *n. pl.*, -ums, -a. sanatorio. Also san·a·to·ri·um.
san·i·tar·y, *a.* sanitario
san·i·ta·tion, *n.* instalación sanitaria
san·i·ty, *n.* juicio sano
sap, *n.* savia. *v.* agotar
sa·pi·ent, *a.* sabio
sap·phire, *n.* zafiro
sar·casm, *n.* sarcasmo
sar·cas·tic, *a.* sarcástico
sar·coph·a·gus, *n. pl.*, -gi, -gus·es. sarcófago
sar·dine, *n. pl.*, -dines, -dine. sardina
sa·ri, sa·ree, *n. pl.*, -ris, -rees. sari, *m.*
sash, *n.* faja; marco de una ventana
sass·y, *a.* descarado
Sa·tan, *n.* Satanás
sa·tan·ic, *a.* satánico. Also sa·tan·i·cal
sate, *v.* saciar; satisfacer
sat·el·lite, *n.* satélite
sa·ti·ate, *v.* saciar; hartar
sat·in, *n.* raso
sat·ire, *n.* sátira
sat·is·fac·tion, *n.* satisfacción
sat·is·fy, *v.* satisfacer; convencer
sat·u·rate, *v.* saturar
Sat·ur·day, *n.* sábado
sa·tyr, *n.* sátiro
sauce, *n.* salsa
sau·cer, *n.* platillo
sau·sage, *n.* embutido; salchicha
sav·age, *a.* salvaje. *n.* salvaje; bárbaro
save, *v.* salvar; conservar; ahorrar. *conj. prep.* excepto
sav·ing, *n.* economía; *pl.* ahorros. *prep.* salvo. *conj.* excepto
sav·ior, *n.* salvador; (*cap.*) Salvador
sa·vor, *n.* sabor. *v.* saborear
saw, *n.* sierra. *v.*, sawed, sawed or sawn, saw·ing. serrar
sax·o·phone, *n.* saxofón
say, *v.*, said, say·ing. decir. *n.* turno
say·ing, *n.* dicho
scab, *n.* costra
scaf·fold, *n.* andamio
scald, *v.* escaldar
scale, *n.* balanza; escama; escala. *v.* escamar; escalar
scal·lop, *n.* venera; festón. *v.* festonear
scalp, *n.* pericráneo; cuero cabelludo
scal·pel, *n.* escalpelo
scan, *v.* escudriñar; mirar rápidamente

scan·dal, n. escándalo
scan·dal·ize, v. escandalizar
scant, a. escaso; corto
scant·y, a. escaso
scape·goat, n. cabeza de turco
scar, n. cicatriz; f. v. marcar con una cicatriz
scarce, a. escaso; poco común
scare, v. asustar. n. susto
scare·crow, n. espantajo; espantapájaros
scarf, n. pl. scarfs, scarves. bufanda
scar·let, n. escarlata
scat·ter, v. esparcir
scav·en·ger, n. basurero
scene, n. escena; vista; escándalo
scen·er·y, n. pl. -ies. paisaje; vista; decoraciones
scent, n. olor; perfume; pista
sched·ule, n. horario; inventario
scheme, v. proyectar; intrigar. n. plan
schism, n. cisma, m.; f.
schiz·o·phre·ni·a, n. esquizofrenia
schol·ar, n. erudito; alumno
schol·ar·ship, n. erudición; beca
scho·las·tic, a. escolar
school, n. escuela. v. enseñar
sci·ence, n. ciencia
sci·en·tist, n. científico
scim·i·tar, sim·i·tar, n. cimitarra. Also scim·i·ter
scis·sors, n. pl. tijeras
scoff, v. mofarse
scold, v. regañar
scoop, n. paleta. v. sacar con pala
scoot·er, n. patinete
scope, n. alcance
scorch, v. chamuscar
score, n. tanteo; cuenta; veinte. v. marcar; orquestar
scorn, n. desdén. v. despreciar
scor·pi·on, n. escorpión
scotch, v. frustrar
scoun·drel, n. canalla, m.; f.
scour, v. fregar; recorrer
scout, n. explorador
scowl, v. poner mal gesto. n. ceño
scrag·gy, a. escarabond
scram·ble, v. revolver
scrap, n. fragmento; sobras
scrape, v. raspar; raer
scratch, v. rayar; rasguñar; rascar. n. rasguño
scrawl, n. garrabatos, garrapatos
scream, v. chillar. n. grito
screen, n. biombo; pantalla. v. esconder
screw, n. tornillo. v. atornillar
scrib·ble, v. garrapatear
scrim·mage, n. arrebatiña
script, n. letra cursiva; guión
scrip·ture, n. (cap.) Sagrada Escritura
scroll, n. rollo de pergamino

scrub, v. fregar. n. maleza
scru·ple, n. escrúpulo
scru·ti·nize, v. escudriñar
scru·ti·ny, n. pl., -nies. escrutinio
scuf·fle, v. pelear. n. pelea
sculp·tor, n. escultor
sculp·ture, n. escultura. v. esculpir
scum, n. espuma
scur·ry, v. darse prisa
scur·vy, n. escorbuto
scut·tle, v. echar a pique
scythe, n. guadaña
sea, n. mar, m.; f.
seal, n. pl., seals, seal. foca
seal, n. sello. v. cerrar
seam, n. costura
sea·man, n. pl., -men. marinero
seam·stress, n. costurera
seam·y, a. asqueroso
sé·ance, n. sesión de espiritistas
sea·port, n. puerto de mar
sear, v. marchitar; chamuscar
search, v. buscar; registrar. n. registro
sea·shore, n. orilla del mar
sea·sick·ness, n. mareo
sea·son, n. estación. v. sazonar
sea·son·ing, n. condimento
seat, n. asiento. v. sentar
sea·weed, n. alga marina
se·clude, v. aislar
se·clu·sion, n. retiro
sec·ond, a. segundo. n. segundo. v. apoyar
sec·ond·ar·y, a. secundario
sec·ond·hand, a. de segunda mano
sec·ond·rate, a. inferior
se·cre·cy, n. pl., -cies. secreto
se·cret, a. secreto; oculto. n. secreto
sec·re·tar·y, n. pl., -ies. secretario; (cap.) Ministro
se·crete, v. secretar; ocultar
se·cre·tion, n. secreción
sect, n. secta
sec·tion, n. sección; porción; división
sec·tor, n. sector
sec·u·lar, a. secular
se·cure, a. seguro. v. asegurar; adquirir
se·cu·ri·ty, n. pl., -ties. seguridad; fianza; pl. valores
se·date, a. sosegado
sed·a·tive, a. calmante. n. sedativo
sed·en·tar·y, a. sedentario
sed·i·ment, n. sedimento
se·di·tion, n. sedición
se·duce, v. seducir
se·duc·tion, se·duce·ment, n. seducción
see, v., saw, seen, see·ing. ver; visitar; ·comprender; percibir. n. sede, f.
seed, n. pl., seeds, seed. semilla; simiente, f. v. sembrar
seed·y, a. desharrapado

seek, *v.,* **sought, seek·ing.** buscar; solicitar

seem, *v.* parecer

seem·ly, *a.* decoroso; correcto

seep, *v.* rezumarse

se·er, *n.* profeta, *m.*

seg·ment, *n.* segmento; sección

seg·re·gate, *v.* segregar

seg·re·ga·tion, *n.* segregación; separación

seis·mo·graph, *n.* sismógrafo

seize, *v.* asir; agarrar; apoderarse de

sei·zure, *n.* asimiento; ataque

sel·dom, *adv.* raramente. *a.* infrecuente

se·lect, *v.* escoger; elegir. *a.* selecto

se·lec·tion, *n.* selección

self, *n. pl.* **selves.** See **my·self, your·self,** etc.

self-cen·tered, *a.* egocéntrico

self-com·mand, *n.* dominio de sí mismo

self-con·fi·dence, *n.* confianza en sí mismo

self-con·scious, *a.* tímido

self-con·trol, *n.* dominio de sí mismo

self-ev·i·dent, *a.* patente

self-ex·plan·a·to·ry, *a.* evidente; obvio

self-gov·ern·ment, *n.* autonomía

self-im·por·tance, *n.* presunción

self·ish, *a.* egoísta; interesado

self·less, *a.* desinteresado

self-re·li·ance, *n.* confianza en sí mismo

self-same, *a.* mismo

self-suf·fi·cient, *a.* independiente

self-will, *n.* terquedad

sell, *v.* **sold, sell·ing.** vender(se)

se·man·tics, *n. pl.* semántica

sem·blance, *n.* parecido; apariencia

se·men, *n.* semen

sem·i·cir·cle, *n.* semicírculo

sem·i·co·lon, *n.* punto y coma

sem·i·fi·nal. *a.* semifinal. *n. usu. pl.* semifinales. *f. pl.*

sem·i·nar, *n.* seminario

sem·i·nar·y, *n. pl.* **-ies.** seminario

sem·i·of·fi·cial, *a.* semioficial

sem·i·pre·cious, *a.* semiprecioso

sem·i·week·ly, *a.* bisemanal. *n. pl.* **-lies.** publicación bisemanal

sen·ate, *n.* senado; (*cap.*) Senado

sen·a·tor, *n.* senador

send, *v.,* **sent, send·ing.** enviar; mandar; dirigir; lanzar

se·nile, *a.* senil

sen·ior, *a.* mayor de edad; superior. *n.* alumno del último año en una universidad o escuela secundaria

sen·ior·i·ty, *n.* antigüedad

sen·sa·tion, *n.* sensación

sense, *n.* sentido; sensación; juicio. *v.* percibir

sense·less, *a.* sin sentido; insensato

sen·si·bil·i·ty, *n. pl.,* **-ties.** sensibilidad

sen·si·ble, *a.* razonable

sen·si·tive, *a.* impresionable; delicado

sen·si·tiv·i·ty, *n. pl.,* **-ties.** delicadeza

sen·so·ry, *a.* sensorio. Also **sen·so·ri·al**

sen·su·al, *a.* sensual; lascivo

sen·su·ous, *a.* sensorio

sen·tence, *n.* frase, *f.;* condena. *v.* condenar

sen·ti·ment, *n.* sentimiento

sen·ti·nel, *n.* centinela, *m.*

sen·try, *n. pl.,* **-tries.** centinela, *m.;* guardia, *m.*

se·pal, *n.* sépalo

sep·a·rate, *v.* separar(se). *a.* separado; distinto

sep·a·ra·tion, *n.* separación

Sep·tem·ber, *n.* septiembre

sep·tic, *a.* séptico

sep·ul·cher, *n.* sepulcro

se·quel, *n.* resultado

se·quence, *n.* sucesión; serie, *f.*

se·ques·ter, *v.* separar; aislar

se·quin, *n.* lentejuela

ser·aph, *n. pl.,* **-aphs, -a·phim,** serafín

ser·e·nade, *n.* serenata

se·rene, *n.* sereno

se·ren·i·ty, *n. pl.,* **-ties.** serenidad

serf, *n.* siervo

ser·geant, *n.* sargento

se·ri·al, *a.* en serie. *n.* novela por entregas

se·ries, *n.* serie, *f.*

se·ri·ous, *a.* serio; grave

ser·mon, *n.* sermón

ser·pent, *n.* serpiente, *f.*

se·rum, *n. pl.,* **se·rums, se·ra.** suero

serv·ant, *n.* sirviente; servidor

serve, *v.* servir; cumplir

serv·ice, *n.* servicio. *v.* mantener

serv·ice·man, *n. pl.,* **-men.** militar; reparador

ser·vile, *a.* servil

ses·sion, *n.* sesión

set, *v.,* **set, set·ting.** poner(se); fijar; arreglar; cuajarse. *n.* juego. *a.* fijo; rígido; establecido. **set a·bout,** ponerse a hacer. **set on,** atacar. **set out,** ponerse en camino

set·back, *n.* revés, *m.*

set·ting, *n.* marco; engaste

set·tle, *v.* resolver; ajustar; arreglar; colocar; establecer(se); calmar(se)

set·tle·ment, *n.* colonización; ajuste

set·tler, *n.* colono

seven, *n.* siete. *a.* siete

sev·en·teen, *a.* diecisiete

sev·enth, *a.* séptimo. *n.* séptimo

sev·en·ty, *a.* setenta. *n.* setenta

sev·er, v. separar; cortar
sev·er·al, a. varios; diversos
se·vere, a. severo; riguroso; duro
se·ver·i·ty, n. pl., **-ties.** severidad; aspereza
sew, v., **sewed, sewn** or **sewed, sew·ing.** coser
sew·er, n. albañal, m.
sex, n. sexb
sex·tet, n. sexteto
sex·u·al, a. sexual
sex·y, a. provocativo
shab·by, a. raído; en mal estado
shack, n. choza
shack·le, n. grillete. v. encadenar
shade, n. sombra; matiz, m. v. sombrear
shad·ow, n. sombra. v. oscurecer; sombrear; seguir
shad·y, a. sombreado
shaft, n. eje; pozo
shag·gy, a. velludo
shake, v., **shook, shak·en, shak·ing.** sacudir; temblar; agitar; estrechar
shak·y, a. poco firme; débil
shale, n. esquisto
shal·low, a. poco profundo. n. often pl. bajío
sham, n. impostura. a. fingido. v. fingir(se)
sham·bles, n. pl. desorden
shame, n. vergüenza. v. avergonzar; deshonrar
shame·less, a. desvergonzado
sham·poo, v. lavar. n. champú, m.
shan·ty, n. pl., **-ties.** choza
shape, n. forma; talle. v. formar
shape·ly, a. bien formado
share, n. parte, f.; acción. v. partir; repartir; compartir
shark, n. tiburón
sharp, a. cortante; agudo; penetrante; vivo. n. sostenido
sharp·en, v. afilar; sacar punta a
shat·ter, v. hacer(se) pedazos
shave, v., **shaved, shaved** or **shav·en, shav·ing.** afeitar(se). n. afeitado, afeitada
shav·er, n. máquina de afeitar
shawl, n. chal, m.
she, pron. ella
shears, n. tijeras grandes
shed, v., **shed, shed·ding.** quitarse; verter. n. barraca
sheen, n. lustre
sheep, n. pl. **sheep.** oveja
sheep·ish, a. tímido
sheer, a. transparente; completo; escarpado
sheet, n. sábana; hoja; lámina
sheik, sheikh, n. jeque
shelf, n. pl., **shelves.** estante
shell, n. cáscara; caparazón; granada. v. descascarar; bombardear

shel·lac, shel·lack, n. goma laca
shell·fish, n. pl., **-fish, -fish·es.** marisco
shel·ter, n. abrigo; resguardo; refugio. v. poner(se) al abrigo
shep·herd, n. pastor
sher·bet, n. sorbete
sher·iff, n. sheriff, m.
sher·ry, n. pl., **-ries.** jerez, m.
shield, n. escudo. v. proteger
shift, v. mover(se); cambiar. n. cambio; tanda
shil·ly-shal·ly, v. vacilar
shim·mer, v. rielar
shin, n. espinilla
shine, v., **shone** or **shined, shin·ing.** brillar; relucir; pulir. n. lustre
shin·gle, n. ripia; tejamanil, m.
shin·y, a. brillante
ship, n. buque; barco. v. transportar
ship·mate, n. camarada de a bordo
ship·ment, n. embarque; envío
ship·shape, a. en buen orden
ship·wreck, n. naufragio. v. naufragar
shirk, v. evitar; esquivar
shirt, n. camisa
shiv·er, v. temblar. n. estremecimiento
shock, n. susto; choque; postración nerviosa. v. escandalizar
shod·dy, a. de pacotilla; falso
shoe, n. pl., **shoes.** zapato. v. herrar
shoe·horn, n. calzador
shoe·lace, n. cordón
shoot, v., **shot, shoot·ing.** disparar; fusilar; lanzarse; espigar. n. retoño
shoot·ing, n. tiro; caza con escopeta
shoot·ing star, n. estrella fugaz
shop, n. tienda; taller. v. ir de compras
shop·keep·er, n. tendero
shore, n. playa
short, a. corto; bajo; breve; insuficiente. n. deficiencia; pl. calzones cortos. v. engañar. **in short,** en resumen
short·age, n. deficiencia; escasez, f.
short cir·cuit, n. corto circuito
short·com·ing, n. defecto
short·cut, n. atajo
short·en, v. acortar(se); reducir(se)
short·hand, n. taquigrafía
short-lived, a. de breve duración
short-tem·pered, a. de mal genio
shot, n. tiro; tirador; inf. inyección
shot·gun, n. escopeta
should, aux. v. past form of **shall**
shoul·der, n. hombro
shout, n. grito. v. gritar
shove, v. empujar
shov·el, n. pala
show, v., **showed, shown** or **showed, show·ing.** mostrar(se); indicar;

enseñar. *n.* exposición; función

show•case, *n.* vitrina

show•er, *n.* ducha; chubasco. *v.* llover; ducharse

show•man, *n. pl.,* -men. director de espectáculos

shred, *v.,* shred•ded or shred, shred•ding. hacer tiras. *n.* triza; fragmento

shrew, *n.* arpía

shrewd, *a.* sagaz; prudente

shriek, *v.* chillar

shrill, *a.* estridente

shrimp, *n. pl.,* shrimps, shrimp. camarón

shrine, *n.* relicario

shrink, *v.,* shrank or shrunk, shrunk•en, shrink•ing. encoger(se)

shriv•el, *v.* encoger(se); secar(se)

shroud, *n.* mortaja

shrub, *n.* arbusto

shrub•ber•y, *n. pl.,* -ies. arbustos

shrug, *v.* encogerse de hombros

shud•der, *v.* estremecerse

shuf•fle, *v.* arrasurar los pies; (*cards*) barajar

shun, *v.* evitar; apartarse de

shut, *v.,* shut, shut•ting. cerrar(se). *a.* cerrado. shut down, cerrar. shut out, excluir. shut up, encerrar; hacer callar

shut•ter, *n.* contraventana

shut•tle, *n.* lanzadera

shy, *a.* tímido; reservado

sic, *v.,* sicked, sick•ing. atacar

sick, *a.* enfermo

sick•en, *v.* hartar; enfermar(se)

sick•le, *n.* hoz, *f.*

sick•ness, *n.* enfermedad

side, *n.* lado; partido; equipo. *a.* lateral

side•burns, *n. pl.* patillas

side•kick, *n. inf.* compañero

side•long, *a.* lateral. *adv.* lateralmente

side•track, *v.* desviar

side•walk, *n.* acera

side•ways, *adv.* oblicuamente

siege, *n.* sitio; cerco

sieve, *n.* coladera; tamiz, *m. v.* tamizar

sift, *v.* tamizar

sigh, *v.* suspirar. *n.* suspiro

sight, *n.* vista; visión; espectáculo. *v.* ver. catch sight of, vislumbrar

sight•less, *a.* ciego

sight•see•ing, *n.* visita de puntos de interés

sign, *v.* firmar. *n.* señal, *f.;* signo; letrero

sig•nal, *n.* señal, *f. a.* señalado. *v.* hacer señas

sig•na•ture, *n.* firma

sig•nif•i•cance, *n.* significación

sig•ni•fy, *v.* significar

si•lence, *n.* silencio. *v.* hacer callar

si•lent, *a.* silencioso; mudo

sil•hou•ette, *n.* silueta

sil•i•ca, *n.* sílice, *f.*

sil•i•con, *n.* silicio

silk, *n.* seda. *a.* de seda

silk•y, *a.* de seda; sedoso

sil•ly, *a.* tonto; absurdo; bobo

si•lo, *n. pl.,* -los. silo

silt, *n.* sedimento

sil•ver, *n.* plata; moneda. *a.* de plata

sil•ver•smith, *n.* platero

sil•ver•ware, *n.* vajilla de plata

sim•i•an, *a.* símico. *n.* mono

sim•i•lar, *a.* parecido; similar

sim•i•lar•i•ty, *n. pl.,* -ties. semejanza

sim•mer, *v.* hervir a fuego lento

sim•per, *v.* sonreírse afectadamente

sim•ple, *a.* sencillo; fácil; simple

sim•pli•fy, *v.* simplificar

sim•ply, *adv.* sencillamente

sim•u•late, *v.* simular

si•mul•ta•ne•ous, *a.* simultáneo

sin, *n.* pecado; transgresión. *v.* pecar

since, *adv.* desde entonces. *prep.* desde; después. *conj.* desde que; puesto que

sin•cere, *a.* sincero

sin•cer•i•ty, *n.* sinceridad

si•ne•cure, *n.* sinecura

sin•ew, *n.* tendón

sing, *v.,* sang or sung, sung. cantar

singe, *v.* chamuscar

sing•er, *n.* cantante, *m., f.*

sin•gle, *a.* soltero; único; sencillo

sin•gle•hand•ed, *a.* sin ayuda

sin•gu•lar, *a.* singular. *n.* singular

sin•is•ter, *a.* siniestro

sink, *v.,* sank or sunk, sunk or sunk•en, sink•ing. hundir(se). *n.* fregadero

sin•ner, *n.* pecador

si•nus, *n.* seno

sip, *v.* sorber. *n.* sorbo

si•phon, sy•phon, *n.* sifón

sir, *n.* señor

sire, *n.* padre. *v.* engendrar

si•ren, *n.* sirena

sir•loin, *n.* solomillo

sis•ter, *n.* hermana

sis•ter•in•law, *n. pl.,* sis•ters•in•law. cuñada

sit, *v.,* sat, sit•ting. sentar(se); posarse

site, *n.* sitio; solar

sit•u•a•tion, *n.* situación; colocación

six, *n.* seis. *a.* seis

six•teen, *n.* dieciséis. *a.* dieciséis

sixth, *a.* sexto. *n.* sexto

six•ty, *n.* sesenta. *a.* sesenta

size, *n.* tamaño; talla

siz•zle, *v.* chisporrotear

skate, *n.* patín. *v.* patinar

skel·e·ton, *n.* esqueleto; armazón

skep·tic, scep·tic, *n.* escéptico

skep·ti·cal, scep·ti·cal, *a.* escéptico

sketch, *n.* esbozo; bosquejo. *v.* dibujar

skew·er, *n.* broqueta

ski, *n. pl.,* **skis, ski.** esquí, *m. v.* esquiar

skid, *n.* patinazo. *v.* patinar

skill, *n.* habilidad; pericia; destreza

skil·let, *n.* sartén

skim, *v.* espumar; desnatar; hojear

skin, *n.* piel, *f.;* cutis, *m. v.* despellejar

skin·ny, *a.* flaco

skip, *v.* saltar; pasar por alto

skir·mish, *n.* escaramuza

skirt, *n.* falda. *v.* ladear

skit, *n.* parodia

skull, *n.* cráneo

skunk, *n.* mofeta

sky, *n. pl.,* **skies.** cielo

sky·rock·et, *n.* cohete. *v.* subir rápidamente

sky·scrap·er, *n.* rascacielos

slab, *n.* tabla; plancha

slack, *a.* flojo; negligente

slack·en, *v.* aflojar

slacks, *n. pl.* pantalones

slag, *n.* escoria

slam, *v.* cerrarse de golpe

slan·der, *n.* calumnia. *v.* calumniar

slang, *n.* argot, *m.;* jerga

slant, *v.* inclinar(se); sesgar(se). *n.* inclinación

slap, *n.* bofetada; palmada. *v.* pegar

slash, *v.* acuchillar

slat, *n.* tablilla

slate, *n.* pizarra; lista de candidatos

slaugh·ter, *n.* matanza; carnicería. *v.* matar

slave, *n.* esclavo

slav·er·y, *n.* esclavitud

slaw, *n.* ensalada de col

slay, *v.,* **slew, slain, slay·ing.** matar

sled, *n.* trineo

sleek, *a.* liso; pulcro

sleep, *v.,* **slept, sleep·ing.** dormir. *n.* sueño

sleep·y, *a.* soñoliento

sleet, *n.* aguanieve, *f.*

sleeve, *n.* manga

sleigh, *n.* trineo

slen·der, *a.* delgado; limitado

sleuth, *n. inf.* detective

slice, *n.* rebanada; tajada. *v.* tajar

slide, *v.,* **slid, slid** or **slid·den, slid·ing.** deslizarse. *n.* resbalón; diapositiva

slight, *a.* pequeño; de poco importancia. *n.* desaire

slim, *a.* delgado. *v.* adelgazar

slime, *n.* légamo

sling, *v.,* **slung, sling·ing.** tirar; suspender. *n.* cabestrillo

slip, *v.* introducir; deslizar(se); resbalar; escaparse. *n.* error; combinación

slip·knot, *n.* nudo corredizo

slip·per, *n.* zapatilla

slip·per·y, *a.* resbaladizo

slip-up, *n. inf.* equivocación

slit, *v.,* **slit, slit·ting.** cortar. *n.* raja

sliv·er, *n.* astilla

slob·ber, *v.* babear; babosear

slo·gan, *n.* mote

slop, *v.* verter

slope, *n.* declive; inclinación. *v.* inclinar(se)

slot, *n.* ranura

slov·en·ly, *a.* descuidado; desaseado

slow, *a.* lento; torpe. *v.* ir más despacio; retardar

slow·ly, *adv.* despacio

slug, *n.* posta. *v.* golpear

slug·gish, *a.* perezoso; lento

slum, *n. often pl.* barrio bajo

slump, *v.* hundirse. *n.* depresión; baja repentina

slur, *v.* comerse palabras; calumniar. *n.* mancha

slut, *n.* pazpuerca; perra

sly, *a.* astuto; disimulado

smack, *n.* manotada. *v.* pegar

small, *a.* pequeño; bajo; chico

small·pox, *n.* viruelas

smart, *v.* escocer. *a.* vivo; listo; elegante; fresco

smash, *v.* romper(se)

smear, *v.* manchar; untar

smell, *v.,* **smelled** or **smelt, smel·ling.** oler. *n.* olfato; olor

smile, *v.* sonreír(se). *n.* sonrisa

smirk, *n.* sonrisa afectada

smith, *n.* herrero. Also **smith·y**

smock, *n.* blusa de labrador; bata

smog, *n.* niebla y humo mezclados

smoke, *n.* humo. *v.* humear; fumar

smol·der, smoul·der, *v.* arder sin llamas

smooch, *v. inf.* besar

smooth, *a.* liso; suave. *v.* allanar

smoth·er, *v.* ahogar(se); sofocar(se)

smudge, *n.* mancha. *v.* tiznar

smug, *a.* papado de sí mismo

smug·gle, *v.* pasar de (o hacer) contrabando

smug·gler, *n.* contrabandista, *m., f.*

snack, *n.* merienda

snag, *n.* obstáculo; rasgón

snail, *n.* caracol, *m.*

snake, *n.* culebra; serpiente, *f.*

snap, *v.* chasquear; romper(se); tratar de morder; sacar una foto. *n.* cierre. *a.* repentino

snap·shot, *n.* foto, *f.*

snare, *n.* trampa

snatch, *v.,* **snatch·es.** fragmento; trocito. *v.* agarrar; arrebatar

snaz·zy, *a. inf.* a la moda
sneak, *v.* moverse a hurtadillas
sneer, *v.* mofarse. *n.* mirada de desprecio
sneeze, *v.* estornudar. *n.* estornudo
sniff, *v.* husmear; oler
snip, *v.* tijeretear. *n.* recorte
snitch, *v. inf.* robar; soplarse
snob, *n.* esnob, *m., f.*
snoop, *v. inf.* espiar. *n.* fisgón
snooze, *v. inf.* dormitar
snore, *v.* roncar. *n.* ronquido
snort, *n.* bufido
snout, *n.* hocico
snow, *n.* nieve, *f. v.* nevar
snow·ball, *n.* bola de nieve
snow·flake, *n.* copo de nieve
snow·man, *n. pl.*, **-men.** figura de nieve
snub, *v.* desairar. *n.* desaire; repulsa. *a.* chato
snuff, *n.* rapé
snug, *a.* cómodo; ajustado
snug·gle, *v.* arrimarse
so, *adv.* tan; así; de este modo. *conj.* por tanto. **so that**, de modo que
soak, *v.* absorber; remojar; empapar
soap, *n.* jabón. *v.* jabonar; enjabonar
soar, *v.* remontarse
sob, *v.* sollozar. *n.* sollozo
so·ber, *a.* sobrio; sereno; serio
so·bri·quet, sou·bri·quet, *n.* apodo
so-called, *a.* llamado; supuesto
soc·cer, *n.* fútbol, *m.*
so·cia·ble, *a.* sociable
so·cial, *a.* social. *n.* velada
so·cial·ism, *n.* socialismo
so·cial·ize, *v.* socializar
so·ci·e·ty, *n. pl.*, **-ties.** sociedad; mundo elegante
so·ci·ol·o·gy, *n.* sociología
sock, *n. pl.*, **socks, sox.** calcetín. *v. inf.* pegar
sock·et, *n.* enchufe; fosa
sod, *n.* césped
so·da, *a.* sosa; bebida no alcohólica
so·da wa·ter, *n.* agua de seltz
sod·den, *a.* empapado
so·di·um, *n.* sodio
so·di·um chlo·ride, *n.* sal, *f.*
sod·om·y, *n.* sodomía
so·fa, *n.* sofá, *m.*
soft, *a.* blando; suave; tierno
sof·ten, *v.* ablandar(se); suavizar(se); mitigar
sog·gy, *a.* empapado
soil, *n.* tierra. *v.* ensuciar; manchar
so·journ, *v.* morar
sol·ace, *v.* consolar. *n.* consuelo; solaz, *m.*
so·lar, *a.* solar
sol·der, *v.* soldar
sol·dier, *n.* soldado; militar
sole, *n.* planta; suela. *a.* solo; único

sole·ly, *adv.* solamente
sol·emn, *a.* solemne
so·lem·ni·ty, *n. pl.*, **-ties.** solemnidad; *usu. pl.* ceremonia
so·lic·it, *v.* solicitar; importunar
sol·id, *a.* sólido; macizo. *n.* sólido
so·li·dar·i·ty, *n. pl.*, **-ties.** solidaridad
so·lil·o·quy, *n. pl.*, **-quies.** soliloquio
sol·i·tar·y, *a.* solitario; solo
so·lo, *n. pl.*, **-los, -li.** solo
sol·u·ble, *a.* soluble
so·lu·tion, *n.* solución
solve, *v.* resolver
sol·vent, *a.* solvente
som·ber, *a.* sombrío
some, *a.* alguno (algún); algo de. *pron.* algunos. *adv.* aproximadamente
some·bo·dy, *pron.* alguien. *n. pl.*, **-dies.** personaje
some·day, *adv.* algún día
some·how, *adv.* de algún modo
some·one, *pron.* alguien
som·er·sault, *n.* salto mortal
some·thing, *n.* algo
some·times, *adv.* a veces
some·what, *adv.* algo; algún tanto
some·where, *adv.* en alguna parte
son, *n.* hijo
song, *n.* canción; cantar
son-in-law, *n. pl.*, **sons-in-law.** yerno
son·net, *n.* soneto
soon, *adv.* pronto
soot, *n.* hollín, *m.*
soothe, *v.* calmar
sop, *v.* empapar; absorber
soph·ist·ry, *n. pl.*, **-ries.** sofistería
soph·o·more, *n.* estudiante de segundo año
so·pra·no, *n. pl.*, **-os, -pran·i.** soprano; tiple
sor·cer·er, *n.* hechicero
sor·cer·ess, *n. fem.* hechicera
sor·cer·y, *n. pl.*, **-ies.** hechicería
sor·did, *a.* asqueroso; vil
sore, *a.* dolorido; *inf.* enojado. *n.* llaga
sor·row, *n.* pesar; dolor; aflicción
sor·ry, *a.* arrepentido; triste; vil; lastimoso
sort, *n.* especie, *f.;* género; clase, *f.;* modo. *v.* clasificar. **out of sorts**, indispuesto
so-so, *a.* mediocre. *adv.* así así
soul, *n.* alma
sound, *n.* sonido; ruido. *v.* sonar. *a.* sano; seguro; bueno
soup, *n.* sopa; caldo
sour, *a.* agrio. *v.* agriar(se)
source, *n.* origen; fuente, *f.*
south, *n.* sur. *a.* del sur. *adv.* hacia el sur
south·east, *n.* sudeste. *a.* del sudeste

south·ern, *a.* del sur; meridional

south·west, *n.* sudoeste. *a.* del sudoeste

sou·ve·nir, *n.* recuerdo

sov·er·eign, *a.* soberano. *n.* soberano; monarca, *m., f.*

sov·er·eign·ty, *n. pl.* **-ties.** soberanía

sow, *v.*, **sowed, sown** or **sowed, sow·ing.** sembrar

spa, *n.* balneario

space, *n.* espacio; sitio; lugar. *v.* espaciar

space·man, *n. pl.* **-men**, astronauta, *m., f.*

space·ship, *n.* astronave, *f.* Also **space·craft**

spa·cious, *a.* espacioso

spade, *n.* pala

spa·ghet·ti, *n.* espagueti, *m.*

span, *n.* lapso. *v.* medir; cruzar

spank, *v.* zurrar

spare, *v.* perdonar; escatimar; pasarse sin. *a.* sobrante; de repuesto; flaco

spark, *n.* chispa

spar·kle, *v.* destellar; centellear

spar·row, *n.* gorrión

sparse, *a.* poco denso

spasm, *n.* espasmo

spas·mod·ic, *a.* espasmódico

spas·tic, *a.* espástico

spat·ter, *v.* salpicar

spat·u·la, *n.* espátula

spawn, *n.* freza; huevas. *v.* desovar; frezar

speak, *v.*, **spoke, spok·en, speak·ing.** hablar; decir

speak·er, *n.* el que habla; orador

spear, *n.* lanza. *v.* alancear

spear·mint, *n.* menta verde

spe·cial, *a.* especial; particular

spe·cial·ist, *n.* especialista, *m., f.*

spe·cial·ize, *v.* especializar(se)

spe·cial·ty, *n. pl.* **-ties.** especialidad

spe·cies, *n. pl.* **spe·cies.** especie, *f.*

spe·cif·ic, *a.* específico; explícito. *n.* específico

spec·i·fi·ca·tion, *n.* especificación

spec·i·fy, *v.* especificar

spec·i·men, *n.* espécimen, *m.;* muestra

spe·cious, *a.* especioso

speck, *n.* manchita; partícula

specs, *n. pl.* gafas. Abbr. for **specifications**

spec·ta·cle, *n.* espectáculo; *pl.* gafas

spec·tac·u·lar, *a.* espectacular

spec·ta·tor, *n.* espectador

spec·ter, *n.* espectro

spec·trum, *n. pl.*, **-tra, -trums.** espectro

spec·u·late, *v.* especular; reflexionar

spec·u·la·tion, *n.* especulación

speech, *n.* palabra; discurso

speech·less, *a.* mudo

speed, *v.*, **sped** or **speed·ed, speed·ing.** acelerar; despachar; apresurarse

speed·om·e·ter, *n.* cuentakilómetros

speed·way, *n.* pista de ceniza

spell, *v.*, **spelled** or **spelt, spell·ing.** deletrear. *n.* hechizo; temporada

spell·bind, *v.*, **-bound, -bind·ing.** encantar

spell·ing, *n.* ortografía

spend, *v.*, **spent, spend·ing.** gastar (dinero); pasar

spend·thrift, *n.* pródigo

sperm, *n. pl.*, **sperm, sperms.** esperma

sperm·whale, *n.* cachalote

spew, *v.* vomitar. Also **spue**

sphere, *n.* esfera

spher·i·cal, *a.* esférico

spice, *n.* especia; picante. *v.* especiar

spic·y, *a.* picante

spi·der, *n.* araña

spike, *n.* clavo; espiga

spill, *v.*, **spilled** or **spilt, spill·ing.** derramar(se); verter(se). *n.* vuelco

spin, *v.*, **spun, spun, spin·ning.** hilar; girar. *n.* vuelta

spin·ach, *n.* espinaca

spi·nal, *a.* espinal

spin·dle, *n.* huso

spin·dle·legs, *n. pl.* zanquivano

spine, *n.* espinazo; púa

spin·ning wheel, *n.* torno de hilar

spin·ster, *n.* soltera; solterona

spi·ral, *a.* espiral, *f.;* hélice, *f.* *a.* espiral

spire, *n.* aguja; chapitel, *m.*

spir·it, *n.* espíritu, *m.;* alma; fantasma, *m.;* energía; *pl.* ánimo; *often pl.* licor

spir·it·ed, *a.* brioso

spir·it·u·al, *a.* espiritual

spir·it·u·al·ism, *n.* espiritismo

spir·it·u·al·ist, *n.* espiritista, *m., f.*

spit, *v.i.* **spit** or **spat, spit·ting.** escupir. *v. t.* **spit·ted, spit·ting.** espetar. *n.* saliva; espetón; asador

spite, *n.* despecho; rencor. *v.* causar pena o indignación. **in spite of,** a pesar de

spit·fire, *n.* fierabrás, *m.*

spit·tle, *n.* saliva

spit·toon, *n.* escupidera

splash, *v.* salpicar; chapotear. *n.* salpicadura

splat·ter, *v.* salpicar

spleen, *n.* bazo; rencor

splen·did, *a.* espléndido; grandioso; magnífico

splen·dor, *n.* esplendor

splice, *v.* empalmar. *n.* empalme; juntura

splint, *n.* tablilla

splin·ter, *n.* astilla. *v.* hacer(se) astillas

split, *v.*, **split**, **split·ting.** separarse; hender(se); dividir. *n.* hendedura; división

splurge, *n. inf.* fachenda

spoil, *v.*, **spoiled** or **spoilt**, **spoil·ing.** estropear(se); arruinar(se); echar(se) a perder. *n. often pl.* botín

spoke, *n.* rayo

spo·ken, *a.* hablado

spokes·man, *n. pl.*, **-men.** portavoz, *m.*

sponge, *n.* esponja. *v.* limpiar con esponja

spon·gy, *a.* esponjoso

spon·sor, *n.* fiador; patrocinador

spon·ta·ne·i·ty, *n. pl.*, **-ties.** espon·taneidad

spon·ta·ne·ous, *a.* espontáneo

spook, *n. inf.* fantasma, *m.;* espectro

spool, *n.* carrete; canilla

spoon, *n.* cuchara

spoon·ful, *n. pl.*, **-fuls.** cucharada

spo·rad·ic, *a.* esporádico

spore, *n.* espora

sport, *n.* deporte; diversión. *v.* divertirse

sports·man, *n. pl.*, **-men.** deportista, *m., f.;* caballero

spot, *n.* punto; mancha; sitio. *v.* manchar. *a.* hecho al azar. **on the spot**, *inf.* en el acto

spot·light, *n.* foco

spot·ted, *a.* moteado

spot·ty, *a.* manchado

spouse, *n.* esposo; esposa

spout, *n.* pitón; chorro; caño. *v.* chorrear

sprain, *v.* torcer(se). *n.* torcedura

spray, *n.* rociada. *v.* rociar

spread, *v.*, **spread**, **spread·ing.** extender(se); diseminar. *n.* extensión; colcha

spree, *n.* juerga; borrachera

sprig, *n.* ramita

spright·ly, *a.* animado

spring, *v.*, **sprang** or **sprung**, **sprung**, **spring·ing.** saltar; nacer. *n.* muelle; fuente, *f.;* primavera. *a.* primaveral

spring·time, *n.* primavera

sprin·kle, *v.* rociar; lloviznar

sprout, *v.* brotar; retoñar. *n.* retoño

spruce, *n.* picea. *a.* apuesto

spry, *a.* ágil; vivo

spue, *v.* vomitar

spume, *n.* espuma

spunk, *n. inf.* valor

spur, *n.* espuela; estímulo. *v.* incitar

spu·ri·ous, *a.* falso; espurio

spurt, *n.* chorro; esfuerzo supremo

sput·ter, *v.* chisporrotear

spy, *n. pl.*, **spies.** espía, *m., f. v.* **spied**, **spy·ing.** espiar; observar

spy·glass, *n.* catalejo

squab·ble, *v.* disputar. *n.* riña

squad, *n.* escuadra; pelotón

squad·ron, *n.* escuadrilla; escuadrón

squal·id, *a.* desaliñado; asqueroso

squall, *n.* ráfaga

squal·or, *n.* miseria e inmundancia

squan·der, *v.* malgastar; desperdiciar

square, *n.* cuadrado. *a.* cuadrado; justo; *inf.* anticuado. *v.* cuadrar

squash, *v.* aplastar(se). *n. pl.*, **squash·es.** calabaza

squash·y, *a.* blando

squat, *v.*, **squat·ted** or **squat**, **squat·ting.** agacharse. *a.* rechoncho

squat·ter, *n.* intruso

squawk, *v.* graznar; *inf.* quejarse. *n.* graznido

squeak, *v.* chillar; chirriar. *n.* chirrido

squeal, *n.* grito agudo. *v.* chillar; *inf.* cantar

squeam·ish, *a.* delicado; remilgado

squeeze, *v.* exprimir; apretar. *n.* estrujón

squid, *n. pl.*, **squids.** calamar

squint, *v.* bizquear; mirar de soslayo. *n.* estrabismo

squirm, *v.* retorcerse

stab, *v.* apuñalar. *n.* puñalada

sta·bil·i·ty, *n. pl.*, **-ties.** estabilidad

sta·ble, *n.* establo; cuadra. *a.* estable

stack, *n.* rimero; niara; cañón de chimenea. *v.* amontonar

sta·di·um, *n. pl.*, **-di·ums**, **-di·a.** estadio

staff, *n. pl.*, **staves**, **staffs.** palo; asta; personal, *m.*

stag, *n.* ciervo; venado; *inf.* para hombres solos

stage, *n.* etapa; escena. *v.* representar

stage·coach, *n.* diligencia

stag·ger, *v.* tambalear; escalonar

stag·nant, *a.* estancado

stag·nate, *v.* estancarse

staid, *a.* serio

stain, *v.* manchar; teñir. *n.* mancha; deshonra

stair, *n.* escalón; peldaño; *pl.* escalera

stair·case, *n.* escalera

stair·way, *n.* escalera

stake, *n.* estaca; apuesta. *v.* estacar; aventurar

sta·lac·tite, *n.* estalactita

sta·lag·mite, *n.* estalagmita

stalk, *n.* tallo. *v.* cazar al acecho; andar con paso majestuoso

stall, *n.* casilla de establo; puesto. *v.* pararse

stal·lion, *n.* caballo padre

stal·wart, *a.* fornido; leal

sta·men, *n. pl.*, **-mens**, **stam·i·na.** es·

tambre

stam·i·na, n. resistencia; fuerza vital

stam·mer, v. tartamudear

stamp, v. estampar; sellar; patear. n. sello

stam·pede, n. estampida

stanch, v. restañar. Also staunch

stand, v., stood, stand·ing. estar de pie; colocar; resistir; tolerar. v. resistencia; puesto; sostén

stand·ard, n. norma; nivel, m.; estandarte. a. normal

stand·ard·ize, v. uniformar

stand·by, n. pl., -bys. persona o artículo digno de confianza

stand·ing, n. posición; duración. a. derecho

stand·point, n. punto de vista

stand·still, n. parada

stan·za, n. estancia; estrofa

sta·ple, n. grapa; producto principal. a. corriente

sta·pler, n. grabadora

star, v., starred, star·ring. presentar como estrella. n. estrella; astro

star·board, n. estribor. a. de estribor

starch, n. fécula; almidón

stare, v. clavar la vista; mirar fijamente. n. mirada fija

star·fish, n. pl., -fish, -fish·es. estrella de mar

star·gaze, v. fig. soñar despierto

stark, a. completo; rígido. adv. en cueros

star·less, a. sin estrellas

star·ry, a. estrellado

start, v. empezar; comenzar; poner(se) en marcha; sobresaltarse. n. sobresalto; comienzo

star·tle, v. asustar; alarmar

star·tling, a. alarmante

star·va·tion, n. hambre, f. a. de hambre

starve, v. morir de hambre; pasar hambre

stash, v. inf. ocultar

state, n. condición; estado. a. de estado. v. exponer; decir

state·craft, n. arte de gobernar

stat·ed, a. establecido; fijo

state·ly, a. majestuoso; elevado

state·ment, n. declaración; estado de cuenta

states·man, n. pl., -men. estadista, m.

stat·ic, a. fijo; estático. n. parásitos

sta·tion, n. puesto; estación. v. situar

sta·tion·ar·y, a. inmóvil

sta·tion·er·y, n. papelería

sta·tis·tic, n. estadístico

sta·tis·ti·cian, n. estadístico

sta·tis·tics, n. pl. estadística

stat·ue, n. estatua

stat·ure, n. estatura

sta·tus, n. estado; posición; prestigio

stat·ute, n. estatuto

staunch, a. firme; fiel. v. restañar. Also stanch

stave, n. duela; estrofa. v., staved or stove, stav·ing. quebrar

stay, v., stayed or staid, stay·ing. quedar(se); sostener; parar. n. estancia

stead, n. lugar

stead·fast, sted·fast, a. firme; constante

stead·fast·ness, n. resolución

stead·y, a. firme; constante; uniforme. v. estabilizar

steak, n. filete

steal, v., stole, stol·en, steal·ing. robar; hurtar. n. inf. ganga

stealth, n. cautela

steam, n. vapor. v. empañar

steam·boat, n. buque de vapor

steam·er, n. buque de vapor

steam·roll·er, n. apisonadora

steam·ship, n. vapor

steam·y, a. vaporoso

steed, n. corcel, m.

steel, n. acero. a. de acero; duro. v. acerar

steep, a. empinado; inf. excesivo. v. saturar

stee·ple, n. campanario

steer, v. guiar; gobernar; conducir. n. novillo

steer·age, n. entrepuente

stel·lar, a. estelar

stem, n. tallo; pie. v. proceder de; represar

stench, n. hedor; tufo

sten·cil, n. estarcido. v. estarcir

ste·nog·ra·pher, n. taquígrafo

ste·nog·ra·phy, n. taquigrafía

sten·to·ri·an, a. estentóreo

step, n. paso; escalera. v. pisar

step·broth·er, n. hermanastro

step·child, n. pl., -child·ren. hijastro; hijastra

step·daugh·ter, n. hijastra

step·fa·ther, n. padrastro

step·lad·der, n. escalera de tijera

step·moth·er, n. madrastra

step·par·ent, n. padrastro; madrastra

steppe, n. estepa

step·sis·ter, n. hermanastra

step·son, n. hijastro

ster·e·o·phon·ic, a. estereofónico

ster·e·o·typed, a. estereotipado

ster·ile, a. estéril

ste·ril·i·ty, n. esterilidad

ster·i·li·za·tion, n. esterilización

ster·i·lize, v. esterilizar

ster·ling, a. esterlina

stern, a. austero; duro. n. popa

stern·ness, n. severidad

ster·num, n. pl. -na, -nums. esternón

steth·o·scope, *n.* estetoscopio

ste·ve·dore, *n.* estibador

stew, *n.* estofado. *v.* estofar

ste·ward, *n.* administrador; camarero

stew·ard·ess, *n. f.* azafata

stick, *n.* palo. *v.,* **stuck, stick·ing.** picar; pegar; clavar

stick·er, *n.* marbete engomado

stick·ler, *n.* rigorista, *m., f.*

stick-up, stick·up, *n. inf.* atraco

stick·y, *a.* viscoso

stiff, *a.* duro; rígido; estirado. *n. inf.* cadáver

stif·fen, *v.* atiesar(se)

sti·fle, *v.* ahogar(se); ocultar

sti·fling, *a.* sofocante

stig·ma, *n. pl.* **-mas, -ma·ta.** estigma, *m.*

sti·let·to, *n. pl.* **-tos, -toes.** estilete

still, *a.* inmóvil; tranquilo. *v.* aquietar. *n.* alambique. *adv.* todavía; sin embargo

still·ness, *n.* quietud

stilt, *n.* zanco

stilt·ed, *a.* hinchado

stim·u·lant, *n.* estimulante

stim·u·late, *v.* estimular

stim·u·la·tion, *n.* estímulo

stim·u·lus, *n. pl.* **-li.** estímulo; estimulante

sting, *v.,* **stung, sting·ing.** picar. *n.* picadura; aguijón

stin·gy, *a.* tacaño; escaso

stink, *v.,* **stank or stunk, stunk, stink·ing.** heder. *n.* hedor

stint, *v.* limitar; restringir. *n.* tarea

sti·pend, *n.* estipendio

stip·u·late, *v.* estipular; especificar

stip·u·la·tion, *n.* estipulación

stir, *v.* agitar; excitar. *n.* conmoción; interés, *m.*

stir·ring, *a.* conmovedor

stir·rup, *n.* estribo

stitch, *v.* coser. *n.* puntada; punto

stock, *n.* valores; acciones; surtido; ganado; caldo. *v.* surtir

stock·ade, *n.* estacada; palizada

stock·brok·er, *n.* bolsista, *m.*

stock·hold·er, *n.* accionista, *m., f.*

stock·ing, *n.* media

stock·pile, *n.* acumular

stock·y, *a.* rechoncho

stod·gy, *a.* pesado

sto·ic, *n.* estoico

sto·i·cal, *a.* estoico

stoke, *v.* echar carbón

stol·id, *a.* impasible

stom·ach, *n.* estómago. *v. inf.* aguantar

stone, *n.* piedra. *v.* apedrear; deshuesar

stone-deaf, *a.* completamente sordo

ston·y, ston·ey, *a.* pedregoso; empedernido

stool, *n.* taburete

stoop, *v.* inclinarse; rebajarse. *n.* cargazón de espaldas

stop, *v.* parar(se); terminar; suspender; tapar. *n.* parada

stop·gap, *n.* tapagujeros

stop·light, *n.* semáforo

stop·page, *n.* cesación

stop·per, *n.* tapón

stor·age, *n.* almacenaje

store, *n.* tienda; almacén; repuesto. *v.* tener en reserva

store·house, *n.* almacén

sto·ried, sto·reyed, *a.* de (el número de) pisos

stork, *n.* cigüeña

storm, *n.* tormenta; tempestad. *v.* asaltar

storm·y, *a.* tempestuoso

sto·ry, *n. pl.,* **-ries.** historia; cuento; piso; *inf.* embuste

sto·ry·tell·er, *n.* cuentista, *m., f.; inf.* embustero

stout, *a.* corpulento; resuelto

stove, *n.* cocina; estufa

stow, *v.* estibar; colocar

stow·age, *n.* estiba

stow·a·way, *n.* polizón

strad·dle, *v.* montar a horcajadas

strag·gle, *v.* extraviarse; rezagarse

strag·gler, *n.* rezagado

strag·gly, *a.* desordenado

straight, *a.* recto; directo; honrado. *adv.* directamente

straight·en, *v.* enderezar

straight·for·ward, *a.* honrado; derecho

straight·way, *adv.* en seguida

strain, *n.* linaje; vena; tensión. *v.* forzar; estirar; filtrar; torcer

strain·er, *n.* colador

strait, *n.* estrecho; *often pl.* apuro

strand, *n.* hebra; ramal, *m. v.* quedarse colgado

strange, *a.* desconocido; raro; extraño

stran·ger, *n.* forastero; desconocido

stran·gu·la·tion, *n.* estrangulación

stran·gle, *v.* estrangular

stran·gler, *n.* estrangulador

strap, *n.* correa; tirante

strap·less, *a.* sin tirantes

strap·ping, *a. inf.* robusto

strat·a·gem, *n.* estratagema

stra·te·gic, *a.* estratégico

strat·e·gist, *n.* estratega, *m.*

strat·e·gy, *n. pl.,* **-gies.** estrategia

strat·i·fi·ca·tion, *n.* estratificación

strat·i·fy, *v.* estratificar

strat·o·sphere, *n.* estratosfera

stra·tum, *n. pl.* **-ta, -tums.** estrato; capa

straw, *n.* paja; pajilla. *a.* de paja

straw·ber·ry, *n. pl.,* **-ries.** fresa

stray, *v.* vagar; extraviarse. *a.* extraviado

streak, *n.* raya. *v.* rayar; listar

stream, *n.* arroyo; corriente, *f.;* torrente. *v.* correr

stream·er, *n.* flámula

street, *n.* calle, *f.*

street·car, *n.* tranvía, *m.*

strength, *n.* fuerza; poder; resistencia; vigor

strength·en, *v.* fortalecer(se); hacer(se) más fuerte

stren·u·ous, *a.* enérgico; arduo

stress, *n.* tensión; compulsión; énfasis, *m.;* acento. *v.* dar énfasis

stretch, *v.* extender(se); estirar. *n.* extensión

stretch·er, *n.* camilla

strew, *v.,* **strewed, strewed** or **strewn, strew·ing.** derramar

strick·en, *a.* afligido; herido

strict, *a.* estricto; severo; riguroso

strict·ness, *n.* rigor

stric·ture, *n.* crítica; censura

stride, *v.,* **strode, strid·den, strid·ing.** andar a pasos largos. *n.* zancada

stri·dent, *a.* estridente

strife, *n.* contienda; lucha

strike, *v.,* **struck, struck** or **strick·en, strik·ing.** golpear; pegar; atacar; encender; declararse en huelga. *n.* huelga

strik·ing, *a.* impresionante

string, *n.* cordel, *m.;* bramante; serie, *f. v.,* **strung, strung** or **stringed, string·ing.** encordar; ensartar

strin·gent, *a.* riguroso

string·y, *a.* fibroso

strip, *v.* despojar(se); desnudar(se). *n.* tira

stripe, *n.* banda; raya. *v.* rayar

striped, *a.* rayado

strip·ling, *n.* mozuelo

strive, *v.,* **strove, striv·en, striv·ing.** esforzarse; contender

stroke, *n.* golpe; ataque fulminante; plumada. *v.* acariciar

stroll, *v.* pasear(se); vagar. *n.* paseo

strong, *a.* fuerte; intenso; robusto; firme

strong·hold, *n.* plaza fuerte

strong-mind·ed, *a.* resuelto; independiente

strop, *n.* suavizador

struc·tur·al, *a.* estructural

struc·ture, *n.* estructura; construcción. *v.* construir

strug·gle, *v.* luchar. *n.* esfuerzo; contienda

strum, *v.* rasguear

strum·pet, *n.* ramera

strut, *v.* contonearse; pavonearse. *n.* tornapunta

strych·nine, *n.* estricnina

stub, *n.* cabo; fragmento. *v.* dar un tropezón

stub·ble, *n.* rastrojo; barba

stub·born, *a.* obstinado; inquebrantable

stub·born·ness, *n.* terquedad; porfía

stuc·co, *n. pl.,* **-coes, -cos.** estuco

stud, *n.* yeguada; tachón; botón

stu·dent, *n.* estudiante; alumno

stud·ied, *a.* premeditado

stu·di·o, *n. pl.,* **-os.** estudio; taller

stu·di·ous, *a.* estudioso

stud·y, *n. pl.,* **-ies.** estudio. *v.* estudiar

stuff, *n.* material, *m.;* cosas. *v.* hinchar; rellenar; llenar

stuff·ing, *n.* relleno

stuff·y, *a.* mal ventilado

stum·ble, *v.* tropezar. *n.* traspié; tropezón

stump, *n.* muñón; tocón. *v. inf.* dejar perplejo

stun, *v.* aturdir

stun·ning, *a.* impresionante; estupendo

stunt, *v.* impedir el desarrollo. *n.* proeza

stu·pe·fac·tion, *n.* estupefacción; aturdimiento

stu·pe·fy, *v.* causar estupor

stu·pen·dous, *a.* estupendo

stu·pid, *a.* estúpido; tonto; necio

stu·pid·i·ty, *n.* estupidez, *f.*

stu·por, *n.* estupor

stur·dy, *a.* fuerte; firme; vigoroso

stur·geon, *n. pl.,* **-geon, -geons.** esturión

stut·ter, *v.* balbucear; tartamudear. *n.* tartamudeo

sty, *n. pl.,* **sties.** pocilgo; *(med.)* orzuelo

style, *n.* estilo; manera; modo. *v.* intitular

styl·ish, *a.* a la moda

sty·mie, *v.* dejar perplejo

styp·tic, *a.* estíptico

suave, *a.* cortés; urbano

sub, *n. inf.* submarino

sub·con·scious, *a.* subconsciente. *n.* subconsciencia

sub·cu·ta·ne·ous, *a.* subcutáneo

sub·di·vide, *v.* subdividir

sub·di·vi·sion, *n.* subdivisión

sub·due, *v.* subyugar; suavizar

sub·head·ing, *n.* subtítulo

sub·ject, *n.* sujeto; súbdito. *a.* sujeto; propenso. *v.* someter

sub·jec·tion, *n.* sujeción

sub·jec·tive, *a.* subjetivo

sub·jec·tiv·i·ty, *n.* subjetividad

sub·join, *v.* adjuntar

sub·ju·gate, *v.* subyugar; sojuzgar

sub·ju·ga·tion, *n.* subyugación; sojuzgación

sub·lease, v. subarrendar
sub·let, v. subarrendar
sub·li·mate, v. sublimar
sub·li·ma·tion, n. sublimación
sub·lime, a. sublime
sub·lim·i·ty, n. pl. **-ties.** sublimidad
sub·ma·rine, a. submarino
sub·merge, v. sumergir(se)
sub·mer·gence, n. sumersión
sub·merse, v. sumergir(se)
sub·mer·sion, n. sumersión
sub·mis·sion, n. sumisión; resignación
sub·mis·sive, a. sumiso
sub·mit, v. someter(se); presentar
sub·nor·mal, a. anormal
sub·or·di·nate, a. subordinado; secundario; dependiente. v. subordinar
sub·or·di·na·tion, n. subordinación
sub·poe·na, sub·pe·na, n. citación; comparendo
sub·scribe, v. subscribir(se); firmar
sub·scrip·tion, n. subscripción
sub·se·quent, a. subsiguiente
sub·ser·vi·ent, a. servil
sub·side, v. bajar; calmarse
sub·sid·i·ar·y, a. subsidiario
sub·si·dize, v. subvencionar
sub·si·dy, n. pl. **-dies.** subvención; subsidio
sub·sist, v. subsistir; existir
sub·sis·tence, n. subsistencia
sub·stance, n. substancia; materia; esencia
sub·stan·tial, a. substancial
sub·stan·ti·ate, v. comprobar
sub·stan·ti·a·tion, n. comprobación; justificación
sub·stan·tive, n. substantivo. a. substantivo
sub·sti·tute, v. substituir. n. substituto
sub·sti·tu·tion, n. substitución; reemplazo
sub·ter·fuge, n. subterfugio
sub·ter·ra·ne·an, a. subterráneo
sub·ti·tle, n. subtítulo
sub·tle, a. sutil; ingenioso; delicado; astuto
sub·tle·ty, n. sutileza
sub·tract, v. substraer
sub·trac·tion, n. substracción; resta
sub·urb, n. often pl. suburbio
sub·ur·ban, a. suburbano
sub·ver·sion, n. subversión
sub·ver·sive, a. subversivo
sub·vert, v. subvertir
sub·way, n. metro
suc·ceed, v. tener éxito; lograr; suceder
suc·cess, n. éxito
suc·cess·ful, a. próspero; afortunado
suc·ces·sion, n. sucesión

suc·ces·sor, n. sucesor
suc·cinct, a. sucinto
suc·cor, n. socorro; auxilio. v. socorrer
suc·cu·lent, a. suculento
suc·cumb, v. sucumbir; morir
such, a. tal; parecido. pron. tal; los que. adv. tan
suck, v. chupar; mamar
suck·er, n. piruli, m.
suck·le, v. lactar; amamantar
suc·tion, n. succión
sud·den, a. imprevisto; repentino; súbito
sud·den·ly, adv. de repente
suds, n. pl. jabonaduras
sue, v. demandar
su·et, n. sebo
suf·fer, v. sufrir; padecer; tolerar
suf·fer·ance, n. tolerancia
suf·fice, v. bastar
suf·fi·cien·cy, n. pl. **-cies.** suficiencia
suf·fi·cient, a. suficiente
suf·fix, n. sufijo
suf·fo·cate, v. sofocar; asfixiar
suf·fo·ca·tion, n. sofocación
suf·frage, n. sufragio
suf·fuse, v. extender; bañar
suf·fu·sion, n. difusión
sug·ar, n. azúcar
sug·ar·y, a. azucarado; almibarado
sug·gest, v. sugerir; indicar; insinuar
sug·ges·tion, n. indicación; sugestión
sug·ges·tive, a. sugestivo
su·i·cide, n. suicida, m., f.; suicidio
suit, n. traje; pleito; (cards) palo. v. acomodar; ir bien
suit·a·ble, a. apropiado
suit·case, n. maleta
suite, n. juego; serie, f.
suit·or, n. pretendiente
sul·fur, sul·phur, n. azufre
sul·fu·ric ac·id, n. ácido sulfúrico
sulk, v. estar de mal humor
sulk·y, a. mohino
sul·len, a. hosco
sul·ly, v. manchar
sul·tan, n. sultán
sul·tan·ate, n. sultanato
sul·try, a. bochornoso
sum, n. suma; cantidad. v. sumar
su·mac, su·mach, n. zumaque
sum·ma·rize, v. resumir
sum·ma·ry, n. pl. **-ries.** resumen. a. sumario
sum·mer, n. verano. a. veraniego; de verano
sum·mit, n. cima; cumbre, f.
sum·mon, v. citar; llamar; convocar
sum·mons, n. pl. **sum·mons·es.** citación
sump·tu·ous, a. suntuoso
sun, n. sol. m. v. tomar el sol

sun·bathe, v. tomar el sol
sun·dae, n. helado con fruta, jarabe, nueces, *etc.*
Sun·day, n. domingo
sun·der, v. hender
sun·down, n. puesta del sol
sun·dries, n. pl. géneros diversos
sun·dry, a. diversos; varios
sun·flow·er, n. girasol, m.
sun·glass·es, n. pl. gafas de sol
sunk·en, a. hundido
sun·light, n. luz del sol
sun·ny, a. expuesto al sol; alegre
sun·rise, n. salida del sol
sun·set, n. ocaso; puesta del sol
sun·shine, n. luz del sol
sun·stroke, n. insolación
sup, v. cenar
su·per·an·nu·ate, v. jubilar
su·perb, a. magnífico; grandioso
su·per·cil·i·ous, a. desdeñoso; arrogante; imperioso
su·per·fi·cial, a. superficial
su·per·flu·i·ty, n. pl., **-ties.** superfluidad
su·per·flu·ous, a. superfluo
su·per·high·way, n. autopista
su·per·hu·man, a. sobrehumano
su·per·im·pose, v. sobreponer
su·per·in·tend, v. dirigir; superentender
su·per·in·tend·ent, n. superintendente, m., f.
su·pe·ri·or, a. superior. n. superior
su·pe·ri·or·i·ty, n. superioridad
su·per·la·tive, a. superlativo. n. superlativo
su·per·mar·ket, n. supermercado
su·per·nat·u·ral, a. sobrenatural
su·per·nu·mer·ar·y, n. pl., **-ies.** supernumerario; comparsa, m., f.
su·per·scrip·tion, n. sobrescrito
su·per·sede, v. suplantar
su·per·son·ic, a. supersónico
su·per·sti·tion, n. superstición
su·per·sti·tious, a. supersticioso
su·per·vise, v. superentender; supervisar
su·per·vi·sor, n. superintendente, m., f.; supervisor, m., f.
su·pine, a. supino
sup·per, n. cena
sup·plant, v. suplantar
sup·ple, a. flexible; blando
sup·ple·ment, n. suplemento. v. suplir
sup·ple·men·ta·ry, a. suplementario
sup·pli·cant, n. suplicante, m., f.
sup·pli·cate, v. suplicar
sup·pli·ca·tion, n. súplica
sup·ply, v. proveer; suministrar; proporcionar. n. pl., **-plies.** provisión
sup·port, v. apoyar; sostener; aguantar; mantener. n. apoyo; sostén

sup·port·er, n. defensor
sup·pose, v. suponer; imaginar
sup·po·si·tion, n. suposición
sup·press, v. suprimir; contener
sup·pres·sion, n. supresión
sup·pu·rate, v. supurar
sup·pu·ra·tion, n. supuración
su·prem·a·cy, n. pl., **-cies.** supremacía
su·preme, a. supremo; sumo
sur·charge, n. sobrecarga
sure, a. seguro; cierto
sure·ly, adv. seguramente
sure·ty, n. pl., **-ties.** garantía; garante
surf, n. oleaje
sur·face, n. superficie, f. v. salir a la superficie
sur·feit, n. exceso; empacho. v. hartar(se)
surge, v. agitarse
sur·geon, n. cirujano
sur·ger·y, n. pl., **-ies.** cirugía
sur·gi·cal, a. quirúrgico
sur·ly, a. áspero; hosco; agrio
sur·mise, n. conjetura. v. conjeturar
sur·mount, v. superar
sur·name, n. apellido
sur·pass, v. exceder; superar
sur·plus, n. excedente
sur·prise, n. sorpresa. v. sorprender
sur·pris·ing, a. sorprendente
sur·ren·der, v. rendir(se); renunciar a. n. rendición
sur·ro·gate, n. substituto
sur·round, v. rodear; cercar; sitiar
sur·veil·lance, n. vigilancia
sur·vey, v. inspeccionar; medir. n. inspección; apeo
sur·vey·or, n. agrimensor
sur·viv·al, n. supervivencia
sur·vive, v. sobrevivir
sur·vi·vor, n. sobreviviente, m., f.
sus·cep·ti·bil·i·ty, n. pl., **-ties.** susceptibilidad
sus·cep·ti·ble, a. susceptible; impresionable
sus·pect, v. sospechar. n. sospechoso. a. sospechoso
sus·pend, v. colgar; suspender
sus·pense, n. incertidumbre, f.
sus·pen·sion, n. suspensión
sus·pi·cion, n. sospecha; sombra
sus·pi·cious, a. sospechoso
sus·tain, v. sostener; sufrir; sustentar
sus·te·nance, n. sustento
svelte, a. esbelto
swab, n. torunda. v. limpiar
swad·dle, v. empañar
swag·ger, v. pavonearse; fanfarronear
swal·low, n. golondrina. v. tragar
swamp, n. pantano; ciénaga. v. inundar
swamp·y, a. pantanoso

swan, *n.* cisne

swap, *v. inf.* cambiar

swarm, *n.* enjambre. *v.* enjambrar; pulular

swarth·y, *a.* atezado

swash·buck·ler, *n.* espadachín

swat, *v.* matar

sway, *v.* bambolearse; inclinar. *n.* influencia

swear, *v.,* **swore, sworn, swear·ing.** jurar; blasfemar

swear·word, *n.* palabrota

sweat, *v.,* **sweat** or **sweat·ed, sweat·ing.** sudar. *n.* sudor

sweat·er, *n.* jersey, *m.;* suéter

sweat·y, *a.* sudoroso

sweep, *v.,* **swept, sweep·ing.** barrer. *n.* extensión

sweet, *a.* dulce. *n. pl.* dulces; bombones

sweet·en, *v.* azucarar; endulzar

sweet·heart, *n.* querida; novia

sweet·meat, *n. often pl.* dulce

swell, *v.,* **swelled, swelled** or **swoll·en, swell·ing.** hinchar(se)

swel·ter, *v.* sofocarse

swerve, *v.* torcer(se); desviar(se)

swift, *a.* veloz

swift·ness, *n.* prontitud

swig, *v.* beber a grandes tragos

swill, *n.* bazofia

swim, *v.,* **swam, swum, swim·ming.** nadar. *n.* natación

swim·mer, *n.* nadador

swin·dle, *v.* estafar. *n.* estafa

swin·dler, *n.* estafador

swine, *n. pl.,* **swine.** puerco

swing, *v.,* **swung, swing·ing.** columpiar(se); balancear(se). *n.* oscilación; columpio

swirl, *v.* arremolinar(se). *n.* remolino

swish, *v.* crujir

switch, *n.* cambio; desviación. *v.* cambiar; (*elect.*) conectar

switch·board, *n.* cuadro de distribución

swiv·el, *v.* girar

swoon, *v.* desmayarse. *n.* desmayo

swoop, *v.* calarse

sword, *n.* espada

sword·play, *n.* maneja de la espada

swords·man, *n. pl.,* **-men.** espadachín

syc·a·more, *n.* sicomoro

syc·o·phant, *n.* adulador

syl·lab·i·cate, *v.* silabear

syl·lab·i·ca·tion, *n.* silabeo

syl·lab·i·fi·ca·tion, *n.* silabeo

syl·lab·i·fy, *v.* silabear

syl·la·ble, *n.* sílaba

syl·la·bus, *n. pl.,* **-bus·es, -bi.** resumen; programa, *m.*

syl·van, sil·van, *a.* silvestre

sym·bol, *n.* símbolo

sym·bol·ic, *a.* simbólico

sym·bol·ism, *n.* simbolismo

sym·bol·ize, *v.* simbolizar

sym·me·try, *n. pl.,* **-tries.** simetría

sym·pa·thet·ic, *a.* compasivo; simpático

sym·pa·thy, *n. pl.,* **-thies.** simpatía; compasión

sym·pho·ny, *n., pl.,* **-nies.** sinfonía

symp·tom, *n.* síntoma, *m.;* indicio

syn·a·gogue, *n.* sinagoga

syn·chro·nize, *v.* sincronizar(se)

syn·di·cate, *n.* sindicato. *v.* sindicar

syn·od, *n.* sínodo

syn·o·nym, *n.* sinónimo

syn·on·y·mous, *a.* sinónimo

syn·op·sis, *n. pl.,* **-ses.** sinopsis, *f.*

syn·the·sis, *n. pl.,* **-ses.** síntesis, *f.*

syn·thet·ic, *a.* sintético

syph·i·lis, *n.* sífilis, *f.*

sy·ringe, *n.* jeringa

syr·up, sir·up, *n.* jarabe; almíbar

sys·tem, *n.* sistema, *m.;* método

sys·tem·at·ic, *a.* sistemático

sys·tem·a·tize, *v.* sistematizar

T

tab, *n.* oreja; cuenta

tab·er·nac·le, *n.* tabernáculo

ta·ble, *n.* mesa; tabla

ta·ble·spoon, *n.* cuchara grande o de sopa

ta·ble·spoon·ful, *n. pl.,* **-fuls.** cucharada

tab·let, *n.* taco; tableta

ta·boo, ta·bu, *a.* tabú. *n.* tabú, *m.*

tab·u·lar, *a.* tabular

tab·u·late, *v.* tabular

tac·it, *a.* tácito

tac·i·turn, *a.* taciturno

tack, *n.* tachuela; virada. *v.* hilvanar; añadir

tack·le, *n.* equipo; carga. *v.* abordar; agarrar

tact, *n.* tacto

tac·tics, *n. pl.* táctica

tad·pole, *n.* renacuajo

taf·fe·ta, *n.* tafetán

taf·fy, *n.* caramelo

tag, *n.* etiqueta; marbete

tail, *n.* cola; rabo; *pl. inf.* cruz de una moneda. *v. inf.* pisar los talones

tai·lor, *n.* sastre

taint, *v.* inficionar(se); corromper(se). *n.* mancha

take, *v.,* **took, tak·en, tak·ing.** tomar; coger; aceptar; asumir; sacar. **take af·ter,** parecerse a. **take back,** retractar. **take in,** admitir; comprender. **take o·ver,** encargarse de. **take up,** acortar

take·off, *n.* despegue

tal·cum pow·der, *n.* polvo de talco

tale, *n.* cuenta

tal·ent, n. talento

tal·ent·ed, a. talentoso

tal·is·man, n. talismán, m.

talk, v. hablar; decir; charlar. n. conversación; charla

talk·a·tive, a. hablador

tall, a. alto

tal·low, n. sebo

tal·ly, n. pl., -lies. cuenta. v. concordar; cuadrar

tal·on, n. garra

tam·bou·rine, n. pandereta

tame, a. domesticado; manso; soso. v. domar

tam·per, v. estropear; falsificar

tan, v. curtir; tostar. n. color de canela; bronceado

tan·dem, adv. en tándem

tang, n. sabor fuerte

tan·gent, a. tangente. n. tangente, f.

tan·ge·rine, n. naranja mandarina o tangerina

tan·gi·ble, a. tangible

tan·gle, v. enredar(se)

tan·go, n. pl., -gos. tango

tank, n. tanque; aljibe

tan·ta·lize, v. atormentar

tan·ta·mount, a. equivalente

tan·trum, n. rabieta; berrinche

tap, n. grifo; golpecito. v. sangrar; golpear ligeramente

tape, n. cinta. v. grabar en cinta

ta·per, v. afilar. n. bujía; cirio

tap·es·try, n. pl., -tries. tapiz, m.

tape·worm, n. tenia

tap·i·o·ca, n. tapioca

ta·pir, n. tapir

tar, v. alquitranar; embrear. n. alquitrán; brea

ta·ran·tu·la, n. tarántula

tar·dy, a. tardío

tar·get, n. blanco

tar·iff, n. tarifa; arancel, m.

tar·nish, v. deslustrar(se); empañar. n. deslustre

tar·ry, v. tardar; detenerse

tart, a. ácido. n. tarta

tar·tar, n. tártaro

task, n. tarea; labor, f.; encargo

task·mas·ter, n. capataz, m.

tas·sel, n. borla

taste, v. saborear; probar. n. sabor; sorbo; gusto

tast·y, a. apetitoso; sabroso

tat·ter, n. andrajo; pl. jirones; andrajos

tat·tered, a. harapiento; andrajoso

tat·too, n. pl. -toos. tatuaje. v. tatuar

taunt, v. mofa; sarcasmo; escarnio. v. mofarse de

taut, a. tieso; tirante

tav·ern, n. taberna

taw·dry, a. charro

taw·ny, a. leonado

tax, n. impuesto; contribución; carga. v. imponer contribuciones; abrumar

tax·i, n. pl., -is, -ies. taxi, m. v., -ied, -i·ing or -y·ing. ir en taxi; rodar por suelo

tax·i·cab, n. taxi, m.

tea, n. té

tea·bag, n. sobre de té; muñeca de té

teach, v., taught, teach·ing. enseñar; instruir

teach·er, n. profesor(a); maestro; preceptor

tea·cup, n. taza para té

tea·ket·tle, n. tetera

team, n. equipo; yunta; tronco

team·mate, n. compañero de equipo

team·ster, n. camionero; camionista, m.

team·work, n. cooperación

tea·pot, n. tetera

tear, n. lágrima

tear, v., tore, torn, tear·ing. romper(se); rasgar(se); desgarrar. n. rasgón

tease, v. tomar el pelo; atormentar; jorobar. n. guasón

tea·spoon, n. cucharilla; cucharita

tea·spoon·ful, n. pl., -fuls. cucharadita

teat, n. pezón; teta

tech·ni·cal, a. técnico

tech·ni·cal·i·ty, n. pl., -ties. detalle técnico

tech·ni·cian, n. técnico

tech·nique, n. técnica

tech·nol·o·gy, n. tecnología

te·di·ous, a. tedioso; aburrido

te·di·um, n. tedio

teem, v. hormiguear; abundar; hervir de

teen·ag·er, n. joven de 13 a 19 años de edad; adolescente, m., f.

teens, n. pl. años o edad de 13 a 19 años

tee·ter, v. balancear(se)

teethe, v. echar los dientes

tel·e·cast, n. teledifusión. v. teledifundir

tel·e·gram, n. telegrama, m.

tel·e·graph, v. telegrafiar. n. telégrafo

te·leg·ra·phy, n. telegrafía

tel·e·pa·thy, n. telepatía

tel·e·phone, v. llamar por teléfono; telefonear. n. teléfono

tel·e·scope, n. telescopio

tel·e·scop·ic, a. telescópico

tel·e·vise, v. televisar

tel·e·vi·sion, n. televisión

tell, v., told, tell·ing. contar; decir; determinar; mandar

tell·er, n. cajero

tell·tale, a. indicador

tem·per, v. templar; moderar. n.

genio; mal genio
tem·per·a·ment, n. temperamento; disposición
tem·per·a·ment·al, a. temperamental; caprichoso
tem·per·ance, n. templanza
tem·per·ate, a. templado
tem·per·a·ture, n. temperatura; fiebre, f.
tem·pest, n. tempestad
tem·pes·tu·ous, a. tempestuoso
tem·ple, n. templo; sien, f.
tem·po, n. pl. -pos, -pi tiempo
tem·po·ral, a. temporal
tem·po·rar·y, a. temporáneo; interino; provisional
tempt, v. tentar
temp·ta·tion, n. tentación
ten, n. diez. a. diez
te·na·cious, a. tenaz
ten·ant, n. inquilino; arrendatario; morador
tend, v. tener tendencia; tender; atender
ten·den·cy, n. tendencia
ten·der, a. tierno; afectuoso; delicado. n. oferta. v. ofrecer
ten·der·ly, adv. tiernamente
ten·don, n. tendón
ten·dril, n. zarcillo
ten·e·ment, n. casa de vecindad
ten·et, n. dogma, m.
ten·nis, n. tenis, m.
ten·or, n. tenor
tense, a. tieso; tenso. v. tensar. n. tiempo
ten·sion, n. tensión
tent, n. tienda de campaña
ten·ta·cle, n. tentáculo
ten·ta·tive, a. provisional
ten·u·ous, a. tenue
ten·ure, n. tenencia
tep·id, a. tibio
term, n. término; plazo; trimestre; pl. condiciones
ter·mi·nal, n. terminal, f. a. terminal
ter·mi·nate, v. terminar
ter·mi·nol·o·gy, n. terminología
ter·mi·nus, n. pl. -nus·es, -ni. término
ter·mite, n. comején
ter·race, n. terraza
ter·rain, n. terreno
ter·res·tri·al, a. terrestre
ter·ri·ble, a. terrible; inf. malísimo
ter·rif·ic, a. terrífico; tremendo; inf. estupendo
ter·ri·fy, v. aterrar; aterrorizar
ter·ri·to·ry, n. pl. -ries. territorio; término
ter·ror, n. terror
ter·ror·ism, n. terrorismo
ter·ror·ist, n. terrorista, m., f.
ter·ror·ize, v. aterrorizar

terse, a. conciso
test, n. prueba; examen. v. examinar
tes·ta·ment, n. testamento; (cap.) Testamento
tes·ti·fy, v. atestiguar; testificar
tes·ti·mo·ni·al, n. recomendación
tes·ti·mo·ny, n. pl., -nies. testimonio
teth·er, n. traba. v. atar
text, n. texto; tema, m.
text·book, n. libro de texto
tex·tile, a. textil. n. textil, m.; tejido
tex·ture, n. textura
than, conj. que; de
thank, v. dar gracias a; agradecer
thank·ful, a. agradecido
thanks, n. pl. gracias
thanks·giv·ing, n. acción de gracias
that, pron. pl., those. ése; ésa; eso; aquél; aquélla; aquello; el cual; la cual. a. ese; esa; aquel; aquella. conj. que
thatch, v. bardar
thaw, v. deshelar(se). n. deshielo
the, def. art. el; la; lo; los; las
the·a·ter, n. teatro
the·at·ri·cal, a. teatral
thee, pron. te; ti (obj. and dat. of thou)
theft, n. robo
their, a. poss. of they. su(s)
them, pron. obj. of they. los; las; les; ellos; ellas
theme, n. tema, m.; ensayo
them·selves, pron. pl. ellos (sí) mismos; ellas (sí) mismas
then, adv. entonces; luego. conj. en tal caso
thence·forth, adv. desde entonces. Also thence·for·ward
the·ol·o·gy, n. pl., -gies. teología
the·o·rem, n. teorema, m.
the·o·ret·i·cal, a. teórico
the·o·rize, v. teorizar
the·o·ry, n. pl., -ries. teoría
ther·a·py, n. pl., -pies. terapéutica
there, adv. allí; allá; ahí
there·a·bout, adv. cerca de
there·af·ter, adv. después de eso
there·by, adv. de ese modo
there·fore, adv. por lo tanto; por esta razón
ther·mal, a. termal
ther·mom·e·ter, n. termómetro
ther·mo·nu·cle·ar, a. termonuclear
ther·mo·stat, n. termostato
the·sau·rus, n. tesauro
these, a. pl. estos; estas. pron. pl. éstos; éstas
the·sis, n. pl., -ses. tesis, f.
they, pron. ellos; ellas
thick, a. grueso; espeso; denso
thick·et, n. espesura
thief, n. pl., thieves. ladrón
thieve, v. robar; hurtar

thigh, *n.* muslo

thim·ble, *n.* dedal, *m.*

thin, *a.* delgado; flaco; ligero; escaso; tenue

thing, *n.* cosa; objeto; *pl.* efectos; trapos

think, *v.,* thought, think·ing. pensar; meditar; creer; imaginar

third, *n.* tercio; tercera. *a.* tercero

thirst, *n.* sed, *f.;* ansia. *v.* tener sed

thir·teen, *a.* trece. *n.* trece

thir·ty, *a.* treinta. *n.* treinta

this, *pron. pl.,* these. éste; ésta; esto. *a.* este; esta. *adv.* tan

this·tle, *n.* cardo

thith·er, *adv.* allá

tho·rax, *n.* tórax, *m.*

thorn, *n.* espina

thorn·y, *a.* espinoso

thor·ough, *a.* completo; concienzudo

thor·ough·bred, *a.* de pura sangre

thor·ough·fare, *n.* vía pública

thou, *pron.* (*poetic, Biblical*). tú

though, *conj.* aunque. *adv.* sin embargo; no obstante

thought, *n.* pensamiento; idea; consideración

thought·ful, *a.* pensativo; atento

thought·less, *a.* descuidado; inconsiderado

thou·sand, *a.* mil. *n.* mil

thou·sandth, *a.* milésimo. *n.* milésimo

thrash, *v.* zurrar; menear; sacudirse

thread, *n.* hilo; rosca. *v.* enhebrar

thread·bare, *a.* raído

threat, *n.* amenaza

threat·en, *v.* amenazar

three, *a.* tres. *n.* tres

three-score, *a.* sesenta

thresh·old, *n.* umbral, *m.*

thrice, *adv.* tres veces

thrift, *n.* economía; frugalidad

thrift·y, *a.* frugal

thrill, *v.* emocionar(se); conmover(se). *n.* emoción

thrive, *v.,* thrived or throve, thrived or thriv·en. prosperar; crecer con vigor

throat, *n.* garganta

throb, *v.* palpitar

throne, *n.* trono

throng, *n.* tropel, *m.;* muchedumbre, *f. v.* venir en tropel

throt·tle, *v.* estrangular. *n.* regulador

through, thru, *prep.* a través de; por; por medio de. *adv.* de parte a parte. *a.* directo

through·out, *prep.* por todo. *adv.* en todas partes; durante todo

throw, *v.,* threw, thrown. echar; arrojar; lanzar; tirar. *n.* tirada; echada; lance

thru, *prep., adv.* See through

thrust, *v.,* thrust, thrust·ing. empujar; clavar. *n.* empuje; ataque

thud, *n.* ruido sordo

thumb, *n.* pulgar

thun·der, *n.* trueno; estruendo

thun·der·bolt, *n.* rayo

Thurs·day, *n.* jueves, *m.*

thus, *adv.* así; de este modo; en esta manera

thwart, *v.* frustrar; desbaratar

thy·roid gland, *n.* tiroides, *m.*

tib·i·a, *n.* tibia

tic, *n.* tic, *m.*

tick, *n.* golpecito; tictac, *m.;* garrapata

tick·et, *n.* billete; entrada; boleto; multa. *v.* rotular

tick·le, *v.* cosquillear; sentir cosquillas

tick·lish, *a.* cosquilloso; delicado

tid·bit, *n.* golosina

tide, *n.* marea

ti·dings, *n. pl.* noticias

ti·dy, *a.* ordenada; *inf.* considerable. *v.* poner en orden

tie, *v.,* tied, ty·ing. atar; ligar; empatar. *n.* corbata; empate

tier, *n.* fila

ti·ger, *n.* tigre

tight, *a.* ajustado; apretado. *adv.* bien

tight·en, *v.* apretar; atiesar

tights, *n. pl.* traje de malla

tile, *n.* baldosa; teja

till, *prep.* hasta. *conj.* hasta que. *v.* labrar. *n.* cajón

till·er, *n.* caña del timón

tilt, *v.* inclinar(se). *n.* inclinación

tim·ber, *n.* madera; madero

tim·bre, *n.* timbre

time, *n.* tiempo; época; hora; vez, *f. v.* cronometrar

time·less, *a.* eterno

time·ly, *a.* oportuno

time·piece, *n.* reloj, *m.*

time·ta·ble, *n.* horario

tim·id, *a.* tímido

tim·id·i·ty, *n.* timidez, *f.*

tin, *n.* estaño; lata

tinc·ture, *n.* tintura

tin·der, *n.* yesca

tinge, *v.* teñir; matizar; tintar. *n.* tinte

tin·gle, *v.* sentir hormigueo

tink·er, *v.* tratar de remendar

tin·kle, *v.* tintinar

tin·sel, *n.* oropel, *m.*

tint, *n.* matiz, *m. v.* teñir; matizar

ti·ny, *a.* muy pequeño; chiquitín

tip, *n.* punta; regatón; propina; aviso; soplo. *v.* ladear; dar propina a

tip·sy, *a.* achispado

tip·toe, *v.* andar de puntillas

ti·rade, *n.* invectiva; diatriba

tire, *v.* cansar(se); fatigar(se). *n.* neumático

tired, *a.* cansado

tire·some, *a.* molesto; pesado

tis·sue, *n.* tejido; tisú, *m.*

ti·tan·ic, *a.* titánico

tithe, *n.* diezmo

ti·tle, *n.* título; nombre. *v.* intitular; titular

tit·ter, *v.* reír a medias

tit·u·lar, *a.* titular

TNT, T.N.T., *n.* explosivo (trinitrotolueno)

to, *prep.* a; hacia; de; hasta. *adv.* hacia

toad, *n.* sapo

toad·stool, *n.* hongo; hongo venenoso

toast, *v.* tostar; brindar. *n.* pan tostado; brindis, *m.*

to·bac·co, *n.* tabaco

to·bog·gan, *n.* tobogán, *m.*

to·day, to-day, *adv.* hoy; hoy día. *n.* hoy

toe, *n.* dedo del pie; punta del pie

tof·fee, tof·fy, *n.* caramelo

to·ga, *n.* toga

to·geth·er, *adv.* juntos; juntamente; simultáneamente

toil, *v.* trabajar asiduamente; afanarse. *n.* trabajo

toi·let, *n.* retrete; wáter; tocado

toi·let·ry, *n.* artículo de tocador

to·ken, *n.* indicio; prenda; señal, *f.;* ficha. *a.* simbólico

tol·er·a·ble, *a.* tolerable; regular

tol·er·ance, *n.* tolerancia

tol·er·ant, *a.* tolerante

tol·er·ate, *v.* tolerar; soportar; permitir

toll, *n.* peaje. *v.* tañer

to·ma·to, *n. pl.,* **-toes.** tomate

tomb, *n.* tumba; sepulcro

tomb·stone, *n.* lápida sepulcral

to·mor·row, to-mor·row, *n.* mañana. *adv.* mañana

ton, *n.* tonelada

tone, *n.* tono; tendencia

tongs, *n. pl.* tenazas

tongue, *n.* lengua; lengüeta; idioma, *m.*

ton·ic, *n.* tónico

to·night, to-night, *adv.* esta noche. *n.* esta noche

ton·nage, *n.* tonelaje

ton·sil, *n.* amígdala; tonsila

ton·sil·li·tis, *n.* amigdalitis, *f.*

too, *adv.* demasiado; también; además

tool, *n.* herramienta; instrumento

tooth, *n. pl.,* **teeth.** diente; muela

tooth·ache, *n.* dolor de muelas

tooth·brush, *n.* cepillo de dientes

top, *n.* cumbre, *f.;* ápice; cima; tapa; peonza. *a.* más alto; primero. *v.* coronar

to·paz, *n.* topacio

top·coat, *n.* sobretodo

top hat, *n.* chistera

top·ic, *n.* tema, *m.*

top·i·cal, *a.* tópico; actual; del día

to·pog·ra·phy, *n.* topografía

top·ple, *v.* venirse abajo

top·sy-tur·vy, *adv.* patas arriba

torch, *n.* antorcha; hacha

tor·ment, *a.* atormentar. *n.* tormento

tor·na·do, *n. pl.,* **-does, -dos.** tornado

tor·pe·do, *n. pl.,* **-does.** torpedo. *v.* torpedear

tor·rent, *n.* torrente

tor·rid, *a.* tórrido

tor·so, *n.* torso

tor·toise, *n.* tortuga

tor·tu·ous, *a.* tortuoso

tor·ture, *v.* torturar; atormentar. *n.* tortura

toss, *v.* echar; agitarse. *n.* cogida; echada

tot, *n.* nene; nena

to·tal, *a.* total; entero. *n.* total, *m.;* suma. *v.* totalizar

to·tal·i·tar·i·an, *a.* totalitario

to·tal·ly, *adv.* totalmente

tote, *v. inf.* llevar

to·tem, *n.* tótem, *m.*

tot·ter, *v.* bambolearse

touch, *v.* tocar(se); palpar; conmover. *n.* toque; tacto

touch·y, *a.* irritable

tough, *a.* duro; resistente; difícil

tough·en, *v.* endurecer(se); hacer(se) correoso

tour, *n.* viaje; excursión. *v.* viajar por

tour·ism, *n.* turismo

tour·ist, *n.* turista, *m., f.*

tour·na·ment, *n.* torneo

tour·ni·quet, *n.* torniquete

tou·sle, *v.* despeinar

tow, *v.* llevar a remolque. *n.* remolque

to·ward, *prep.* hacia; cerca de; con respecto a. Also **to·wards**

tow·el, *n.* toalla

tow·er, *n.* torre, *f.*

town, *n.* ciudad; pueblo

tox·ic, *a.* tóxico

tox·in, *n.* toxina

toy, *n.* juguete. *v.* jugar (con)

trace, *n.* indicio; huella; rastro. *v.* seguir la pista de; trazar

tra·che·a, *n.* tráquea

track, *n.* vía; pista; senda. *v.* rastrear; seguir la pista de; manchar con huellas

tract, *n.* extensión; tratado

trac·tor, *n.* tractor

trade, *n.* comercio; negocio; profesión. *v.* comprar; vender; comerciar; trocar

trade·mark, *n.* marca de fábrica;

marca registrada
trade un.ion, n. sindicato
tra.di.tion, n. tradición
tra.di.tion.al, a. tradicional
tra.duce, v. calumniar
traf.fic, n. tráfico; movimiento. v. traficar
trag.e.dy, n. pl., -dies. tragedia
trag.ic, a. trágico
trail, v. arrastrar(se); rastrear. n. pista; rastro; estela
trail.er, n. remolque
train, n. tren; hilo; serie, f.; comitiva. v. adiestrar; entrenar
trait, n. característica; rasgo
trai.tor, n. traidor
tra.jec.to.ry, n. pl., -ries. trayectoria
tramp, v. andar con pasos pesados. n. vagabundo
tram.ple, v. pisotear
trance, n. arrobamiento; estado hipnótico
tran.quil, a. tranquilo
tran.quil.li.ty, n. tranquilidad
tran.quil.ize, v. tranquilizar; aquietar
tran.quil.iz.er, n. tranquilizante
trans.act, v. despachar
trans.ac.tion, n. transacción; negocio
tran.scend, v. sobresalir; exceder
tran.scribe, v. transcribir
tran.script, n. trasunto
tran.scrip.tion, n. transcripción; copia
trans.fer, v. transferir; trasladar. n. transferencia; transbordo
trans.fer.ence, n. transferencia
trans.form, v. transformar
trans.for.ma.tion, n. transformación; metamorfosis, f.
trans.form.er, n. transformador
trans.fu.sion, n. transfusión
trans.gress, v. traspasar; pecar
trans.gres.sion, n. transgresión; pecado
tran.sient, a. transitorio; pasajero. n. transeúnte, m., f.
tran.sis.tor, n. transistor
trans.it, n. tránsito
tran.si.tion, n. transición
tran.si.tive, a. transitivo
tran.si.to.ry, a. transitorio; fugaz
trans.late, v. traducir
trans.la.tion, n. traducción; interpretación
trans.lu.cent, a. translúcido
trans.mis.sion, n. transmisión
trans.mit, v. transmitir
trans.mit.ter, n. transmisor
trans.om, n. travesaño
trans.par.ent, a. transparente; claro; obvio
tran.spire, v. transpirar; suceder;

ocurrir
trans.plant, v. trasplantar
trans.port, v. transportar. n. transporte
trans.por.ta.tion, n. transportación; transporte
trans.pose, v. transponer; (mus.) transportar
trans.verse, a. transversal
trap, n. trampa. v. entrampar; atrapar
trap door, n. escotillón
tra.peze, n. trapecio
trap.e.zoid, n. trapezoide
trap.pings, n. pl. adornos; arreos
trash, n. hojarasca; basura
trau.ma, n. trauma, m.
trau.mat.ic, a. traumático
tra.vail, n. afán; dolores del parto
trav.el, v., -eled or -elled, -el.ing or -el.ling. viajar; recorrer. n. pl. viajes
trav.erse, v. atravesar; recorrer
trav.es.ty, n. pl., -ties. parodia
tray, n. bandeja; cubeta
treach.er.ous, a. traicionero; traidor; incierto
treach.er.y, n. traición
tread, v., trod, trod.den or trod, tread.ing. pisar; hollar. n. paso; huella
trea.son, n. traición
treas.ure, n. tesoro. v. atesorar; guardar
treas.ur.er, n. tesorero
treas.ur.y, n. pl., -ies. tesorería; tesoro
treat, v. tratar; curar; invitar. n. placer
trea.tise, n. tratado
treat.ment, n. tratamiento
trea.ty, n. pl., -ties. tratado; pacto
tre.ble, a. triple. n. (mus.) tiple, m., f. v. triplicar(se)
tree, n. árbol, m.
trek, v. caminar
trel.lis, n. enrejado; espaldera
trem.ble, v. temblar; estremecerse
tre.men.dous, a. inf. tremendo
trem.or, n. temblor
trench, n. foso; trinchera
trench.ant, a. mordaz
trend, n. dirección; tendencia. v. tender
tres.pass, v. infringir; pecar; entrar sin derecho
tress, n. trenza
tri.al, n. proceso; prueba; desgracia
tri.an.gle, n. triángulo
tri.an.gu.lar, a. triangular
tribe, n. tribu, f.
trib.u.la.tion, n. tribulación; aflicción
tri.bu.nal, n. tribunal, m.
trib.u.tar.y, n. pl., -ies. afluente. a.

tributario

trib·ute, *n.* homenaje; tributo

trick, *n.* truco; trampa; engaño; (*cards.*) baza. *v.* engañar

trick·le, *v.* gotear

tri·cy·cle, *n.* triciclo

tried, *a.* probado

tri·fle, *n.* bagatela. *v.* desperdiciar

tri·fling, *a.* sin importancia

trig·ger, *n.* gatillo

trig·o·nom·e·try, *n.* trigonometría

tril·lion, *n.* billón

trim, *v.* recortar; guarnecer. *a.* en buen estado

trin·ket, *n.* dije

tri·o, *n. pl.* **-os.** trío

trip, *n.* viaje; tropiezo; traspié; paso falso. *v.* tropezar; coger en falta

tri·ple, *a.* triple. *v.* triplicar(se)

trip·let, *n.* trillizo

trip·li·cate, *v.* triplicar. *a.* triplicado

tri·pod, *n.* trípode

trite, *a.* gastado

tri·umph, *v.* triunfar. *n.* triunfo

tri·um·phant, *a.* triunfante

triv·i·al, *a.* trivial; frívolo

triv·i·al·i·ty, *n. pl.* **-ties.** trivialidad

trol·ley, *n.* tranvía

trom·bone, *n.* trombón

troop, *n.* tropa; escuadrón

troop·er, *n.* soldado de caballería

tro·phy, *n. pl.* **-phies.** trofeo

trop·ic, *n.* trópico

trop·i·cal, *a.* tropical

trot, *v.* ir al trote; hacer trotar. *n.* trote

trou·ba·dour, *n.* trovador

trou·ble, *v.* molestar(se); inquietar(se); agitar. *n.* dificultad; pena; disturbio

trou·ble·some, *a.* molesto

trough, *n.* abrevadero

troupe, *n.* compañía

trou·sers, *n. pl.* pantalones

trous·seau, *n.* ajuar

trout, *n.* trucha

trow·el, *n.* paleta; desplantador

tru·ant, *n.* novillero

truce, *n.* tregua

truck, *n.* camión; carretilla. *v.* acarrear

true, *a.* fiel; verdadero; genuino

tru·ly, *adv.* verdaderamente; realmente

trump, *n.* triunfo. *v.* fallar

trum·pet, *n.* trompeta

trun·cate, *v.* truncar

trunk, *n.* tronco; baúl, *m.;* portaequipaje(s); línea principal; trompa

truss, *v.* empaquetar

trust, *n.* confianza; obligación; fideicomiso. *v.* confiar en; esperar

trus·tee, *n.* fideicomisario

trust·wor·thy, *a.* fidedigno; confiable

trust·y, *a.* seguro

truth, *n.* verdad

truth·ful, *a.* veraz

try, *v.,* **tried, try·ing.** intentar; probar; juzgar. *n.* tentativa

try·ing, *a.* difícil; penoso

tryst, *n.* cita

T-shirt, *n.* camiseta. Also **tee shirt**

tub, *n.* baño; tina

tu·ba, *n.* tuba

tube, *n.* tubo

tu·ber·cu·lo·sis, *n.* tuberculosis, *f.*

tuck, *v.* alforzar

Tues·day, *n.* martes, *m.*

tuft, *n.* copete

tug, *v.* tirar con fuerza; remolcar. *n.* tirón

tug·boat, *n.* remolcador

tu·i·tion, *n.* enseñanza

tu·lip, *n.* tulipán

tum·ble, *v.* voltear; caer(se). *n.* caída

tum·bler, *n.* volteador; vaso

tu·mor, *n.* tumor

tu·mult, *n.* tumulto

tu·mul·tu·ous, *a.* tumultuoso

tu·na, *n.* atún

tun·dra, *n.* tundra

tune, *n.* aire; afinación. *v.* afinar; sintonizar

tu·nic, *n.* túnica

tun·nel, *n.* túnel, *m.*

tur·ban, *n.* turbante

tur·bid, *a.* túrbido

tur·bine, *n.* turbina

tur·bu·lence, *n.* turbulencia; confusión

tur·bu·lent, *a.* turbulento

tu·reen, *n.* sopera

turf, *n.* césped

tur·key, *n. pl.* **-keys.** pavo

tur·moil, *n.* alboroto; tumulto

turn, *v.* girar; dar vueltas a; volver(se); convertirse. *n.* vuelta; turno. **in turn**, por turnos. **turn down**, doblar; rechazar. **turn out**, apagar; producir

turn·coat, *n.* traidor

tur·nip, *n.* nabo

turn·out, *n.* concurrencia; producción

turn·pike, *n.* autopista de peaje

turn·stile, *n.* torniquete

tur·pen·tine, *n.* trementina

tur·quoise, *n.* turquesa

tur·ret, *n.* torrecilla

tur·tle, *n.* tortuga

tusk, *n.* colmillo

tus·sle, *n.* agarrada

tu·te·lage, *n.* tutela

tu·tor, *n.* preceptor, tutor. *v.* enseñar

tux·e·do, *n. pl.* **-dos.** smoking, *m.*

TV, *n. pl.* **TVs, TV's.** televisión

twang, *n.* tañido; timbre nasal

tweed, *n.* mezcla de lana
tweez·ers, *n. pl.* bruselas
twelfth, *a.* duodécimo
twelve, *n.* doce *a.* doce
twen·ty, *n.* veinte. *a.* veinte
twice, *adv.* dos veces
twig, *n.* ramita
twi·light, *n.* crepúsculo
twill, *n.* tela cruzada
twin, *n.* gemelo. *a.* gemelo
twine, *n.* guita; bramante. *v.* enroscarse
twinge, *n.* dolor agudo
twin·kle, *v.* centellear. *n.* centelleo
twirl, *v.* girar; piruetear. *n.* giro
twist, *v.* enroscar(se); torcer(se); retorcer(se). *n.* torsión
twitch, *v.* crisparse. *n.* contracción nerviosa
twit·ter, *v.* gorjear. *n.* gorjeo
two, *n.* dos *a.* dos
two-faced, *a.* falso; hipócrita
ty·coon, *n.* (fin.) magnate
type, *n.* tipo; género. *v.* escribir a máquina
type·write, *v.,* -wrote, -writ·ten, -writ·ing. escribir a máquina. Also **type**
type·writ·er, *n.* máquina de escribir
ty·phoid, *n.* fiebre tifoidea. Also **ty·phoid fe·ver**
ty·phoon, *n.* tifón
ty·phus, *n.* tifus, *m.*
typ·i·cal, *a.* típico; característico
typ·i·fy, *v.* simbolizar
typ·ist, *n.* mecanógrafo
ty·pog·ra·phy, *n.* tipografía
ty·ran·ni·cal, *a.* tiránico; déspótico
tyr·an·nize, *v.* tiranizar
tyr·an·ny, *n.* tiranía
ty·rant, *n.* tirano
ty·ro, *n.* novicio

U

u·biq·ui·tous, *a.* ubicuo. Also **u·biq·ui·tar·y**
u·biq·ui·ty, *n.* ubicuidad; omnipresencia
ud·der, *n.* ubre, *f.*
ug·ly, *a.* feo; repugnante
ul·cer, *n.* úlcera
ul·te·ri·or, *n.* ulterior
ul·ti·mate, *a.* último; fundamental
ul·ti·ma·tum, *n. pl.* -tums, -ta. ultimátum, *m.*
ul·tra, *a.* ultra
ul·tra·son·ic, *a.* ultrasónico
ul·tra·vi·o·let, *a.* ultravioleta
um·bil·i·cal, *a.* umbilical
um·brage, *n.* resentimiento
um·brel·la, *n.* paraguas, *m.*
um·laut, *n.* diéresis, *f.*
um·pire, *n.* árbitro
ump·teen, *a. inf.* muchos

un·a·bashed, *a.* desvergonzado; descarado
un·a·ble, *a.* incapaz
un·a·bridged, *a.* íntegro
un·ac·count·a·ble, *a.* inexplicable
un·ac·cus·tomed, *a.* desacostumbrado
un·af·fect·ed, *a.* sin afectación; sincero
un·af·fect·ed·ly, *adv.* sin afectación
u·nan·i·mous, *a.* unánime
un·ap·proach·a·ble, *a.* inabordable
un·armed, *a.* desarmado
un·as·sum·ing, *a.* modesto; sencillo; sin pretensión
un·at·tached, *a.* soltero; suelto; no embargado
un·a·void·a·ble, *a.* inevitable
un·a·wares, *adv.* de improviso
un·bal·anced, *a.* desequilibrado
un·be·com·ing, *a.* que sienta mal; indecoroso
un·be·liev·a·ble, *a.* increíble
un·be·liev·er, *n.* escéptico; descreído
un·bend, *v.,* -bent or -bend·ed, -bend·ing. desencorvar; aflojar
un·bend·ing, *a.* inflexible
un·bi·ased, *a.* imparcial
un·blem·ished, *a.* sin tacha; puro
un·born, *a.* no nacido
un·bos·om, *v.* revelar
un·break·a·ble, *a.* irrompible
un·bri·dled, *a.* desenfrenado; ingobernable
un·called-for, *a.* inmerecido
un·can·ny, *a.* extraño; misterioso
un·ceas·ing, *a.* incesante
un·cer·e·mo·ni·ous, *a.* informal; descortés
un·cer·tain, *a.* incierto; indeciso
un·char·i·ta·ble, *a.* implacable; duro
un·cle, *n.* tío
un·clean, *a.* sucio
un·com·fort·a·ble, *a.* incómodo
un·com·mon, *a.* poco común; extraordinario
un·com·mu·ni·ca·tive, *a.* poco comunicativo
un·com·pro·mis·ing, *a.* inflexible; intransigente
un·con·cern, *n.* indiferencia
un·con·cerned, *a.* despreocupado
un·con·di·tion·al, *a.* incondicional
un·con·scion·a·ble, *a.* desrazonable
un·con·scious, *a.* sin sentido; inconsciente
un·con·sti·tu·tion·al, *a.* inconstitucional
un·con·strained, *a.* voluntario
un·con·trol·la·ble, *a.* ingobernable
un·con·ven·tion·al, *a.* no convencional; original
un·couth, *a.* grosero; rudo
un·cov·er, *v.* descubrir; destapar

unc·tion, *n.* unción

unc·tu·ous, *a.* zalamero

un·de·cid·ed, *a.* indeciso

un·de·ni·a·ble, *a.* innegable

un·de·pend·a·ble, *a.* poco confiable

un·der, *prep.* debajo de; bajo. *adv.* debajo. *a.* inferior

un·der·brush, *n.* maleza

un·der·class·man, *n. pl.,* -men. estudiante de primer o segundo año

un·der·clothes, *n. pl.* ropa interior

un·der·cov·er, *a.* secreto

un·der·cur·rent, *n.* corriente submarina

un·der·es·ti·mate, *v.* subestimar

un·der·go, *v.,* -went, -gone, -go·ing. sufrir

un·der·ground, *adv.* bajo tierra. *a.* subterráneo

un·der·hand·ed, *a.* secreto

un·der·line, *v.* subrayar

un·der·ling, *n.* subordinado

un·der·ly·ing, *a.* fundamental

un·der·mine, *v.* socavar

un·der·neath, *prep.* bajo. *adv.* debajo

un·der·priv·i·leged, *a.* desamparado

un·der·rate, *v.* menospreciar

un·der·score, *v.* subrayar

un·der·side, *n.* cara inferior

un·der·stand, *v.,* -stood, -stand·ing. comprender; entender

un·der·stand·ing, *n.* entendimiento; acuerdo

un·der·stud·y, *n. pl.,* -ies. sobresaliente, *m., f.*

un·der·take, *v.,* -took, -tak·en, -tak·ing. emprender

un·der·tak·er, *n.* director de pompas fúnebres

un·der·tak·ing, *n.* empresa

un·der·wear, *n.* ropa interior

un·do, *v.,* -did, -done, -do·ing. deshacer; anular; desatar

un·dress, *v.* desnudar(se)

un·due, *a.* excesivo

un·du·ly, *adv.* indebidamente

un·earth, *v.* desenterrar; descubrir

un·eas·y, *a.* incómodo; intranquilo

un·em·ployed, *a.* sin empleo; sin trabajo

un·e·ven, *a.* desigual

un·ex·pect·ed, *a.* imprevisto

un·faith·ful, *a.* infiel

un·fa·mil·iar, *a.* poco familiar

un·fin·ished, *a.* incompleto

un·flinch·ing, *a.* resuelto

un·fold, *v.* abrir; desplegar; extender; revelar

un·for·get·ta·ble, *a.* inolvidable

un·for·tu·nate, *a.* desgraciado; infeliz. *n.* desgraciado

un·furl, *v.* desplegar

un·gain·ly, *a.* desgarbado

un·guent, *n.* ungüento

un·hand, *v.* soltar

un·hap·pi·ness, *n.* desdicha; infelicidad

un·hap·py, *a.* desdichado; infeliz

un·health·y, *a.* enfermizo; insalubre

un·heard·of, *a.* inaudito

un·hurt, *a.* ileso

u·ni·corn, *n.* unicornio

u·ni·fi·ca·tion, *n.* unificación

u·ni·form, *a.* uniforme; constante

u·ni·form·i·ty, *n. pl.,* -ties. uniformidad

u·ni·fy, *v.* unificar

u·ni·lat·er·al, *a.* unilateral

un·in·ter·est·ed, *a.* desinteresado

un·ion, *n.* unión; junta; sindicato

un·ion·ize, *v.* agremiar(se)

u·nique, *a.* único; sin igual

u·ni·son, *n.* unisonancia. in u·ni·son, al unísono

u·nit, *n.* unidad

u·nite, *v.* unir(se); aliarse

u·nit·ed, *a.* unido

u·ni·ty, *n. pl.,* -ties. unidad; unión

u·ni·ver·sal, *a.* universal

u·ni·ver·sal·ize, *v.* universalizar

u·ni·verse, *n.* universo

u·ni·ver·si·ty, *n. pl.,* -ties. universidad

un·just, *a.* injusto

un·kempt, *a.* despeinado

un·known, *a.* desconocido

un·law·ful, *a.* ilegal

un·less, *conj.* a menos que. *prep.* excepto

un·like, *a.* distinto. *prep.* a diferencia de

un·like·ly, *a.* improbable

un·lim·it·ed, *a.* ilimitado

un·load, *v.* descargar

un·looked·for, *a.* imprevisto; inopinado

un·luck·y, *a.* desgraciado; desdichado

un·mask, *v.* desenmascarar

un·mer·ci·ful, *a.* despiadado

un·mis·tak·a·ble, *a.* inequívoco

un·mit·i·gat·ed, *a.* no mitigado

un·nat·u·ral, *a.* anormal; cruel; afectado

un·nec·es·sar·y, *a.* innecesario

un·num·bered, *a.* innumerable

un·pack, *v.* desempaquetar; deshacer

un·par·al·leled, *a.* sin par

un·pleas·ant, *a.* desagradable; molesto

un·pop·u·lar, *a.* impopular

un·prec·e·dent·ed, *a.* sin precedente

un·prin·ci·pled, *a.* sin conciencia

un·ques·tion·a·ble, *a.* incuestionable; indudable

un·ques·tioned, *a.* incontestable; indisputable

un·rav·el, *v.* desenredar(se); des-

mara·ñar(se)
un·re·al, a. imaginario
un·rea·son·a·ble, a. irrazonable; inmoderado
un·re·lent·ing, a. inexorable
un·rest, n. desasosiego; inquietud
un·roll, v. desenrollar
un·ru·ly, a. ingobernable
un·sa·vor·y, a. desagradable
un·scathed, a. sano y salvo; ileso
un·scru·pu·lous, a. sin conciencia; sin escrúpulos
un·seem·ly, a. indecente; indecoroso
un·set·tle, v. descomponer; agitar
un·sight·ly, a. repulsivo; feo
un·skilled, a. inexperto
un·snarl, v. desenredar
un·so·phis·ti·cat·ed, a. ingenuo; cándido
un·sound, a. falso; defectuoso
un·sta·ble, a. inestable
un·stead·y, a. poco firme; inseguro
un·sung, a. celebrado
un·think·a·ble, a. inconcebible
un·think·ing, a. irreflexivo; desatento
un·til, conj. hasta que. prep. hasta
un·time·ly, a. inoportuno; intempestivo
un·to, prep. archaic. a
un·told, a. incalculable
un·truth, n. falsedad
un·truth·ful, a. mentiroso
un·u·su·al, a. poco común; raro
un·var·nished, a. sin adornos
un·veil, v. descubrir
un·war·y, a. incauto
un·whole·some, a. insalubre
un·will·ing, a. desinclinado; de mala gana
un·wit·ting, a. inconsciente
un·wor·thy, a. indigno
un·wrap, v. deshacer; desempapelar; desenvolver
un·yield·ing, a. inflexible; terco
up, adv. arriba; hacia arriba; acabado. a. ascendente; en pie. prep. en lo alto de; subiendo
up·braid, v. reprender
up·bring·ing, n. crianza
up·date, v. modernizar; poner al día
up·heav·al, n. cataclismo
up·hill, adv. cuesta arriba. a. ascendente; penoso
up·hold, v., -held, -hold·ing. sostener; defender
up·hol·ster, v. entapizar; tapizar
up·hol·ster·y, n. pl., -ies. tapicería
up·keep, n. manutención
up·on, prep. encima de; sobre
up·per, a. superior; alto. n. pala de zapato
up·per·most, a. (el) más alto. adv. principal; primero

up·pish, a. inf. arrogante; engreído
up·raise, v. inf. levantar
up·right, a. vertical; recto; derecho
up·ris·ing, n. insurrección; sublevación
up·roar, n. alboroto
up·roar·i·ous, a. tumultuoso
up·root, v. desarraigar
up·set, v., -set, -set·ting. volcar; trastornar. n. contratiempo; trastorno. a. perturbado
up·shot, n. resultado
up·side down, adv. de arriba abajo; al revés
up·stairs, a. arriba. n. pl., usu. sing. in constr. piso superior
up·stand·ing, a. honrado
up·to-date, a. moderno
up·turn, v. volver hacia arriba
up·ward, adv. hacia arriba. Also up·wards
u·ra·ni·um, n. uranio
U·ra·nus, n. Urano
ur·ban, a. urbano
ur·bane, a. urbano; fino
ur·chin, n. pilluelo
urge, v. impeler; instar; incitar. n. impulso
ur·gen·cy, n. pl., -cies. urgencia
ur·gent, a. urgente; apremiante
u·ri·nate, v. orinar(se)
u·rine, n. orina
urn, n. urna
us, pron. nos; nosotros, nosotras
us·a·ble, use·a·ble, a. utilizable
us·age, n. uso; usanza; costumbre, f.
use, v. usar; emplear; utilizar. n. uso; empleo. be of no use, no servir para nada. use up, agotar
used, a. usado
use·ful, a. útil
use·ful·ness, n. utilidad; provecho
use·less, a. inútil; inservible
ush·er, n. acomodador. v. acomodar
u·su·al, a. usual; habitual
u·su·al·ly, adv. por lo general; usualmente
u·surp, v. usurpar
u·sur·y, n. pl., -ries. usura
u·ten·sil, n. utensilio
u·ter·us, n. pl., u·ter·i. útero
u·ti·lize, v. utilizar; aprovechar
ut·most, a. sumo; mayor; más lejano. n. grado supremo
u·to·pi·a, n. utopía, utopia
ut·ter, a. absoluto; total. v. pronunciar
ut·ter·ance, n. pronunciación

V

va·can·cy, n. pl., -cies. vacante, f.
va·cant, a. vacío; libre; vago
va·cate, v. dejar vacante

va·ca·tion, n. vacación; vacaciones
vac·ci·nate, v. vacunar
vac·ci·na·tion, n. vacunación
vac·cine, n. vacuna
vac·il·late, v. vacilar
vac·il·la·tion, n. vacilación; fluctuación
va·cu·i·ty, n. pl., -ties. vacuidad
vac·u·ous, a. mentecato; necio
vac·u·um, n. pl., -ums. vacío. v. limpiar con un aspirador de polvo
vag·a·bond, a. vagabundo. n. vagabundo
va·gar·y, n. pl., -ies. capricho
va·gran·cy, n. vagancia
va·grant, n. vagabundo
vague, a. vago; indistinto; incierto
vain, a. vanidoso; vano. in vain, en vano
vale, n. valle
val·e·dic·to·ry, n. pl., -ries. discurso de despedida
val·en·tine, n. novia o novio en el día de San Valentín
val·id, a. válido; valedero
val·i·date, v. validar
va·lid·i·ty, n. pl., -ties. validez, f.
va·lise, n. maleta
val·ley, n. pl., -leys. valle; arroyada
val·or, n. valor; valentía
val·u·a·ble, a. valioso; costoso; precioso; n. usu. pl. objetos de valor
val·u·a·tion, n. valuación; tasación
val·ue, n. valor; precio; importancia; estimación. v. valorar; valuar; apreciar
val·ued, a. estimado
valve, n. válvula
vam·pire, n. vampiro
van, n. vanguardia; camión de mudanzas
van·dal, n. vándalo
van·dal·ism, n. vandalismo
vane, n. veleta
van·guard, n. vanguardia
va·nil·la, n. vainilla
van·ish, v. desvanecerse; desaparecer
van·i·ty, n. pl., -ties. vanidad
van·quish, v. vencer; conquistar
van·tage, n. ventaja; provecho
vap·id, a. insípido
va·por, n. vapor
va·por·ize, v. vaporizar(se)
va·por·ous, a. vaporoso
var·i·a·bil·i·ty, n. pl., -ties. variabilidad
var·i·a·ble, a. variable; vario. n. variable
var·i·ance, n. variación; desacuerdo
var·i·ant, a. variante; diferente. n. variante, f.
var·i·a·tion, n. variación
var·i·cose, a. varicoso

var·ied, a. variado; diverso
var·i·e·gat·ed, a. abigarrado
va·ri·e·ty, n. pl., -ties. variedad
var·i·ous, a. vario; variado; diverso
var·nish, n. barniz, m. v. barnizar; paliar
var·si·ty, n. pl., -ties. equipo principal de una universidad
var·y, v. variar; desviarse; cambiar
vase, n. jarrón; florero
vas·sal, n. vasallo
vast, a. vasto; inmenso
vat, n. tina; cuba; depósito
vault, v. saltar. n. bóveda; sepultura; cámara acorazada
veal, n. ternera
vec·tor, n. vector; radio vector
veer, v. virar
veg·e·ta·ble, n. legumbre, f.; vegetal, f.
veg·e·tar·i·an, n. vegetariano
veg·e·tate, v. vegetar
veg·e·ta·tion, n. vegetación
ve·he·mence, ve·he·men·cy, n. vehemencia
ve·he·ment, a. vehemente; apasionado
ve·hi·cle, n. vehículo; medio
veil, n. velo
vein, n. vena; veta; filón
veined, a. veteado
vel·lum, n. vitela
ve·loc·i·ty, n. pl., -ties. velocidad
vel·ours, vel·our, n. pl., -lours. velludillo
vel·vet, n. terciopelo
vel·vet·y, a. aterciopelado
ve·nal, a. venal
ve·nal·i·ty, n. venalidad
vend, v. vender
ven·det·ta, n. odio de sangre
vend·i·ble, a. vendible. n. usu. pl. artículo de comercio
ve·neer, n. chapa
ven·er·a·ble, a. venerable
ven·er·ate, v. venerar
ven·er·a·tion, n. veneración
ve·ne·re·al, a. venéreo
ven·geance, n. venganza; retribución
ve·ni·al, a. venial
ven·i·son, n. carne de venado
ven·om, n. veneno; rencor; virulencia
ven·om·ous, a. venenoso
vent, n. salida; orificio. v. descargar
ven·ti·late, v. ventilar
ven·ti·la·tion, n. ventilación
ven·tral, a. ventral
ven·tri·cle, n. ventrículo
ven·tril·o·quism, n. ventriloquia
ven·tril·o·quist, n. ventrílocuo
ven·ture, n. empresa arriesgada. v. aventurar(se)
ven·ture·some, a. aventurero; arriesgado

Ve.nus, n. Venus, m., f.
ve.ra.cious, a. veraz
ve.rac.i.ty, n. veracidad
ve.ran.da, ve.ran.dah, n. galería
verb, n. verbo
ver.bal, a. verbal
ver.ba.tim, adv. palabra por palabra
ver.bi.age, n. verbosidad; palabrería
ver.bose, a. verboso
ver.bos.i.ty, n. verbosidad
ver.dant, a. verde
ver.dict, n. veredicto; juicio; fallo
verge, n. borde
ver.i.fi.ca.tion, n. verificación
ver.i.fy, v. verificar; comprobar
ver.i.si.mil.i.tude, n. verosimilitud
ver.i.ta.ble, a. verdadero; real
ver.i.ty, n. pl., **-ties.** verdad
ver.mil.ion, ver.mil.lion, n. bermellón. a. bermejo
ver.min, n. pl., **ver.min.** sabandijas
ver.mouth, n. vermut, m.
ver.nac.u.lar, a. vernáculo. n. lengua vulgar
ver.nal, a. vernal
ver.sa.tile, a. adaptable; polifacético
ver.sa.til.i.ty, n. adaptabilidad
verse, n. verso; versículo
ver.si.fy, v. versificar
ver.sion, n. versión
ver.sus, prep. contra
ver.te.bra, n. pl., **-brae.** vértebra
ver.te.brate, a. vertebrado
ver.tex, n. pl., **-tex.es, -ti.ces.** ápice; vértice
ver.ti.cal, a. vertical. n. vertical
ver.ti.go, n. pl., **-ti.goes, -tig.i.nes.** vértigo
verve, n. brío; vigor
ver.y, adv. muy; sumamente. a. mismo; mero
ves.pers, n. vísperas
ves.sel, n. embarcación; vasija; vaso
vest, n. chaleco
ves.ti.bule, n. vestíbulo
ves.tige, n. vestigio; rastro
ves.try, n. pl., **-tries.** sacristía
vet, n. inf. veterinario
vet.er.an, n. veterano
vet.er.i.nar.i.an, n. veterinario
vet.er.i.nar.y, n. pl., **-ies.** veterinario. a. veterinario
ve.to, n. veto. v. vetar
vex, v. molestar; enojar; vejar; irritar
vex.a.tion, n. contrariedad; molestia
vi.a, prep. por
vi.a.duct, n. viaducto
vi.al, n. frasco pequeño
vi.brant, a. vibrante
vi.brate, v. vibrar; oscilar
vi.bra.tion, n. vibración
vic.ar, n. vicario
vi.car.i.ous, a. substituto
vice, n. vicio

vice-pres.i.dent, n. vicepresidente
vice.roy, n. virrey, m.
vice ver.sa, adv. viceversa
vi.cin.i.ty, n. pl., **-ties.** vecindad; proximidad
vi.cious, a. depravado; vicioso; cruel
vic.tim, n. víctima
vic.tim.ize, v. hacer víctima; estafar
vic.tor, n. vencedor
vic.to.ri.ous, a. victorioso
vic.to.ry, n. pl., **-ries.** victoria; triunfo
vict.ual, n. usu. pl. víveres, m. pl.
vie, v., **vied,** vy.**ing.** competir
view, n. vista; escena; panorama, m.; propuesta; opinión. v. ver; contemplar
view.point, n. punto de vista
vig.il, n. vigilia
vig.i.lance, n. vigilancia
vig.i.lant, a. vigilante; alerta
vi.gnette, n. viñeta
vig.or, n. vigor
vig.or.ous, a. vigoroso
vile, a. vil; despreciable; horrible
vil.la, n. casa de campo
vil.lage, n. aldea
vil.lain, n. malvado
vil.lain.y, n. pl., **-ies.** maldad
vim, n. vigor
vin.di.cate, v. vindicar
vin.dic.tive, a. vengativo
vine, n. vid, f.
vin.e.gar, n. vinagre
vine.yard, n. viña
vin.tage, n. vendimia. a. antiguo; clásico
vi.ol, n. viola
vi.o.la, n. viola
vi.o.late, v. violar; forzar
vi.o.la.tion, n. violación
vi.o.lence, n. violencia
vi.o.lent, a. violento; intenso; vehemente
vi.o.let, n. violeta. a. violado
vi.o.lin, n. violín
vi.o.lon.cel.lo, n. violonchelo, violoncelo
vi.per, n. víbora
vi.ra.go, n. pl., **-goes, -gos.** fiera
vir.gin, n. virgen. a. virgen
vir.gin.i.ty, n. virginidad
vir.ile, a. viril
vi.ril.i.ty, n. virilidad
vir.tu.al, a. virtual
vir.tu.al.ly, adv. virtualmente
vir.tue, n. virtud, f.
vir.tu.os.i.ty, n. pl., **-ties.** virtuosismo
vir.tu.o.so, n. pl., **-sos, -si.** virtuoso
vir.tu.ous, a. virtuoso
vir.u.lent, a. virulento
vi.rus, n. pl., **-rus.es.** virus, m.
vi.sa, n. visado

vis·cos·i·ty, n. viscosidad
vis·count, n. vizconde
vis·count·ess, n. vizcondesa
vise, n. tornillo
vis·i·bil·i·ty, n. visibilidad
vis·i·ble, a. visible; conspicuo
vi·sion, n. visión; vista
vi·sion·ar·y, n. pl., -ies. visionario. a. visionario
vis·it, v. visitar; ir a ver. n. visita
vis·it·a·tion, n. visitación
vi·sor, n. visera
vis·u·al, a. visual
vis·u·al·ize, v. representarse en la mente
vi·tal, a. vital; de suma importancia
vi·tal·i·ty, n. pl., -ties. vitalidad; brío
vi·ta·min, n. vitamina
vit·re·ous, a. vítreo
vit·ri·ol, n. vitriolo
vi·tu·per·ate, v. vituperar
vi·va·cious, a. vivaz; animado; vivaracho
vi·vac·i·ty, n. pl., -ties. vivacidad; animación
viv·id, a. vivo; intenso; gráfico
vix·en, n. arpía; zorra
vo·cab·u·lar·y, n. pl., -ies. vocabulario
vo·cal, a. vocal; de la voz
vo·cal·ist, n. cantante, m., f.
vo·cal·ize, v. vocalizar
vo·ca·tion, n. vocación; profesión
vod·ka, n. vodka
vogue, n. moda; boga
voice, n. voz, f. v. expresar
void, a. nulo; vacío. v. vaciar; invalidar. n. vacío
vol·a·tile, a. volátil
vol·can·ic, a. volcánico
vol·ca·no, n. pl., -noes, -nos. volcán
vo·li·tion, n. voluntad; volición
vol·ley, n. pl., -leys. descarga; voleo. v. volear
volt, n. voltio
volt·age, n. voltaje
vol·u·ble, a. hablador
vol·ume, n. volumen; tomo; cantidad; volumen sonoro
vo·lu·mi·nous, a. voluminoso; extenso
vol·un·tar·y, a. voluntario
vol·un·teer, n. voluntario. v. ofrecerse a
vo·lup·tu·ar·y, n. pl., -ies. voluptuoso
vo·lup·tu·ous, a. voluptuoso
vom·it, v. vomitar. n. vómito
vo·ra·cious, a. voraz
vor·tex, n. pl., -tex·es, -ti·ces. vórtice
vote, n. voto; votación; sufragio. v. votar
vot·er, n. votante, m., f.

vouch, v. confirmar; garantizar
vouch·er, n. comprobante
vow, n. promesa solemne; voto. v. jurar
vow·el, n. vocal, f.
voy·age, n. travesía; viaje. v. viajar
vul·can·ize, v. vulcanizar
vul·gar, a. vulgar; grosero
vul·gar·i·ty, n. pl., -ties. grosería; cursilería
vul·gar·ize, v. vulgarizar
vul·ner·a·bil·i·ty, n. vulnerabilidad
vul·ner·a·ble, a. vulnerable
vul·ture, n. buitre
vul·va, n. pl., -vae, -vas. vulva

W

wack·y, a. inf. loco; chiflado
wad, n. fajo; taco; rollo; bolita
wad·dle, v. anadear
wade, v. vadear; pasar con dificultad
wag, v. menear(se)
wage, n. often pl. salario; jornal, m. pl., sing. or pl. in constr. salario. v. hacer
wa·ger, n. apuesta. v. apostar
wag·on, n. carro
waif, n. niño abandonado
wail, v. lamentarse; sollozar. n. gemido
wain·scot, n. friso de madera
waist, n. cintura
waist·coat, n. chiefly Brit. chaleco
waist·line, n. talle
wait, v. esperar; estar listo; servir. n. espera
wait·er, n. camarero
wait·ress, n. fem. camarera
waive, v. renunciar a; abandonar
waiv·er, n. renuncia
wake, v., waked or woke, waked, wak·ing. despertar(se). n. vela; estela
wake·ful, a. vigilante
wak·en, v. despertar(se)
walk, v. andar; caminar; ir a pie. n. paseo; caminata
walk·out, n. huelga
walk·o·ver, n. inf. triunfo fácil
wall, n. pared, f.; muro; muralla. v. emparedar
wall·board, n. cartón de yeso
wal·let, n. cartera
wal·lop, v. inf. zurrar. n. inf. golpazo
wal·low, v. revolcarse
wall·pa·per, n. papel pintado
wal·nut, n. nogal, m.
wal·rus, n. pl., -rus·es, -rus. morsa
waltz, n. vals, m. v. valsar
wan, a. pálido
wan·der, v. vagar; errar; desviarse
wan·der·lust, n. deseo de viajar
wane, v. disminuir; menguar
want, v. requerir; necesitar; desear;

querer. *n.* falta; carencia

want·ing, *a.* deficiente. *prep.* sin

wan·ton, *a.* lascivo; desenfrenado; inconsiderado

war, *n.* guerra. *v.* guerrear; hacer la guerra

war·ble, *v.* trinar. *n.* trino; gorjeo

war·cry, *n.* grito de guerra

ward, *v.* desviar. *n.* pupilo; distrito electoral; crujía

war·den, *n.* guardián; alcaide

ward·robe, *n.* guardarropa; vestuario

ware, *n. usu. pl.* mercancías

ware·house, *n.* almacén

war·fare, *n.* guerra

war·lock, *n.* hechicero

warm, *a.* caliente, cálido; caluroso. *v.* calentar(se)

warm·heart·ed, warm·heart·ed, *a.* afectuoso

war·mon·ger, *n.* belicista, *m., f.*

warmth, *n.* calor; entusiasmo

warn, *v.* advertir; avisar

warn·ing, *n.* advertencia; aviso; admonición

warp, *v.* alabearse; pervertir. *n.* comba

war·rant, *n.* autorización; garantía; orden; cédula. *v.* justificar

war·ran·ty, *n. pl.,* **·ties.** garantía

war·ren, *n.* conejera

war·ri·or, *n.* guerrero

wart, *n.* verruga

war·y, *a.* cauteloso

was, *pret.* of **be**

wash, *v.* lavar(se); fregar. *n.* lavado; estela

wash·cloth, *n.* paño para lavarse

wash·er, *n.* lavadora; arandela

wash·ing, *n.* lavado

wash·out, *n.* derrumbe de aluvión; fracaso

wash·room, *n.* lavabo

wash·stand, *n.* lavamanos

wash·tub, *n.* tina o cuba de lavar

wasp, *n.* avispa

wast·age, *n.* desgaste; merma

waste, *v.* malgastar; desperdiciar. *n.* desgaste; pérdida; yermo; *pl.* excremento. *a.* sobrante

wast·rel, *n.* derrochador

watch, *v.* vigilar; guardar; observar; mirar. *n.* vigilia; reloj, *m.*

watch·ful, *a.* vigilante; desvelado

watch·man, *n. pl.,* **·men.** vigilante

watch·word, *n.* santo y seña

wa·ter, *n.* agua. *v.* regar; aguar

wa·ter·col·or, *n.* acuarela

wa·ter·course, *n.* corriente, *f.;* lecho

wa·ter·fall, *n.* cascada

wa·ter·fowl, *n. pl.,* **·fowls, ·fowl.** ave acuática

wa·ter·front, *n.* terreno ribereño

wa·ter·lil·y, *n. pl.,* **lil·ies.** nenúfar

wa·ter·logged, *a.* anegado

wa·ter·mark, *n.* nivel de agua; filigrana

wa·ter·mel·on, *n.* sandía

wa·ter·proof, *a.* impermeable. *n.* impermeable

wa·ter·side, *n.* orilla del agua

wa·ter soft·en·er, *n.* ablandador químico de agua

wa·ter·spout, *n.* tromba marina; manga

wa·ter·tight, *a.* estanco; seguro

wa·ter·way, *n.* canal, *m.*

wa·ter·y, *a.* acuoso; insípido

watt, *n.* vatio

wave, *n.* ola; onda; ondulación. *v.* ondear; ondular; hacer ademanes

wa·ver, *v.* oscilar; vacilar

wav·y, *a.* ondulado

wax, *n. pl.,* **wax·es.** cera. *v.* encerar; aumentarse; crecer

wax·en, *a.* de cera; pálido

wax·work, *n.* figura de cera

way, *n.* modo; manera; dirección; distancia; vía; camino; método. **under way,** en marcha

way·far·er, *n.* viajero

way·lay, *v.,* **·laid, ·lay·ing** acechar; asaltar

way·side, *n.* borde del camino

way·ward, *a.* voluntarioso; travieso

we, *pron.* nosotros; nosotras

weak, *a.* débil; flojo; ineficaz

weak·en, *v.* debilitar(se)

weak·ling, *n.* alfeñique

weak·ly, *a.* achacoso. *adv.* débilmente

weak·mind·ed, *a.* sin voluntad; irresoluto

weak·ness, *n.* debilidad

wealth, *n.* riqueza

wealth·y, *a.* rico

wean, *v.* destetar

weap·on, *n.* arma

weap·on·ry, *n.* armas, *f. pl.*

wear, *v.,* **wore, worn, wear·ing.** llevar; usar(se); desgastar(se). *n.* ropa; desgaste; uso

wear·ing, *a.* penoso

wea·ri·some, *a.* fastidioso

wea·ry, *a.* fatigado; aburrido

wea·sel, *n. pl.,* **·sels, ·sel.** comadreja

weath·er, *n.* tiempo. *v.* desgastar(se); aguantar

weath·er·beat·en, *a.* curtido por la intemperie

weath·er·glass, *n.* barómetro

weath·er·man, *n. pl.,* **·men.** pronosticador del tiempo

weave, *v.,* **wove** or **weaved, wov·en** or **wove, weav·ing.** tejer. *n.* tejido

web, *n.* tela; membrana

web·bing, *n.* cincha

wed, *v.,* **wed·ded** or **wed, wed·ding.**

casar(se); casarse con

wed·ding, *n.* boda

wedge, *n.* cuña. *v.* acuñar

wed·lock, *n.* matrimonio

Wednes·day, *n.* miércoles, *m.*

wee, *a.* pequeñito

weed, *n.* mala hierba. *v.* escardar

week, *n.* semana

week·day, *n.* día laborable o de trabajo

week·end, *n.* fin de semana

week·ly, *a.* semanal. *adv.* cada semana

weep, *v.,* **wept, weep·ing.** llorar

wee·vil, *n.* gorgojo

weigh, *v.* pesar

weight, *n.* peso; pesa. *v.* cargar

weight·y, *a.* pesado; importante

weird, *a.* fantástico; extraño

wel·come, *a.* bienvenido; agradable. *n.* bienvenida. *v.* acoger

weld, *v.* soldar

wel·fare, *n.* bienestar

well, *n.* pozo; fuente, *f. adv.,* **bet·ter, best.** bien; pues. *a.* bien de salud. *int.* vaya; pues

well-be·ing, *n.* bienestar

well-bred, *a.* bien criado

well-dis·posed, *a.* bien dispuesto

well-known, *a.* conocido; famoso

well-off, *a.* adinerado

well-read, *a.* leído

well-thought-of, *a.* bien mirado

well-timed, *a.* oportuno

well-to-do, *a.* acaudalado

welt, *n.* verdugón

wel·ter, *v.* revolcar(se). *n.* conmoción

wench, *n.* moza

were, *pret. of* be

were·wolf, wer·wolf, *n. pl.,* **-wolves.** hombre que puede transformarse en lobo

west, *n.* oeste; occidente. *a.* del oeste. *adv.* al oeste

west·ern, *a.* occidental. *n.* película del oeste

west·ward, *adv.* hacia el oeste. Also **west·wards**

wet, *a.* mojado; húmedo; lluvioso. *v.,* **wet** or **wet·ted.** mojar(se)

whack, *v. inf.* golpear. *n.* golpe ruidoso

whale, *n.* ballena

whale·bone, *n.* ballena

wharf, *n. pl.,* **wharves, wharfs.** muelle

what, *pron. pl.,* **what.** lo que; qué. *a.* que; qué; cuál. *int.* qué. **what if,** y si

what·ev·er, *pron.* todo lo que. *a.* cualquier

what-not, *n.* estante; juguetero

wheat, *n.* trigo

whee·dle, *v.* engatusar; halagar

wheel, *n.* rueda. *v.* dar una vuelta

wheel·bar·row, *n.* carretilla

wheel·chair, *n.* silla de ruedas

wheeze, *v.* respirar asmáticamente; resollar

when, *adv.* cuándo. *conj.* cuando

whence, *adv.* de dónde; de qué

when·ev·er, *adv.* siempre que; todas las veces que

where, *adv.* dónde; adónde. *conj.* donde

where·a·bouts, *n. pl., sing. or pl.* in *constr.* paradero

where·as, *conj.* mientras que; visto que

where·up·on, *adv.* con lo cual

wher·ev·er, *adv.* dondequiera que

where·with·al, *n.* medios

whet, *v.* afilar; estimular

wheth·er, *conj.* si

whey, *n.* suero de la leche

which, *pron.* cuál; que; el, la, lo que; el, la, lo cual. *a.* cuál; qué

which·ev·er, *a.* cualquier. *pron.* cualquiera

whiff, *n.* olorcillo

while, *n.* rato. *conj.* mientras (que). *v.* pasar; entretener

whim, *n.* capricho; antojo

whim·per, *v.* lloriquear

whim·si·cal, *a.* caprichoso

whine, *v.* gimotear. *n.* quejido

whin·ny, *n. pl.,* **-nies.** relincho *v.* relinchar

whip, *v.* **whipped** or **whipt, whip·ping.** azotar; batir. *n.* azote; látigo

whir, whirr, *v.,* **whirred, whir·ring.** zumbar; batir

whirl, *v.* girar rápidamente

whirl·pool, *n.* remolino

whirl·wind, *n.* torbellino

whisk·ers, *n. pl.* barbas; bigotes

whis·key, whis·ky, *n. pl.,* **-keys, -kies.** whisky, *m.*

whis·per, *v.* cuchichear. *n.* cuchicheo; susurro

whis·tle, *v.* silbar. *n.* silbido; pito

white, *a.* blanco. *n.* blanco; clara de un huevo

white-col·lar, *a.* oficinesco

whit·en, *v.* blanquear

white·wash, *n.* jalbegue. *v.* enjalbegar; *inf.* encubrir

whith·er, *adv.* adónde. *conj.* adonde

whit·tle, *v.* cortar poco a poco

whiz, whizz, *v.,* **whizzed, whiz·zing.** silbar; rehilar. *n. pl.,* **-zes.** silbido

who, *pron.* quien; quién; que; el, la, lo que

who·ev·er, *pron.* quienquiera que

whole, *a.* entero; todo. *n.* todo; totalidad

whole·heart·ed, *a.* sincero; incondicional

whole·sale, *n.* venta al por menor. *a.* al por mayor. *adv.* en masa

whole·some, *a.* saludable

whol·ly, *adv.* completamente

whom, *pron.* a quién; a quien; que

whom·ev·er, *pron.* a quienquiera

whoop, *n.* alarido. *v.* gritar

whore, *n.* puta; prostituta

whose, *pron.* de quién; cuyo

why, *adv.* por qué. *n. pl.,* **whys.** causa; porqué

wick, *n.* mecha

wick·ed, *a.* malo; malicioso; inicuo

wick·er, *a.* de mimbre

wide, *a.* ancho; amplio; extenso. *adv.* lejos

wide·a·wake, *a.* despabilado

wid·en, *v.* ensanchar(se)

wide·spread, *a.* extendido; difuso

wid·ow, *n.* viuda

wid·ow·er, *n.* viudo

width, *n.* anchura

wield, *v.* ejercer; mandar; manejar

wife, *n. pl.,* **wives.** esposa; mujer

wig, *n.* peluca

wig·gle, *v.* menear(se); cimbrearse

wild, *a.* salvaje; silvestre; descabellado; loco. *n. often pl.* yermo

wild boar, *n.* jabalí, *m.*

wil·der·ness, *n.* yermo; desierto

wile, *n.* ardid

will, *aux. v., past* **would.** *aux. del futuro.* querer

will, *n.* voluntad; albedrío; testamento. *v.* legar

will·ful, wil·ful, *a.* voluntarioso; terco; premeditado

will·ing, *a.* dispuesto; complaciente

wil·low, *n.* sauce

wil·low·y, *a.* esbelto

wil·ly-nil·ly, *adv.* de grado o por fuerza

wilt, *v.* marchitar(se)

win, *v.,* **won, win·ning.** ganar; triunfar; lograr. *n.* victoria

wince, *v.* estremecerse; respingar. *n.* mueca de dolor

winch, *n.* torno

wind, *n.* viento

wind, *v.,* **wound, wind·ing.** serpentear; arrollar(se); devanar

wind·fall, *n.* ganancia inesperada

wind·mill, *n.* molino de viento

win·dow, *n.* ventana

win·dow·pane, *n.* cristal, *m.*

wind·shield, *n.* parabrisas, *m.*

wind·y, *a.* ventoso; expuesto al aire

wine, *n.* vino

win·er·y, *n. pl.,* **-ies.** lagar; candiotera

wing, *n.* ala

wink, *v.* guiñar; pestañear. *n.* guiño

win·ner, *n.* ganador

win·ning, *n. usu. pl.* ganancias. *a.*

victorioso; encantador

win·now, *v.* aventar

win·some, *a.* atractivo; alegre

win·ter, *n.* invierno. *a.* invernal. *v.* invernar

win·try, *a.* glacial; invernal

wipe, *v.* enjugar; secar; borrar. *n.* limpión

wire, *n.* alambre; *inf.* telegrama, *m. v.* telegrafiar

wire·tap, *v.* intervenir

wir·ing, *n.* instalación de alambres

wir·y, *a.* nervudo

wis·dom, *n.* sabiduría

wise, *a.* sabio; sagaz; juicioso; acertado

wise·crack, *n.* cuchufleta; pulla

wish, *v.* desear. *n.* deseo

wish·ful, *a.* deseoso

wish·y-wash·y, *a.* soso

wist·ful *a.* pensativo; melancólico

wit, *n.* sal, *f.*; ingenio; juicio

witch, *n. pl.,* **witch·es.** bruja; hechicera

witch·craft, *n.* brujería

with, *prep.* con; de

with·draw, *v.,* **-drew, -drawn, -draw·ing.** retirar(se); sacar

with·draw·al, *n.* retirada

with·drawn, *a.* ensimismado

with·er, *v.* marchitar(se); secarse

with·hold, *v.,* **-held, -hold·ing.** retener

with·in, *prep.* dentro de; en. *adv.* dentro

with·out, *prep.* sin; a falta de. *adv.* por fuera

with·stand, *v.,* **-stood, -stand·ing.** resistir

wit·less, *a.* tonto

wit·ness, *n.* espectador; espectadora; testigo; testimonio. *v.* ver

wit·ti·cism, *n.* dicho gracioso

wit·ty, *a.* salado; ingenioso

wiz·ard, *n.* hechicero

wob·ble, *v.* bambolear; bailar

woe, *n.* aflicción; infortunio. *int.* ay de mí

wolf, *n. pl.,* **wolves.** lobo

wom·an, *n. pl.,* **-en.** mujer

wom·an·kind, *n.* sexo femenino

womb, *n.* matriz, *f.*; útero

wom·en's rights, *n. pl.* derechos de la mujer. Also **wom·an's rights**

won·der, *v.* desear saber; asombrarse. *n.* maravilla; milagro

won·der·ful, *a.* maravilloso

woo, *v.,* **wooed, woo·ing.** cortejar

wood, *n.* madera; *pl.* bosque

wood·en, *a.* de madera; sin expresión

wood·land, *n.* monte

wood·peck·er, *n.* picamaderos, *m.*; pito

wood·work, *n.* madraje

wood·y, a. leñoso
wool, n. lana
wool·en, wool·len, a. de lana
wool·ly, wool·y, a. lanudo
word, n. palabra; vocablo; recado. v. expresar
word·ing, n. fraseología
word·y, a. verboso
work, n. trabajo; labor, f.; empleo; obra. v. trabajar; operar; funcionar; obrar. **the works,** inf. todo lo posible
work·book, n. cuaderno
worked-up, a. emocionante
work·er, n. obrero; trabajador
work·man·ship, n. habilidad; destreza
work·shop, n. taller
world, n. mundo
world·ly, a. mundano
world-wide, a. mundial; universal
worm, n. gusano
worn, a. raído; usado
worn-out, a. gastado; rendido
wor·ri·some, a. aprensivo
wor·ry, v. preocupar(se); inquietar(se). n. pl., **-ries.** preocupación
worse, a., irreg. compar. of **bad** and **ill.** peor; inferior
wors·en, v. empeorar
wor·ship, n. culto; adoración. v. venerar; adorar
worst, a., irreg. superl. of **bad** and **ill.** peor. n. el, lo peor. adv. del peor modo posible
wor·sted, n. estambre
worth, n. valor; mérito. a. que vale; que merece
worth·less, a. sin valor; despreciable
worth·while, a. digno de atención
wor·thy, a. benemérito; digno de
would-be, a. supuesto
wound, n. herida. v. herir
wraith, n. fantasma, m.
wrap, v. envolver; arropar. n. pl. abrigo. **wrapped up in,** inf. absorto en. **keep un·der wraps,** inf. guardar el secreto
wrath, n. ira; furor
wreak, v. descargar
wreath, n. pl., **wreaths.** guirnalda
wreck, n. naufragio; desastre; ruina. v. destruir; naufragar
wreck·age, n. restos, m. pl.
wrench, n. torcedura; arranque; llave inglesa
wring, v., **wrung, wring·ing.** torcer(se); retorcer; exprimir
wrin·kle, n. arruga; pliegue. v. arrugar(se)
wrist, n. muñeca
write, v., **wrote, writ·ten, writ·ing.** escribir
writ·er, n. escritor; escritora

writ·ing, n. escritura; let. a; escrito
wrong, a. erróneo; equivocado; malo. n. mal, m.; agravio. adv. mal; injustamente. v. agraviar

X - Y - Z

x-ray, n. radiografía. v. radiografiar
yank, v. sacar de un tirón
Yan·kee, n. yanqui, m., f.
yard, n. yarda; patio
yard goods, n. tejidos
yard·stick, n. vara de medir
yarn, n. hilaza; inf. cuento
yar·row, n. milenrama
yawn, n. bostezar. n. bostezo
ye, pron. vosotros
yea, adv. sí
year, n. año
year·ling, n. primal, m.
year·ly, adj. anual. adv. anualmente
yearn, v. suspirar; anhelar
yearn·ing, n. anhelo
yeast, n. levadura
yell, v. gritar. n. grito
yel·low, a. amarillo; inf. cobarde. n. amarillo
yes, adv. sí
yes·ter·day, n. ayer
yet, adv. todavía; aún. conj. sin embargo
yew, n. tejo
yield, v. producir; rendir(se); someterse. n. rédito
yolk, n. yema
yon·der, adv. allí; allá
yore, n. antaño
you, pron. tú; vos; vosotros; vosotras; usted; ustedes
young, a. joven; nuevo. n. jóvenes; hijuelos
young·ster, n. jovencito
your, poss. a. tu(s); su(s); vuestro(s); vuestra(s)
yours, pron. de usted(es); el tuyo; el suyo
your·self, pron. pl., **-selves.** tú mismo; usted mismo; sí mismo
youth, n. pl., **youth, youths.** juventud; jóvenes
youth·ful, a. juvenil
zeal, n. celo; ardor
zeal·ous, a. celoso; entusiasta
ze·bra, n. pl., **-bras, -bra.** cebra
ze·nith, n. cenit, m.
ze·ro, n. pl., **-ros, -roes.** cero
ze·ro hour, n. hora de ataque
zest, n. entusiasmo; gusto
zone, n. zona
zoo, n. pl., **zoos.** jardín zoológico
zo·o·log·i·cal, a. zoológico
zuc·chi·ni, n. pl., **-ni, -nis.** cidracayote de verano
zy·gote, n. cigoto